CRITICAL COMPANION TO

The Bible

The Bible

A Literary Reference

MARTIN H. MANSER

ASSOCIATE EDITORS
David Barratt
Pieter J. Lalleman
Julius Steinberg

☑️ Facts On File
An imprint of Infobase Publishing

Critical Companion to the Bible

Copyright © 2009 by Martin H. Manser

Facts On File, Inc.
An imprint of Infobase Publishing
132 West 31st Street
New York NY 10001

Library of Congress Cataloging-in-Publication Data

Manser, Martin H.
Critical companion to the Bible : a literary reference / Martin H. Manser ;
associate editors, David Barratt, Pieter J. Lalleman, Julius Steinberg.
p. cm.
Includes bibliographical references and index.
ISBN 978-0-8160-7065-7 (hc : alk. paper) 1. Bible as literature. 2. Bible—
Criticism, interpretation, etc. I. Barratt, David. II. Lalleman, Pieter J. III.
Steinberg, Julius, 1972–   IV. Title.
BS535.M34 2009
220.6'1—dc22   2008029257

Facts On File books are available at special discounts when purchased in bulk
quantities for businesses, associations, institutions, or sales promotions.
Please call our Special Sales Department in New York at (212) 967-8800
or (800) 322-8755.

You can find Facts On File on the World Wide Web at http://www.factsonfile.com

You can find Martin H. Manser on the World Wide Web at
http://www.martinmanser.com

Text design by Erika Arroyo
Cover design by Cathy Rincon

Printed in the United States of America

VB Hermitage 10 9 8 7 6 5 4 3 2 1

This book is printed on acid-free paper and
contains 30 percent postconsumer recycled content..

CONTENTS

INTRODUCTION

From its first printing in 1450 C.E. to the present day, the Bible has consistently been a best seller. It has been translated into more languages than any other book—currently more than 2,000. No book has influenced the Western world more than the Bible, and, probably, no book has triggered more controversies than the Bible.

This title in the Critical Companion series examines the Bible as a masterpiece of literature. A literary reading of the Bible looks particularly at the language and verbal structures of the text and at the imaginative quality of its thought. This approach entails study of the Bible's imagery, diction, patterns of words, and striking expressions, as well as its use of dialogue, monologue, and various genres. For example, many readers do not appreciate how much of the Bible is poetry and, therefore, needs to be read as poetry. This guide of study can give a more subtle reading and understanding of the text and sensitize us to how the words on the page affect us.

Part I of this book, Reading the Bible as Literature, gives an overview of various approaches scholars have taken to interpreting the Bible. It also comments on the approach taken in this book, that is, a specifically literary approach, in which the biblical books are appreciated as works of ancient Near Eastern and Jewish-Hellenistic literature, with the aim of listening carefully to what the texts want to communicate. Of course, historical and theological issues are also discussed, where appropriate. Part I also comments on other general issues, such as the authorship of the biblical books and the historical development of the biblical canon.

Part II contains in-depth entries, arranged alphabetically, on each of the books of the Bible. (Many reference works on the Bible follow the traditional order of its books, but this can be confusing to those unfamiliar with the Bible or with the traditional order. See Part IV for lists of biblical books arranged according to different traditions.) Apocryphal or deuterocanonical portions that are associated particularly with a canonical book are listed with that book. For example, at the end of the entry on the book of Daniel are entries on the Prayer of Azariah and the Song of the Three Jews, Susanna, and Bel and the Dragon.

Within each book of the Bible in Part II, the material is structured as follows:

- general introduction to the book, including the dating of the book
- concise synopsis of the book, describing its major events
- commentary on the book, focusing on how it can be interpreted from a literary point of view, including a description of important themes, literary techniques, forms, and characterizations
- an alphabetical listing of significant figures appearing in the narrative of that book

Entries on some books employ a somewhat different structure, appropriate to the nature of the book. For example, the entry on Psalms discusses the poetry, different genres, and various themes of the psalms in general before considering certain individual psalms.

Part III provides entries, also arranged in alphabetical order, on the important people, places, concepts, genres, and themes that relate to the Bible but are not covered extensively in Part II. For example, people who are significant across the biblical narrative are included in this section, whereas people whose importance is limited to one Bible book are included in the relevant book in Part II. Longer entries in this section include God, Hebrew Bible worship and ritual, Jesus Christ, formation of the canon, genres, poetry, and women of the Bible.

Part IV contains appendixes: lists of books of the Bible, a chronology, and a list of secondary resources, including Web sites, that are important to the literary study of the Bible.

This edition also includes about 50 illustrations that complement the verbal commentaries. These depict various understandings and interpretations of biblical events and characters.

Literary study of the Bible is immensely valuable and not limited to devout readers. A scholar once compared the Bible to a great lake. Children splash and play in it, but even the most educated scholars have not yet been able to fathom its depths fully. The contributors to this volume hope that it may help readers find their own way of appreciating the literature of this unique book.

PART I

Reading the Bible as Literature

In other volumes in the Critical Companion series, Part I contains a biography of the great writer who is the subject of the book. For the Bible, however, the issue is more complex. The Bible was written by many human authors, some of whom are known with certainty and some of whom are disputed. What is more, if you were to ask believing Jews or Christians, they would name a different author of the Bible: God is said to have "inspired" the writing of the Scriptures. Therefore, in this introduction we need to take some time to consider the question of the authorship of the Bible.

The Bible is a religious book, not just for one community of faith, but for several: Jews and Christians of different denominations, including both Catholic and Protestant traditions. These groups disagree as to which books actually belong in the Bible. In addition, over time, several different approaches to interpreting the Bible have been developed by these groups. The introduction will also give an overview of these issues.

In this volume, the Bible is examined mainly from a literary point of view. A literary approach to this unique book, however, will only be successful if we are conscious of the fact that it is not to be judged according to the rules of modern literature but rather as a document of the ancient Near Eastern and Jewish-Hellenistic cultures. The introduction, therefore, will also discuss the nature and some distinctive features of biblical literature.

One Book, Many Books: Which Texts Belong to the Bible

The Bible is not a single, unified work but a compilation of individual texts commonly called books. Which books belong to the Bible? This question is answered differently by different religious communities.

The Hebrew Bible is the Holy Scripture of the Jews. It contains books originally written in the ancient Hebrew and partly in the ancient Aramaic languages. The five books of Moses, also called the Pentateuch, or Torah, belong to it, as well as some

books dealing with the history of ancient Israel. These are followed by the books of the prophets, some books of wisdom, and the Psalms (a complete list of the books of the Bible is given in Part IV of this volume).

The first Christians were Jews, and so the Jewish Holy Scripture became the Holy Scripture of the Christian Church as well. However, in the first century of the common era, a group of specifically Christian texts came into being that were later collected and named the New Testament, whereas the previous Jewish Scriptures were renamed the Old Testament by the Christians. The New Testament consists of four so-called Gospels that document the ministry of Jesus. These are followed by a book on the history of the early Christian Church, a series of letters written by apostles (the first Christian missionaries) to Christian churches in Asia Minor and Greece, and the book of Revelation, which foretells mainly events at the end of time.

Somewhere between the third and the first centuries B.C.E., the Hebrew Bible/Old Testament books were translated into Greek, the Greek translation being called the Septuagint, often written as LXX. In the Septuagint, some additional books were included that had not been part of the Hebrew Bible. These books date mostly from late pre-Christian times and were not considered to be of equal authority to the books of the Hebrew Bible. They are therefore termed deuterocanonical, i.e., of secondary canonical importance. (The word *canon* denotes a fixed group of recognized books, in our case, the books of the Bible.) Nevertheless, these books became part of the Septuagint and in religious practice were often used together with the canonical books. Deuterocanonical books include, for example, Sirach, Wisdom, Maccabees, Judith, and Tobit.

In the first century, Christians as well as Jews used the Hebrew Bible and the Septuagint side by side. Before long, however, the Christians increasingly looked on the Septuagint as "their" Old Testament. In a counterreaction, the Jews decided in favor of the Hebrew Bible. This is the reason why the Catholic Old Testament contains more books than the Hebrew Bible of the Jews. The number of deuterocanonical books included in their Bible varies even among Roman Catholics and Greek and Russian Orthodox.

Moreover, the church reformer Martin Luther endorsed keeping only those books in the Old Testament that are also part of the Hebrew Bible and thus belong to the inner circle of inspired Scripture. So he removed all the deuterocanonical books from the Bible. In some editions of the Protestant Bible, the additional books are arranged in a separate group called the Apocrypha. According to Luther, the books of the Apocrypha are "not on the same level as the Holy Scriptures, but still good and useful to read." It has to be mentioned that the inclusion or exclusion of the deuterocanonical/apocryphal books has no direct bearing on the most fundamental aspects of Christian teaching.

In Part II of this book, you will find entries on all books of the Jewish, Protestant, and Catholic Bible. (Less space, however, is devoted to the deuterocanonical/apocryphal books.) Entries for each of the books explain which part of the Bible it belongs to. Comparative lists of canonical books are given in Part IV. For further information on this subject, see also the entries in Part III on APOCRYPHA AND PSEUDEPIGRAPHA; BIBLE, LANGUAGES OF; BIBLE, EARLY TRANSLATIONS OF; FORMATION OF THE CANON: THE HEBREW BIBLE; FORMATION OF THE CANON: THE NEW TESTAMENT.

One Author, Many Authors: Who Wrote the Bible

The Bible was written over the course of many centuries. Conservative scholars date the formation of the Hebrew Bible from about 1400 to 350 B.C.E., while liberal scholars estimate a time span from about 900 to 160 B.C.E. The terms *liberal* and *conservative* here do not denote a political point of view but, rather, attitudes to the study of the Bible adopted by scholars and theologians. Basically, conservative scholars tend to adhere to what the biblical text specifically states, believing in its divine inspiration, whereas liberal scholars tend to view the biblical texts as engendering the best human ideas about God, but ideas that may be questionable or have been revised at a later date by others.

Both groups assume that the origins of some of the traditions reach much further into the past (about 2000 B.C.E. and earlier). The New Testament texts were written about 50–100 C.E.

THE HUMAN AUTHORS

Concerning the authors of the biblical books, the Hebrew Bible gives the following details: Moses (15th century B.C.E.) is said to be the author of the Pentateuch, or at least his authority is claimed for large parts of it. The prophetic books consist mainly of the words of the eponymous prophets. They can therefore be seen as the authors of their books, respectively. But it is also possible that others, for example, their disciples, did the final editing. Of the psalms, many are ascribed to individual authors, mostly King David (whose reign was 1010–971 B.C.E.). The books of Proverbs and the Song of Songs give King Solomon as their author (he reigned from 971 to 931 B.C.E.). In the books of Ezra and Nehemiah, certain passages are written in autobiographic style (fifth century B.C.E.). The other books are anonymous. In the later Jewish and Christian tradition, certain books are attributed to specific writers, but these attributions are speculative.

The extent to which the biblical author designations can be trusted is questionable. Conservative scholars tend to see these details as reliable, whereas liberal scholars have doubts about these designations. Instead of speaking of individual authors, a longer editorial process is often assumed, whereby the books developed only step-by-step into the form in which we know them now. Scholars are in no doubt that there was some reworking of earlier material (see, for example, the editorial information in Proverbs 25:1). However, the extent of these activities is disputed.

Authors of the New Testament are, according to the text itself, the apostles Paul, Peter, John, James, and Jude. The four Gospels make no mention of their respective authors. However, superscriptions in the early manuscripts, as well as the witness of the early church, strongly suggest that Matthew, Mark, Luke, and John wrote the gospels assigned to their respective names. Luke also is thought to have written Acts. In the New Testament, only the Letter to the Hebrews is anonymous. All named authors belong to the first century C.E. Christian Church.

As with the Old Testament, also with the New Testament, the given authors are mostly accepted by conservative scholars, whereas liberal scholars tend to doubt the origins, especially of some of the letters of Paul.

Some deuterocanonical or apocryphal books are attributed to specific writers. However, some texts exhibit evidence of pseudepigraphy. That is, because the texts came into being relatively late, they did not have a natural authority, as the texts of the Hebrew Bible have. In order to heighten their importance, those texts were ascribed to well-known biblical persons. This is true, for example, for the book of Wisdom, which is attributed to King Solomon (10th century B.C.E.) but reflects first-century Hellenistic thinking. Other examples are the book of Baruch and the Prayer of Manasseh. Conversely, the author ascribed to the book of Sirach, Jesus Ben Eleazar Ben Sirach, is generally considered to be historical. Anonymous works are also included in the Apocrypha: the books of the Maccabees, Judith, Tobit, and some others. For a more detailed discussion of the authorship of the individual biblical books, see Part II.

GOD AS THE INTENDED AUTHOR OF THE BIBLE

One of the biblical authors has not yet been discussed. He is the one who is said to be the original author guiding all the human authors: God himself.

In the Hebrew Bible, long passages of the five books of Moses are presented as being the recorded speech of God. Moses is commanded by God to write down the law God gave him (Exodus 17:14; Deuteronomy 31:24–26). Moses knows God "face to face" (Deuteronomy 34:10–12) and therefore can reliably write down God's words; the entire Torah is seen as God-given; disobedience results in punishment by God (Deuteronomy 29:20).

The prophets understand themselves as being led by the Spirit of God (e.g., Micah 3:8; Jeremiah 1:1–2; 30:2; Ezekiel 1:1). The Spirit of the Lord also speaks through David when he writes psalms (2 Samuel 23:1–3), and Solomon's wisdom again is

given by God (1 Kings 3:12; 5:7). Therefore, divine inspiration is explicitly claimed for the known authors.

The anonymous works, in turn, are written from the perspective of an omniscient narrator who can describe events that took place in distant locations as well as the inner thoughts and feelings of the human characters and even of God. In modern literature, such a perspective is used for fictional texts only, making the omniscience a fictional one. The Bible, however, uses it for its historical narratives, thus assigning the narrator divine knowledge.

The New Testament expresses the conviction in many places that the Hebrew Bible is divinely inspired. According to Jesus Christ, the Hebrew Bible is valid without any exception (Matthew 5:18; John 10:35); Paul is convinced that all Scripture is inspired by God (2 Timothy 3:16).

For the New Testament itself, Jesus Christ claims to speak in the name of God, and, even more, he is said to be the word of God incarnate (John 1:1–14). Paul also speaks with divine authority (Galatians 1:11–12). Matthew calls his gospel "the book of the genesis of Jesus" and so places it side by side with the "book of the genesis of Adam" (Genesis 5:1). This suggests that he was conscious of writing a holy book. Matthew especially, but other New Testament texts as well, demonstrates that many Old Testament prophecies find their decisive fulfillment in the person and work of Jesus Christ.

However, even many believers insist that these claims of divine authority do not suggest that the writing of the Bible happened as a kind of heavenly dictation. Rather, it suggests that there was a coworking of the human and the divine in the process of writing the Holy Scriptures. The Bible is seen as the word of God expressed through the words of human beings. In theology, this phenomenon is called inspiration.

Deciding on the Bible's claim for inspiration, lies, of course, with each individual reader. In theology, the issue of whether, how, and how much the Bible is based on divine inspiration is hotly disputed. However, it has to be recorded that belief in the Bible as the "word of God" is not a dogma put up by any ecclesiastical institution but is based on a claim that the biblical texts themselves make.

Many Readers,
Many Readings: How the
Bible Is Approached

How should the Bible be interpreted? In the course
of history, several approaches have been developed.
Different Jewish and Christian groups acknowledge
the Bible as Scripture but differ fundamentally in
their methods of exegesis. It could be said that,
historically, there are three main streams of biblical
interpretation, as follows:

THE AGE OF SYSTEMATIC APPROACHES

Until the Enlightenment (that is, until the 18th
century), the focus of interest in biblical study did
not lie so much in literary interpretation as in systematic theology. Systematic theology is an attempt
to develop a system of statements of belief. The aim
is to erect an edifice of ideas that represent the
contents of the Christian faith in a logical, ordered
manner. Main categories typically used in such an
edifice are "the doctrine of God," "the doctrine of
man," "the doctrine of sin," "the doctrine of salvation," "the doctrine of the church," and others.
In such an approach, the Bible is mainly used to
develop theological constructions. From all over the
biblical text, statements are collected that support
the doctrine under consideration. This approach
is therefore also called "proof text method." Using
this method, the Bible effectively becomes a collection of universally applicable sentences that can be
freely combined in order to support a theologian's
thesis. This way of using the Bible is justified by
a high view of inspiration: Each of the individual
biblical statements is given by God and therefore
contains divine truth.

The theologians of this age also assumed that the
Bible's historical statements were valid. However,
they did not have a strong interest in the historical
dimension of the Bible. In fact, quite the opposite:
The fact that the books of the Bible speak into different times, cultures, and even religious contexts
makes their application much more difficult. As
a solution to this problem, medieval theologians
assigned different layers of meaning to a text. The
system of the fourfold sense of Scripture was devel-

oped. The word *Jerusalem*, for example, in the *literal
sense* meaning the historical city of Jerusalem, was
interpreted in the *tropological* (psychic) sense as the
soul of the believer. In the *spiritual* or *mystical* sense
it symbolized the Christian Church, while in the
anagogical or *eschatological* sense it represented the
new world of God. Another example: In the flood
story, the ark symbolizes the church, Noah is Jesus,
the dove is the Holy Spirit. Using this kind of allegorical approach, virtually any text can be made fit
into the theological system.

In the Jewish realm, the Bible was also used in
a deductive and nonhistorical manner. Although
the Jewish scholars of this time do not seem to
have been interested in an overall theological system, they nevertheless approached the Bible thematically. An example of this would have occurred
when they wanted to define exactly what the term
work meant in the context of the Sabbath commandment. When they used Bible verses for their
argumentation, they often applied very specific
techniques of interpretation to them. In a way comparable to the Christian approaches of that time,
the Jews differentiated between Pshat, the literal
meaning, and Drash, the "looked for" meaning.
According to Pshat, for example, an eye has to be
given for an eye (Exodus 21:23–24). According to
Drash, however, the injured person has to be given
a financial compensation. Next to Pshat and Drash,
the Jewish scholars also developed Remez, an allegorical interpretation, and Sod, a mystical-esoteri-
cal interpretation. A certain rule of interpretation
says, for example, that two Bible verses containing
the same words or phrases have to be understood
in the light of each other. Another of these rules
explains how to go to the general from the specific,
so, for example, the statement "You shall not boil a
kid in its mother's milk" (Exodus 23:19) has been
interpreted as meaning that it is forbidden to have
milk and meat in the same meal.

THE AGE OF HISTORICAL APPROACHES

During the Enlightenment, a fundamental skepticism arose against any form of supernaturalism.
Human reason was set up as the final criterion
and chief source of knowledge; that meant that
the idea of the divine inspiration of the Bible was

questioned. In addition, a new view on history developed, called historism. According to that view, each historical epoch has to be understood in its own light without judging it from a normative outside standpoint.

These developments had a very strong impact on biblical studies. March 1787 is seen as the "birthday" of historical theology. At that time a German theologian, Johann Philipp Gabler, asserted in his inaugural lecture that theology should not work from a systematic, but from a historical, point of view. The biblical statements of belief should not be analyzed on the basis of an overarching system, but rather the individual thoughts of the different human authors should be examined by themselves. In doing so, the individual periods of Old Testament and New Testament religion should be carefully differentiated.

The approach to the Bible that has dominated theology since that time is called the historical-critical approach. The word *critical* here stands for human reason as the final criterion; the inspiration of Scripture is denied or at least set aside. People believed that biblical study could only be academic if based on the assumption *etsi deus non daretur,* "as if God were not given." Where the Bible speaks about God's supernaturally intervening in human history, this was generally doubted. Theologians working from this basis doubt, for example, the historicity of the exodus from Egypt, the historicity of the wonders of Jesus, his resurrection, the sense of his mission in general, and so on. It has to be added, however, that some scholars use this criterion more rigidly than others.

The word *historical,* in the historical-critical approach, stands for historical interest. It very much includes evolutionary thinking, which also became prominent in the Enlightenment era. Historical-critical theology focuses mainly on the reconstruction of historical developments. Having removed the supranatural aspects from the biblical history, it asks: How did the history of Israel *really* happen? What are the real lines of historical development that stand behind the biblical texts?

Even the interpretation of the biblical literature was mainly seen from an evolutionary perspective. Texts are explained by reconstructing their histori-

cal development. There is often the assumption that the texts underwent a long process of reworking before they reached their final form. There are many sophisticated but also highly speculative reconstructions of the textual history of biblical books that are discussed controversially among historical-critical scholars. However, one model accepted by many in the 19th and 20th centuries is the so-called documentary hypothesis for the Pentateuch. Its basic assumption is that in the Pentateuch, four different types of texts can be detected, assigned the letters *J, E, D,* and *P. J,* the Yahwist (German: *Jahwist*), is said to be a storyteller of the ninth century B.C.E., who, when speaking about God, used the name *Yahweh* (translated as the Lord). *E,* another storyteller, from the eighth century, mostly uses *Elohim* for "God." An anonymous redactor is said to have taken up the stories of J and E and drawn them together in order to form a unified narrative. In the seventh or sixth century, the material of "D," the Deuteronomist, was added. His name is derived from the book of Deuteronomy. He has a more theological point of view of Israel's history, comparable to the message of the prophets. Finally, P, the so-called Priestly source, is added in the fifth century. All the passages on laws, offerings, Sabbath, clean and unclean animals, and so forth, are ascribed to him. For example, the creation account in Genesis 1, with its tidiness, its emphasis on separation, and its formal seven-day structure, is said to stem from the Priestly source, whereas the beautiful paradise narrative of Genesis 2:4ff. is ascribed to the storyteller J. Alleged discrepancies between these two creation accounts are explained by pointing out that they were originally two independent texts.

The JEDP model expresses the conviction that the Israelite religion developed toward a prophetic high point (the prophets being understood in the sense of the "romantic genius") and afterward declined again into a priestly, law-based religion. This reconstruction stands in strong opposition to the biblical self-presentation that places the priestly element at the very beginning of Israel's history as a people. The main proponent of this model was the German theologian Julius Wellhausen (1844–1918).

For analyzing redactional layers (or parts written or revised by different authors) in texts, the historical-critical approach uses a set of methods. For example, by *source criticism* is meant the dissection of a text, searching for its original sources and redactional layers. The method looks for inner tensions, unexpected repetitions, and other signs of unevenness in the text that provide evidence that some reworking was done. However, texts that do not exhibit such unevenness are also taken apart, on the basis of assumptions concerning religious developments: Which religious conviction expressed in the text has to be assigned to which period of the (reconstructed) history of religion?

Another method is *Form Criticism*. It identifies smaller literary forms in texts and tries to find their "Sitz im Leben," i.e., in what life setting the text was originally used. *Tradition Criticism* tries to reconstruct older written or oral traditions behind a given text. Here, it is assumed that some of the biblical content once had the status of folktales transmitted orally from one generation to the next, before being incorporated into the big historical narrative of the Bible. *Redaction Criticism*, finally, is the counterpart to source criticism. Redaction criticism asks in which way and for what purpose different sources were combined to build the final form of the text we now have and which views the final editor or redactor imposed on the source materials.

In the Christian world, from the time of the Enlightenment until today, there has existed alongside the historical-critical approach an approach that can be called historical-biblical. Both approaches agree in their emphasis on historical questions. The historical-biblical approach, however, belongs to the realm of conservative scholarship. Here, the biblical self-presentation of history is more or less accepted. It is believed that from an academic point of view, the trustworthiness of the biblical witness can be maintained. Jewish scholars have always been hesitant to accept the historical-critical approach.

LITERARY AND CANONICAL APPROACHES

Beginning in the 1970s, a new tendency developed in both Jewish and Christian biblical scholarship. The Bible began to be looked upon from more of a literary point of view. Historical questions were pushed into the background, and scholars began to read and interpret biblical texts as they might secular literature.

In the secular study of literature, historic-diachronic approaches (approaches that focus on historical developments) were also favored until the beginning of the 20th century, but they were abandoned in secular literary study much earlier than in biblical studies. In the 1920s, the so-called *New Criticism* was developed, putting an emphasis on the text itself, trying to free interpretation from historical questions. The search for the author's intention was denied; texts were interpreted ahistorically. In its radical form, this approach only had a short lifetime. However, it has had considerable impact on all later literary studies.

In the 1960s, literary study was dominated by the philosophy of *structuralism*. Its main aim was to understand language and literature as a system of relationships. The subjects and objects of a text, their relationships, and their transformations were analyzed and described using a notation system that looked quite similar to mathematical equations. By using such systems, scholars wanted to show how narratives are built upon recurring patterns and structures. Other studies tried to find fundamental binary oppositions that underlie narrative texts, for example, "water/dry land" or "wish for eternal life/finality of death" in Genesis 1–4.

Related to this is *semiotics*, with its approach to language as a sign system, a code, and the two concepts *langue* and *parole*, where *langue* stands for the language system and *parole* for the concrete acts of speech. Any *parole* is, on the one hand, an extract of the *langue*, but on the other hand, it also contributes to the forming of the *langue*. In his work *The Great Code*, Northrop Frye, the Canadian literary critic, analyzes the literary *parole* of the Bible in terms of its contribution to the literary *langue*. He demonstrates how the myths, metaphors, images, and typologies of the Bible became elements of the European language system, literature system, and cultural system. In other words, Frye describes the Bible as an "alphabet of literary forms and images."

In the wake of structuralism and semiotics, approaches were developed for biblical interpretation that follow a similar direction but set aside the full philosophical background of these methods. For example, *Discourse Analysis* tries to discover the rules according to which stories are constructed, how the elements of the plot follow one another. *Rhetorical Criticism* and the *Composition Criticism* work out the intention of a given text by carefully analyzing the textual structure and the development of the argument. *Archetypal Criticism* is an approach concentrating on the basic building blocks of literature. Finally, *Biblical Poetics* analyzes literary features such as the presentation of characters, the narrative plot, or the point of view, not primarily in order to interpret an individual text, but rather to understand how meaning is transmitted in texts. The interest is not in what the text means but *how* the text means. The results of such studies can in turn be applied to the interpretation of individual texts.

These approaches overlap and cannot be fully separated. As an overall category, the term *Narrative Criticism* or *Narrative Theory* is probably best, but *Rhetorical Criticism* sometimes is also used as an umbrella term.

In literary study, the approach of structuralism was followed by different postmodern approaches. These are applied to the Bible as well. One example is the *reader response theory*. In its weak variant, it asks which reactions a text provokes in the reader and how texts deliberately use rhetoric to provoke such reactions. It discusses the problem of different readers' reacting differently to the same text. In its strong variant, the theory denies the idea that a text has a fixed meaning. Each cultural or subcultural group of readers assigns a different meaning to the text, reading it from its own point of view. Different "readings" of a text stand side by side and are of equal value. This is the basis of, for example, feminist, psychoanalytical, or liberation theology interpretations of biblical texts.

Out of all these, and even more, literary approaches and methodical tools that literary study offers, we have to decide which ones to use for our approach to the biblical texts. We have to look for methods that are appropriate and that do justice to the distinctive type of literature we find in the Bible. One of the prominent features that certainly has to be considered, even from a literary point of view, is that the Bible is a canon of Holy Scripture.

As a counterreaction to the emphasis on historical reconstruction, scholars not only started reading the Bible from a literary point of view again but also wanted to do more justice to the fact that the Bible is Holy Scripture for Jews and Christians. Therefore, alongside the newer literary approaches, so-called canonical approaches have been developed. These examine, for example, the mutual relationship between the biblical texts and the faith communities that transmit these texts. For the Hebrew Bible, it is assumed that a group of priests and scribes of the Jerusalem temple was assigned to give the biblical books their final form. The question is asked how biblical texts were finalized so that they could speak not only to the current generation but also to coming generations of believers as well. A main proponent of this kind of thinking was the American theologian Brevard Childs (1923–2007). Whereas the historical-critical approach tries to find the truth in the (hypothetically) earliest layers of a text, the canonical approach points to the fact that the final form of the text is the one relevant for the faith community. In order to grasp the intention of the texts, they have to be read from the perspective of the first readers of the faith community, for which they were intended. *Canonical Criticism* also points out that the texts have to be read in the light of the whole biblical canon as their literary context.

Canonical approaches help us to overcome the historical-critical fragmentation of the biblical witness and to understand the Bible as a theological unity again. It has to be added, however, that the canonical approach does not see itself as stepping backward into a pre-Enlightenment state of theology. The results of historical study are not rejected completely. Rather, they are critically evaluated and, if positive, integrated into the overall picture. Today, canonical approaches are favored by liberal as well as by conservative scholars.

How to Read the Bible as Literature

How do we best approach the Bible as a literary work? First, our task should not be to read the Bible *as* literature, as if this were one of several possible options. Rather, it is about reading the Bible and, in doing so, recognizing its literary features (in the same way it would not make sense to read Shakespeare *as* literature).

The Bible *is* literature. However, it exceeds literature. Its books are literary works of art, but they also attempt to communicate divine truth. As discussed, the Bible is a canon of Holy Scripture for Jews and for Christians. Whether a reader accepts this claim or not, the literary method should still do justice to this specific aspect of the Bible. If you want to understand the Bible as it understands itself, as it wants to be understood, then the best way is to look at it through the eyes of the people from whom and for whom it was written.

The Jewish literary specialist Meir Sternberg takes the view that there are three different interests that the biblical texts support: a historical, an ideological or theological, and an aesthetic interest. The three interests are interwoven in a very artistic manner. Narrative texts, for example, claim to give an account of historical facts. However, the events are not presented in the form of purely factual information, as is in a chronicle. Rather, they are shaped into stories, with a beginning and an ending, a plot and a climax, foreground and background characters, and so on. Some of the historical events are presented in detail, while others are only summarized or are completely skipped; the chronological order of events is sometimes abandoned for thematic or other reasons. The purpose of all this literary shaping of history is not only its entertainment value. Rather, through the shaping, the author communicates how he wants the history to be understood, what he sees as important or less important, and what clues readers should draw from it for themselves. In short: *History* is shaped into *story* in order to transmit a *message*.

To give an example: From the Gospel of John we know that Jesus on his journeys through the country traveled to Jerusalem at least three times. In Luke, chapters 9:51–19:28, however, the material is structured in such a way that it looks as if the whole ministry of Jesus consisted more or less of one long journey to Jerusalem. The purpose of this shaping of history is to demonstrate that, even if Jesus traveled back and forth throughout the country, in some sense his whole ministry was leading to the final events that happened in Jerusalem, namely, his crucifixion and resurrection.

In approaching the biblical text, it follows that it is important to recognize the forms and structures according to which the narratives are shaped. If we understand the logic of presentation, we can infer the authorial intention from it. And only if we understand the logic of presentation do we have a sound basis on which to reconstruct the exact order of the historical events, if necessary.

People often hold the view that the Bible's truth should not be looked for on the historical level but rather on the level of the statements of belief it makes. However, the analysis of Sternberg shows that it is not an "either/or." The Bible claims both at the same time. The different truth levels are connected inseparably to each other by way of literary shaping: Theology is developed out of history by way of narrative.

In the texts of the Hebrew Bible, the literary shaping of the material was done according to techniques prevailing in the ancient Near Eastern literary culture. In some respects, these techniques differ from those that we are accustomed to in modern literature. In particular, texts were designed in sections or blocks, arranged according to certain patterns. A typical technique is that of concentric structures, where the first block of the text corresponds to the last, the second to the second last, the third to the third last, and so on. The center of such a structure can consist of either a single text or a pair of text blocks. Structures of that kind can extend for a few verses, a couple of chapters, or even whole biblical books.

An example of a concentric structure is 2 Chronicles 1–9. The capital letters that follow—A, B, C, D, C', B', A'—demonstrate the concentric pattern:

1:1–17	A	Solomon's wealth and wisdom
2:1–18	B	Solomon's international relations
3:1–5:1	C	Solomon's building projects
5:2–7:22	D	Dedication of the temple
8:1–16	C′	Solomon's building projects
8:17–9:12	B′	Solomon's international relations
9:13–28	A′	Solomon's wealth and wisdom

Structures like this help to give the text an over-arching meaning in two ways.

First, the structure clarifies which sections of the text are the most important for interpretation. Mostly, these are the beginning and ending and, in concentric structures, the central text. In the Solomon narrative in 2 Chronicles 1–9, for example, the building of the temple is marked as the most important activity of Solomon. Moreover, in the central section are found a long prayer of the king and a long speech of God dealing with the significance of kingdom and temple. The fact that the other sections are arranged symmetrically around these two speeches underscores the importance of their theological content.

Second, the structure defines relationships among text sections, so that analogies, contrasts, or developments that implicate a message on a higher level become visible. For example, in the book of Ruth, Elimelech stands at the beginning and Boaz at the end. The acts of Elimelech result in barrenness and death, whereas the acts of Boaz result in happiness and new life. Although the text does not state any direct evaluation of Elimelech or Boaz, the literary structure implies that these two should be compared to each other.

Literary structures built into the texts of the Hebrew Bible are not made visible through subheadings or the like. Rather, the literary structures have to be worked out by careful interpretation of the text. In some texts, agreed-on structures have been found. Other texts are still disputed. The texts of the New Testament employ literary techniques akin to the ancient Greek literary culture, which is more like our own and therefore less problematic.

Another distinctive feature of biblical literature is its poetry. About 40 percent of the Hebrew Bible is shaped as poetry; in the New Testament there are several short poetical sections inserted in the prose text. The main feature of the biblical poetry is so-called parallelism: In each pair of successive lines, the second line repeats the thought of the first line in different words. It is a "rhyme of thoughts" instead of a rhyme of words. An example from Psalm 8:4:

> What is man that you are mindful of him,
> And the son of man that you care for him?

The main issue of biblical poetry is that the two lines of a parallelism should not be interpreted independently of each other but should be seen as a conceptual unity.

For more information on the literary features of biblical texts, see POETRY, BIBLICAL; STRUCTURES, LITERARY.

Many Books, One Book: How Everything Fits Together

THE CANON OF THE HEBREW BIBLE/ OLD TESTAMENT

Canonical approaches not only read individual passages in the light of the canon but also try to see the whole canon as a unified whole. For the Hebrew Bible, this can best be done by following the order of books as it is given in the Jewish tradition.

The first part of the Hebrew Bible consists of the five books of Moses: Genesis, Exodus, Leviticus, Numbers, and Deuteronomy. It is also called Pentateuch, Law, or Torah. The book of Genesis relates the prehistory of Israel, from the creation of the world until Jacob, whose name is also Israel, and his family. The books Exodus, Leviticus, and Numbers should probably be seen as a unified literary work. It deals with the call of Moses and the liberation of the Israelites from slavery in Egypt. At Mount Sinai, God makes a covenant with Israel. From now on, Israel stands in a unique relationship with God. Deuteronomy is fashioned as a long speech of Moses, containing his last will for the people. Moses repeats the essential events and contents of the Sinai covenant, preparing the people for entering the land of Canaan.

The Pentateuch is closed by a text pointing to the overarching authority of Moses (Deuteronomy 34:10–12). Apart from the historical statement made, a canonical statement is also implied: As no human being could ever be nearer to God than Moses, so no biblical author could ever claim to have higher authority than Moses. The passage therefore has the function of a seal underscoring the authority of the Pentateuch. According to this function, the passage is called a *canonical phenomenon*.

The next four books are the so-called Former Prophets of the Hebrew Bible: Joshua, Judges, Samuel, and Kings. These books describe the conquest of Canaan and then the era in which Israel was ruled by the so-called judges. After that was the era of the Israelite kingdom. The people's disobedience toward the Lord finally led to the destruction of the kingdom by the Assyrians and the Babylonians.

These four books are each a literary work on its own. At the same time, they stand in a strong chronological and thematic relationship to each other. It is even possible to understand the books from Genesis to Kings as a great unified narrative comprising the whole history of Israel from the creation of the world until the Babylonian exile.

Interestingly, the beginning of the book of Joshua contains a passage that is a counterpart to the ending of the Pentateuch discussed previously. Joshua is admonished there to keep strictly to the "book of the Law" of Moses in all his ways (Joshua 1:7–8). This statement again carries a canonical overtone: The Pentateuch forms the basis for all subsequent events. Blessing and curse in the history of Israel are already preordained in the Sinaitic covenant. The history of Israel as related in Joshua, Judges, Samuel, and Kings can only be understood properly on the basis of the book of the covenant.

After this block of historical narrative in the Christian Old Testament, there follow more historical books: Chronicles, Ezra, Nehemiah, and Esther. However, these books obviously do not join the preceding books, either chronologically or thematically, and only for formal reasons (genre) are they put in this sequence. The Hebrew Bible, in contrast, maintains the inner logic by continuing instead with the prophets who are, according to

the tradition, called the Latter Prophets: Isaiah, Jeremiah, Ezekiel, and the books of the Twelve Prophets.

The prophetic books form a homogeneous group from a literary and thematic point of view. The prophets accompany the people of Israel from the time of the kingdom onward. They criticize disobedience toward the Lord. They announce God's judgment and salvation over Israel but also over the other nations. The prophetic message is fully based on the announcements of blessing and curse in the Pentateuch.

At the end of the last prophet book there is a text that points out the importance of Moses and Elijah (Malachi 4:4–6). Analogous to the conclusion of the Pentateuch, this text can be seen as a canonical phenomenon binding together and concluding the first two canon parts, the Law and the Prophets, with Moses and Elijah the representatives of each.

The third canonical part of the Hebrew Bible is called the Writings. The order of books in the Writings varies considerably in the different editions. In the Jewish tradition, the following order is said to be authoritative: Ruth, Psalms, Job, Proverbs, Ecclesiastes, Song of Solomon, Lamentations, Daniel, Esther, Ezra-Nehemiah, Chronicles.

The Psalter, the first extensive work of the Writings, begins in Psalm 1 with a reference to the Law of Moses, which is very similar to that found in Joshua 1:7–8. In this way, the Psalter, and in a way also the Writings in total, refers to the Pentateuch. Therefore, the Law forms the basis of the whole Hebrew Bible, and the Prophets and the Writings rest on it, sharing the same importance. Today, several scholars see Psalm 1 as a canonical phenomenon, independently of the fact that the Psalter is not always placed at the beginning of the Writings. (In the talmudic order given, the small booklet of Ruth can be seen as an introduction to Psalms because it prepares for the role of David and his kingdom, which is a prominent theme in the Psalter.)

In most of the Hebrew tradition, the book of Chronicles forms the conclusion of the Bible. Since Chronicles virtually comprises the whole biblical history from Adam until the return from exile in

Egypt; it functions there as a concluding summary of the whole Hebrew Bible. Several scholars see Chronicles as a canonical phenomenon and suggest that the book was written with the deliberate purpose of summarizing, concluding, and sealing the canon of the Hebrew Bible. This thesis cannot be proven historically—as we do not have any knowledge of the people who closed the canon—but it is plausible from the textual considerations: A book such as Chronicles put at the end of the Hebrew Bible would almost automatically be understood in such a way.

The other books of the Writings, according to the Talmud, can possibly be structured into a "wisdom series" Job-Proverbs-Ecclesiastes-Song of Solomon and a "national-historical series" Lamentations–Daniel–Esther–Ezra-Nehemiah. Both sequences consist of four books (Ezra-Nehemiah is one book in the Hebrew Bible). Both start with sorrow and end with joy. The first series describes the way of the individual with God; the second series describes the way of the people back to God.

THE CANON OF THE NEW TESTAMENT

Whereas the Hebrew Bible is structurally and theologically based on the Sinaitic covenant, the New Testament centers on the "new covenant" (Luke 22:20) that Jesus makes through his crucifixion and resurrection with all who believe in him. From this new covenant, Christians derived the term *New Testament* (via the Latin *testamentum*).

The Hebrew Bible, in turn, is called the Old Testament. This term, however, is sometimes used in a derogatory manner. From the New Testament itself, this cannot be justified. For the first Christians, the Old Testament was the revelation of God and therefore of highest authority. For example, the New Testament letters often quote Old Testament passages even when they explain the New Testament faith. The New Testament understands itself, not as replacing the Old, but rather as demonstrating how the Old has achieved its definite fulfillment in Jesus Christ.

The unity of the New Testament mainly consists in its message. All texts have as their subject Jesus Christ and his mission, in one way or another.

The New Testament begins with the four so-called Gospels: Matthew, Mark, Luke, and John. These texts relate the teaching and the ministry of Jesus, putting an emphasis on the Passion of Christ. The first three gospels are very similar to one another. They often report the same incidents, sometimes with slight variations. Therefore, they are called the Synoptics (literally, "see them together"). The Gospel of John is of a different character. The interpretative and spiritual moment is stronger in John than in the other three Gospels. However, some incidents of the ministry of Jesus are reported in all four Gospels.

After the four Gospels is a text dealing with the beginnings of the Christian church, the Acts of the Apostles. This book was written by Luke. Originally, it was the sequel to Luke's gospel. In the canon, however, the two works have been separated to keep the four Gospels together, making the more interpretative John the last.

Detailed theological explanations of the life, suffering, and resurrection of Jesus are found in the New Testament letters. First are the letters of the apostle Paul addressed to churches: Romans, 1 and 2 Corinthians, Galatians, Ephesians, Philippians, Colossians, and 1 and 2 Thessalonians. Then follow letters of Paul addressed to individuals: 1 and 2 Timothy, Titus, and Philemon. Then follow letters written by other authors: Hebrews; James; 1 and 2 Peter; 1, 2, and 3 John; and Jude.

The central idea conveyed in the letters is that Jesus Christ, although he was without any sin, freely chose to die on the cross, in order to redeem the sins of humanity on their behalf. He rose from the grave and ascended into heaven, being the head of the church of all who believe in him. Additionally, the letters contain instructions on how to be a Christian in everyday life.

The New Testament is closed by the Revelation of John. The book deals with the final judgment day and the beginning of God's new creation. In its last chapters, it contains many allusions to the first chapters of the Hebrew Bible, thus forming an INCLUSIO framing the whole Bible.

See also in Part III: NEW TESTAMENT, HEBREW BIBLE, RELATIONSHIP WITH THE QUOTATIONS; SYNOPTIC GOSPELS.

PART II

Books of the Bible
A–Z

Acts of the Apostles

The book of Acts describes some foundational events in the history of the Christian movement between the years 30 and 62 C.E. As the author indicates in his opening words, it is the second volume of two books. There is general agreement that the earlier book is the Gospel according to Luke. Not only are both books dedicated to the same person, Theophilus, but the resemblances between them in theological outlook, in narrative style, and in plot device are overwhelming. Because Acts is the second volume of Luke to Theophilus, according to ancient conventions the preface to the first book (Luke 1:1–4) is the prologue to the twofold work.

In the canon of the New Testament, Acts is most important as a bridge between Jesus and the Gospels on the one hand and the earliest church and the epistles on the other. It introduces us to Paul, the author of the 13 epistles that follow it.

Although it was already known at the end of the second century, the title "Acts of the Apostles" is not original. In fact, this title is quite deceptive as it leads readers to expect stories about many or all apostles, whereas in actual fact the narrative focuses on Peter and Paul alone. The author leaves many things unsaid, such as how the gospel was transmitted to ROME, EGYPT, or PERSIA. No wonder that in later times many stories were written to supplement the "facts" Acts did not include; most of these, however, are legendary. In view of the opening words in 1:1–2 it has been suggested that "Acts of the exalted Jesus" would have been a better title. These words create the impression that Jesus is still as much the protagonist here as in the first volume. After his ascension he acts in absentia via apostles such as Peter and Paul. It has also been suggested that Acts is about the acts of the HOLY SPIRIT, who is frequently mentioned as the driving force behind the growth of the church.

To its later readers Acts is anonymous, but the dedication to Theophilus implies that the intended readers knew the author. (On Theophilus, see Luke.) Over Theophilus's head the author is surely addressing a generally Christian audience. The author is usually given the name Luke on the basis of the title of the third gospel. Later tradition associates him with the towns of Antioch (see on 11:28 below), Troas (16:8–9), and Rome (28), but that is little more than speculation. The date of writing is hard to determine, but considerations given in the entry on Luke lead us to prefer a date before 70 C.E., not long after the last events described.

Acts is well written; the author consciously imitates the style of existing biblical narratives such as Deuteronomy, Ezra, and Nehemiah. It is not easy to point out any one reason for its composition. There are apologetic elements in the book, such as the emphasis on the church's continuity with Judaism and the behavior of its members as citizens of the Roman Empire. Another aim may have been the strengthening of the church in the face of opposition.

It is likely that in writing a long historical narrative such as this the author used preexistent sources, but the uniform style of Acts gives nothing away about this. Many scholars argue that the author of the Gospel of Luke used Mark's gospel and probably the lost source Q. In writing Acts, Luke probably had existing documentation in particular for the first part of the book. As Paul's traveling companion, he may have been with the apostle during his imprisonments in Jerusalem and Caesarea, as suggested by the use of the we-form in chapters 21 and 27. (The we-passages are discussed in the commentary that follows.) During that period of several years (58–60 C.E.) Luke would have been able to meet eyewitnesses to the events of Acts 1–15, which had taken place some 25–30 years before. The summary passages that are identified later would have been added by Luke to connect the material he found in his sources and to impose his theological outlook. As an eyewitness to most of the events in the second half of the book, Luke may not depend on written sources for that part.

As does the gospel, Acts makes use of the Hebrew Bible in several ways. There are some 60 quotations, most of which follow the Septuagint (see BIBLE, EARLY TRANSLATIONS OF) verbatim or closely. Some 45 of those are introduced by formula expressions. There are specific concentrations of quotes in chapters 1–4, 7, and 13.

The Hebrew Bible as such is Luke's *model* for writing, and Luke-Acts can be seen as a conscious sequel to the Hebrew Bible: Luke's Greek resembles that of the Septuagint; the *we*-passages are modeled on the books of Nehemiah, Ezra, and Daniel; the Hebrew historiography in general has influenced the use of speeches and refrain lines and the emphasis on the visibility of God's hand in all that transpires.

The use of the Hebrew Bible serves at least four goals, the first of which is to show the continuity between Israel's history and the history of the church. Luke demonstrates that the church is the true people of God. Second, Jesus is shown to be the fulfillment of the Scriptures, in particular with respect to his death and resurrection. Most texts Luke uses were already seen as messianic in contemporary Judaism. Third, Luke uses quotations from Scripture to typify his main characters, and, fourth, he also uses quotations to justify events and decisions in the life of the church. All of this gives new relevance to the ancient text, as can be seen for example in 1:20 (Psalm 69:25 and 109:8) and in 2:34–35 (Psalm 110:1).

The text of Acts is more problematic than that of most other books. There exists a so-called Western version of the Greek text that is some 10 percent longer than the text that is translated in modern Bibles. The Western text has more historical and theological detail, for example, a more explicit version of the Apostolic Decree (chapter 15), and it is sexist (antiwoman). It was already known in the second century, and different explanations of its existence are given. Although some scholars argue that both versions stem from Luke, and a few even that the Western text is the original, the vast majority assume that it is a later edition. The internal evidence in fact suggests that this version was the result of revision by one or a few persons.

Acts was traditionally seen as history. In the ancient world, history normally contained supernatural elements such as miracles and prophecy. Luke mentions many names of people, areas, and nations, as well as events from secular history, and whenever his accuracy can be checked against other sources, he appears to be remarkably accurate. He correctly handles complicated Roman job titles like *governor* and *proconsul* as they were used in each city and province around the middle of the first century. Acts is even a major source for the reconstruction of the history of first-century Judaism and of Roman Asia. Comparison with the work of the Jewish historian Flavius Josephus has led to the more specific genre designation "apologetic history." Others would see the book as an ancient biography, much like the Gospels. This genre was very popular in the period in which Acts originated. Still others think of Acts as a historical monograph.

The plot of Acts is determined by the progress of the gospel from Jerusalem to Rome. The book contains many subjects and themes, such as the careers of Peter and Paul; the reliability of the Christian message; the work of the Holy Spirit; the life, growth, and organization of the church; the relationship between Israel and the emerging church; and the relationship between the church and the Jewish and Roman authorities. Different interpreters make different themes the main theme, and a conclusion is not easy to reach. The most important theological question in Acts concerns the relationship of the church to Israel and the Gentiles.

Acts is not a simple success story. Many people convert to Jesus, but many do not; Jews are less responsive than Gentiles. Luke reports on dangers and even losses such as persecution, imprisonment, martyrdom (Stephen, James), attempted murder, and storm. He is quite realistic in his picture of the early church and does not shy away from describing deceit, misunderstandings, and conflicts.

Modern research has shown that all history has its particular point of view, and it also points to the presence of novelistic aspects in Acts. As all good historians do, Luke does his best to entertain his readers, and the episodic style reflects acquaintance with novelistic story writing. Novelistic elements of Acts are the presence of elaborate courtroom scenes, dreams, suicide and apparent death, and miracles. At the same time the courtroom speeches convey an important part of the text's message, the legitimate status of Christianity and the innocence of Paul. Other novelistic elements, such as love and marriage and the proverbial happy end, are absent from Acts.

Probably the most important novelistic element in Acts is travel. Luke also pays much attention to travel in his gospel (Luke 9–19). The author shares this interest with much contemporary pagan literature, whereas the Jews hated the sea and Paul's letters hardly mention the topic. Many Greek authors wrote descriptions of sea voyages, e.g., Scymnus of Chios and Arrian. For the Jewish view of the sea, see "Water" in C. Brown, ed., *The New International Dictionary of New Testament Theology* III, Grand Rapids: Zondervan, 1971, 983; also D. E. Aune, *Revelation 17–22*, Word Biblical Commentary, Nashville: Nelson, 1998, 1,119–1,120. Luke's vocabulary for travel is enormous (see, e.g., 20:6, 20:13–15; 27), and Acts has elements in common with narratives about the founding of colonies. In Acts travel does not assist a literary motif such as separation and recovery, but it records the advance of the gospel. Paul is presented as a "man on the move." However, the idea that he makes three missionary journeys was imposed on the text by interpreters. In actual fact he spends long periods in cities such as Corinth and Ephesus (18:11, 18; 19:10).

Other cities that play a major part in the narrative are Jerusalem, Antioch, and Rome. Antioch is the first strong church with believers from a non-Jewish background, and it becomes Paul's sending church to which he returns after his first two journeys. Jerusalem and Rome are in a kind of polar tension as Luke documents how the gospel moves from the one to the other. Yet this polarity should not be exaggerated, for the two cities do not exclude one another: Luke never reports the destruction of Jerusalem in 70 C.E., and he is quite positive about its church.

The style of Acts is expressed in good but not overly complicated Greek. Many events are not dated, and careful study shows that there are large gaps between some episodes. The book contains some repetition, the most obvious example of which is the story of Paul's conversion, which occurs in chapters 9, 22, and 26. Yet Luke never just repeats information; he always introduces variation and places different emphases. He makes much use of pairs, which enables the reader to compare charac-ters in the narrative (see earlier discussion on Peter and Paul).

Greek historians normally included speeches in their narratives. No less than a quarter of Acts consists of long speeches (sermons) by Peter (six), Stephen and James (one each), and Paul (seven) and many shorter speeches. In other places (e.g., 4:33; 14:1, 3) Luke refrains from including a speech and just summarizes the activities of the apostles. Together these summaries add considerably to our knowledge of the content of the apostolic preaching.

The speeches are often the focal point of an episode. The majority of the long speeches are missionary in outlook, but several are spoken in defense against false accusations. In view of their length—even the longest can be read in a few minutes—and of their stylistic similarities with the rest of the text, the speeches can be seen as summaries of what was actually said. This, too, is in line with Greek historians' practice, which did not always include verbatim reporting. It is nonetheless striking how in every situation appropriate words are spoken: In a synagogue Paul argues from the Jewish Scriptures (chapter 13), with simple pagans he finds common ground in talking about nature as God's creation (chapter 14), but in Athens he interacts with the belief in numerous gods and raises philosophical issues (chapter 17). All missionary speeches mention the love and the mighty deeds of God, whereas the coming judgment has a place in no more than half of them. All mention the Resurrection.

In terms of narrative perspective, the narrator is an all-knowing person. At certain stages he steps into the story in the form of a *we*-passage, but only as an unidentified member of a group. The pace of the narrative shows considerable variation. Much detail is provided in most of the longer episodes, which can take up to an entire chapter. Yet whole periods are only briefly summarized, e.g., the activity of the scattered believers (8:1, 4; 12:24) and Paul's years in Ephesus and beyond (19:10). No details are provided about major events such as the death of James (12:2) and the way Paul and Barnabas survive a stoning (14:19–20).

Very interesting are the so-called *we*-passages, which occur in 16:10–17, 20:5–15, 21:1–18, and

27:1–28:16. Here the third-person narrative suddenly changes into first-person plural narrative, so that it seems that the narrator becomes a character in the story he is telling. Just as suddenly as these transitions occur, they come to an end again. There is no equivalent to this in the entire world literature, because narrators always introduce themselves at the moment they enter their own story. In several respects, though, what happens in Acts reminds the reader of the books of Ezra, Nehemiah, and Daniel in the HEBREW BIBLE, where we find similar alternation. The difference is that in those books the name of the *I*-person is known to the readers. It has often been thought that the *we*-passages are the result of the incorporation of a preexistent source by a later author, but stylistically and theologically the *we*-passages cannot be distinguished from the rest of the book. The best explanation is that the author in a modest way intimates that he was involved in the actual events, that is to say that at certain stages he was a traveling companion of the apostle Paul and journeyed with him to Rome.

In the commentary—and in the synopsis earlier—the words *church* and *Christian* are used, but it should be borne in mind that in Acts the followers of Jesus still form one of the numerous groups within Judaism, that the name *Christians* is first mentioned as late as 11:26, and that they only began to construct their own buildings in the third century.

SYNOPSIS

For the sake of convenience we include a short chronology of the events described in Acts (all years are in the common era):

Pentecost (chapter 2)	30 or 33
Conversion of Paul (9)	ca. 35
First visit to Jerusalem (9)	ca. 37
Second visit to Jerusalem (11:30)	ca. 45
First missionary journey (13–14)	46–47
Council at Jerusalem (15)	48
Second missionary journey (15:36–18:22)	50–53
Third missionary journey (18:23–21:16)	54–58
Prisoner in Jerusalem/Caesarea	58–59
Prisoner in Rome	60–62+

There is general agreement that Acts consist of two main parts, which have many parallels. In the first part (chapters 1–12) Peter is the leading character, so it has been called Acts of Peter. The second part (13–26) focuses on Paul and could be called Acts of Paul. Here are some examples of parallels:

- Peter (5:15–16) and Paul (19:11–12) perform miracles in similar ways, their first miracle the healing of a lame person (3:1–10; 14:8–10).
- Both bring people back to life (9:36–43; 20:9–12).
- Both are involved in supernatural punishment that involves knowledge of hidden thoughts (5:1–11; 13:8–12).
- Both see a vision that calls them to preach to new people (10:17–19; 16:9–10).
- Similar summaries are used for both (2:43 and 5:12; 14:3 and 15:12).

The numerous similarities between the two parts and the two apostles are not the result of authorial inventions but of a careful selection from the traditions; they probably serve to vindicate Paul's apostleship.

Overall, Acts consists of a long string of loosely connected episodes, and numerous suggestions for further subdivision exist, with up to eight sections. We have opted for a division into four main parts.

The Beginnings of the Church (Chapters 1–5)

Luke begins with a brief preface that connects his second book with his first and repeats the dedication to Theophilus. This flows over into a much expanded repetition of the final scene from the gospel, the story of Jesus' ascension. The new elements are a dialogue between Jesus and his disciples, his commission to spread the gospel, and the appearance of angels to comfort the disciples. After a short section that lists the core group of followers (verses 13–14), the rest of chapter 1 is the story of how the unfaithful Judas is succeeded as an apostle by Matthias.

Chapter 2 contains the events on the day of PENTECOST, when the Holy Spirit descends on the followers of Jesus. As a result, Peter gives a long speech about Jesus Christ. The narrative is rounded off by a summary that states that 3,000

Peter and John healing the cripple at the gate of the temple (Acts 3:1–10), etching by Rembrandt

people become believers and describes the life of the earliest community. One day Peter and John heal a crippled person near the temple entrance, an opportunity for Peter to deliver another message to a Jewish audience (chapter 3). The Jewish leaders have the two apostles arrested, and Luke records Peter's words in their defense. In the end, the apostles are released unharmed (4:1–22), and Luke reproduces the subsequent prayer of thanksgiving of the believers.

A positive summary about great generosity within the community (4:32–35) is followed by the positive example of Barnabas and the very negative example of Ananias and Sapphira. Another summary tells about the miracles performed by the apostles, in particular by Peter (5:12–16). The apostles are arrested and tried, but at the recommendation of the Pharisee Gamaliel the only action taken is a flogging. This part of the story concludes with a short summary that emphasizes the forceful proclamation of the gospel.

Expansion in and around Israel (Chapters 6–12)

A new phase in the history of the Jerusalem church begins when seven Greek-speaking men are chosen to look after the distribution of goods to the poor (6:1–7). One of them, Stephen, turns out to be an excellent speaker, who is such a challenge to the Jews that he is arrested and put on trial. Stephen defends himself in a lengthy speech that is basically a very critical rehearsal of the history of Israel as recorded in the Hebrew Bible (chapter 7). Unlike previous occasions, this trial has no happy ending, for Stephen is stoned to death without a formal sentencing process. At this point the future apostle Paul is briefly introduced into the story as Saul (7:58; 8:1, 3): He supports Stephen's execution and begins to persecute the followers of Jesus in a very bloody way. Consequently, many believers are scattered over the country, with the unintended effect of increasing the spontaneous proclamation of the gospel.

Two episodes focus on this expansion of the church outside Jerusalem; both have Philip, another of the seven Greek-speaking leaders, as their protagonist. The first takes place in SAMARIA, where many people are converted through Philip's preaching and accompanying miracles. However, a magician called Simon fails to understand what it is really about (8:5–13). In the second episode, Philip preaches the gospel to an Ethiopian eunuch on the way back to his country, in all likelihood the first black Christian (8:26–40). Both episodes include the BAPTISMS of the converts. In between Luke narrates how the apostles Peter and John travel from Jerusalem to authorize the church formally in Samaria.

Attention shifts back to Saul's persecution of believers (9:1–31). He now travels to Damascus to capture them, but on his way there he is stopped by an appearance of Jesus himself. Saul is blinded by a bright light and hears the Lord's voice. His companions have to take him into Damascus, where God sends a Christian, Ananias, to visit him. His eyesight is restored, he receives the Holy Spirit, and he is baptized. He immediately starts proclaiming Jesus in the town, but under threat from the Jews he leaves for Jerusalem and later for his hometown of Tarsus.

Peter is the main character in the rest of this section. He is shown traveling to the coastal region of Israel, where there are already disciples, and performing miracles (9:32–43). The narrator introduces us to the non-Jewish officer Cornelius, who will be the second pagan convert to Christianity after the Ethiopian eunuch (10:1–8). It takes some efforts to persuade Peter, go to Cornelius's home, for pious Jews considered such a visit a defilement, as verse 28 explicitly tells the readers. A divine vision and an invitation from Cornelius combine to convince the apostle that he has to take this step (10:9–23). Once he arrives there, his preaching is highly effective: The Holy Spirit is given to Cornelius and his companions, who are subsequently baptized (10:24–48). Back in Jerusalem Peter is forced to defend his behavior, and the readers get a summary of the preceding story (11:1–18). An intermezzo tells us that in the meantime a Christian church, which consists largely of non-Jews, is established in Antioch. The apostles send Barnabas to take a pastoral and evangelistic role; he in turn secures the help of Saul, who is still in Tarsus. Later the church in Antioch provides help for the Jerusalem church when it is afflicted by a severe famine (11:19–30; 12:25).

Chapter 12 tells how the apostle James is martyred. Peter is once more arrested as well but has a miraculous escape from prison. As a result he nonetheless leaves Jerusalem. His captor, King HEROD Agrippa, dies not much later. The "word of God continued to increase and spread" (verse 24).

Paul's Missionary Journeys (Chapters 13–20)

Another major step forward is taken when the church in Antioch releases Barnabas and Saul to be traveling missionaries. They first sail to Cyprus together with John Mark (13:1–5). Luke's brief report focuses on the conversion of the local proconsul and the punishment of a sorcerer (13:6–12). The missionaries then cross to Asia Minor, where they visit another Antioch, called Pisidian Antioch. A long speech by Paul in the local synagogue is included. The Jews who are the majority do not believe in Jesus, but many Gentiles are converted (13:13–48). However, the Jews make life so hard on Paul and Barnabas that they move on to Iconium, which they then have to flee for their lives again (13:49–14:7). After a healing miracle, the pagan population of Lystra wants to venerate Paul and Barnabas, who narrowly prevent this from happening. But no sooner have Jews arrived than the same population stones the two apostles, who only just survive. On the return journey to Antioch they strengthen the new churches (14:21–28).

A conflict breaks out over the necessity for believers who have a pagan background to observe the Jewish law, and in particular the law on circumcision. A meeting is convened in Jerusalem at which Peter, Barnabas, and Paul speak, but it is James who reaches the final verdict. The meeting records the result in a letter to the church in Antioch (15:22–35). While planning for a second missionary trip, Barnabas and Paul split up over the role of a helper, so Paul sets off with a new companion, Silas, and chooses Timothy as third man (15:36–16:5). Unable to work in Asia Minor, Paul is called in a dream to cross over into Macedonia (see GREECE) and arrives in Philippi, where a small group of people accept the new faith. When Paul heals a female slave, her owners have Paul arrested, and after torture he is locked up. During the night an earthquake opens the prison doors, but Paul does not run off. This so impresses the jailer that he converts to Jesus Christ. The next morning Paul is rehabilitated by the city magistrates before he leaves Philippi (chapter 16).

In Thessalonica Paul's work is quite successful, but jealous Jews cause him to leave the town rather quickly. The same happens in the next city, Berea: All too soon Paul and Silas have to move on. In Athens Paul wakens the interest of some philosophers and is invited to address a meeting at the Areopagus. Luke has recorded the speech, but the results are very limited, and Paul's stay is short (17:16–34). His next station is Corinth, where he lives for two years (18:1–17). A church starts to grow, including Jews and Gentiles. Nonconverted Jews ask the proconsul Gallio to declare the new movement illegal, but Gallio decides that it is an internal Jewish affair.

After a short stop in Ephesus Paul returns to Antioch—and soon sets out on his third journey (18:18–23). In an aside Luke provides some details about Apollos, who first works in Ephesus and then moves to Greece (18:24–28). Arriving in Ephesus himself, Paul first sorts out some believers who have not advanced beyond the baptism of John (19:1–7). He then begins a three-year ministry that reaches the entire province of Asia. Just when he is about to move on, a row breaks out, which Luke reports in much detail: In the city's theater the silversmiths accuse the Christian movement of threatening their business, but thanks to a shrewd city leader it all ends peacefully (19:23–41). Paul indeed departs for Macedonia and Greece, and on his way back to his base he visits Troas (20:1–6). His sermon in this town is so long that a young man falls asleep and falls to his death, but Paul restores him to life (20:7–12). At Miletus he meets with the leaders of the church in Ephesus and gives a farewell speech (20:13–37).

Jerusalem, Caesarea, Rome (Chapters 21–28)

From here the narrator focuses on five defense speeches by Paul (in Jerusalem before the crowd and the Sanhedrin; in Caesarea before Felix, Festus, and Agrippa) and two travelogues (to Caesarea and to Rome). Both journeys lead Paul to another trial in dangerous circumstances but with divine promises of protection (23:11; 27:23–25). In the speeches the resurrection of the dead plays a large role.

Paul continues his journey via Tyre and Caesarea to Jerusalem, despite repeated warnings not to go there, to which he replies that he is ready to die for his faith in Jesus (21:1–16). In Jerusalem he reports to James and the other leaders. On the final day of a seven-day stay in the temple area, Paul is attacked by a mob as a result of a misunderstanding; a group of Roman soldiers arrives in time to save his life (21:27–36). The commanding officer allows Paul to address the multitude with an apology, and he tells the story of his life up to his conversion on the road to Damascus (22:1–21). The Jews are unconvinced, and the Romans have to continue to protect Paul; at the same time they want to torture him, but his Roman citizenship comes to his rescue (22:22–30).

Paul is taken to the Sanhedrin, the Jewish council, in which he manages to set PHARISEES AND SADDUCEES against each other. A number of Jews plot to kill him, but his nephew hears about it, and the Romans are warned; as a result Paul is taken to a safer place, the Roman provincial headquarters in Caesarea (23). Here a formal trial takes place, but the Roman governor, Felix, is unable to reach a verdict, and Paul is left in prison for two years (24). Felix's successor, Festus, is faced with a Jewish request to have Paul returned to Jerusalem, which would be extremely dangerous to Paul; as a precaution Paul demands that the emperor hear his case so his trial must take place in Rome (25:1–12).

Before Paul can be sent there, Festus has a visit from King Agrippa and Queen Bernice, who are interested to hear Paul. Festus allows this as Agrippa can help him to formulate a letter to the emperor regarding Paul (25:14–27). So Paul is once more able to tell his life's story. Neither Festus nor Agrippa is impressed, but they agree that Paul is innocent (26).

Paul is sent to Rome by sea in the custody of a humane Roman officer who changes ship in Myra (Asia Minor). After slow progress, they are caught by a fall storm, which Luke describes in much detail. In the end the ship breaks up on the rocks of Malta, and all passengers are saved (27). On the island Paul survives the bite of a viper and heals the father of the Roman ruler (28:1–10). Then follows the final lap of the journey; Paul is met by Christians from Rome and escorted to the town, where he is allowed to live by himself. A trial does not take place, so over two years Paul is able to meet with many Jews and to proclaim Jesus Christ unhindered (28:11–31).

COMMENTARY

The Beginnings of the Church (Chapters 1–5)

Chapter 1 prepares the way for the breakthrough in chapter 2. Jesus' appearances (1:3) serve to prove the Resurrection. The disciples' question in 1:6 is quite understandable in light of the fact that Jesus had completed his mission and had promised the coming of the Spirit, which was a sign of the end times. Yet Jesus gives them the wider perspective of the whole world as part of God's purpose (1:7–8). The expression "the ends of the earth" does not refer to Rome but was applied to outlying countries such as Spain, Ethiopia, India, and Scythia (present-day Bulgaria). In contrast, the people present in Jerusalem at Pentecost are from the civilized world, from countries on all sides of Israel (2:9–11).

The fact that Luke never again mentions Matthias and that he was elected before the outpouring of the Spirit suggests that in fact the disciples' decision that he would succeed Judas was premature.

Some suggest that God had intended Paul to be the 12th apostle.

Luke can refer to Pentecost as a fixed festival day because it is the Jewish Feast of Weeks, which took place seven weeks after Easter/Passover (Leviticus 23:15–16; Deuteronomy 16:9–12). The Greek word *pentecost* means "fifty," referring to the 50 days after Easter. The outpouring of the Holy Spirit that took place on the day of Pentecost in the year 30 or 33 C.E. led to a radical change in character of the festival for Christians, which is still celebrated by the church. The new meaning of Pentecost surpasses that of the old festival in the same way that the Resurrection of Jesus surpasses the previous meaning of Easter. Yet whereas for the celebration of Christmas there are at least two foundational passages (the birth stories of Jesus in Matthew and Luke) and for Easter there are the Resurrection stories in all four Gospels and 1 Corinthians 15, the only foundational story for Pentecost is Acts 2.

The speech of Peter is notable for saying little about the Holy Spirit (2:15–21) and much about Jesus Christ, in particular about his resurrection (2:22–36). Acts 2:17–21 is a long prophetic reinterpretation of Joel 2:28–32; among the changes is that Joel's "dreadful day" (Joel 2:30) is replaced with "glorious day" (Acts 2:20). Luke records the tremendous growth of the church (2:41) and its health (verse 42–47); "breaking bread" is a figure of speech for the celebration of the LORD'S SUPPER (EUCHARIST, COMMUNION).

Chapters 3–5 are framed by the nearly identical summaries in 2:46 and 5:42. Acts 3:1 shows that initially the Christians continued to worship with the other Jews. Toward the end of his speech in 3:12–26, Peter refers to Jesus as the prophet promised by MOSES in Deuteronomy 18. The consequence of this identification is the threat of judgment of those who reject him, but the speech still ends on a positive note. On the role of the high priest Annas (4:5–6), see John 18:13–24.

Although the sharing of possessions is not explicitly commanded in Acts, the repeated references (2:44; 4:32–35; 4:36–37; 6:1) show that Luke sees it as a good thing to do; in his gospel he also pays much attention to issues of wealth and stewardship.

The story about the punitive death of Ananias and Sapphira, the married couple who tried to deceive the church and the Holy Spirit, is among the hardest passages in the whole Bible because upon their conviction by Peter they are not given the opportunity for repentance. It illustrates that under the new dispensation God's requirements of church life and honesty are no less stringent. Yet it is emphatically a unique event. Paul's parallel interference in 13:8–11 only results in blindness. Other New Testament passages do report grave sins, e.g., 1 Corinthians 5:1; 2 Timothy 4:14; and James 2:6–7, but there are no more reports of divine retributive intervention. The New Testament thus suggests that any retribution will take place at the final judgment (see LAST THINGS). In this sense this event at the very beginning of the history of the church parallels the deluge at the beginning of the history of the world (Genesis 6–9; see FLOOD, THE) and the death of Nadab and Abihu at the beginning of the covenant between God and Israel (Leviticus 10).

Expansion in and around Israel (Chapters 6–12)

Acts 6:1–8 describes a conflict between Greek-speaking Jewish Christians (Hellenists) and Aramaic-speaking Jewish Christians (Hebrews). It was the Hellenists who took the lead in spreading the gospel to the Samaritans and the Gentiles (8; 11:19–20), after their leader, Stephen, had been murdered. It might be intentional that 6:2 is the last time we hear about "the Twelve" apostles as a group. The seven men chosen here are often referred to as "deacons" because the word for "to serve" (*diakoneō*) corresponds to the noun *deacon*, but Luke himself never uses that label. As these seven are gifted people, their roles include much more than simple service, and they appear as the leaders of the Greek-speaking part of the church. The distribution system set up is similar to that of the Jewish group of the Essenes, whose officers combined a teaching role with care for the poor.

The fact that Stephen's face is like that of an angel (6:15) is not a romantic characterization but puts him at the level of prophets like Moses (Exodus 34:29–35) and Jesus (Luke 9:29). His speech in chapter 7 is the longest in Acts. It consists of a selective historical résumé in the tradition of Psalms 78, 106, and 135, and it is in line with the travel motif of Acts in focusing on the wandering of God's people (see PILGRIMS AND WANDERERS). After brief sections on Abraham and Joseph, verses 17–43 focus on Moses. By severely criticizing the temple (44–50) and the murder of Jesus (51–53), Stephen seals his own fate. Speeches of this type are not anti-Semitic but a form of internal Jewish polemic like that of the prophets in the Hebrew Bible. Stephen's final words echo those of Jesus (Luke 23:34, 46).

Chapters 8–11 contain a series of conversion stories. The one in 8:9–25 had an interesting effective history: It led to the term *simony* for attempts to buy and sell ecclesiastical offices for money, and it gave rise to numerous legends about Simon the Sorcerer and his conflict with Peter. In some of these Simon has become the archenemy of Peter and the founder of the sect of the Gnostics, which was very dangerous for the church in subsequent times (see EARLY CHURCH).

It is remarkable that the Samaritan (see SAMARIA) converts only received the Holy Spirit through the mediation of Peter and John (8:14–17). This does not signify that the Spirit is a second blessing given only to some Christians (see Romans 8:9), but this gift marks the formal incorporation of the first non-Jewish church into the church universal under the leadership of the apostles whom Jesus had appointed. Without this, ethnic churches might have sprung up apart from the apostolic authority.

The call and conversion of Saul (chapter 9) form the next major turning point, although its potential is only fulfilled in the second half of the book. Whereas the Jewish leaders somehow just barked at the disciples but never bit, young Saul single-handedly was a great danger to the Christian movement. This very person is now turned around and made God's best man in the first century. The narrative combines elements of an appearance story, a vision, and a call story. With its elements of divine confrontation, objection, commissioning, and reassuring sign, it reflects the call narratives of the prophets of the Hebrew Bible. Paul also steps into the footsteps of Jesus as a servant of God

(Isaiah 49:1–7), and the persecutor becomes persecuted (9:23–24, 29).

A key word in the story about Peter and Cornelius (chapters 10–11) is *send*. Peter's role as an apostle ("one sent") is on the line when in Joppa (cf. Jonah 1:3) he has to decide whether he will heed the Lord's command and let himself be sent to preach to Gentiles. The fact that he is staying in the home of a tanner (9:43, repeated 10:6) is no insignificant detail. A tanner worked with dead animals, which were ritually defiling, and Peter's staying with him reflects an initial break with Jewish legalism. Inviting Gentile visitors into the home of his host to stay for the night (10:23) was a further step in the right direction but not quite as hard as accepting hospitality from a Gentile (10:28). The main criticism leveled at Peter is exactly about this "eating with uncircumcised men" (11:3).

Acts 11:26 tells that the name *Christians* was first used in Antioch, although Luke does not specify when. As the word *christianos* is of Latin origin, it was probably invented by Roman authorities. The earliest evidence of its use stems from later times and can be found in Acts 26:28, 1 Peter 4:16, and the Roman historian Tacitus. These texts have in common that they deal with persecution of believers and that non-Jewish outsiders use the word. Luke prefers the expression "the Way" to refer to the Christian faith, as in 9:2; 19:9, 23; 22:4; 24:14, 22.

The spectacular narrative of Peter's escape from prison is surrounded by shorter stories about how King Herod kills (12:1–2) and how he is killed (12:20–25). The main story is funnily realistic, with the freed Peter banging on the door, the servant girl in her excitement forgetting to open the door to him, and the church leaders not believing the poor slave girl.

Paul's Missionary Journeys (Chapters 13–20)

Modern readers can be surprised at the slow progress made by the proclamation of the gospel. When Paul and Barnabas set out on the first organized mission trip, it is the year 46 C.E., some 15 years after the resurrection of Jesus. This lack of planned progress is largely due to the attitude of the Jewish believers who were not ready to take the gospel to Gentiles;

their negative response to Cornelius's conversion in chapter 11 is highly indicative of their attitude. In the end Barnabas and Paul are sent out by the first largely Gentile church, and in many places he visits Paul is hindered by Jews who do not want to accept Gentiles as legitimate believers.

The makeup of the leadership of the Antioch church is symbolic for times to come: It includes two people from Africa, Simon, whose other name, *Niger,* shows he was black, and Lucius from present-day Libya; Barnabas was from Cyprus and Saul from Tarsus in present-day Turkey.

When Paul is confronted with a pagan sorcerer who impedes the effects of his proclamation of the gospel, he announces a severe punitive miracle: The man becomes blind (13:9–12). The positive side effect of this judgment is that the Roman proconsul becomes a believer. God's powerful intervention suffices to convince him and probably many others with him. The remainder of chapter 13 and chapter 14 are situated in inland Turkey, not far from Paul's hometown of Tarsus. To make sense of 14:11–15, one should know about the local legend according to which the gods Zeus and Hermes had once before visited Lystra. At that time they had been ignored by all inhabitants except an elderly couple, and they had dished out appropriate punishment and reward. The inhabitants obviously do not want to make the same mistake again. As Hermes was the messenger god, Paul as main speaker would be seen as Hermes. The appointment of "elders" (14:23) means the new churches are organized according to a Jewish pattern (cf. 4:5, 11:30).

The description of the meeting in Jerusalem, known as the Apostolic Council (15), has been prepared by the story of Cornelius (10–11), which is center stage in the deliberations. Here is the main theological issue in Acts: How can Christians from a Gentile background be full members of the church? The leading role of James at the council comes as a surprise and suggests that the 12 apostles are now traveling missionaries (see also 21:18); Luke clearly has not told us all about the developments in the Jerusalem church. James's argument in 15:16–18 combines Leviticus 17–18 with Jeremiah 12:16 and Zechariah 2:11; the argument only works in Greek, not in Hebrew. In 15:23

(and again in 23:26) we see the original form of a Hellenistic letter; the other New Testament letters are Christian modifications of that form (see EPISTLE). The four requirements agreed by the council (15:20, 29) are meant to ascertain that Christians from Gentile backgrounds make a clean break with pagan religion and practice, not to impose Jewish food laws on Gentiles. That Paul has Timothy circumcised immediately after the council (16:3) may be surprising, but it is due to the fact that Timothy is legally a Jew and therefore not affected by the council's decisions, which relate to believers with a Gentile background.

In modern terms, when sailing from Troas to Philippi, Paul and his group cross over from Asia into Europe (16:11–12). As shown in 16:16, when there were insufficient Jews in a locality to have a synagogue, the Jews would meet in the open air. In this chapter and in 19:18–19 we find examples of popular divination and magical practices.

The "public accusation scenes" in Acts 16–21 (Philippi, Thessalonica, Corinth, Ephesus, Jerusalem) follow a fixed pattern: The missionaries are dragged before a sort of tribunal, charges are uttered, and there are violent protest and punishment from the crowd or the authorities.

At the heart of the story about Paul in Athens (17:16–34) is his address (verses 22–31) surrounded by audience responses (17–21 and 32–33). The address shows a good awareness of the philosophical systems of the Epicureans and Stoics, who are mentioned in verse 18. For centuries Athens had been the philosophical capital of the world, and the town's citizens are obviously proud of that legacy, although by that time Alexandria was the cultural capital of the eastern Mediterranean.

When Paul arrives in Corinth, Luke initially presents us with the exceptional situation that his work is entirely in vain (18:4–7; only paralleled in 28:23–28). In response Paul pronounces judgment on the unbelieving Jewish audience and turns to the Gentile population of the city. The Roman historian Suetonius provides confirmation of the edict of the emperor Claudius that expelled the Jews from Rome in 49 C.E.; his motive was internal strife among the Jews about a certain Chrestus, who must be Jesus Christ. This shows that by this time the gospel had arrived in Rome but that Claudius did not distinguish between traditional Jews and believers in Jesus Christ.

There is independent evidence in the form of an inscription that Gallio (18:12–17) was proconsul of Achaia in 51–52 C.E. Thanks to this we are able to date Paul's stay in Corinth and, consequently, all his journeys.

Acts 18:22–23 marks Paul's return from his second missionary journey and the beginning of the third, but the briefness of the notes shows how artificial the separation is. In fact, Paul has already begun work in Ephesus, which he has left in the care of Priscilla and Aquila (18:19–21) and to which he returns immediately (19:1). Otherwise from now on he merely revisits existing churches to strengthen them (chapter 20). The narrative about Paul's stay in Ephesus contains some quick summaries as well as longer descriptions in a way that is typical of Acts. It is evident that Paul's ministry must have had an enormous impact in Asian society.

The brief episode 20:7–12 is full of historical details. In many cities the poor lived in high-rise apartment buildings, and falling from a window was always possible. But Luke also intimates that the Christians meet "to break bread" on the first day of the week, that is, Sunday. This shows that early on the Christians moved away from observing the SABBATH, at least outside Jewish areas.

Paul's farewell speech to the Ephesian elders is the only speech in Acts to an audience of Christians (20:18–35). It can be read as an apology but also as a set of valuable instructions for Christian leaders. In all this it follows the conventions of the ancient farewell address.

Jerusalem, Caesarea, Rome (Chapters 21–28)
In these final chapters, nothing is said about physical suffering; in fact, the reader has the impression that Paul is safe and quite comfortable in prison. He appears to have a high social status, which is not easy to square with his occupation as a lowly tentmaker (18:3). His speeches in self-defense turn into opportunities for unhindered proclamation of the gospel, and the Romans who hear him all agree that he is innocent.

At the end of his "third missionary journey," Paul does not return to Antioch. He knows he has to travel to Jerusalem and face major problems there (20:22–24). "The brothers" listen to his enthusiastic reports (21:17), but the leadership ("James and the elders") coldly tell him that many Jewish Christians do not believe that his mission has been faithful to the Jewish law. Paul is asked to prove himself at considerable financial cost, and he does indeed humiliate himself in order to be to the Jews as a Jew (1 Corinthians 9:20). All goes well until non-Christian Jews from Asia wrongly assume he has taken a non-Jew into a restricted part of the temple (Acts 21:28–29; the temple had several different courtyards, and only the outer one was accessible to non-Jews). Much as Stephen, whom he helped to kill, had, he now finds himself faced with a bloodthirsty Jerusalem mob. Unlike many times before, on this occasion Paul does not manage to escape his Jewish foes, whose "Away with him" (21:36) resembles the cries against Jesus (Luke 23:18, 20).

In Paul's own version of his conversion story (chapter 22; chapter 9 is in the third person) the emphasis is on the objective, visual aspects of the event. In 21:40 and 22:2 Luke calls the language spoken by Paul Hebrew, but it is probable he means Aramaic, which was the common language of the Middle East from 539 B.C.E. till 630 C.E. As a Jew Paul spoke and wrote Greek but also Aramaic (cf. Philippians 3:5; see BIBLE, LANGUAGES OF).

After rescuing him, the Roman officer does not know what to do with Paul: The Jews want him dead, but he appears to be innocent (22:30; note the similarity with Pilate's position vis-à-vis Jesus). Moreover, as a citizen by birth, Paul is higher in status than the officer, who had bought his citizenship (22:26–29). The officer takes Paul to the Sanhedrin not to be tried but to understand the accusation leveled against him; however, the behavior of the Sanhedrin is no better than that of the mob in the temple. Paul's failure to recognize the high priest (23:5) might be due to bad eyesight but is more probably mock-ironic: Somebody who behaves so badly cannot be the high priest of Israel. As a consequence of this failed hearing, the Romans keep Paul in precautionary custody.

The harbor town of Caesarea, which is the setting of 23:31–26:32, had been built by HEROD the Great, and from the first century C.E. it was the capital of the Roman province of Judaea. For that reason, the governors such as PILATE, Felix, and Festus resided in the town. Remains of the Roman palace in which Paul was held captive (23:35) have been found. The language used by the lawyer Tertullus (24:2–8) is excellent judicial Greek.

Chapter 25 contains an interesting narrative order: What is briefly related by the narrator in verses 7–12 is repeated in more detail in the words of one of the characters in verses 14b–21. Paul's appeal to the emperor is neither an act of great trust in the Roman judicial system nor an easy way to get to Rome but a desperate attempt to escape lynching by the Jews in Jerusalem. Luke calls the king who visits Caesarea "Agrippa" to distinguish him from the "Herod" in chapter 12. They were father and son, otherwise known as Herod Agrippa I and Herod Agrippa II, respectively. The son was a good king over areas north of Israel at the time when Judaea was ruled by incompetent Roman procurators, among them Felix (52–60 C.E.) and Festus (60–62). Bernice was the sister of the younger Agrippa and later the mistress of the future emperor Titus.

In chapter 26 we have the third version of Paul's Damascus road conversion story, this time with extra emphasis on the threat he posed to the Christians and with an added proverb in verse 14—a proverb known from Classical Greek literature. Ananias is omitted this time.

In chapter 27 Paul shows skills as a seafarer, a characteristic more common of Greeks than of Jews. With his great gifts and personal skills, he actually controls the ship and the entire progress of the trek to Rome. Ancient geographers have left us detailed information about the sailing season, which was strictly limited to the summer period. During the winter months the Mediterranean was effectively "closed," and 27:9 suggests a date too late in the year to guarantee a safe journey. The three months spent on Malta mentioned in 28:11 must roughly be November and December 59 C.E. and January 60 C.E. From Malta the journey is the normal one.

At the historic level, the gospel had preceded Paul to Rome, as can be seen not only from verse 15 but also from 18:1–2 and from the Epistle to the Romans. It is unknown how this had happened, but there is no authoritative evidence that the apostle Peter had been involved. At the narrative level, the end of Acts is a masterpiece. No doubt the first readers knew the outcome of Paul's trial, but Luke never tells us. Instead he focuses on Paul's freedom to speak the word of God in the heart of the Roman Empire; the Greek word for "without hindrance" is in fact the last word of the text (therefore correct in the New Revised Standard Version). The final episode both looks back to 1:3 and 1:8 and forward to God's future. Acts 28:23–28 is only the second time Luke tells about persistent unbelief in Paul's entire audience (cf. 18:4–7). In response, Paul quotes the harsh words from Isaiah 6:9–10 that were also on the lips of Jesus in Matthew 13:14–15. Yet the judgment here is only a threat and later repentance remains an option.

CHARACTERS

In Acts nearly 100 people are introduced by name, and many more by their office or role only. Several women play positive minor roles, such as Mary the mother of Mark (12:12), Lydia (16:14–15, 40), and the four daughters of Philip, who are prophetesses (21:9).

Barnabas   Barnabas is a totally positive and supportive person from the moment he first appears at the end of chapter 4 until his silent exit at the end of chapter 15. He is a great help to the churches in Jerusalem and Antioch as well as to Saul and John Mark. He is mentioned before Saul until that person becomes Paul in chapter 13 and takes the lead. Luke's realism can be seen in the fact that he tells us frankly about the split between Paul and Barnabas over John Mark, in which Barnabas is the more forgiving person.

James   James is the brother of Jesus who is mentioned in Matthew 13:55 and is to be distinguished from James, the brother of John, who was one of the TWELVE DISCIPLES (Acts 1:13; 12:2). Initially he has a small role, and Acts 1:14 does not even give his name. Acts 12:17 signals his importance, and in chapter 15 and in 21:18 he appears as the leader of the Jerusalem church; see also 1 Corinthians 15:7 and Galatians 1:19; 2:9, 12. The historian Josephus tells us that he was killed by the Jews in 62 C.E. The New Testament contains a letter written by him.

Paul   In Acts the "Apostle of the Gentiles" is first introduced under his Hebrew name *Saul,* which is changed into the Latin *Paul* at the beginning of his first missionary journey (13:9). Luke does not explain the change.

Luke describes Paul as a Roman citizen and someone who easily mingles with the higher classes (13:12; 19:31; 24:24; 25:22–23). These characteristics contribute to the rise of Christianity to a position as a respected religion. Unlike what a first reading of Acts suggests, Paul does not just travel around aimlessly; he plants churches in strategic cities where he spends much time and that he revisits in a strategic way. Sometimes, but not always, the narrator notes that Paul's plans were led by the Holy Spirit.

The final section of the book shows up many parallels between Paul and Jesus, as it describes Paul's entry in Jerusalem, his arrest, his trial (despite his innocence), and his suffering and (near-) death. The introductory 21:11–14 resembles Jesus' struggle in Gethsemane: "The Lord's will be done" (21:14 = Luke 22:42). The shipwreck is Paul's passing through darkness, and in Rome he is as resurrected. One-fourth of Luke's gospel and of Acts is taken up by the respective "trial and death" stories.

Peter   In the first part of Acts Peter is the leading apostle and the spokesperson of the church on numerous occasions. This role is in line with the task Jesus Christ gave him (Matthew 16:18). The events culminate in his preaching of the gospel in a pagan house (chapters 10–11) and his miraculous release from prison (chapter 12). When Paul takes center stage, Peter disappears from sight.

Philip   One of the seven leaders chosen in chapter 6 who are often called "deacons," he is not to be confused with the apostle Philip, who is not mentioned in Acts after chapter 1. Philip plays a key role in the early period of the church when it struggles to begin its missionary activity.

Priscilla and Aquila   In Corinth Paul meets Priscilla and Aquila, a Jewish couple who have just arrived from Italy, having been ordered to leave the city of Rome by the emperor Claudius. Almost certainly Priscilla and Aquila were Christians at that time, because they immediately become Paul's helpers. This implies that they were already converted in Rome. After 18 months of cooperation they depart together with Paul for Ephesus, where Priscilla and Aquila teach the learned Jew Apollos about the gospel. It is remarkable that Luke consistently mentions the woman, Priscilla, before her husband, implying her superior position. For this reason a famous theologian suggested that she was the author of Hebrews. According to Romans 16:3, the couple had returned to Rome by the time Romans was written, about 57 C.E.

Romans   For Luke the Roman Empire forms a beneficial environment for the development of the Christian movement. Persecution originates from pagan crowds (16:19–24; 19:23–41) and more often from the Jews, not from the Roman authorities. Many Romans in the story are "good characters," such as Cornelius (chapters 10–11); the proconsul Sergius Paulus, "an intelligent man," who becomes a Christian (13:7–12); and the tribune Claudius Lysias, who saves Paul from the Jerusalem mob (21:31–36).

On the other hand, Luke shows how the Roman authorities consistently fail to protect the weak and to provide justice (3:13; 13:28; 18:17). In 4:25–28 he is negative about existing authorities, and in chapters 21–26 he exposes the authorities as lazy and incompetent, Felix as corrupt (24:26), and Festus as a liar (compare 25:9 with 20). In sum, there is a variety of perspectives on the Romans, and Luke paints a rather nuanced picture, steering a middle course between the positive attitude of Romans 13 and the negative view of Revelation 13.

Some scholars see Acts as an apology to the Roman government that was written to show that the church is harmless and that, as a legitimate development of Judaism, it deserves the same respect and freedom that the Romans granted the Jews. Gallio's verdict (18:14–16) would seem to support this idea: The Christians have just left the synagogue (verse 7), but Gallio still regards the issue as an internal Jewish matter. This opinion is confirmed in 23:29 and 25:19.

Amos

The PROPHECY of Amos stands third among the Minor or Lesser PROPHETS in the Hebrew Bible. However, there is considerable internal evidence that Amos was the first of the "writing prophets," as opposed to those earlier prophets, such as Samuel, ELIJAH, or Elisha, whose deeds and words are recorded as part of the historical accounts of Samuel-Kings.

The prophecy is set in the reigns of Jeroboam II of the northern kingdom of ISRAEL (793–753 B.C.E.) and Uzziah of the southern kingdom of JUDAH (792–740 B.C.E.). The only other clue as to the date of the prophecies is that the southerner Amos went north "two years before the earthquake" (1:1). We do not know exactly when this was, but the quake was so massive it was remembered 200 years later by Zechariah (Zechariah 14:5). Clearly, his mission was of limited duration—he was actually told to leave the country—and the prophecies were not written down till after the earthquake. It may well be that the original prophecies were added to—earthquake imagery is quite marked in the written text—and also applied to the southern kingdom in places (2:4; 6:1).

Most scholars, therefore, posit a date around 760 B.C.E., which would make Amos almost a generation ahead of Hosea, and longer for Isaiah and Micah. There would thus have been a gap of 40 years between the last recorded prophet to the northern kingdom, Elisha, whose death is recorded in 2 Kings 13:14–20, and the arrival of Amos. In Elijah and Elisha's day, the threat was the substitution of Baal worship for the worship of the Lord, a threat that they saw overcome (2 Kings 11:18f.). For Amos, the threat is an empty and purely ritu-

alistic worship of the Lord, together with growing social injustice, as the gap between poor and rich grew wider.

The northern kingdom was enjoying a period of prosperity, since the defeat of its northern neighbor, SYRIA, by the Assyrian Empire had given it freedom to trade and expand its borders. Prosperity seems to have led to moral decline and to a growth of ritualistic religion. Amos sees all this will lead to punishment if there is no reform. He is horrified at what he sees and prophesies destruction, and that is why he is told to leave. In fact, Amos was proved right: The northern kingdom was overrun and its capital, SAMARIA, captured and torn down in 722 B.C.E. by a resurgent Assyria.

The language is primarily poetry, highly imagistic and dramatic, using many forceful parallelisms. There are some brief prose passages, including a brief narrative interlude detailing Amos's confrontation with Amaziah, the high priest of the Bethel shrine (7:10–17).

SYNOPSIS

The prophecy falls into three sections: chapters 1–2, 3–6, and 7–9. The first two chapters consist of a brief introduction, and then a series of attacks or "woes" against neighboring countries, finishing with those against his own country of Judah and his guest country of Israel. Such WOES AND DENUNCIATIONS against neighboring countries became a feature of prophetic writing. We find similar woes in Isaiah 13–23, Jeremiah 46–51, and Zephaniah 2:4–15. The woes here are against Syria (1:3–5); the PHILISTINES (1:6–8), Tyre (1:9–10), Edom (1:11–12), the Ammonites (1:13–15), Moab (2:1–3), Judah (2:4–5), and Israel (2:6–16).

The last denunciation leads into the second section, which is a series of oracles, mainly woes but also a LAMENT (5:1–2), against various features of Israelite life, especially its social injustices and formal religion. To Amos, God is a god of righteousness and judgment, which includes the notion of justice. This is paramount, and he is appalled at how the people, especially the richer classes, seem to have lost all moral sense. On the one hand, he urges them to change their ways and see true religion as a moral activity, and, on the other, he warns them of the dire consequences of not changing. Basically, the consequences are the withdrawal of God's protection, so that they will experience economic disaster followed by military devastation and ultimately exile. However, he sees that God will restore a remnant. This "remnant theology" is one that is taken up and expanded by later prophets.

The third section is a series of visions: of locusts (7:1–3), fire (7:4–6), a plumb line (7:7–9), a basket of ripe figs (8:1–3), and shaking of pillars (9:1–4). Within the section, too, are warnings of judgment, rather more in the style of APOCALYPTIC WRITING than in the previous section (8:9–14). The conclusion, however, is a promise of future restoration (9:13–15) and the end of judgment.

Scattered throughout are also declarations of the Lord's greatness, his cosmic power, and his control over all the nations (4:13; 5:8–9; 9:5–6). Though Israel may be "chosen," there is ultimately no good reason why it should see itself as special and beyond the reach of that same punishment that will come on all unrighteous and proud nations (9:7–10).

COMMENTARY

The prophecy begins dramatically, "The LORD roars from Zion" (1:2), a phrase picked up again later as "Does a lion roar in a thicket?" (3:4) and "the lion has roared—who will not fear?" (3:8). The lion roars because there is prey (3:4), here Israel. Zion is significant, since as a southerner, Amos would see that as the true dwelling place of God, rather than the northern shrines of Bethel and Dan, set up as substitutes when the northern kingdom split off from the southern (1 Kings 12:29–33). He would be very aware, too, as a shepherd, of the "pastures of the shepherds" drying up, seeing this as an early warning of his displeasure.

The opening introduces a series of woes against the nations. They are formulaic, beginning with "Thus says the LORD," continuing with "For three transgressions . . . and for four, I will not revoke the punishment, because" and "I will set fire upon . . . that shall devour its strongholds." The woes are both specific and general: specific in the place-names and geographical features of the places, general in the sins (several are the same, as 1:6 and 1:9) and the punishment. We expect the same

formula for Israel, but after 2:6 Amos breaks the formula for other rhetorical moves.

Such formulae are common in the prophecy. "Hear this word" is one such (3:1, 4:1, 5:1); "On that day" another (3:14, 8:3, 9, 13, etc.). The prophet's intercession on behalf of Israel and God's relenting are similarly formulaic (7:2–3; 7:5–6). They are part of a deliberate and careful patterning of language that belies Amos's apparent manual occupation. His insistence he does not belong to the professional prophets is intended to distance him from their falsehood and lack of authenticity in God's sight, not to be modest about his rhetorical abilities. It raises for us the question of literary as well as divine inspiration. Some scholars would like to include here questions of editorial intervention, but, within most literatures, there are well-documented cases of apparently uneducated writers who produced poetry full of powerful rhetoric. The only evidence of editing is in two passages that could be seen as inserted later (5:8–9; 7:10–17).

Such examples of patterned rhetoric can be found in abundance in Amos. The passage already quoted about lions roaring (3:2–9) consists of a series of rhetorical questions leading up to the climax: "The LORD God has spoken / who can but prophesy?" Then follow other rhetorical moves: calling other nations to witness (3:9–10), an elaborate simile (3:12), and an "on that day" formula, describing in detail the luxury of the prosperous Israelites, which will become a sign of their punishment (3:15).

The warnings God has sent them already are arranged as lists, using parallel structures that build up powerful resonances. Amos 9:2–4 is one example; chapter 4 is another. Amos 4:1 forms a dramatic opening to the chapter, "You cows of Bashan," echoing Psalm 22:12 and turning it into an insult. The luxury demanded by the women stands in antithesis to their eventual degradation (4:2–3). Then is the first list, their empty religious rituals (4:4–5), but paralleled ironically by "go and sin": The very act of carrying out the ritual so well *is* sin, not salvation, as they suppose. Then follows the list of warnings already delivered (4:6–11): Details of natural disasters become metonymies of warning, a second series of Egyptian plagues (4:10).

Amos's ability to make telling historical allusions shows a thorough grasp of the PENTATEUCH (cf. 2:9f.; 3:1; 4:11; 5:25; etc.). The chapter is then climaxed by one of the declarations of God's cosmic power that we have already noted (4:13).

As opposed to this elaboration, Amos is able to make absolutely concise statements that resonate because we feel he has got to the very center of God's heart. Thus 5:15, 24 give us exactly what God does want, as opposed to the elaboration of the ritual God does not want: thus 3:7, the authenticity of his activity as God's messenger, as opposed to the silencing of the northern prophets (2:12).

Other rhetorical moves include plays on words. The vision of the summer fruit plays with the Hebrew word *qayits* and *qets,* meaning "the end." The New International Version tries to get the sense of this by using the word *ripe* as in "ripe fruit" but also "ripe for judgment." The place-name *Kir* (1:5) also means "nothing," while *Aven* (1:5) means "wickedness"; *Beth Aven* is a parody of *Bethel* (House of God).

The imagery works in two ways. First, we get little cameos of Israelite society in its practice of social inequality and luxury (e.g., 2:6; 3:15; 5:11; 6:4–7) and in its ritualistic worship (2:7–8; 4:4–5; 5:21–23). The two are linked in 8:4–6. Amos must have visited the country before he delivered his prophecies to have such a thorough and well-documented knowledge of its practices, as well as some of its natural disasters (4:7–10).

Second, we have images as figures of speech, metonymy, metaphor, and simile. Much of the imagery is natural: lions, bears (5:19), horses (6:12), birds in traps (3:5), shepherds and sheep (3:12), floods (5:8; 8:8), and so on. Some of it seems particularly centered on earthquake images: roaring and thundering (1:2), fire (5:6; 7:4), unnatural darkness (5:8, 18), walls and buildings flattened (5:9), the land itself heaving and shaking (9:5, 9), and flooding (9:6). As has been suggested, these images may have been added after the experience of the real earthquake. Or they could have reflected Amos's experience of seeing military devastation. He is very aware of military defense and how it can be torn down (e.g., 1:4; 2:5; 3:10, 11).

It has been said that Amos has "rhetorical mobility and thematic restraint." The result is an intense and dramatic presentation of human sin and God's greatness.

CHARACTER

Amos A shepherd from the southern kingdom, from the village of Tekoa, in the high plateau country south of Bethlehem, he also describes himself as a shepherd and a tender of sycomore-figs, a small variety of fig that usually grows at a lower altitude than that of Tekoa. It is surmised, therefore, that he was somewhat itinerant in his lifestyle. He makes it clear that he is not a professional prophet. Such people did exist in "schools of prophets," and certainly such schools are mentioned in connection with Elijah and Elisha. He was therefore a southerner sent to prophesy to the northern kingdom, especially to the religious shrine of Bethel (see 1 Kings 12:29–33). His preaching was considered subversive, and he was told to leave (7:12). He is considered the first of a series of "prophets of righteousness," who include Hosea and Micah.

Baruch

Baruch is a book of the Apocrypha, recognized as deuterocanonical (i.e., belonging to the secondary canon, by the Catholic and Orthodox Churches; see APOCRYPHA AND PSEUDEPIGRAPHA). There is no Hebrew version of it at all. It appears first in the Septuagint, and from there it was taken into the Vulgate, located between Jeremiah and Lamentations (see BIBLE, EARLY TRANSLATIONS OF). It has proved impossible to date. It purports to be written shortly after the first EXILE from JERUSALEM under Nebuchadnezzar (2 Chronicles 36:6–10), perhaps at the time of Zedekiah's visit, recorded in Jeremiah 51:59–64 around 593 B.C.E. But references to Belshazzar (1:12), the last king of BABYLON, suggest a later date. The time covered by the book is the exile, as in the books of Daniel and Esther. Parts of Baruch are very similar to parts of Daniel, in fact. It could have been written either later in the exile or some time thereafter. The other reason to remove it from the time of the fall of Jerusalem becomes obvious if we compare it to Jeremiah or Lamentations. The ordered calm and emotional distance, the theological maturity and vision of Baruch are light-years away from the chaotic distress occasioned by the last days of Jerusalem as recorded by Jeremiah.

SYNOPSIS

The book falls into two parts: 1:1–3:8 are prose; 3:9–5:9 is poetry. They may have been written by different individuals and compiled together later. The first part purports to be a letter to those left in Jerusalem. In fact, it turns out to be a rather magnificent PRAYER of confession of the sins that led the Israelites into exile. The second part can be divided further into two separate poems. The first (3:9–4:4) is a HYMN of praise to Wisdom (see WISDOM LITERATURE). The second poem (4:5–5:9) is prophetic, looking forward to the return to Jerusalem and full reconciliation with God.

COMMENTARY

The prose part appears to be a letter (1:10) from the exiles to be sent back to the inhabitants of Jerusalem, together with gifts of money and some of the temple equipment taken by Nebuchadnezzar. But the letter soon merges into a full confession by the writer, made on behalf of all Jews, with the devastation of Jerusalem and a total exile now assumed as having happened. There are also confessions in the Hebrew Bible, most notably Daniel 9; and statements of what would happen if the covenant with God were breached, as in Leviticus 26:27–45 and Deuteronomy 28 in the PENTATEUCH, and 1 Kings 8:22–61, Solomon's prayer of dedication of the temple. Baruch's confession appears to be a very well composed prayer taking elements from all the passages cited. And although the writer may not, after all, have been close to Jeremiah, there are significant references or echoes of his prophecy also. The same phrase is used by Jeremiah at least four times (7:34; 16:9; 25:10; 33:11).

Much of the prayer has the feel of ritual, as there are a number of repetitive patterns, as in a litany (e.g., 1:18; 2:10; 3:2). It maintains an elevated style and is suitably general, in complete contrast to the detailed descriptions and images to be found in Lamentations. Only references to mothers eating their own children (2:3) have that sort of vividness, but even here, the language suggests they are taken from Leviticus 26:29 rather than Lamentations 2:20. However, there are a few passages that seem original to the book, such as 3:5–8, that suggest an actual situation.

The first poem, in praise of Wisdom, reflects several other apocryphal books also devoted to Wisdom, namely, The Wisdom of Solomon and Sirach (or Ecclesiasticus). In the Hebrew Bible, Proverbs 8:1–9:6 is the main passage that is a PERSONIFICATION of Wisdom. The poem is carefully structured: It is book-ended by an actual problem and an actual solution (3:9–14; 4:2–4). Then there are two blocks of verse, the first starting and ending with rhetorical questions "Who?" (3:15, 29–31). The first question then gives three groups of people who have not found wisdom (3:16–19, 20–23, 24–28). The second block answers: It is God the Creator who has found Wisdom and who has enshrined it in the Law.

The second poem is prophetic, consisting of a complaint (4:9–29) made by a personified Jerusalem, though in far different tones from Jerusalem's LAMENT in Lamentations 1. The remainder of the book is the prophetic reply, which echoes Isaiah 65:18–25 particularly, also Isaiah 35:10, 51:11; and Jeremiah 31:8–9. The tone rises to a glorious climax of hope in a full restoration of Jerusalem's children to her. In both poems, the typical Hebrew structuring of parallelism (see POETRY, BIBLICAL) is evident, though the imagery is either generalized or borrowed.

CHARACTER

Baruch The supposed author, Jeremiah's secretary (Jeremiah 36:4, 32). There is no biblical evidence he ever went to Babylon, though one tradition suggests he died there. However, his probable brother, Seraiah (both are named sons of Neriah), did go to Babylon with King Zedekiah as quartermaster, ca. 593 B.C.E. Jeremiah had given Seraiah a scroll to be read to those already in exile. Other works were attributed to Baruch, such as the Apocalypse of Baruch.

Bel and the Dragon

See Daniel.

1 and 2 Chronicles

The book of Chronicles is a historical-theological narrative combining all of biblical history from the CREATION of the world to the restoration of Israel after the EXILE in one coherent picture. The task of the chronicler is to explain to the postexilic community who they are and what "Israel" should mean to them.

Chronicles in large part consists of material that can also be found in 1 and 2 Samuel, 1 and 2 Kings, and some other books of the Hebrew Bible. This often leads to confusion among readers who plan to read through the whole Bible from the beginning. The continuous flow of narrative from Genesis to Kings suddenly stops when one arrives at Chronicles. Here the story starts all over again with Adam, and after nine awkward chapters of genealogies, the history of the kings, which one thought one had just dealt with, is presented in detail again.

This duplication of content raises the question as to the nature and purpose of the book of Chronicles. Why has this book been written at all? In scholarship, three different positions have been taken:

First, traditionally, Chronicles was understood as a parallel historical tradition that was kept in the Bible because it has some *additional* material that is not covered by Samuel and Kings. In the tradition of the Septuagint (see BIBLE, EARLY TRANSLATIONS OF), the book therefore has been given the title "the things omitted." The placing of Chronicles after Kings corresponds to this, making it a supplement or appendix to the preceding history books.

Second, in critical scholarship, Chronicles was seen by some as an alternative account of the history of Israel deliberately written to *replace* the account of Samuel and Kings. However, it is unlikely that two works contradicting each other would become part of the same canon of Holy Scripture.

According to the third position—which is gaining more and more support today—Chronicles is a work *interpreting* other biblical texts. By putting together different passages into a new structural framework, the chronicler uncovers some overarching theological concepts and connection lines. Moreover, Chronicles extends over the whole of biblical history from creation to restoration and therefore can be seen as a theological summary of the whole Hebrew Bible. This corresponds to the Jewish order of books in the canon, where in most of the editions Chronicles does not follow Kings but rather forms the last book in the Hebrew Bible.

Chronicles starts with an allusion to Genesis, the first book of the Bible, and it ends with a quotation from Ezra-Nehemiah, the last book of the Hebrew Bible apart from Chronicles (Ezra and Nehemiah were originally one book rather than two). By this the chronicler brackets biblical literature from its beginning to its end. Some scholars therefore hold the view that Chronicles was written not only as a summary but also as the intended conclusion and sealing of the whole Hebrew canon.

It is difficult to give an exact date when the book was written. The last events recorded can be dated to approximately 515 B.C.E. Since the radical political changes of the Hellenistic age (see INTERTESTAMENTAL PERIOD) are not reflected in the book, it can be assumed that it was written before 300 B.C.E. The oldest extant manuscripts have been found at Qumran (see DEAD SEA SCROLLS).

The book of Chronicles was originally a single book and was only later divided into 1 and 2 Chronicles. The book consists of four large sections: the genealogies of Israel (1 Chronicles 1–9), the David narrative (1 Chronicles 10–29), the Solomon narrative (2 Chronicles 1–9), and the narrative of the kings of Judah until the exile in Babylon (2 Chronicles 10–36). The last two verses of the book (2 Chronicles 36:22–23) can be seen as a separate fifth section alluding to the return from exile.

SYNOPSIS

The Genealogies of Israel (1 Chronicles 1–9)
Chronicles opens with an extensive genealogical prologue covering the first nine chapters of the book.

The first section, 1:1–2:2, comprises the history of the human race from Adam onward, the spreading of the nations after THE FLOOD, and the line of descendants down to the 12 sons of Israel. The collateral lines are presented before the main lines, respectively: Japheth and Ham before Shem, Ishmael before Isaac, Esau before Jacob (Israel).

Chapters 2–8 contain genealogies of the 12 tribes of the people of Israel, ordered along a geographical round-trip, starting in the west and going southward counterclockwise. The tribe of Judah is dealt with first and in most detail of all the tribes. Chapters 2 and 4 present genealogies of Judah, framing, in chapter 3, a list of descendants of David and Solomon, who are the two main characters of Chronicles stemming from the tribe of Judah.

Advancing to the south, the next genealogy recorded is of Simeon (4:24–43). After Simeon follow the east Jordan tribes Reuben, Gad, and the eastern half of Manasseh, proceeding from south to north (5:1–26).

After about half of the geographical round-trip, the tribe of Levi is dealt with (6:1–81). Since the Levites were occupied with the worship service, they did not possess their own tribal territory. Instead, they were allocated cities throughout the country (6:54–81). The treatment of Levi is second in length only to that of Judah.

Chapter 7 continues to present the remaining tribes in the northwest and the center of the country. However, the genealogies of Dan and Zebulun are missing, though these tribes are mentioned in other passages in the book; furthermore, for the remaining tribes the rationale of the presentation order is not at all clear. Possibly, this text passage was corrupted in an early stage of its transmission. Whatever is the case, the presentation in chapter 8 closes with the tribe of Benjamin, which is located immediately north of Judah. In this way the geographical round-trip is completed.

Chapter 9 contains a list of inhabitants of Jerusalem after the Babylonian Exile. The section closes with a genealogy of the family of Saul, thus providing a transition to the following narrative.

The David Narrative (1 Chronicles 10–29)

*The Kingdom Transferred from Saul to David
(1 Chronicles 10–12)*
The narrative starts in chapter 10, in the midst of the last battle of King Saul and his army against the Philistines. Heavily wounded by the archers of the enemy, Saul takes his sword and falls on it, in order not to be taken prisoner. In the same battle, the three sons of Saul also die. God has ended Saul's kingdom, because Saul has not been obedient to him. Therefore, the kingdom is being transferred to David, God's chosen king.

Chapters 11:1–3 and 12:38–40 deal with David made king over all Israel at Hebron. There is a feast of three days' eating and drinking, and even the tribes far away in the north of the country send presents.

The report on the coronation ceremony forms a literary frame around some material thematically connected to David's kingship: a narrative on David's conquering Jerusalem, the new capital of David's kingdom, and some lists of supporters and warriors of David (11:4–12:37).

*David Prepares the Temple Service
(1 Chronicles 13–16)*
David is very much concerned about the worship of the Lord according to the Law of Moses. Therefore, he decides to take the ark of the covenant back to Jerusalem. The ark had been standing at a remote place and had been neglected for some time during the reign of Saul. On the way to Jerusalem, however, a misfortune happens. When the cart shakes, a man called Uzzah reaches out his hand to steady the ark. But God becomes angry with him for touching the ark and lets him die. David is very alarmed about what has happened. He does not want to continue taking the ark to Jerusalem and stores it at a nearby house.

The next group of events documented shows that despite the accident, the kingdom of David is still blessed by God: A foreign king sends material and carpenters to build a palace for David. As a king, David takes more wives, and he is blessed by sons and daughters. David goes into battle twice against the Philistines who had raided the country. On both occasions he defeats them. As a result, David's fame spreads throughout the neighboring countries.

Now David prepares a place in Jerusalem for the ark. He gives the order that, according to the Mosaic Law, no one except the priests and Levites are allowed to carry the ark. Also, the priests and Levites have to consecrate themselves beforehand. Furthermore, David appoints singers and musicians to accompany the procession. After all these preparations are completed, the ark is taken to its place in Jerusalem successfully. The event is celebrated with singing and burnt offerings. After that, David installs a regular worship service at the ark according to the Mosaic Law.

Nathan Announces God's Promise about Kingdom and Temple (1 Chronicles 17)

David is not satisfied with having the ark of the covenant kept inside a tent while he himself lives in a palace. So he decides to build a temple. God, however, sends him word that he should not build a house for the Lord; rather it would be the other way round: The Lord wants to build a house for him, meaning that he would establish the dynasty of David so that his offspring would reign for all time. Furthermore, God sends David word that one of his sons would be commissioned to build the temple. David is delighted at this promise and answers with a long prayer of thanksgiving.

David's Kingdom Established and Extended (1 Chronicles 18–20)

The chronicler now describes some of David's campaigns. David is victorious and subdues the surrounding countries. His power and his wealth are growing steadily. David keeps a large amount of the plunder carried off from the subjugated peoples for the construction of the temple.

The Kingdom Transferred from David to Solomon (1 Chronicles 21–29)

David decides to count the people of Israel. The census, however, is not to serve a particular purpose but only David's pride. David ignores the fact that Israel is the people of God and not his own. So God is displeased and sends a plague on Israel, reducing the number of the people. God also sends an angel to destroy Jerusalem. But as the angel is doing so, God takes pity and puts an end to it. The place where the avenging angel of the Lord stops is a threshing floor belonging to a certain Ornan. David decides that this place of mercy should be the site where the temple will be constructed. He

buys the land from Ornan, erects an altar there, and offers sacrifices.

In chapters 22:2–23:2 and 28–29 the chronicler describes Solomon made king. David entrusts Solomon with the construction of the temple and makes many preparations in order to support his son for his great task.

The report on the coronation ceremony forms a literary frame around some material of a documentary kind demonstrating that David hands over to Solomon an orderly kingdom. Chapters 23–26 deal with the personnel needed for the temple service; chapter 27 contains details on army divisions, officers of the tribes, and officials of the king.

The Solomon Narrative (2 Chronicles 1–9)

Solomon summons all his government officials at the old sacrificial altar at Gibeon in order to worship God there. At night, God appears to him and asks him what he would like to receive from him. Solomon asks him for wisdom in order to be able to rule the people of Israel. God is pleased that Solomon has not made a selfish request, so he grants him great wisdom as well as abundant riches and honor.

Solomon decides to build a temple in Jerusalem and a royal palace as well. For this he conscripts a large number of laborers and stonecutters. He asks King Huram of Tyre to send him a master craftsman to join the skilled workers of Jerusalem. He asks him also for high-grade wood from Lebanon. Solomon offers to pay him in food. King Huram agrees.

Solomon starts building the temple at the place provided for it by David. The temple house is 30 meters long and 10 meters wide. Its height is 10 meters. In front of the house, there is a vestibule. The house itself is divided into the holy and the most holy. Inside, the walls are lined with cypress, covered with fine gold, and decorated with palms and chains. For the Most Holy Place, two carved cherubim are made and overlaid with gold. The extended wings are each 2.5 meters long, so that the two figures standing beside each other extend over the whole width of the hall. Between the Holy Place and the Most Holy Place, there is a curtain of blue, purple, and crimson fabrics and fine linen with cherubim worked into it. In front of the house,

Solomon makes two giant pillars. The house is surrounded by an inner and an outer court.

Solomon also makes a large altar for burnt offerings and the so-called molten sea, a large basin for ritual ablutions. Additionally, 10 smaller basins are made, 10 golden lamp stands, and 10 tables for standing inside the temple. Many other temple vessels are also manufactured.

In the seventh month, the month of the great religious feasts, the ark of the covenant is carried into the temple in a ceremonial act. A cloud fills the temple, symbolizing the presence of God. In a solemn prayer, Solomon thanks God that the temple could be erected according to his promise. He asks God to fulfill his other promise as well, making the Davidic kingdom an everlasting dynasty. He also asks God to make the temple a place where God would answer the prayers of the people and where God would forgive sin. Even for foreigners, the temple would become a place where they could know the Lord. The dedication of the temple is celebrated for seven days. After that, the Feast of Tabernacles is celebrated for another seven days.

At night, God appears to Solomon. He confirms that the temple would be the place where he would answer prayers and forgive sins. He also confirms his promise about the Davidic kingdom. But he warns Solomon that he will reject the people if they turn away from him.

The construction of the temple takes 20 years in total. Solomon also builds a palace for himself. He rebuilds and fortifies several cities throughout the country and builds storehouses. He marries a pharaoh's daughter and builds a palace for her as well. After the temple is built, Solomon takes care to maintain a regular temple service according to the instructions and preparations of his father, David.

Solomon continues trading with King Huram. The queen of Sheba hears of the fame of Solomon and visits him. She tests Solomon's wisdom, and she is very impressed by him.

Solomon has large amounts of gold at his disposal. His merchant fleet supplies him with gold, ivory, and different kinds of monkeys. He excels all the other kings in riches and in wisdom. He reigns over a vast empire between the Euphrates River, the land of the Philistines, and Egypt. In total, Solomon reigns over Israel for 40 years. His son, Rehoboam, succeeds him.

The History of the Kings of Judah (2 Chronicles 10–36)

Rehoboam wants to be made king over Israel at Shechem. The 10 tribes of northern Israel, however, want to accept him only when he reduces the burden of taxation and compulsory labor his father, Solomon, had laid on them. But Rehoboam refuses their request, and so the northern tribes break away from him. Rehoboam becomes king only over the southern kingdom of Judah comprising the tribes of Judah and Benjamin, and the Levites, who join him.

Rehoboam and the people are not obedient to God. Therefore, God sends a punishment: In the fifth year of Rehoboam, Pharaoh Shishak of Egypt conquers Jerusalem and takes away all the treasures of the temple and of the king's palace. Rehoboam humbles himself before God, and God establishes his kingdom again. In total, Rehoboam reigns for 17 years. His son, Abijah, succeeds him, reigning for three years. After him follows his son, Asa.

Asa does what is right in the sight of God. He takes away the foreign altars and calls the people of Judah to return to the Lord. When Zerah the Ethiopian opposes him, he fully relies on the help of God. God gives him victory and a great quantity of plunder. Asa also renews the covenant with God in a ceremonial act.

The king of the empire of northern Israel opposes Judah. In order to protect himself, Asa pays the Aramites for attacking Israel so that they have to give up fighting against Judah. God, however, criticizes Asa for relying on the king of Aram instead of God. Asa is struck by a severe disease, but still he does not seek the Lord. After having reigned for 41 years, Asa dies. His son, Jehoshaphat, succeeds him.

Jehoshaphat reigns according to the commandments of God. He destroys the altars of foreign gods. He sends his officials together with Levites to teach the people the Law of Moses. Therefore, God blesses his kingdom. Jehoshaphat also establishes diplomatic relations with the northern Israelite kingdom. In doing so, however, he is partly responsible for the wrongdoing of the Israelite king, Ahab. Ahab wants to attack the city of Ramon with the help of Jehoshaphat. Jehoshaphat asks him to inquire for the word of God first. Ahab gathers 400 prophets, predicting that he would be victorious. But Jehoshaphat is still not sure about the battle. Another prophet, Micaiah, son of Imlah, is summoned. He predicts that the king would die during the fight. Ahab becomes angry and puts Micaiah into prison. Preparing himself for the battle, King Ahab disguises himself as an ordinary soldier, in order not to be attacked directly. However, during the fight, a man draws his bow at random and strikes King Ahab. Ahab dies the same evening. Jehoshaphat returns safely, but God rebukes him for having allied himself with Ahab. From that time on Jehoshaphat breaks off his relations with the northern kingdom. Now he is faithful to the LORD again. He appoints judges and urges them to obey the Mosaic Law fully.

Jehoshaphat learns that Moabites, Ammonites, and other people groups have joined in order to enter into war with Judah. In the temple, Jehoshaphat prays to God for help. Through a prophetic word, God tells him that he will protect him. The next morning, Jehoshaphat goes into battle. In the front of the army he places a group of temple singers. When they begin to praise God, God confuses the enemy troops so that they attack each other. When the army of Judah finally reaches the battlefield, they find only dead bodies and a lot of booty. In total, Jehoshaphat reigns for 25 years. His son, Jehoram, succeeds him.

After Jehoram's death, his son, Ahaziah, is made king by the people but killed after only one year of reign. Now Athaliah, Ahaziah's mother, seizes the kingdom for herself. She destroys all the royal family of the house of Judah. However, Ahaziah's small son Joash is saved. The priest Jehoiada takes care of him and raises him secretly in one of the temple buildings. After seven years, Jehoiada takes courage and summons the heads of the families of Judah. He proclaims Joash legitimate king. Athaliah is put to death. At the age of seven, Joash becomes king. He reigns for 40 years in Jerusalem. His counselor is Jehoiada the priest. As long as Jehoiada lives, Joash does what is right in the eyes of the Lord. He

decides to restore the temple and reinstates the giving of the tithes. After the death of Jehoiada, however, Joash turns to foreign gods. Jehoiada's son intervenes, but the king orders his death. He dies at the outer court of the temple. Soon after that, the Aramites rise up against Jerusalem. Although they are relatively weak, God delivers the great army of Judah into their hands. Joash is badly wounded; lying on his bed, he is killed by some of his officials. His son, Amaziah, succeeds him. He is followed by his son, Uzziah.

Uzziah reigns for 52 years. He is obedient to the Lord. He is very successful, especially in military campaigns. In the end, however, he grows proud, and that pride leads to his destruction. He enters the temple in order to make an offering that only the priests are allowed to make. For that, God punishes him with leprosy. For the rest of his life, he has to live in a separate house, and he is not allowed to enter the temple anymore. After him his son, Jotham, and his grandson, Ahaz, follow as kings of Judah.

Ahaz reigns for 16 years. He does not do what is right and turns to foreign gods. So Judah has to suffer several military attacks. Since the gods of the foreign people seem so strong, Ahaz shuts up the doors of the house of the Lord and makes altars for the foreign gods instead. When Ahaz dies, he is not buried with the other kings of Israel. His son, Hezekiah, succeeds him.

Hezekiah reigns for 29 years. He is faithful to God, reigning according to the standards of his predecessor, David. He summons the priests and Levites in order to cleanse the temple. In a ceremonial act, the temple is newly dedicated, and the regular temple service is installed again. For the first time in many years the Feast of Tabernacles is celebrated. Hezekiah even invites to the feast the people from the north, who remain after their kingdom has been destroyed by the Assyrians. But only a few answer the call. Hezekiah also destroys pagan shrines in the country and reorganizes the priests and Levites.

When Hezekiah learns that Sennacherib of Assyria is planning to attack Judah, he takes the necessary military measures to protect Jerusalem. But he also urges his military leaders to trust fully in the Lord. Sennacherib mocks the God of Israel and tries to make the people feel unsure. But God sends an angel, who kills many of Sennacherib's soldiers while they are in the camp, so that Sennacherib has to return home in shame. He goes into the temple of his god and is assassinated by some of his own sons, who had waited for him there.

Except for one single incident, Hezekiah is always faithful to the Lord. After his death, his son, Manasseh, succeeds him.

Manasseh reigns for 55 years. He does not obey the Lord. Instead, he worships other gods, following heathen practices; making his son pass through fire; practicing all kinds of soothsaying, augury, and sorcery; and dealing with mediums and wizards. He even places an idol of a foreign god inside the temple of Jerusalem. God punishes Manasseh for his disobedience: The army of Assyria captures him and takes him to Babylon. But in this time of great distress, Manasseh turns back to the Lord and humbles himself before him. God shows mercy to him and allows him to return to Jerusalem and to continue his reign. Manasseh now takes away all the foreign gods and restores the altar of God. After his death, his son, Amon, succeeds him but is assassinated after only two years.

Josiah becomes king when he is only eight years old. He reigns for 31 years. Josiah follows in the footsteps of his ancestor David, being faithful to God. He destroys the images and altars of foreign gods in Judah. He also travels into the areas of the former northern kingdom and destroys foreign idols there. After that, he repairs and restores the temple. While renovating, one of the priests finds the book of the Law of Moses. The book is read aloud to the king. Josiah informs the people of Judah about the book, and he renews the covenant between God and the people. Afterward, the Passover is celebrated according to the Law.

When Pharaoh Neco crosses the land of Judah in order to attack Babylon, Josiah unnecessarily joins battle against him. Josiah is badly wounded and dies. All Judah and Jerusalem mourn.

Jehoahaz, Josiah's son, is made king, but after three months, Pharaoh Neco deposes him and makes his brother, Jehoiakim, king instead. Jehoiakim reigns for 11 years, but he is unfaithful to God.

Nebuchadnezzar, king of Babylon, moves against Judah. Jehoahaz is taken captive to Babylon. His son, Johoiachin, succeeds him, but after three months he is also taken to Babylon by Nebuchadnezzar, who makes his brother, Zedekiah, king instead.

Zedekiah reigns for 11 years. He is disobedient to God. He rebels against Nebuchadnezzar. In Judah, foreign gods are worshipped. Time and again, the warnings of the prophets have been cast to the wind. Now the wrath of God against his people becomes so great that there is no remedy. Nebuchadnezzar destroys Jerusalem, burns the temple, robs all the treasures and vessels of the temple, and takes the people into exile in Babylon. There they have to stay and to serve him and his successors until the time of the Persians.

The Decree of Cyrus (2 Chronicles 36:22–23)

Cyrus, the king of Persia, proclaims that the God of heaven had appointed him to build a temple for him in Jerusalem. He allows the people of Judah to return to Jerusalem.

COMMENTARY

The Genealogies of Israel (1 Chronicles 1–9)

For the modern reader, genealogies are not usually very appealing, but on closer examination, they often prove to have considerable literary, theological, and sociological interest.

Genealogies, first of all, tell the individual where he or she belongs. They provide an individual of rank or office with connection to a worthy family. They define the social relationships of individuals, tribes, and peoples to one another. Biblical genealogies, in particular, demonstrate the fulfillment of God's blessing to be fruitful and multiply (Genesis 1:28); they trace lines of divine promises, for example, the promise to the descendants of Abraham (Genesis 12:2) or of David (2 Samuel 7:16); they exhibit a sense of movement within history toward a divine goal. To the informed reader, some of the genealogies even recall whole historical epochs (see 1 Chronicles 1:1–4).

The large genealogical section of 1 Chronicles 1–9 deals particularly with the identity of the people of Israel. The first chapter contains the genealogy from Adam to Israel, which is taken from the book of Genesis. The genealogy locates the history of the people of Israel in the frame of human history in general and thereby clarifies the relationship of Israel to the other nations. The theological concept of the chosen line is indicated by distinguishing it from the collateral lines and by placing the collateral lines before the main lines, respectively: Japheth and Ham before Shem, Ishmael before Isaac, Esau before Israel.

Chapters 2–8 describe the preexilic people of Israel as a mighty nation consisting of 12 tribes. Although in postexilic times only the two tribes of Judah and Benjamin formed the Jewish community, the chronicler throughout his book is interested in the totality of the 12 tribes. Two of the tribes are emphasized by length of presentation: Judah, the tribe in which the Davidic kings originate, and Levi, the tribe occupied with the ritual service.

Chapter 9, finally, contains a list of the inhabitants of Jerusalem after the EXILE (see Nehemiah 11). The postexilic community, which is the present-day community from the point of view of the chronicler, is thus put in direct continuity with the preexilic Israel.

After half a century of Babylonian captivity, the identity of the Jewish people was severely threatened. The postexilic community was very small and in danger of mixing with the neighboring nations. People felt that their present sad state of affairs was due to God's having abandoned them. To these people the genealogies of Chronicles explain who they were and where they belonged. To establish a connection between the present and the past was crucial for maintaining the identity of Israel as God's chosen people.

The David Narrative (1 Chronicles 10–29)

The chronicler presents the era of David and Solomon as the formative age of Israel's history. According to the chronicler, all later generations have to be judged against this era.

For his presentation of David, the chronicler makes use of biblical sources from 1 Samuel 31; 2 Samuel 1–24; 1 Kings 1; and some other texts. However, he does not just repeat his sources but rather arranges the material into an entirely new form. He leaves out many historical details; he likes to combine texts from different sources for thematic reasons. In some places he abridges his sources; in other places he even adds whole chapters. All this revision is done in order to draw out two theological themes considered to be decisive for this epoch: the house that the Davidic kings build for the Lord, i.e., the temple and the worship service, and the house that the Lord builds for the Davidic kings, i.e., establishing their kingdom and their dynasty.

The David narrative can be divided into five sections. The first of these, 1 Chronicles 10–12, deals with David made king over Israel. From the reign of King Saul, as it is documented in 1 Samuel 9–31, the chronicler retells only chapter 31, the last battle of King Saul, his defeat and death. The chronicler begins in the middle of the story, without any kind of introduction. He alludes to the events that had led to the rejection of Saul in only a few words (1 Chronicles 10:13–14). In places like this it becomes apparent that the chronicler assumes that his readers are familiar with the biblical history books. His interest is not to retell but to interpret: By repeating the passage about Saul's death he, in a way, gives a conclusion to the whole story of 1 Samuel 9–31: Saul is rejected by God because of his sin, but David is chosen.

After the death of Saul, David is made king over Israel in a ceremonial act. The report of the coronation ceremony is divided into two parts, 11:1–3 and 12:38–40, that form a literary frame around the rest of the text in 11:4–12:37. The material enclosed is taken from different places of the book of Samuel and joined for thematic reasons. For example, 2 Samuel 5:5 and 1 Chronicles 29:27 show that David reigned in Hebron for seven years before he took Jerusalem. Nevertheless, the chronicler places the report of conquering Jerusalem into the literary frame of the coronation ceremony, because the choosing of the capital stands in relation to the kingdom theme, regardless of the chronological sequence. The lists of David's warriors are placed here for the same reason.

The second section, 1 Chronicles 13–16, demonstrates David's interest in building the "house of the LORD," which in this instance means taking the ark of the covenant to Jerusalem and setting up regular worship there. The chronicler's report is based on 2 Samuel 6, to which, however, substantial portions of text are added that deal with the consequences of Uzzah's death. In chapter 14, the chronicler gives an answer to the possible question of whether David is to be blamed for Uzzah's accident or not. This he does by combining different accounts that all indicate that David's kingdom is still blessed by God and has not been disgraced. In chapter 15, the chronicler explains why the second attempt to transfer the ark is successful rather than the first: He reports a lot of the preparations undertaken, which show that David is now concerned to transfer the ark fully according to the Mosaic Law. In particular, only the Levites are allowed to carry the ark (see Numbers 4:1–15). After the ark is transferred to Jerusalem successfully, David institutes regular worship there. Again the emphasis is on David's concern to worship the Lord according to the Law.

The third section, chapter 17, consists mainly of two speeches: a speech of God through the prophet Nathan and an answering prayer by David. The speeches treat the two main themes of the David narrative: the house that God wants to build for David and the house that David's son is to build for God. The source text for this section is 2 Samuel 7.

The fourth section, chapters 18–20, demonstrates God's building the "house of David" by establishing his kingdom. For this purpose, the chronicler reports successful military campaigns undertaken by David, taken from 2 Samuel 8, 10, 12, and 21. The episode with Mephibosheth from 2 Samuel 9, however, is omitted, because it does not serve the chronicler's purpose. For the same reason, David's act of adultery with Bathsheba from 2 Samuel 11–12 is also left out; only the allusion "but David remained at Jerusalem" is retained (1 Chronicles 20:1; see 2 Samuel 11:1), recalling the context to the learned reader. It should not be concluded from this omission that the chronicler wants to show David in a better light; in chapter 21 the sin of David in counting his people is judged even more grave than in the Samuel source.

The fifth section, chapters 21–29, begins as the first does with a negative incident as the starting point for the further developments. The purpose of the account is to show that the threshing floor of Ornan is a symbolic place where the grace of God overcomes his wrath. David chooses this place as the appropriate site for building the temple. In the source text of 2 Samuel 24 it is said that God incited David to count the people. In 1 Chronicles 21:1, however, it reads, "Satan . . . incited David." Although at first sight the contrast between these two statements could not be stronger, the formulation of the chronicler is not meant as a contradiction of the source but rather as a comment on the source. By his alteration, the chronicler explains that 2 Samuel does not mean that God himself would entice anyone. Rather he would test human beings by allowing Satan to act.

Chapters 22–29 are about David's transferring his duties of kingdom and temple to his son, Solomon. As in the coronation account of David in chapters 11 and 12, the report on Solomon's coronation is also split in two (22:2–23:2 and 28–29), framing material of a documentary kind, which demonstrates that David hands over to Solomon an orderly kingdom and that he does everything conceivable to help his son with his great task of building the temple.

The Solomon Narrative (2 Chronicles 1–9)

The chronicler's Solomon narrative is based on the account of 1 Kings 1–11. The chronicler has shaped the material according to his own purposes, however. For instance, he leaves out the struggle for the succession of David (1 Kings 1–2) and the sin of Solomon at the end of his life (1 Kings 11). Instead, the act of building the house of the Lord is made the focal point of the whole story.

The Solomon narrative is formed as a concentric structure (see example on page 11) framed by the sections 2 Chronicles 1:1–17 and 9:13–28. Both sections document Solomon's wealth and wisdom. Parallel statements on Solomon's horses in 1:14 and 9:25 and the note that Solomon "made silver and gold as common in Jerusalem as stone" in 1:15 and 9:27 enhance the framing effect.

The second ring of the concentric structure consists of the two sections 2:1–18 and 8:17–9:12. Both texts deal with the international relations of Solomon. Trading with Huram is a motif common to both texts (2:3; 8:18). It is noticeable that Huram and the queen of Sheba both express the opinion that God must love Israel very much (2:11–12; 9:7–8). The parallel is deliberately fashioned by the chronicler. In his source, only the queen of Sheba makes such a statement (see 1 Kings 5:7; 10:9).

The third ring consists of the sections 2 Chronicles 3:1–5:1 and 8:1–16. Both sections deal with Solomon's building projects. While chapters 3 and 4 are about the building of the temple, chapter 8 describes other building activities. However, the chapter begins and ends with a reference to the building of the temple.

The three rings are formed around a center comprising 5:2–7:22, the dedication of the temple. The section contains a long royal prayer and a long speech of God, as is the case with the center of the David narrative.

According to the literary structure, the message of the Solomon narrative can easily be developed: The basis of the narrative is Solomon's faithfulness to God, which is rewarded by God with wisdom and wealth. In Solomon's kingdom, God's great love for Israel becomes visible. These prerequisites form the appropriate frame for the most important work of Solomon, the construction of the house of God. The decisive theological statements are found in the prayer of Solomon and in the speech of God placed at the center of the structure: The "house of David" is chosen by God as the means through which God would reign over his people. Likewise, the "house of God," the temple of Jerusalem, is chosen by God as the place where God answers prayer and forgives sin.

However, God also threatens to reject kingdom and temple, if Israel turns away from God. The exile and the destruction of the temple are therefore indicated in advance. According to the chronicler, the kingdoms of David and Solomon constitute the formative era of Israel's history. Both kings reign over all Israel. Both are very much committed to the house of God. David and Solomon assume complementary roles: David founds the kingdom and the temple ritual; Solomon completes both of them.

The History of the Kings of Judah (2 Chronicles 10–36)

The third main part of Chronicles opens with a report on the separation of the 10 northern tribes of Israel. After that follows a series of longer and shorter sections dealing with the individual kings of the southern kingdom of Judah in chronological order.

The main source for the chronicler's account is the narrative in 1 Kings 12–2 and Kings 25. (For a timetable and other historical issues on the individual kings, see KINGS.) The book of Kings deals with the northern kingdom as well as with the southern kingdom. For the chronicler, however, the "true Israel" is only the southern empire, the Davidic kingdom of Judah. In his account, the northern kingdom is only mentioned in those instances when there is a point of contact with Judah. To understand the chronicler's hints on the northern kingdom, however, the reader has to be familiar with the books of Kings.

Notice that in the book of Chronicles, the word *Israel* is used in three different ways. It can mean (1) the whole of Israel, i.e., the 12 tribes; or (2) the northern empire of the 10 tribes, which is called "Israel" in opposition to the southern empire of "Judah"; or (3) in the sense of "true Israel," the southern empire. The chronicler's retelling of the history of the kings serves one particular purpose: He wants to demonstrate a theology of immediate retribution: Good acts lead to reward; bad acts lead to punishment. Reward and punishment follow their precipitating events rather quickly. The principle is expressed in the text at various places. One of the best-known passages of the book is 2 Chronicles 7:14. It expresses the positive side of the principle:

> If my people who are called by my name humble themselves, pray, seek my face, and turn from their wicked ways, then I will hear from heaven, and will forgive their sin and heal their land.

In the section on the individual kings, certain elements that express the principle of immediate retribution appear time and again. Kings are obedient: For instance, they "seek God," they "humble themselves," when they support the temple service and destroy the altars of foreign gods. The opposite act is to "abandon" or "forsake" the Lord by worshipping foreign gods, by trusting in alliances with foreign people instead of trusting in the Lord. God rewards obedience with success and prosperity, building programs, victory in warfare, progeny, popular support, large armies, and more. God's punishment, in turn, is expressed in military defeat, the disaffection of the population, and illness. These are the aspects of history the chronicler wants to emphasize. For everything else he refers the reader to the source texts. His aim is not to give an alternative account of Israel's history but to demonstrate what can and should be learned from history.

The theological purpose of the book of Kings is to show how guilt and injustice accumulated until the point of God's great judgment through the Babylonian exile. The book of Kings therefore gives a theological explanation of the exile. But for the postexilic people it was important to notice that God's punishment does not only occur after several hundreds of years. Rather, each generation has to take the responsibility for its own acts. Hence, the book of Chronicles demonstrates that the good or bad behavior of a king has consequences in his own period of office.

The Decree of Cyrus (2 Chronicles 36:22–23)

The last two verses of Chronicles define the point of view from which the whole work needs to be read. They are a quote from the beginning of the book of Ezra-Nehemiah, alluding to the return from exile and to further developments in postexilic times. The final verses request the postexilic reader to compare his own time with the formative era of the first temple. Again, a king is installed by God. Again, a temple has to be built. With 2 Chronicles 36:22–23, the history of Israel begins anew.

Chronicles is a sort of full historical and theological stocktaking. The work presents a universal concept of history, revealing its principles. In this way, it functions as the basis for the continuance of Israel after the exile. The history is made the binding pattern, the formative era, the identity on which the present age can rest.

CHARACTERS

David After the kingdom of Saul has failed, David establishes the first stable kingdom over the 12 tribes of Israel according to the will of God. He combines military strength with a deep obedience toward the Lord. His military power can be seen in numerous successful military campaigns, such as the conquest of Jerusalem, his victories over the Philistines, and the occupation of Edom. The lists of David's warriors also support this impression. However, because he is a man of war, God does not allow him to build the house of God. Instead, God promises that he will build "the house of David," establishing an everlasting Davidic dynasty. Nevertheless, David engages in preparations for the building of the temple. He takes the ark of the covenant to Jerusalem, he chooses the site where the temple should be built, he provides materials in great quantity, and he organizes the priests and Levites, preparing for the temple service according to the Law of Moses.

David's act of adultery with Bathsheba (2 Samuel 11–12) is not recounted in the book of Chronicles. The fact that the chronicler wants to show David in a better light, however, should not be assumed from this omission; in 1 Chronicles 21 the sin of David counting his people is judged even more seriously than in the Samuel source. Rather, the reason for omitting the incident is that it does not stand in a relationship to the theological themes of kingdom and temple that the chronicler wants to highlight.

Solomon Son of David, king over Israel. In the beginning of his reign, God asks him what he would like to receive from him. Solomon demonstrates his uprightness by not making a selfish request. Instead, he asks God for wisdom in order to be able to rule the people. God is pleased, and he blesses Solomon with exceptional wisdom as well as exceptional wealth. During Solomon's reign, the area of Israel is larger than it has ever been before or will be after. In Jerusalem, gold and silver are as common as stone. Even non-Israelite kings and the queen of Sheba admire Solomon's wealth and wisdom and praise God's love for Israel. Solomon engages in many building projects, the most important of which is to build the "house of the LORD" in Jerusalem, as a place where "the name of God would be" and where God would answer the prayers and forgive the sins of his people.

The downfall of Solomon at the end of his life (1 Kings 11) is not reported in the book of Chronicles. It would have distorted the picture of the "golden age" of Israel under David and Solomon that the chronicler wants to paint. Instead, at the end of the Solomon narrative, the chronicler refers his readers to other written sources on the life of Solomon (2 Chronicles 9:29). A negative aspect of Solomon's reign is, however, alluded to in 2 Chronicles 10:4. The passage mentions the "heavy yoke" of taxes and compulsory labor that Solomon laid on the people.

Colossians

Ancient letters began with the identity of addressees and senders. The opening of this letter mentions as the senders the apostle Paul and his young helper Timothy. The actual writing will have been done by a paid secretary, with the senders dictating the letter together (cf. 1 Thessalonians 1:1). In 4:18, however, Paul adds a greeting in his own hand.

This letter was addressed to Christians in Colosse, a town in the heartland of Asia Minor that Paul had never visited (2:1). Colosse was close to the cities of Laodicea (2:1) and Hierapolis, which had overtaken it in importance and which are mentioned in 4:13, 15. Paul's reference to his associate Epaphras in 1:7 and 4:12 suggests that Epaphras was the founder or at least the spiritual father of the Christian church in the town. The mentioning of Epaphras links Colossians to Paul's letter to PHILEMON, where he is mentioned in verse 23. Moreover, Onesimus, who according to Colossians 4:9 will deliver the letter, is the main character of Philemon. The logical conclusion is that Paul wrote and dispatched Philemon and Colossians at the same time. The most likely time of writing is sometime in the fifties C.E., during an imprisonment (1:24; 4:18) of Paul in Ephesus. Acts 19:10 says that during Paul's period in Ephesus all of Asia heard the gospel, and this will include Colosse. Alternatively, both Colossians and Philemon could be dated during Paul's imprisonment in Rome in 60–62 C.E., the same period when he presumably wrote a third letter, Ephesians. Colossians has formal and theological similarities with Ephesians, but whereas the latter does not address a specific local or personal situation, Colossians is addressed to a real church. The best explanation of this state of affairs is that Paul was so pleased with Colossians that he made it the basis for the more general letter known as Ephesians. See also EPISTLE.

SYNOPSIS

After the formal opening salutation (1:1–2), Paul pays attention to the faith of the church, indicating that he both thanks and prays for it. His reference to salvation by Christ in 1:14 takes him to a hymn in praise of Christ (1:15–20), which he subsequently applies to the readers. In 1:24–2:7 he discusses his own efforts as messenger of the good news about Christ; the final two verses of this passage are transitional as Paul moves on to the issues at stake in the church, which he discusses in 2:8–23, the central passage of the letter.

The second half of the letter is the practical application. In 3:1–17 we find general guidance for the life in Christ in contrast to the readers' old lifestyle, followed in 3:18–4:6 by specific guidance for different groups of people. Finally, 4:7–18 is a long section with greetings and personal notes.

COMMENTARY

Colossians addresses the problem of wrong ideas and ensuing wrong practices in a young church, formed of Christians who until very recently were pagans. Epaphras must have told the imprisoned Paul that the church was under threat from strange teachings that undermined the position of Jesus Christ as the sole Savior and Lord, and Paul must have felt obliged to help the church by sending them a letter. Chapter 2 contains numerous allusions to the views of the heretics yet does not allow us to associate them with a known Christian sect. As they have no known parallels, the particular problems the church faced are hard to reconstruct.

Paul mentions "philosophy and empty deceit, according to human tradition, according to the elemental spirits of the universe" (2:8) and "self-abasement and worship of angels" (2:18). Fear of spiritual powers seems to occupy a large place in the thinking Paul opposes. Some scholars use the term *Gnosticism* for it, but Gnosticism is a Christian heresy that only developed in the second century C.E. It is best to think of a local mixture of Jewish and pagan ideas, a folk religion that cannot be reconstructed. Whatever it was, it did not give Christ the honor he deserves.

What is crystal clear is Paul's reply: Jesus Christ is put at the center of the stage as creator and Lord of the universe and as founder and Lord of the church. Faith in him is all a person needs in order to be happy and secure, and there is no room for legalism (2:13–18). The role of the Hebrew Bible in Colossians is limited, presumably because the readers were young Christians with a pagan background and as-yet little knowledge of the Hebrew Bible.

Chapter 1:3–14 is a typical prayer report of Paul's. In 1:4–5 he mentions the triad hope, love, and faith, as in 1 Thessalonians 1:3 and 1 Corinthians 13:13. The structure and tone of 1:15–20 are hymnal; Paul may have used an existing Christian HYMN or written one himself. The hymn, characterized by the word *all,* first describes the involvement of Christ in the creation of the universe, his existence before time began, and his role as supreme revelation of God. It then considers his role in relation to the Church. Verse 16 is based on the assumption that the universe is filled with angelic powers and prepares for the discussion in chapter 2. The imagery of the body is here used in a different way from that in 1 Corinthians: Christ is the head of the body, which is the universal Church rather than the local church (1:24; 2:19). In 3:15 the members of the body also come in view. This image is used together with that of the Church as a building (1:23; 2:7). *Blood* (verse 20) is a reference to the sacrificial value of the death of Christ (see SALVATION). The implication of the hymn is that Christ is superior and the readers need not fear any spiritual or physical powers. These implications are spelled out in the following sections.

Colossians 1:24 may seem to suggest that the suffering of Christ was deficient, but what Paul means is that the suffering of Christ's body, the Church, is yet incomplete, and that he can in prison carry his share of it. As in Ephesians, *mystery* (1:26; 2:2; 4:3) refers to something that was hidden from previous generations but has become known in and through the ministry of Jesus Christ. Its content is the role of Christ in saving humanity.

As was said, we cannot reconstruct the ideas that Paul combats in 2:8–23. As an antidote, Paul reminds the readers of their connection with Jesus, which was formally established in their Christian initiation (verses 9–12). The false teachers presumably insisted on the need for the readers to be circumcised, that is, to undergo the Jewish initiation rite, but Paul calls their BAPTISM a spiritual circumcision, enacted by Jesus himself. In 3:9–10 their Christian initiation is likened to putting off an old garment and putting on another one. Colossians 2:16 and 21–22 suggest that the Colossians had embraced a form of asceticism that made the quality of a person's faith dependent on abstinence from certain joys. In contrast, verses 13–15 are a positive statement of salvation in Christ; the latter verse uses the image of a general leading his captives in a triumphant procession.

The thrust of the second half of the latter is characterized as "become what you are" by Howard Marshall: Put your old life to death and stop yielding to the power of sin. The theological motives include the fact that the readers are God's chosen people (3:12) and members of one body (3:15). The idea that Christ sits on the right side of God in heaven (3:1) occurs also in Ephesians 1:20 and in Hebrews (e.g., 10:13). Usually Paul talks about "the word of God," but in 3:16 he uses "the word of Christ"; this will include teaching by Christ (as transmitted orally and later preserved in the Gospels) as well as teaching about him.

In 3:18–4:1 scholars recognize the genre of the "household code," an ancient type of ethical instruction also at the basis of Ephesians 5:21–6:9 and 1 Peter 2:13–3:7. Paul is adamant that the readers' faith will affect the way they relate to each other and to outsiders in diverse relationships. The remainder of chapter 4 is an attempt to forge a link with the addressees who do not know the author by mentioning people known to both parties. As if in passing, Paul highlights the importance of prayer in the Christian life.

Colossians 4:14 is the one verse in the New Testament that suggests that Luke, the author of the third gospel and of Acts, was a medical doctor. The letter sent to the church in Laodicea (4:16) has not been preserved; centuries after Paul, a fake letter was produced and gained no recognition in the Church.

CHARACTERS

The apostle Paul is the author of the letter, but it does not contain much personal information about him. At the time of writing he is imprisoned (4:10). In 4:7–17 many people get a brief mention that shows that Paul, although an outstanding personality, was by no means a soloist. People "of the circumcision" (verse 11) are Jewish Christians as opposed to Christians from a pagan background.

1 Corinthians

Corinth was an important city in Greece, a commercial center and the capital of a Roman province. As it was a Roman colony, its citizens were primarily Romans augmented by Greeks and Jews. The city leadership was in the hands of freemen and other self-made men who would never have been leaders in a more traditional city. This situation of upward mobility encouraged the citizens to boast of their achievements. Corinth was notorious for its decadence and has been described as the "Vanity Fair" of the ancient world, a combination of contemporary Los Angeles, New York, and Las Vegas. The Greek neologism *to corinthianize* meant "to fornicate."

The Christians in Corinth arguably formed PAUL's most difficult church. They were a divided church (chapters 1–4), with huge differences between rich and poor (chapters 10–11). Among the members must have been Roman citizens (the upper class), dependent servants, and slaves.

Paul had founded the church while staying in the city for more than a year (Acts 18), and this letter was written from Ephesus (16:8) a few years later, probably in 55 C.E. The present letter is not the first Paul wrote to this church, for in 5:9–11 he refers to a previous letter that they had misunderstood and that is since lost. Paul has now received oral reports (1:11) as well as a letter from the church to him (7:1) that may have been delivered by the people mentioned in 16:17 but that, again, we no longer have. The introduction "Now concerning . . ." in 7:25; 8:1; 12:1; and 16:1, 12 indicates places where Paul addresses a new issue from the Corinthians' letter. It appears that Paul regularly quotes it, but it is difficult to know where exactly. (Ancient manuscripts do not contain quotation marks or any other device to mark quotes.) The New International Version uses quotation marks in 1:12; 3:4; 6:12–13; 8:1; 10:23, but the New Revised Standard Version *also* uses them in 7:1 and 8:4, 8. This discrepancy is a clear illustration of the unavoidable interconnectedness of translation and interpretation. See also EPISTLE.

Compared to letters of Paul's contemporaries, this is a very long letter; the average letter those days was shorter than one chapter in 1 Corinthians. In terms of genre this letter could be classified as a friendship letter. Ancient letters always opened with the identity of both the addressee and the sender. This one mentions Paul and Sosthenes as authors; the latter is also mentioned in Acts 18:17 as the ruler of the Corinthian synagogue who must since have become a Christian and have traveled with Paul. The actual writing will have been done by a paid secretary.

As with all letters, the title did not originate with its authors. It must have been added when the early churches started collecting the letters Paul had written to several of them, in order to distinguish these letters from each other. As soon as we find evidence for the existence of a collection of Paul's letters in the early church, 1 Corinthians is an undisputed part of it. As far as we know, it later made its way into the canon of Scripture without any discussion.

This letter does not have an overarching theme or theological subject; Paul is simply addressing divisions and faults in many areas of the life of the church and responding to issues that they raised in their letter to him. Yet it is striking that the apostle relates each practical issue to the Christian message, asking every time what the mind of Jesus is. For this reason this letter has proved valuable for the church throughout the ages, even when it struggles with issues not specifically addressed here.

A key concept in this letter is that of *body*, which is mentioned more than 30 times. It can refer to a person's physical body such as Paul's (5:3; New International Version "physically") or that of any person (chapter 6), but also to the church as a gathering of diverse people (chapter 12) and to the new body we receive at the Resurrection (15). At times Paul's expression can be deliberately ambiguous as in 11:24, 27, 29. Other recurrent images are those of planting and seed (3:6–8; 9:7, 11; 15:36–37) and yeast (5:6–8).

Exceptionally in his letters, three times Paul refers to things that Jesus had said during his life on earth: In 7:10 he alludes to words on divorce later recorded in Matthew 5:32 and 19:9; 9:14 contains an allusion to what Luke 10:7 records about laborers' wages; and Paul's recollection of the Last Supper in 11:23–25 is close to that in Luke 22:14–20.

A recurrent literary technique in this letter is the use of the A-B-A' form, which is also found in the Gospel of Mark and is known as sandwich structure or interpolation. The most obvious example is that chapter 13 (B) interrupts the discussion of the use of spiritual gifts in chapters 12 (A) and 14 (A'). The B elements are only apparently digressions, and in fact they shed light on the surrounding discussion. Thus the role of chapter 13 is to argue that spiritual gifts are only meaningful and constructive if used in love. Other instances of the sandwich are the interpolation about gospel values (1:18–2:16) in the discussion of the divisions (1:10–17 and 3:1–23); the placing of the passage on the lawsuit (6:1–11) within the discussion of sins of a sexual nature (5 and 6:12–20); and the position of the personal chapter 9 in the middle of the discussion of (un)lawful food (8 and 10).

SYNOPSIS

Despite the many difficult issues Paul needs to discuss, he opens the letter with a very positive section of greetings and thanksgiving that repeatedly uses the phrase "the Lord Jesus Christ" (1:1–9). The first issue he tackles is that of the party strife within the church (1:10–4:21). This is followed by matters relating to sexuality and marriage (5–7), legal disputes between Christians (6:1–11), the attitude toward idolatry (8–10), women in Christian worship, the LORD'S SUPPER (EUCHARIST, COMMUNION) (11), the use of spiritual gifts in particular in worship (12–14), and the resurrection of Jesus Christ (15). The final chapter contains brief notes on the collection for the church in Jerusalem, personal plans, and greetings.

COMMENTARY

The first issue Paul discusses is that of the divisions (1:10–17), and he returns to it after a principled discussion (3:1–5). The members of the church met in different houses (1:11–12; 16:15), and the rival groups mentioned were perhaps home groups. Paul suggests that they followed either him, Apollos, Cephas (= Peter; see TWELVE DISCIPLES), or Christ (1:12). As we cannot assume that there was a Christ party in the church, Paul's list is probably rhetorical rather than historical. (On the role of Apollos, see below.)

As the alternative to strife, Paul presents the cross of Jesus (1:18), and he develops this subject first in general terms (1:19–25), then in terms of the readers (1:26–31), and finally in terms of himself (2:1–5). The preaching of the cross does create an entirely different division from that which occurred in Corinth, between believers and unbelievers. This part of the letter contains at least two major paradoxes. Whereas in 1:18–25 Paul denies the importance of secular wisdom, in 2:6–16 and again in 3:18–23 he explains that he preaches God's wisdom. The second paradox is that in very eloquent words Paul denies the relevance of eloquence. Sandwiched between the sections on wisdom is one on the building of the church as a fruit of wise leadership (3:1–17).

The lack of respect for ethical values as seen in chapters 5–7 may have to do with misplaced loyalty to patrons even if they behaved unacceptably. A sexual relationship with one's stepmother as implied in chapter 5 was illegal under both

Roman and Jewish law. Paul's severe treatment of the case qualifies his previous insistence on unity in the church. Going to court (chapter 6) was only open to the rich in the church as large bribes were normally involved. The word translated "body" in 6:12–20 can also refer to the whole person. Chapter 7 is characterized by Paul's careful and uncommon distinction between his own opinion and God's. Careful study of the chapter shows that Paul is not the misogynist he is often taken to be.

Behind the Corinthians' question that Paul answers in chapters 8–10 lies the reality that meat was a luxury for all except the wealthy. However, meat was widely available at public festivals in the temples and in the meat markets associated with the temples. Paul's renunciation of his rights (chapter 9) resembles the renunciation that he is asking of the "strong" Corinthians (= the wealthy) in chapters 8 and 10. Among the narrative devices Paul uses are highly effective rhetorical questions (chapter 9) and analogies from the Hebrew Bible (10:1–13).

In chapters 11–14 we see Paul attempting to restore order and respectability to the Corinthian worship gatherings. His main aim is that God should be central in meetings and that nothing should divert attention from the reading of the Scriptures and the preaching, but he also has in mind the reputation of the church in society. In this vein he deals with the behavior of women (11:2–16 and 14:33b–35), the celebration of the Lord's Supper (11:17–34), and speaking at the meetings (12–14). The chapters as a whole show that women did speak in the gatherings and that Paul issues guidance for them to do so in a decent, edifying way.

Chapter 13 is well known for its use at weddings, but this eloquent text with its beautiful parallelisms is really about divine love, not love between husband and wife. The "speaking in a tongue" that is questioned in chapter 14 is the utterance of unknown languages (see also Acts 2:1–13; 10:46; 19:6), whereas prophecy was readily intelligible. The fact that the Corinthians placed such high value on all spiritual gifts can be explained by the social makeup of the church: For members from the lower classes the use of such gifts, especially of "tongues," would have increased their status—in a society in which such mobility was possible.

Chapter 15 is another display of Paul's eloquence. For reasons that are hard to clarify some Corinthians denied the resurrection of Jesus Christ, and Paul counters them in a masterly way. Historically very important is his recital of the earliest traditions about the Resurrection and Jesus' appearances, many of which are not recorded in the Gospels (verses 1–11). Paul then points out that the ultimate consequence of denying the Resurrection is that humans would not be saved. He argues that without the Resurrection, the perils of apostleship would be a waste of time, as would being baptized for the dead (a rite only known through this passage). More seriously, a "sin as much as you like" attitude would become the best advice for living. On the positive side, in verses 35–58 Paul proclaims Christ's resurrection as the model for all believers, the "first fruits from the dead." He uses a series of analogies—seed; Sun, Moon, and stars; the first and last Adams (cf. Romans 5:12–14)—all to show that the resurrected state will be much more glorious than our present earthly state. And as he did in Romans 8:31–39, Paul produces a rhetorical climax, which is read at many funeral services: Quoting Hosea 13:14, he asks, "Where, O death, is your victory? Where, O death, is your sting?"

At the end of the letter Paul raises the matter of the collection for the Christians in Jerusalem (16:1–4). This is one of the few things he does not write in response to Corinthian issues.

CHARACTERS

Apollos A learned person from Alexandria, a Christian teacher who is mentioned in Acts 18:24–19:1, where he is said to have stayed in Ephesus as well as in Corinth. Paul's close associates Priscilla and Aquila needed to "explain the Way of God to him more accurately" (Acts 18:26). His role in the Corinthian Church is clouded in mystery: The church obviously made him one of their champions and a rival of Paul, but we do not know whether he himself encouraged this situation. Paul wanted him to travel to Corinth at the time of writing, but he refused (16:12).

Paul   In the church in Corinth Paul's authority is at stake. In response he plays a double act. On the one hand he argues that church leadership is not about human leaders and that the cross of Christ should be central. On the other he does assert his authority as an apostle and as the founder and spiritual head of the church. As 2 Corinthians shows, the present letter did not resolve all issues and the resulting conflict was of a more personal nature.

2 Corinthians

2 Corinthians is the most personal of all PAUL's letters. Under heavy attack, even in the face of death (5:1–10), he passionately defends his ministry and himself. The letter is a fascinating mixture of doctrine and practice. It is not always easy to understand but has given us well-known Christian sayings such as "Where the Spirit of the Lord is, there is freedom" (3:17), "For the love of Christ urges us on" (5:14), and "We entreat you on behalf of Christ, be reconciled to God" (5:20). Because so much of it deals with the Christian ministry, this letter has a special appeal for Christian workers. (See also EPISTLE.)

See 1 Corinthians for an introduction to the city of Corinth, to its church, and to previous correspondence exchanged by Paul and the church. The writing of 2 Corinthians follows a painful visit that Paul made in haste, his second to the city (2:1; 12:14; 13:1). This visit is not mentioned in Acts, and we have few details about it, but see below on 2:5–11. A further letter from Paul, written between 1 and 2 Corinthians, also preceded our text and is referred to in 2 Corinthians 2:4, 9 and 7:8–12. What we call 2 Corinthians is thus the fourth letter Paul wrote to this church, probably from somewhere in Macedonia (see GREECE) in the year 56 C.E.

SYNOPSIS

This letter readily falls into three main parts, chapters 1–7, 8–9, and 10–13. Some scholars think that these three units originally were (parts of) separate Pauline letters that were combined after his death, but that is not necessarily the case. (More radical scholars even distinguish fragments of some six letters within 2 Corinthians.) The main argument of the source critics is that, whereas chapters 2 and 7 suggest that peace has been agreed between Paul and the Corinthian church, chapters 10–13 have a different tone and presuppose a background of (renewed) hostilities. Those who defend the unity of the letter usually assume that some time passed between the completion of chapters 1–9 and 10–13. Here the unity of the letter will be assumed.

In the first main part, 1:1–11 forms the greeting and thanksgiving section. Between 1:12 and 2:4 Paul is on the defense about his recent behavior: The Corinthian church is obviously annoyed that he did not pay them the visit he had promised. He explains that he had good reasons for changing his plans. 2 Corinthians 2:5–11 form a small digression about somebody who offended Paul during his recent visit. Paul sets out on a recital of more recent events in 2:12–13, which is soon interrupted and only resumed at 7:5. In the long intermezzo 2:14–7:4 he discusses the nature of his ministry as an apostle of Jesus Christ, and in 7:5–16 he writes about the return of Titus from his visit to Corinth.

In the intermezzo Paul defends his apostolic ministry, arguing that he is not afraid to speak out (2:14–17); that the Corinthians themselves should be his recommendation (3:1–4), although it is God who made him competent for the work (3:5–6); and that the ministry of the new COVENANT in Jesus Christ is superior to that of the covenant with MOSES (3:6–18). After these grand words Paul focuses on his own problems, and the long passage 4:1–5:10 is a dialectic discussion of the power of the gospel and the perceived weakness of its apostle. 2 Corinthians 5:11–6:2 make clear that the core of the gospel is the reconciliation of God and humankind thanks to the work of Jesus Christ, while 6:3–13 returns once more to Paul's precarious position as apostle.

The passage 6:14–7:1 does not easily fit into its context, and those who regard 2 Corinthians as a combination of letters often think this short passage was part of yet another letter. However, it can also be seen as the conclusion of the explanation of the gospel, pointing to its radical demands. Its tendency resembles that of 1 Corinthians 10:14–22.

The positive tone of the end of chapter 7 opens the way for the next main part, chapters 8 and 9, which discusses Paul's collection for the church in Jerusalem ("the saints," 8:4; 9:1; for this designation cf. 1 Corinthians 16:1, 3). The churches in Macedonia are praised for their giving, and the Corinthians are encouraged to follow this example of their own free will. Titus's role in the operation is clarified (8:16–24). In a careful piece of rhetoric, the Macedonians are once again used as examples (9:1–5), but more theological arguments for charitable giving are also brought to bear.

The transition to chapter 10 is loose, and the third main part of the letter is not easily subdivided. Paul engages is strong polemic with new and allegedly pretentious newcomers to the church. In what experts regard as the hardest Greek of all his letters, he calls for obedience in faith and condemns the arrogance of the adversaries. He reminds the readers that meekness is a virtue of Christ, and he defends himself against the charge of cowardice (10:1–11), condemns boasting (10:12–18), identifies and warns against the false teachers (11:1–15), gives an account of himself (11:16–12:13), and tries to make plans for a new, third visit to Corinth (12:14–13:10). The ending 13:11–14 is not unlike his other letters.

COMMENTARY

The letter reveals how Paul makes use of a range of methods to serve the church in Corinth: He pays visits himself, he sends envoys such as Titus, and he writes several letters. In the present letter he uses numerous rhetorical questions. Metaphors from the world of business occur in 1:22; 2:17; 5:5; and 8:9. The word *boast* plays a large role in the letter as a whole but in particular in its third main part; 10:3–6 is based on military metaphors (cf. 6:7), and 11:2 contains the metaphor of marriage. On the other hand, in this letter the word *body* is used literally (chapters 4, 5, 7, and 12), so in a more limited way than in 1 Corinthians it typifies Paul's vulnerability and mortality as a servant of Jesus Christ, but he also employs metaphors such as "clay jar" and "tent" to refer to it.

Timothy is mentioned as coauthor in the letter's opening, but his role will have been marginal. He had made a visit to Corinth on his own (1 Corinthians 4:17; 16:10), which probably had been unsuccessful. 2 Corinthians 1:3–7 is an elaborate and clever word-play on the word *console*. In the first chapters Paul basically looks back on a chain of nasty situations both in Asia Minor, where he had stayed until recently, and in Corinth, which he had visited briefly. The enormous problems Paul had faced in Asia Minor, most probably in the church at Ephesus, had nearly finished him off (1:8–11). The apology 1:12–14 is encircled by the words "our boast."

In 2:5–11 Paul picks up an incident that must have happened during his brief and painful visit to the church. Apparently somebody offended him (hit him?), and it is to the credit of the church that they had actually reprimanded the wrongdoer (cf. 7:12). The trip mentioned in 2:12–13 is the one mentioned in Acts 20:1; the metaphor "an open door" is also used for missionary opportunities in Acts 14:27; 1 Corinthians 16:9; Colossians 4:3; and Revelation 3:8. Paul's discussion of the nature of his ministry in 2:14–6:13 makes use of a series of eloquent metaphors:

- The triumphal entry of an army officer (2:14).
- Spreading a good scent (2:15–17).
- Preparing letters of recommendation (3:1–3); the latter two emphasize that the church should be attractive to outsiders.
- Reflecting God's glory (3:6–18). Paul engages in a lengthy comparison of the COVENANT conducted at Sinai and the covenant in Christ in the form of a kind of sermon on Exodus 34:29–35, where Moses is said to have worn a veil. The sermon revolves around antithetical parallelisms (see POETRY, BIBLICAL) and around the comparative "if . . . how much more. . . ." Paul argues that the new covenant is much more glorious and that it enables human change to glory.
- Having a treasure in a clay jar (4:1–18). Paul's weakness, described as "bearing the death of Jesus in his body" (verse 10), is evidence that whatever power the gospel has is God's power and not Paul's. Clay jars were a common packaging of wares and also a common metaphor for the frailty of the human body. In 4:4 "the god of this world" is a unique title for Satan; 4:13 is derived from Psalm 116:10.

- Living in a perishable tent (5:1–10). Other metaphors in this passage are the house and clothing; all were common in Paul's days and are used here to point to the temporary nature of the present life over against the eternity of the future life with God, to which the apostle looks forward.
- The job of an ambassador (5:11–21 and 6:3–13). These passages are full of paradoxes, as Paul in all his weakness still is a representative of the greatest power in the universe. Although 5:16 has sometimes been taken to mean that Paul is not interested in factual knowledge about the life of Jesus, it rather says that any knowledge of Jesus must be spiritual. The most explicit teaching on the atonement in the letter appears in 5:17–21. Paul literally writes that Christ "was made sin for us" (verse 21), meaning that he was made the atoning sacrifice for the sins of humanity (cf. Isaiah 53:10), so that they can be reconciled to God and can even become a new creation in Christ (verse 17; cf. Galatians 6:15). 2 Corinthians 6:4–10 is a highly personal rhetorical outburst about Paul's circumstances, which foreshadows chapters 10–13, in particular 11:23–32.

The position of 6:14–7:1 has been discussed in the Synopsis. In 6:16–18 we have a free rendering of ideas from a range of passages in the Hebrew Bible that can be compared to Romans 3:10–18. The ideas stem from Leviticus 26:11–12; Isaiah 52:11; Ezekiel 20:34, 41; and 2 Samuel 7:8, 14.

Chapter 8 is bound to the preceding chapters by the fact that Paul continues to use words such as *comfort, trial,* and *boast.* He also discusses the collection for Jerusalem in 1 Corinthians (16:1–4) and in Romans (15:25–29). The churches of Macedonia mentioned in 8:1 will have included Thessalonica and Philippi. Paul shows his rhetorical skills by only mentioning his actual request in verse 6. Although 9:1 looks like a new beginning, it introduces an explanation of what preceded in 8:16–24. In 9:6–10 he employs Proverbs 11:24 (for the imagery of sowing and reaping), Psalm 112:9, and Isaiah 55:10 from the Hebrew Bible.

The whole of chapters 10–13 is a piece of judicial rhetoric built on the polarity of weak versus strong.

Whereas until now Paul had labored carefully to remove misunderstandings and prejudices, in these closing chapters he launches a frontal attack on a group of new and apparently unforeseen obstacles to his ministry. These opponents must have been powerful people with strong claims to authority based on miracles and eloquence. As a skilled debater, Paul employs irony and sarcasm, as in the label *superapostles* (11:5; 12:11) to describe these adversaries. For himself, he rejects all boasting, arguing that although weak from a human perspective, he is strong in Jesus Christ. Several times the reader is reminded of the prophet Jeremiah, who is quoted in 10:17 and whose key theme of building up and tearing down is alluded to in 13:10.

For 11:7 compare 1 Corinthians 9, where Paul argues that he will not be paid by the church. The "forty minus one" lashes (11:24) were given to be certain that the number stated in Deuteronomy 25:3 was not exceeded. In 12:1–5 Paul hints at a visionary experience that must be his own, in the period before his ministry, but he disappoints the eager readers by not providing any details. 2 Corinthians 12:7 intimates that Paul had a physical weakness, probably a chronic disease, which we cannot identify with certainty. Yet he received a special word from God, "My grace is sufficient for you, for my power is made perfect in weakness" (12:9; cf. what is said about Jesus in 13:4). One of Paul's aims in bringing the letter to a close is to prepare the way for another visit to Corinth. The text alluded to in 13:1 is Deuteronomy 19:15; compare Matthew 18:16.

The letter's final verse is a trinitarian (see TRINITY) formula that is often used as blessing in church services.

CHARACTERS

Paul   2 Corinthians contains Paul's most elaborate defense of his apostleship, in particular in 2:14–6:13 and chapters 10–13. He faces complaints about his behavior in certain situations, but also more generally about his unimpressive speech and his weak presence (10:10). Yet simplicity, integrity, authenticity, and willingness to suffer are Paul's hallmarks (cf. 1 Thessalonians 2:1–13). He regards suffering and weakness not as disqualifications but as natural consequences of the message he bears, which is about the crucified Christ. There are parallels not only between Paul and Jesus but also between the apostle and the prophets, particularly Jeremiah. They all suffer on behalf of those they serve.

The list of his experiences in 11:22–29 includes many events not included in Acts. Some have suggested that Paul suffered from depression on the basis of verses such as 1:3–7 and 7:6, but that assertion goes beyond the evidence.

Paul's opponents   Whereas in 1 Corinthians the opposition to Paul arose from within the church, the final part of 2 Corinthians gives evidence that false teachers have arrived from outside the church (11:5; 12:11) and that Paul is challenged on his record as a performer of miracles (12:1, 12). It is hard to ascertain the identity and ideas of these people; some scholars suggest that they may have had a Jewish background (11:22).

Titus   This helper of Paul, to whom he sent a letter that is in the New Testament, is mentioned 11 times outside that letter, eight of which occur in 2 Corinthians. As he is not mentioned in Acts, little is known about him. He enjoys Paul's full confidence and acts as his envoy to Corinth.

Daniel

The interpretation of the book of Daniel is one of the most fraught of all the Bible. An example of this is where it is to be placed. In the Hebrew Bible, it is not considered a prophetic writing but is placed in the section known as the Writings, along with the WISDOM LITERATURE, the historical narratives including those of Ezra-Nehemiah, and Esther. However, the Septuagint, the early Greek translation of the Hebrew Bible, places it after Ezekiel as one of the major prophets, as opposed to the Twelve, or Minor Prophets. The Christian Old Testament has preserved this place.

So the question may be asked, In what sense is this a prophetic book? The most conventional argument is to suggest it is one of just two books of APOCALYPTIC WRITING in the Bible (the other

being Revelation). The apocalyptic genre is usually seen as a subgenre of the prophetic, the two occurring side by side at times (e.g., in Ezekiel 38–39). Whereas the prophetic addresses the here and now behavior of God's people and God's dealings with them and messages to them, the apocalyptic seeks to describe God's future intervention in his people's catastrophic situations. There is a good deal more prediction in the apocalyptic. The prophetic traces the future both as consequences of wrong action and hope for restoration after punishment, while the apocalyptic looks very little at God's people's actual behavior, rather exhorting them to patience, perseverance, and faithfulness in the face of overwhelming suffering and persecution.

Certainly, in these distinctions, Daniel is largely apocalyptic in its second part. However, the term used by certain Christian groups for understanding the LAST THINGS is "biblical prophecy," and so further confusion sets in. In any case, the first part of Daniel does not seem unduly apocalyptic at all but a series of narratives, not dissimilar to the book of Esther, on the one hand, or of Jonah, on the other. The former is seen as historical, the latter prophetic. So what do the stories establish? And what is their connection to the apocalyptic visions of the second part? One way of answering such questions is to see the book as a mix of wisdom and dream literature, to be interpreted symbolically. But a more satisfying way, perhaps, is to see the book as a rather remarkable way to write history, both present and future.

Another major source of disagreement is the actual date of the book. Those aspects of the disagreement that are more theological than literary we shall avoid considering. There are two major dates posited: one, that stated in the narrative of the book, that is, the EXILE in BABYLON, and its continuance under the Persians in the sixth century B.C.E. The other is in the second century B.C.E. during the period of the Maccabean revolt (167–164 B.C.E.); that would make it one of the last to be written in the canon of the Hebrew Bible. Both periods were times of great suffering and discouragement for the Jews, so the message is equally relevant to both periods. There is good evidence for both sides, and major difficulties for both sides to argue over, including historical facts and inaccuracies, details that may be known at one time but forgotten or not known at the other, and linguistic features. Most of these are technical and not literary. But the last, the linguistic, reminds us of another strangeness about the book: Half of it is not written in Hebrew at all, but in Aramaic (from 2:4–7:28), the common language developed through the Middle East, which was spoken by Jews in New Testament times. Only conjectures can be made for the reason for this.

Whatever the provenance of the book, some understanding of the historical background is needed to make sense of the apocryphal material. The exile was in Babylon—or Chaldea, as the sixth-century revival of Babylonian power (636–539 B.C.E.) is often called in the Hebrew Bible. That was ended suddenly (as Daniel 5:30 correctly states) by Persian invasion. Technically, the latter empire (539–331 B.C.E.) was a dual one, that of the Medes and Persians, though the Persians were the stronger partner. This in turn succumbed to the Macedonian Greeks under Alexander. His premature death in 323 B.C.E. led his huge empire to be divided into four, partitioned among his four leading generals. One inherited EGYPT and Palestine; another SYRIA and Asia. Palestine passed from one to the other over the next few centuries. Finally, because of extremely tyrannical suppression of the Jewish religion, a degree of independence was won by the Maccabean revolt (see INTERTESTAMENTAL PERIOD). Finally, ROME entered the arena, controlling Judea in 63 B.C.E., establishing its empire throughout the Mediterranean world, and incorporating most of the old Greek empire, and some of the Persian.

SYNOPSIS

Six Narratives (Chapters 1–6)
The six narratives (one per chapter) can all be seen as tests for the eponymous hero, Daniel, and his three friends. Three of the tests are ordeals they undergo through their unwillingness to compromise their faith and its practices in the light of pagan demands (chapters 1, 3, and 6). The ordeals are eating a vegetarian diet, being thrown into a

The writing on the wall (Daniel 5:1–30), engraving by Julius Schnorr von Carolsfeld

furnace, and being thrown into a pit of lions. The other three tests are for Daniel to interpret dreams or signs (chapters 2, 4, and 5), for instance, mysterious writing that appears on the wall at a sacrilegious feast. In every case, the tests are undergone successfully, and the lives of the characters are not only spared but honored. There is a sense of competition with or antagonism from the native wise men or officials. Their defeat leads to God's name's being acknowledged as that of the only true god by the king, and the Jewish refusal to compromise totally vindicated.

Four Visions (Chapters 7–12)
The four visions that follow link back to chapter 2, where Daniel's apocalyptic interpretation is the right one, where the future of four great empires and their downfall is predicted, as God's final kingdom bursts in violently. The four visions here are all variations of this, with the final vision being extended over the last three chapters and giving a detailed summary of the period surrounding the Maccabean revolt. In every case, Daniel's role is reversed from the first section: He dreams the dreams rather than interprets others' but in every case needs an angelic interpreter. The force of each revelation devastates him. In terms of a time sequence, these four visions are intermixed with the earlier section.

COMMENTARY

Six Narratives (Chapters 1–6)

The six narratives are all remarkably memorable. They are six perfectly structured stories with dramatic climaxes and happy endings. Even casual readers of the Hebrew Bible are likely to find that the stories from Daniel stay with them. Although each story can be viewed separately, there are references from one to the other, they are placed sequentially, and they all have basically the same structure. The structure for the three ordeals can be set out thus:

	chapter 1	3	6
Story setup, part i	verses 1–2	verses 1–7	verses 1–5
Story setup, part ii	verses 3–7	verses 8–15	verses 6–9
The Jewish response	verses 8–14	verses 16–18	verses 10–15
The ordeal	verse 15	verses 19–26	verses 16–22
The result: climax and coda	verses 16–20	verses 27–30	verses 23–28

In every case, the midpoint is the Jewish response by Daniel or his three friends. As the result, God is always glorified and declared to be the only true god, and the Jewish men are honored in some way. In chapter 1, the ordeal seems much less dangerous for the men themselves: The refusal to compromise their Jewish diet and eat unclean food would merely lead to loss of career opportunity, whereas the official may be in some danger. What emerges here, and is consistent all the way through, is Daniel's tact. Even when confrontation cannot be avoided, it is still handled politely and in as peaceable a way as possible.

Chapters 3 and 6 are close parallels and perhaps the most famous of the tests. 1 Maccabees 2:59–60 shows that these two stories were already well known by the second century B.C.E., even if it is held the rest of the book was compiled about then. The setup of the story always falls into two parts: the paraphernalia of the foreign court is established in the first part, often with repeated lists (officials, instruments), which give a rhythmic memorability to the narrative. The second part then involves some accusation or entrapment against the Jewish heroes, whether Daniel or Shadrach, Meshach, and Abednego. The link between chapters 2 and 3 is that those three have just received promotion, and there is thus the motivation of jealousy. That foreigners should hold senior positions is by no means unusual in any empire where individual merit is recognized; biblical examples include Joseph at the court of Pharaoh, and Nehemiah and Esther in the Persian court. Interestingly, Joseph also has the ability to interpret dreams. That native-born colleagues should become jealous is totally believable, given human nature. Chapter 6 is a parallel account featuring Daniel, here in a new empire, but jealousy seems again probably the motive (6:3), although his honesty preventing the rigging of accounts has also been suggested.

The midpoint of the chapter, its turning point, is always exactly the same: the summoning of the Jews and their response, which is invariably not to compromise. This leads inevitably to the ordeal, whether fire or wild animals, two typical punishments. This is then followed by some sort of response on the part of the spectators. In chapter 3 it is the observation of a fourth person (3:25), who is translated variously as having the appearance of a god, or a son of the gods. Christian commentary has tended to see this as a "preincarnation" appearance of Christ, though this interpretation in itself poses further theological difficulties. Jewish commentary would suggest an angelic personage, and there is plenty of evidence in Daniel of a growth in angelology compared to earlier writings (e.g., 4:17; 9:21; 10:5, 21; 12:1; see ANGELS). In chapter 6 the interest lies more in the emotions of Darius, who clearly has given in to the ordeal against his better nature and is a divided man.

The final stage is the proving of the Jews, and the public acknowledgment of their god (3:28–29; 6:26–27) and further promotion or honors (1:19; 3:30). The theological issue behind this refusal to compromise is God's ability to deliver in even the most dire situation as a result of such faithfulness.

The structure for the tests of interpretation (chapters 2, 4, and 5) is not dissimilar:

	chapter 2	4	5
Setup, part i	verses 1–11	verses 4–8	verses 1–9
Setup, part ii	verses 12–16	verses 9–18	verses 10–12
Daniel's response	verses 17–24	verse 19	verses 13–23
The dream/ sign	verses 25–35	verses 20–27	verses 24–25
The interpretation	verses 36–45		verses 26–28
Result	verses 46–49	verses 28–33	verses 29–31

The only major difference is that the ordeal is displaced by a two-part division of dream/sign plus interpretation, though in chapter 4, the two are run together. Chapter 4 also has a framing device around it (4:1–3, 34–37) since, unusually, it is Nebuchadnezzar himself telling the story. Otherwise, all the features remain the same. As before, Daniel's enemies meet their comeuppance in narrative reversal. The dream interpretation is significant in a culture where astrology, omens, occultic signs, and so on all form part of the mainstream culture. Even in such a hostile environment, Daniel is granted supernatural as well as natural wisdom, in order that his God is honored above all others.

Other literary devices are hyperbole (e.g., the 10-fold wisdom of the youths, the heating of the fire seven times), repetition, and parallelism; Psalm-like poetic utterances; symbolism (e.g., the huge tree); and delayed anticipation. Nebuchadnezzar's refusal to tell his dream is an example of this last feature: We too wait eagerly to hear what it is, just as we wait to know what the writing on the wall is.

Unlike the audience, we modern readers are not threatened; our lives are not at stake in this bizarre world of absolute monarchy, and we can afford to quibble about historical or theological details. But the original readers of the stories could well have felt they were in exactly the same situation as Daniel and his friends. Such stories resonate in times of persecution and distress.

Four Visions (Chapters 7–12)

The carefully balanced structure of the book continues into the second half. One way to see this structure is that just as in the first part there were two sets of three chapters, so are there three in the second part. Chapters 7–9 give us three discrete apocalyptic visions in fairly general terms, while chapters 10–12 give us one extended apocalypse in tremendous detail. Chapter 12 functions both as a conclusion to that apocalypse and as an epilogue for Daniel himself.

The first three visions have been anticipated already by chapter 2 and Nebuchadnezzar's dream of the four empires. While it could be argued that that chapter is not primarily apocalyptic but intended to prove God's supremacy, the symbolic framework of it fits these three visions well. Two main lines of interpretation have been taken for the empires of chapter 2: first, the Babylonian, Persian, Greek, and Roman Empires, which are then superseded by the Kingdom of God. In Christian interpretation this latter kingdom has traditionally been seen as the spread of the church and the reign of Christ, while in Jewish interpretation this would be the messianic kingdom. Another common interpretation is to subdivide the Persian Empire into two, the Medes and the Persians, and then omit the Romans. This might seem more strained, but it would mean the messianic kingdom immediately follows the fall of the Seleucid Empire that was oppressing the Jews in the second century B.C.E. This would then tie it in with the time framework of the final vision of chapters 10–12.

Such time frameworks have proliferated in Jewish and Christian thinking of the end times but are beyond the scope of this commentary. It is of the symbolic nature of apocalypse to give rise to continuing reinterpretations according to the age in which any interpreter lives.

Chapter 7 continues the use of huge objects seen in the first part: huge statues, figures, rocks, overheated furnaces, and so on. This is all much larger than life! The chapter is the only one in the second half to be in Aramaic, as was chapter 2, to which it bears obvious similarities: the four beasts paralleling the four body parts. The final beast is not named but is identified in terms of horns, symbolic of power. The structure of the chapter, as of the following two chapters, is much simpler than in the first part: The first half is the vision, followed by a request for interpretation, then the interpretation given by an angelic figure. Unlike in the first part, Daniel is unable to interpret for himself and is left ill and exhausted by the actual visionary impact on him. In fact, the interpretation given needs an interpretation! Daniel 7:21 actually seems to extend the original vision rather than interpret it. What we carry away as readers is a sense of the theophany given to Daniel (7:9–10) and the assurance that in the end God will intervene and establish an eternal kingdom (7:27).

Chapter 8 is patterned in much the same way, though the language switches to Hebrew. The horns are again symbols of the power of Persia and Greece (8:20–21). The question "How long?" becomes persistent (8:13), and the sense of angelic help more pronounced. Again, the interpretation does not yield understanding (8:27), though, generally, the figure of the Seleucid ruler Antiochus Epiphanes is accepted as being the referand.

Chapter 9 is the chapter in this section that breaks the patterns somewhat, just as chapter 2 does in the first part. We seem to move back into prophetic writing, as the sins of God's people are rehearsed rather than the evils of foreign empire. However, it is better to see Daniel's prayer of repentance as a parallel to Nehemiah's in Nehemiah 1 or Ezra's in Nehemiah 9: an inclusive prayer of repentance asking God to intervene on the Jewish nation's behalf, or, as here, to ask for revelation. Daniel includes himself in the "us," unlike the typical prophetic utterance of "you." So it does not become one of the WOES AND DENUNCIATIONS. (But see Jeremiah 14:7–9; 19–22 for another inclusive prayer.)

After the prayer, what emerges is a reinterpretation of Jeremiah's prophecy of a 70-year exile (Jeremiah 25:11, 12; 29:10). We arrive at another feature of apocalyptic writing here: the apocryphal arithmetic. Jeremiah's prophetic time may have been meant either historically or symbolically, but the writer here takes a hidden meaning from it, revising it to 70 weeks of years, that is, 490 years, with the Babylonian exile itself reduced to 49 years, a span that would actually fit the 586–537 B.C.E. historical time frame better. That then leaves 434 years for the return "in a troubled time" (9:25), though, of course, that shoots well over the period of the sacrilegious Antiochus Epiphanes (175–163 B.C.E.). This has led some Christian interpreters to place the final week into the period of Christ's crucifixion and the destruction of the temple in 70 A.D. The final week of years is then divided into two, three and a half years each, a figure that is then reconfigured into days and into the phrase "a time, times and half a time." Because it is half the perfect number, there is clearly some symbolism present. The difficulty with apocalyptic arithmetic is to know whether the numbers are to be considered literally or symbolically.

The final three chapters have a very different feel about them, especially in the very detailed timetable given. Most of the events of chapter 11, the main part of the vision, can be read against the events of 1 Maccabees. Thus they seem to be direct predictions rather than symbolic: No interpretation as such is needed. The three chapters seem curiously detached from the previous chapter, and there is perhaps a feeling of a later addition about them, even though they complete the total structure well. They also complete the sense that God is in full control of history, and that his rule will eventually be established.

Chapter 10 gives us further insight into the developing angelology of the book: the idea of angelic conflict between "the prince of the kingdom of Persia" and one of the chief angelic princes, Michael. This conflict allowed Daniel's angelic visitor to "get through" in the end. The idea of angels' being prevented from giving their message by hostile forces is a new one.

Another new development, though only briefly referred to, is that of resurrection from the dead, found in the closing of chapter 12 (12:2), with Daniel being assured of such resurrection (12:13).

This final verse sounds like a benediction: Daniel has completed his task, his book, and now can rest. If the historical references to the time of each vision or test are added up, he would certainly have been an old man, well into his eighties, since this final section is dated the third year of Cyrus's reign, that is, 535 B.C.E. (10:1).

The tone of the section is more deterministic than that of previous sections, "for what is determined shall be done" (11:36), pointing to another major difference with the prophetic, which is provisional, while apocalyptic seems determined.

Much of the apocalyptic language and imagery found in the book of Daniel is to be found in other apocalyptic writings from the intertestamental period, and later in Christian apocalyptic, especially Revelation. As brief examples, the beast and 10 horns are found in Revelation 13:1; 17:3f.; the unnamed beast also appears in Revelation 19:19–20. Michael appears in Revelation 12:7. Jesus himself refers to "the desolating abominations" of 8:13 and 9:27 in the apocalyptic gospel passages of Matthew 24:15 and Mark 13:14, a phrase also used in 1 Maccabees 1:54.

CHARACTERS

Belshazzar Last ruler of Babylon. His outrageous and sacrilegious using of vessels from the destroyed temple brings about the mysterious writing on the wall, predicting his sudden downfall as the Persian army overcome Babylon by night.

Daniel We have no other references to Daniel as a person outside this book. References to a "Daniel" in Ezekiel (Ezekiel 14:14; 28:3) must refer to a mythological figure of wisdom, Danel. Even if Daniel did live as a contemporary of Ezekiel's, he would have been slightly younger, with no time to have yet established a reputation for wisdom. In the first chapter he is seen as a youth, trained in the king's court for royal service, and renamed Belteshazzar ("Bel protects his life"). His Hebrew name means "God is my judge." His visions and interpretations span the zenith and sudden fall of the Babylonian Empire, under Nebuchadnezzar and his grandson, Belshazzar; and then into the Persian Empire under a ruler called Darius the Mede (of whom there is no historical record), and Cyrus. He exemplifies the belief that Jews can prosper in a hostile environment without compromising beliefs.

Hananiah, Mishael, Azariah Three other Jewish youths, Daniel's companions at court, where they are renamed Shadrach, Meshach, and Abednego. They, too, achieve high office, and they, too, undergo ordeal for their beliefs.

Nebuchadnezzar Or Nebuchedrezzar, in Babylonian documents, sole ruler of the Babylonian Empire. He is shown in Daniel as alternating from a beneficent ruler to a hubristic tyrant, a madman, and a believer in Yahweh. But he is not basically an opponent of the Jews. It is only his jealous subordinates who are.

The Prayer of Azariah

The full title of this work from the Apocrypha is The Prayer of Azariah and the Song of the Three Jews. It is one of three additions to the book of Daniel that are to be found in the Septuagint and various versions of the Christian Old Testament, though the versions found in the latter are usually derived from a different Greek source than the Septuagint. These books are recognized as deuterocanonical, i.e., as belonging to the secondary canon, by the Catholic and Orthodox Churches; see APOCRYPHA AND PSEUDEPIGRAPHA. The Greek versions may have had Hebrew or Aramaic originals. Both languages are used in Daniel itself. The other two additions are Bel and the Dragon and Susanna and the Elders, both of which feature Daniel himself, while this addition features his three companions.

This addition is placed in some versions of the Bible between Daniel 3:23 and 3:24, that is to say, in the middle of the story of Shadrach, Meshach, and Abednego (or Hananiah, Mishael, and Azariah, to give them their Hebrew names), when they are thrown into the fiery furnace for not bowing down to the huge statue of himself that Nebuchadnezzar, the Babylonian king, had erected (see BABYLON).

SYNOPSIS

The single chapter falls into three sections:

- verses 1–22: Azariah's PSALM of confession
- verses 23–28: A short prose copula enlarging on Daniel 3:19–23
- verses 29–68: A second psalm, this time of praise, sung by all three men

COMMENTARY

Verses 1–22

Although Azariah is suffering for his righteousness, nevertheless he makes a corporate prayer of confession for the sins of the nation that have brought about the Exile and destruction of JERUSALEM. This parallels Daniel's prayer of Daniel 9:3–19, but this is in verse form and reads as a penitential psalm. The exiles have been stripped of all outward religious forms, and so all that is left are a "contrite heart and a humble spirit" (verses 15–16; see Psalm 51:17).

Verses 23–28

The joining prose section adds some details to the Daniel story: The fourth man is identified specifically as an angel, rather than "like a son of man." The angel causes cooling winds to blow the heat away from the three men. And the song is sung within the furnace.

Verses 29–68

The second psalm is a wonderfully organized psalm, asking the whole of creation to bless God (see Psalm 148 for a similar psalm). It is creation praise that begins in the throne room of God himself, moves systematically through his creation, finishing in deliverance praise, as the three men have been rescued from the fire (66). In faith, the hope is that the Jews, too, will be delivered from the fire of exile and restored, their enemies destroyed.

Susanna

This chapter is one of three apocryphal additions to the book of Daniel and is known more fully as Susanna and the Elders. For a fuller introduction to these additions, see The Prayer of Azariah. In some versions of the Christian Old Testament and the Septuagint, this becomes Daniel 13.

SYNOPSIS

The story falls into four sections:

- verses 1–14: The two corrupt Jewish judges lust after the beautiful Susanna, Hilkiah's daughter, a virtuous woman.
- verses 15–27: They seize her while she is bathing in her garden, but she screams out rather than give in to their threats.
- verses 28–44: The two judges concoct a story about a secret liaison with a young man that they foiled. Susanna is given a show trial by the judges and condemned to death.
- verses 45–64: The youthful Daniel is inspired to intervene, reopen the trial, and prove the falsity of their testimony. The judges are thereupon put to death.

COMMENTARY

This story and the following Bel and the Dragon are both stories about the exposure of fraud by Daniel, at the very beginning and the very end of his career. This story appears to be the first recognition of the supernatural wisdom given him: not the wisdom he had been taught at the court of Nebuchadnezzar (Daniel 1) but divine wisdom to expose falsity—here, false justice. Interestingly, in the book of Daniel we do not see this sort of Solomonic wisdom in action at all. It is also an ordeal story, as are many others in the book of Daniel, but here the ordeal is that of the virtuous woman Susanna. The combination of virtue and beauty reminds us of Esther, another Exile story.

The main difference of this story is that it is set purely within the Jewish exilic community, which seems to be largely self-governing. This has led many scholars to set it at a later date, in the second century B.C.E., when the Jews were back in their homeland. The prosperity of the Jews and their social cohesion also stand out. But the judges act as judges and witnesses, both marks of a mock trial. The ordeal at court involves unveiling her, which may be a polite version of semistripping her (see Ezekiel 16:37–38). The ease with which the judges can touch her in the very act of supposedly administering justice shocks us and prepares us for the justness of the death penalty (62). The judges' lies are punningly connected to their sentence (vv. 54–55, 58–59), as the Greek words are very similar.

Bel and the Dragon

This chapter is one of three apocryphal additions to the book of Daniel, in some versions of the Hebrew Bible being numbered as Daniel 14. For further details, see the introduction to The Prayer of Azariah.

SYNOPSIS

The chapter consists of three stories, all dealing with Daniel under King Cyrus of PERSIA, during the Exile.

- verses 1–22: Daniel exposes the falsity of the worship of the Babylonian god, Bel.
- verses 23–30: Daniel exposes the falsity of another object of worship, a great snake.
- verses 31–42: A different account of Daniel's ordeal in the pit of lions is given.

COMMENTARY

The stories are set at the end of Daniel's life, after the Persians had overrun the Babylonian kingdom. However, it appears they took over the Babylonian gods, under Cyrus, the Persian king, who is mentioned only in passing in the book of Daniel (Daniel 6:28). In Daniel, it is Darius who threw Daniel to the lions. This is the Cyrus of Ezra 1, who gave permission for the Jewish exiles to return to their homeland.

Daniel, by now an elder statesman, and Cyrus are on good terms. So what could be seen as an ordeal story turns out to be more of a joke story, the exposure of simple cheating by the priests of Bel, by a simple device of Daniel's. Bel is identified with Marduk, the main Babylonian god.

The second story follows on naturally. If Bel is a fake, then surely the great snake cannot be. That really does eat what it has been thrown. The Greek word *drakon* usually does mean "dragon," but in the Septuagint it is used also to describe other monsters. The snake/dragon is very easily disposed of, and so the element of danger and ordeal is very much lessened.

However, as in the book of Daniel, Daniel's success leads to jealousy among the king's subordinates, which then leads to a real ordeal. Unlike the parallel story in Daniel 6:16–24, an element straight out of a fairy story is substituted: The prophet Habakkuk is air-lifted with food, not for the lions, but for Daniel, as he has to stay in the lions' den six days. The hyperbole and fablic dimension of the story again forbid us to take it seriously, unlike the Daniel story. All elements of real danger are removed, suggesting the writing of these three stories was done in more harmonious times than the book of Daniel.

Deuteronomy

The book of Deuteronomy is the last will and testament of Moses. After 40 years of wilderness wandering (see Numbers), the Israelites are now at the threshold of the HOLY LAND, ready to cross the RIVER JORDAN. Moses himself, however, is not allowed to enter the land because of an act of disobedience (see Numbers 20). Therefore, at this critical moment he explains for a last time the significance of the COVENANT that God has made with the previous generation of Israel. He urges the people to love God and to be faithful to him, and he warns them about the consequences of violating the covenant. In the canon of the Hebrew Bible, the book of Deuteronomy forms the conclusion of the Pentateuch (which consists of the books Genesis, Exodus, Leviticus, Numbers, and Deuteronomy). The traditional name of the book, *Deuteronomy*, meaning "second law," is appropriate insofar as Moses repeats in his farewell speech some of the events and of the legal material that are already covered in the books Exodus, Leviticus, and Numbers.

From its form, Deuteronomy fulfills the pattern of the ancient Near Eastern vassal treaty. Archaeological excavations have brought to light many Hittite vassal treaties stemming from the second millennium B.C.E. Typically, these contain six elements, which can also be found in Deuteronomy:

1. The preamble, in which the king is introduced (see 1:1–5; 4:1)
2. The historical prologue, in which past relations between the two parties are reviewed (either chapters 1–3 or the historical illustrations in chapters 5–11)
3. The treaty stipulations: (a) general principles (chapters 4–11); (b) detailed stipulations (chapters 12–26)
4. The treaty sanctions, curses, and blessings (chapters 27–30)
5. The witnesses—gods who will guarantee the treaty (the biblical text, instead, calls heaven and earth as witnesses: 4:26; 30:19; 31:28)
6. The provision for deposit of the treaty document in the temple and periodic public reading (31:9–13)

Therefore, Deuteronomy contains all elements that are typical of this kind of treaty (see DOCUMENTS). As a whole, however, it is not a treaty in its "pure" form but rather a treaty embedded in a farewell speech of Moses, which is, in turn, embedded in an overall frame locating the book in its narrative context.

The book's structure consists of an outer frame, chapters 1–3 and 31–34. These two sections basically form the historical framework, and they may be read as a single document: Chapter 3 ends announcing the death of Moses and the appointment of Joshua as his successor; chapter 31 begins with the same subject.

The inner frame, chapters 4–11 and 27–30, has the function of an appeal to keep the covenant. Again, the two sections may be read together: Chapter 11 ends announcing a covenant ceremony on Mount Gerizim and Mount Ebal; chapter 27 begins with the same topic. The inner frame can be further divided into two rings: introducing and summarizing exhortations of Moses in chapters 4 and 29–30, and the exhortations of the covenant document proper in chapters 5–11 and 27–28.

Chapters 12–26 form the core of the book, containing the detailed covenant stipulations.

Regarding the dating of the book, scholars take two different standpoints. The first is the traditional historical-critical dating, the Wellhausen school, which originated in Germany in the 19th century. According to this position, Deuteronomy has to be seen in connection with the Mosaic law book that is reported to be found while renovating the temple in the time of King Josiah (around 622 B.C.E.; see 2 Kings 22). Scholars put forward the insinuation that this book, which is seen as an original form of Deuteronomy, was actually not an old Mosaic document rediscovered but rather a text recently written and deposited there in order to be "discovered" and thereby feigning old age and great authority. By doing so, it is said, Josiah or the priests wanted to carry out some reforms, for example, banning all local sanctuaries, restricting the ritual service to the temple at Jerusalem (see chapter 12). According to this model, Deuteronomy would have been the first book canonized and therefore the beginning and the core of the canon of the Hebrew Bible. Scholars also try to find elements of the "Deuteronomistic Theology" in some of the prophetical texts of this time. The books of Deuteronomy, Joshua, Judges, Samuel, and Kings taken together are, according to this position, called the Deuteronomistic history. The position that the actual beginning of the biblical canon was based on a deception has, of course, wide-ranging implications.

The second position is also taken up by many scholars. According to this position, Deuteronomy, or at least large parts of it, originated toward the end of the second millennium B.C.E. As already mentioned, Deuteronomy has the form of an ancient vassal treaty. Comparison reveals that it very much resembles treaties found from the second millennium B.C.E. but differs from those from the first millennium B.C.E. In addition, the structure of Israel's society that can be inferred from the legal passages in Deuteronomy 12–26 fits into the premonarchic time (before roughly 1000 B.C.E.) better than into the monarchic time.

According to the biblical text's own witness, the speech of Moses took place around 1400 B.C.E. At the same time, the covenant text (but not necessarily the whole of Deuteronomy) was written down.

SYNOPSIS

Historical Retrospect: The Journey from Sinai to the Plains of Moab (Chapters 1–3)

After a short introductory passage, the book starts with a historical retrospective view by Moses, summarizing the events from the departure from MOUNT SINAI until the present situation. First, Moses tells how he has organized the people by appointing experienced persons as officers and judges over the individual tribes and families of the people. After that, he relates about the 12 spies the people had sent into Canaan after they had arrived at its border. The spies report that the land is very fertile but also that strong nations live in it. The Israelites are very much discouraged. They do not trust that God has power to make his promise come true. God punishes the people for their disbelief: They have to travel around in the wilderness for 40 years (see PILGRIMS AND WANDERERS).

It is the next generation that attempts the conquest of Canaan. They plan to enter the land not from the south, as the preceding generation had tried, but from the east. Therefore, they first have to travel around the territories of the Edomites and Moabites in the southeast of Canaan, moving into the eastern Jordan regions. After a few battles, the Israelites gain control over the whole eastern Jordan region, which is only sparsely populated. Then they move to the plains of Moab, in the northeast of the DEAD SEA, opposite Jericho, in order to prepare for crossing the Jordan and conquering Canaan. Moses now recalls that he himself will not be allowed to enter the land. God will allow him to climb a mountain from which he will see the whole land. After that, he will die. Joshua is appointed to be Moses' successor.

The Nature of Covenant Faith (Chapters 4–11)

But before the end of his life, Moses urges the younger generation of Israel to keep the covenant with God. He admonishes them neither to add anything to the covenant nor to take away anything from it. He emphasizes the great wisdom that is in the law. He warns the people not to leave the true God and to worship idols. He announces that God will punish those who violate the covenant. But he also predicts that after the judgment, repentance and a new beginning will be possible (chapter 4).

Now comes the actual text of the covenant that is made in the plains of Moab (4:44–49). First of all, Moses recalls the covenant that God had made at Mount Sinai with the previous generation. He describes the appearance of fire and smoke on the mountain, and he repeats the TEN COMMANDMENTS. Then he explains that the people have invited him to be the mediator between God and Israel. Moses tells the younger generation that they have to keep the Sinai covenant as the previous generation had (chapter 5).

After that, Moses turns from the past to the future. He talks about the coming conquest of the Promised Land and about the importance of continuing to keep the covenant after the conquest and in generations to come. When the Israelites enter the fertile land, they are—even with all their riches—not to forget that it was God who has taken them there. Moses forbids the Israelites to contact the former inhabitants of Canaan, so that they will not be seduced into idolatry, abandoning the true God. On the contrary, all idols and shrines have to be destroyed. If the people will keep the covenant, God will give many blessings. However, above all the blessings they should not forget to honor God (chapters 6–8).

Moses also warns the Israelites against becoming too proud of their election. The former inhabitants of Canaan will not be driven out because Israel is particularly faithful, but because the inhabitants are particularly godless. Moses retells the story of the golden calf, reminding the people that they are themselves always in danger of renouncing God (9:1–10:11).

Moses finishes his exhortation again by urging the Israelites to trust God and to obey his commandments. He speaks about God's majesty. He sets before the people blessing and curse: blessing, when the people are obedient; curse, when they are disobedient. Moses instructs the people to conduct a ceremony in which the blessings are to be called out in the direction of Mount Gerizim and the cursings in the direction of Mount Ebal (10:12–11:32).

The Detailed Covenant Stipulations (Chapters 12–26)

The core of the book consists of a series of legal and religious regulations. Moses begins by giving instructions on the proper worship of God. In the land, God will choose one place for a sanctuary, but local shrines will not be allowed. People who seduce others into idolatry are to be killed. After that are other laws on different subjects: tithes; holidays; limitations of royal authority; rules on warfare; laws on murder and manslaughter, marriage and divorce; and more, covering a wide range of areas of civil and cultic life.

The Covenant Ceremony, Blessings, and Curses (Chapters 27–30)

The covenant ceremony already announced in 11:29–30 is now described in more detail. As soon as the Jordan is crossed, an altar will have to be erected, and the words of the covenant engraved on its stones. There the Israelites are to celebrate the ratification of the covenant. After that, six of the tribes are to proclaim the words of blessing in the direction of Mount Gerizim; the other six tribes are to proclaim the curses in the direction of Mount Ebal. The Levites are to call out 12 words of curse, each to be answered by the people with the word *Amen* (chapter 27).

In the following chapter, the actual blessings and curses are given. First, Moses lists all the blessings God will give to the people, as long as they are obedient. After that, Moses lists the curses that will come over the people when they violate the covenant (chapter 28).

The book of the covenant actually ends at 29:1. However, Moses continues the subject by adding a couple of admonitions. He appeals to the people not to forget the great deeds of God and not to leave the covenant. Again he warns of the curse. But he also predicts that after all the curses have been fulfilled, there will still be the possibility of a new beginning. Moses sets before the people blessings and curses, life and death, and he urges them to choose the blessing and the life, by loving God and keeping his covenant.

Historical Prospect: The Last Acts of Moses and His Death (Chapters 31–34)

Moses announces to the people that he, at the age of 120 years, will die soon. God had forbidden him to enter the Promised Land. God has appointed Joshua as his successor. Ultimately, however, it is God himself who will give success to the conquest of the land. As ordered by God, Moses encourages Joshua in his mission.

With these words, the speech of Moses ends. Now Moses writes down the book of the covenant and hands it over to the priests and elders of Israel. He instructs them to let the book be read before the whole people every seven years at the Festival of Booths. Now God calls Moses to encounter him for a last time in the tent of meeting, together with Joshua. In the tent, God tells Moses that the people of Israel will violate the covenant in the future. He instructs Moses to compose a song of warning and teach it to the people (chapter 31).

The content of the song is given in the next chapter. The song is about the power and the faithfulness of God, who elected and blessed his people; about the disobedience of the people, hurting God's feelings with idolatry; about the judgment God will bring on his people by a hostile people; and about the final deliverance of Israel from its adversaries (chapter 32).

Now God commissions Moses to climb Mount Nebo, where he will die. Before he does so, Moses speaks out words of blessing over the 12 tribes of Israel. Then he climbs the mountain. From its top, God lets him see in a vision the whole land of Canaan, the land that he had promised to Israel's ancestors Abraham, Isaac, and Jacob. After that, Moses dies. God himself buries him. Joshua succeeds him in his office. In Israel there will never be any prophet so near to God, experiencing so many powerful signs and wonders of God, and being able to announce words of God with an authority as high as Moses (chapters 33–34).

COMMENTARY

Historical Retrospect: The Journey from Sinai to the Plains of Moab (Chapters 1–3)

This first main part is an abstract of the events told in Numbers 10–36. It summarizes the incidents that happened during the 40 years of Israel's wandering in the wilderness, beginning with the departure from Mount Sinai. The function of the section is to establish a connection between the Sinai covenant that has been made with the preceding generation of Israel 38 years before and the covenant that is now being made with the present generation, just before the conquest of the Promised Land begins. Since Moses is not allowed to take part in the conquest (see Numbers 20), this is his last chance to speak to the people.

The Nature of Covenant Faith (Chapters 4–11)

Moses takes the opportunity to urge the people to keep the covenant. The actual covenant document begins in chapter 5 (see 4:44–49), where Moses retells how he received the Ten Commandments on Mount Sinai 38 years before. In the course of the narrative, the Ten Commandments themselves are given (5:6–21), repeating almost word for word the text of Exodus 20 (For detailed comment on the Ten Commandments, see the commentary there).

Moses points to the fact that the covenant made at Mount Sinai is valid not only for the past generation but also now. The covenant that is made in the plains of Moab is therefore not a new, independent contract but rather a confirmation of the Sinaitic covenant.

The following chapters, 6–11, specifically address the generation that is about to occupy the land. This can be seen from the introductory sentences of the individual sections—6:1, 3; 7:1; 8:1; 9:1—as well as from the concluding statement in 11:31. It is important for those living in the Promised Land in the future to keep the covenant of God. The argument is illustrated by describing past events in the relationship between God and Israel. This is a typical element of ancient Near Eastern treaties.

The Detailed Covenant Stipulations (Chapters 12–26)

The core of the book consists of legal material from the political as well as from the ritual realm. Some of the texts repeat laws that are already given in the books of Exodus, Leviticus, and Numbers. However, concrete case laws with corresponding penalties are fairly rare. In contrast, overarching ethical principles are explained and illustrated. One can

probably say that the section is a SERMON on obeying the Lord more than an actual law book used in court.

As noted, the foregoing chapters 6–11 set the covenant very much in the context of occupying the Promised Land. Accordingly, the detailed stipulations from chapter 12 onward often deal with aspects of living in Canaan. For example, the collection starts with instructions for a central place of worship and a central sanctuary in the land (chapter 12). In contrast, the book of Exodus does not deal with this subject since it did not have any relevance for the wilderness generation. The legal collection closes with a text on tithes (chapter 26). The text emphasizes that by giving the tenth the people should remember that all yields of the land are ultimately given by God, who has delivered his people out of EGYPT and led them into this fruitful region. This background of living in the land can also be seen with many of the other laws, e.g., the laws on royal authority, the rules of warfare, and the cities of refuge. Therefore, the organizational principle of Exodus, Leviticus, and Numbers, according to which the legal sections are always thematically connected to the surrounding narrative, also applies to Deuteronomy.

The internal ordering of the individual sections in Deuteronomy 12–26, however, seems rather haphazard, at least at first sight. Some scholars indeed hold the position that the sections are organized in the order of the Ten Commandments. This can be clearly shown especially for the first half of the Commandments:

The first section, 12:1–14:21, contains instructions about the proper worship of God and the ban of idolatry. In the Ten Commandments, this corresponds to the first three commandments (according to the Jewish numbering; see the commentary to Exodus 20). In more detail, chapter 12 deals with the proper worship of God and therefore is an application of the sentence "I am the Lord, your God"; chapter 13 warns of seduction to idolatry and therefore corresponds to the commandment that bans idolatry; 14:1–21 is against a heathen way of dealing with food and against Canaanite ritual practices that were probably executed while worshipping the Lord and can therefore be understood as an application of the commandment not to misuse the name of the Lord.

The second section, 14:22–16:17, deals with holy times, such as the sabbatical year and the yearly holidays, and with holy taxes, and is therefore an illustration of the fourth commandment on keeping the Sabbath.

The third section, 16:18–18:22, mostly consists of laws concerning the authorities of Israel: judges, kings, priests, and others. This can be seen as an extension of the fifth commandment to honor father and mother—which is, in a more general sense, a commandment regarding authority.

Deuteronomy 19:1–13 and 21:1–9 deal with murder and manslaughter and therefore correspond to the sixth commandment. However, after 19:13, a clear grouping of subjects is not discernible. The topics of the remaining commandments, murder, adultery, robbery, and coveting, are all dealt with in Deuteronomy 19–25 but not in a strict order. Rather, the subjects are woven into one another. Probably this is due to the fact that they are all based on the same principle, that is, to respect the neighbor.

The Covenant Ceremony, Blessings, and Curses (Chapters 27–30)

The proclamation of curses and blessings as part of the ratification ceremony is another element typical of ancient Near Eastern treaties. Parts of this ceremony are described in chapter 27. The content of the proclamation, the blessings and curses, are given in chapter 28. That the curses receive much more space than the blessings is also common for this Near Eastern form. The blessings should not just be understood as a reward for good behavior—the issue at stake is rather the personal relationship of God to his people. Since God is the source of all blessing, being in fellowship with him will result in blessing, and separating from him will necessarily result in the loss of the blessing. The text of the covenant proper ends in 29:1. However, Moses continues the topic in chapters 29–30, again urging the people to keep the covenant. These concluding words very much correspond to Moses' opening words in chapter 4: In both instances, Moses warns the people about the curses, but he also announces that after the curses have been fulfilled, there will be the possibility of returning to the Lord and making a new beginning (4:29–31; 30:1–10). The statement "I call heaven and earth to witness against you this day" is also common to both sections (4:26; 30:19).

Historical Prospect: The Last Acts of Moses and His Death (Chapters 31–34)

The last main part begins by taking up the subject that ended the first part: Moses will die soon. This is the issue that gives tension and motivation to the whole book and especially to the last main section: When the moment of farewell is near, one has to concentrate on what is really important. So the whole book, but especially the last section, expresses the last will and testament of Moses.

The narrative sections of the last main part that move the action forward are 31:1–2, 14–16; 32:48–52; and 34:1–12. The important farewell topics embedded in this framework are the appointment of Joshua as Moses' successor (31:3–8) and the finishing of the book of the covenant, handing it over to responsible persons and commissioning them to read the book to the whole people every seven years (31:9–13, 24–26). In a final encounter with God in the tent of meeting, God tells Moses that the people will violate the covenant soon. Therefore, Moses composes the Song of Moses as a closing warning (chapter 32). It is, however, not a song in the proper sense but rather a didactic poem (see 32:2) based on the ancient literary form of the lawsuit (*rib*, in Hebrew), which was common for a suzerain confronting an erring vassal. The poem, presented immediately before the crossing of the Jordan, also forms a counterpart to Moses' first psalm sung after the crossing of the Red Sea (Exodus 15). Before Moses leaves the people for the last time, he speaks out a blessing over the 12 tribes (chapter 33).

The coda in 34:10–12 underscores the paramount authority of Moses. The text functions as a canonical seal pointing to the overarching authority of Deuteronomy and of the Pentateuch as a whole: No one can impart words of God with the same authority as Moses. Therefore, in the Hebrew Bible the Pentateuch, the Torah, has the highest authority. All other biblical books depend on it and have to be read on the background of the Pentateuch (see, for example, Joshua 1:7–8).

The statement that there will be no prophet like Moses has, however, a counterpart in Deuteronomy 18:15, where Moses announces that "the LORD your God will raise up for you a prophet like me from among your own people; you shall heed such a prophet." The writers of the New Testament apply this to Jesus Christ, who is presented as the "new Moses," the new authority, the new mediator between God and humanity.

CHARACTER

Moses Moses has become very old. Moreover, because he has been disobedient in one instance (Numbers 20), God has forbidden him to enter the land of Canaan together with his people. Therefore, Moses addresses himself to the people with a last great speech. He introduces himself as the mediator between God and the people of Israel. God as well as Israel have appointed him for this office (5:22–31). On the basis of this authority, Moses renews the covenant between God and Israel. With many words he urges and encourages the people to love and trust God and keep the covenant he has made with them to be his holy people.

Ecclesiastes

What is the meaning of life? This, in modern words, is the theme of the book of Ecclesiastes. The book belongs, together with Job, Proverbs, and the Song of Solomon, to the so-called WISDOM LITERATURE of the Hebrew Bible. Like the other wisdom books and especially Proverbs, Ecclesiastes bases its wisdom reflections on the observation of nature and society. Unlike Proverbs, however, Ecclesiastes is concerned with the exceptions rather than with the rules. The book is especially interested in situations that *cannot* be explained according to tried and tested patterns. In particular, the book deals with the bounds of life and the bounds of knowledge, and it asks how it can be possible to live a meaningful life despite these limitations.

The name of the book is derived from its main speaker, Qoheleth, in the Septuagint (see BIBLE, EARLY TRANSLATIONS OF) rendered as *Ecclesiastes.* The Hebrew word, as well as the Greek, probably means someone who has an office associated with an assembly. The traditional rendering "the preacher," however, is overspecific.

Traditionally, Qoheleth is identified with the king, Solomon. Although the book itself does not mention Solomon's name, the wisdom context and the description of a rich king of Jerusalem, descendant of David (1:1, 12ff.), very much give the book a Solomonic aura. Two aspects, however, have to be considered. The first is that Qoheleth is not to be identified with the author of the book. Rather, from a literary point of view, there is an anonymous narrator who quotes the words of Qoheleth (see the "says the Preacher" in 1:2; 7:27; 12:8). Second, the expression "I was king over Israel" in 1:12 does not necessarily imply that Qoheleth actually was the king. There is at least the possibility that this sentence wants to express a literary, fictional identification: Qoheleth appears in the role of the king in order to make certain reflections on the king's life as if it were his own. Three observations support this position: (1) The Solomonic identity is not explicitly stated but rather given in a veiled form, unlike, for example, in the title of the book of Proverbs. (2) The Hebrew past tense in "I was king" in 1:12 sounds enigmatic, since the historical Solomon was king until the moment of his death, and he could not have spoken about himself in that way. (3) The specific royal viewpoint ends after the second chapter of the book.

The date of the book is directly related to the question of authorship. Solomon reigned from 971 to 931 B.C.E. If Solomonic authorship is not assumed, then any date between 931 and approximately 190–170 B.C.E. is possible, since from that time we have the first extant manuscripts of the book, found in the caves of Qumran (see DEAD SEA SCROLLS). Current scholarship is inclined to favor the Hellenistic era, around 250 B.C.E., though there are no compelling reasons for this. Influences of Greek philosophy in the book are assumed by some.

The language of the book is distinctive. It is difficult to decide whether its overall style is prose or poetry. Although most of the text does not show the typical features of Hebrew poetry, e.g., strophic parallelism, its style is nevertheless very dense, even formulaic. Among Qoheleth's favorite words are *do* (62×), *wise* (51×), *good* (51×), *see* (46×), (*all is*) *vanity* (38×), *time* (37×), *trouble* (33×), *evil* (30×), and *under the sun* (29×). Together, the favorite words and phrases make up even about 20 percent of the text. In some places, Qoheleth also employs traditional wisdom proverbs supporting his argument (e.g., 1:15, 18; 7:1–12). Two of the most powerful biblical poems can be found in the book of Qoheleth: the poem on time (3:1–8) and the poem on death (12:1–7).

The book's message is complex and very much disputed. Even totally opposite interpretations have been proposed. The interpretation given here is based on a close following of the literary structure of the book, as proposed in more recent scholarship. The literary structure has the function of defining the relationships among the individual parts of the text, which very much enhances the understanding of the whole argument.

The main part of the book is framed by the statement "Vanity of vanities, says Qoheleth, vanity of vanities," which appears in 1:2 and 12:8. Inside that frame Qoheleth speaks in the first person; outside the frame Qoheleth is spoken of in the third person (but see 7:27). The main part of the book is seen to consist of three large blocks (1:3–3:9; 3:10–8:17; 9:1–12:7), which each consist of a major train of thought of Qoheleth.

SYNOPSIS

In his first train of thought (1:3–3:9), Qoheleth looks at life from the perspective of the most wealthy King Solomon, who can fulfill any wishes for himself. He conducts, as it were, an investigation into the whole of life, choosing the very promising life of Solomon, searching for anything in life that lasts. His finding, however, is that human beings cannot gain any lasting profit. In particular, death as the supreme leveler puts an end to all human ambitions. Nevertheless, it is possible to be happy for those who take their life as a gift from the hand of God and enjoy it.

A second train of thought of Qoheleth (3:10–8:17) is based on various observations of the uncertainties and inequities of life. Qoheleth demonstrates that the ways of God are often incomprehensible to human beings. Therefore he appeals for respect before God. "God is in heaven and you upon the earth, therefore let your words be few" (5:2). Even wealth often leads to misfortune, whether for others or for the rich. Nevertheless, there is the possibility of living a rich and happy life from the hand of God.

In a third train of thought (9:1–12:7), Qoheleth asks how it is possible to live a meaningful life despite all its limitations. He discusses life in the face of death. He analyzes how unforeseen circumstances and the ups and downs of everyday life distort the outcomes of human efforts. He instructs his readers to take those scattering effects into consideration right from the start, to be ready for all eventualities, and, despite uncertainties, to act bravely, and enjoy their lives.

COMMENTARY

The Limits of Life (1:3–3:9)

The first main train of thought is framed by the question "What do human beings gain from all their toil under the sun?" in 1:3 and 3:9. A direct answer is found at the center of the section in 2:11. The subject of the section, therefore, is the limits of living a successful life, expressed through the futile attempt to achieve for oneself a profit that survives.

In the body of the first section, 1:12 to 2:26, Qoheleth imagines being the wealthy King Solomon, with all life's options open before him. In his experiment, he concentrates on three areas, namely, works, wisdom, and pleasure, trying to gain a lasting profit in his life in any of these areas. Looking back, however, he sees that none of them can yield the profit he sought. In particular, he finds death to be the ultimate limitation on all human efforts.

Choosing Solomon as an example has a special significance. According to the narrative of 1 Kings 1–11, Solomon was very wise, wealthy, and successful. He had all the possibilities human beings could have at that time. Nevertheless, in the end he failed. He had too many foreign wives, he turned to foreign gods, and the Israelite kingdom split after his death.

Qoheleth's experiment is framed by two poems. The first poem (1:4–11) shows, on the basis of ecological cycles, that things that are apparently new have in fact existed before. Things are in a continuous rotation. Everything is balanced; there is no lasting profit, no surplus in one or the other direction.

The second poem, "Everything has its time" (3:1–8), surely is one of best-known passages of the book. People like to interpret it to indicate that one has to recognize when it is the right time for doing something. Taken in itself, this interpretation is valid. Seen in the context of the question of lasting profit, however, the following, more pessimistic interpretation is to be preferred: In the poem, Qoheleth lists pairs of contrary acts. Each deed has its opposite. Everything that happens at a certain time is balanced by its opposite at another time. Again, there is no surplus in one or the other direction.

Qoheleth's result in 2:11 is that life "under the sun" has no "gain," or, to express it in modern words: Life does not have any meaning without God.

Qoheleth is often deemed to be a confirmed skeptic. He is, however, not skeptical about belief in God but about belief in human beings *without* God. As soon as contact with God is established, a happy life out of God's hand is possible, beyond all profit aspirations. "Happiness is not founded in man, when he eats and drinks and finds enjoyment in his work. Rather, I saw, this is from the hand of God" (2:24, translation according to Ludger Schwienhorst-Schönberger). The apparent contradiction in the assessment of pleasure in 2:1–2 and 2:24–26 can be resolved by distinguishing between the concepts of "profit" and "portion," both used throughout the book. By seeking pleasure, people cannot achieve a lasting *profit* for their lives, but they can enjoy the happiness that is given to them as their *portion* from God.

In total, there are seven passages in the book where Qoheleth calls upon people to enjoy their lives as given to them by God (2:24–26; 3:12–13; 3:22; 5:17–19; 8:15; 9:7–10; 11:9–10).

To summarize the first main part: There is no lasting profit for human beings under the sun, whether in works, wisdom, or pleasure. People can achieve happiness, however, by taking their lives as a gift out of the hand of God and enjoying it.

The Limits of Knowledge (3:10–8:17)
While the first main section of the book deals with the limits of life, the second train of thought devotes itself to the limits of knowledge. The first and the last passage (3:10–22 and 8:9–17) make up a frame around the second main part. They have the following main statements in common:

- Basic message: Human beings cannot comprehend the work of God (3:11; 8:17).
- Example: There is injustice on earth (3:16; 8:10–11, 14), but God will bring justice (3:17; 8:12b–13).
- First conclusion: There is nothing better for human beings than to enjoy life (3:12, 22; 8:15).
- Second conclusion: God is to be revered (3:14, see 8:12b–13).

These four basic statements are further expounded in the inner part of the second main section; 4:1–16 and 7:15–29 contain case studies demonstrating the incomprehensibility of the divine world order. In the face of this, 4:17–5:7 and 6:10–7:14 call for humility, respect for God, and contemplation; 5:8–17 and 6:1–9 deal with wealth leading to misfortune. The two passages can be understood as flanking warnings to the positive statement in 5:18–20, which says that wealth is a gift of God to be enjoyed. The second main section is seen by some as forming a concentric structure (see STRUCTURES, LITERARY), the pairs of passages given earlier forming concentric rings around the central passage of 5:18–20. This call to enjoy life is the fourth of seven such calls in the book, underscoring its central position.

The message of the second main section can therefore be summarized as follows: People cannot comprehend the work of God under the sun. Many things seem to be meaningless or unjust to them. In view of that, however, they should not remonstrate but rather learn to accept their own limitations, learn humility, contemplation, and respect before God. For human beings there is nothing better than to take the life that is given to them by God with all its mysteries and enjoy it.

Living in the Face of Death (9:1–12:7)

While the first main section deals with the bounds of life and the second with the bounds of knowledge, the third main section examines how life can be led successfully despite these limitations. The section can be described as an A–B–A′ form. The very touching passages of 9:1–12 and 11:7–12:7, A and A′, deal with life in the face of death. The message here is to seize the opportunities of life as long as it is possible, since old age and death are inevitable, and no one knows when his or her time will end. When it comes to the subject of death, Qoheleth is far from glossing over this matter. Rather, he talks about death in a harsh, pessimistic, but ultimately realistic manner.

The middle part, 9:13–11:6, deals with managing the ups and downs of everyday life. Qoheleth starts here with an example of a wise man whose wisdom could have delivered a city—but no one remembered him (9:13–15). On that basis he discusses the problem that actions do not always have their envisaged consequences. Traditional wisdom assumes the principle of retribution, saying that every action has its corresponding consequence. Qoheleth, however, widens this principle in order to include the scattering effect to which all human work is subject. Unforeseen circumstances, as well as a lack of wisdom, can distort the outcome. Sometimes what happens is the opposite of what is intended, or side effects occur (9:13–10:1; 10:8, 9, 11); sometimes complicating conditions slow one's work (10:10); sometimes consequences are unexpectedly far-reaching (10:20).

Qoheleth, therefore, asks the reader to take these scattering effects into consideration from the start, to be ready for all eventualities, and, despite uncertainties, not to hesitate but to act and seize all opportunities.

To sum up the message of the third main section: Enjoy your life, as long as you have it, and make the best of it; in the ups and downs of life act wisely; enjoy the time of your youth—in respect before God—before old age and death.

The Framing Motto Verse (1:2; 12:8)

Qoheleth's thoughts are framed by the statement "All is vanity" in 1:2 and 12:8. Literally, the text speaks of a "breath of wind." Everything that happens under the sun is a "breath of wind." It is insignificant, transitory, and meaningless from the perspective of death and eternity.

It is important to consider two points here. First, the word *all* does not include God and the heavenly realm. It rather refers to the human world, or, in Qoheleth's words, the living "under the sun." Second, the sentence does not make up the book's total message. It rather denotes the context in which Qoheleth puts his thoughts. All false senses of security, all false hopes and vain dreams, have to be done away with before the path to true joy can be found.

The Epilogue (12:9–14)

The book of Qoheleth has a peculiar literary frame. The author, or narrator, does not directly communicate with the reader. Instead, he lets "Qoheleth" speak for him. For most of the time, the author leaves open whether he agrees with Qoheleth or not. Through this technique, faithful readers do not feel obliged to accept all that they read right from the beginning. Rather, they are challenged to find their own position. Only in the epilogue does the auctorial narrator himself take a stand on Qoheleth, giving an overall confirmation.

The last two verses of the book have some particular implications. The call to obey God can, first of all, be understood as a protection against misunderstanding. Readers of Ecclesiastes who end up rather confused are on the safe side when they follow this last call to obey God.

Second, the last verse expresses the important theological idea of the last judgment. This idea directly follows from Qoheleth's observations of injustice on earth paired with his assumption that God will finally effect justice. Although Qoheleth opposes religious speculation on death and the afterlife (see 3:21), he is sure that there will be a life after death, at least for the purpose of effecting justice.

Third, in the book of Proverbs, the "fear of the LORD" is said to be the beginning of all wisdom

(Proverbs 1:7). In Qoheleth, it rather forms the end. All intellectual efforts in the end lead one back to fearing God.

CHARACTERS

God   God is, according to the book of Ecclesiastes, the source of true life. Without him, life has no meaning. If human beings take their life as a gift from God, they can enjoy it. However, human beings cannot comprehend the work of God. Therefore, they should be humble before him. But they can trust that God will effect justice in the end.

Qoheleth   The main speaker of the book. The Hebrew word *Qoheleth* probably means someone who has an office associated with an assembly. Most of the English versions therefore render his name as *preacher* or *teacher*. In 12:9 he is said to be a wise man teaching the people and arranging many proverbs. In 1:12 he says, "I, the Preacher, was king over Israel in Jerusalem." But this identification may well be a literary, fictional one (see the introduction). Qoheleth is surely an independent thinker. His arguments are not so much based on traditional wisdom as his own observations and reflections.

Ecclesiasticus

See Sirach.

Ephesians

Among the letters of PAUL, Ephesians has its own characteristics. In the original Greek it has unusually long sentences, especially in the first half, although this is obscured in the translations. It uses extended prayer forms. Its conceptual world includes unusual ideas such as power, "the heavenly places," and "fullness," as well as more familiar ones such as "in Christ" and the plan of God. Here Paul has more to say about the universal Church than in most other letters, and we might say that

the letter's theme is "the Church as God's new society." Among the images used to describe the church are those of a temple, household, body, and bride. Issues such as the LAW and justification by faith—the key ideas of Romans and Galatians—are hardly found here.

Ephesians has many similarities with Colossians, including a similar outline, but it lacks the specifics of a local or personal situation. The best explanation of this state of affairs is that some time after Paul had written Colossians, which is a real letter to a particular church, he used the same material once again in a more general text. By the time of writing, toward the end of Paul's life, there may have been several house churches in the large town of Ephesus with its up to half a million inhabitants. Alternatively, the letter we call Ephesians may have been sent as a circular letter to a range of churches in Asia Minor. Ephesus was the capital of Asia Minor. Evidence for this origin is found in the absence of the phrase "in Ephesus" from several old, good MANUSCRIPTS in 1:1 together with the absence of church-specific data in the letter as a whole. It is best to see Ephesians as a general letter by Paul to an audience of Christians from a Gentile background. Whenever the church is mentioned, it is the universal Church rather than a specific local church.

Paul is in prison as he writes (3:13; 4:1; 6:20), and this is probably in Rome so that we date the letter in the years 60–62 C.E. See also EPISTLE.

SYNOPSIS

Ephesians falls neatly into two equal parts: Chapters 1–3 have doctrinal content, whereas chapters 4–6 are ethical. The letter includes many topics that would have been treated in an introduction to the Christian faith but at quite a high level.

After a brief introduction and greetings (1:1–2) Paul praises the grace of God in Jesus Christ, then he mentions the Holy Spirit (verses 13–14). The second half of chapter 1 addresses God directly in prayer, asking for the work of the Holy Spirit and for certainty of the believers' hope of the future. In chapter 2 attention shifts further to the position of the believers, with verses 1–10 spelling out how they were saved and verses 11–22 explaining that they belong to God's holy people, the Church, which consists of believers from Jewish and Gentile backgrounds. Paul then discusses the contribution of his own ministry to the Church (3:1–13) and prays once more for it (3:14–21).

The second half of the letter addresses the unity, growth, and development of the Church (4:1–16) before it moves on to the individual believer. Here Paul considers the consequences of being a Christian. Specific topics include the roles of husband and wife (5:21–33) and of other groups (6:9). The letter ends with a discussion of spiritual armor (6:10–20) and the usual personal notes and blessings (6:21–24).

COMMENTARY

A frequent word in Ephesians is *mystery* (1:9; 3:3, 4, 5, 9; 5:32; 6:19), which always refers to something that has become known in Jesus Christ: His saving work of death and Resurrection was as yet unknown in the period of the HEBREW BIBLE, and Paul and the other apostles are now proclaiming it.

Another common term is "heavenly places" (1:3, 20; 2:6; 3:10; 6:12), which originated from a worldview that distinguished multiple heavens. It suggests that believers live a spiritual life as well as a natural life, and to modern readers it evokes the superiority of Jesus as well as the believers over the entire world.

Ephesians makes limited use of the Hebrew Bible, largely in the second half. In 5:14 Paul introduces the words "Sleeper, awake! Rise from the dead, and Christ will shine on you" as a quote. As they are not found in a known document, they are probably an early Christian saying.

In lofty terms 1:3–14 discusses God's way with the world in Jesus Christ in the form of a benediction (blessing) of God. Much emphasis falls on God's initiative in sending Jesus to the world and in calling humans to follow him, even before they were created. The phrase "redemption through his blood" (verse 7) alludes to the death of Jesus on the cross, where his blood flowed as a sacrifice. Paul also spells out the "inheritance" Christians have, which is their eternal salvation. The importance of Jesus is brought out in the claim that the entire universe will be united in or under him (verse

10). At the end of the passage the HOLY SPIRIT is introduced as well so that we have a trinitarian benediction (see TRINITY). He is called a seal, alluding to the believers' BAPTISM, which in church language became known as "seal of the Spirit," and also "deposit" or "pledge," which indicates that his presence in the lives of believers guarantees their resurrection to eternal life (cf. 4:30). In verse 21 as in 6:12 the word *power* reflects the Jewish belief in powerful ANGELS, good and bad, who are all being subjected to Jesus Christ (cf. 1 Corinthians 15:24–27). In verse 23 Paul attempts to squeeze three metaphors into one short sentence: God fills everything, Christ is the fullness of God, and the Church is the body of Christ. Paul here applies the body metaphor that he used in 1 Corinthians 12 to the universal Church, while including Jesus as the head (leader) of the Church. Ancient people knew enough of the body to realize that it was controlled by the head.

The two parts of chapter 2 run in parallel, with the first half discussing the position of individual believers and the second half that of the Church. Both parts emphasize the change brought about by the coming of Jesus into the world by using words such as *then* and *but now*. What it means that unbelievers are "dead through . . . sins" (2:1) is explained in verses 2–3; "children (or: objects) of wrath" is a Jewish way of saying that people deserve God's anger against sin. As in chapter 1, the emphasis is entirely on God's initiative and grace, to which humans cannot add anything of their own: Although God prepared good deeds for them to do, they do not earn their salvation (verse 10). The "dividing wall" (verse 14) is the LAW as a symbol of national identity that set the Jews apart from the other nations and led to reciprocal hostile feelings. Scholars disagree over whether the "cornerstone" (verse 20) is in the foundation or in the top of the building, but this unclarity does not affect the force of the metaphor. The "apostles and prophets" (2:20; 3:5) are probably the two leading groups in the Church.

In 3:1–13 the theme of the unity of Jewish and Gentile believers continues as Paul discusses his own role as the apostle who was instrumental in breaking down the ethnic barriers in the earliest churches. Paul's prayer in 3:14–21 is for more faith and spiritual knowledge for the readers. The "every family" (3:15) must be the entire Church. Unity is still the central thought in 4:1–6, after which Paul discusses the diverse roles of the members of the Church in its upbuilding. The Church has received ample gifts from God to enable growth to maturity. In 4:8 Psalm 68:18 is quoted. As in John 3:13, Jesus' descent is his incarnation (see JESUS CHRIST); his ascension allowed the coming of the Holy Spirit with his gifts. In its critical description of the misguided thinking of unbelievers, 4:17–5:5 parallels Romans 1:18–32 and offers renewal of the mind as alternative.

The prohibition of drunkenness (not of all drinking!) in 5:18–20 turns attention to the collective, for Paul suggests fulfillment with the Spirit as alternative to filling up with spirits. In 5:21–6:9 scholars recognize the form of the "household code," an ancient type of ethical instruction also found in the New Testament in Colossians 3:18–4:1 and 1 Peter 2:13–3:7. The entire instruction is to be read in the light of the self-giving love of Jesus (5:2). Some Bible translations are wrong to take verse 21 with the preceding verses because the command to be subject to one another introduces the instructions for the wives (verses 22–24) and the husbands (verses 25–33). The washing in verse 26 is BAPTISM, and in verse 31 Paul quotes Genesis 2:24. In 6:1–4 the husband-and-wife pattern is repeated for parents and children, 6:5–9 for masters and slaves. By emphasizing the lordship of Christ over all aspects of life, and a lifestyle in imitation of his, Christianity gradually transformed society.

In 6:10–20 the cosmic undercurrent of the letter recurs a last time as believers are encouraged to partake in the spiritual battle with spiritual armor (cf. Isaiah 11:4–5; 59:16–17), of which the sword (the word of God) is the only offensive weapon. Holy war is here a metaphor for the struggle the Church faces with evil forces.

CHARACTER

Jesus Christ   Apart from Paul and Tychicus (6:21), no human characters are mentioned in this letter. The person who dominates the entire argument is Jesus Christ, who is depicted as the center

The ascension of Jesus, engraving by Julius Schnorr von Carolsfeld

of God's dealings with the world, the head and equipper of the Church, and the example of a good life. The believers live in the light with him (5:8).

1 and 2 Esdras

Using the name or pseudonym of Ezra (*Esdras* is the Greek spelling), several books are named and numbered differently in the Hebrew, Greek, and Latin traditions, respectively. The most important can be seen in the following table:

English Bibles	Septuagint (Greek)	Vulgate (Latin)
Ezra (canonical)	Esdras B, 1–10	1 Ezra
Nehemiah (canonical)	Esdras B, 11–23	2 Ezra
1 Esdras	Esdras A	3 Ezra
2 Esdras	—	4 Ezra

More apocryphal "Ezra" books came into being up until the ninth century C.E. In this entry, the books of 1 and 2 Esdras are discussed.

1 Esdras belongs to the deuterocanonical (i.e., being of secondary canonical rank) books of the

Orthodox Churches. The Roman Catholics as well as the Protestants reckon the book among the Apocrypha (see APOCRYPHA AND PSEUDEPIGRAPHA).

From its content, 1 Esdras is in large parts compiled of sections of the books of Chronicles, Ezra, and Nehemiah. It is a narrative stretching from the destruction until the restoration of the Jerusalem temple. Of the nine chapters, only chapters 3 and 4 are not based on canonical texts.

The book is extant in Greek and Latin versions. It dates from about 100 B.C.E. to 100 C.E.

The first chapter of the book deals with the final days of the kingdom of Judah, from Josiah's reforms until the conquest of Jerusalem by the Babylonians (2 Chronicles 35–36). The second chapter deals with the return from the Babylonian Exile (see RETURN FROM EXILE) and the beginning of the restoration of the temple. However, opposition arises against rebuilding the temple, and the work stops soon after the laying of the foundation stone (Ezra 1:1–11; 4:7–24).

Chapters 3 and 4 of the book tell about a bet three guardians of King Darius make. They decide to hold debate about what thing is the strongest. The one who argues his case best would be rewarded by the king. Topics discussed are the wine, the king, and the women. The third guardian happens to be Zerubbabel, a Jew and leading figure in the restoration process. His speech is about the power of women, but then he turns to praising truth as the highest. He wins the debate. As a reward, he asks King Darius to fulfill his promises to Judah and support the rebuilding of the Jerusalem temple. This section of the story is not based on a canonical text. Motifs are used, however, from the biblical books of Daniel and Esther.

Chapters 5–7 describe the continuation of the work at the temple according to Ezra 2–7. Finally, chapters 8–9 report the arrival of Ezra in Jerusalem, his actions against the mixed marriages, and his reading of the Law to the people (Ezra 7–10; Nehemiah 7:38–8:12).

Since the book quotes from the book of Ezra-Nehemiah but omits the passages dealing with Nehemiah, it was assumed to be based on an earlier version of Ezra-Nehemiah. In the same way, since the book combines sections from Chronicles as well as from Ezra-Nehemiah, it was assumed that Chronicles, Ezra, and Nehemiah originally were a single book.

However, it rather seems to be the case that 1 Esdras combines different biblical passages with the purpose of telling the story of the Jerusalem temple from its destruction until its rebuilding. Possibly this was done in order to give the story of the three guardians' bet a historical framework. In any case, 1 Esdras is a deliberate rearrangement of biblical material and so does not give a hint to an earlier version of the biblical text.

2 Esdras belongs to the deuterocanonical books of the Russian Orthodox Church. All other churches reckon the book among the Apocrypha.

The book consists of three parts that originated in different times. Chapters 3–14 probably stem from a Palestinian Jew around 100 C.E. and were originally written in Hebrew but are today extant only in Greek (fragmentary) and other translations. About 50 years later, a Greek-speaking Christian added chapters 1–2. Another century later, chapters 15–16 were added. The three parts sometimes appear independently of each other, called the fourth, fifth, and sixth books of Ezra.

Chapters 1 and 2 of the book describe Ezra's being called as a prophet for God and relate an initial prophetic message. Its major point is that God now has rejected Israel and turns to other nations. In a vision, Ezra sees the "Son of God" among a great multitude placing a crown on each of the people.

The main section, chapters 3–14, consists of seven so-called visions. The first three are rather dialogues Ezra has with the angel Uriel about the problem of suffering (3:1–9:25). Ezra laments that the ways of God are incomprehensible to human beings. Uriel explains to him the greater concept of the work of God using the teaching of the two ages. According to this teaching, the present age is only an intermediate stage and a time of proof preparing human beings for the age to come. The course of history runs as God has determined it; it cannot be quickened or slowed. However, the end of the present age will occur soon. That people will have access to the coming age is an act of God's grace. However, it also depends on how people commit their life in the present age. In this age, people decide for life or death of the coming age. The Law of Moses gives orientation in the present age and leads to eternal life in the coming.

This teaching is then illustrated in three visions: Zion's grief and splendor (9:26–10:59); the eagle from the sea (11:1–12:51), symbolizing the Roman Empire; and the human being from the sea, the Son of God, redeeming the world (13:1–58).

In the seventh vision, Ezra laments before God that Holy Scriptures had been lost (during the EXILE). As an answer, God commissions him to call five scribes. Then Ezra is filled with God's spirit, and in 40 days he dictates all the Scriptures to the five scribes. Ninety-four books are written, 24 of them for the public and 70 only for the wise and worthy. Obviously, the account is legendary. Interesting, however, is the number of books given. Twenty-four is the number of books in the Hebrew Bible (the 12 small prophets are counted as one book; 1 and 2 Samuel, 1 and 2 Kings, 1 and 2 Chronicles, and Ezra-Nehemiah are taken as one, respectively, thereby arriving from the Protestant 39 books at the Hebrew 24 books). This means, from the end of the first century C.E., we have a clear statement that the canon of the Hebrew Bible was closed (see FORMATION OF THE CANON: THE HEBREW BIBLE). The other 70 books probably belong to the realm of the Apocrypha.

Chapters 15–16 talk about the coming judgment day. God's wrath is announced over different nations, and the people of God are admonished to prepare for the end. A time of intense tribulation will come, but God will deliver his people from their enemies' hands.

Esther

Full of tragedy and at the same time full of humor and irony, the book of Esther depicts the dangerous and uncertain character of life for the Jewish people in the DIASPORA of the Persian Empire. It records an imminent pogrom and its warding off, and God who is seemingly absent but still acts even though he is hidden, holding his guiding hand over his people and changing the evil plans of the Jews' enemies into their opposite. The book also forms the historical basis for the Jewish feast of Purim.

The book of Esther can be subsumed under the broad biblical genre of "historical-theological narrative." Its style, however, is quite different from that of the older narratives on Israel's history, Joshua, Judges, Samuel, and Kings. The Jews are no longer a collective nation but scattered groups, and that lack of a cohesive background of kingdom and sacrificial system does give a quite different feel. There are differences from the literary point of view as well. The conception of the book is very artistic. The concreteness and vividness of the descriptive detail are striking, especially in the introductory part. The book uses literary devices like suspense, elements of surprise, humor, and sarcasm much more than other biblical books. More specific genre designations that have been given to the book are "diaspora story" and even "carnivalesque."

More than with any other book of the Hebrew Bible, the canonicity of Esther has been disputed. Many early Christian church fathers either rejected the book or at least seem to have ignored it. The reason for that may be the strong national-Jewish flavor of the story, the seemingly cruel acts of revenge the Jews do to their enemies, and the fact that God does not appear in the book. However, in old Jewish lists of the canon, e.g., in the Talmud and in a text from Josephus, the book is listed. It makes an important contribution to the overall message of the Hebrew Bible. The Septuagint (see BIBLE, EARLY TRANSLATIONS OF) translation of Esther is very free and paraphrastic and has considerable textual extensions adding to the religious dimension of the book that was felt to be missing (see Esther, Greek Additions, below).

The author of the book is anonymous. From his wealth of accurate knowledge about the Persian world and court, we can reason with some certainty that he was a member of the eastern diaspora depicted in the book. He may have been a resident of the city of Susa. The story is written from the perspective of an omniscient narrator standing outside the story. The narrator does not himself give any comments or other direct evaluation of the events reported. Evaluations and theological statements, however, are indirectly given through the literary shaping of the story.

The book is dated somewhere between the fifth and the second centuries B.C.E. The Ahasuerus mentioned in the book is the Persian Xerxes I, who reigned 486–465 B.C.E. The title information given to the Septuagint version of Esther establishes a latest possible date some time before 100 B.C.E. Different considerations make the fifth or fourth century B.C.E. the most probable date of writing.

From a literary point of view, the book consists of three parts: introduction (chapters 1–2), main action (3:1–9:5), and conclusion (9:6–10:3). The introduction and conclusion stand opposite to each other, while the main action is in itself built as a series of reversals.

SYNOPSIS

The Persians Feasting (Chapters 1–2)

Ahasuerus, king over the vast Persian Empire, invites his officials and ministers from all over his 127 provinces to a great banquet. He wants to display to them the great wealth of his kingdom. The banquet takes place in the citadel of Susa and lasts for six months. After that, all the people of Susa are also invited to a feast for seven days. At the same time, Queen Vashti gives a banquet for the women of the palace. During the feast, Ahasuerus sends for Vashti, because he wants to show the guests her beauty. But Vashti refuses. The king becomes very angry, and he asks his seven counselors what to do. They decide to take away the royal position from Vashti and to issue a royal order and proclaim it to every province and every people of the empire as a warning to all women, declaring that every man should be master in his own house.

Some time after that, Ahasuerus and his officials decide to gather beautiful young virgins from all over the country to the harem in the citadel of Susa. In this way Ahasuerus wants to find a new queen instead of Vashti. In the citadel itself, there lives a Jew named Mordecai together with Esther, his foster daughter. Since Esther (*Hadassah*, in Hebrew) is very beautiful, she also is taken into the king's palace. The king loves Esther more than all the other women of his harem and decides to make her queen instead of Vashti. In honor of Esther, the king gives a great banquet.

Mordecai is serving at the gate of the king's citadel. Two of the king's eunuchs conspire to assassinate Ahasuerus. But Mordecai hears of it and tells Queen Esther, who in turn informs the king. The affair is investigated, and the two eunuchs are hanged. The incident is recorded in the book of the annals.

Fortunes Change (3:1–9:5)

After some time, Ahasuerus promotes a certain Haman to be above all the officials of the king. He commands that all the king's servants have to bow down before Haman. But Mordecai refuses to do so. Haman becomes very angry. He is not satisfied with destroying Mordecai alone, but, since he knows that Mordecai is a Jew, he plots to destroy all the Jews throughout the whole kingdom. He persuades, or tricks, the king into issuing a decree for their destruction. The day for the pogrom is decided by drawing lots, which is the 13th of the month of Adar. The order is proclaimed in every province for the people to prepare themselves for that day.

When the Jews learn what has happened, there is great mourning and weeping among them. Mordecai sends to Esther informing her about Haman's plan and asking her to intercede with the king on behalf of the Jews. Esther hesitates at first, because going to the king inside the inner court without being called could mean that she would receive the death penalty. But finally she decides to stand up for her people.

Esther's plan is to invite the king and Haman to a banquet. After the meal, the king asks Esther what her request is. But Esther does not yet tell him. Instead she invites the king and Haman to another banquet the next day.

Haman feels very much honored having been invited by Esther and the king. But on his way home, he passes Mordecai at the gate. Again he does not bow down before him. At home, his wife and his friends suggest letting a gallows be made and asking the king to have Mordecai hanged on it.

On that same night, the king cannot sleep. He reads in the book of annals and finds out that

Mordecai had uncovered a plot against him. He also finds out that Mordecai has not been rewarded for his loyalty. In that moment the proud Haman enters the court. He wants to request that Mordecai be hanged. But before he can say anything, the king asks him, "What shall be done for the man the king wishes to honor?" Haman is convinced that he himself is the person under consideration. So he suggests giving that man royal robes to wear and allowing him to sit on one of the king's horses with a crown on his head. One of the highest officials should conduct the man on horseback through the city so that everyone could see him being honored by the king. It is a moment of great shame for Haman and the turning point of the whole action when the king instructs Haman to do as he suggested to Mordecai.

So Haman is forced to honor Mordecai instead of Mordecai's having to honor him. After that, Haman returns home with his head covered, a sign of grief, as in 2 Samuel 19:4 and Jeremiah 14:3–4. He tells his wife and his friends what has happened.

Esther accusing Haman (Esther 7:6), engraving by Gustave Doré

They predict to him that since Mordecai is a Jew, Haman would surely fall before him.

Haman now has to hurry off to the second banquet Esther has prepared. After the meal, the king again asks Esther what her request is. Now she tells him about the pogrom that is planned against her people. She also tells him about the role of Haman in it. The king becomes very angry with Haman. Haman is hanged on the same gallows that he has prepared for Mordecai.

The decree that Haman has issued is part of the laws of the Persians and the Medes, which means that it cannot be altered. In order to save the Jews from the pogrom, a counterdecree has to be issued. It allows the Jews to assemble at the 13th of Adar and to defend their lives and destroy any armed force that might attack them.

Then the 13th of Adar comes. The enemies of the Jews have hoped to gain power over them, but the opposite happens: The Jews attack those who seek to do them harm. The Persian officials aid the Jews, so they can put all their enemies to the sword.

The Jews Feasting (9:6–10:3)

In the 127 provinces, the Jews kill 75,000 of their enemies at the 13th of Adar, and they make the 14th of Adar a day of feasting. In Susa, however, the Jews kill 500 men on the 13th and 300 more on the 14th of Adar. So they feast only on the 15th.

Mordecai sends letters to all the Jews obliging them to celebrate annually the 14th and the 15th of Adar as joyful days of feasting, the sending of food to one another and of gifts to the poor. Since Haman cast the lot, the (Babylonian) *pur*, in order to decide the day of the pogrom, the feast is called *Purim*.

COMMENTARY

The Persians Feasting (Chapters 1–2)

The introduction characterizes the pagan world in which the Jews of the Diaspora have to live. In a satirical manner, the wealth and the power, the arrogance and pomp of Ahasuerus and his Persian Empire are depicted. The situation is ridiculed in the moment when the only solution to Vashti's "No" is to set into motion the whole administrative machine and the famous huge Persian postal system. Ahasuerus is master over 127 provinces, but not over his own wife.

Where power is exercised without true authority and wisdom, there is the danger of subversive elements' gaining control. This becomes visible especially with Haman's plot against the Jews. Haman persuades the king to issue the decree without even telling him the name of the people under attack. The ruler over the Persian Empire seems to be always at the mercy of his counselors.

In Daniel 3 and 6 there is also a ruler who himself is not hostile to the Jews but is influenced by people who are. The similarities make it possible to define a genre "diaspora story" or "diaspora agenda" for the book of Esther as well as for Daniel 1–6 and the apocryphal book of Tobit.

The introduction not only deals with the characterization of the diaspora situation. It also depicts two events that precede and prepare the main action of the book. One is the choosing of Esther as the Persian queen. The other is the plot against Ahasuerus that is uncovered by Mordecai.

Fortunes Change (3:1–9:5)

The cornerstones of the main action are the two decrees. They are formulated very much in parallel to each other. At the same time, however, they stand opposite to each other, because the first decree gives the order to destroy the Jews, and the second allows the destruction of the Jews' enemies. What is true for the two decrees also applies to most of the other scenes of the main action (except 4:4–17): The scenes are formed as complementary pairs of two. In each instance, there are strong parallels in content and language as well as an element of opposition, or reversal. For example, there are two banquets of Esther, the king, and Haman. After the first banquet, Haman feels honored; after the second, he is unmasked and brought down (5:1–8; 6:14–7:10). There are two discussions of Haman with his wife and his friends. In the first discussion, they suggest having Mordecai hanged; after the second, they expect Haman to be destroyed. Haman wants Mordecai to honor him, but, to the contrary, Haman has to honor Mordecai (5:9–14; 6:11–13).

The pairs of opposite scenes make visible one of the main themes of the book, which is the reversal of fortunes. Toward the end of the main section, this is also expressed explicitly: "but now the tables were turned" (9:1, New International Version).

The pairs of opposite scenes are built around the nocturnal scene at the king's court (6:1–10), making it the turning point of the whole story. In this scene, several coincidences are apparent. It is on this night between the two banquets of Esther that the king cannot sleep; it is on this night that he reads about Mordecai's uncovering the plot against him; it is on this morning that Haman appears at the court; and so on.

There is only one scene in the main section that does not have a counterpart: the discourse between Esther and Mordecai in 4:4–17. While the rest of chapters 3–9 describes the reversal of circumstances in the Persian Empire, 4:4–17 deals with a reversal in the relationship of Esther and Mordecai. Before, Esther obeyed Mordecai in all things (2:20); now it is Mordecai who obeys Esther in all things (4:17). The section depicts the development of the character of Esther from a beautiful but passive young woman into a powerful advocate of her people.

The section 4:4–17 also contains the interpretative key passage of the book. Mordecai tells Esther: "Do not think that in the king's palace you will escape any more than all the other Jews. For if you keep silence at such a time as this, relief and deliverance will rise for the Jews from another quarter, but you and your father's family will perish. Who knows? Perhaps you have come to royal dignity for just such a time as this" (4:13–14).

In the whole book, God is not mentioned even in a single instance. But that does not make Esther a nonreligious book. On the contrary: The book emphatically deals with the hiddenness of God. Beyond the world order of Ahasuerus and his 127 provinces, a greater power is at work but is hidden. The book asks its readers to act in the knowledge of this providential power. Not only Mordecai but also the advisers of Haman are convinced of the fact that the Jewish people is, even in the diaspora, under the protection of divine providence and cannot be destroyed (4:13–14; 6:13). The "reversal of fortunes," which is expressed in the literary structure, points in the same direction. From the inner-biblical perspective, the reversal of fortunes is one of the trademarks of the work of God (e.g., 1 Samuel 2:1–8; Psalm 7:14–16; 9:15–16; Matthew 19:27–30; Luke 1:52–53). The power of God turns the Persian world upside down.

Another case is the accumulation of "coincidences" in 6:1–10 that again reveals providential guidance. All the individual events—Esther's being chosen queen, Mordecai's overhearing the plot, the king's sleeplessness, Haman's entering the court, and the moment of dramatic irony when Haman misunderstands the king's question—suddenly combine in order to give the story its decisive turn. God is at work but not through powerful signs and wonders or authoritative prophetic utterances. Rather, he directs the strings behind the scenes, coworking with human activities. Even such small matters as the king's insomnia become part of his plan of salvation.

The Jews Feasting (9:6–10:3)

Some interpreters see the section 9:6–19 as part of the main story. But the details about the different dates for the feast in Susa and in the provinces do not contribute to the plot of the story itself. Furthermore, there is no place for 9:6–19 in the symmetry of the main part. Rather, from 9:6 on the narrator is concerned with the inauguration of the Purim feast.

The book deals with a couple of feasts and banquets. The analysis shows that they are again structured according to the theme of the "reversal of fortunes." So the feasts of the Persians of the provinces and of Susa (chapter 1) stand in opposition to the feasts of the Jews in the provinces and in Susa (chapter 9). In the beginning, the pagans are feasting; in the end, the Jews. In the introductory section, the feast of Vashti and the feast of Esther form another pair (1:9 and 2:18), framing the events from the dismissal of Vashti to the appointment of Esther. They depict a reversal of fortunes on a small scale that prepares the reversal of fortunes on a larger scale. The main section contains four feasts that are arranged in pairs of oppositions. After the first banquet of Esther, Haman feels honored; after

the second, he is brought down (5:1–9a and 6:14–7:10). After the first decree, the Persians feast; after the second, the Jews feast (3:15 and 8:17).

To sum up the message of the book: In a dangerous world, controlled by despotic and foolish pagan rulers, whose lack of authority is used by enemy forces in order to threaten the lives of the diaspora Jews, the Jews can trust in the protection of divine providence and, in interaction of human wisdom and initiative with the hidden actions of providence, can turn their lot to their advantage and strengthen their position in the pagan world. The Jews shall remember this experience by the annual feast of Purim.

CHARACTERS

Ahasuerus (Xerxes) Ahasuerus is king over the Persian Empire with its 127 provinces. He rules over a vast state machinery and a huge postal system. He is lawgiver contributing to the famous and irrevocable "laws of the Persians and the Medes." But all this cannot give him true authority. When his wife says "No" to him, he becomes completely helpless. At the mercy of his counselors, he is always in danger of letting subversive elements gain control over the empire.

Esther Esther (Hadassah, in Hebrew) is a beautiful young Jewish woman who has lost both her parents and has been adopted by Mordecai. She is very friendly and obedient and wins the favor of all who meet her. She is chosen by Ahasuerus to be queen instead of Vashti. When it comes to her taking over responsibility for her people, however, she has to learn to step out of her role of the handsome but passive beauty. With brilliance she manages to turn the king's attention to her request, to unmask and bring down Haman, and to save the Jews from the imminent danger.

Haman Haman is the enemy of the Jews par excellence, the irrational evil personified. He is a descendant of Agag. A person of the same name was the king of the Amalekites defeated by King Saul, a precursor of Mordecai (1 Samuel 15). Haman's motivation is not a political one. Rather, he is driven by his vast ego, based probably on a deep feeling of inferiority. After Mordecai has not bowed down before him, Haman's wounded pride can only be healed by attacking the whole Jewish people. Esther is playing with his pride, giving him the deceptive impression of being honored. In the end, his pride causes him to misunderstand the king's question, and from the highest honors he is lowered to the deepest shame.

Mordecai   Mordecai is a Jew, a descendant of a certain Kish. A person of the same name was father of King Saul, who defeated Agag, a precursor of Haman (1 Samuel 15). As the narrator tells us, Mordecai is "the Jew," i.e., the ideal diaspora Jew. This qualifies not only his nationality but even more his attitude, which is, first of all, characterized by loyalty to the Jewish people and to its customs and laws. His loyalty extends to seeking the good of the Persian king, saving him from being assassinated, but not to bowing down before people like Haman. Mordecai is the foster father of Esther and the initiator of the events leading to the saving of his people.

Esther, Greek Additions

The Septuagint (see BIBLE, EARLY TRANSLATIONS OF) version of the book of Esther is a rather free translation from the Hebrew that also contains additional material. These "Greek additions" are counted as deuterocanonical (being of secondary canonical rank) by the Catholic and Orthodox Churches, while the Protestants reject them as apocryphal (see APOCRYPHA AND PSEUDEPIGRAPHA).

Additions A + F: The Greek version of the book begins with a dream of Mordecai, in which the coming threat and deliverance of the Jewish people are predicted to him. At the end of the book, the dream is referred to a second time.

Additions B + E: The contents of the two decrees against and in favor of the Jewish people are reported in great detail in the Greek. In the second decree, the heathen king acknowledges God as the "living God, most high, most mighty," and the Jews he calls "chosen people"—i.e., the king has apparently become a believer.

Addition C: After the dialogue between Esther and Mordecai, the Greek version reports two lengthy prayers of Esther and Mordecai, respectively.

Addition D: The scene where Esther appears before the king the first time is very much embellished and dramatized in the Greek version.

The main interest behind the additions can easily be determined. It is to add to the religious dimension of the story, which was felt to be missing. In the Hebrew version, for example, the words *God* and *the Lord* do not appear even a single time, but in the Greek version they appear more than 50 times. By this means, the message of the book is shifted: The tension created by the difficult problem of God's apparent absence is resolved in the Greek version.

Besides the Septuagint text, there exists another Greek version of the book, the so-called Alpha-text. Regarding the six Greek additions, the texts match each other. However, the rest of the Alpha-text seems to be translated from a different Hebrew original. What is distinctive about the Alpha-text is that it does not refer to the feast of Purim. Some scholars think that the Alpha-text (without the six additions) is even older than the canonical version of the book.

Exodus

The book of Exodus describes the beginnings of the history of Israel: The Lord delivers the Israelites from slavery in EGYPT with mighty deeds. He reveals himself to his people and makes a covenant with them at Mount Sinai, declaring them to be his own treasured possession, a kingdom of priests, and he installs the tabernacle as the place where he would live directly among his people.

From a literary point of view, the book of Exodus should probably not be seen as a book on its own. Rather, the books of Exodus, Leviticus, and Numbers together form a literary entity. So Exodus 1–18 deals with the deliverance from Egypt and the journey to Mount Sinai. The section encompassing Exodus 19–40, the whole of

Leviticus, and Numbers 1–9 deals with the covenant between God and Israel made at Mount Sinai. Numbers 10–36, finally, describes the journey from Mount Sinai to the borders of the Promised Land. Seen this way, the books of Exodus, Leviticus, and Numbers together form the core of the PENTATEUCH. This core is framed on one side by Genesis, narrating the prehistory of Israel, beginning with the creation of the world. On the other side is Deuteronomy, consisting of the farewell speeches of Moses held at the threshold of the Promised Land. The whole Pentateuch, in turn, forms the basis of the Hebrew Bible. In the Pentateuch, all the essential features of the relationship between God and human beings in general, and between God and Israel in particular, are defined. All biblical books that follow relate themselves to the Pentateuch in one way or another. A special affinity can be seen with the books Joshua, Judges, Samuel, and Kings following the Pentateuch. The books from Genesis to Kings together can be seen as a closed literary work narrating the history of Israel from the CREATION of the world until the Babylonian Exile.

From their literary genre, the narrative sections of the three books Exodus, Leviticus, and Numbers can best be described as "historical-theological narrative." That means the text claims to be based on history, which is, however, shaped into a narrative style, in order to develop some theological points from it (see Part I).

However, modern readers are sometimes irritated by the fact that sections containing legal material often interrupt the narrative. This is felt to be a violation of the rules of genre. However, detailed analysis reveals that the legal sections are always inserted in such places where they are needed in the context of the narrative. For example, the covenant laws are given where the covenant is made in the narrative; laws on sacrifices are given before the first sacrifices are made in the narrative; laws concerning the journey are given just before the journey to Canaan begins in the narrative. So the text still forms a unity, although it is different from what is expected by the modern reader. Concerning the legal sections themselves, again the reader might be surprised to find secular laws beside religious laws and festal calendars beside descriptions on how to build the tabernacle. The book of Exodus-Leviticus-Numbers bears witness to a holistic view on life that does not make modern analytical distinctions between politics and religion, between the immanent and the transcendent.

Regarding the date of writing of the books Exodus, Leviticus, and Numbers, opinions differ greatly. Many scholars assume that the text went through several literary stages before it gained its final form. Others see the whole work or major parts of it as written by Moses (15th century B.C.E.) or under his authority. From the ancient Near East, several examples of vassal treaties and of law codes are extant. When the "book of the covenant," Exodus 19–24, is compared to these, it can be shown that it resembles documents of the second millennium B.C.E. better than those of the first millennium B.C.E. This is at least a hint pointing to an old age of the material.

Together with the date of writing, the historical reliability of the book is disputed. First of all, the text relates many amazing miraculous deeds of God, which, by nature, can neither be proven nor disproven by scientific method. However, the experience of the Exodus of Egypt is so foundational to Israelite thinking and to the Hebrew Bible that even more skeptical scholars argue that there must be some historical core to the story. In addition, unlike in the other ancient Near Eastern people groups, there were no class distinctions in Israelite society; this indirectly supports the Exodus narrative, according to which Israel came into being as a society of freed slaves. More generally, the fundamental biblical skepticism of human rule points in a similar direction. Remarkable are also some typical Egyptian names in the biblical narrative: the name of Moses himself, and also *Merari* (6:16), *Phinehas* (6:25), and some others.

For the dating of the Exodus of Egypt, scholars propose two different dates: either the 15th century B.C.E., relying on a literal understanding of numbers given in the biblical text (especially 1 Kings 6:1), or the 13th century, relying on certain interpretations of archaeological observations made in the country of Canaan (cities that were destroyed as a result of Israel's conquest of the land).

According to the 15th-century dating, Ameno-phis II of the Eighteenth Dynasty would have been the pharaoh of the Exodus (time of reign around 1450–1425 B.C.E.). Interestingly, he reigned in Memphis, in the northern part of Egypt, whereas the other pharaohs of his dynasty lived in Thebes in the south, a location that would have made the frequent visits of Moses and Aaron to the pha-raoh impossible. The predecessor of Amenophis II was Tutmosis III. He reigned more than 50 years; this would explain why Moses had to hide in the desert for 40 years, waiting for the death of the pharaoh before he returned (see Exodus 2:15, 23; 4:19). Tutmosis III was the only pharaoh in the whole dynasty who reigned for such a long time. If the dating is correct, then Hatshepsut, Tutmosis's mother-in-law, may possibly have been Moses' adoptive mother. Since Tutmosis was very hostile to her, this would also explain the strong rivalry between Moses and Tutmosis pointed to in Exodus 4:19. Another interesting detail is that the successor of Amenophis II was not, as usual, the firstborn son. This is in accordance with the biblical narrative, according to which the firstborn son of the pharaoh died before the Exodus (Exo-dus 12:29). According to the 13th-century dating, in turn, Rameses II of the 19th dynasty (time of reign 1304–1236 B.C.E.) would have been the pha-raoh of the Exodus. More detailed connections to the Egyptian history can, however, not be drawn with this dating. The 40 years of Moses' hiding in the desert would have to be taken in a figurative rather than in a literal sense.

In Egyptian sources, the Exodus of Israel is not documented. From this, however, nothing can be inferred, since the pharaohs in general only doc-umented their achievements, not their failures. In turn, the biblical narrative does not give any names of pharaohs, as this was custom in that time of the Egyptian history. In the end, the historical issues cannot be fixed with certainty—more "con-servative" and more "liberal" positions are possible as well.

The structure of the book of Exodus is seen differently by different scholars. This discussion follows the analysis of the Dutch theologian H. Koorevaar (in H. Klement and J. Steinberg, eds.,

Themenbuch zur Theologie des Alten Testaments, Wuppertal: Brockhaus, 2007, pp. 87–131).

SYNOPSIS

Slavery in Egypt and Preparation of Moses (1:1–6:27)

The family of Israel that has settled in the Nile Delta (see Genesis) is constantly growing. After some time, they become so many that the Egyptian pharaoh begins fearing them as a political threat. So he decides to hold them down by inflicting forced labor on them. But still the people increase. An attempt of the pharaoh to enlist the Hebrew midwives on his side so that they might secretly kill the Israelites' newborn sons fails. Finally, the pharaoh gives the official order that all newborn sons of the Hebrews have to be drowned in the Nile (chapter 1).

A son is born. For three months, his mother hides him at her home. When this becomes impos-sible, she produces a watertight basket, lays the baby in it, and places the basket in the reeds at the bank of the RIVER NILE. The older sister observes the scene from a hidden place.

The pharaoh's daughter goes to the Nile and finds the crying Israelite baby. She does not have the heart to drown it. The sister of the baby talks to her and asks her whether she should look for some-one to raise the child for her. The pharaoh's daugh-ter agrees, and so the sister takes the baby back to his mother. After some time, the boy is taken to the pharaoh's court. The pharaoh's daughter takes care of him and gives him the name *Moses*.

Some time after that, Moses observes an Egyp-tian slave driver beating some one of his own peo-ple. When he thinks that nobody is looking, he kills the Egyptian and buries him in the sand. But the deed is made known, and Moses has to flee in order to escape the anger of the pharaoh. He settles in the land of Midian and marries there (chapter 2).

The pharaoh who tried to kill Moses dies. One day, when Moses is taking care of the sheep of Jethro, his father-in-law, he sees a flame of fire rising out of a bush. When he decides to have a closer look at it, God speaks to him out of the bush. God wants to deliver the people of Israel from

Egypt and lead them into the land he promised to their ancestors (see DELIVERANCE; SALVATION). He wants Moses to be their leader. God also reveals his name to Moses. The name is *Yahweh*, which means "I am who I am" or "I am there" (modern Bible translations mostly render the name as *the Lord*, often written with small caps [the] LORD; see GOD). God also informs Moses that the pharaoh will not cooperate, and that God will perform mighty miraculous acts in order to free his people. Moses, however, has doubts. He does not feel prepared for such a great task. God answers his worries by enabling him to perform some miracles with his staff and by giving his brother, Aaron, to him as support (chapters 3–4).

Moses returns to Egypt and meets Aaron. They appear before the pharaoh for the first time and ask him to allow the Israelites to travel into the desert for a couple of days in order to prepare a feast and worship the Lord. But the pharaoh refuses. He even increases the amount of forced labor for the people—so that they may "pay no attention to deceptive words" anymore. The people become very angry with Moses and Aaron. But God assures Moses again that he will deliver Israel from the Egyptian bondage (chapters 5–6).

The block ends, as it has begun, with a genealogy. The genealogy concentrates on the descent of Moses and Aaron.

Deliverance from Egypt and Journey to Mount Sinai (6:28–18:27)

Now the Lord reveals his power in a series of 10 plagues. As a first plague, God makes the water of the Nile turn into blood. However, the Egyptian magicians are able to perform a similar trick, so the pharaoh does not prove to be impressed. A week later, there is a plague of frogs. This time the pharaoh asks Moses to pray that God might take away the frogs. And he also promises that he will let the Israelites go. The frogs die, but the pharaoh does not keep his promise. In the third plague, a plague of gnats, the magicians see the "finger of God," but the pharaoh still does not change his mind. Similar are his reactions to the following plagues: flies, a livestock disease, festering boils on the skin of humans and animals, thunder and hail, locusts, and a deep darkness lasting three days. Time and again, the pharaoh gives way until the plague ceases, but afterward he again refuses (chapters 7–10).

Now Moses announces to the pharaoh the 10th and last plague: the dying of all firstborn humans and animals at midnight. All the Egyptian officers and the people are already on Moses' side, and they give a lot of golden and silver jewelry to the Israelites. But the pharaoh remains hard. Meanwhile, the feast of Passover is instituted among the Israelites. In each family, a lamb is to be slaughtered in the evening. Some of the lamb's blood is to be sprinkled on the doorposts and the lintel. The lamb is to be roasted over the fire and be eaten; anything that remains is to be burned until morning. While eating, the people are to be clothed ready for the journey with sandals on their feet as a sign that the deliverance is coming. This feast is to be held annually as a remembrance of the Exodus.

The Israelites feast according to the instructions given. In the night, the Lord strikes down all the firstborns of the Egyptians. But he passes over all doors of the Israelites, which are sprinkled with the blood of a lamb.

The same night the pharaoh gives way. The Israelites leave. On departing, they prepare unleavened cakes of dough (chapters 11–12).

In the text, there follows a block of thematically related cultic material regarding the feast of the Passover, the Festival of Unleavened Bread, and the consecration of the firstborn (chapters 12–13).

So the exodus out of Egypt commences. More than 600,000 Israelite men, plus women and children, leave the land, accompanied by other groups of people and by a vast amount of livestock. They also take the coffin with Joseph's mummified corpse (see Genesis 50:26) with them. God himself is leading the people, in the form of a pillar of cloud at day and a pillar of fire at night.

But soon afterward, the pharaoh regrets his decision. He has all his chariots and horses prepared and begins pursuing the Israelites with his army. At the bank of the Red Sea, the Israelites seem to be trapped. But God commands Moses to lift up his staff and stretch his hand over the sea. A strong wind rises and drives back the water, so that the Israelites can cross the inlet without getting wet.

The Egyptians follow them. But the water returns, and so the whole army of pharaoh is destroyed. This mighty act of divine deliverance is then celebrated in a song (chapters 14–15).

The people continue traveling into the desert, in the direction of the SINAI Peninsula. In the desert, God supplies the people with water and food several times. As a daily provision of food, God lets a fine flaky substance rain onto the ground at night, which the Israelites call manna. Jethro, Moses' father-in-law, joins the people. He observes Moses' trying hard to be counselor for all the people. He gives the advice to organize this work better by finding able men and setting them as officers over thousands, hundreds, fifties, and tens. Moses follows Jethro's advice (chapters 16–18).

God Gives the Law at Mount Sinai (Chapters 19–34)

Now the people reach the Sinai mountain range and camps at its foot. God asks the people to form a covenant with him making the nation of Israel the special possession of God. The people agree. They prepare to encounter God. God appears in the form of a cloud with thunder and lightning on top of the mountain. The mountain smokes and shakes. The people stay at the foot of the mountain; Moses climbs it to approach God (chapter 19).

On top of Mount Sinai, God gives Moses the TEN COMMANDMENTS. After that are other regulations elaborating on the Ten Commandments (chapters 20–23). The covenant is inaugurated in a ceremonial act, as Moses, Aaron and his sons, and 70 elders have a banquet in the presence of the Lord (chapter 24).

Moses then climbs Mount Sinai again for another 40 days. He receives the tablets of the covenant, and he also receives detailed instructions on how to build the tabernacle, the transportable sanctuary of Israel, and how to install a regular ceremonial service in it (chapters 25–31).

While Moses remains on the mountain, the people become impatient. They ask Aaron to make an idol. Aaron agrees and makes a golden calf. The next day the people make a great feast worshipping the calf. God informs Moses about this, he is very angry and wants to destroy all the people. Moses, however,

Moses coming down from Mount Sinai (Exodus 32:15), engraving by Gustave Doré

intercedes before God on behalf of his people. He climbs down the mountain, with the covenant tablets in his hands. When he sees the people feasting, his anger burns intensely and he throws the tablets from his hands so that they break. As a punishment for their disobedience, God sends a plague on the people. Furthermore, he instructs Moses to place the tent of meeting outside the camp, since he does not want to be in the middle of the people anymore. But Moses continues interceding on behalf of his people. So God agrees to renew the covenant. He makes two new tablets. God also reveals himself to Moses as "The LORD, the LORD, a God merciful and gracious, slow to anger, and abounding in steadfast love and faithfulness" (34:6).

After 40 days, Moses leaves Mount Sinai for the last time, holding the new tablets of the covenant in his hands. His face shines, reflecting the glory of God.

The Building of the Tabernacle (Chapters 35–40)

Moses relates the commandments that God has given to him on Mount Sinai to the people. The tabernacle is constructed exactly according to his instructions. When it is finished, the cloud of the glory of the Lord fills the sanctuary, so it is impossible for Moses to enter the tent.

COMMENTARY

Slavery in Egypt and Preparation of Moses (1:1–6:27)

The attempt of the pharaoh to suppress and to decimate the people of Israel has to be evaluated against the theological background that God had given Abraham the promise to make him become a great nation (Genesis 12:2). That means that the pharaoh is trying to fight against a divine promise and makes way for a conflict that escalates in the course of the narrative and, in the end, can only be resolved by a mighty act of God.

Into the middle of this situation of distress, Moses, the liberator, is born and saved from death in a wonderful way. Later in Midian, he meets the God of his ancestors in a burning bush. God reveals himself to him with his name, meaning "I am who I am" or "I am there." And this is what he is going to prove in the course of the events: God will show that he is the one with whom everyone, even pharaoh, will have to reckon.

The first encounter between Moses and Aaron and the pharaoh does not have a positive effect on Israel, however. From a literary perspective, the episode rather functions as a retarding moment: The pharaoh can still say, "Who is Yahweh, that I should heed him and let Israel go?" (5:2). He can still arbitrarily harden the labor of the Israelites, who cannot mount resistance against him. There is still no sign of divine intervention. Even the people of Israel themselves turn away from Moses and Aaron. This adds considerably to the tension of the narrative, and an act of divine deliverance is expected even more urgently.

Before this finally happens, however, the narrator takes his time to repeat the announcement of the divine plan of deliverance and present a genealogy of Moses and Aaron. Distinctive in this genealogy is that it begins as a list of the sons of Israel, like the list in Exodus 1:1ff., but when it reaches Levi, the third son, the interest suddenly turns to Moses and Aaron, and the other sons of

Israel are not mentioned again. The person named last in the genealogy is Phinehas, a Levite, who will play a special role in Numbers 25 and whom God will promise an everlasting priesthood there. So the genealogy has three functions: forming an INCLUSIO with Exodus 1:1ff., locating Aaron and Moses in the genealogical tree, and giving a prospect of some events occurring later (probably the name of Phinehas was well known to the first readers of the book).

Deliverance from Egypt and Journey to Mount Sinai (6:28–18:27)

The first short section 6:28–7:7 summarizes again the call of Moses and Aaron and at the same time gives an overall interpretation of the following events: The Lord wants to reveal himself with mighty deeds and miracles as the true God, he wants to bring judgment on Egypt, and he wants to deliver the people of Israel out of slavery in Egypt. The fact that the heart of the pharaoh is hardened will be an occasion for God to demonstrate his power so that all other people will trust him even more deeply.

The narrative on the 10 plagues has often puzzled readers. Some try to explain the plagues in a natural way, seeing them as the consequences of a strong disturbance in the environment. Others see in each of the plagues a humiliation of one of the Egyptian gods. In any case, the plagues have the character of signs demonstrating God's power over nature.

It is possible to see an intensification from plague to plague. Especially with the first plagues, an element of the comic can also be discerned: In the first plague turning water into blood, the Egyptian magicians can perform the same "trick"; however, they do not seem able to undo it. In the second plague, the frogs hopping everywhere reveal an element of the comic. They are even hopping on pharaoh's bed and on pharaoh himself! So the first plagues serve as kinds of warning showing that God is able to take total control. The comic element vanishes, however, as the plagues become more and more severe.

In the section on the 10th plague and on the Passover, ritual and narrative are strongly interwoven.

Not only are some religious regulations attached to the narrative, even more so, the event itself is liturgy. The blood spread at the doorposts is the symbol of life given in order to redeem the firstborn of the Israelites. As the attached religious text explains, all firstborn, not only the Egyptians', belong to the Lord. Therefore, all human firstborn in Israel have to be redeemed by animals.

The crossing of the Red Sea is probably the greatest of all the miracles—and it is also one of the most well-known stories of the Hebrew Bible. The whole event seems to be orchestrated by God. He uses it as a final demonstration of his power, totally depriving the pharaoh of his military power. The Israelites can do nothing but marvel. Moses' Song of Deliverance in chapter 15 is exemplary Hebrew POETRY.

The "Red Sea" literally is the "Sea of Reeds." It is probably to be identified with one of the smaller bodies of water in the delta region that are to the north of the Red Sea proper.

God Gives the Law at Mount Sinai (Chapters 19–34)

With Exodus 19, the Israelites begin their stay at Mount Sinai, which extends through the whole book of Leviticus, to Numbers 10.

At Mount Sinai, the covenant between God and Israel is made, forming the basis for the relationship between God and Israel and therefore the basis for the whole religion of the old Israel as presented in the Hebrew Bible. After God has delivered the people from Egypt, he wants to make it his own possession and "a kingdom of priests." As priests are mediators between God and human beings, speaking out the divine blessing over the congregation, the whole nation of Israel is asked to be a mediator of the divine blessing for the other nations. Theologically speaking, it therefore has to be pointed out that the election of Israel does not imply a rejection of the other nations; rather, the election of Israel is the means with which God wants to reach the other nations as well. With this, the Sinai covenant continues the Abraham covenant, according to which Abraham's family would be a mediator of blessing for "all the families of the earth" (Genesis 12:1–3).

The Sinai covenant is a voluntary covenant that only takes force after both parties have agreed. God introduces an advance concession: He has already delivered the people out of Egypt. The Sinai covenant includes obligations for both sides: God commits himself to leading the people into the Promised Land, to blessing it, and to living in its midst. The people, in turn, are obliged to live as holy people, according to their divine election. From its form, the Sinaitic covenant resembles ancient Near Eastern vassal treaties known to us from the second millennium B.C.E. from all over the region. Typical of this kind of treaty is a section on blessings (for keeping the treaty) and cursings (for breaking the treaty). In the biblical text this can be found in Leviticus 26 and in Deuteronomy 28–30. A short version is also given in Exodus 23:20–33.

The central legal text of the Sinaitic covenant, which is at the same time one of the most well-known and most influential passages of the whole Bible, are the Ten Commandments. The Ten Commandments set out the fundamental values for the Israelites in order to live as a holy nation. (For the numbering of the Ten Commandments, different traditions exist, as can be seen in the table on the following page.)

At the beginning of the Ten Commandments, God introduces himself as "Yahweh," the God "who is there," as a very personal God ("your God") and as the deliverer of Israel out of the slavery in Egypt. This statement is instructive since it points out that keeping the commandments is an answer to divine redemption, not a prerequisite to it. So the old Israelite religion is not a "legalistic" religion of salvation by works.

The commandment not to have other gods has had a special significance in the world of the ancient Near East, where it was custom to worship a multitude of gods. The monotheism requested by this first commandment also draws a sharp distinction between the Jewish and Christian faiths on the one side and any type of syncretism on the other side. In a figurative sense, "other gods" may be anything that captures the heart of the believer more than God. The church reformer Martin Luther commented on it, "Where your heart is, there is your god."

Numbering of the Ten Commandments	Catholic, Lutheran	Orthodox, Reformed	Jewish
I am the Lord, your God, who delivered you . . .	1	1	1
You shall have no other gods before me . . .	1	1	2
You shall not make for yourself an idol . . .	1	2	2
You shall not take the name of the Lord in vain . . .	2	3	3
Remember the Sabbath day, and keep it holy . . .	3	4	4
Honor your father and your mother . . .	4	5	5
You shall not murder	5	6	6
You shall not commit adultery	6	7	7
You shall not steal	7	8	8
You shall not bear false witness against your neighbor	8	9	9
You shall not covet your neighbor's house	9	10	10
You shall not covet . . . anything that belongs to your neighbor	10	10	10

The commandment not to make idols is not directed against making pictures or images per se but against making an image of God and worshipping it (see Deuteronomy 4:15–19). The creator of the world cannot be represented by an image of any of his creatures.

The commandment not to misuse the name of the Lord directs itself against a careless "Oh, my God!" and against curses and oaths using the name of God in an inappropriate way, as well as against presumptuously pretending to speak in the name of the Lord.

The Sabbath commandment calls to mind that success in life is not just a matter of one's own efforts. The Sabbath is to be kept "holy," to be reserved for God. It is to be kept free from ordinary daily work, for having rest and for worshipping the Lord. The commandment to honor one's parents addresses itself not only to small children but also to adults who are to take care of their parents when they are getting old.

The commandment not to kill expresses the high value the Hebrew Bible assigns to the life of the individual. With this, the Sinaitic covenant stands out positively against other ancient Near Eastern law codes, where, for example, the life of slaves had a relative low value.

The Hebrew word for "kill" used here refers to the killing of human beings in the sense of murder

or manslaughter. The law cannot be used as an argument against the death penalty—in the book of Exodus itself, the death penalty is requested for capital offenses. Neither does the commandment address the slaughter of animals, which is allowed according to Genesis 9:2–4.

Regarding the "false witness," a court situation is primarily in mind. In a wider sense, the regulation is about not doing anyone an injustice using words, for example, spreading slander.

The commandment about coveting seems to overlap partially with the regulations against stealing and adultery. However, it has to be seen as a more general rule concerning the respect to be shown toward other people. The privileges of the individual end where the privileges of other persons are concerned. As the commandments begin with a general command to respect God, they end with a general command to respect the other.

In the Hebrew Bible, the Ten Commandments are related two times, namely, in Exodus 20:2–17 and Deuteronomy 5:6–21. The two sections differ slightly. In the Sabbath commandment, the explanatory text is different, and in the double commandment of coveting the words *house* and *wife* are exchanged—without influencing the content. According to the reformed and to the Jewish tradition, the two commandments are counted as one.

The Ten Commandments play an important role not only in the Jewish but also in the Christian tradition. The central importance of the Ten Commandments is underscored by the literary feature of placing thunder and lightning directly before and after them in the text.

After the Ten Commandments are several chapters containing additional laws. Other than the Ten Commandments, most of these regulations are case laws fashioned according to the pattern "if . . . then." The collection displays a concern for ordering a wide range of issues in daily life. The laws are probably not to be understood in the sense of a complete law code but rather as representatives of a larger body of material, giving some basic guidelines. The collection is framed by the two sections 20:22–26 and 23:20–33, dealing with Israel's loyalty to God and God's loyalty to Israel. After the commandments are presented in chapters 20–23—this section is also called the "book of the covenant" (see 24:7)—in chapter 24 the covenant is put into operation in a ceremonial act. Participants at the banquet are Moses as the leader, Aaron and his two sons as representatives of the (future) clergy, as well as 70 elders as representatives of the whole people.

The following, very detailed instructions for the erection of the tabernacle may seem arduous for today's readers. However, the detail is justified by the theological significance of the tabernacle: It is about having fellowship between God and humanity, about God's living in the midst of his people Israel. From the introductory passage in 25:1–9, some guidelines emerge: (1) The decision to support the building of the tabernacle is voluntary. (2) But if the tabernacle is built, it has to be built from the best materials available and exactly according to the divine plan. (3) The tabernacle and the ceremonial ritual installed in it are the means by which God will live among his people.

The instructions begin with the objects of the Most Holy that symbolize God's presence. From then, the description moves outward, describing the sanctuary itself and then the court around it with all its holy objects. To have a portable sanctuary was not unique to the people of Israel. Unique, however, was the fact that in the Israelite tabernacle there was no idol.

The incident with the golden calf (chapters 32–34) is again very dramatic. While God installs a great covenant with Moses and prepares to live among the people himself, the people thoughtlessly reject all that has been achieved. They are in imminent danger of losing their God, their identity as a nation, and even their lives. Only by the courageous intervention of Moses, who intercedes before God on behalf of the people, is the catastrophe averted. However, the innocence is gone; God wants to have the tent of meeting put outside the camp. Nevertheless, God makes a new beginning possible. The broken tablets of the covenant are replaced by new ones. God even allows Moses to see his glory, assuring him of his continuing presence with the people.

The incident with the golden calf somehow serves as a paradigm for the whole history of Israel, as it is presented in the Hebrew Bible: Time and again, there are situations when the covenant is endangered or actually broken. But time and again, there is also the hope that God will make a new beginning possible.

The Building of the Tabernacle (Chapters 35–40)

The last chapters describe the erection of the tabernacle. In long passages, the description of the erection forms an exact counterpart to the instructions given in chapters 25–31. Everything is done exactly "as the Lord had commanded Moses" (Exodus 39:1, 5, 7, 21, 26, 29, 31, 32, 42, 43; 40:19ff.). By this it is shown that after the act of disobedience and the necessary covenant renewal have taken place, the people are now fully obedient to the Lord. Moreover, God accepts the new beginning by taking possession of the tabernacle in the form of a cloud filling the whole place.

However, from the instructions given in chapters 25–31, not everything is carried out yet, especially the inauguration of Aaron and his sons and the beginning of the regular cultic service prescribed in chapter 29. These instructions will be executed only in Leviticus 9–10. Before that, a legal block about making sacrifices is inserted in

Leviticus 1–8, which must be followed to ensure that the regular service at the tabernacle is performed correctly.

CHARACTERS

Aaron   Brother of Moses, installed as Moses' spokesperson by God. Therefore, in the narrative Aaron appears most of the time together with Moses. At the banquet that is held on the occasion of making the covenant, Aaron and his two sons are allowed to participate in their function of representatives of the (future) priesthood. However, while Moses is on the mountain receiving more of the divine instructions, Aaron lets himself be persuaded to form a golden calf and to make a feast in order to worship it—however, at this time the people seem to be more in charge than Aaron.

Moses   A son of parents from the tribe of Levi. Moses is raised at the Egyptian court. Eventually, he kills an Egyptian slave driver and has to flee to Midian, where he marries. There, God calls him to deliver the people of Israel out of Egypt. Moses at first does not feel prepared for such a great task. He objects that he is not eloquent. Therefore, God gives him his brother, Aaron, to support him in order to be the spokesman. After Moses has taken the people to Mount Sinai, God makes him his close confidant. God reveals the Law to him. Moses is trustworthy. He is very faithful to God, but he also intercedes with God on the people's behalf, after they have sinned, in order to avert or mitigate the divine punishment on them.

Pharaoh (of Exodus 5ff.)   The pharaoh is a very arrogant and stubborn person. Without scruples, he takes advantage of the forced labor of the Israelites; he even increases it just to demonstrate his power. When God starts demonstrating his power, the pharaoh does not give way. He remains obstinate until the bitter end. He therefore provokes the mightiest acts of God, even to the killing of all firstborn Egyptians and to the total destruction of the Egyptian army in the Red Sea. In the New Testament, the pharaoh is taken as an example of a hardened person (Romans 9:14ff.).

Ezekiel

In the Hebrew Bible, the book of Ezekiel stands third in the Latter Prophets in most manuscripts. In the Christian Old Testament, it stands fourth among the Prophetic Books. It is the third longest of the prophetic books, after Isaiah and Jeremiah, and divided into 48 chapters. Its author, Ezekiel, prophesied between 593 and 570 B.C.E. and was thus a younger contemporary of Jeremiah. Unlike those of Jeremiah, however, Ezekiel's prophecies were delivered in the EXILE in BABYLON, where he had been deported in 598 or 597 B.C.E., after the first siege of JERUSALEM.

At that time, Nebuchadnezzar had taken the king, Jehoiachin, into exile, and a large number of the ruling class, priests, and others. He had settled them in Babylon, they hoped temporarily. But further rebellion by King Zedekiah of Judah, against Jeremiah's advice, had led to a further siege of Jerusalem, resulting in its destruction in 586 B.C.E. and almost total deportation of the remaining inhabitants. Ezekiel's earlier prophecies, like Jeremiah's, were largely directed to Jerusalem during this rebellious and disastrous period. We must presume the prophecies were not only heard by the first exiles but also by those still in Jerusalem. The book of Jeremiah gives evidence of frequent letters passing between the first exiles and those remaining (Jeremiah 29:29–32).

Ezekiel's prophecies also included, again like Jeremiah's, Isaiah's, and others', those directed against surrounding nations. After the fall of Jerusalem, these were directed particularly at those neighbors of Judah who had rejoiced over its fall. But Ezekiel, as the other great writing prophets of the period, also looked forward to a time of restoration, to a time when God would bless his chosen people again in their own land. As a priest, Ezekiel was particularly concerned in his prophecies with a restored temple and priesthood, and the layout of the new regime.

At times his style becomes what came to be called APOCALYPTIC WRITING. The imagery of his visions becomes symbolic or allegorical and was to be repeated in the books of Daniel, Zechariah, and Revelation. His prophetic imagination and language take on a different note from previous prophets'. The book has often been seen, as with the book of Isaiah, as transitional from preexilic to postexilic times (see RETURN FROM EXILE), when not only the experience of exile, but the experience of living in a strange and alien culture added new dimensions to the religious language of the Bible, and, more importantly, new insights into the greatness and universality of Yahweh.

The book is carefully dated. There is some scholarly disagreement whether later editors added material to Ezekiel's prophecies, but generally speaking, the book has a unity of thought and language that persuades most scholars it is the work of one man, the prophet-priest Ezekiel. The text has had a confused transmission, and some passages are difficult to translate.

Ezekiel's vision of the glory of the Lord (Ezekiel 1:1–28), engraving by Julius Schnorr von Carolsfeld

SYNOPSIS

Commission, Visions, and Prophecies (Chapters 1–7)

The first seven chapters of Ezekiel are as strange as any seven chapters in any of the prophetic books of the Bible. The first chapter contains an amazing vision that sounds as if it should belong to a science fiction story, with the sighting of a glorious spacecraft. In fact, it is an appearance of God in his majesty, appearing to the exiled Ezekiel, to commission him to speak out as a prophet (chapters 2–3). The message will be difficult to give because of the intransigence of the hearers, who will be both the exiled Jews and those still back in Jerusalem.

He returns to them and is told to enact a series of prophecies by building a model of a besieged Jerusalem, by lying on his side immobile and bound, and by shaving his hair with a sword (4:1–5:4). In a further three spoken prophecies, these enactments are explained: Jerusalem will be laid waste because of its continuing rebellion against God (5:5–7:27). The initial vision remains with Ezekiel throughout this first section.

Laments and Prophecies over the Jerusalem Temple (Chapters 8–19)

The next 12 chapters focus on the Jerusalem temple, from which Ezekiel had been exiled. In a vision similar to that of chapter 3, he is taken to Jerusalem

and shown abominable practices being performed there. Ezekiel hears words of judgment pronounced (chapters 8–9). In a second vision of the cherubim, more like that of chapter 1, the prophet sees the LORD's glory leaving the temple (chapter 10); in a third, he hears both judgment on the people and a hope of restoration (chapter 11).

The remaining chapters of the section are a series of oracles dealing with specific aspects of this judgment. There is a further enacted prophecy (chapter 12) depicting the coming exile and attacks, similar to Jeremiah's, on false prophets and false prophecies of peace (chapters 12–14). Three prophecies are given as extended analogies or allegories (chapters 15–17), the first of Judah as a vine, the second of Judah as a naked and faithless woman, the third of eagles and vines, depicting Judah caught in the trap of power politics between EGYPT and Babylon. Chapter 18 is an exposition of a proverb, which is now altered to propound individual responsibility for one's own sin or righteousness; the last chapter of the section consists of two laments over the princes of JUDAH now in exile.

Prophecies and Allegories over Punishment and Restoration (Chapters 20–24)

This short section completes the first half of the book. The focus widens slightly, from the temple to the city of Jerusalem itself, taking us up to its moment of fall. The first oracle in the section sets up a parallel between Israel's exile in the wilderness after being taken out of Egypt, and its forthcoming exile, having been taken out of their sinful city and state. Eventually, after its evil is purged, the exiles will reenter Israel, as previously in their history. Ezekiel then turns to the actual invasion under the Babylonians. They will be guided to attack Jerusalem before other cities (chapter 21). Chapter 22 is a vehement attack on the moral degradation of Jerusalem, and thus the extent to which it will need to be cleansed. The sexually explicit chapter 23 is an allegory of the two kingdoms in their faithlessness, while chapter 24 dramatically draws Ezekiel directly into his oracles. The death of his own wife is to be a sign of the death of Jerusalem. But there is to be no mourning by Ezekiel or the exiles.

Oracles against Other Nations (Chapters 25–32)
As in Isaiah and Jeremiah, there is a group of hostile prophecies concerning surrounding nations. The list of nations differs slightly from prophet to prophet. In Ezekiel, the list begins with four short oracles against Ammon, Moab, and Edom, on the west side of the RIVER JORDAN, and Philistia on the Mediterranean coast (chapter 25). They were all Israel's near neighbors. Then follows a much longer series of oracles against the city-state of Tyre (see LEBANON), including its allied city-state, Sidon (chapters 26–28). Finally, as a climax, there is an even longer and more sustained series of seven oracles against Egypt (chapters 29–32). Most of the prophecies are precisely dated to around the time of the fall of Jerusalem, and it is these nations' attitude to that fall that determines the nature of the denunciation for the most part.

Fall and Restoration of God's People (Chapters 33–39)
This section returns to Israel, but now after the fall of Jerusalem, which is reported in chapter 33. This chapter acts as a bridge or transition, picking up previous themes of individual responsibility and the justice of Israel's downfall. This is followed in the next chapter by a denunciation of Israel's leaders, and in chapter 35 by a further denunciation of Edom. However, parts of chapter 34 and all of chapter 36 provide a generous promise of full restoration. This is symbolized in the famous vision of the valley of dry bones in chapter 37, which is followed by a promise of a new unity between the divided nations under a Davidic king. The section closes with an apocalyptic account of a final assault on the restored nation, an assault that is decisively defeated by divine intervention (chapters 38–39).

Vision of a New Jerusalem (Chapters 40–48)
The final section deals with an extended vision of what a restored and rebuilt Jerusalem will look like, focusing particularly on a new temple and a new temple ritual. In the vision, Ezekiel is given an angelic guide (see ANGELS) who gives detailed instructions as to design and architecture of the temple and measurements of how the whole HOLY LAND is to be reallocated among the restored 12 tribes. There are also detailed instructions as to ritual and dress for the new priesthood, as well as for "the prince," who will have sacred as well as secular duties. Ezekiel also sees in the vision the glory of the LORD returning to the temple through the east gate.

COMMENTARY

Commission, Visions, and Prophecies (Chapters 1–7)
The opening of the book of Ezekiel dates it exactly. In fact, all through the book, exact dates are given for various oracles, nearly all in chronological order. This is in contrast to the confused order of much of Jeremiah, and the ambiguity of the second part of Isaiah, where times and dates are highly conjectural.

The fifth year of the exile would date to 593 B.C.E., and the fifth day of the fourth month would date it around midsummer. The opening phrase "in the thirtieth year" is best taken as a reference to the prophet's age. Significantly, priests of the Zadokite order were not allowed to take up their office till they were 30, serving till they were 50 (see Numbers 4:3).

The place of the initial vision is also given: "by the river Chebar." This was a canal that ran south of the Euphrates, branching from it above Babylon and running through the city of Nippur. Babylonian records indicate a settlement of Jews in the area at the time. Ezekiel, therefore, had been in exile five years—long enough to accustom himself to the strange land, with its foreign deities and architecture, but not long enough really to grasp the enormity of the religious challenge posed to him as a priest. The whole of Israelite religion had centered on the temple of Jerusalem and its rituals. God was seen as having his footstool there. How could he be served and worshipped in a foreign land? What validity would any ritual have? Would it be possible to return to Jerusalem anytime soon?

It cannot be emphasized too strongly how significant this opening vision was for Ezekiel. It was a theophany, that is, a revelation of God's glory and presence at the place where he was. Like Isaiah's vision in the Temple (Isaiah 6), it was a commissioning vision, but unlike Isaiah's, it was in the open air, in a foreign land. The vision was saying that God's power and control were universal; his glory could manifest itself where he pleased.

The substance of the vision and the language in which it is expressed were also quite new. It has been suggested its elements could all derive from the temple worship, but it would seem more likely that features of Babylonian religious motifs and architecture melded themselves into Ezekiel's mind and imagination. The "four living creatures" (1:5) are later identified as cherubim, as were carved over the ark of the covenant in the Holy of Holies in the temple, its innermost shrine. As such, they are majestic angelic beings, stretching up to the sky. Each of the four creatures has four aspects, man, lion, eagle, and ox, representing the four orders of created beings: men, domestic animals, wild animals, birds. But majestic as they are, they only surround "something that looked like burning coals of fire" (1:13), reminding us of Isaiah's vision, and supporting a dome (1:22). Over the dome there was a throne (1:26) on which is seated "something that seemed like a human form" (1:26). Yet so awe-inspiring is the vision that we, as readers, know as well as Ezekiel that it is the very presence of God in his glory.

Equally striking to this visualization is the description of its sound (1:24) and movement (1:15–21). The huge wheels within wheels allow it to move in whatever direction it wishes. The rims of the wheels themselves have eyes in them (see Revelation 4:6, 8). The sounds vary between thunder and rushing waters, imagery that the writer of Revelation was also to use.

These sorts of description, though found in part elsewhere in earlier writings, are so dense in imagery and symbolism as to represent a new sort of writing, one that became later associated with apocalyptic writing. Ezekiel constantly uses the phrase "was something like," conveying at the same time the likeness and the unlikeness of what he is describing: that it exists both in its indescribable force, and yet as symbolically a word that needs to be understood.

Though the word *glory* is used only half as many times as in Isaiah, this sense of the glory of God runs throughout the book more consistently than anything else. The symbolism represents God's omniscience (the eyes), his omnipresence (the wheels), and his omnipotence (the cherubim and the throne). It is a vision Ezekiel finds sustaining as he is commissioned to deliver a message that, like Jeremiah's, will not be heard nor received (2:1–7).

The significant image for this message is the written scroll that he has to eat (2:8–3:3), which is "sweet as honey" to eat at first but becomes bitter (3:14; cf. Jeremiah 15:16; Revelation 10:8–10), suggesting the double-edged nature of the prophetic in terms of utterance and reception. Commission and vision are then repeated.

Ezekiel takes seven days of stunned silence to absorb this vision (3:15). The third word of commissioning follows (3:16–21) in terms of the "watchman" image used typically of the prophetic ministry (e.g., Isaiah 21:6–12; 56:10; Jeremiah 6:17; 31:6), though it has been suggested that as a priest, Ezekiel might have linked it more to the doorkeepers employed in the temple than to watchers on the walls. The idea is prophetic responsibility: If words are not spoken and people perish, their blood is held to the prophet's account.

The fourth commissioning word (3:25–27) becomes the first of a series of enacted prophecies, in the manner seen also in Isaiah and Jeremiah (e.g., Jeremiah 13, 16, 19). The prophet has to act out his prophecy; only when this has made a significant impact is he allowed to speak. In this first one, he will be mute, and he will not be allowed out of his house to speak unless he has a message from God. It has been suggested that Ezekiel was in such shock that he could not speak or that he was in some kind of paralytic state.

The next four enactments, however, are quite deliberate: the model of Jerusalem (4:1–3), the lying on his side bound with cords (4:4–8), the rationing out of seed for bread making (4:9–17), and the shaving of his head and weighing out the hair (5:1–4). Each symbolizes the siege and eventual destruction of Jerusalem, thus dashing the hopes of the exiles that they would be able to return home quickly. Interestingly, Ezekiel goes along with the sheer physical discomfort of all this. Unlike Jeremiah, at only one point does he argue with God, who allows him to use cow dung rather than human excrement (4:14–15). The precise symbolism of the length of time involved in the lying on his side (4:5) has been debated. Most scholars opt for seeing it as representing the time of the divided kingdom leading up to the final destruction of Jerusalem.

The enacted prophecies are then followed by three prophecies expounding their meaning (5:5–17; 6:1–14; 7:1–27). The parallels with Jeremiah 32:24–36 are strong: The same message comes from exile and from home. As with Isaiah, a remnant theology emerges (6:8; and see 7:16; 11:16–21; 12:15–16; 16:60–63; compare also Isaiah 4:3; 10:21; 11:11; Jeremiah 23:3; Zechariah 8:12). As important is the recurring phrase "then you shall know that I am the LORD," which climaxes this section (7:27).

Chapter 7 is the first chapter set as poetry and rises to new rhetorical heights. Basically it repeats the message of the previous chapter but introduces the prophetic genre of WOES AND DENUNCIATIONS, on the one hand, and of the lament, on the other (see 2:10). And while chapter 6 stresses sins of idolatry, chapter 7 stresses the sins of materialism and injustice. Both stress the cataclysmic nature of the day of God's wrath in the repeated "See, the day! See, it comes!" (7:10, and compare Amos 5:18, 20; 8:1–14; Isaiah 2:6–13; Zephaniah 1:17–18).

Laments and Prophecies over the Jerusalem Temple (Chapters 8–19)

The second section opens with a second series of visions, precisely dated to the sixth year, the sixth month, and the fifth day, some 14 months after the first series, thus around September 592 B.C.E. The language is also much the same: "cherubim," "wings," "brightness," "what appeared to be," "the appearance of."

As before, Ezekiel is not addressed by name but as "mortal" or "Son of Man." The Hebrew is literally "son of Adam," a term used elsewhere in the Bible, but here particularly with the sense of "mere man," as opposed to a transcendent God. In the visions, he is carried to Jerusalem, around which the whole section centers. The three visions in the first half describe the idolatry within the temple, which leads to the removal of the *shekinah* glory, the presence of God that entered the temple at its dedication under Solomon (2 Chronicles 5:14). That such idolatries were happening is well attested by Jeremiah, who was actually living in the city (Jeremiah 16:10–21).

In the first vision he is shown a series of four "abominations." The first is the "image of jealousy," which is not hidden. The other three are manifested by symbolically "digging through the wall" (8:8). The second abomination consists of engravings of creeping animals, suggesting some sort of Egyptian or Sumerian religion, with 70 elders worshipping them, one of whom is Jaazaniah. His father, Shaphan, is mentioned elsewhere as being a worshipper of Yahweh, so here we have a significant body of leaders who have reneged on true worship of God. Then follow women weeping for Tammuz, a Middle Eastern goddess, whose rituals enacted the dying of fertility in the winter and rebirth in spring. Last are the sun worshippers. King Josiah had previously cleansed the land of such pagan rituals (2 Kings 23:4–14), but in the degenerate last days of Jerusalem, they were free to return.

The second part of this vision consists of six angelic executioners, accompanied by a recording angel (9:1–2). Such well-structured details of this vision were new to Hebrew prophecy and anticipate a new apocalyptic note rather than just isolated dramatic imagery. The putting of a mark on the foreheads of the righteous (9:4) is another such detail. The book of Revelation reverses its symbolism in its apocalyptic descriptions of a final judgment (Revelation 20:4).

The second vision follows immediately from the first. His gaze is returned to the cherubim, which are described much as in his initial vision. Out of them emerges a voice "like the voice of God Almighty when he speaks." The term for the deity here is *El Shaddai* and is used rarely in the book; the usual name is *Yahweh Adonai* ("the Sovereign LORD"). The vision depicts the final removal of the glory from the temple, again in stages. Once God's presence leaves, then the city is in truth defenseless before its enemies, who become God's instruments of justice, and is open to natural catastrophes (14:12–20). God dwelling among his people was a foundational belief (Exodus 29:45–46; 2 Chronicles 6:20–21; etc.), but the inhabitants of Jerusalem had taken it to mean automatic protection. They should be under no illusions now. In fact, the recurring use of *face* as in the phrase "set his face against" is used here more than in any other book of the Bible. The glory from the temple is reunited with the glory above the cherubim (10:19).

The third vision (chapter 11) returns him to the temple, but this time in the vision Ezekiel is no longer an observer but a prophetic participant. We need to realize how different these visions are from, say, the literary dreams of medieval literature or Bunyan's *Pilgrim's Progress*. They are ecstatic experiences, even theophanies, as was suggested earlier. To be able to participate in them was a major privilege. Part of this participation is to refute a series of proverbs uttered by the Jerusalem leaders suggesting security (11:3, 7, 11; 12:21–28; 18).

Ezekiel 11:19 reminds us of Jeremiah 32:36–39, in the promise of "a new spirit within them," and in the image of "hearts of flesh" for "hearts of stone." As the glory departs finally (11:23), there is therefore a hope of a remnant to be restored, at least among the exiles to whom Ezekiel is finally returned.

The second part of this section (chapters 12–19) continues to focus on Jerusalem and its temple, though more obviously spoken from Babylon in the form of oracles, enacted prophecies, and laments. Wise utterances (see WISDOM LITERATURE) of false security are refuted alongside denunciations of false prophecies (13:10). The false prophets are attacked in the metaphor of whitewashing (13:11–16; and see 22:28; the Authorized (King James) Version has "untempered mortar"). The oracles develop as a denunciation against the prophetesses (13:17–23) who seem mere fortune-tellers. Ezekiel 14:21 establishes the pattern of 4s running throughout the book so far: four cherubim with four faces, four commissioning words, four abominations and woes, four acts of judgment.

The most important message of these chapters concerns individual responsibility, paralleling the earlier teaching on prophetic responsibility (chapter 3). Individuals are saved by individual acts of righteousness (14:14, 18). Generational righteousness or punishment as laid out in Exodus 20:5 has to be subordinated to individual accountability, as Deuteronomy 24:16 also suggests. The proverb of sour grapes is one Jeremiah also uses in the same context (Jeremiah 31:29–30).

More obviously striking than this, though no more significant, is the imagery of Jerusalem as a naked woman, taken in and protected in a COVENANT relationship by God, yet then turning to prostitution. Such sexual imagery is to be found elsewhere, as in Hosea, but its explicitness and force suggest a new depth of despair (chapter 16, and see comments on chapter 23). Further figurative language occurs in the extended analogy or parable of chapter 15, one of the few chapters to be written as verse, where the imagery of Israel as a vine is used, but only in terms of uselessness as wood (cf. Isaiah 5:1–10). A further poetic section in chapter 17 deals with the allegory of eagles and cedars, representing hope for the future in the transplanting of sprigs in lands of exile. The cedar image is used again in chapter 31. The metaphor of the branch as messianic occurs in Isaiah 11:1, Jeremiah 23:5, and Zechariah 3:8. This allegory is balanced by chapter 19, which becomes a lament in *qinah* form for the two young kings, Jehoahaz and Jehoiachin, who were removed to Egypt and Babylon, respectively, but as marks of punishment.

Prophecies and Allegories over Punishment and Restoration (Chapters 20–24)

The section, as the previous two, opens with a precise dating—the seventh year, the fifth month, the 10th day. It has been worked out that this will be July or August 591 B.C.E., nearly a year after the previous oracle. As in 14:1, the elders went to Ezekiel, since he was neither allowed to move out of his house or to prophesy unless clearly commanded by God (3:24). Ezekiel gives them a lukewarm welcome, developing a history lesson for them. As in chapter 16, it is an allegory followed by an interpretation. This rehearsal of national history is to be seen in the Psalms right up to Stephen's defense in the New Testament (Acts 7:1–53). As with Stephen later, Ezekiel uses national history as denunciation of the people's unfaithfulness, rather than as a memorial of God's faithfulness to them. They are now in a new wilderness, which will become the place of purging.

While this first oracle section is not in poetry, the prose is heightened, as it is being spoken directly by God. It is as powerful a historical denunciation as any to be found in the Hebrew Bible. It is followed by two shorter oracles (20:45–49; 21:1–7) beginning, "Set your face toward." The first is an extended image of the south burning, especially the forests of the Negev, much more wooded then than now. Ezekiel is troubled by the response from this (20:49): For his hearers, "allegory" has become no more than "fantasy." What is a living prophetic image has become for them fanciful rhetoric.

In fact, the threat of fire is followed by that of the metonymic sword, continued in what is sometimes referred to as the Song of the Sword in 21:9–17, which is in verse form. An equally powerful "sword song" follows in 21:18–27, with its dramatic reenactment of how the Babylonian king will seek divine guidance through heathen means of divination, yet find himself being used as God's instrument to strike Jerusalem first. This is followed by a third sword song (21:28–32), which picks up the earlier fire imagery (21:32). There are no fewer than 86 references to swords in Ezekiel.

Chapter 22 is a straightforward woe and denunciation against Jerusalem, which has Leviticus 17–26 as its subtext. Every single area of the moral and social law is being abused. The smelter image of 22:17–22 renews the fire imagery, but in terms of fire as used in smelting and refining of metals by totally destroying their original form. In the list of corrupt leaders of 22:23–31, the image of whitewashing is again used, and the famous phrase "I sought for anyone who would . . . stand in the breach . . . but I found no one." Later readers of the Hebrew Bible would doubtless see Nehemiah as someone who would finally stand in the breach in the walls (Nehemiah 2:13).

Chapter 23 repeats the sexual imagery of chapter 16 but names two erring women, allegorically called Oholah (literally, "her tent"), referring to SAMARIA or the northern kingdom, and Oholibah (literally, "my tent in her"), referring to Jerusalem and the southern kingdom. The allegory, as before, is to be understood historically, in terms of making foreign alliances in order to buy protection, rather than trusting God to protect them. Both women are later hauled into slavery by the men to whom they sold them. It is shocking language to convey a shocking spiritual reality.

The final chapter is equally shocking in another way. In terms of enacted prophecy, this is the ultimate. Ezekiel has to lose his own wife and not mourn her death as an enactment of the "death" of Jerusalem and the prohibition to weep for its fall. The date of the prophecy is given as the ninth year, the 10th month, and the 10th day, which is both the day of his wife's death and the date when the final siege of Jerusalem begins, January 15, 588 B.C.E. In fact, priests, especially the high priest, were not allowed to mourn outwardly (Leviticus 21:1–6). But as soon as news verifying his prediction is received, the prophet will be allowed to speak freely.

Before that (24:3–13) is an allegorical woe that uses many of the previous images: meat in a cauldron, fire, purification of corruption, and blood shed unjustly.

Oracles against Other Nations (Chapters 25–32)

The small kingdoms of Ammon, Moab, and Edom run north to south, respectively, along the west bank of the Jordan. Ammon is also denounced by Jeremiah (Jeremiah 49:1–6) and Zephaniah (2:8–11). Ezekiel has referred to it once before (21:20), in that Nebuchadnezzar was divinely guided to attack Jerusalem rather than Rabbah, its capital. It thus escaped immediate destruction but as its two neighbors did, then proceeded to gloat over the fall of Jerusalem (25:3). This may refer to the first siege of Jerusalem, when Ezekiel was made an exile, or to its final fall. Similar denunciations for similar reasons follow against Moab, Edom, and Philistia.

The conventional denunciations in chapter 25 do not prepare us for the powerful and strikingly detailed woes, denunciations, taunts, and laments over Tyre that follow in the following three chapters, which are a mixture of poetry and highly rhetorical prose. At one level, there seems little reason for Ezekiel to denounce the city-state. Isaiah and Joel do (Isaiah 23; Joel 3:4–8) but not Jeremiah. In fact, after Jerusalem fell, Tyre was the next one on Nebuchadnezzar's list, and it endured a 13-year-long siege, 586–573 B.C.E. However, the city, being partly built on an island, was able to reinforce itself by sea and withstand the Babylonians, who could do no more than raze the land-based part of the city.

So powerful are the oracles, however, that some interpreters have read them allegorically as referring to either Satan himself and his fall or typologically as the city of trade and commerce that reappears as Babylon in Revelation 17. Isaiah 14 taunts Babylon in very similar language, and perhaps Ezekiel is projecting onto Tyre some of his own feelings about Babylon, though outwardly he sees Babylon as God's instrument for punishment (26:7; 29:18–20; 30:25) and refuses to denounce it directly, unlike Isaiah or Jeremiah (see Isaiah 13; Jeremiah 50–51).

One of the striking features is the detailed knowledge of the ships and materials the Tyrians use (27:2–11) and of their trade (27:12–25). In this respect, Ezekiel seems to have a wider knowledge of the Middle Eastern commercial systems than other prophets. The two laments (27:2–11, 26–36) are among the most poetic sections of the book and equal the poeticality of any other prophetic utterance in the Hebrew Bible. When we consider that Ezekiel is typically a prose writer, this is even more significant. Two passages of equal poeticality are 28:1–10, a denunciation or taunt, and 28:12–23,

another lament. The other striking feature is Ezekiel's use of Canaanite mythology, linking it with that of Genesis: Thus the garden of Eden becomes a central image, especially its trees and its guardian cherubim. The "mountain of God" (28:16) probably refers to Canaanite mythology, being Mount Sapon, north of Ugarit. References here and elsewhere to "Daniel" are probably to be interpreted as "Dan-el," a character in this mythology. "Day Star" and "Dawn" are actual names of Canaanite deities.

Another systematic set of mythological references unusual for the prophets is to the underworld, or "Sheol," or "the pit" (see 31:14–17; 32:21–28). Usually such references occur in passing in other books. The reason for Tyre's fall is the hubristic pride of the rulers, seeing themselves as gods (28:8). This is renewed again in 31:16 in reference to Egypt. In many ways the denunciations of Egypt are in line with Isaiah's (Isaiah 19) and Jeremiah's (Jeremiah 46): They have been a false support, a delusion to Israel. Some of the imagery, of crocodiles, fish, "a dragon in the seas," refers obviously to Egypt's dependence on the Nile. But some (e.g., 31:2–18) have more to do with the mythological imagery just referred to, as well as building on imagery taken from chapter 17. In Ezekiel's last dated prophecy (29:17), Egypt becomes Nebuchadnezzar's reward for his long, profitless siege of Tyre.

Fall and Restoration of God's People (Chapters 33–39)

After the denunciations and laments against surrounding nations, Ezekiel needs to return to the collapsing southern kingdom and the exiles already taken to Babylon. He does this by reiterating some of the major prophecies in the first half of the book. Just as he began by references to his own calling, so he begins here by his being reminded by God of this calling and its responsibilities, tying up specifically with 3:16–21. The image, as before, is of the prophet as sentinel or watchman, ready to sound the trumpet (33:1–9).

This personal responsibility is then widened into the individual responsibility of all the people (33:12–20), again using a major theme from chapter 18. As before, the underlying principle is "I have no pleasure in the death of the wicked" (33:11, repeating 18:23). No judgment made in life is final: There is always the possibility of repentance just as there is the possibility of falling away.

The unfinished episode from 24:27 is then completed in 33:21–22. The date given for this (12th year, 10th month, fifth day) would put the message of the actual fall of Jerusalem a full 18 months later—rather too long a time perhaps for the news to travel, so some manuscripts suggest it is the 11th year that is meant. Ezekiel is now free to speak.

Ezekiel 33:23–29 repeats the reasons behind God's judgment from chapters 5 and 6, and three of the means of death, sword, wild animals, and pestilence, echoing 14:21 and 21:3–5, where famine is mentioned as the fourth death (cf. Jeremiah 5:6; 14:12; 32:36). Such punishments were threatened in Leviticus 26:22 and Deuteronomy 28:15–20 (cf. 2 Kings 25:8–9; Habakkuk 1:5–11). "Sword" is mentioned 86 times in the book. Another recurring phrase is "the mountains of Israel" (33:28), echoing 6:2, which will take on greater significance. Following the destruction of the city, the "waste places" are particularly noted.

The final theme is in 33:30–33: People do actually go to hear him, but only because of his rhetorical prowess, not to take notice of the message—a complaint made earlier in 20:49. The scene is then set for two further denunciations, one against "the shepherds" (chapter 34) and one against "mount Seir," that is to say, the country of Edom (chapter 35). Just as the prophet is held personally accountable, so are the shepherds (34:10)—and in this they have failed miserably. Ezekiel gives a detailed list of their failings, keeping, however, strictly to the sheep/shepherd imagery. The shepherds here should be seen as the nation's leaders in general, secular and spiritual. However, the oracle is not entirely denunciatory. Verses 11–16 give a promise of the future: God will become their shepherd; there will be a gathering of the remnant, and a new (under) shepherd, a new Davidic king, will be appointed (cf. Jeremiah 33:15f.)

The imagery from 34:15 becomes particularly rich in terms of a "covenant of peace," which will bring "showers of blessing." The final verse is quite psalmlike, with echoes of Psalm 23, and anticipating

in turn Jesus' use of the good shepherd image in the Gospel of John in the New Testament. Although the passages are all prose, it is a highly poetic prose, using parallelisms, repetitions, imagery, and other rhetorical devices freely—essentially prose poems.

It may seem odd for Ezekiel to round on just one country, Edom, when he had previously denounced a whole range. In fact, Edom had only been briefly mentioned (25:12–14). It was Edom, however, that after the fall of Jerusalem not only hindered escape efforts (for which, see Obadiah; Jeremiah 49:7–22; Psalm 137:7) but coveted the territory of Judah (35:10). For these very specific reasons were they condemned, the construction "as . . . so" suggesting the justice of that condemnation.

However, it has been suggested there is a rhetorical reason also for delaying the denunciation: to bring out a parallel between the mountains of Edom (35:8) and the "mountains of Israel" addressed in chapter 36. The two countries were traditionally related (Genesis 25:23), and that relation is remembered as late as Malachi 1:2–5. The chapter falls into two halves: the nadir now reached by the broken and desolate land, and the future hope in its full restoration. The anthropomorphism of God's "jealous wrath" works both ways: in judgment but also in rescue, since his honor is at stake. "For the sake of my holy name" (36:21, 22) echoes throughout the Hebrew Bible.

The heart of the restoration lies exactly where Jeremiah also put it: in renewed hearts and spirit (36:26–27; cf. Jeremiah 31:33–34; 32:38–41) and later a new covenant (37:26). Such spiritual renewal goes along with material prosperity in terms of the fertility of the land. These detailed images of fertility are thus both literal and figurative, forming a new Eden (36:35). The echo of the lost Eden of 28:13 resounds optimistically.

The most striking image of the restoration, however, is in the next chapter, where in a vision, the prophet is shown a valley of bones and graves. These symbolize the deadness of the Israelites and the kingdom. But as Ezekiel prophesies to them in the vision, so God's spirit blows new life into them. The Hebrew word *ruah* means "spirit," "breath," and "wind," and the prophet plays with each meaning. The winds from the four quarters suggest the universality and extent of this change. The concept of resurrection becomes stronger than just renewal. The revivifying occurs in two stages: the bones, symbolic of the body politic, and the breath, symbolic of a new spirit. A further symbolic image follows: the two sticks becoming one. Israel and Judah will be reunited, and the promise of Davidic kingship is repeated in the shepherd imagery.

The final two chapters are clearly apocalyptic, and it has been suggested they do not easily belong here, apart from 39:25–29, which return to the prophetic. However, they refer to the "latter days" after the previous restoration. The fact that the opening references to Gog and Magog and God's divine intervention in the face of overwhelming military force were taken up by the writer of Revelation in the New Testament (Revelation 20:7–10) has opened up a whole raft of so-called prophetic interpretation about the end times (see LAST THINGS). What do these names represent? The easiest interpretation is to see the countries' names as representing the whole known world of the time, all joining to wipe God's country off the map. Most of the countries named are to Israel's north, but some are to its south.

The style is certainly typical of much apocalyptic writing: "be ready," "keep ready," "after many days," "in the latter days," "a great shaking," plus God's direct intervention in a hopeless situation. The actual slaughter takes on unimaginable proportions, though Ezekiel's details help to concretize it. This defeat echoes other defeats, as in Isaiah 29:5–8; 66:15f.; Zechariah 12:1–9; 14:1–15, for example. The modes of death pick up from earlier references—sword, pestilence, wild animals, fire—but the apocalyptic intervention adds the natural phenomenon of "mountains being thrown down" and the phenomenon of self-destruction as enemy fights enemy (38:21). The section thus ends dramatically, final victory instead of present defeat, with everyone knowing "that I am the LORD their God"—the refrain that above every other refrain is the one that matters.

Vision of a New Jerusalem (Chapters 40–48)

This section has been seen as a kind of appendix. However, it has also been argued that it perfectly rounds off a book that began in profanation and the departure of glory and now at the end insists on a new holiness and sees the return of that glory. The final vision is deliberately compared to the initial vision of Ezekiel also. It was given 25 years after his first going into exile, that is, in April 573 B.C.E. Commentators have linked this to either the Day of Atonement or the Passover of that year.

The future it depicts is not directly linked to the previous chapters of restoration, though it gives concrete form to what the restored land would look like. It is, of course, an idealization, and no attempt was made by the eventual returnees from exile under Ezra and Nehemiah to put this plan into practice. Because of this, perhaps, the chapters in the section have been seen either symbolically or allegorically, or apocalyptically, as the shape of the future land during the last days. The section certainly reminds us that Ezekiel was priest as well as prophet, and his priestly knowledge of temple ritual is most clearly seen as he envisages its future form. It is both a radical and at the same time a very conservative vision. The temple design is traditional through the Middle East, but the perfection of land division radical.

It is not possible to discuss the many details of the plans for the new temple and its rituals. One scholar, Walther Zimmerli, in his commentary on Ezekiel, part 2, suggests that 25 is the crucial number for the measurements. Many others have commented on possible symbolic patterns in the numbers and design. As for the rituals, there are parallels to the very explicit instructions given in the Pentateuch for the tabernacle rituals and its priesthood (e.g., Exodus 25–30; 35–39; Leviticus 1–8; Numbers 18–19; 28–29) and the details of the Solomonic temple (2 Chronicles 3–5). But there are significant differences: There is no mention of any high priest, there is no ark of the covenant (which presumably had disappeared when Jerusalem fell), only a small number of rituals and festivals are described, and there are other significant absences. The holy of holies (the Most Holy Place) is not entered, and without a high priest, there would technically be no one to enter it. It has been suggested that when God's glory does return, he will make sure the temple is never defiled again. Human participation in it is thus lessened, and his people will recognize the reason as a chastening one.

Most significantly, the new priesthood is restricted to the Zadokite priesthood (40:46). Zadok was high priest in the latter years of David (2 Samuel 15:24–29) and into Solomon's reign (1 Kings 1:45). Ezekiel, a Zadokite himself, feels strongly that the ordinary Levitical priesthood has betrayed its calling beyond redemption and is now only fit for minor temple duties (44:5–27). Only the Zadokites kept some sense of the due holiness needed for God's service. Interestingly, in the absence of a high priest, the prince or secular ruler is called upon to take an active part in ritual and provision for the needs of the priests. There is certainly no separation of church and state in Ezekiel's vision! Most of the section is angelic instruction, but, interestingly, in one section, the prince is directly addressed as "you" (45:9–15).

The description of the new temple places it on a terraced east-west axis, within a square enclosure, but with no west gate (chapters 40–42). The east gate is the "holy" gate, through which a vision of the returning glory enters (43:1–12), just as it departed through the same gate (10:18–19; 11:22–23). Ordinary entrance into the outer courtyard is through the north and south gates, which penetrate a thick wall. Once the glory has returned, a sacred river breaks out of the temple, flowing in an increasingly deeper channel, till it reaches the Dead Sea, which it will cause to become fresh, apart from the preservation of salt in the marshes (47:1–12; compare the river in Zechariah 14:8).

The final two chapters (47–48) see the temple as the center of the new holy city, called *Yahweh Shammah* ("The LORD is there") rather than Jerusalem. The city itself sits in the center of the new Holy Land. The traditional 12 tribes are reinstated but in a new sacred geography, each tribe given a strip of land running east-west from the Jordan to the Mediterranean, and the northern border stretched up into Syria. Natural geographical borders are ignored. The book closes, as does the book of Zechariah, on the note of the restored holy city.

CHARACTER

Ezekiel Meaning "God strengthens." He was a married priest of the Zadokite order, who was taken into exile at the first siege of Jerusalem by the Babylonians. Unable to carry out his priestly duties, he was still consulted by the elders, though he was not allowed for a time to speak at will, and his message did not appear to be heard. His vivid and powerful visions, which began at the age of 30, predicted the fall of Jerusalem, which occurred at the same time as his wife's death. His first prophecy is dated to July 593 B.C.E., his last to April 571 B.C.E. He is not mentioned elsewhere in the Bible.

Ezra-Nehemiah

The book of Ezra-Nehemiah is a historical-theological narrative. It relates the story of Israel's restoration after the terrible experience of the Babylonian Exile. The individual historical events of reestablishment of the temple, the people, and the city of Jerusalem are combined, by means of literary design, into a unified overall picture. This is done in order to show that behind the individual events there is an overarching plan of salvation. God makes it possible for a new Jewish community to be founded, a continuation of the preexilic Israel.

In the Christian Bible, Ezra and Nehemiah are two separate books. From a literary point of view, however, they form a unified narrative. One proof for this unity is the mission of Ezra, which is announced in Ezra 7 but carried out in its main parts only in Nehemiah 8–10. Correspondingly, the Hebrew tradition only knows one book, which is called Ezra-Nehemiah, or, simply, Ezra.

In the Christian Bible, the order of books, namely, Chronicles, Ezra, and Nehemiah, suggests that these three together form a continuous work of history. For this, the expression *chronistic history* has been invented. Today, however, scholars tend to see Chronicles and Ezra-Nehemiah as two independent works again. The Hebrew Bible certainly sees them as independent by placing Chronicles not before, but after, Ezra-Nehemiah, thus breaking up the chronological line. (For a description of the unique character of Chronicles as a conclusion to the Hebrew Bible, see CHRONICLES.)

The author of the book of Ezra-Nehemiah is anonymous. For his narrative, he uses a great deal of material from historical sources. In Ezra 1–6, these are a list of returned exiles and four official letters reflecting the political circumstances of the time. The letters and some of the text that binds them together are written in the Aramaic language, as this was the official language of Israel's neighbors at this time (Ezra 4:8–6:18; 7:12–26; see BIBLE, LANGUAGES OF). First and foremost, however, the author uses texts that are written in the first person by the main characters of the book, Ezra and Nehemiah. The so-called Ezra Memoir is used mostly in Ezra 7–10 and Nehemiah 8. The Nehemiah Memoir extends over Nehemiah 1–7, 12, and 13. The Nehemiah Memoir especially is quite vivid and even confrontational, and it reveals much of Nehemiah's personality. Other forms integrated into the narrative are royal decrees (e.g., Ezra 1:1–4; 7:12–26), prayers and confessions (e.g., Ezra 9:5–15; Nehemiah 1:4–11; 9:1–37), and other legal documents (Nehemiah 10:1–39).

The historical reliability of the sources is generally acknowledged. The author, however, does not present his material in a strict chronological order. Especially in Nehemiah 7–12, different historical horizons are melded together in order to give a unified theological picture. This makes historical reconstruction more difficult. Interestingly, although less than 10 percent of the text are the author's own words, the book does not present itself as an anthology but rather as a unified whole.

Persian Kings and Events of Ezra-Nehemiah

559–530	**Cyrus II**
538	Cyrus's decree
536	First return under Zerubbabel
530–522	**Cambyses II**
522	**Gaumata**
522–486	**Darius Hystaspes**
520	Rebuilding of temple starts
516	Temple completed
486–465	**Xerxes (=Ahasuerus)**
464–424	**Artaxerxes I**
458	Second return under Ezra (date disputed)
445	Third return under Nehemiah
423–404	**Darius II**

It is not possible to state an exact date for the composition of the book. It is reasonable to assume that it was written not long after the last events reported, which would be around 400 B.C.E.

The book is structured as follows: The restoration of the temple (Ezra 1–6); the restoration of the people (Ezra 7–10); the restoration of the city (Nehemiah 1–6); the completion of the restoration of temple, city, and people (Nehemiah 7:1–13:3); the ongoing threat to the restoration of temple, people, and city (Nehemiah 13:4–39).

SYNOPSIS

The Restoration of the Temple (Ezra 1–6)

Cyrus, king of Persia, is moved by God to issue a decree (538 B.C.E.). In it he permits the Jews captured in Babylonia to return to their home country. He gives them the task of rebuilding the temple of Yahweh in Jerusalem. He hands over to them the temple vessels of the first Jerusalem temple, which Nebuchadnezzar had carried away after the destruction of Jerusalem and had been kept in Babylonia.

The total number of returnees is about 50,000 (2:64–65). The leaders of the first track (536 B.C.E.) are Jeshua and Zerubbabel, but a certain Sheshbazzar also plays a role (1:11; 5:16).

In the seventh month, the month of the major religious feasts (see Leviticus 23:23–36), the returnees gather in Jerusalem. Under the leadership of Jeshua and Zerubbabel, the altar for the burnt offerings is reerected, and the daily burnt offerings are reinstalled according to the Law of Moses. The people begin to make preparations for the rebuilding of the temple. As a ceremonial act, the foundation of the temple is laid. This is a moment of great emotions. Many of the older people weep, because they remember the old temple, but the others shout joyfully. The sound of both the weeping and the shouting is heard far away.

The surrounding people, however, do not want Judah to become strong again. By using different political strategies, they interrupt the work of rebuilding that just has begun. The quarrels continue for almost two decades (4:4–5). For example, these people write a letter to King Artaxerxes telling him that Jerusalem always has been a rebellious city and should not be allowed to gain strength again. Artaxerxes finds this confirmed by the royal annals and issues an order to stop rebuilding Jerusalem.

However, the Jews can also make use of the royal annals to their own benefit. When they write a letter to Darius, the king searches and finds in the annals the record of Cyrus's decree to rebuild the temple. In this way the Jews are politically strengthened again. Additionally, the prophets Haggai and Zechariah give spiritual encouragement. So the Jews can finally complete the temple and dedicate it in a ceremonial act of great joy (516 B.C.E.).

The Restoration of the People (Ezra 7–10)

The second stimulus for the restoration originates with Ezra. Ezra is a scribe and a priest descended from Aaron, the first priest. He is authorized by the Persian king, Artaxerxes, to put into force the Mosaic Law in the Judean community and to install the regular temple service. The king also gives financial support for this. Ezra assembles a delegation of Jews, including some priests and Levites, who will be needed for the maintenance of the temple service. In the seventh year of the reign of King Artaxerxes (458 B.C.E.), the group journeys to Jerusalem.

The first problem Ezra is confronted with in Jerusalem is that many of the Jewish returnees have entered mixed marriages. Even some of the political and spiritual leaders are affected. Through mixed marriages foreign religion can find its way into the Jewish community, and this is a case of disobedience of the Lord. Furthermore, the identity of the small Jewish community is endangered.

Ezra is shaken. Together with some of the elders, he offers a prayer of confession, weeping and throwing himself down in front of the temple. While he does so, more and more people assemble and join him. After the praying and weeping have ended, they decide together to send away the foreign wives and children.

The Restoration of the City (Nehemiah 1–6)

Nehemiah is a Jew and court official of the Persian king, Artaxerxes, in the citadel of Susa. In the 20th year of Artaxerxes' reign (445 B.C.E.), a traveling Jew informs Nehemiah about the miserable state of Jerusalem. Nehemiah is alarmed. After some time of spiritual preparation, he tells the king about his concerns. The king commissions him to travel to Jerusalem in order to rebuild the city.

Having arrived in Jerusalem, Nehemiah at first examines the state of the walls. After that, he wins over the leading Jews for his plan of rebuilding. The individual segments of the wall are assigned to different families and groups, and together the people start rebuilding the wall.

However, Nehemiah has to face various kinds of opposition. The people living around Judah do not want Jerusalem to become an independent city again. They join in order to stop the rebuilding of Jerusalem by force. Fortunately, the Jews are warned early enough. Nehemiah commands that from this time on, half of the people continue building the walls while the other half are ready to fight any attackers.

But there are not only threats from outside the city but also conflicts inside. Nehemiah learns that the rich Jerusalem upper class is oppressing the poor Jews. Nehemiah achieves a remission of debts and a return of property for them. Nehemiah himself sets a good example by relinquishing his right as a governor to collect taxes from the people.

Nehemiah is also threatened personally. His adversaries set traps for him in order to catch him and to discredit him. But he sees through all their attempts. Finally, after only a little over seven weeks, the wall is finished.

The Completion of the Restoration of Temple, People, and City (Nehemiah 7:1–13:3)

The fourth main part of Ezra-Nehemiah is formed as a concentric structure.

The first, outer ring is made of the sections 7:1–3 and 12:27–43. After the city wall is finished, the gates are set up and the gatekeepers are appointed. After that, the wall is dedicated in a ceremonial act. Two great companies go in procession along the new wall. They start in opposite directions, each walking around half of the city, meeting each other again at the temple. There is a lot of joy and feasting, and the shouting of the people is heard far away.

The second literary ring is made of the sections 7:4–73a and 11:1–12:26. Nehemiah notices that Jerusalem is sparsely populated and many houses have not been rebuilt. From the list of returnees he gains an overview of the people living in the cities around Jerusalem. Then the people cast lots to invite one family out of 10 to live in Jerusalem. The people bless all those who willingly offer to move into the city.

The core of the concentric structure consists of the section 7:73b–10:39. On the first day of the seventh month, the people gather in Jerusalem. Ezra stands on a wooden platform reading to them from the Law of Moses. Some of the Levites explain the passages read, so that the people understand what they mean to them. When the people hear the words of the Law, they weep. But Ezra, Nehemiah, and the Levites tell them that this ought to be a day of joy and feasting and a holy day.

The next day, the people again assemble in order to hear of the Law. On this day Ezra reads the regulations concerning the Feast of Tabernacles. The feast is then celebrated for eight days in accordance with that law.

On the 24th of the same month, the people gather a third time to hear the Law, this time in connection with a national confession. So a long prayer of confession is offered. The prayer describes the whole story of God and his chosen people. It deals with all the good things God has given to Israel and all wonders he has performed for them, from the creation of the world, the election of Abraham, the delivery out of Egypt, the making of the covenant at Mount Sinai, the leading into the Promised Land, up to the living in the land in the time of the judges and kings. On the other hand, the prayer describes the ongoing disobedience of the people. God had shown patience and mercy for a long time, but finally the people had to go into the Babylonian Exile. Nevertheless, the grace of God has not ended, for God has allowed his people to return home, even if it is a time of great distress.

After the prayer, the priests, the Levites, and the people make an agreement in writing to obey the Law of Moses and to maintain the temple service properly.

The concentric structure ends with two short notes. The first, 12:44–47, describes the organization of the tithes for the priests and Levites. The second, 13:1–3, deals with separation of foreign people from the religious community of Israel. With these final arrangements, the restoration of Israel is completed.

The Ongoing Threat to the Restoration of Temple, People, and City (Nehemiah 13:4–39)

Nehemiah leaves Jerusalem and returns only after some time. He discovers that in the meantime some irregularities have taken place. A large room of the temple scheduled for tithes is occupied by a private person named Tobiah, and the portions of the Levites have not been given to them. Nehemiah throws all the private furniture out of that temple room and makes new arrangements for the maintenance of the tithes.

Also, the Sabbath day is profaned by some. The non-Jewish traders in particular are selling their products on the Sabbath. Nehemiah commands that the city gates should not be opened on the Sabbath anymore.

Some Jews have again married foreign women. Nehemiah intervenes vigorously in order to resolve these matters.

COMMENTARY

The Restoration of the Temple (Ezra 1–6)

In order to understand the significance of the restoration, one has to recognize that the destruction of the temple in 587/6 B.C.E., the end of the Davidic kingdom, and the Exile of the people in Babylon were the most distressing experiences Israel had suffered in its whole history. This discontinuity could easily have led to a total loss of identity by the Jewish people. In order to prevent this, efforts of restoration had to be made very consciously, not only in a literal, but also in a theological, sense. One document of this is the book of Ezra-Nehemiah.

The first three parts of the book (Ezra 1–6, Ezra 7–10, Nehemiah 1–6) describe the restoration of temple, people, and city in three large historic-thematic blocks. All three parts are formed according to the same pattern: God ordains in each case that a group of Jewish exiles return to Jerusalem under Persian authorization. They undertake a project of restoration and have to face opposition from outside and from inside before they finally succeed.

The new postexilic Jewish community derives its legitimacy and its identity by putting itself into continuity with the preexilic Israel. Ezra 1:1 shows that not only the exile but also the restoration after exile are already preordained in the prophetic message of Jeremiah (Jeremiah 29:10–14). It is one and the same Lord who caused both. Furthermore, the return from Babylon is presented as a second Exodus, e.g., in 1:6, where the neighbors aid the Jews with gifts as they leave (see Exodus 3:21–22). Like the deliverance from Egypt, the deliverance from Babylon is an act of God continuously caring for his chosen people. Another important point of continuity are the temple treasures. Although the temple has to be rebuilt completely, at least the temple vessels are physically the same as in preexilic Israel (Ezra 1:7–11).

The promised people and the Promised Land are the two most precious elements in God's promises to Israel (see Genesis 12:1–3). Against this background, the list of exiles returning to their individual cities in the land of Judah (chapter 2) is especially highlighted. Some of the priests could not find their entries in the genealogical records and therefore could not be priests anymore (Ezra 2:62–63). This has to be understood against the background, however, that most of the returnees obviously *could* trace back their family lines into preexilic times.

The prophetic message of obedience and disobedience, of judgment and salvation, given in Jeremiah, for example, makes it clear that the first and most important tasks of the returnees are to reestablish their relationship to God, and, in concrete forms, to reestablish the temple and the temple service.

Therefore, the first act reported of the returnees was to reerect the altar for the burnt offerings and to resume the daily offerings according to the Law of Moses. This uniform daily rhythm is again a strong symbol of continuity.

The people living in the neighborhood of Judah, however, are hostile to the returnees. Some of them belong to ethnic groups that had been imported into the territory of the old northern Israel kingdom by the Assyrians in the eighth century B.C.E. These people to some extent adopted the Israelite religion and understood themselves as being Israelites, but those who returned from Babylon did not recognize them as such. The people living in the vincinity of Judah had brought the rebuilding of the temple to a standstill shortly after it began. Concerning the opposition to the rebuilding of the temple, there are some chronological issues at stake: According to Ezra 4:4–5, the opposition extends from the time of Cyrus to the beginning of the reign of Darius, i.e., to 522 B.C.E. Accordingly, 4:24 and 6:15 inform us that the temple was rebuilt between the second and the sixth year of Darius, i.e., between 520 and 516 B.C.E. However, the letter that the adversaries write and that is quoted in 4:7–16 addresses itself to Artaxerxes, a king who reigned about half a century later. Additionally, the letter does not even deal with the rebuilding of the temple but with the rebuilding of the city wall. Its date, as well as its content, suggest that the letter originally belonged to the time and the mission of Nehemiah, not those of Zerubbabel and Jeshua.

This chronological deviation should not, however, be seen as a historical error. The writer of Ezra-Nehemiah knew that Artaxerxes reigned after Darius (see 6:14). Furthermore, the fact cannot have escaped him that the letter deals with the city wall and not with the temple.

The reason for the chronological deviation is rather to be understood from a literary point of view: Initially, the author introduces in 4:4–5 the theme of opposition in a summarized form and with correct dates. After that, he quotes a letter from a later time in giving an example illustrating the general situation for the reader. He wants to leave appropriate room to the theme of opposition, which occurs in all three restoration cycles. In 4:24 the writer explicitly returns to the original historical horizon.

In 6:14, in a somewhat confusing statement, the writer again gives the name of Artaxerxes for dating the completion of the temple. In the same sentence in 6:15, however, he makes clear that the real finishing of the temple took place long *before* Artaxerxes. This tension can be resolved by referring to the fact that Artaxerxes indeed played a major role in supporting the temple (7:15–20)—but only at a later time. In places like this it is apparent that for the writer of Ezra-Nehemiah thematic connections are sometimes more prominent than the strict historical-chronological order.

The Restoration of the People (Ezra 7–10)

Ezra is introduced to the reader as priest and as scribe. Before the EXILE, it was mainly the priests who had been responsible for the Law. With the development of Judaism in postexilic times, however, the class of scribe as student and teacher of the Holy Scriptures became more and more important. With increasing historical distance, the Law could not be directly executed anymore but first had to be interpreted, in order to translate its meaning into the new historical setting. Ezra is portrayed as the first and great example of this new class. In the later Jewish tradition, he is therefore sometimes depicted as a second Moses.

Ezra travels to Jerusalem with a double commission: He has to set into force the Law of Moses concerning the lives of the people, on the one hand (7:14, 25–26), and that concerning the temple service, on the other (7:15–24).

It was part of the Persian policy to allow subordinated peoples to have their own local laws and temple service. This can be substantiated from extrabiblical sources as well. About 520 B.C.E., for example, a certain Udjahorresnet was sent from the Persian king, Cambyses, to Egypt with a commission very similar to that of Ezra. The purpose of this policy was probably to increase the political stability of the subordinated peoples.

The list of the people who returned with Ezra begins with two priestly descendants and one royal descendant, followed by 12 lay families. This list is, therefore, to be seen as a small-scale representation of Israel with its 12 tribes, seen from a priestly perspective. However, Levite families are missing

and have to be added by Ezra. Ezra needs Levites in order to install the regular temple service according to the Law.

Ezra and his fellow Jews travel to Jerusalem under the protection of the grace of God (8:18, 22, 31). In Jerusalem, they hand over all the gifts for the temple.

The first difficult problem Ezra has to consider are mixed marriages. For many of today's readers, the chapters on the mixed marriages certainly belong to the less-loved passages of Scripture. In order to assess this properly, however, one has to see that although Ezra seems to stress racial aspects, the issue at stake is a spiritual or religious one. According to the Mosaic Law, Israel was called by God to be a kingdom of priests, a witness to the nations for God and his standards (see Exodus 19:5–6). This could not be achieved without maintaining a distinctive self-identity. On the other hand, mixed marriages in those times normally meant mixed religions as well. The marriages of the political and religious leaders to foreign women especially posed a severe threat to the identity of the Jewish community—which, one must not forget, was small and weak at that time.

Nevertheless, dissolving more than 100 marriages seems tough. As a mitigating factor one should consider that Ezra does not impose his solution from above; rather, the initiative rises from the community itself. Furthermore, a passage from about the same time in Malachi 2:10–16 points to the possibility that at least some of the men had released their Jewish women before marrying other foreign women. All these circumstances make it possible to say that divorcing the foreign wives could at that time be considered the lesser of the two evils.

In any case, dissolving the mixed-religion marriages was only a small aspect of Ezra's mission. However, his tasks of setting into force the Law on a large scale and of installing the temple service are held back as the crowning glory for the last stage of restoration in Nehemiah 7–12.

The Restoration of the City (Nehemiah 1–6)

The third aspect of restoration is the reestablishment of the city of Jerusalem. Nehemiah 1–6 particularly deals with the construction of a new city wall.

When Nehemiah is informed about the sorry state of affairs in Jerusalem, this is a call of God to act on behalf of his people using the position that has been given to him. In his behavior he shows that he is a man of prayer and of action at the same time. Typical of Nehemiah are also his skills in dealing with people. When he arrives in Jerusalem, he inspects the walls secretly. He wants to be informed but without giving the impression of making decisions over the people's heads.

Nehemiah 3 just lists the individual sections of the wall together with the groups of builders that have been assigned to them. The message of this list is twofold: First, it demonstrates the unity of intention with which the people rebuild the wall together. Second, the list shows Nehemiah's talent for organization.

The adversaries, however, endanger the project by using political propaganda and direct military threats. Nehemiah responds by taking military measures and encouraging the people to trust in divine protection. Again, human activity and trust in God do not stand opposite to each other.

The Completion of the Restoration of Temple, People, and City (Nehemiah 7:1–13:3)

In Ezra 1 to Nehemiah 6, the restoration of temple, people, and city is treated in three individual sections. In Nehemiah 7–13, however, all the aspects are combined into one historical-thematic overall picture. The purpose of this is to express that behind the individual events, which in total stretch over more than a century, there is an overarching unity. It is the fulfillment of God's plan of salvation to restore Israel.

The first ring is made of the sections 7:1–3 and 12:27–43. These two sections belong to the theme of Nehemiah's mission, which is the restoration of the city. From a chronological point of view, we can assume that the dedication of the wall took place shortly after its completion. They are separated only from a literary point of view. This can also be seen from the fact that the first-person reports of Nehemiah end in 7:5 and resume only in 12:31. In between, the text speaks of Nehemiah

in the third person: 8:9; 10:1; 12:26. The reason for this arrangement of the sources certainly lies in the message that derives from it: As important as the city wall may be, bricks and mortar can never provide more than a framework; the city is nothing without the people living in it.

Therefore, the next inner ring, 7:4–73a and 11:1–12:26, deals with regulations increasing the number of inhabitants of the city. This section belongs to the theme of restoration of the people. Again the source material is divided into two parts. In 7:4 it is recorded that the city is wide and large, but the people within it are few. After that, however, the text deals with different matters. Only in 11:1–2 does the narrative resume with that theme. So the city is nothing without the people living in it. The people, in turn, are nothing without God living in it.

The core of the structure, 7:73b–10:39, deals with a new self-commitment of the people to the Mosaic Law, and, in particular, to the maintenance of the temple service, so that the communion with God can take place anew in the temple.

The core section is made of three scenes (7:73b–8:12; 8:13–18; 9:1–10:39) that each follow the pattern of time reference, assembly, encounter with Law, application, and response. Each scene culminates in the response of the people, particularly in celebrating a feast of joy, in celebrating the Feast of Tabernacles, and—accentuated by its length—in the confession of the people and their new commitment to the Law.

The record of Ezra's mission, the enforcement of the Law of Moses, is therefore placed at the most prominent position of the book's literary structure. This conveys the message that the Law should be the most important foundation of the postexilic community. A reason for this is given in the recapitulation of Israel's history in Nehemiah 9, which shows the consequences of obeying or not obeying the Law.

The ring structure is closed with some short notes that demonstrate the completion of the acts of restoration. After the restoration of the city is completed in 12:27–43, 12:44–47 reports a final act concerning the restoration of the temple, and 13:1–3, of the people. Now, in all areas, the restoration has reached its final conclusion.

The Ongoing Threat to the Restoration of Temple, People, and City (Nehemiah 13:4–39)

The coda, the last chapter of the book, however, deconstructs this picture of a perfect new community. It gives the book an antiheroic twist. In each of the three areas of restoration, after some time new problems arise and have to be solved: In 13:4–14 Nehemiah settles irregularities in the temple, in 13:15–22 he uses the city wall for protecting the Sabbath, and in 13:23–31 the problem of mixed-religion marriages occurs again.

With these short notes, the coda points to the fact that the status of the community is never fixed. In order to protect what has been achieved, a steady, daily effort is needed. The eschatological kingdom of God is not yet achieved.

CHARACTERS

Ezra   Ezra is priest and scribe. His main interest is to promulgate and to put into force the Law of Moses among his people and to install a regular temple service according to the Law. For him, it is very important to trust in the Lord and to obey the Lord. For his journey to Jerusalem, for example, he relies on divine rather than on military protection. He is very concerned about people who disobeyed the Law by marrying women of foreign religion. In his prayer of confession, he unites himself humbly with the sins of his people. In the later Jewish tradition, Ezra becomes a very prominent figure and is sometimes referred to as a second Moses.

Nehemiah   Nehemiah is a very competent leader. He has practical and organizational skills. When the king asks him what he needs for his task, he is able to tell him in detail. He organizes the rebuilding of the city wall in a very effective manner so that it is finished after no more than 52 days. Nehemiah also has a great emotional sensitivity, and he knows how to deal with people. He wins most of the Jerusalem families for his task, and he effectively encourages people to continue their work in spite of hostile propaganda and military threats. Nehemiah's emotional sensitivity can also be seen when he weeps and mourns for days after having heard about the sorry state of affairs in Jerusalem. Sometimes he acts very emotionally. For example,

he throws the private furniture of Tobiah out of the temple, and he curses and beats people who have married foreign women and pulls out their hair. Finally, Nehemiah is also a man of faith. When he makes decisions, they are accompanied by intense prayers. Even in writing down his memoirs, as they are quoted in the book, he works little prayers into the text, reflecting what he has achieved before God. His trust in God, however, does not replace his own actions (as is the case with the journey of Ezra). For Nehemiah, praying and acting belong together. For example, he prepares the people to defend themselves militarily and at the same time tells them, "Our God will fight for us" (Nehemiah 4:20). In this he is a model of the balance that must be maintained between the sovereignty of God and human responsibility.

Sanballat; Tobiah   From extrabiblical documents we know that Sanballat was governor of Samaria in 408 B.C.E. Samaria was the former capital of the northern Israelite kingdom, as Jerusalem was for the southern kingdom. Tobiah was possibly a junior colleague of Sanballat. Sanballat and Tobiah are jealous of Nehemiah. They are afraid of losing their influence in the region when Jerusalem is rebuilt. By means of political intrigues and military threats, they try to stop the rebuilding of the wall. They also try to do harm to Nehemiah personally. But Nehemiah sees through all their attempts.

Galatians

The original territory of Galatia was situated in the heart of present-day Turkey, in what is called Anatolia. Its capital was Ancyra, modern-day Ankara. The Romans formed a province, Galatia, that extended far to the south. The apostle PAUL visited the southern part of this province on his first missionary journey, which is described in Acts 13–14, and was able to plant churches in the cities of Pisidian Antioch, Iconium, Lystra, and Derbe. On his second trip, described from Acts 15:36, Paul revisited Derbe and Lystra, after which Luke specifically mentions that Paul passed through Galatia, meaning the original territory (Acts 16:6). Paul's third journey again began with a trek through Galatia on the way to Ephesus (Acts 18:23; 19:1).

It is not easy to determine exactly to whom this letter is addressed. The name *Galatians* is more appropriate for the inhabitants of the old territory; this would place the writing of the letter after Paul's second missionary journey and thus after the meeting in Jerusalem, known as the Apostolic Council (Acts 15, in the year 48 C.E.). Yet exactly the issues at stake in Galatians were discussed and solved at that meeting, so that the letter fits better into the time just before the council. Assuming this is correct, we date Galatians in 47–48 C.E., making it the earliest extant letter by Paul. Those addressed were the new Christians in towns such as Antioch, Iconium, Lystra, and Derbe. Paul had preached the gospel to them, but soon afterward other people had arrived and had twisted his message. Paul's reason for writing immediately is not so much his anger with those who preach the alternative version of the gospel as his concern that the new churches will adopt an incorrect form of Christianity.

The theme of this letter is similar to that of Romans: the fact that God accepts human beings on the basis of their faith in Jesus Christ and not on the basis of anything they do or contribute. Romans and Galatians thus have much in common, but whereas Romans is a well-planned and considered discussion of these and related issues, Galatians appears to have been written on the spur of the moment. Galatians is also his most autobiographical letter. Its message is that Christians are not obliged to observe the Jewish laws, such as circumcision and the dietary laws, as found in the Hebrew Bible. See also EPISTLE.

SYNOPSIS

Whereas most of Paul's letters begin with praise to God and thanksgiving for the readers and their faith, Galatians has only a short introduction (1:1–5), after which Paul immediately goes on the attack and states his point: What others after him have preached in Galatia is not the true gospel (1:6–9). He takes much time to establish his credentials as an apostle, the credentials of

the gospel that he received from Jesus Christ himself (1:10–2:10). He recalls an earlier controversy over the issue of the law, an incident in Syrian Antioch that put him head to head with his fellow apostle Peter (2:11–14), and he rounds off the first part of the letter with a statement of the gospel (2:15–21).

A second round of polemics begins with the blunt address "You foolish Galatians" and continues to remind them of the work of the Holy Spirit among them as evidence for the truth of the gospel as preached by Paul (3:1–5). Twice Abraham is introduced as an example of true faith (verses 6–14, 15–18). Paul explains that the role of the law was to prepare the Jewish people for the gospel (verses 19–29) so that Christians by definition are not subject to it (4:1–7). A series of personal utterances of concern for the readers follows in 4:8–20, underscored once more with reference to Abraham, this time in relation to his wives, Hagar and Sarah (4:21–31). Galatians 5:2–6 applies the entire argument to the specific issue of circumcision, and 5:7–12 is one more personal appeal. A principled discussion of the relation between the law and the freedom in the Spirit follows in 5:13–26, with 6:1–10 offering practical suggestions for mutual relations within the fellowship. A final time Paul sums up his appeal (6:11–15) before he closes with a few words of blessing (verses 16, 18), which surround a repetition of the argument that Paul is being persecuted for the message he preaches.

COMMENTARY

This letter can be read in at least three ways, which are not mutually exclusive: It is a personal, emotional appeal by a pastor to his congregation; it is a clever piece of judicial rhetoric; and it is an interpretation of the Abraham stories in Genesis 12–25. Paul makes no attempt to hide his extreme disappointment over the young church, which has lent its ears to people who preach a gospel tainted by legalism. In places the first two chapters are quite aggressive in tone, and the letter lacks the usual introductory thanksgiving section.

Paul had taught the church that non-Jewish Christians need not obey specifically Jewish precepts, in other words, that one does not have to become a Jew in order to become a Christian. Other Jewish Christians, however, wanted the new converts to observe the entire Law. These opponents of Paul had apparently traveled after him to Galatia to twist his message after his departure (1:6–7).

Paul's autobiographical notes in chapter 1 complement what is known about his early life from Acts 9: Arabia (1:17) here stands for the area south of Damascus, modern-day Jordan; and Syria (verse 21) is the area north of Damascus. The visit in 1:18 is probably the same as that described in Acts 9:26–30, the visit in 2:1–10 parallels Acts 11:29–30, whereas the conflict in 2:11–14 is not mentioned in Acts, probably to protect Peter. Paul tells how Peter during a stay in Antioch first ate with all Christians but subsequently withdrew from the non-Jews after receiving a warning from Jerusalem (Acts 15:1). Paul took this as moral weakness and rebuked his fellow apostle.

Paul employs his favorite imagery of running a race in 2:2 and 5:7; compare 1 Corinthians 9:24–27. Galatians 2:16–21 is one of the fullest statements of the Christian message and shows how as a message of grace and forgiveness it differs from legalism; it has parallels in Romans 3:20, 28 and 6:5–10. According to Paul, all that is necessary to be a follower of God in Jesus Christ is faith (2:16, 20; 3:6, 8, 26). This thesis is illustrated with several appeals to the story of Abraham. Long before God gave the Law to Moses, he had accepted Abraham on the basis of his faith alone. What Paul does in 3:6–14 is quite acceptable to modern readers as he employs the literal meaning of the texts in Genesis 12:3; 15:6; 18:8; Leviticus 18:5; Deuteronomy 27:26; and Habakkuk 2:4. His exegesis in 3:15–18 is harder to follow, for it is merely based on the occurrence of the singular *seed* (= offspring) in Genesis 13:15; 17:8; and 24:7, which Paul sees as referring to Jesus Christ. The number 430 is derived from Exodus 12:40.

It is again easy to follow Paul in his demonstration that the dispensation of the Law was an interim period from Moses to Jesus Christ, made obsolete by the coming of Jesus (3:22–24). The Law is compared to a disciplinarian (King James Version schoolmaster, Greek *paidagōgos*) such as

a minor would have in Paul's time. The image is continued in 4:1–7, which argues that the coming of Jesus Christ marks the coming of age of God's people. Consequently, the lives of Christians are not determined by obedience to the Law (the disciplinarian) but by the power of the Holy Spirit, who works in them. The rule of life is in their hearts, not in a book of law codes. The Aramaic word *abba* (4:6; Romans 8:15–16) means "father" and was first used for God by Jesus (Mark 14:36); that Christians can also use it is indicative of the intimate relation between God and humans brought about by God's Son. Becoming like Paul (4:12) means becoming free of the Mosaic Law. Paul's illness (4:13) is not mentioned in Acts.

In 4:21 *law* refers to the Pentateuch, more specifically the story in Genesis 16–17 about Abraham's two wives and their sons, Ishmael and Isaac. Paul calls his interpretation of this material an allegory (NRSV), that is, a story with a deeper meaning, but he leaves the historical reality of Genesis intact. It is likely that Paul's opponents had used this story to argue their case by saying that all Abraham's descendants were physical descendants so that the Galatians physically had to become Jews, that is, by means of circumcision.

Galatians 5:9 quotes a proverb also found in 1 Corinthians 5:6. 5:11 interrupts the flow of thought and can be explained as a counterargument against a totally misguided accusation. Another sign of Paul's frustration is his exclamation that "those agitators" should have themselves emasculated (5:12).

In one of the best-known phrases of the letter, Paul sums up the work of the Holy Spirit in believers as "love, joy, peace, patience, kindness, generosity, faithfulness, gentleness, and self-control" (5:22–23). It occurs in an extended comparison between the spiritual and the unregenerate life, typified by the Holy Spirit and the human flesh.

The expression "the Israel of God" (6:16) is without parallels that could explain its referent; this could be Jewish Christians, all Jews, or rather all Christians as the new people of God. The argument in 6:17 presupposes that those who are persecuted are right, as in 5:11. In ancient times, runaway slaves had a mark branded on their bodies.

CHARACTERS

Abraham   Abraham is the father of the Jewish people (see Genesis). Important for Paul is that Genesis mentions his faith in God (Genesis 15:6) as something that preceded his submission to God's commandments, such as the sign of circumcision (Genesis 17:11). Paul leaves the historicity of the stories intact while deriving spiritual lessons from them.

Galatians   As the name suggests, the original inhabitants of Galatia were Gauls, a Celtic tribe. Yet the recipients of this letter are probably the churches in the south of the Roman province of Galatia, such as Pisidian Antioch, Iconium, Lystra, and Derbe.

James   Initially James, a brother of Jesus, had a small role in the new Christian movement, yet from Acts 12:17 onward he appears in a leading position in the Jerusalem church (cf. Galatians 1:19 and 2:9). Galatians 2:12 shows him as the leader of those who demanded circumcision and observance of the Law of all Christians. This position was discussed and abandoned at the Jerusalem Council shortly after Galatians had been written (Acts 15).

Paul   Galatians is the letter par excellence that shows why Paul is called the apostle of freedom. Despite his great respect for the Hebrew Bible and the Jewish laws, he makes the bold claim that Christians who have a Gentile background do not need to become Jewish.

The first two chapters of Galatians provide numerous details about Paul's early life. In an attempt to establish his credentials, he writes at length about his relationship with the church in Jerusalem. No doubt having been helped by a secretary for most of the letter, he personally writes the final part from 6:11 onward. The fact that he makes large letters may point to a problem with his eyesight, for as a trained Pharisee (Philippians 3:5) writing as such would have been normal for him.

Peter   In this letter Paul calls the apostle Peter *Cephas,* his Aramaic name, although many translations use the more familiar *Peter* regardless.

Peter was the leading follower of Jesus who after PENTECOST largely worked among the Jews. From Acts 10–11 we know that God had shown him that racial boundaries and the observance of certain laws were irrelevant for Christians. This letter shows how he nonetheless submitted to Jewish pressures to have segregated meals with Jews and how Paul openly rebuked him (2:11–14). Peter resembles the Galatians: Both began with a spirit of freedom but subsequently shrank back, to be called to task by Paul.

Genesis

Genesis is the first book of the Hebrew Bible. It deals with the creation of the world, the prehistory of the human race, and the prehistory of the people of Israel. Its narratives are generally thought to be among the most beautiful of the Bible. The power of its symbolism and the vividness of its characters make it famous in world literature—quite apart from the paramount theological importance it has for Jewish and Christian believers.

The book of Genesis is the introduction to the PENTATEUCH and to the great narrative work of the Hebrew Bible, which consists of the Pentateuch and the books Joshua, Judges, Samuel, and Kings, narrating the history of Israel from the creation of the world until the Babylonian EXILE. In the book of Genesis, many of the later events of Israel's history are introduced prophetically or typologically (see TYPES); all the important theological subjects of the Hebrew Bible are already discernible in Genesis. Regarding the dating of the book, there are no direct clues. All dating attempts are based on suggestive historical reconstructions. Many scholars assume that the Book of Genesis passed through several literary stages before it assumed its final form. Liberal research dates the oldest textual layer into the 10th and the final redaction of the book into the fifth centuries B.C.E. Conservative research, to the contrary, sometimes assumes even a 20th-century B.C.E. origin for the oldest traditions. Some assign the final redaction to Moses (15th century B.C.E.); others assume a later date.

The book is a historical-theological narrative. This genre is based on historiographic material, which is shaped into a narrative in order to develop some theological points from it (see Part I). The historiographic interest of Genesis can, for example, be seen in the genealogical chain that embraces the whole book, reaching from the first primeval human beings to the historical time of the people of Israel. On the other hand, many of the narratives, especially in the first half of the book, function very much on a symbolic level. Symbols used are, for example, the garden, the tree of life, and the snake. So there is a complex relationship between history and theology in these texts, which cannot always be clearly resolved. However, one should resist the temptation to reduce the text to either its historical or its symbolic meaning alone.

The book is structured by so-called Toledoth-formulas that occur in 11 places throughout the narrative, so dividing the book into 12 main parts. The Toledoth-formulas all use the Hebrew word *toledoth*, meaning "descendants" or "follow-up." A translation that works in all places is "This is what came of. . . ." So, after the creation of heaven and earth, the text tells "what came of heaven and earth" (2:4); after THE FALL narrative, the text tell, "what came of Adam" (5:1). This chain is continued until "what came of Jacob" (37:2), namely, the people of Israel. Therefore, the Toledoth-formulas join the main parts of the book to each other and draw historical as well as theological connection lines. The prehistory of Israel is unfolded historically; at the same time, the relationships of human beings and creation, the nations and the chosen people of Israel, are defined theologically.

The 12 main parts of the Genesis account can be further divided into two blocks of six parts. The first block consists of the so-called primeval history, comprising mainly the creation, THE FALL, the fratricide, THE FLOOD, and the Tower of Babel. The second block deals with the patriarchs and their families: Abraham, Isaac, and Jacob, who is also called Israel, and his 12 sons, especially Joseph.

SYNOPSIS

Part I: Creation of Heaven and Earth (1:1–2:3)

The first main part of the book of Genesis deals with the creation of the world. At the beginning, the earth is in a chaotic and unfinished state. During seven days, God shapes and orders the earth and creates all living beings.

On the first day, God creates the light. He separates the light from the darkness. So, day and night come into existence.

On the second day, God creates the sky, or the atmosphere. He separates the water above the atmosphere from the water below the atmosphere.

On the third day, God makes the water gather so that the dry land becomes visible. On the dry land, he brings forth all kinds of plants and trees.

On the fourth day, God creates the Sun, the Moon, and the stars. Sun and Moon are made to reign over day and night and to structure the time.

On the fifth day, God creates the animals living in the water and the birds. God blesses the animals and commands them to multiply and to fill their habitats.

On the sixth day, God creates the animals living on the dry land. He creates human beings "in his image"; he creates them as man and woman, and he commissions them to multiply and to rule the earth. To the human beings and the animals, God assigns the plants for food.

On the seventh day, God rests, and he makes it a holy day.

Part II: "This Is What Came Of Heaven and Earth": Paradise and Fall (2:4–4:26)

At a time when there are not yet any plants from farming, God creates the man from the soil of the ground. He breathes the breath of life into his nostrils, so the man becomes a living being. Then God plants a garden. In the middle of the garden, there are two trees: the tree of life and the tree of knowledge of good and bad. God puts the man into the garden in order to cultivate it. He allows him to eat from all the trees in the garden. Only the tree of knowledge is forbidden to him on pain of death.

God creates human beings (Genesis 1:24–31), engraving by Julius Schnorr von Carolsfeld

Adam is lonely. God brings all the animals he has created to him, so that Adam can name them. However, a complementing person is not found for him. Therefore, when Adam sleeps, God takes a rib from him and fashions it into a woman, called Eve. The institution of marriage is introduced.

The snake appears. It persuades the woman to take the fruit of the tree of knowledge. It promises Eve that she will become like God. So, Eve and Adam eat from the fruit. At once they realize that they are naked. They sew fig leaves together and make loincloths for themselves. When God walks in the garden, they hide.

But God calls Adam over. Adam, however, lays the blame on Eve. Eve, in turn, blames the snake. God punishes the snake, cursing it to crawl on the ground and to eat dust. He imposes pain in childbearing on the woman and toil in farming on the man. As man is made from soil, he will turn into soil again. God drives Adam and Eve out of the garden so that they do not have access to the tree of life anymore.

Adam and Eve have two sons, Cain and Abel. One day, both make an offering. God accepts the offering of Abel but not that of Cain. Cain becomes jealous. On a pretext, he lures Abel into a field. There he beats him to death. God curses Cain so that he is expelled from his family and becomes a fugitive on earth.

Adam and Eve have a third son, Seth. A son is born to Seth, named Enosh. In his time, people begin to worship God.

Part III: "This Is What Came Of Adam": Adam's Genealogy; The Human Race Increasingly Good and Bad; Noah (5:1–6:8)

The third main part begins with a GENEALOGY from Adam to Noah, comprising 10 generations. The people live for around 900 years each, and then they die. Enoch, however, the seventh in the genealogy, does not die, but, since he walks with God, God takes him up.

After that, the text deals with the sexual union between male angelic beings and human women. From these unions, giants and mighty warriors are born. As a reaction, God decides to reduce the age of human beings to 120 years.

The wickedness of human beings increases more and more. Finally, God regrets having created them, and he decides to destroy them. Only Noah and his family find favor before him.

Part IV: "This Is What Came Of Noah": The Flood; A New Beginning; Noah's Sons (6:9–9:29)

God decides to destroy the human race through a flood. But he wants to save Noah's family and all the animals. He commissions Noah to form a box-like ship of 300 cubits length, 50 cubits width, and 30 cubits height (ca. 450 × 75 × 45 feet, 120 × 20 × 12 meters), having three floors. At the top it should have a window, and at the side a door. Noah is to collect and prepare food for the animals to take with him.

Noah and his family enter the ark. From each animal species, one pair is taken on board, but seven pairs each from the clean animals. Then it starts raining for 40 days, until all dry land is covered by water and all people and animals on the dry land die. After 150 days, the waters subside, and the ark comes to rest on the mountains of Ararat. Noah sends out a raven and a dove from the window of the ark, in order to see whether the waters are gone. The dove returns with a freshly plucked olive leaf in her beak. Then Noah, his family, and all the animals leave the ship.

Noah makes a burnt offering of one of the clean animals. God promises that despite all human wickedness he will never bring a flood over the whole earth again. God allows the human beings to eat animals. The blood, however, is not to be eaten. Human life is protected: The one who sheds human blood will have his or her blood shed by human beings. As a sign of his new covenant, God puts the rainbow into the cloudy sky. Noah plants a vineyard. He becomes drunk and lies uncovered in his tent. His son Ham, the father of Canaan, behaves improperly by watching his father's nakedness. His brothers, Shem and Japheth, carry a garment between them and walk backward into the tent to cover their father's nakedness without looking at him. When Noah awakes and hears what has happened, he speaks a curse on Ham and declares that Ham will be the servant of his brothers.

Part V: "This Is What Came Of Noah's Sons": The Table of Nations; The Tower of Babel (10:1–11:9)

The fifth main part begins with a genealogy of the three sons of Noah and the peoples and tribes that stem from them.

After that, the story of the Tower of Babel is given. The people move to the east and decide to build a city and inside it a tower that reaches into the heavens. God, however, confuses their language, so they cannot understand each other anymore. They stop building the tower, and they scatter over the whole earth.

Part VI: "This Is What Came Of Shem": Shem's Genealogy (11:10–26)

The sixth main part consists of a genealogy stretching from Shem, Noah's son, to Abraham, the ancestor of the people of Israel, comprising 10 generations.

Part VII: "This Is What Came Of Terah": The Story of Abraham; Ishmael and Isaac (11:27–25:11)

Together with his family, Terah leaves his hometown, Ur of the Chaldeans, in order to move to the west into the land of Canaan. About halfway, in Haran, the family settles. After Terah's death, God calls Abraham, whose name is *Abram* at that time,

and commands him to leave his father's house and move into a land God will show to him. God promises that the descendants of Abraham will become a great nation and that he will receive God's blessing. Abraham shall be a mediator of blessing: Whoever blesses him will be blessed, whoever curses him will be cursed, and in him all families of the earth shall be blessed.

Abram is obedient to God. Together with his family, he travels to Canaan. With him is Lot, his nephew. Because of a famine, they move on to Egypt, into the Nile delta. Abram's wife, Sarai, is very beautiful. Abram is afraid he will be killed because of her, so he passes her off as her sister. The pharaoh hears about Sarai's beauty and has her taken into his house. God, however, afflicts pharaoh and his family with great plagues. Pharaoh understands. He reprimands Abram for deceiving him and returns his wife. He assigns his soldiers to escort Abram's family as long as they are in his land.

Back in Canaan, the herdsmen of Lot and Abram have a quarrel with each other because of the pastureland. Abram decides to divide the land between them. He asks Lot to make his choice first. Lot decides for the better land and settles in Sodom (probably situated at the southwestern edge of the Dead Sea). But God appears to Abram, telling him that he would surely own the *whole* land.

Some Canaanite city-states make war against other city-states. Sodom is one of the cities involved. In the course of the war, Lot and his family are captured and deported. With 318 men, Abram chases after the withdrawing troops and rescues Lot. A priest of the Lord from Salem (the later Jerusalem), Melchizedek, blesses Abram for what he has done. Abram gives him the 10th part of all his property.

After that, God renews the promise to Abram that he will make him a great nation and give them their own land. However, he also tells Abram that the land will only be taken after the descendants of Abram have been oppressed in a foreign country for 400 years.

Sarai does not give birth to a child. In order to help bring about the divine promise, she suggests that Hagar, her Egyptian maid, give birth to a son on her behalf. This was an ancient custom. Hagar becomes pregnant by Abram. However, this makes her arrogant toward her mistress. When Sarai wants to humiliate her, she flees into the wilderness. There she meets the angel of the Lord. The angel commissions her to return to Sarai and let herself be humiliated by her. But he also tells her that she will give birth to a son and should call him Ishmael. Ishmael will become the father of a great nation. Hagar is obedient to the LORD and returns to Abram and Sara. Eventually, Ishmael is born.

Thirteen years later, God again appears to Abram and renews his covenant with him. He renames Abram as *Abraham* ("father of a multitude") and Sarai as *Sarah* ("princess"). He orders that all male members of the family have to be circumcised, as a sign of the covenant. God confirms his promise to Ishmael, but he also promises that Sarah herself will give birth to a son named Isaac, who will be the bearer of the divine promise.

God appears to Abraham in the form of three angels. They announce to him that one year later he will have a son. Sarah listens to them, sitting in the tent. She laughs because she cannot believe it.

After that, two of the angels turn to Sodom, for God has decided to destroy the city. Abraham, however, objects, saying that God should not kill the righteous citizens together with the godless. Because of Abraham's persistent prayers, God promises him that he will not destroy the city if there are at least 10 righteous people in it. The two angels arrive in Sodom in the evening. Lot invites them into his house. The citizens, however, pester Lot to give the two men to them so they can abuse them. But Lot refuses. The citizens attack him, but the two angels intervene. They urge him to leave the city together with his family. They should hurry and not look back.

Lot, his wife, and his two daughters flee from the city. God lets sulfur and fire fall from the sky, destroying Sodom, Gomorrah, and the region around the two cities. Lot's wife, however, looks back and turns into a pillar of salt. God had taken care of Lot because Abraham had insisted that the righteous should not be killed together with the godless.

Lot stays in a cave in the mountains, together with his two daughters. In order to get offspring, the daughters decide to make their father drunk and sleep with him. From the two sons born, the Moabites and the Ammonites stem.

Abraham travels to Gerar, into the area of the Philistines. Again, he passes off his wife as his sister. Abimelech, the king of Gerar, has her taken to his home. In a dream, however, God tells him that she is a married woman. Abimelech reprimands Abraham for having deceived him and gives his wife back to him. He also gives them livestock, slaves, and money, in order to preserve Sarah's honor. Abraham prays for Abimelech, so God takes the impending curse from him.

When Abraham is 100 years old, Isaac is born. On the eighth day, he is circumcised. The Egyptian maid Hagar and her son, Ishmael, are driven out of the family at Sarah's instigation. However, in the wilderness, God takes care of them.

Abraham casting out Hagar and Ishmael (Genesis 21:14), etching by Rembrandt

After some time, God tests Abraham. He asks him to travel to a certain mountain and take his son, Isaac, as a burnt offering there. Abraham obeys. He chops wood and travels to the place, together with his son and two servants. They leave the servants behind and climb the mountain, Isaac carrying the wood. Isaac asks his father where the sheep for the burnt offering is. Abraham answers him that God himself will provide the lamb. At the top of the mountain, Abraham erects an altar, puts the wood on top of it, and binds his son. At the moment he takes the knife to kill him, the angel of the LORD puts a stop to it. Abraham discovers a ram caught in the thicket by his horns. He sacrifices the ram instead of his son. Since Abraham has obeyed the Lord and has put all his trust in him, God blesses him and confirms his covenant with him.

Sarah dies at the age of 127. In order to lay her to rest, Abraham buys a piece of land in Canaan from the Hittites, making it a family tomb.

Abraham wants Isaac to marry a woman from his own family and not a Canaanite woman. Therefore, he sends his servant with 10 camels and dowry to Haran, where his brother, Nahor, lives. The servant prays to God to give him a sign to find the right woman. At the well, he encounters Rebekah, a granddaughter of Nahor. She offers to give him and his camels a drink and therefore behaves the way the servant had prayed for. She invites the servant to meet her family. There he explains his reason for coming. Rebekah and her family agree to the marriage. The servant takes Rebekah and her maidens back to Canaan. There, Isaac and Rebekah marry.

Abraham marries again and more children are born to him. At the age of 175, he dies. Isaac and Ishmael lay him to rest at the family tomb.

Part VIII: "This Is What Came Of Ishmael": Ishmael's Genealogy (25:12–18)

This short section names the 12 sons and tribal leaders of Ishmael. The people of Ishmael live as Bedouins in the deserts south and east of Canaan.

Part IX: "This Is What Came Of Isaac": Jacob and Esau (25:19–35:29)

Rebekah becomes pregnant with twins. God announces that she has two nations in her womb, and that the older would eventually serve the younger. Esau becomes a skilled hunter and a man of the fields. Jacob, the opposite, becomes a peaceful and well-mannered man.

One day, Esau returns home very hungry. Jacob has prepared a lentil stew. He offers Esau the meal in exchange for his birthright, i.e., his right as the firstborn to receive a double inheritance and a special blessing from his father. Esau, who does not care about his birthright, agrees.

Because of a famine, Isaac and his family move into the area of the Philistines. There, God appears to him, telling him that they should not move farther to the south into Egypt. God also renews the covenant with him.

Isaac is afraid he will be in danger because of his wife, Rebekah, and shows her off as his sister. On one occasion Abimelech, king of Gerar (possibly the son of the abovementioned Abimelech), sees Isaac and Rebekah caressing each other. He becomes afraid and consults Isaac: Someone could easily have taken her as a wife. Abimelech gives an order to protect Isaac and Rebekah.

Isaac enters into conflict with some Philistine shepherds. They are jealous of Isaac's property and stop up the wells Isaac needs. But God appears to Isaac and promises to protect him. Then Abimelech and Isaac make a peace treaty.

When Isaac has became very old and nearly blind, he wants to give his blessing to Esau. He sends him out hunting, for on this occasion he wants to have some savory food, which is his favorite. Rebekah, however, learns about it. When Esau is out in the fields, she instructs Jacob to go out to the herds and take two kids from the goat. She prepares a meal from them. Jacob puts on Esau's best garments. Since Esau is a very hairy man, Jacob binds the skins of the kids of the goats around his arms and on his neckline. Jacob takes the meal to his father and passes himself off as Esau. At first, Isaac is suspicious, but then he becomes a victim of the delusion. He gives his blessing to Jacob. Shortly afterward, Esau returns, and the swindle is seen for what it is. However, the blessing has been pronounced, and Isaac cannot take it back.

Esau plans to kill Jacob. Rebekah, however, learns of it. She tells Jacob and sends him to Haran, where her family lives, to save his life.

One night during the journey, Jacob dreams of a ladder set up on the ground, the top of which reaches to heaven; angels are ascending and descending on it. And above, the Lord stands. He renews his covenant with Jacob. The next day, Jacob erects a stone there and calls the place *Bethel* (house of God).

Jacob moves on to Haran. He meets Laban and falls in love with his daughter, Rachel. He works for seven years for Laban, serving for Rachel. Finally, the day of the wedding arrives. Laban, however, deceives him: The bride under the veil is the older, less beautiful sister of Rachel, Leah. Jacob complains to Laban. One week later, Jacob is allowed to marry Rachel as well. However, he also has to work for Laban for seven more years.

Because Leah is unloved, God makes her, but not Rachel, fertile. Leah gives birth to four sons: Reuben, Simeon, Levi, and Judah. Then she stops childbearing. Rachel is very jealous of her. She gives her maid, Bilhah, to Jacob so that she might conceive children on her behalf. Bilhah gives birth to Dan and Naphtali. Then Leah also gives her maid, Zilpah, to Jacob. Zilpah gives birth to Gad and Asher. After that, Leah herself becomes pregnant again, and she gives birth to two more sons and one daughter: Issachar, Zebulun, and Dinah. Finally, Rachel becomes pregnant and gives birth to Joseph. She asks God to give her one more son.

Jacob wants to leave Laban. As a payment for his work, he wants to take some of the livestock with him. After some discussion, he suggests to Laban that he will take only the speckled and black of the newborn sheep, and the speckled of the newborn goats (herdsman were usually paid with a percentage of the offspring). All other animals should belong to Laban. But Laban separated all the multicolored animals from the herds and took them away on a three-day journey so that Jacob would not be able to cheat him. However, Jacob has a plan to increase the number of multicolored offspring: He puts multicolored rods of wood into the water troughs when the strong and healthy of the sheep and goats go there to mate. So they produce speckled offspring. When weak animals arrive, he takes away the rods, so they get one-colored offspring. In this way, Jacob becomes very rich

in livestock. God had promised to help Jacob, after Laban had cheated him so badly.

Laban's sons become hostile to Jacob. Jacob decides to leave with his family and all his property in a furtive manner. But Laban chases him. An argument blows up, but finally Laban and Jacob make a covenant.

Jacob sends messengers to his brother, Esau, announcing his return. The messengers return and tell Jacob that Esau is moving in his direction with an army of 400 men. Jacob becomes frightened. He prepares a large gift of livestock, together with herdsmen, and sends them on ahead. If Esau receives all these gifts, Jacob hopes he will be mollified. Jacob himself stays at the very end of the long trek.

During the night, a man wrestles with him, until dawn. Jacob's hip is put out of joint. When the man is leaving, Jacob suspects that he is the angel of the LORD. He asks him to bless him before he leaves. The man gives the blessing to Jacob and renames Jacob as *Israel*, "God-wrestler," because he has wrestled with human beings and with God and has won. Jacob calls the place *Penuel*, "the face of God."

Jacob and Esau meet and are reconciled. Esau returns to the land of Seir; Jacob buys a piece of land near Shechem and stays there.

Shechem, the son of Hamor, the lord of the city of Shechem, rapes Dinah, Jacob's daughter. Afterward, he falls in love with her and wants to marry her. Jacob's sons, however, are very angry about it. Hamor goes to Jacob and asks for the hand of his daughter to give her to his son. He also offers to allow Jacob to settle fully in his area. Jacob's sons explain to Hamor that they could not give Dinah to an uncircumcised man. But if Hamor, Shechem, and all the men and boys of the city would let themselves be circumcised, Jacob's family could join them, and Shechem could marry Dinah. Hamor agrees, not only because of his son, but also because of economic considerations: Jacob has taken great possessions into his area. So the whole people are circumcised. On the third day, however, when all the men are weakened from pain due to the operation, Jacob's sons attack the city. They take back Dinah, kill all male citizens, and plunder the city.

Jacob does not like the fact that his sons have put his family in disrepute. He orders that all statues of foreign gods should be buried. Then he leaves the region, moving to Bethel, according to a commission from God. God appears to him, confirming his new name *Israel* and his covenant with him.

Rachel becomes pregnant again. At the birth, however, complications arise. In dying, she names her son *Ben-oni*, "son of my misfortune." Jacob, however, renames him *Benjamin*, "son of fortune." Finally, Jacob returns to Hebron, to his father's place. Isaac dies at the age of 180 years. His sons Esau and Jacob lay him to rest.

Parts X and XI: "This Is What Came Of Esau": Esau's Family and Tribe Genealogy (36:1–8 and 36:9–37:1)

The genealogy of Esau is presented in two sections. A Toledoth-formula (the main structuring device of the book) occurs in 36:1 and 36:9. The first section gives the name of Esau's descendants in the land of Canaan. After that, the family moves to the mountains of Seir, where they further increase and form the people of Edom.

Part XII: "This Is What Came Of Jacob": The Story of Joseph (37:2–50:26)

Joseph is Jacob's favorite son. Therefore, his brothers are hostile to him. Joseph has received a special multicolored garment from his father. He also has peculiar dreams. In one of the dreams, the sheaves bound by the brothers bow to the sheaf of Joseph. In another dream, the Sun, the Moon, and 11 stars bow before Joseph. These dreams further anger his brothers.

Eventually, Joseph is sent to the herds of his brothers. When they see him approaching, they decide to kill him. Reuben, however, defends him because he is afraid of his father's reaction. When Joseph arrives, they take his garment from him and throw him into a pit. When a caravan moves across, they sell him as a slave to them. They slaughter a billy goat and spread its blood over Joseph's garment and send the garment back to his father. Jacob, believing a wild animal has killed his son, is deeply hurt. Joseph, however, is taken to Egypt and there sold to Potiphar, pharaoh's official.

Joseph telling his dreams (Genesis 37:5–10), etching by Rembrandt

In the house of Potiphar, Joseph is promoted rapidly, because God gives him success. Potiphar's wife falls in love with Joseph. But he resists her. One day, she stands very close and catches him by his garment. But he leaves his garment in her hand and flees out of the house. The woman, however, shows the garment to her husband and accuses Joseph of having tried to sleep with her. Joseph is put into prison.

Even in prison, Joseph's talents soon become visible. The keeper of the prison hands over many of his duties to Joseph. Joseph also interprets the dreams of two fellow prisoners. After three days, Joseph's predictions become true.

Two years later, Pharaoh has a dream: He sees seven cows walking out of the Nile River, fine-looking and fat. After them, seven ugly and thin cows emerge from the river, swallowing the seven fat cows. In another dream, Pharaoh sees seven ears of grain on a single stalk, plump and good. After them, seven thin and blighted ears sprout, swallowing up the good ears.

The next morning, Pharaoh calls his wise men to have his dreams interpreted, but they cannot do it. Then the chief cupbearer, who had been in prison, remembers Joseph. He is taken before Pharaoh. With the help of God, he can interpret the dreams of Pharaoh. Both dreams mean that there will be seven years of abundance, and after that seven years of hunger. Joseph suggests that Pharaoh should appoint a man to take care that in the next seven years the agricultural surplus is collected into storehouses in order to prepare for the following years of hunger. Pharaoh installs Joseph himself for this duty.

During the next seven years, Joseph takes care that in the whole country the yields are collected into storehouses. During this time, he also marries. Two sons are born to him: Ephraim and Manasseh. When the period of crop failure begins, Joseph starts to sell from the stocks.

In Canaan, there is also a lack of food. So Jacob sends 10 of his sons, except his youngest, Benjamin, to Egypt in order to buy food. They go before Joseph. However, they do not recognize him. He treats them harshly, pretending he believes they are spies. They protest to him that they all belong to a family of 12 brothers. Joseph requests proof from them: They shall take the youngest brother, Benjamin, to Egypt. For the time being, one of the other brothers, Simeon, is taken hostage. The nine brothers buy grain and return home. In the grain bags they eventually find the money that they had given to Joseph. At home, they tell Jacob the whole story. But Jacob refuses to let Benjamin go.

However, when all the grain is consumed, Jacob realizes that he has to let Benjamin go to Egypt together with his brothers. When they arrive, Joseph speaks in a friendly manner to his brothers. When he sees Benjamin, he has to hurry to another room, crying secretly.

Joseph sells food to his brothers and sends them home. Again, he puts their money back into their grain bags, and he puts his silver cup into the grain bag of Benjamin. When the brothers are leaving the city, Joseph sends soldiers after them. They are accused of theft. The cup is found in Benjamin's bag. Joseph asks to keep Benjamin as his slave. The other brothers, however, do not dare return

to their father without Benjamin. Judah makes a confession of sin. Finally, Joseph sheds his disguise. Joseph lets the whole family go to Egypt, in order to take care of them during the time of famine. The family of Jacob has increased to 70 members in the meantime. Jacob is very happy to see Joseph again.

When the famine continues, the Egyptians run out of money. So they start selling their livestock, their land, and, finally, themselves, to Pharaoh. The whole land turns into the personal property of Pharaoh. The only exception is the land of the priests. When Jacob is 147 years old and about to die, he makes Joseph promise not to bury him in Egypt but in Canaan in the family tomb. Jacob gives a blessing to the two sons of Joseph, Manasseh and Ephraim. In doing this, however, he crosses his arms so that his right hand lies on top of the head of Ephraim, the younger brother. In this way he places Ephraim before Manasseh. Then Jacob calls all his sons and gives a prophetic word to each of them, concerning their future as a tribe of Israel. After that, Jacob dies and is embalmed. Joseph transports his corpse to Canaan to the family tomb.

After Jacob's death, Joseph's brothers are afraid that Joseph may take revenge. But Joseph deals kindly with them, because he sees in the situation the plan of God: "You intended to do harm to me, but God intended it for good."

Finally, Joseph dies at the age of 110 years. He is embalmed and put into a coffin in Egypt.

COMMENTARY

Part I: Creation of Heaven and Earth (1:1–2:3)

The creation narrative first of all states that God created the world. So, from the very first sentence, the specific biblical philosophy is expressed: Everything in the universe has to be seen in relation to the one God, who created it.

Second, the fact has to be recorded that the text does not in the first instance describe the creation of the world out of nothing but rather the forming and shaping of the earth so that it becomes a place for animals and human beings to live. The introductory sentences can be interpreted in different ways. One variant is that the first sentence, "At the beginning God created the heavens and the earth," speaks about the creation of the world out of nothing, and from the second sentence onward, "the earth was formless and void," the focus lies on the shaping of the earth.

The second variant is a traditional Christian interpretation. It is argued that God would not create anything formless and void, and therefore, between the first and the second sentence of the text, the fall of Satan (see Luke 10:18) is to be placed. After God had created heaven and earth, Satan rebelled against God and devastated the earth. After that, God recreated the earth. This interpretation, however, is not supported by the text. Rather, the text has to be seen in contrast with ancient creation myths. In those myths, the world originates from a struggle of different gods, or the good god has to gain control over the powers of evil before he can create the world. Genesis 1, on the contrary, radiates the calmness of an omnipotent God in absolute control over the world he creates.

The third variant sees the first sentence as a superscription or announcement for the whole chapter. The proper report starts in verse 2 with the earth in a raw state, corresponding to the image of a clod of clay the potter puts on his wheel and then starts forming and shaping.

As the narrative progresses, the topic of shaping and forming is prominent. The first three days, God makes divisions and makes habitats or living spaces: On the first day, God separates light and darkness. Therefore, day and night are set up as living spaces. On the second day, God creates the atmosphere and separates the water in the atmosphere from the water on the ground. Therefore, the sea and the sky are set up as living spaces. On the third day, God separates water and dry land and creates all the plants. Therefore, the dry land is set up as a living space.

Interestingly, the second group of three days corresponds to the first group: The fourth day to the first, the fifth to the second, and the sixth to the third. The living spaces are now filled with the living beings, respectively: On the fourth day, the inhabitants, or "rulers" of day and night, are created: the Sun and the Moon. On the fifth day, the inhabitants of the sea and the sky are created: the animals of the water and the birds. On the sixth

day, the inhabitants and rulers of the dry land are created: the land animals and the human beings.

One could ask why God created the light on the first day but the Sun only on the fourth day. What do *day* and *night* mean if there is no Sun yet? But by asking such questions we are overlooking the literary-theological shaping of the material. The intention of the text is more than simple history. The text does not only tell *how* but rather *for what purpose* the world was created: God created the world as a living space. To be more exact, he created different living spaces and living things that fit into these living spaces, respectively.

Modern natural science correspondingly uses the concept of the ecological niche: Each species is adapted to a certain specific environment. It can live best in the environment it is made for: a zebra in the prairie, a frog in the pond, and so forth. Modern psychology correspondingly points to the fact that in order to live a full life, human beings need a living space where they can develop, and that they can shape and tend.

Therefore, on the level of the text's message, there is no real contradiction between the biblical creation account and the findings of modern science, and the intense debate of seven-day creationism versus Darwinism seems to be at least partly off the point.

The creation of human beings is considered in more detail in the creation account. A lot of discussion has arisen about the statement that man and woman are created "in the image of God" (Genesis 1:26–27). Several interpretations have been given: (a) physical resemblance; (b) mental faculties that humans share with God, e.g., reason, personality, or free will; (c) the capacity to relate to God; (d) humans seen as God's representatives on earth.

The first interpretation seems improbable, not only from a modern point of view, but also from old Israelite thinking. The variants (b) and (c) cannot be excluded and may be part of the meaning. From ancient Near Eastern thinking, however, interpretation (d) is the most probable: Ancient Near Eastern kings were described as "image" of the god. This last interpretation also explains why in verse 26 the command to rule the earth follows directly after the statement concerning the image. According to the text, not only kings, but all human beings are God's representatives on earth and shall rule it, shape it, dress it, and keep it in an ordered and purposeful way.

To a certain extent, the creation account is to be seen in its role as a foreword to the history of Israel, especially the Sinai covenant with its laws. In the creation, there are ordered spaces to live in. The same is true for the Law. The TEN COMMANDMENTS, for example, create living spaces; they make room for the individual to develop and at the same time give protection from breaking into other people's living space: the space of the individual life (Exodus 20:13), the space of the family (Exodus 20:12, 14), the space of earning one's living (Exodus 20:8–11, 15), and so on. Human beings are commissioned to make room for each other. The connection between the creation account and the Ten Commandments is further strengthened by the fact that the phrase "God said" occurs 10 times throughout the creation narrative: With 10 words God orders nature, and with 10 words he orders society.

While the creation of man and woman is surely the climax of the narrative, the final words of the text direct the reader's attention back to God. The seventh day is the day of God's rest. Rest also receives its space in life. The seventh-day space is at the same time a holy space reserved for God. The Sabbath commandment in Exodus 20:8–11 directly relates to the creation account. The importance of 7 is also expressed numerically: The phrases "and it was so," "and God made," "and God saw that it was (very) good" each occur seven times throughout the text. The first sentence of the text consists of seven Hebrew words. Each of the six days is mentioned once, but the seventh day is mentioned three times, using three sentences of seven Hebrew words each. In total, the section on the seventh day, Genesis 2:1–3, consists of 35 (= 5 × 7) words. These more hidden numerical patterns underscore the notion of divine perfection in creation.

Therefore, the creation account is a text that is theologically greatly loaded. Its main message is to be derived on a symbolic level. Despite its literary-theological shaping, however, the historical interest of the text should not be neglected, namely, the fact that God created the world.

Part II: "This Is What Came Of Heaven and Earth": Paradise and Fall (2:4–4:26)

The second main part of Genesis is introduced by the Toledoth-formula "This is what came of heaven and earth" (Genesis 2:4). The sentence resumes the creation of heaven and earth in the first main part and leads to the continuation of the story. All Toledoth-formulas have this double function of introducing a new main part as well as connecting it to what occurred before.

The second main part begins with a chronological overlap with the first part. For a second time, the creation of human beings is described. This story is very rich in symbolism. Again, there is an intertwining of historical and paradigmatic interests that cannot easily be resolved.

According to 2:5–7, God makes man (Hebrew *adam*) of dust from the ground (Hebrew *adamah*) in order to cultivate the ground (*adamah*). However, he does not put him on a field to plow as might be expected and as other ancient Near Eastern creation narratives say. Rather, he places him into a garden that is rich in fruits. The garden is symbolic of God's wanting to give human beings a status higher than earth bound creatures. He wants to enter in a specific relationship to them, giving blessing to them, even eternal life.

Eve, the first woman, is created out of Adam's rib. This is not to be understood biologically as an act of cloning. The point rather is that Eve is not made from Adam's head, in order to surpass him, nor from his foot, to serve him, but from his rib, in order to be at his side, protected by his arm, and near to his heart.

In the garden stand the tree of life and the tree of knowledge. The tree of life symbolizes perfect, eternal life. Whereas in ancient Near Eastern belief, eternal life is reserved for the gods—so human beings can be called "mortals"—the biblical text interestingly points to the fact that human beings originally had free access to life in community with God. The boundary between God and man is not defined by life but by knowledge. "Knowledge of good and evil" in the Hebrew Bible also means "majority" or "responsibility"—in our context, it stands for all-encompassing knowledge making one independent of God. When Adam and

Adam and Eve's expulsion from Paradise (Genesis 3:23–24), woodcut by Albrecht Dürer

Eve take from the fruit, however, they first find out something much less lofty: They are naked and feel ashamed they are. Innocence has gone. Adam and Eve are driven out of paradise. So direct communion with God as well as the access to eternal life are lost.

In conservative interpretation, this so-called Fall is understood as a unique historical event changing the face of the earth. Through the Fall, illness, suffering, and death have befallen not only all human beings but also the animals and the whole creation. This expresses the instinctive feeling that the creation is not functioning as it should be (see Romans 8:21). Other interpretations, however, put their emphasis on the story's interest in explaining the present state of affairs, saying that all human beings are subjugated by sin and transience and are therefore cut off from community with God and from life.

The snake persuading Eve is a symbol of evil. Surprisingly, the origin of evil is not explained. The snake just exists. The conflict between snake and people, as it is described in Genesis 3:15, has a symbolic meaning besides its literal meaning: It depicts the human race as continually wrestling with sin. From a Christian point of view, Genesis 3:15 is understood typologically as relating to Jesus Christ: Jesus, the true descendant of Eve, will crush the head of the snake, i.e., break the devil's power. But the snake will strike his heel: i.e., Jesus has to die in order to gain the victory (see Revelation 12:1–9). In the New Testament, Jesus Christ is also depicted as the second Adam, who was tested as Adam was but overcame (Luke 4; Romans 5:12–19).

Because of the Fall, divine blessing is followed by the divine curse. Three blessings, on the animals, on human beings, and on the Sabbath, are followed by three curses: on the snake, on the ground, and, later, on Cain. Humans are condemned to wrestle with evil; the typical tasks of man and woman, farming and giving birth, respectively, are loaded with toil, and humans (*adam*) finally have to return to the ground (*adamah*) from which they are made.

The garden of Eden is also a symbol, or type, of the Promised Land of Canaan, which would be entered and which would have to be left again at the Babylonian Exile.

After the primary sin against God has been committed, the primary sin against the brother follows: Cain kills Abel. That God accepts the offering of Abel but not that of Cain is probably a foreshadowing of the later ceremonial system: God is not satisfied with just any kind of offering. Rather, the right attitude is needed as well as the right kind of sacrifice. Cain is punished by being expelled from his family. Therefore, he becomes a fugitive on earth. However, God protects him with a "sign," whose precise nature is unknown. The one who kills him has to bear sevenfold revenge. The genealogy of Cain that follows gives the origin for handicraft and music. At the same time, it demonstrates the development of evil. A first negative climax is reached in the seventh generation, where Lamech announces that he will revenge himself 77-fold (see, in contrast, Matthew 18:22, where Jesus requests that one forgive 70 times 7 times).

The main part closes with a glimpse of hope: Eve gives birth to a third son, Seth. Under his son,

Enosh (a Hebrew word for "human being"), people "begin to call upon the LORD." Interestingly, God is named in the first and in the second main parts 35 times each. In the sentence quoted from the end of the main part, the name of God appears for exactly the 70th time. A kind of divine fullness is reached: Genesis 1:1–4:26 fulfills a pattern of "creation," "uncreation," and "recreation," or in other words: "blessing," "curse," and "new hope." The creation account in Genesis 1 describes the blessing. Genesis 2:4ff. again deals with the creation, but this time the curse is added. The section ends with Seth and Enosh as a glimpse of new hope.

The pattern of blessing, curse, and new hope is of central importance for the covenant God makes with Israel: From obedience follows blessing, from disobedience follows curse, but in the end there is still hope for a new beginning (see Leviticus 26; Deuteronomy 28–30). This pattern is the paradigm along which the history of Israel is presented in the books of Genesis to Kings.

The primeval history is fashioned in this way, preparing the reader for the patterns along which God will conduct his further history with his chosen people.

Part III: "This Is What Came Of Adam": Adam's Genealogy; The Human Race Increasingly Good and Bad; Noah (5:1–6:8)

The third main part of Genesis is introduced by the Toledoth-formula "This is what came of Adam" (Genesis 5:1). So the further development of the human race is presented. The main part starts with a linear genealogy stretching over 10 generations, from Adam until Noah and his three sons. The genealogy mainly reports the fulfilling of the divine command to be fruitful and multiply.

For each of the people, three numbers are given: the age at which the first son is born, the remaining years, and, as a sum of the two, the total number of years. These detailed numbers invite the reader to calculate the year of Adam's creation from them. In order to achieve that, we first have to find a later event whose date is known and from that reckon back to the time of Abraham. On the basis of the information that Solomon reigned from 971 B.C.E. onward, and of the numbers given in Genesis 21:5;

25:26; 47:9; Exodus 12:40; and 1 Kings 6:1, the birth year of Abraham can be calculated as 2166 B.C.E. If the numbers from the genealogies of Genesis 5 and 11 are added, the creation of Adam would fall in the year 4113 B.C.E. A number often given, however, is 4004 B.C.E. This number was calculated in the 17th century when the dates of the Israelite kings were not known as well as they are today (the number is often assigned to a Bishop Ussher, but in fact it stems from a certain John Lightfoot). In any case, the number of 4113 B.C.E. is only valid for the Hebrew text. The Greek tradition (the Septuagint; see BIBLE, EARLY TRANSLATIONS OF) gives different numbers in Genesis 5 and 11, so that the date of Adam's creation computes to about 1,000 years earlier.

Many scholars, however, deny that the numbers of the genealogies are made to be used for this kind of calculation. Among others, they point to the fact that in ancient genealogies generations can be skipped.

At any rate, the high numbers transmit a theological statement: The divine blessing on humanity is still very strong, and death is still far away. However, the number 1,000 seems to be a final limit for humanity: The oldest biblical person is Methuselah, who lived for 969 years.

Also, the names of the genealogies carry a symbolic overtone. In the Hebrew, every letter also has a numerical value (e.g., aleph = 1, beth = 2, . . . , jod = 10, kaph = 20, etc.). All the letters of all the names of the genealogy from Adam to Israel (= Jacob) add up to exactly 7,000. The symbolism again implies a kind of divine fullness. In the person of Israel, the plan of God has its fulfillment.

As with Cain's genealogy, so, too, in the genealogy of Genesis 5, the seventh position is of special interest. This time, it is in a positive way: Enoch "walks with God." He does not die, but after 365 years (again a symbolic number?) he is taken up to God. This is, after Genesis 3:15, another hint that death will not have the last word.

After the genealogy there follows a section dealing with sexual relationships between "sons of God" and daughters of man. For the sons of God, different explanations have been given. The most probable is that angelic beings are meant. As a counterreaction,

God announces a reduction of the age of human beings to 120 years, so they cannot infinitely plague each other. This number is, however, reached only step by step. The age of the people decreases rapidly, until at the end of Genesis, Joseph, with 110 years, falls into the envisaged limit.

The sequence of blessing, curse, and new hope can again be detected in the order of events. Noah, named in the last verse (6:8), is that glimpse of hope with which the story is concluded.

Part IV: "This Is What Came Of Noah": The Flood; A New Beginning; Noah's Sons (6:9–9:29)

From the third millennium B.C.E. until today, the story of a great Flood has captured human imagination. Flood narratives can be found in the traditions of many peoples spread over the whole world. In Mesopotamia, for example, such a story is contained in the Gilgamesh Epic.

In the Gilgamesh Epic, the gods send the Flood because the humans are too noisy for them. In the biblical interpretation of the event, however, the reason for the Flood is human sinfulness. As evil increases beyond all measure, God, in his justice, as a last resort destroys the whole human race. Only Noah is saved. After the Flood, however, God decides not to do this a second time. Instead, he makes a covenant promising that he will not destroy the earth through a Flood again.

The Flood story is giving a partial answer to the question why God allowed a Hitler or Stalin to do all the evil they did: If God were to punish immediately all the evil that is done, no one would survive. Since this does not make sense, God rather allows the righteous as well as the wicked to live their lives and carry out what they want according to their own will, with reward and punishment delayed.

The prophecy Noah utters on his three sons is a foreshadowing of the relationships among the peoples stemming from them (see below).

Part V: "This Is What Came Of Noah's Sons": The Table of Nations; The Tower of Babel (10:1–11:9)

The fifth main part starts with a segmented genealogy comprising the majority of the then-known peoples of the earth, connecting them to the three

The dove sent out from the ark (Genesis 8:8), engraving by Gustave Doré

sons of Noah. First are the descendants of Japheth. These have fewest points of contact with Israel. As far as they can be identified, they belong to the area in the north and west of Israel, e.g., Cyprus, Greece, and Turkey. Historically, Japheth has been associated with the Indo-European languages.

Among the descendants of Ham are those who are in most conflict with Israel: the Babylonians, Egyptians, and Canaanites. (Some linguists and anthropologists would rather include them with the Semites, i.e., belonging to Shem.) The sons of Ham, especially Canaan, are those standing under Noah's curse (see Genesis 9:25–27). Finally, the nations stemming from Shem are given. These stand in closest relationship to Israel. Most of them have, according to the biblical presentation, an overall good relationship to Israel: the Arameans and Arab tribes. However, the Assyrians and Elamites are also descendants of Shem.

Altogether, 72 descendants are listed. Possibly the list originally contained only 70 members, or two of the names given that are not connected genealogically have to be left out while counting. However, the fullness symbolism of the number 72 (6 × 12) is the same as that of 70.

While Genesis 10 describes the community of nations in a positive or, at least, neutral way, the same facts are presented from an entirely different perspective in the Tower of Babel narrative. As is the case several times within primeval history, the same facts are first presented from a perspective of blessing and then from a perspective of curse.

Once more, God performs an act of punishment on all humanity. The different languages and people groups are separated from each other because of their arrogance. As presented in the primeval history of Genesis 1–11, human action begins and ends with the sinful wish to be like God.

The story of the Tower of Babel, of course, contains a polemic on Babel and the ziggurat erected there. The Babylonians' own popular etymology of the word *Babel* as "gate of the god" is here contrasted by a pun with the Hebrew word *balal,* which means "to confuse." In Christian interpretation, Pentecost undoes the curse of Babel (see Acts 2:4–11).

Part VI: *"This Is What Came Of Shem"*: *Shem's Genealogy (11:10–26)*

The last main part of the primeval history consists of a genealogy forming a bridge to the following history of Abraham. A wordplay with the Tower of Babel narrative is possibly employed, since the Hebrew word *Shem* also means "name": In Babel, the nations try to make themselves a "Shem," a name. But God continues salvation history with his own "Shem."

For the numbers given in the genealogy, see the comments on Genesis 5 above.

Part VII: *"This Is What Came Of Terah"*: *The Story of Abraham; Ishmael and Isaac (11:27–25:11)*

The first six main parts of the book, 1:1–11:26, are the so-called primeval history. With the seventh main part, a new kind of history starts. Up to this point, the narrative has dealt with the prehistory of all nations; from now on the text concentrates on the ancestors and the origin of the people of Israel. While in the primeval history, at least in some of its

stories, the symbolic overtones are very much in the forefront, in the following narratives the historiographic interest becomes more clear. However, no fundamental distinction regarding the truth claims of the two halves of the book can be made—even if modern readers doubting the historicity of Genesis 1–11 would like to make it. From a literary point of view, there is no major division between Genesis 11:26 and 11:27. On the contrary, the genealogies as well as the Toledoth-formulas connect all sections of the book very tightly.

There is a division, however, from a theological point of view: The primeval history is dominated by the attempt of God to direct his history with the whole human race. From Abraham onward, however, God takes a different route: He chooses a family, or rather a people, to make his history with them in an exemplary manner. Others should be able to learn from the example and join the people of God. However, people rejecting God are not immediately punished for their sins (as, for example, in the Flood story and the Tower of Babel story). The curse rather consists in the fact that God leaves those people alone with their sins. In theology, this is called "election."

The election of Abraham is described for the first time in Genesis 12. There, God promises Abraham that he will become the father of a great nation and that he will obtain his own land, where this nation will eventually live. And God makes Abraham and his offspring mediators of the blessing: Abraham shall be blessed and he shall be a blessing, the one who blesses Abraham will be blessed, the one who curses Abraham will be cursed, all nations of the earth shall receive blessing through Abraham. This promise is repeated several times in Genesis, also in the form of a covenant God makes with Abraham, Isaac, and Jacob. As a sign for this COVENANT, circumcision is introduced.

The Abraham covenant is of the greatest importance for understanding the role and destiny of the people of Israel as they are depicted in the Hebrew Bible. And in most of the Genesis narratives, at least one of the aspects of the covenant is the theological clue to the story.

Concerning offspring, the promise of God is countered at first by the barrenness and then by the old age of Sarah. Sarah wants to help the divine promise with human methods by giving her maid Hagar to her husband. This way of having offspring was an ancient Near Eastern custom. However, the attempt fails in more than one respect: First, the honor given to Hagar goes to her head, and she enters into conflict with her mistress. Second, God does not accept Ishmael as bearer of the divine promise. However, as compensation, he makes a separate covenant with him. It is 13 more years before Abraham and Sarah finally conceive their own son, Isaac.

But then, as a test of faith, God asks Abraham to sacrifice this son to him. God wants to see whether Abraham really loves God or only the gifts of God. From the Christian point of view, the story is also foreshadowing the sacrifice of Jesus. "God himself will provide the lamb" (Genesis 22:8). Abraham did not have to sacrifice his only son, but God sacrificed his only son—so faithful is he to the human race (John 3:16). The offspring continues to be a topic of the Genesis narrative, for example, in the rivalry of Esau and Jacob, which is not only about the birthright but also about which of the two will become the bearer of the divine promise. Also, the Toledoth-formulas go along the elected family line, giving the collateral lines before the main lines, respectively: Terah, Ishmael, Isaac, Esau, Jacob.

The second topic of the Abraham covenant is the possession of the land of Canaan as Israel's living space. A text that deals especially with this topic is, for example, the quarrel between Abraham and Lot: Abraham divides the land for Lot's sake, but God tells Abraham that he would own the whole land (Genesis 13). Another important theme is the family tomb bought from the Hittites in Canaan. Again, the reason that Abraham does not allow Isaac to move to Haran, choosing a woman for himself, is that he does not want Isaac to leave the Promised Land. At the end of Genesis, the traveling of the whole family to Egypt is another aspect of the topic.

The third topic of the covenant is the mediation of the blessing. This again becomes apparent in some of the stories. In three different situations, for example, the patriarch's wives are passed off as sisters. In each of the cases the truth of the sentence

"I will curse the one who curses you" is demonstrated: The people who take (without knowledge) the patriarch's wife receive the divine curse. The mediation of blessing can be seen mostly in the Joseph story, where Joseph saves the Egyptian people from a famine.

The promise theme involving offspring, land, and blessing is common to all three large patriarchal cycles. Besides that, however, each of the cycles has its own specific subject. Within the Abraham cycle, this is surely the subject of trusting in God or doubting him. Two examples of Abraham's extraordinary faith are his obedience when he is called to leave his family and move into a foreign country (Genesis 12:1–7) and his willingness to sacrifice even his only son if God demands it (Genesis 22). Before that, however, Abraham and Sarah lack trust in God's promise, when they try to obtain offspring through Hagar, which leads to the birth of Ishmael (Genesis 16). In the New Testament, Abraham is cited as an example of faith several times (Romans 4; Galatians 3; Hebrews 11:8–19). For the specific subjects of the Jacob and the Joseph cycles, see below.

Regarding the historical reliability of the patriarch narratives, there is no direct extrabiblical evidence to compare with the texts. However, it can be shown that the cultural and historical context information given in the narrative fits well within the archaeological picture of that time. For example, the forms of the names of the patriarchs Isaac, Jacob, Joseph, and Ishmael are typical for the Middle Bronze Age (ca. 2150–1550 B.C.E.). Many of the names explicitly occur on archaeological inscriptions of that time, e.g., Jacob, Abram, Nahor, Benjamin, Zebulon, and others. Egyptian consecration texts of the 19th and 18th centuries B.C.E. also refer to several Canaanite cities mentioned in the Genesis narrative. Furthermore, the possibility of the patriarchs' traveling freely among Mesopotamia, Palestine, and Egypt reflects the political circumstances of the early second millennium B.C.E., when the population was sparse and there were no strong kingdoms hindering people from traveling. The names given in Genesis 14, the narrative on the war of the city-states, are also interesting from an archaeological point of view. Some of the names given there are so old that the biblical writer has to explain them to his readers. Only in around 2000 B.C.E. did Elam control parts of Palestine, as is mentioned in the text (14:1, 4). And a final observation may be given: Joseph is said to have been sold as a slave for 20 shekels of silver (Genesis 37:28). As can be shown from several extrabiblical witnesses, this was the usual price for a slave between the 19th and 16th centuries B.C.E., but neither before nor after.

The mentioning of PHILISTINES in Genesis 21 and 26, on the other hand, has often been said to be an anachronism, because the sea people known as Philistines arrived only around 1200 B.C.E. A possible explanation for this is that a group called "Philistines," already living there in the early second millennium, was joined by the sea people at a later time. Another alleged anachronism, the mentioning of camels as domesticated animals in several of the stories, has been resolved in the meantime. For a long time it was believed that camels were only domesticated in the first millennium B.C.E. In recent decades, however, several findings have been made throughout the ancient Near East that support the domestication of camels at a much earlier time.

Part VIII: "This Is What Came Of Ishmael": Ishmael's Genealogy (25:12–18)

Ishmael has been born because Abraham and Sarah wanted to fulfill blessing of God by human methods, so Ishmael is not the bearer of the divine blessing. Yet because he is Abraham's son, God makes him, as well as Israel, the father of a nation of 12 tribes.

The Ishmaelites were a Bedouin people living in the deserts south and east of Canaan. Generally, the Israelites and the Ishmaelites were not in conflict with each other in ancient times. However, a certain tension, already present between the two brothers Isaac and Ishmael, existed in the two nations' relationship.

Part IX: "This Is What Came Of Isaac": Jacob and Esau (25:19–35:29)

As with the Abraham cycle, the Jacob cycle has the divine promise of offspring, land, and blessing as its main topic. The more specific subject of the Jacob story itself, however, is the conflict between the twin brothers Jacob and Esau, and the question of which of them will receive the divine blessing: The one who has the natural right to it, as the firstborn, but does not care or the one who has no natural right but the right attitude and longs for the blessing with all his heart? While Jacob is being born, he is grabbing the heel of his twin brother, Esau. From this, a wordplay on his name is derived: *Jacob,* "he clutches the heel," "the tricky one." Already at the moment of his birth, he, the second, wants to become the first. Negotiating, deceiving, wrestling—these are the marks of Jacob's story, in the active as well as in the passive sense.

First of all, Jacob buys the birthright from Esau. Their father, Isaac, however, does not know about it. Through an act of deception he has to be made to bless Jacob instead of Esau. Thereby, the bad intention of the father, to bless *only* his beloved son, Esau, is turned back against him, when he unwittingly gives his entire blessing to Jacob. When he learns of it, it is too late: He does not have any blessing left for Esau. But does God approve what Jacob does? Jacob has to flee from Esau, leaving the Promised Land. Laban, his father-in-law, cheats him badly. As Jacob had deceived Isaac into blessing the wrong brother, now Jacob is himself deceived into marrying the wrong sister. Through this act of poetic justice, God makes Jacob learn and mature.

Jacob's seven years serving Laban turn to 20 in the end (Genesis 31:41). Jacob, however, gets his just deserts when he again cheats Laban, this time with the help of God, making sure more multicolored sheep and goats are born than usual.

Then occurs the final act of Jacob's wrestling. One night, on his way back to Esau, Jacob literally wrestles with God, or rather with an angel of God. Jacob does not want to let him go before being blessed by him. Finally, he receives the divine blessing he has longed for so long. A new name is given to him: *Israel,* explained as "God-wrestler." He reenters the Promised Land and is reconciled with his brother, Esau.

From his two wives and their two maids, 12 sons have been born to Jacob. Possibly, he also had several daughters. However, only one is named, Dinah, because she plays a role in one of the stories, namely, in the conflict with Shechem.

Jacob wrestling with the angel (Genesis 32:24, 30), engraving by Gustave Doré

Parts X and XI: "This Is What Came Of Esau": Esau's Family and Tribe Genealogy (36:1–8 and 36:9–37:1)

In the genealogy of Esau, the Toledoth-formula appears twice: in 36:1 and in 36:9. This can be justified by the observation that 36:1–8 contains the family genealogy of the time Esau lives in the land of Canaan, while 36:9–37:1 concentrates on the people of Edom in the mountains of Seir. The doubling of the formula may suggest that just as Esau is the brother of Jacob, Edom is the brother people of Israel (Genesis 25:23; 27:38–40). Often in history, the two people are in conflict. The Edomites refuse to allow the Israelites to cross their land when entering into Canaan (Numbers 20:14–21). In the prophetic books and in other texts, Edom is mentioned as mocking Israel when they are oppressed by the enemy (see, for example, Obadiah; Lamentations 4:21–22; Psalm 137:7).

Part XII: "This Is What Came Of Jacob": The Story of Joseph (37:2–50:26)

Sometimes, this part is seen as just the story of Joseph, and chapters 38 and 48–50, which do not deal with Joseph, are excluded as of secondary character. Properly speaking, however, the Toledoth-formula does not announce the story of Joseph but of Jacob. The whole family is in view. Therefore, chapter 38 and especially chapters 48–50 make sense the way they are.

From a theological point of view, the story is again to be understood against the background of the divine covenant with Abraham, Isaac, and Jacob. At the end of Genesis, the promise that Abraham's offspring would become a great people is at least partly fulfilled. Jacob's family consists of 70 members—a microcosm of the 70 nations given in Genesis 10. What is more, the prophecies of Jacob given to each of his 12 sons take into view the coming time of Israel as a nation and therefore point to the final fulfillment of the promise. That Abraham's name would become great is already fulfilled in Joseph, who becomes a very famous person.

The promise of the mediation of blessing is especially demonstrated in Joseph. Through divine providence and organizational talent, he is a blessing for Potiphar's house and for the prison, and he is even able to save a whole nation from a severe famine. His blessing is said to extend even to the point that the "whole world" buys food from him (Genesis 41:57). Surely this has to be seen in the light of the promise given to Abraham to bless all families of the earth in 12:3. But the statement "I will bless those who bless you" from the same verse is also exemplified: Pharaoh very generously offers all Egypt for Jacob's family to live in (47:5–6) and thereby "blesses" them. For this, he receives blessing of the same kind: Joseph makes all Egyptians sell their land to Pharaoh, so that Pharaoh in the end possesses all Egypt and is able to impose a 20 percent tax on all agricultural yields (Genesis 47:13–26).

One of the aspects of the promise, however, is not fulfilled at the end of Genesis: the land promise. The Joseph story explains why Abraham's family moves to Egypt instead of living in the Promised Land. But reproach is not made. Rather, God confirms the decision to move to Egypt (Genesis 46:3–4), since it is part of his plan.

Besides the promise theme, the Joseph cycle has its specific subject, which is expressed in one of the last verses of the book, where Joseph says to his brothers, "You intended to do harm to me, God intended it for good" (Genesis 50:20). It is a story of divine providence, and its counterpart, human responsibility, especially in a family context. The story teaches how unwise it is for parents to treat their children unequally. Jacob makes Joseph and Benjamin, the two sons of his beloved wife, Rachel, his favorite sons. That Joseph is preferred makes his brothers literally hate him. Joseph's arrogance in telling the family about his dreams heightens the tension even more. His brothers make him face hard facts again, selling him as a slave. Put into prison in Egypt, Joseph arrives at the lowest point of his career. There he has to learn and to grow, becoming ready for true greatness.

The second part of the statement quoted becomes visible when God turns the cruel act of the brothers into a good ending. In his position at the Egyptian court, Joseph is now able to provide his family with food and a fertile land to live in—even if it is outside the Promised Land, in Egypt.

CHARACTERS

Abel Son of Adam and Eve, and the world's first victim of murder. His name means "vapor" or "vanity."

Abraham Ancestor of the people of Israel, married to Sarah, and father of Ishmael and Isaac. God gives him a promise that he will become a great nation, that his descendants will receive a land to live in, and that he and his family will be blessed and become a blessing even for the whole world. Abraham obeys God and leaves his family and his home region, moving into the land of Canaan. Abraham is an example of what it means to trust in God. However, that does not mean that he is exempted from difficult situations or from times of doubt and sin. His name means "father of a multitude."

Adam The first human being, and at the same time a symbol of the human race. Adam is put in the garden of Eden to be in a close relationship with God and to have access to eternal life. After an act of disobedience, however, he and his wife are expelled from the garden. See ADAM AND EVE.

Cain Son of Adam and Eve, and the world's first murderer. When he sees that God does not accept his sacrifice as he does the sacrifice of his brother Abel, he kills Abel in an act of jealousy. As a punishment, he is driven out from his family, and he becomes a fugitive on earth.

Esau Son of Isaac and Rebekah, and brother of Jacob. Esau does not care much about his right as the firstborn and sells it to Jacob for a bowl of stew. He marries two Canaanite women, again indicating that he does not esteem the divine election of his family. In the end, not he, but his brother, Jacob, becomes the bearer of the divine blessing.

Eve The first woman, made of Adam's rib while he is asleep. Eve is named twice throughout the narrative in order to express her roles: The first name is *Ishah*, meaning "woman," derived from *Ish*, "man." This naming expresses her role of being related to the man as his counterpart or complement. The second name *Eve*, Hebrew *Chawwah*, means "life," since she becomes the "mother of all life." See also ADAM AND EVE.

Isaac Son of Abraham and the second bearer of the divine promise after him. He is married to Rebekah and is the father of Esau and Jacob. In the narrative, he is a rather passive figure, overshadowed first by his father and then by his sons.

Jacob Son of Isaac and Rebekah, brother of Esau. Although he is not the firstborn, he wants to become the bearer of the divine promise. He struggles with his brother, his father, with Laban, and even God himself, until he finally receives the blessing from him. His name is explained as "he clutches the heel," "the tricky one."

Joseph Son of Jacob and his beloved wife, Rachel. Jacob makes him his favorite son. This preference leads to intense conflicts among the brothers. Being sold as a slave and being imprisoned, Joseph has to mature before God finally exalts him and makes him a blessing for all Egypt and for his family.

Noah Noah is faithful and obedient to God. When God decides to annihilate the whole human race by means of a Flood, he instructs Noah to build a ship, so that he, his family, and all the land animals will be saved.

Leah   The first wife of Jacob. Jacob does not love her, a fact she suffers from all her life, as the name giving of her sons shows (Genesis 29:31 ff.).

Lot   Nephew of Abraham, traveling into the Promised Land together with him. As long as Lot is with Abraham, he also takes part in Abraham's blessing and becomes very wealthy. But he decides to become independent and settles in Sodom, among very wicked people. From then his decline begins. Twice Abraham saves Lot, but Lot does not return to him. Fleeing from Sodom, Lot's wife looks back and becomes a pillar of salt. Lot ends up alone with his two daughters in a cave, sliding into an incestuous situation.

Rachel   The second wife of Jacob. Since Jacob loves her and rejects Leah, God, in an act of poetic justice, makes her barren for a number of years. So Jacob and Rachel have to wait a long time until they have their first son, Joseph. During the birth of her second son, Benjamin, Rachel dies.

Rebekah   Wife of Isaac and mother of Esau and Jacob. Rebekah loves Jacob more than Esau and supports him in his plan to obtain the right of the firstborn instead of Esau.

Sarah   Wife of Abraham. She is promised a son, but she cannot imagine becoming pregnant in her old age. Therefore, she gives her maid, Hagar, to Abraham, and Hagar gives birth to Ishmael. However, eventually Sarah becomes pregnant herself and gives birth to Isaac, who becomes the bearer of the blessing.

Habakkuk

The book of Habakkuk is the eighth book of the 12 Minor Prophets in the Hebrew Bible. Nothing at all is known about its writer, and his name occurs only once outside the book, in the apocryphal book of Bel and the Dragon. One of the early finds of the DEAD SEA SCROLLS was a commentary on the first two chapters of Habakkuk, but not the third. Internal dating suggests it was written before the Babylonian invasion of 598 B.C.E., but at some point when their invasion seemed a possibility. Babylonian (called here Chaldean; see BABYLON) supremacy of the region was gained at the battle of Carchemish, which can be dated to 605 B.C.E. The date must be approximately correct, probably when Jehoiakim was king of Judah. The third chapter suggests a temple connection, so we can suppose Habakkuk was writing from Jerusalem. This would make him a contemporary with Jeremiah, with whose prophecies there are similarities.

SYNOPSIS

The prophecy falls into three sections:

- 1:1–2:5: A dialogue, or argument, between Habakkuk and the Lord. The prophet sees injustice around him and asks God how long he has to cry against this. God's reply is that he is sending the Chaldeans to inflict punishment. The prophet is aghast at this: However wicked his own people are, surely the Babylonians are far more wicked? God tells him he must take the long view and, meanwhile, live by faith.
- 2:6–20: A taunt song, with five woes directed at the invaders, who will ultimately be overcome themselves.
- 3:1–19: A PSALM that can be divided into two subsections: first, a dramatic psalm of praise as God comes sweeping in cosmic dislocation to deliver his judgment (3:1–15); second, in great contrast, a psalm of trust, that he, the prophet, will trust God whatever happens (3:16–19).

God is seen in the book as a God whose ultimate purposes are never fully revealed. They are, however, just and ultimately brought about in powerful ways. He is able to summon nations and dismiss them. He looks above all for faith in his people.

COMMENTARY

This is one of the most poetic of all the minor prophetic books. Its imagery is dense and memorable, and its use of parallelisms is complex, suggesting a writer well accustomed to writing verse. In 2:2 he is told to "write the vision," rather than just utter it orally and for someone else to write it down, perhaps some time later. The writing has all the force of immediate verbal utterance, just as Jeremiah's did, as his secretary, Baruch, recorded his prophecies.

The carefully wrought verbal structure can be seen from the beginning, with three questions being followed by three statements to support the questions. Each question and statement is constructed as a parallelism, except the last line: "Therefore judgment comes forth perverted." This statement is the key to the first section—the prophet's struggle to find justice anywhere. It is not in his own society, just as his contemporary Jeremiah proclaimed. But it also does not appear to be in God's response, which follows in 1:5–11. The depiction of the Babylonian army is a brilliant description of military force and its self-sufficiency. The images are of wild animals, leopards, wolves, eagles, and of wind and unstoppable force.

God is going to raise up the Chaldeans to effect justice. It is an unbelievable message (1:5, quoted in the New Testament in Acts 13:41). It is not the first revelation of God's using alien nations to fulfill his purpose. Jeremiah knew this (Jeremiah 5:15–17; 27:5–11), as did Ezekiel (Ezekiel 7:24). Before them, Isaiah had realized this about the Assyrians (Isaiah 10:5–10). An individual, Cyrus, was later seen similarly (Isaiah 44:28; 45:1). But these three prophets had seen that Israel's sins warranted the most severe punishment. Habakkuk did not see this: However sinful God's people were, the Babylonians were far worse. So how can two wrongs make a right? Of all the prophets of the period, he had least sense of his own people's sin and thus a greater sense of God's apparent injustice. Jeremiah had also argued with God (Jeremiah 12:1–4), but it was at a more personal level: God was asking him to do the impossible, though, as did the Psalmist, he, too, asked why the unrighteous appeared to prosper.

This type of questioning can be called *complaint* (as 2:1), a literary subgenre. It can also be seen as working toward a theodicy, trying to see God's justice in apparent injustice. Theodicies are never easy to construct. John Milton used 12 books in his epic *Paradise Lost*; Job uses 42 chapters. Habakkuk condenses his complaint into just six verses (1:12–17). He bases his complaint on what he knows of God—"Your eyes are too pure to behold evil" (1:13)—and on what seem to be the implications, that the Babylonians, as voracious fishermen, will never end their destruction if God allows them leave (1:17). The fishing image is an extended simile, running from 1:14–17. Fish have no leadership, and this is how the Babylonians' victims seem: helpless and leaderless. Where is God in all this?

The prophet then evokes on a traditional prophetic image, that of the prophet as watchman (2:1; see Isaiah 21:8–12; Ezekiel 3:17, 33:1ff.). But rather than watch for the enemy, Habakkuk is going to watch for God's answer, which comes at once (2:2–5). It is a kinder response than God's to Jeremiah (Jeremiah 12:5). Basically, it says there is a vision still to come, and "If it seems to tarry, wait for it" (2:3). In other words, God's announcement about the Babylonians is only part of the picture, but God only reveals one thing at a time. What matters is not revelation but righteous faithfulness (2:4). Many commentators have seen this as the key verse to the whole book, and certainly the New Testament writers used it no fewer than three times (Romans 1:17; Galatians 3:11; Hebrews 10:38–39). Ultimately, faith is the key to theodicy, not more revelation or more argument.

The last few verses contrast the faithful to the unrighteous. The next section picks up this theme in a classic taunt song. Isaiah 14:4f. is another such taunt song, also against the Babylonians. It is somewhat different from WOES AND DENUNCIATIONS in that the tone is more lament than anger, and it is more carefully structured. Here the five taunts are marked by an "Alas!" (2:6, 9, 12, 15, 19). Each "alas!" has its own theme and image. The first is that of plunder. The second is the image of a house, with the marvelous phrase "the plaster will respond from the woodwork." Each thing the Babylonians have done will be a witness against them. The third contains the much-quoted verse "But the earth will be filled / with the knowledge of the glory of God / as the waters cover the sea," echoing Isaiah 11:9. Habakkuk rises from mere taunt to affirmation of his faith. The fourth taunt centers on the image of drinking, and the fifth on idols. The whole is gathered in 2:20, "Let all the earth keep silence before him!" a phrase used later by Zechariah (Zechariah 2:13). Verses 6 and 20 can be seen as marking an INCLUSIO, verses marking off the beginning and end of a particular genre passage. Verses 1:12/2:1 have also been seen as inclusio.

The final chapter has all the marks of being written to be sung: "According to Shigionoth" (3:1, see Psalm 7); the "selah" of 3:13; and the final instruction "To the choirmaster with stringed instruments" (3:19). This has led some commentators to suppose that Habakkuk was perhaps a temple singing prophet, as 1 Chronicles 25:1 mentions. Certainly the psalm is fairly similar to Psalm 68. Some have even supposed this was added later, but the themes in it seem to round off the first two chapters neatly.

3:2 is probably most familiar in its King James Version wording: "O LORD, revive thy work in the midst of the years, in the midst of the years make known; in wrath remember mercy." The New Revised Standard Version has "in our time." The verse emphasizes Habakkuk's seeking renewal rather than further punishment for God's people. The following verses use the Exodus as subtext: God's marvelous deliverance is described in images of sun and storm, flood and earthquake, building up a sense of a cosmic dislocation far greater than anything the Babylonians could cause in chapter 1. The passage climaxes in the almost apocalyptic 3:12, gradually stilling to 3:16: "I wait quietly."

But even despite this outburst of confident praise, Habakkuk returns in his conclusion to the faith of 2:4. The contrast is stark. A number of delaying parallel constructions begin "though . . . not . . ." (3:17), involving images of thwarted fertility: figs, vines, olives, flocks. Even though these fail, he bursts out, "Yet . . . I will rejoice in the LORD." This faith is what will keep him buoyant, not dramatic visions. Again, the King James Version is the more familiar: "He will make my feet like hinds' feet, and he will make me to walk upon my

high places." What better way to finish a prophetic word!

CHARACTER

Habakkuk Habakkuk appears a literate and sophisticated writer, well aware of literary forms of psalm, taunt, and complaint. He expects his psalm to be sung in the temple, suggesting a close connection to its musical life. He is aware, too, of the Babylonian menace, suggesting he lived at much the same time and place as Jeremiah.

Haggai

The book of Haggai is the 10th of the Minor or Lesser Prophets in the Hebrew Bible. The Hebrew form is *Chaggay*, from the Hebrew word *hag*, meaning a feast. The name thus means either "the festive man" or a contraction of "My Feast is Yahweh." Haggai is linked with another prophet, Zechariah, as the first prophets of the postexilic period described in the Ezra-Nehemiah narrative. They are mentioned several times there (Ezra 5:1–2; 6:14) as well as in the parallel apocryphal text of Esdras (1 Esdras 6:1–2), both credited with revitalizing the rebuilding of the second temple after the return of the first exiles in 520 B.C.E.

According to Ezra, these first returnees, led by Zerubbabel and Joshua, had begun laying the foundations for a new temple on reaching Jerusalem. They had received permission from the Persian emperor Cyrus to do this and even to requisition materials (Ezra 1–3). But then opposition to the project had grown from the local populace, who had at first been friendly (Ezra 4:1–5). Their discouragement effectively stopped the rebuilding for the next 16 years, until the second year of the Persian king Darius (522–486 B.C.E.).

At this point, the two prophets felt sufficiently inspired to challenge this failure of purpose. The two prophets could not have been more dissimilar. Haggai is brief, to the point, logical, and practical; Zechariah is visionary, idealistic, and poetic. Together, however, they succeeded. Rebuilding began again, and the temple was completed five years later, in 516 B.C.E.

SYNOPSIS

The book of Haggai is the second shortest in the Hebrew Bible. Nevertheless, his ministry was among the most successful of the prophets, and only Jonah was as successful. Part of the reason for this was that its aim was limited, highly focused, and motivational, using equal quantities of carrots and sticks.

The two chapters consist of four oracles:

- 1:1–11, 13: addressed to Zerubbabel and Joshua, arguing that the reason for their poor standard of living and the general failure of all their worldly efforts is that they have neglected to prioritize the building of the temple.
- 2:1–9: addressed to Zerubbabel, Joshua, and "the remnant," encouraging them that the new temple would be more glorious than the old, even though at present it looked quite the opposite. They needed to see the project with the eyes of faith.
- 2:10–19: addressed to the priests, arguing that the present ruins had "defiled" the spiritual life of the returnees but now was the turning point in their fortunes.
- 2:20–23: addressed to Zerubbabel, assuring him of his election by God and the collapse of his enemies.

COMMENTARY

First Oracle and Its Effect: Wrong Priorities (1:1–15)

In postexilic times, events become precisely dated. Here the prophecies are dated to the very day of their utterance, in marked contrast to, say, Jeremiah, whose prophecies are somewhat chaotically arranged. Here, as we also see in Ezra-Nehemiah, the rule of law and the power of logic give a different feel to events. This does not mean the spiritual is relegated. Far from it: Haggai's message seems to have led to a minirevival of hope and effort. Haggai continues to emphasize, even more than other Hebrew prophets, that he is only the mouth-piece for God. In only 38 verses, phrases underlining God's ownership of the words spoken occur 24 times, as "the word of the LORD by the prophet Haggai" (1:1, 3; 2:1, 10, 20), or "Haggai, as the LORD their God had sent him" (1:12), or equivalent phrases.

The date of the first message is given as "the second year of King Darius, in the sixth month, on the first day." In modern chronology this would be August 29, 520 B.C.E. Zechariah began his prophecies just two months later (Zechariah 1:1). We need to remember that the great reformers, Ezra and Nehemiah, were not to appear on the scene for another 60 years. The two prophets were on their own at first. Haggai challenges the prevailing apathy: "These people say the time has not yet come to rebuild the LORD's house" (1:2). By contrast, Haggai's message is "It's high time!"

Although the book is translated as a prose document, there do appear to be poetic structures in the oracles. For example, 1:6 contains marked parallelism (see POETRY, BIBLICAL) and could easily be set out as verse:

> You have sown much, and harvested little;
> you eat, but never have enough;
> you drink, but you never have your fill;
> You clothe yourselves, but no one is warm;
> and you that earn wages
> earn wages to put them into a bag with holes.

Similar parallel structures may be seen in 1:9–11; 2:4–5, 6–9, 16–17.

Haggai's style is poetic in its rhetorical force—the piling up of parallel examples—but at the same time prosaic in its sense of cause and effect. Thus we have "Consider" (1:7), "Why?" (1:9), followed by "Because" (1:9), and "Therefore" (1:10). As in a court case, the jury is asked to look at the evidence and find the logical pattern. The lawyers may use persuasive rhetoric, but only for a reasoned conclusion. Here Haggai offers a logical reason for their total lack of success: They have their priorities completely wrong. "Because my house lies in ruins while all of you hurry off to your own houses" (1:9). The details are specific. It is, theologically, a breaking of the first commandment, since in Hebrew ritual, worship implied a place in which to worship. God has been directly punishing them: "I have called for a drought" (1:11).

The writer records the impact of the prophecy in 1:12–15: "The people feared the LORD" (1:12), using the word *fear* to mean "give due respect to." But more than that: "The LORD stirred up the spirit of Zerubbabel . . . and Joshua . . . and the remnant of the people" (1:14). The book balances finely what is said and what is not said. We have just enough to imagine the scenario with Haggai's ability to assure them they had made the right choice: "I am with you, says the LORD" (1:13). The details of the action they took are condensed into another date, "the twenty-fourth day of the month." It took them just over three weeks to become organized.

Second Oracle: Be Encouraged! (2:1–9)

Haggai's ability to motivate is seen here. A month after work has begun, he has another oracle from God. It addresses the one issue that could potentially discourage more than any other: the realization that for all their efforts, what they build would be a poor replica of the first temple built by Solomon, with all its years of preparation and collection of materials, which was destroyed 66 years ago. The same source of discouragement is seen in Ezra-Nehemiah (Ezra 3:12–13). Here Haggai rises from everyday actuality to a vision of the future, as was given to prophets (e.g., Isaiah 60:5, 11; 61:6; Zechariah 14:14), in terms of the wealth of the nations pouring into Jerusalem, as it had, of course, in Solomon's day (1 Kings 10:25ff.). Haggai takes them back further into their history, to the other great return out of Egypt, when the Egyptians' wealth came to them (Exodus 3:21–22). Hence the covenant reference in 2:5: That covenant was still in force.

Third Oracle: Turning Point (2:10–19)

The third oracle has more of the form of a Socratic dialogue: The logic is established by asking one's opponent a series of questions. Here, Haggai addresses the priests, one of whose concerns was to prevent defilement and maintain ritual purity. Verses 2:12–13 are two technical questions, which the priests have no difficulty answering. As with Jesus, Haggai then delivers the punch line as a surprising analogy, drawing on the logic of the first oracle: You did not prosper before, because the temple ruins were a defilement too. And then he clinches his case with a rhetorical question: "Do the vine, the fig tree . . . still yield nothing?" But rhetorical questions can be ambivalent: Is the answer yes or no? The sense seems to be, up to now they have been unfruitful. But from now on, their fortunes will change, as the defilement has been removed. It finishes with an appropriate promise, therefore (2:19).

Fourth Oracle: Zerubbabel Exhorted (2:20–23)

The last oracle occurs on the same day as the previous one but is for Zerubbabel alone; a somewhat terse, visionary, almost apocalyptic, message is given. God is about to shake heavens and earth, and especially the surrounding kingdoms, repeating 2:7. But more detail is given, "every one by the sword of a comrade" (2:22), suggesting civil war in the Persian Empire, leaving Jerusalem in peace. But Zerubbabel needs more than that: He needs, psychologically, to know that he has God's approval, despite the lack of leadership shown in previous years (cf. Zechariah 4:9). This is what Haggai, encourager and motivator, gives him, "Make you like a signet ring" (2:23), a phrase also used in Sirach 49:11, a metonymy, symbolizing God's authority being given him (cf. Esther 8:8). It echoes and undoes the words used in Jeremiah 22:24, when Jehoiachin's authority was removed. The sense of God's choosing him echoes God's choosing Solomon in 1 Chronicles 28:10. As temple builder, he is among the greats.

CHARACTERS

Haggai Haggai and Zechariah were presumably among the first returnees. In a spiritual vacuum, he rose briefly to spiritual authority, speaking out the prophecies, which may have been written down somewhat later. The force of his delivery and their encouragement seems to have galvanized the leaders and people to action.

Joshua (or Jeshua) The high priest, a post inherited from his father Jehozadak. He is not described here, though in Zechariah 3, he becomes a significant individual in the drama of salvation. Haggai's prophecy suggests he had not so far been as proactive as he could have been.

Zerubbabel   The grandson of King Jeconiah (1 Chronicles 3:19; Matthew 1:12), appointed governor of the first exiles to return to Jerusalem. A tremendous amount of work is placed on him by Haggai as a royal representative, though there is little evidence he fulfilled these expectations in his own person. Jewish royalty had disappeared by the time Nehemiah arrived as governor.

Hebrews

One of the aspects that make Hebrews special among the letters in the New Testament is that for a long time it was attributed to the apostle PAUL, despite the fact that the text does not mention Paul as the author. In Paul's actual letters, to the contrary, he always introduces himself as author and as an apostle. In the early church Paul's alleged authorship was used as an argument to include Hebrews in the canon of the New Testament, for anonymous texts were regarded with some suspicion (see FORMATION OF THE CANON: THE NEW TESTAMENT). As a result, Hebrews was indeed accepted as canonical but for at least partly the wrong reasons. The letter is included in the oldest extant manuscript of Paul's letters, which dates from about 200 C.E.

So Hebrews does not belong to the letters of Paul, but neither is it part of the group of the so-called Catholic epistles, that is, the group of seven non-Pauline letters in the New Testament (James, 1 and 2 Peter, 1–3 John, and Jude). Most of these are addressed to a general audience, hence the name *catholic*, which means "general." The author of Hebrews has in mind a specific audience whose problems he attempts to solve by writing this letter. The impression is created that he is a leading person among his audience who is temporarily away from them. Hebrews 13:24 suggests that the church is in Italy and the author not, but the reverse interpretation is not impossible. The fact is that Hebrews was known to Clement of Rome when he wrote a letter at the end of the first century C.E.

As to the date of writing, it is hard to be specific. Had the letter been written after the year 70 C.E., the destruction of the temple in JERUSALEM would probably have been mentioned as an additional argument against reverting to Judaism. Hence a date before 70 C.E. seems quite likely.

So who was the letter's author? He was a Christian who had not personally been an eyewitness to Jesus, somebody therefore from the so-called second generation. This is clear from 2:3, which rules out as authors the apostles who had been eyewitnesses. (Contrast Paul in Galatians 1:12 and 1 Corinthians 15:8–10.) The author refers to himself with a masculine grammatical form in 11:32, but that is about all we know. Among the suggestions are New Testament characters such as Barnabas, Luke, Apollos, and—despite the said masculine form—Priscilla, who is mentioned before her husband, Aquila, in Romans 16:3 and Acts 18:18, 26. It is best to acknowledge that nobody really knows.

Hebrews is probably the best planned of all New Testament texts, with an intricate structure that surprises even the scholars (see below). It is also a determined attempt to read the Hebrew Bible as Christian Scripture, as pointing to JESUS CHRIST. The author sees God's new revelation in Jesus foreshadowed in his revelation of the Hebrew Bible, which he considers as "obsolete and aging" (8:13). God's history with his people Israel plays a vital role in the argument.

The author reads the Hebrew Bible in its Greek translation (the Septuagint; see BIBLE, EARLY TRANSLATIONS OF), an indication that he probably does not live in Israel. Greek must be his native language, and his style of writing is the best of the entire New Testament. He uses about 150 words that do not occur elsewhere in the New Testament and several new coinages. Some of his one-liners can hardly be translated. Yet on occasions some knowledge of the Hebrew language is evident as well, as when he explains a Hebrew name for his readers (7:2).

In literary terms Hebrews is in fact not a real letter but a written SERMON with a short appendix in a simpler style (13:22–25). This can, for example, be seen in the frequent use of words for speaking and the absence of words for writing, and in the virtual absence of personal notes.

The Hebrew Bible in Hebrews

The argument of Hebrews includes six large sections of text from the Hebrew Bible, which are regarded as references to Jesus and the new covenant initiated by him:

Psalm 8:4–6 is quoted in 2:6–7 and expounded in 2:5–18

Psalm 95:7–11 is quoted in 3:7–11, 15; 4:7, and expounded in 3:1–4:13

Psalm 110:1–4 with Genesis 14 is quoted in 5:6; 7:17, 21 (cf. 1:13), and expounded in 4:14–7:28

Jeremiah 31:31–34 and Psalm 40:6–8 are quoted in 8:8–12 and 10:5–7, respectively, and expounded in chapters 8–10

Habakkuk 2:3–4 is quoted in 10:37–38 and expounded in chapter 11

Proverbs 3:11–12 is quoted in 12:5–6 and expounded in chapters 12–13

In addition to these core quotes there are other citations as well as allusions and summaries (e.g., 1:1; 10:1–4). In the Hebrew Bible the author hears God's voice (e.g., 1:5), but also that of the HOLY SPIRIT (e.g., 3:7) and of Christ (2:12, 13). Sometimes he can take the Hebrew Bible literally (e.g., in 11:18), but more often he finds a deeper meaning beneath the words. As does Paul, the author argues that God's covenant with Abraham (Genesis) and his descendants remains intact but that the later covenant with Moses (Exodus) has been superseded by Jesus.

SYNOPSIS

Hebrews 1:1–4 is the grand prologue to the letter, which in elevated style announces all major themes. The first two verses focus on God, the latter two on Jesus. In the Greek of verse 1 there is beautiful alliteration as the five key words all begin with *p*. The prologue is followed in 1:5–14 by three comparisons between Jesus and the angels. Verse 2:4 shows that just as in the churches founded by Paul, the Holy Spirit had worked visible signs and

miracles in this community. After the emphasis on Jesus' divinity, the attention shifts to his humanity (2:10–5:10). The readers are urged to press on to the rest that God has prepared for them.

The emphasis on a single priesthood in chapter 7 is Jewish because in the Greco-Roman world there were multiple priesthoods. Whereas in 4:14–5:10 similarities with Aaron, the first high priest, predominate, we now, to the contrary, learn that Jesus replaces the Levitical priesthood. Chapter 7 develops the role of Melchizedek (see below) and emphasizes Jesus' perfect sacrifice of himself as a once-and-for-all event; chapter 8 contrasts Jesus with the Levitical priesthood. Chapter 9 focuses on the tabernacle and the Day of Atonement (see Leviticus 16); the implication of the argument is that those who would return to Judaism have something to which to return.

In 10:19–25, which forms one sentence in Greek, the sermon's main themes are joined. Prefigured in 10:39, chapter 11 is a well-known listing of believers under the old covenant who now serve as examples of faith; as they are, the readers are regarded as resident aliens (11:8–9). The frequent repetition of "by faith" is highly effective. The exhortations in chapters 12–13 flow straight from the preceding argument and can be summed up as "being faithful to Jesus, the mediator of the new covenant." The postscript of 13:22–25 follows after a benediction in verses 20–21.

COMMENTARY

As stated, this sermon is well structured, but on the surface this structure is not immediately visible. The larger structure of Hebrews is concentric: A central element is flanked by two parallel elements, which are in turn flanked by two more parallel elements, and so on. Hebrews has the following structure:

1:1–4 Introduction
  1:5–2:18 Jesus superior to the angels
    3:1–5:10 Jesus' faithfulness and compassion
      5:11–10:39 Central exposition
    11:1–12:13 The believers' faithfulness
  12:14–13:19 Living in service of the superior one
13:20–23 Conclusion

Within the larger structure, the central portion ("Central exposition") is also concentric, with the following structure:

5:11–6:20 Warning and encouragement
7:1–28 The perfect high priest
8:1–9:28 The meaning of Jesus' sacrifice
10:1–18 The perfect sacrifice
10:19–39 Warning and encouragement

Chapters 8 and 9, therefore, form the core of the letter.

Another important structural element is that a theme that will be considered later on is usually announced beforehand. For example, in 1:5–2:18 the topic is a comparison of Jesus and the angels; this is announced by the deliberate use of the word *angels* in 1:4. The theme of the faithfulness of Jesus Christ is announced in 2:17 and developed in 3:1–4:14, whereas 2:18 already anticipates the idea that Jesus is the high priest, which is discussed in 4:15–5:10. A final example is the announcement of Melchizedek in 5:6, 10, and 6:20.

Another characteristic of Hebrews is that the application of the message does not follow in the second half of the letter, as often in Paul's letters, but in several scattered passages, of which 2:1–4; 5:11–6:12; and 10:26–39 are the most important.

Hebrews makes much use of three traditional biblical methods of scriptural interpretation. In the first place, there is the idea that what is true for the lesser is also true of the greater; see, e.g., 2:2–4; 9:13–14; 10:28–29; and 12:25. Second, the author exploits the occurrence of the same word in different contexts on the assumption that the entire passages are therefore related. Examples are *rest* in 4:1–11 (building on Genesis 2:2 and Psalm 95:11) and the emphatic use of *you* in 5:5–6 (combining Psalm 2:7 with Psalm 110:4). In the third place, Hebrews contains TYPES, for example, in 3:12–19 and 8:1–5. Each of these methods gives expression to the view that through Scripture God speaks to his people today. At the same time, the author employs some Greek logic, and he also appeals to the hearers' emotions. As a true preacher, he includes himself with the hearers to make his words more acceptable (e.g., 2:3; 3:1; 4:13; 6:1). His language is so vivid that the hearers can picture items

such as the tabernacle and the high priest. He uses the Greeks' metaphors of the anchor (6:19) and the footrace (12:1–2). In 13:10 "altar" is a synecdoche for Christ's sacrifice, and God is described, e.g., as "the throne of grace" (4:16; cf. 1:4; 2:10; 5:7; 10:23).

The main character and the hero of this text is Jesus Christ. To bring out his greatness he is compared to and contrasted with ANGELS, Moses, Joshua, and the high priest in a very effective way. What the author in 13:22 modestly calls "a word of exhortation" is much more than a list of requests: It is a rich treatise of the person and work of Jesus Christ, intended to persuade the readers, who are in danger of lapsing, that the Christian faith is worth holding fast. A key word in Hebrews is *persevere* (10:36 New International Version; 11:27), but the author also expects Christians to grow because stagnation would be detrimental to their faith (5:12–6:3).

Hebrews makes a unique contribution to the New Testament in describing Jesus Christ as the high priest of the new covenant, who intercedes with God for humankind. The middle chapters compare and contrast the worship of the old and new covenants, to conclude that the new is better because the high priest is of a different order and because he made his sacrifice once for all. At the same time Hebrews has much to say about the humanity of Jesus and his resulting ability to feel with humankind in their hardship. There is strong emphasis on Jesus' sinlessness in 7:26–28.

Problematic for certain modern readers are the strong warnings against falling away in 6:4–8 and 10:26–31. Some interpreters solve the apparent tension with the rest of the New Testament, which has much to say about the perseverance of believers, by assuming that the people addressed here are not real Christians, just churchgoers.

CHARACTERS

angels The discussion of angels in chapters 1 and 2 is not an aim in itself; they merely serve as a foil to bring out Jesus' superiority and glory: Whereas angels are created servants, he is God's Son and cocreator. In 2:2 it says that angels were instrumental in delivering God's law to the people of Israel.

This is a tradition that goes beyond the Hebrew Bible but can also be found in Acts 7:53 and Galatians 3:19. After chapter 2 angels are mentioned only in 12:22 and 13:2.

Jesus Christ Hebrews describes Jesus through concepts that are in part familiar from the rest of the New Testament, in part unique. He is seen as God's Son and God's equal, but there is equal emphasis on his humanity (chapter 2; 5:7–9). As in Paul's letters, Hebrews points to Jesus as the key character in world history (1:1–2; 7:25; 9:28). There are allusions to his preexistence, the reality of his suffering, his resurrection, and ascension. He is said to be immutable (13:8).

Hebrews agrees with the Gospels, Peter's letters, and Paul that Jesus made the perfect sacrifice for human sin. Unique to Hebrews is the typology of the high priest, so that Jesus is both priest and sacrifice. We also come across the designation "heir of all things" (1:2) and comparisons with persons from the Hebrew Bible such as Moses, Joshua, and Melchizedek that bring out Jesus' superiority.

Melchizedek This enigmatic person occurs in Genesis 14 and was the subject of speculation in the INTERTESTAMENTAL PERIOD. The DEAD SEA SCROLLS mention him, but Hebrews is independent of these texts in making the ancient priest and king a prototype of Jesus Christ. Some inspired comparisons between Melchizedek and Jesus help the author to justify how one who did not descend from Aaron can nonetheless be high priest.

Hosea

The book of Hosea stands first among the Minor or Lesser PROPHETS in the Hebrew Bible, since it used to be considered the earliest of the "Written Prophets." It is also the longest of the 12 prophecies composing the Minor Prophets. Its 14 chapters are slightly longer than Zechariah's 14.

There is very little stated about the prophet Hosea apart from his strange marriage. It would seem best to consider him a younger contemporary of Amos, whose prophecy was probably given prior to Hosea's. Both prophets spoke to the northern kingdom of ISRAEL (also referred to as Ephraim and Jacob) during the reign of its king Jeroboam II (793–753 B.C.E.), though Amos was from the southern kingdom of JUDAH. Hosea, a northerner himself, as dialect features of his language indicate, continued to preach after Jeroboam's death. In fact, the list of the Judean kings he was contemporary with (1:1) is the same as listed for Isaiah (Isaiah 1:1). However, as there is no internal mention of the fall of SAMARIA, the capital of the northern kingdom, which occurred in 722 B.C.E., we must conclude his prophecies were completed before that date. While his actual marriage occurred before Jeroboam's death, there is no absolute reason to suppose his actual preaching ministry began immediately. The book contains oracles given over a number of years, woven together as a unity.

The historical account of the demise of the northern kingdom is given in 2 Kings 15 and 17:1–6, which should be read in conjunction with the prophecy. This will show the relevance of the end of Jehu's lineage in the assassination of Jereboam's son, Zechariah, and the subsequent period of political turmoil, especially as the threat of ASSYRIA grew. Alliances with Assyria alternated with ones with Egypt instead, none of which Hosea supported.

It is also helpful to compare Hosea's ministry with Amos's. Amos, the visiting prophet, focused on the twin themes of social injustice and empty religion or ritualism in a series of powerful WOES AND DENUNCIATIONS. He is full of a sense of God's righteousness and the imminent punishment that will follow for Israel's faithlessness. By contrast, Hosea has the actual experience of being the faithful partner in a faithless marriage, which from its origin was to be constructed as an extended analogy with Israel's faithlessness to the Lord. It is in the form of a *complaint,* containing a much more extended list of failings. Although punishment is threatened, there are many dramatic reversals, since God also pleads with Israel, through Hosea, to turn back to him and renew the broken "marriage" covenant he originally had with them.

The Hebrew word *hesed* is central here, meaning covenant keeping, righteousness, and justice.

Idolatry, faithlessness, and arrogance are Hosea's concerns. Given the later threats and actual invasions by Assyria in 734–732 B.C.E., the prosperity that blighted Israel's spirituality in Amos's day would have disappeared, only being mentioned once (12:7). What stands out are Hosea's reconciliatory tone and the prominence of his assurance of God's heart cry of love and mercy: "My compassion grows warm and tender" (11:8).

SYNOPSIS

The only obvious division in the book is between chapters 1–3 and 4–14. Scholars have subdivided the last 11 chapters further, but there is no general agreement as to those subdivisions. The last four chapters do take on a somewhat different tone, but there is continuity in theme and imagery, and it is best to see the 11 chapters as a general complaint, with interwoven themes and imagery and a final appeal.

The first three chapters contain the only two prose sections of the prophecy. They give the dramatic narrative of God's call to Hosea to marry and have children. But this is no ordinary marriage: His wife is, or will become, faithless, possibly even being or becoming a prostitute. Hosea is told to rescue her from her faithlessness, but he finds he has to buy her back (3:2). Having done that, he stipulates a period of celibacy before marital relations can be resumed (3:3). Previously, he had two sons and a daughter by her, each one symbolically named.

The whole experience then becomes, in a literary sense, an analogy of God's dealings with Israel, her faithlessness, and God's seeking to restore covenant relations with her, if only she has a change of heart. This is set out in brief in the poetic chapter 2, inserted between the two prose narratives, and then expanded upon as a commentary in the second section, in which chapter 11 particularly parallels the movement of chapter 2, climaxing in the heart cry of 11:8.

The main themes of these chapters may be categorized as follows:

Israel's failings:
- Israel's faithlessness and covenant breaking: 4:1; 5:7; 6:4, 7; 8:1; 9:1, 10; 11:2, 12
- Israel's "spirit of whoredom (prostitution)": 4:12f.; 5:4; 6:10

- Israel's arrogance and self-reliance: 5:5; 10:13; 12:8; 13:1
- Israel's idolatry and religiosity: 4:12f.; 8:4, 6, 11, 13; 9:4; 10:1; 13:1–2
- The failure of its priests: 4:6–9; 5:1f.; 6:9; 10:5
- Her disregard for prophets: 9:7–8; 12:10
- Her rejection of knowledge and her lack of understanding: 4:6, 14; 13:3
- Her failure to repent truly: 6:1–3; 7:14; 8:2, 11; 10:3; 11:5, 7
- Her seeking outside help: 5:13; 7:11; 8:9; 9:3; 12:1; 14:3

God's response:
- God's longing to redeem and be merciful: 6:11; 7:13; 11:4, 8–9; 14:3f.
- God's anger and punishment: 5:10, 14; 6:5; 9:7, 9; 10:2, 10–15; 12:2, 14; 13:7–8
- Specific punishment: ecological disaster: 4:3; 5:7f.; 8:7; 9:2; 13:15
- Specific punishment: military defeat: 5:8–9; 10:14; 11:5–6; 13:16
- Specific punishment: exile: 9:17; 10:5–6
- Promise of better things: 11:9–11; 14:5f.

Hosea includes a number of historical reviews to show God's covenant dealings with the nation: 9:10; 10:9; 11:1–3; 12:3–4, 9–10, 12–13; 13:4–6. He also is aware that the southern kingdom of Judah is not exempt from many of the same sins and so addresses her also: 4:15; 5:5, 10; 6:11; 8:14; 10:11; 11:12; 12:2.

COMMENTARY

The happenings and language of the first three chapters have always grabbed readers and make the book's opening the most memorable of all the prophets. What can God be doing telling a prophet to marry a whore? It would appear to be one of those strange "enacted prophecies" that we find also in Isaiah (20:2–4), Jeremiah (13:1–11; 16:1–4; 19), and Ezekiel (12:3–7). The acting out of the prophecy reinforces it to the listeners as well as giving greater insight to the prophet.

Nevertheless, the first three chapters have been a site of great controversy. For example, it has been argued that for the analogy to fit exactly, Hosea would have needed to marry a pure wife, who then became unfaithful, drifting into desertion and prostitution, since Israel was pure when God chose her. But there is nothing in Hosea's historical reviews that suggests Israel was originally pure, and in Ezekiel's great development of the image, she is anything but (Ezekiel 16).

Other suggestions are that chapters 1 and 3 are parallel narratives of the same event, rather than one following another. But the two-stage narrative parallels chapter 2, the commentary, with its unexpected antithesis after 2:13. This suggests the tension of the prophet, torn between hatred of his wife's unfaithfulness and his continuing and God-given love for her. We must not water down the strong, even unorthodox presentation of God as lover and husband, however shocking it might seem. Hosea does not mention divorce, only separation and redemption. Some discussions have confused the issue by suggesting divorce, but Deuteronomy 24:4 forbids remarrying a divorced wife.

Sexual and marital images of God are used elsewhere in the prophets. We have quoted Ezekiel 16. Ezekiel 23 is another example, as are Jeremiah 3:14 and Isaiah 8:3, including violent images of stripping and nakedness. We need to understand that the term *Baal,* used for the chief cultic fertility god, also means "Master." Hosea 2:7–8, 16 have plays on the words *master* and *husband.* This language of adultery runs throughout the Hebrew Bible in connection with idolatry.

The analogue of faithless wife leads, as we would expect, to a whole range of sexual imagery. "Prostitution" is an ambiguous image, since much Baal worship did involve sexual practices, which to the prophets of the Lord literally entailed prostitution, which, therefore, become synecdochic for all idolatry, as in 4:10–11; 5:3; 6:10. *Adultery* is a term used similarly in 4:14 and 7:4, and *illegitimacy* in 5:7. Other related images are of birth, miscarrying, and infanticide (9:12–16; 13:13). Antithetically, God as the good parent is imaged in 11:1–4, as opposed to the bad mother (Israel) in 2:2; 4:5.

The symbolic naming of children is also a prophetic move, an enacted, unmistakable sign of future hopes or disasters. Isaiah names his son as a sign of impending judgment (Isaiah 8:3), for example. Hosea's naming of his children then forms a play on words to reverse their meaning (2:1, 23). There is a problem with the naming of *Jezreel,* which is seen metonymically as a punishment on the royal house of Jehu (1:4). The historical account is to be found in 2 Kings 10, but there is no suggestion the massacre is to be punished (v. 17). Ironic wordplay also occurs with place-names. *Jezreel* (1:5) actually means "God plants," whereas its opposite is implied; *Achor* (2:15) means "trouble," whereas again, its opposite is meant.

The complaint, a subgenre briefly mentioned in the Introduction, typically uses forensic (legal) terms within a quasi-courtroom scenario, as we see in Isaiah and Jeremiah. Hosea 4:1, 4; 12:2; and 13:12 are good examples. Moving boundary stones is another crime (5:10). Powerful parallelisms of lawlessness are built up in 7:1, leading into the unusual image of fires of passion being likened to a baker's oven (7:4–5). There is always a correspondence established between evil behavior and the consequences, even if only by a simple *so* or *therefore.* God is not arbitrary.

Otherwise, the imagery is largely natural in a poetry that has a vast amount of figurative language, particularly similes. Images of wind (4:19; 8:7; 12:1; 13:15) jostle with those of wild and domestic animals (5:14; 8:9; 10:11–12; 13:7–8). The latter are applied to Israel's behavior, the former to the consequences of that behavior. Sowing and reaping imagery is the logical expression of this (8:7; 10:12–13). God's activity, however, is also merciful, expressed in disease and curing images (5:13; 6:1; 7:1). Rot and blight are other images of disease (5:12; 9:16).

Interestingly, rain, dew, and mist are used ambiguously, as in the antithesis between 6:3 and 6:4. Spring rains express the hoped-for mercy of God, as the dew of 14:5. But the dew of 6:4 and 13:3 is a metonymy for transience and faithlessness, as is the morning mist of 13:3. The point seems to be the distinction between true and false repentance: They can look alike, and some scholars have even argued that 6:1–3 represents true repentance, when the context must surely suggest its superficiality. Other natural images include birds, wine and grapes, trees, and weeds. Urban imagery is almost entirely lacking.

CHARACTER

Hosea The name means "the LORD's salvation" or "May the LORD save." Apart from his marriage to Gomer and his three children by her, nothing is told of him. The use of natural rather than urban images would suggest perhaps a countryman. He is not well acquainted with the court or politics, except in a general way. His message is not denunciatory but pleading; his experience of marriage suggests a merciful, loving, and patient man.

Isaiah

The PROPHECY of Isaiah is the longest of all the prophetic books in terms of chapters. In the Christian Old Testament and in most versions of the Hebrew Bible it stands first of the prophetic books.

The prophet Isaiah was active in the period 750–700 B.C.E. The first verse (1:1) puts him as living through the reigns of four kings of the southern kingdom of JUDAH: Uzziah (or Azariah, 792–740 B.C.E.), Jotham (740–735 B.C.E.), Ahaz (735–716 B.C.E.), and Hezekiah (716–687 B.C.E.). This was the period of Assyrian domination. Tiglath-Pileser III reigned 745–727 B.C.E.; Shalmaneser V, 727–722 B.C.E.; Sargon, 722–705 B.C.E.; and, most sig-

Isaiah prophesies the suffering servant (Isaiah 53:4–12), engraving by Julius Schnorr von Carolsfeld

nificantly, Sennacherib; 705–681 B.C.E. For part of that time, Babylonia was an independent kingdom that became a factor in the political machinations of Judean foreign politics.

These are well-documented facts. The area of controversy is the book's authorship. Was the prophet Isaiah the author of all 66 chapters, or did he, in fact, only write the first 39 chapters, and a later prophet or prophets continue the book? The general scholarly opinion is that there was a so-called Deutero-Isaiah (Second Isaiah) writing somewhat later, but in the tradition of first Isaiah, after the Assyrian Empire had fallen to the Babylonians in 612 B.C.E. and during the Babylonian EXILE. The date of Cyrus I of PERSIA, who reigned 559–530 B.C.E. and was the conqueror of the Babylonians and the restorer of the exiles to Israel in 538 B.C.E., is crucial to such discussions. It would suggest a period of writing between 559–539 B.C.E. for chapters 40–55, where Cyrus is mentioned. This places its writing some 150 years after Isaiah. There is also considerable support for a "Trito-Isaiah" as the author of chapters 56–66, as they seem to refer to an even later period than those of Deutero-Isaiah, after the first return of the exiles.

These arguments about authorship have been conducted at various levels. For instance, there is the theoretical concern that if the book is divided between a known author and unknown authors claiming to be someone they are not, then the authenticity, even the inspiration, of the book is compromised. Historically, the book had always been regarded as a unity from the earliest Qumran manuscripts (see DEAD SEA SCROLLS) till historical-critical methods were developed in the nineteenth century. One of these methods developed the more literary argument that the style seems to change after chapter 39. But even if this is true—and it is debatable—it is not a clinching argument. Shakespeare's style changed considerably over 20 years, and his last play looks very different from his first.

Fundamentally, the real debate is the literary-theological one over the very nature of prophecy. There is always a tension in biblical prophecy between the immediate situation of the utterance and its first audience; the actual reference of that utterance, whether present or future; and the reading of that utterance for us now as present-day readers. Great literature is universal, speaking to every generation, not a historical museum piece awaiting carbon dating. But does its universality lie in the depiction of God and his dealings with his people in a historic context? Or in a timeless future? Or, more narrowly, in its "correctness" at depicting then-future but now-past events, especially concerning the coming of the Messiah?

The best way to resolve these questions lies in considering the sense of urgency of the prophecies. To be urgent is to speak to the present of the first hearers, here the inhabitants of Jerusalem and Judah, either in situ or in exile, even though the fullness of the truth of that speaking may not be fully apparent till later. And Isaiah is nothing if not urgent. The direction of this emphasis is certainly to see the later part of Isaiah to have been delivered later, but by someone or some others who see themselves in the tradition of Isaiah and who understand his vision. The anxiety over discontinuity should not blind us to the essential continuity in prophetic emphasis on a righteous God who loves his people but who will not compromise the present or the future in order to achieve his purposes. These purposes are universal, beyond the narrow confines of Judah, but nevertheless, God's people have a central role to play in them.

This unity of message and urgency, rising toward a cosmic vision, achieved for the book a place of supreme importance in the New Testament, where it is quoted more times than any other prophetic book, and in the historic formulations of christology.

SYNOPSIS

Section I: Present Despair and Future Hope (Chapters 1–12)

This first section of 12 chapters can be further subdivided into five units:

1. Chapters 1–5: a rehearsal of some of the main themes that are going to run through the whole book:
   - God is a holy God. (The phrase "The Holy One of God" is generally only to be found in this book.)
   - The moral behavior of his people at present offends him deeply, especially in the lack of social justice, idolatry, and insincere worship.
   - There will be punishment for this in an invasion and subsequent devastation of the land.
   - After the devastation, there will be restoration and good governance.

2. Chapter 6: an account of Isaiah's calling to be a prophet and the message he is to deliver.

3. Chapters 7–9: an account of the northern kingdom of ISRAEL (Jacob) threatening Judah in the time of King Ahaz (ca. 735 B.C.E.). Prophecies are given against Israel of a similar nature to those against Judah.

4. Chapters 10–11: the theme of restoration is put in the context of Assyria, which is seen both as an instrument of God's purposes and as an object of his anger. The concept of a righteous remnant is elaborated. This will be a united remnant, consisting of representatives from both the northern kingdom and the southern.

5. Chapter 12: the section is concluded with a psalmlike hymn of praise.

Section II: Oracles against Other Countries (Chapters 13–24)

WOES AND DENUNCIATIONS against Israel's neighboring countries are a commonplace among the Hebrew prophets. For example, the prophecy of Jeremiah contains a long section (Jeremiah 46–51) containing a series of woes against most of the countries Isaiah also addresses. Section I contained one against Assyria (10:24–34). In this second section, there is a more organized list.

- 13:1–14:23
  21:1–10   Babylon
- 14:24–27   Assyria
- 14:28–32   The PHILISTINES
- 15:1–16:14   Moab
- 17:1–3, 9–14   Damascus (SYRIA, Aram)
- 17:4–8   Israel (i.e., the northern kingdom)
- 18:1–7   Cush (Ethiopia)
- 19:1–20:6   EGYPT, with a historical note
- 21:11–12   Edom
- 21:13–17   Arabia (Kedar)
- 23:1–18   Tyre and Sidon (Phoenicia, LEBANON)

In chapter 22, Isaiah turns his denunciation back on his home city of Jerusalem, and in the final chapter of the section, chapter 24, there is a concluding apocalyptic scenario of a worldwide devastation as part of God's judgment and his reign in Jerusalem.

Section III: Judgment and Blessing (Chapters 25–35)

Section III should be seen in continuity with the preceding section, since it contains a number of further woes against nations or certain foreign policies. However, these are balanced by chapters of promise of future blessing and divine intervention. In this balance it is more akin to Section I, but this time it has less to do with the moral state of Judah and Jerusalem.

Chapters 25–26 form a bridge between the two sections. The sense of judgment gives way to an apocalyptic vision when God "will swallow up death forever." This naturally leads into a song of praise. Of the other nations, only Moab is briefly mentioned. The vineyard imagery seen in Section I is reintroduced in chapter 27, with the idea of returning from exile to "worship the LORD on the holy mountain in Jerusalem."

Chapter 28 is the first of the woes: against the northern kingdom, here called Ephraim. This is balanced by chapter 29 against the southern kingdom, especially Jerusalem, here called Ariel. Chapters 30–31 are denunciations against its foreign policy of relying on Egypt. A further woe occurs in Chapter 34, which begins as if a summarizing woe, as in chapter 24, but turns into a particular one against Edom, much longer than the one of 21:11–12.

The remaining chapters (32–33; 35) deal with various aspects of the future kingdom, where peace and righteousness will be restored, together with a just king, prosperity, and the return of the redeemed, when "everlasting joy shall be upon their heads."

Section IV: Isaiah's Interventions with King Hezekiah (Chapters 36–39)

We now turn to a short mainly narrative section, relating three dramatic interventions made by Isaiah at a time of national emergency. The first such intervention was made at the time of the approach of a huge Assyrian army to Jerusalem itself in 701 B.C.E. Chapter 36 gives us a detailed account of the message delivered by the Assyrian commanders to King Hezekiah and the people of Jerusalem: basically, surrender or else.

In chapter 37, Isaiah is sent for; he tells the king not to be afraid. The Assyrian commander is then called away to rejoin the main Assyrian army under King Sennacherib on hearing of the approach of an Egyptian army. Isaiah then delivers a much fuller denunciation of the Assyrians, who are mysteriously struck down by "the angel of the LORD," 185,000 men dying overnight. That ends the Assyrian campaign, and the last we hear of Sennacherib is his death at the hands of his two eldest sons.

Chapter 38 tells of another encounter, probably occurring a year or so before the last one. King Hezekiah was mortally ill. Isaiah is sent for, and he intercedes for the king, who then recovers. The chapter ends with Hezekiah's psalm of praise. The final chapter of the section deals with a mistaken attempt by Hezekiah to enlist Babylonian help, again probably a few years before the other incidents. Isaiah tells Hezekiah of God's displeasure at this act and announces that everything Hezekiah showed off about will eventually be taken to Babylon.

Section V: A New Beginning (Chapters 40–55)

The next two sections contain no narrative by which we may date them. The name of Isaiah is not even mentioned. Many of the themes of the first 39 chapters are continued, but a significant number of new themes emerge.

In this section, the prophet writes of a present Babylonian captivity, from which he is utterly certain God will deliver them and give them a wonderful new start as they return to Jerusalem. But the new start will not be in terms of a new secular domination of the world but as a servant who will witness to God's mercy.

Eight predominating themes can be singled out. The sections marked (*) are the key sections to look at, though all other references help to build up the total picture. As can be seen, the themes are interwoven throughout the section.

1. New things: "See, the former things have come to pass, and new things I now declare" (42:9;

also 43:18–19; 44:3–5; 48:6b). This will primarily be in terms of new blessings and an outpouring of God's Spirit.

2. DELIVERANCE: God's desire is for the future welfare of his people. This is a theme continued from the first part, which absolutely predominates here, giving a very positive message of hope (40:11, 29–31; *41:10f.; *43:2, 18f.; 44:26–28; *46:3–4; *49:8f.; *51:3f.; 52; 54:1f.; 55:6–7). In this deliverance, God is sometimes seen as *Rescuer* (42:22; 46:4; 49:24–26; 51:15); sometimes as *Gatherer* (43:6; 49:12); and sometimes as *Comforter* (51:12; 52:9).

3. REDEMPTION: This could be seen as a part of deliverance, but it does mark a much greater emphasis than in the first 39 chapters, where redemption is mentioned only occasionally. There is an idea of buying back, enshrined in the ritual sacrifices of the PENTATEUCH. Here perhaps it is more of God as the "kinsman-redeemer," buying back his people out of slavery (43:1, 14; 44:6, 23–24; 47:4; 48:17; 49:26; 52:3, 9; 54:5). In the Hebrew Bible, it was the responsibility of the nearest relative or kinsman to readjust past family wrongs or disasters (Numbers 5:5–8; Ruth 3:12).

4. The past is forgiven: The punishment threatened in the first 39 chapters has been given, and the promise is that God will no longer be angry. A line has been drawn under the past (40; 42:23–25; 44:22; 48:1–6, *8–11; 49:19f.; 50:1f.; 51:17f.).

5. God's sovereignty: The sense of God's holiness and power is continued from the previous sections. The phrase "The Holy One of Israel" is one of the book's great unifying phrases, though in this section it is often linked to the term *Redeemer*. His sovereignty is seen in six ways:

   (a) He is Creator of the whole world (42:5; 44:24; 45:7, 12, 18; 48:13; 51:16).

   (b) This means he is Lord over the whole world (40:15, *21–31; 45:7; 50:2–3; 54:5). This emphasizes the insignificance of humans (40:15–17, 22–24; 45:9).

   (c) He is the *only* God (43:10; 44:5–6; 45:5–6; 46:9).

   (d) He plans or ordains everything that happens (41:1–4; 45:13, 21; *46:10–13; 48:3, 14; 55:9).

   (e) These plans and God's nature are beyond human comprehension (40:12–14; 55:8–9).

   (f) He uses secular kings in his plans, specifically Cyrus (44:28; 45; 46:11; 48:14–15).

6. Israel is his servant: This is quite a new theme and is developed in wholly new ways, in fact quite uniquely at times. No longer is there a messianic emphasis on a righteous king, but of a humble, even suffering servant (41:8–9; *42:1–7; 43:10; 44:1–2, 21; 48:20; *49:2f.; 50:4–10; *52:13–53:12).

7. God continues to establish a covenant with his people, who are here called Israel, rather than Judah, as in the earlier sections. In other words, the prophet resumes using the earlier name for the whole people of God (42:6; 49:8; 54:10; 55:3). The covenant is seen as a "Covenant of Peace," with *peace* a word that is carried over from earlier (here seen in 48:18, 22; 52:7; 54:10; 55:12).

8. The futility of idolatry: a theme that continues from the earlier sections (40:18–20; 41:5–7, 21–24; 42:17; *44:6–20; 46:1–2, 5–7).

Section VI: Universal Peace, Justice, and Deliverance (Chapters 56–66)

A good deal of the thematic material of the previous section is continued in this one. However, there is no mention of exile or captivity, and what little historical context there is suggests a period immediately after the return of the exiles to Israel and the initial reconstruction of Jerusalem. Chapters 58; 63–64; 66 all suggest a period when exiles have returned but have not yet started any sort of rebuilding program. Chapter 56 suggests the temple has been rebuilt, 60 that the walls are not yet rebuilt, while 61 and 62 suggest the walls are being rebuilt or have been completed. The remaining three chapters (57; 59; 65) give us no sort of context at all.

The prophet expresses similar concerns to those voiced by Zechariah and Haggai, both of whom can be dated to the reign of Darius (522–486 B.C.E.). As the first returnees can be dated at 536 B.C.E., this could well be the sort of period of these prophecies.

Many scholars want to suppose a third or more prophets as author of these chapters. But there is no need to: The circumstances have changed, but if Section V is anything to go by, the prophet of that section would have been the first to sign up to return to Israel. This would make him an older contemporary of Haggai, therefore. In view of the maturity of much of the writing, it would be difficult to imagine many other prophets with the ability to write at this sort of theological and literary level. Much later dates for these chapters seem unnecessary.

There is, however, some new thematic material, especially concerned with "the nations." There is a brief reference in 2:2–4 to the surrounding nations' seeing Jerusalem as the moral and spiritual center of the world. The prophet now revives this vision in many of the chapters (56:7; 60:3–12; 61:6; 62:2; 63:6; 66:12, 19). There are two facets of this vision: first, that "the wealth of the nations" will pour into Jerusalem in a new material prosperity that will be part of a wider era of peace, social justice, and righteousness. Chapter 60 is the fullest expression of this and can be paralleled by passages in Haggai (2:7–9) and Zechariah (2:5; 6:15). This is also allied to previous Isaianic hopes of a full return and restoration, also expressed here in 57:18; 59:20–21; 61:4; 62; and 66:20.

But the other facet is that here will be a place of judgment (cf. 59:18–19; 66:14–16, 22–24). The two facets are not deliberately balanced, since the judgment will also fall on those within Israel who have not reformed. Another new theme, only hinted at, is an enlarged community (56:4–8) and an enlarged priesthood to serve in the temple (61:6; 66:21). Unlike Ezekiel, the prophet otherwise has little interest in the membership or worship of the new temple, except negatively; that too much store should not be put on the system of sacrifices (58; 66:3–4).

Most of the themes of the previous section or sections are resumed:

- God as the Holy One of Israel (57:15; 60:9, 14)
- God as Redeemer (and Savior in 60:16; 63:8)
- The centrality of righteousness, since God is righteous above all (*57; 59:16; 60:17; 61:10; *62:1–2; 66:2b)
- The covenant (56:4, 6; 59:21; 61:8)
- Peace (57:2, *19–21; 59:8; 60:17; 66:12), to which may be added joy (61:7), a new thing, especially a "new heaven and a new earth," and including a "never again such punishment" clause (62:8; *65:17; 66:22)

Moreover, we return in places to the world of the first three sections, to the "bad old days," where there is a general state of unrighteousness, manifested in idolatry (57:1–13; 65:3–7, 11f.; 66:17), false worship (58; 66:3–4), and failure to keep the Sabbath meaningful (56:2–6; 58:13). Significantly, there is only one reference to the great new theme of the previous section, servanthood, in 65:8, 13–14, where servants and a remnant become conflated; nor to the earlier theme of a righteous king. God is the only sovereign. Israel's witness and salvation are not so much through servanthood as through being a "light to the nations" (60:3) in the sense of showing the righteous nature of God and the blessings that brings. Chapter 59 gives us the best summary of the overall message of this section.

COMMENTARY

Section I: Present Despair and Future Hope (Chapters 1–12)

One of the more dramatic chapters in a dramatic opening section is chapter 6, detailing Isaiah's vision, call, and commissioning as a prophet. In fact, the calling is more dramatic even than that of Jeremiah (Jeremiah 1:4–19) or of Ezekiel (1:1–28). What surprises us is that it is not placed first, as with Jeremiah and Ezekiel. It is perhaps symptomatic that Isaiah never emerges as a forceful individual in his own right. We never see him arguing with God, as Jeremiah does, nor in many confrontations with opponents. He is very much a mouthpiece for God, and personal details are limited to the fact that he was married and had two sons, who were both named in an act of symbolic reenactment (8:1–4, 18; 7:3). Chapter 5 represents one of the few cases where Isaiah speaks in the first person (others are 8:1–5, 18).

So it is his message that is placed first. Only then does an account of his calling authenticate him personally as the messenger. The vision of a holy God is central to our understanding of his message, however. The phrase "the Holy One of Israel" has to be seen in the context of this vision. It occurs seven times in this opening section (1:4; 5:19, 24; 8:13; 10:17, 20; 12:6) but then echoes throughout the rest of the book (17:7; 29:23; 30:11f.; 31:1; 37:23; etc.), occurring as many times after chapter 39 as before it: one of the book's great unifying phrases.

Another recurrent phrase of central importance is "on that day," with variations in the form of "the last days," "a day," and "latter time." The last variant is in antithesis to "former time" (9:1), and whether stated or not, this is the antithesis that has to be understood. *Now* is a time of failure and unrighteousness; *then* God is going to act decisively to restore the balance in terms of righteousness and good government (2:2, 12, 17, 20; 3:7; 4:2; 7:18, 20–21, 23). The last few references in chapter 7 form a particularly rhetorical parallelism, with vivid images of flies from Egypt, bees from Assyria, shaving heads, and metonymies of plenty (curds and honey) and desolation (briers and thorns). See also IMAGERY, BIBLICAL.

The failure of the present is conveyed in a series of short parallel images. For example, 1:2–3 contrasts the natural obedience of domestic animals to the rebelliousness of God's people. The result is similarly expressed in a series of similes: "like a booth in a vineyard," "like a shelter in a cucumber field," and "like a besieged city" (1:8). Interestingly, the doom in this first chapter suggests a country already devastated, whereas the country portrayed in 2:1–4:1 suggests some considerable prosperity, attested by historians as being the result of a period of peace before Assyria began its expansionist policies under Sennacherib. The incidents recorded in chapters 7–9 suggest Judah was put under considerable pressure by its neighbors, which may have resulted temporarily in conditions described in chapter 1. It is interesting that the writers of the historical books of 2 Kings and 2 Chronicles judge that only Ahaz was a completely bad king of the four kings Isaiah lived under (2 Chronicles 27:2; 28:1–2, 22; 29:2). The judgment of Uzziah's reign was mixed (2 Chronicles 26:5, 16). The view of

Isaiah in this first section is that every reign was a moral failure (but see 2 Chronicles 27:2).

The prosperity of chapters 2–3 merely led to wasteful and luxurious living by the rich (3:16; cf. 5:9). It did nothing to redress the underlying moral failures of injustice (1:17, 21–23; cf. 5:8), idolatry (1:29; 2:6, 20), and formal worship (1:11–15). Jeremiah, almost 150 years later, complained of exactly the same failures (e.g., Jeremiah 5:26–31; 7:1–11; 10:1–16).

The simile of the vineyard (1:8, referred to again in 3:14) grows in importance in 5:1–7, where it becomes a symbol for God's people themselves, made explicit in 5:7. This is one of the many instances of the New Testament's picking up on Isaianic imagery, in this case, Jesus' using the vineyard in a parable of the failure of Israel to recognize him as its Messiah (Matthew 21:33–44; Mark 12:1–9; Luke 20:9–16). Jeremiah makes a similar allusion (Jeremiah 12:10). The use of this symbolic analogy is as if there were a courtroom in which God was pleading a case against his people (5:4), a move picked up from 1:18–20: "Come now, let us argue it out, says the LORD." In the latter, God is still hopeful of persuasion; in the former, he asks whether he could do anything else but punish. There follows a vivid series of woes against the rich, especially the rich women, graphically describing their fate—an extension of 3:18–24. The detailed lists of sin and punishment suggest both firsthand observation and an exact sense of punishment, like for like. In 9:8–21, the thrice-repeated refrain "Yet for all this his anger has not turned away" (9:12, 17, 21) underscores God's anger. Zephaniah also uses the courtroom scenario (Zephaniah 3:8).

Counterbalancing the failure of the present are, first, the promise of the future in a renewed temple to be the central worship focus for the nations (2:1–4), and, second, the return of a righteous remnant (10:20–27; 11:10–16). Both are concepts central to the message of the prophets, for example, of Isaiah's contemporary, Micah (Micah 2:12–13; 4:6; 5:7; etc.).

The opening section is remarkable historically in the number of passages that have been interpreted messianically in the New Testament and, subsequently, by the Christian Church. The vineyard image has been mentioned. A similar image, that of the branch (4:2), is picked up again in 11:1 as a prophecy of a future Davidic king (Jesse was David's father) and the nature of his peaceful reign ("the wolf shall lie down with the lamb"). It must be noted that first the image had entered prophetic tradition, as in Jeremiah 23:5–6; Zechariah 3:8; 6:12. Other parts of a vine or tree figuratively mentioned are "stump" (6:13) and "shoot" (11:1). The seven attributes of the Spirit (11:2) have found their way into early Christian formulations of the Holy Spirit, and the verse is echoed at Jesus' baptism (John 1:32). The vine imagery stands in contrast to the tree images of 1:29–30; 10:33–34, which signify pride.

Even more interesting is the case of 7:14. Many scholars see the figure used in the paragraph to mean that if Ahaz trusted the Lord for his foreign policy, then a child just born would grow up in peace and plenty. But the New Testament writers took the symbolic name of this child, *Immanuel* (God with us), as one of the titles of Jesus Christ. They also saw in one of the possible meanings of the Hebrew word for "young woman" as "virgin," a prediction of the virgin birth of Christ (Matthew 1:23; cf. Luke 1:34). Isaiah repeats the name in 8:8, addressing him directly and calling the land "your land," and in 8:10, where the NRSV translates it "for God is with us."

The third messianic passage is 9:1–7. The mention of the word *Galilee* in 9:1 is striking. Although this term for northern Israel goes back to Joshua 20:7, it is not a common term. It can be understood why it was used as a reference to Jesus Christ, whose parents were from Galilee and who lived and ministered there for a significant portion of his life (Matthew 4:12–16; Luke 1:26; 2:4). But it is 9:6–7 that is the passage used messianically in later Jewish and Christian thinking: the promise of a Davidic reign of righteousness, but in terms of a child. In the gospel of Luke, the angel's annunciation to Mary of her pregnancy specifically mentions this Davidic throne (Luke 1:32).

Section II: Oracles against Other Countries (Chapters 13–24)

The first denunciation against Babylon seems surprising, as Section I has focused on Assyria, the major power of Isaiah's time and the one that was both to be God's instrument of punishment and the recipient of his judgment. Some scholars have felt this was a later addition, when Babylon had actually become the dominant power, as it was in Jeremiah's and Ezekiel's time, some hundred years later. Certainly, the language used is very similar to Jeremiah chapters 50–51, and there is a second, much vaguer woe against Babylon in 21:1–10, more in keeping with its contemporary status as a weaker power. However, these oracles are not arranged in any specific chronological order, and Babylon was for a time acting independently of Assyria under Merodach-Baladan from 721 to 711 B.C.E., as chapter 39 shows.

Certainly, the language of Isaiah 13 is powerfully apocalyptic: the first 13 verses describing the devastation of battle and the next three verses the chaos afterward. These scenes are seen as "the day of the LORD" (6, 9, 13). Isaiah 13:17–22 predicts the destruction of Babylon by the Medes (Persians). The image of owls as a sign of devastation in 13:21 is repeated in 14:23 and 34:11,13, and used by other prophets, such as Jeremiah (Jeremiah 50:39) and Zephaniah (Zephaniah 2:14). Other wild animals, including hyenas, jackals, and goats, become metonymies of an uninhabitable land.

Chapter 14 is introduced by the promise of restoration and reunion with the northern kingdom, as in 11:12. Then follows a pure example of the "taunt song," which could be seen as a subgenre of the woes genre. It follows dramatically the entry of the Babylonian rulers into the underworld, climaxing in 14:13–16, which describes in terms worthy of Greek tragedy the hubris or overweening pride that sought to reach the heavens only to be brought down to hell, or Sheol. Jesus half quotes it in Luke 10:18, where he applies it to SATAN.

The following woes are less dramatic, but some are noteworthy for various features. For example, within the woe against Assyria, there is a sense of a cosmic vision in 14:26. Isaiah is not rehearsing local grudges against bad neighbors: He has a sense of God's plan for the whole political system of earth. The oracle against Philistia can be exactly dated, one of the few examples of specific dates. The year that King Ahaz died would have been

716 B.C.E. A similar woe is to be found in Jeremiah 47 and Zephaniah 2:4–7.

The long oracle against Moab (chapters 15–16) contains what would seem firsthand accounts of what a defeated nation would look like in those days. It is the details that startle us today. The prophet is caught up in the tragedy of Moab's destruction (15:5; 16:9). Unlike the Babylonian oracle, Isaiah is not rejoicing over Moab's defeat, even though Moab's hubristic pride is mentioned (16:6). It was obviously a beautiful and fertile country. Isaiah 16:13–14 seems to be an addition, dating the prediction to three years in the future. The parallel woe in Jeremiah 48 similarly mentions its fertility, especially in terms of its vineyards, but is far less sympathetic. Zephaniah 2:8–11 has a similar woe against Moab and Ammon.

The woe against Damascus, paralleled in Jeremiah 49:23–27, is mixed in with one against the northern kingdom (17:3). This may be because of the Syria-Israel alliance mentioned in Isaiah 7:1–9, dated to 734 B.C.E. For a period, the two countries had locked their fortunes together. Isaiah 17:12–14 is a poetic generalization, typical of the Psalms. Isaiah is truly as much a poet as a prophet. His handling of imagery and facility in switching from specific to general are a poet's abilities.

The oracle against Cush (Ethiopia) probably refers not so much to Ethiopia itself as the Ethiopian rulers of Egypt at the time. There does seem to be some specific geographical knowledge here (18:2) that again suggests Isaiah was a well-educated man with access to travelers. Other specific references are to the racial features of the Ethiopians, though the rest of the woe is fairly generalized to failures of harvest. Many of the woes finish with a final prediction of acknowledgment of the LORD and of Zion as his dwelling (18:7; cf. 14:32; 16:5; 17:7).

The oracle against Egypt, paralleled by Jeremiah 46, is given in terms of civil war and drought. The language switches to prose from 19:16–20:6 and is structured by paragraphs beginning "in that day" (19:16, 19, 23). Chapter 20 stands apart from the woe structure of the surrounding chapters, giving a precise dating (20:1), the Assyrian king Sargon's attack on Philistia, where he crushed an Egyptian-

Philistine coalition in 711 B.C.E. Judah had had the wit to keep out of this coalition, and it is Isaiah's advice, as it was Jeremiah's, to avoid any reliance on Egypt. Isaiah demonstrates this by an enacted prophecy of going naked and barefoot (20:3) for three years. In a society where nakedness was considered deeply shameful (47:1–3), this must have been an excruciatingly difficult enactment to make. Ezekiel has to make a similar embarrassing enactment, which he does manage to modify a little (Ezekiel 4:1–5:4).

The image of the prophet as a watchman is a recurring one, used in the oracle against Babylon (21:8) and Edom (21:11; elsewhere 52:8; 56:10; 62:6; cf. Ezekiel 3:17; 33:1–9). Isaiah fills out the prophecy against Edom in 34:5f. Obadiah also denounces Edom, as does Jeremiah (Obadiah 1–14; Jeremiah 49:7–22), doubtless inspired by Edom's faithlessness in the siege of Jerusalem. The oracle against Tyre (or Phoenicia) and its trading colonies has no equivalent in Jeremiah. Isaiah sees her trade as prostitution (23:16–17) and predicts a 70-year period of oblivion, the same period Jeremiah predicts for the EXILE in Babylon for the Judeans.

The oracle against Jerusalem reminds them that God's judgment comes on all nations: There are no exemptions, as Jeremiah also has to emphasize. Mixed in with predictions of a siege are specific names of officials, as though Isaiah is well aware of palace corruption (22:15, 20).

The final chapter of the section is a summary of the preceding woes. The powerful parallelisms of 24:2 suggest the universality of judgment as Isaiah's language again takes on apocalyptic proportions. The imagery of earthquakes is typical of such language, as is that of revelry brought suddenly to an end (24:7–12 anticipates the language of Lamentations). But again, it finishes with the focus on the Lord's reign on Mount Zion in Jerusalem.

Section III: Judgment and Blessing (Chapters 25–35)

After the woes and denunciations of the preceding section, it is something of an oasis to reach chapters 25–26, which at times sound like psalms in their praise and lyricism. The two chapters, besides being a bridge passage, demonstrate the twofold voice of the prophet. He is not only the voice of God, the bearer of divine oracles, but also a human representative of his people, offering praise or petitions to God. It is in the latter voice as praise giver and intercessor that we see his personality (see also chapter 33).

The prophet is responding in his own, at times passionate voice to the cosmic vision of God's righteousness. Although this may have seemed to be expressed predominately in terms of judgment hitherto, Isaiah's apocalyptic vision and sense of God's holiness are tempered by his sense of God's grace and mercy, by the vision of peace in the future just reign of God. The word *peace* echoes through this subsection, for example, 26:3, 12 (cf. 30:15), as do natural images of fertility (25:6).

This future vision is well seen in the parallel structures of chapter 25, marked by the refrain "On this mountain" (25:6, 7, 10). So we have promises of feasts and banquets, the end of death itself and sorrow, and the removal of human pride exemplified in the defeat of Moab. The apocalyptic nature of the language of the end time is picked up by the writer of Revelation (Revelation 7:17; 21:4) in the New Testament.

The main imagery, however, relates to fortified cities. There is an antithesis between cities torn down (25:2, 12; 26:5) and cities built up (26:1). The "this mountain" reference is to Mount Zion, that is, Jerusalem, so in a way, that is another city reference. The broken city is a metonymy of hubristic pride; the secure city, of peace and security (25:4, 9; 26:3). Isaiah 32:2 picks this up as part of the righteous king's rule. The central idea of refuge and security, also central in the Psalms (e.g., Psalm 18:2; 42:9), takes form also in the image of the "rock" (26:4; 30:29; 32:2; and later 44:8; 51:1).

One of the other noteworthy features of this whole section is the prophet's developing sense of death, resurrection, and hell. Isaiah 26:19 suggests resurrection. This may be merely figurative: the people who have lived in poverty ("dust") will now experience new life in the messianic kingdom. But with the reference to 25:8, "he will swallow up death for ever"; the reference in the last section to the underworld (14:9–15); and the

later reference to this as "Topheth" (30:33), it would be more natural to see all such references as the beginnings of a developed view of the afterlife and God's control over that. It may be surprising to know that a concept of the afterlife in earlier Hebrew literature was not well developed, but a look at Job 17:16 or Psalm 88:4–5 would be enough to demonstrate this.

Chapters 27–28 return to the northern kingdom, variously called Israel, Jacob, or Ephraim. The vineyard image from chapter 5 is now applied to Israel (25:6) and the promise of return from exile from Assyria and Egypt to worship at Mount Zion. At the time of writing, of course, the northern kingdom had set up its own shrines for worship. But the promise is followed by a denunciation against "the drunkards of Ephraim" (28:1, 3, 7–8). It would seem that literal fact is used metonymically for confusion of truth. This would parallel the otherwise strange image of covering in 25:7. Later references to sight and hearing also suggest the prophet's concern that people discern the truth correctly. That, after all, is the prophetic duty.

From 28:14 he turns to those "who rule this people in Jerusalem." They have made a "covenant with death" rather than one with God (28:14, 18). The image he sets against this is that of the "precious cornerstone," another metaphor of building, so that "One who trusts will not panic"—the peace motif again.

There are two images of stones in the Bible that need concern us at this point: the cornerstone metaphor here (28:16) and the capstone or "chief cornerstone" one of Psalm 118:22. Some versions use the term *cornerstone* for both stones, but what is meant here is the foundation stone, whereas the Psalms reference is to the locking stone that holds an arch in place at its highest point. Isaiah has previously used the image of a "stone of stumbling" in 8:14 (Authorized [King James] Version). All refer to God. The New Testament quotes all three images, applying them to Christ. Matthew 21:42 quotes the Psalm, as do Acts 4:11 and 1 Peter 2:7. But Peter also quotes the other two verses: 1 Peter 2:6 quotes the Isaiah verse here, while 1 Peter 2:8 quotes the earlier Isaiah verse. Romans 9:33 combines both Isaiah verses into one, while Romans

10:11 quotes the second half only, "No one who believes in him shall be put to shame." Last, Ephesians 2:20 uses the image as part of another image of the church as building. This is a good example of both the importance of the image to New Testament writers and the way imagery is adapted from the Hebrew Bible to the New Testament.

Further building images of "measuring line" and "plumb line" occur in the next verse, echoing Amos 7:7–8.

The woe against Jerusalem continues in chapter 29, when it is addressed as *Ariel*. This is not a name that occurs elsewhere, and the suggestion is that it is a play on words, since the Hebrew sounds like "altar hearth," as in Ezekiel 43:15. This is the chapter where the prophet's concern about the lack of spiritual understanding is most fully expressed. The unreadability of the sealed scroll (29:11–12) is one taken up in Revelation 5:1–5, via Daniel 12:4, 9.

Chapters 30–31 deal with Judah's foreign policy. The temptation always seems to have been to rely on Egypt when there was a threat from the north. Both Isaiah and Jeremiah denounce such an alliance, correctly seeing the Egyptians as unreliable. For both, the underlying failure is a lack of trust in God's sovereignty. In 30:15 Jeremiah returns to his theme of peace. Only trust in God can yield the inward peace that will lead to wise decisions (30:21). The external enemy, Assyria, will be shattered soon enough (30:31).

The apocalyptic reference to "streams of water" (30:25) is picked up in the next two chapters (32–33). The promise of a messianic king (32:1) carries similes of inner spiritual resources: "like streams in the desert" (32:2). At this stage we need to consider the centrality of this image in Isaiah, and see how it runs throughout the whole book. Whether by one, two, or three authors, we have to acknowledge the unity of imagery here. Up to this point, only 8:6 and 12:3 have mentioned waters. But from here on, the references are more frequent, as in 33:21 ("a place of broad rivers and streams"); 35:6, 7; 41:18–19; 43:19–20; 44:3; 48:21; 49:10. Isaiah 58:11 is similar (a well-watered garden), as is Jeremiah (e.g., Jeremiah 31:12). Isaiah 48:21 refers to the wilderness experience under Moses. In the New Testament, John gives Jesus quoting 12:3 in

John 7:38, picking up on John 4:14, but John 7:39 suggests the writer had Isaiah 32:15 in mind.

The messianic king's reign, then, is marked by fertility, both literal and spiritual. It is also marked, as we have seen previously, by peace (32:17–18) and wisdom (32:3). Chapter 33 represents a heartfelt prayer that this vision soon be accomplished. We feel the tension between the *now* and the *then*.

The last two chapters can be seen antithetically. Chapter 34 deals with fertility becoming desert (as also 33:7–9); chapter 35, with desert becoming fertile. The former chapter begins apocalyptically (34:1–4) but then becomes focused as a woe on Edom, perhaps synecdochic for all such nations. Images of desertification are seen in terms of Sodom and Gomorrah (34:9–10), and images of wild beasts (we have already noted owls and hyenas) as metonyms.

The reverse of chapter 35 is noteworthy in two aspects. First, the image of highways through the desert (35:8) ("the Holy Way") parallels that of streams in the desert. It, too, links all parts of Isaiah: 11:16; 19:23; 33:8; 40:3; 49:11; and 62:10. Second, the use of the term *redeemed* (35:9) rather than *remnant* is significant. The term is mainly used in the Hebrew Bible in the Pentateuch and in Isaiah. In the Law it refers either to the laws concerning redemption, which do not concern us here, or to the idea that Israel has been "redeemed" out of Egypt, the land of slavery, as in Exodus 15:13 (the Song of Moses); Deuteronomy 7:8; 9:26; 15:15; and so on. In Isaiah we have some 13 references, beginning with 1:27 and going through 63:4, 9. Necessarily perhaps, the term *Redeemer* also features, though only after chapter 40. Thus, the new reign will be a new deliverance from Egypt, and the land flowing with milk and honey will be renewed both literally and as metonymies for inward graces and resources by God, who will buy back Israel (not just bring back, as with a remnant) for a second time.

Section IV: Isaiah's Interventions with King Hezekiah (Chapters 36–39)

Most of this material is to be found word for word in 2 Kings 18:17–20:19. This parallels the final chapter of Jeremiah, which again is word for word the same narrative as is found in 2 Kings 24–25. It suggests the editing of Isaiah and the editing of 2 Kings proceeded at much the same time, with materials used for both. Indeed, the complementary account in 2 Chronicles 32 suggests this (2 Chronicles 32:32). We have, in fact, four sources for these events: Isaiah, 2 Kings, 2 Chronicles, and Sennacherib's Assyrian account recorded in the Assyrian capital of Nineveh, one version of which is to be found on the Taylor Prism in the British Museum.

Isaiah's account details only those parts in which he was involved directly or indirectly. The 2 Kings account also details Hezekiah's earlier dealings with the Assyrians, where he asserts his independence and then is made to regret it (2 Kings 18:5–16); and the 2 Chronicles account details Hezekiah's elaborate defense of the city and preparations for war (2 Chronicles 32:1–8), mentioned earlier by Isaiah in 22:8–11. It also spends two chapters on Hezekiah's religious reforms (2 Chronicles 29–31). Both the Kings and Chronicles accounts are united in their high praise of Hezekiah as a person, in his moral and religious stature. Isaiah gives us no sense of this at all. In fact, Isaiah warns against an Egyptian alliance (30:1–4), a warning that may well have been directed against Hezekiah. And his last conversations with the king are all of warning and disaster.

The Assyrian accounts give great details of Sennacherib's conquests, including earlier campaigns, and the siege of Lachish, the second city of Judah, and refer to the Egyptian army. But they give no account of the deaths in the army or the hasty retreat back to Assyria—as we would expect.

Most of the material, therefore, is narrative, possibly not written by Isaiah at all but by the writer of 2 Kings. The detail is so vivid and precise (e.g., "the highway to the Fuller's Field," Isaiah 36:2) that we are talking about an eyewitness account. Chapter 36 is structured around three challenges: The first is that by the Assyrians to Hezekiah: Submit or take the consequences; second, the challenge of language, the first challenge to be made in Aramaic, the common language of the empire, though not understandable at that time to the Judeans, or in Hebrew, the language of the city? The third

challenge is theological: Are Hezekiah's reforms reforms at all or have they merely displeased God? In other words, is God really a fertility god in the shape of the pagan rituals followed by the Assyrians, or is he a single cosmic deity, as worshipped by the Judeans?

Isaiah's prophetic interventions take up this last challenge (37:22–29). Far from being displeased by Hezekiah's reforms, God is insulted by Sennacherib's hubristic pride. In 37:26 God reminds him that he is only an instrument in God's hands (cf. 8:6–8), but now the infamous cruelty of the Assyrians will be turned back against him (37:29).

The other nonnarrative material consists of Hezekiah's psalm of praise on his recovery, the one passage not to be found elsewhere (38:9–20). Its figurative language of sickness is certainly very similar to several psalms, the similes of 38:12–14 especially. It also consists of Isaiah's prophecy to Hezekiah (37:30–35) and brief denunciation of Hezekiah's exhibitionistic display of his wealth to the Babylonian envoys (39:6–7).

It is worth noting, in passing, the importance Isaiah attaches to giving a "sign" to his utterances (37:30; 38:7; cf. 7:11, 14; 19:20; 55:13). The first sign (37:30) will not be immediately apparent but merely the natural result of the fulfillment of his prophecy of rescue and deliverance and is made in terms of natural fertility. But the second sign (38:7) is clearly miraculous and is immediately fulfilled. Symbolically its meaning is that time will indeed go backward and Hezekiah will be granted a longer life span. Compared to Elijah or Elisha, the written prophets are noticeably short on miracles, so this one stands out by its rarity. Needless to say, elaborate accounts have been given of either its fictiveness or, conversely, how it might have literally happened, just as they have for the miracle of the Assyrian deaths. The literary-theological point is that prophetic words are not "just" words; they are signifiers of God's power and have a significance that from time to time needs a sign.

Section V: A New Beginning (Chapters 40–55)
Both thematically and figuratively, these chapters are among the densest of all the prophetic writings. They are also among the most quoted in the New

Testament, some 25 direct quotations and some further 12 echoes or indirect quotations. Some of these quotations identify predictions of, or allusions to, Jesus Christ; others are used more theologically to determine the nature of Christian salvation. They had a dominant effect in the formulation of early Christology.

In a guide such as this, we have to set aside questions of prophetic and literary inspiration that naturally arise. The question, To what extent was the prophet writing beyond what he believed to be true? has to be laid aside with that other question, How did his audience understand his message? With no narrative passages given here, we have no clue as to the prophet, how he came to be speaking in such magnificent language, with such conviction, or how he was received. How did he grasp such hope for the future; how did he formulate concepts not formulated before or, for that matter after?

The synopsis indicated some of the themes that are interwoven throughout this section. Some are picked up from earlier chapters, such as God's holiness and righteousness, peace, and the return from exile and subsequent restoration of Jerusalem (chapter 40). Others are new: God as Redeemer, his redemption, and especially servanthood. We need to examine this latter concept particularly, especially in the so-called Servant Songs (42:1–7; 49:2f.; 50:4–10; 52:13–53:12).

The earliest reference is to Israel as "my servant," paralleled by "Jacob, whom I have chosen" (41:8), repeated in the next verse. This refers the term to the whole nation, and their being elected by God to be his people. The following servant song in chapter 42 proceeds to spell out the features of this servanthood, especially in relation to giving sight (again, a theme from the earlier chapters) and release (42:7). But this is to be done in gentleness ("a bruised reed he will not break" 42:3) rather than in terms of messianic power. "He" is "the servant" in the singular, so the question arises, Does the prophet mean the nation as a collective person, or does he mean a real individual, equivalent to the righteous king of 32:1? The New Testament understood it as referring to the individual Christ (Matthew 11:18–21), and hence the privileging of these

Servant Songs in Christian theology. But in some sense, servanthood must be understood to be part of the prophet's vision for God's people redeemed to fulfill such a role.

The servant song of 49:1–7 could be seen autobiographically: The prophet himself as the servant, as in 20:3. If so, it would be one of the very few personal references by the prophet in this section. The final servant song (52:13–53:12) raises this question again more urgently. Not only does the singular form remain emphatically throughout, but there other voices are introduced: *I/my, we/our, he/his, they*. Who are all these voices? Throughout, the servant is *he*. *I/my* seems to be the voice of God, speaking directly through the prophet, as he does almost the whole section. The *we* seems to be the prophet here speaking as the representative of the people, who become almost onlookers, an audience who misunderstand what they are seeing. The *they* (as in 53:9) seem to be others who are not God's people, perhaps the kings of 52:15. Thus the servant cannot be the people here but rather a representative for the people, the actor of God's will for his people.

His main action is to suffer and be put to death (53:3, 5, 8, 12). But in doing that, he bears away the sins of his people (53:5, 12) and even their diseases (53:4). In this, he is being equated with the sacrifice made as a guilt offering (53:10, referring to Leviticus 5:1–19; 7:1–10), made in the old temple ritual, or even as the "scapegoat" of the Day of Atonement ritual (Leviticus 16:7–10, 15–22, 26–28). The point of the latter ritual was substitutionary atonement, as it is technically called: The sacrifice substitutes for the sinner and bears away his guilt, leaving the individual free of sin.

This is a radical new thinking paradoxically expressed by the prophet in several ways. First, he has ceased to think apocalyptically and in terms of power—quite the reverse. Second, he is looking at the old sacrificial system, which in exile would have been largely abandoned in the absence of a temple, and seeing quite a new way of thinking about it: that instead of animals, a human substitute could be called by God to deal with sin. Isaiah 53:7 likens him to a sacrificial sheep, to answer our sheeplike errors (53:6). This is certainly how the passage was interpreted in the New Testament (Matthew 8:17; Acts 8:32–35; Romans 5:19; 1 Peter 2:24–25).

Having looked at themes, we now need to look briefly at language, especially the richness of the imagery. Images that continue through from the earlier chapters include those of the highway in the desert (40:3; 49:11); water in the desert or deserts becoming fertile (41:18–19; 43:19–20; 44:3; 48:21; 49:10); deafness and blindness (42:7, 16, 18–19; 43:8; 49:9; 50:10); and the Rock (44:8; 51:1). Also continued is the courtroom idea, of God's pleading a case with his people (41:21; 43:26; 45:21).

Of the images introduced for the first time, we have a cluster of female images, especially maternal ones (46:3; 49:15f.; 50:1) of God as mother. Also women in childbirth (42:14), barrenness (54:1), and God as husband (54:5–8)—these are not unique to Isaiah by any means, however. Clothing images occur in 50:9; *51:6 (quoted in Hebrews 1:11–12 and similar to one in Psalm 102:25–27); 51:8. Other images of ephemerality are in 44:22 (morning mist) and 40:6–8 (grass, as in Psalm 102:11, and as there, in antithesis to the enduring Word of God). There are many other nature images: eagles (40:31), antelopes (51:20), willows by flowing streams (44:4), rivers and waves (48:18). There are many appeals to those who live in the coastlands, perhaps of the Mediterranean or the Persian Gulf (41:1; 42:10; 49:1; 51:5). Urban imagery is strangely missing; instead we have nomadic images, such as tents (54:2) and, of course, sheep and shepherds (40:11). Only in chapter 54 do we find urban references in the rebuilding of Jerusalem, where precious stones become metonymies for permanence and richness (54:11–12, echoed later in Revelation 21:11, 19–21). Jerusalem is personified in this strikingly figurative chapter.

As we might expect in a section that deals with return, the Exodus story is a source of imagery, as in 43:16–17; 48:21; 51:9–11; and 52:12. In the latter, the imagery is as much how it will be unlike as how much it will be like ("you shall not go out in haste"). Noah's Flood is also mentioned (54:9). The tone is consolatory more than anything. Much-quoted passages, such as 40:1; 43:1, 4; 49:15–16; 55:1–2, all bear this out in their lyricism.

But there are other tones: the taunt song against Babylon (chapter 47), for example, or exasperation (43:22–28) and sarcasm (44:12–20).

Section VI: Universal Peace, Justice, and Deliverance (Chapters 56–66)

The previous section is written entirely as poetry; hence its nonnarrative arrangement and its dense figurative texture. This section is written similarly, apart from two very brief prose sections (59:21; 66:18–21, 24), with very similar linguistic and structural features. However, the tones and subgenres to be found are much more mixed, as is the imagery, reflecting the much more mixed thematic material. Wonderful visions of the future dawn of righteousness exist now side by side with the reality of a newly emergent society, where many of the faults of the bad old society of preexilic days are manifesting themselves again. This raises questions for the prophet: If God has promised not to punish again as he did in the past, how are these old unregenerate sins to be handled? The same problems confronted the righteous priest and the righteous administrator in the Ezra-Nehemiah narrative, as well as the contemporary prophets, Haggai and Zechariah.

Thus, we have chapters or part-chapters of the same transcendent and universal vision as in the last section, such as chapters 60, 61, and 62. By contrast, we have chapters that are more like woes and denunciations (for example, chapter 58) or are confessions or laments (for example, 59:12–15; 63–64, where the deliverance from Egypt is highlighted, as in earlier sections). And then we have mixed chapters, which probably show most truly the state of the prophet's mind, where he despairs of human reform but then catches at the vision of divine intervention to restore true righteousness, as chapters 56, 57, 59, 65, or 66.

Structurally, the chapters are mixed, going from one subgenre to another, one theme to another. However, the last chapter of the book, which seems to end so negatively with fiery judgment, does bookend the whole prophecy with chapter 1, with which it shares close parallels. For example, heaven and earth are invoked (1:2; 66:1), false offerings are condemned (1:11; 66:3), social injustice is attacked (1:17, 23; 66:5), blessing and judgment are promised (1:19–20; 66:6), as is restoration (1:26–27; 66:10–13). Destruction and judgment by fire are then mentioned, in the same order in both chapters (1:28; 66:15–16), then a further attack on idolatry (1:29–30; 66:17), concluding with the threat of the unquenchable fire of judgment (1:31; 66:24). This structure does suggest some shaping editorial work.

The latter feature of chapter 66 suggests the return of more apocalyptic features to this section, and these are certainly glimpsed, in contrast to their absence in the previous section. However, the two sections do share more obviously a general eschatological vision, which is not expressed in specifically apocalyptic language (e.g., 65:17f.). Much of the imagery is continued from the previous section or sections too. Particularly do we have images of light and darkness (58:8, 10; 59:9; 60:1–3, 19–20; 61:1) and of blindness (56:10; 59:10). Female imagery recurs as figures of childbirth and labor (66:7–9), maternal suckling (60:16; 66:11–12), and marriage (61:10; 62:4–5). Sexual imagery is also linked to idolatry (57:7–8). Other repeat images are to clothing (61:10; 64:6), clay/potter (64:8), and natural images such as oaks, doves, bears, dogs, and reptiles (59:5–6, 11, etc.). A reference to harmony among the animals (65:25) goes back to early Isaiah (11:6–8), one of the eschatological signs.

What does not recur is fertility imagery in terms of water in the desert. Only 58:11 refers to a watered garden; otherwise the imagery begins to be more urban, as we might expect with rebuilding programs: walls, gates, watchtowers, and so on, as in chapter 60.

Other rhetorical devices include the dialogue/argument form also used in earlier courtroom scenarios (58:5–6), with the use of rhetorical questions. The complaint question of 63:17 is quite a theological back-hander! Antithetical parallelisms are particularly noticeable; 65:13–15 is a good example ("My servants . . . but you . . ."); 61:7, another. Examples of metonymy include the conventional one of God's "glorious arm" (63:12).

Voice is again divided, between the prophet as mouthpiece of God and the prophet speaking in his own persona. Direct prayers to God ("O that you would tear open the heavens" 64:1) are dramatically interposed with what appears to be a direct reply ("I was ready . . ." 65:1), though we do not have to read this chapter as a reply to the confession of the last. Examples of the conventional prophetic signal "Thus says the LORD" (66:1) are set against direct rhetorical devices such as "Who is this that comes from Edom . . ." (63:1). The prophet clearly has a range of rhetorical moves at his command, which we are in no way able to predict. We are kept on our toes as readers.

Last, we need to look at reception, at least in terms of the New Testament. We have seen how widely these prophecies were taken up in the New Testament, not just as christological markers, but as theological insights into human sinfulness, salvation, and the end of time. The chapters in this section are just as influential. Verses from these 11 chapters are quoted directly 19 times and indirectly a further seven times, for example, in Revelation, a book that never quotes directly but where chapters 21–22 are heavily dependent on Isaianic imagery. A good example of how pervasive the image transmission is would be 59:17: "He put on righteousness like a breastplate, and a helmet of salvation on his head," which is used by Paul in Ephesians 6:14, where the parallelism has been smoothed out into part of a longer list of figures.

The book of Isaiah has often been seen as a highwater mark for prophetic insight, vision, and prediction. The anxieties over its authorship should not be allowed to cloud what are essentially universal, undated, though not timeless oracles. They speak to us both about the human situation of failure and about a God who allows tremendous revelation into his character and purposes and who desires his people's salvation.

CHARACTERS

Hezekiah   King of Judah 716–687 B.C.E. Though he is regarded by the historians of the Kings and Chronicles narratives to have been an exemplary king, we only see him in three crises with Isaiah, in one of which he has made a serious mistake. Isaiah himself makes no other independent judgment on him, merely reporting God's verdict.

Isaiah   Son of Amoz. He may well have been from the upper class, having free access to the various kings as political adviser or court prophet. He is mentioned a number of times in the historical books of the Hebrew Bible (2 Kings 19:2, 5–7, 20–34; 20:1–11, 14–19; and much more briefly in the parallel account as in 2 Chronicles 26:22; 32:20, 32). He was married to "the prophetess" (8:3) and had two sons, both named symbolically. His initial calling to be a prophet was through a tremendous vision of a transcendent God in the temple, and his message echoed that initial vision of transcendence and holiness. We know little of him as a person except the events surrounding the invasion of the Assyrian army under Sennacherib, where he acts even-handedly as adviser as well as messenger of God to King Hezekiah. He is traditionally presumed to have died in unfavorable circumstances in the reign of Hezekiah's successor, Manasseh.

James

This book begins as a letter by mentioning its author and addressees and as a greeting. It lacks, however, other characteristics of a letter (see EPISTLE) such as references to solidarity between writer and readers, a proper closure, and an overarching theme. For this reason it is considered a tract or a circular letter. Of the books of the New Testament, it is most like the genre of WISDOM LITERATURE in the Hebrew Bible, in particular Proverbs, as well as the apocryphal books Sirach and Wisdom of Solomon. These books all contain collections of pithy sayings with little apparent connection or progress of thought. Yet the contents of James's book can be captured under some overarching headings, as we will see. It also has the directness and the radicalism of the PROPHETS of Israel, for example, in its criticism of the rich and defense of the poor.

The introductory verse refers to the author only as James, prompting the question of who of the several people called James in the Bible is meant here. The one serious candidate for the authorship is James, the brother of Jesus, who was also the leader of the church in Jerusalem. As such, he had the position to refer to himself simply as "James" without further introduction. Because it seems that James reacts to (misrepresentations of) the teaching of the apostle Paul, the letter probably stems from the last part of his life, so the late 50s or early 60s of the first century C.E. The letter was probably known to the author of 1 John. It is written in good Greek, and its imagery reflects the influence of Hellenistic culture (see CULTURES OF THE BIBLE), so it is likely that James received help from a trained secretary.

Within the New Testament, James is the first of the so-called Catholic Epistles, that is, the group of seven non-Pauline letters: James, 1 and 2 Peter, 1–3 John, and Jude. Most of these are addressed to general audiences, hence the name *catholic,* which means "general." In James, the addressees are called the 12 scattered tribes, by which the author alludes to the tribes of ancient Israel, and he probably has the entire Christian Church in mind. The letter contains no further details about particular churches and is thus truly "catholic."

SYNOPSIS

Because of the nature of the letter, which touches on many apparently loosely connected subjects, interpreters are not agreed on an outline. The one given here is just one among many suggestions, which does have the virtue of being based on the wording of a verse in the letter itself (1:19).

After an introductory verse James discusses the issue of testing and temptation, arguing that God is not the author of sinful desires. This section commends the two virtues of patience and prayer (1:2–18). Chapter 1:19 is seen as the indication of the author's plan: The phrase "quick to listen" is dealt with in the rest of chapter 1 and chapter 2, "slow to speak" is the subject of chapter 3, whereas "slow to anger" is the theme of chapter 4 with 5:1–6. In the concluding section (5:7–18), some of the initial subjects return, in particular patience and prayer.

COMMENTARY

James avails himself of rhetorical techniques such as the introduction of imaginary adversaries and misunderstandings, with words that help him to move from subject to subject. Numerous rhetorical questions and the repeated address "brothers and sisters" give the letter a very lively character. Several people of the Hebrew Bible are mentioned as authoritative examples, such as Abraham (2:21–24), Rahab (2:25), Job (5:11), and Elijah (5:17–18). Quotations from the Hebrew Bible occur in 2:8, 11, 23, and 4:6, but there are many more allusions to it. James 4:5 looks like a quote, but the source is unknown. Psalm 12 and Leviticus 19 are regarded as the deep-level influences of the letter. In addition, James seems to allude to the words of Jesus as contained in the Gospels, especially his radical teaching in the Sermon on the Mount (Matthew 5–7), e.g., in 1:12. It is possible that sections of traditional Jewish material are included in the letter, e.g., in 2:20–26; 3:14–18; and 4:4–10, but this cannot be proven.

Jesus himself, however, is only mentioned twice in the entire letter (1:1; 2:1), and he is simply called Lord. This sets James in contrast to the letters of Paul, Peter, and John. Key elements of the Christian faith are not mentioned at all by James, such as the life of Jesus (his brother!), the cross, the Resurrection, and the institutions of BAPTISM and the LORD'S SUPPER. Nonetheless, Richard Bauckham (*James* [London: Routledge, 1999]) lists several areas of similarity between Jesus and James, such as their unusually radical ethics; their vision of a new, countercultural community; their lively expectation of God's future; and their emphasis on God's grace and generosity. The lack of references to Jesus is made up by James's use of the teaching of Jesus.

The reason for James's omissions is simple: He is writing an entirely practical letter. His book is theocentric, and his concern is that his readers will adopt a more radical and consistent lifestyle. Unlike Paul, Peter, and John, he does not feel the need to provide penetrating theological thoughts to motivate them.

Within the letter, several subjects that recur from time to time can be discovered:

- Suffering and testing. This is the element that occurs at the beginning and at the conclusion (chapters 1; 2; 4:1–10; and 5:19–20). It is unclear whether James is aware of active perse-

cution of believers, but the fact that their lives are not always easy leads to spiritual conflicts in which James seeks to extend a helping hand.

- Poverty and piety. Correct use of possessions is a core concern for James as it was for Jesus. He follows the Hebrew Bible and in particular Jews of the INTERTESTAMENTAL PERIOD in regarding the poor in the communities as the god-fearing, righteous group. There are wealthier members as well (2:1–4; 4:13), but their very presence creates tensions in communities, and riches are looked at with some suspicion (5:1–6).

- The law. James assumes that the law is a valid norm for believers (1:25; 2:8–13; 4:11–12), but he does not enforce the entire law of the Hebrew Bible. It is a moral law, as in the Sermon on the Mount. In the Christian era, the word of God is in the hearts of the believers (1:21). In this way, James balances indicative and imperative in good Christian style and demonstrates God's demand of total allegiance. The word *perfect* occurs several times to indicate the right integration of words and deeds. The perfection of the readers' faith is James's concern.

- Justification by faith. Although it seems that in 2:14–26 James contradicts what Paul writes about the relationship between faith and good works in Romans and Galatians, he is probably responding to certain popular misunderstandings. There is no real contradiction because the key words *faith* and *works* are used in different ways. Whereas for Paul *faith* is entrusting one's all to Jesus, for James it is mere verbal assent to facts (2:19). And whereas Paul uses *works* for meritorious good deeds that form a road *to* salvation, for James they are the expected results *of* salvation and the essence of the Jewish-Christian lifestyle. Both Paul and James use the example of Abraham from Genesis and both are correct, albeit slightly one-sided, in what they say about it (Romans 4; Galatians 3:6–9; James 2:20–23).

- Sins of speech are dealt with in chapter 3, which may include much Jewish traditional material. James uses the synecdoche "tongue" to refer to speech.

- James uses the concept of wisdom (1:5–8; 3:13–18) in roughly the same way as the Holy Spirit occurs in Paul's letters, as the guiding person of believers in their lives as Christians.

- Prayer is the theme of the final section of the letter. James particularly mentions prayer for healing, which could be accompanied by anointing with oil. Jews and Gentiles used oil as medication; but here it is being given a ceremonial function.

The expression "If the Lord wishes" (4:15) has found its way into our language via the Latin *Deo volente* as "God willing."

CHARACTER

James   James (Greek Iakōbos) is one of the brothers of Jesus who during Jesus' lifetime did not believe that his brother was anything special. It is likely that Jesus' appearance to him after the Resurrection (1 Corinthians 15:7; see JESUS CHRIST) changed his life radically. After the departure of most apostles, he led the church in Jerusalem until he was executed by a high priest of the Sadducees in the year 62 C.E., a tragic event recorded with disdain by the contemporary Jewish historian Josephus. In his radicalism, evidenced both in this letter and in Acts, he differs much from later generations of Christian authors such as the apostolic fathers. He is also mentioned in the Synoptic Gospels, in Acts, and in Galatians.

Jeremiah

The book of Jeremiah takes its name from its main character, the prophet Jeremiah. In the Christian Bible, it belongs to the final section of the Old Testament, "The Prophets." These in turn are subdivided into five books of "Major Prophets," of whom Jeremiah is one, and the "Minor Prophets." The book is placed after Isaiah and before Lamentations, which many people think was also written by Jeremiah. At 52 chapters, it is the second longest of the prophetic books after Isaiah. In the Hebrew Bible, the arrangement is somewhat different. It occurs there in the second section, also named "Prophets," but this time Jeremiah

Jeremiah's Lament (Lamentations of Jeremiah 1:1–5, 11, 12), engraving by Julius Schnorr von Carolsfeld

forms part of the second group, known as the "Latter Prophets," and is placed between Isaiah and Ezekiel.

As his life, Jeremiah was based in JERUSALEM, the capital of the remaining part of ISRAEL (see HOLY LAND) that remained independent after the Assyrian invasion of 722 B.C.E. and was variously called Judah or the southern kingdom. He prophesied during the reigns of no fewer than five kings (see MONARCHY), from Josiah, continuing through the reign of Josiah's two sons, Jehoahaz and Eliakim, renamed Jehoiakim by his Egyptian overlords; then through the reigns of Jehoiachin and the last king of the southern kingdom, Zedekiah. The period covered by his ministry is from around 627 B.C.E. till around 580 B.C.E.

The book of Jeremiah is one of the most dramatic of the prophetic books. Jeremiah lived in dramatic times, during the last years of Jerusalem and the southern kingdom of Judah before they fell to the Babylonians (see BABYLON) under King Nebuchadnezzar in 586 B.C.E. after a two-year-long siege. He was in conflict with the religious and secular leadership of the city and at one stage was thrown into a well and left to die. Another time, a fellow prophet was summarily executed for speaking out, and Jeremiah could easily have suffered the same fate. But perhaps what makes this book so dramatic is that, as with the prophet Jonah, we see the interaction between the prophet and God, which fills the first 20 chapters.

In the book of Jeremiah, God (usually referred to as the Lord, *Yahweh* in Hebrew, but also as the Lord of Hosts, the Lord God, and the God of Israel) is the one who called Jeremiah to be his prophet and who gives him the words to speak. He is the true God, not just of the Israelites, but of the whole cosmos. All other gods are idols, unreal. He is prepared to argue with Jeremiah but not the people or their leadership. He is bound to them by a covenant, but because of their breaking this covenant, he has to punish them by allowing the Babylonians to conquer them. Nevertheless he promises a new covenant with them as their restorer. The term *Redeemer* is used of him several times in this connection (50:34; cf.15:21).

The very writing of the book is dramatic. The prophecies were first given orally. But at some stage Jeremiah feels he should write them down and present them to the king, a risky move. The king thereupon reads them. After he has read one page, he cuts it with his knife and throws it into the fire—a sign of his defiance and contempt not only for the prophet but for the message. So, the lost prophecies have to be reconstructed and then protected through the siege and escape from a burning city. After Jeremiah's death, they are somehow preserved and edited during deportation and exile. The burning city is the backcloth for what emerges as a message of continuation: God still has a future for his people, however unlikely that appears on the surface.

It is possible that some editing went on in EGYPT, to which Jeremiah was kidnapped and where he died, but probably most of it occurred in Babylon, to where most of the inhabitants were marched. At any rate, we are left with two slightly different versions: the one we use today and the one in the Septuagint (see BIBLE, EARLY TRANSLATIONS OF). What is certain is that the order of the book is not chronological, though there is some logic in its ordering. Certain themes gradually emerge, then are repeated emphatically. The drama lies in the urgency of the repetitions: Time is running out; the situation is desperate.

To his immediate audience, whether they were the Judeans in general, as in chapters 1–20, or their leader, most of what Jeremiah said was all nonsense, but history proved Jeremiah right. The intended readers of the edited book, the Jews in exile and then in a reconstituted nation, knew Jeremiah was right. And we, too, as modern-day readers, read it with the hindsight that he was. Christians who read it also in the light of the Christian Bible certainly see Jeremiah's prediction of a new covenant amply fulfilled.

We need to add a note on the type of writing that is found in Jeremiah. Prophecy is a literary GENRE in its own right. Within it, other literary genres are to be found: poetry (see POETRY, BIBLICAL), SERMON, PARABLES, NARRATIVE, dialogue, LAMENTS, complaint, and so on. We see all of these in the book of Jeremiah. Besides Jeremiah's own words, we have the narrative account of his personal assistant, Baruch, which fills out the parallel historical narrative given in 2 Kings 25 and 2 Chronicles 36 and constitutes a book in the Apocrypha (see pages 385–386). See also Letter of Jeremiah (pages 237–238).

See also time line page 156.

SYNOPSIS

Section I: Jeremiah's Pleadings and Warnings to a Deaf City (Chapters 1–10)

Chapter 1 is an account of Jeremiah's youthful calling, giving him a historical and spiritual setting. The next nine chapters fall roughly into four subsections (2:1–3:5; 3:6–4:4; 4:5–6:30; and 7:1–10:25). Each subsection begins with some sort of command from God to Jeremiah to speak out the messages he has been given. However, each subsection is really a group of separate prophecies given at different times, so there is a good deal of apparent repetition. Nevertheless, the messages are consistent with each other and become increasingly urgent.

The main themes covered in this first section of 10 chapters are:

1. The people of Jerusalem and Judah have worshipped and put their trust in idols and have syncretized the true worship of God: That is, they worship God *and* idols. Child sacrifice is the most horrifying aspect of this worship (2:1–3:6; 7:16–8:17).

2. The people still have a false sense of security in the presence of Solomon's temple in the city and the ritual that surrounds it (see HEBREW BIBLE, WORSHIP AND RITUAL). They see it as the place where God literally dwells (7:1–15).

3. There are all sorts of social injustice; class divisions are exploited in favor of the well-off (5:1–31; 6:13–21; 9:3–26).

4. In some prophecies, there is a sense that there is still time to repent (see SIN) and turn back to true worship and create a more just society (3:11–4:4; 5:18).

5. If there is no repentance, then God has no option but to allow invaders from the north to destroy Jerusalem and disperse its people (4:5–31; 6:1–12, 22–30).

6. This is not a pleasant message for Jeremiah or God to deliver. Both their hearts are broken, because God intended so much blessing for his people (4:19; 8:18–9:2; 10:19–25).

Although in this section no specific mention is made of "COVENANT," the thought of it underlies all Jeremiah says. There is a "special relationship" that God wants to keep but that the people misunderstand. We have to wait till chapter 11 for specific covenant references.

Section II: Jeremiah's Inner and Outer Conflicts (Chapters 11–20)

This second section can be divided into five groups (chapters 11–12, 13, 14–15, 16–17, and 18–20). As before, each section begins with some phrase such as "The word of the LORD came to me." Some of the same prophetic material is repeated, in terms of conditions or judgments, but there are also specific historical incidents that show the opposition Jeremiah received and that are causing him grief enough to voice a series of complaints to God.

Each of the six points made in the synopsis of Section I is repeated. However, God uses much more specifically covenant-related language in chapters 11–12. In the same chapters, we also hear about plots by Jeremiah's fellow villagers against him, Jeremiah's complaint, and God's judgment on them. Later, we hear about a drought (14:1–6) and then about one of the priests' attacking Jeremiah

physically, again causing a complaint and a word of judgment (20:1–18). Even more dramatic are the enacted prophecies, where the prophet is told to do something or go somewhere, and only when he has done so is God's word heard, usually a symbolic understanding of the action performed. Thus Jeremiah is told to bury a linen cloth (13:1–11), not to marry (16:1–4), to go to a potter's workshop (18:1–11), to buy a jug and take it to one of the city gates (19:1–13). This, again, is in the prophetic tradition: Isaiah was told to walk around naked; Hosea, to marry a loose woman; Ezekiel, to make a model of Jerusalem. Such actions make an impact and trigger clear memories of the symbolic message that emanates from them.

Section III: Denunciation of Faithless Kings and False Prophets (Chapters 21–29)

Jeremiah's message is bleak and uncompromising to the ears of the Israelites, who want only to hear that they will be saved from Nebuchadnezzar's power. Jeremiah makes it clear that Nebuchadnezzar is God's chosen instrument for justice and punishment over the surrounding nations, not just over Judah. It is useless, therefore, to try to resist him. It will only lead to a worse situation. To those who are already in exile, he writes that they should expect a 70-year exile before a return (see RETURN FROM EXILE). Jerusalem will inevitably fall to the Babylonians.

This section is much more specific in the objects of Jeremiah's denunciations. Each of the four kings who followed Josiah is addressed, and his fate spelled out. But the greatest force of denunciation is reserved for the false prophets. They are preaching peace where there is no peace, and an easy SALVATION out of their troubles, with no commitment to moral or religious reform. They are assuming that God's promise of protection over Jerusalem and the Davidic kingship are givers. Jeremiah's understanding of the covenant is that it is conditional. His denunciation of four false prophets in the last two chapters of the section is powerful, with specific punishment predicted for them, and one of them is reported as having happened. The whole integrity of Jeremiah's prophetic message is challenged by such falsity in the way nothing else has challenged it.

TIME LINE FOR JEREMIAH

Date B.C.E.	King	Events	Bible References	References in Jeremiah
722		Fall of Northern Kingdom	2 Kings 17:5–18	30–31(part)
701	Hezekiah	Assyrian siege of Jerusalem	2 Kings 18:9–19:37; 2 Chronicles 32:1–22	
639	Josiah	Begins reign at 8 years old	2 Kings 22:1–2; 2 Chronicles 34:1–7	
627		Jeremiah begins his ministry		1:2, 5
621		Book of the Law found in temple	2 Kings 22:3–20; 2 Chronicles 34:8–35:19	
612		Babylonians defeat Assyrians		
609		Josiah attacks Egyptians and dies	2 Chronicles 35:20–24	
	Jehoahaz (also known as Shallum)	Reigns 3 months; deported to Egypt	2 Kings 23:31–33; 2 Chronicles 36:1–3	22:11–12
	Jehoiakim (also known as Eliakim)	Reigns as Egyptian puppet	2 Kings 23:34–37; 2 Chronicles 36:4–6	
		Jeremiah's Temple sermon		ch. 26
605		Battle of Carchemish; Babylonians defeat Egyptians		25; 46:2–12
		Jeremiah's first book burned		chs. 36, 45
604		Babylonians attack Philistines		ch. 47
602		Jehoiakim rebels against Babylonians; raids	2 Kings 24:1–4	ch. 35
598		First siege of Jerusalem; Jehoiakim dies	2 Kings 24:5–6	
597	Jehoiachin (also known as ([Je]coniah)	Jehoiachin surrenders. First deportation to Babylon	2 Kings 24:8–17; 2 Chronicles 36:9–10	22:24–30; 24; 52:28
	Zedekiah	Installed as Babylonian puppet	2 Kings 24:18–25:7	52:1–2
596		Jeremiah's letter to exiles		ch. 29
595		Unrest in Babylonia		
594		Spreads to Judah; Babylonian campaign to suppress unrest	Ezekiel 1	ch. 27–28
593		Zedekiah goes to Babylon to swear allegiance		51:59
587		Zedekiah rebels; Jerusalem besieged by Babylonians	2 Chronicles 36:11–16	39:1–10
		Egyptians attempt to relieve siege, but fail	Ezekiel 17:11–21	chs. 21, 32

Date B.C.E.	King	Events	Bible References	References in Jeremiah
		Babylonians resume siege		34, 37–38
586		Fall of Jerusalem; city burned	2 Kings 25:8–21; 2 Chronicles 36:17–21	33; 39:1–8
		Zedekiah taken to Babylon; Edomites obstruct escape of refugees	Obadiah	52:3–27; 49:7–22
		Gedeliah governor; assassinated	2 Kings 25:22–26	chs. 40–42
		Second deportation and exile	Psalm 137	39:9; 52:29
		Remnant flee to Egypt		chs. 43–44
582		Third deportation		52:30
580		Jeremiah dies in Egypt?		
561		Jehoiachin released in Babylon	2 Kings 25:27–30	52:31–34
560		Final text of "Jeremiah" put together?		
539		Persians defeat Babylonians	Daniel 5:30	
536		First of several returns by the exiles	2 Chronicles 36:22–23	

The defeat of Judah by the Babylonians does raise the question of just how powerful the Lord is. Is the Babylonian god Marduk more powerful? Jeremiah makes it quite clear that the Lord is supreme. In his time, when he has finished using the Babylonians, they, too, will go down to defeat (see also chapters 50–51).

At a practical level, such messages seemed defeatist and even treasonable to the hearers. Jeremiah is attacked and abused verbally (26:7–11). On the other hand, this section shows God and Jeremiah on the same side: There is no inner conflict between Jeremiah and God as we saw earlier.

Section IV: The Promise of Restoration (Chapters 30–33)

After answering the question "Who is to blame?" Jeremiah faces the next obvious questions: "Is it all over, then?" The false prophets said, "Peace, peace . . ." and were obviously wrong. So does "Judgment, judgment . . ." mean "the end"? The next four chapters supply the answer, and in the most dramatic circumstances. In most of the prophecies here, the city is under siege, and Jeremiah is under detention at the king's orders—an unlikely scenario in which to offer hope. The essence of the prophecies can be set out in five statements:

1. God's punishment is real and decisive, and for real reasons. It is not done out of vengeance but out of love, and therefore, it is not final (30:1–17).

2. God still wanted to establish a covenant with his people, but it would need to be a new sort of covenant, one that was "written on their heart," that is to say, involving their willing love, which was to be in response to God's grace (30:18–31:37).

3. Jeremiah posits such a new covenant as part of a wider restoration, which would include a return from exile of those deported not only at the fall of Jerusalem, but from earlier deportations too (31:18–40; 32:36–41).

4. Such a restoration would include a restoration of the civil and sacred leadership in the form of a Davidic king capable of administering justice and a priesthood capable of conducting spiritual worship (32:42–33:26).

5. The city itself would be rebuilt, and the lands and their fertility restored. Jeremiah buys a field as a symbolic act of his faith (32:1–15). The city would become a world city, recognized by every nation.

Section V: The Last Days of Jerusalem (Chapters 34–45; 52)

We arrive now at the major narrative section and the climax to the historical events: the capture of Jerusalem by the Babylonians, the destruction of the temple, and the deportation. The account is from Jeremiah's viewpoint and explains how his final years were probably spent in Egypt.

From chapter 36 the section is more or less chronologically arranged, beginning back in 605 B.C.E., in Jehoiakim's reign. Chapter 36 (and chapter 45) deals with Jeremiah's writing down his prophecies through his personal assistant, Baruch, in order to present them to the king. Although his officials see the significance of the prophecies, the king, in a dramatic act of defiance, shreds and burns the scroll. Jeremiah and Baruch take a year to rewrite and add to it, but here lie the beginnings of the written text.

The narrative then skips to 587 B.C.E., to the siege of Jerusalem. In chapter 37 we read the rest of the account of Jeremiah's buying the field from chapter 32. On his return, Jeremiah is arrested as a traitor. Zedekiah is shown to be a weak and vacillating king, shuttling between Jeremiah and his Egyptian-leaning officials. At one point, Jeremiah is in danger of losing his life, being thrown into a cistern of sinking mud, but he is rescued by an Ethiopian eunuch, one of the hidden band of Jeremiah's sympathizers (38:7–13).

Finally, the city is captured. Two parallel accounts in chapters 39 and 52 give us the details. The king and his courtiers try to escape, are captured, and most are put to death; the king is (merely!) blinded after watching his sons being killed. A second deportation takes place, and the city appears to be depopulated. The Babylonians appoint a civil governor, Gedaliah, and they treat Jeremiah well, giving him the choice to go with them or stay. He chooses to stay (40:6).

On the departure of the Babylonian army, chaos breaks out. The naive Gedaliah is assassinated, but his Judean assassins, fearing Babylonian wrath, flee to Egypt, much against Jeremiah's counsel (42:7–22). As ever, Jeremiah's counsel is disregarded, but he is forced to go with the band. Clearly, other Judeans join them in Egypt. We next hear from Jeremiah a year or two later, when he addresses them, reprimanding them for their continued idolatry (chapter 44) and emphasizing that Egypt is no safe haven.

The account finishes with the exiles in Babylon, a section presumably added by the same hand that appended the last chapter of 2 Kings. The Babylonians had carried off many of the smaller items from the temple, and they had melted down the larger ones. So some bits of the temple did remain. And the former exiled king, Jehoiachin, was still alive, to be released eventually by King Nebuchadnezzar's successor. There is one of the Davidic line still alive and free (52:28–34).

Section VI: Judgments against Surrounding Nations (Chapters 46–51)

A number of the prophets address sections to surrounding nations, almost always in terms of their impending demise as a result of God's judgment against them (e.g., Amos 1:3–2:16; Isaiah 13–23; Ezekiel 25–31). Jeremiah's "oracles" or prophetic utterances against the nations may be divided into two:

1. Smaller prophecies addressed to Judah's neighbors: Egypt (ch. 46), the PHILISTINES (ch. 47), Moab (ch. 48), the Ammonites (49:1–6), Edom (49:7–22), Damascus (SYRIA) (49:23–27), the Arabs (49:28–33), Elam (49:34–39).
2. A major prophecy, or series of prophecies, directed against Babylon (chs. 50–51).

The typical features of the smaller prophecies are the cause of judgment, usually pride; the downfall of the nation's gods; the devastation of the judgment, usually in terms of military defeat; and, in some cases, the promise of restoration.

Against Babylon, the features are emphasized through constant repetition: The pride of Babylon is the main cause. Its defeat will be from the north, it will be catastrophic and sudden, and it will make Babylon a wilderness forever. There is no possibility of restoration. At the same time, Jeremiah tells the exiles there to be ready to leave quickly and announces that there is a future back in Israel for them.

COMMENTARY

Section I: Jeremiah's Pleadings and Warnings to a Deaf City (Chapters 1–10)

Jeremiah is introduced in chapter 1. In Hebrew, his name is *Yirmeyah,* which means "God throws." Certainly, Jeremiah is thrown about a good deal, both by God and by the people to he whom preaches. He was born in the territory of Benjamin (see ISRAEL, TWELVE TRIBES OF), a little to the north of Jerusalem, but still part of the southern kingdom. His father was a priest in Anathoth (1:1), where a former high priest, Abiathar, lived (1 Kings 2:26–27).

His calling (see CHOSEN PEOPLE) to be a prophet was quite specific. He dated it in the 13th year of King Josiah, which would be 627 B.C.E. It was a long calling, continuing through the next four kings, surviving the fall of Jerusalem. There are actually four references to Jeremiah in the historical account in 2 Chronicles. First, in 2 Chronicles 35:25, he composes a song of lament for the untimely death of King Josiah in an ill-advised attack on the Egyptian army. Jeremiah and the form of the lament are closely linked. Though we do not have the particular lament for Josiah, there are several others in the book of Jeremiah. He probably wrote the book of Lamentations, also, over the fall of Jerusalem. Second, in 2 Chronicles 36:12 the narrative of Jeremiah concerning King Zedekiah's refusal to listen to him is reinforced; last, in two references in 2 Chronicles 36:21–22, the chronicler refers to Jeremiah's prophecy as to the length of the exile. By the time Chronicles was written, Jeremiah's reputation as an important prophet was well established.

Other prophets indicate the time and nature of their calling by God. In Jeremiah's case, he has a sense that it is "from the womb," echoing Psalm 139:13, and a lifelong vocation. But despite such a sense of destiny, Jeremiah's call was met with some reluctance and excuses. "Ah, LORD God! Truly I do not know how to speak for I am only a boy" (1:6). It could have been that, like the prophet Samuel,

he was indeed only a boy (1 Samuel 3:1–14); or it may have been an exaggeration, such as MOSES' claim that he could not speak (Exodus 4:10–16).

The interesting point is that at the time, something of a religious revival was occurring. 2 Kings 23 describes how King Josiah restored some of the temple ritual that had been forgotten, as well as tore down the idols that his father had erected. So Jeremiah could hardly have met with much hostility to begin with; rather, it gave him a good foundation. We only have a few prophecies from this period.

God gives him authority, touching his mouth, as with Isaiah (1:9), but perhaps more intimately. In this language of profound religious experience, it is hard to decide whether the terms used are metaphorical or whether they actually represent some sort of literal physical sensation (see REVELATION, GOD'S). The "commission" (1:9–10) is set out formally, as if it were a public ceremony: "Today I appoint you." He also gives Jeremiah a confirmatory sign (1:11): an almond branch. The force of this is lost in English, but in Hebrew, the word for almond tree is *shaqed.* There is a playing with language, since a near-sounding word, *shoqed,* means "I am watching." It is God's responsibility to "watch" over his word; the prophet's, to utter it. The second sign of commission is either a literal or a mental image, a boiling pot an enemy will "pour over" the land, "scalding" it.

The language of the remaining paragraph exemplifies this. God says: "An enemy is coming to attack and besiege the city. The people you are to speak to will attack and besiege you. If you break before them, I will break you. But if you stand against them as a wall, you will prevail." The military language of spiritual conflict is immediately and dramatically established.

In the section from 2:1 to 3:5, one of the striking features is its restrained legal format and language (see DOCUMENTS). The use of rhetorical questions, for example, is similar to the language of the law court: "What wrong did your ancestors find in me?" (2:4) God asks. "Therefore" (2:9) suggests God's actions, his punishment, are logical and a measured response, not the acts of an irrational tyrant. "Why do you complain against me?"

(2:29); "Have you not brought this upon your-self?" (2:17), which is ambiguously the dramatized voice of God or his spokesperson. The accused is allowed to plead a defense: "I am not defiled" (2:23), though it is put into a wider rhetorical question: "How can you say . . .?" Putting dialogue within dialogue suggests a skilled use of dramatic speech (see STRUCTURES, LITERARY).

In terms of imagery, there are three strands that we shall find constantly recurring. First is the imagery of *wilderness* (see PILGRIMS AND WANDERERS), which is based on the actual wilderness history of Israel at the time of the EXODUS from Egypt (2:6). Just as God's salvation was out of the wilderness (2:7), so his punishment will be back into wilderness (2:15). God even dramatically asks, "Have I been a wilderness to Israel?" (2:31). Later examples are to be found in 4:23; 7:34; 9:12; and many more.

Second is the image of the *vine*, as in Isaiah 5. Here God states, "Yet I planted you as a choice vine" (2:21) and asks, "How did you turn . . . into a wild vine?" This image runs throughout the Old and New Testaments, a basic agricultural image. Linked to this are *water* images: cisterns and fountains (2:13) and the phrase "the fountain of living water," an image that Jesus (see JESUS CHRIST) took up later to refer to spiritual life (John 4:10; 7:38).

Third, we have a network of *sexual* images, particularly appropriate since much of the idol worship involved sexual fertility practices, with cult prostitutes, and so on (see CULTURES OF THE BIBLE). Hosea had earlier lived an enacted version of this image in taking a faithless wife who turned to prostitution. Jeremiah emphasizes on this image too: "your love as a bride" (2:2); "I have loved strangers and after them I will go" (2:25); and the analogy of "If a man divorces his wife . . ." (3:1), which leads to strong sexual language. Jeremiah is nothing if not an intimate prophet, and the breaking of marital intimacy appalls him. The image of bride is taken up in the New Testament with the church as "the bride of Christ" (Revelation 19:7; 21:2; etc.). Ezekiel uses the image of unfaithfulness too (Ezekiel 23), echoing Jeremiah's trope of the bride in the wilderness as opposed to Israel as a wanton woman in the luxury of city life (5:7–8).

The prophecy beginning 3:6 is the only one that definitely states it is from Josiah's reign (3:6), addressed to the remnant of the northern kingdom, Israel, sometimes also referred to as "Ephraim"(31:9) or "Jacob"(30:18). This is God's olive branch to them, to return home from an Assyrian captivity dating back to 722 B.C.E.; "home" is defined as Jerusalem (3:14, 17). As such, it is one of the more peaceable prophecies and seems to suggest a real possibility of a future, a note missing from the later prophecies. Jeremiah 3:17–18 especially promise the true presence of God. Jeremiah may well have been thinking of the restored temple of King Josiah.

Particularly to be noticed are two series of phrases: First, the "I thought's" of 3:7, 19: God allows Jeremiah, and us, to see his thinking. He is not an inscrutable, unknowable God. And he can be disappointed! Second, the "if's" of 4:1–2: the list of conditions builds up to a climax, "Then nations shall be blessed." Prophecy is conditional, so the language tends to structure itself into parallel conditional clauses. The parallelisms (see POETRY, BIBLICAL) here are both insistent and pleading.

The section 4:5–6:30 is far more emotional and dramatic than anything before, giving us a sense of the prophet's total engagement in his ministry. It also reflects: like God, like prophet—a God totally engaged with his people. There is also, in chapter 5, a new element in Jeremiah's message, that of social injustice. "See if you can find one person who acts justly and seeks truth" (5:1). The answer is obvious. The failure to find a just person is as significant as the failure to worship God single-mindedly: Indeed, the two are related.

The drama is expressed in a number of ways. The language itself is violent, even exclamatory: "Blow the trumpet" (4:5); "My anguish! My anguish!" (4:19), translated in the King James Version as "My bowels! my bowels!"; "a cry of a woman in labor" (4:31); "Run to and fro" (5:1); "Flee for safety" (6:1) are just a few of the examples that could be given. The imagery is equally violent. *Wild animal images* of lions (4:7; 5:6) and wolves and leopards (5:6) mingle with *martial images* of weaponry: "bow and javelin" (6:23); "(war) horses swifter than eagles" (4:13); "the noise of horseman and archer" (4:29); and the dramatic similes of "his chariots like the whirlwind" (4:13) and "Their quiver is like an open tomb" (5:16), which take on apocalyptic significance. Dramatic imagery is applied to the prophet himself: He is "a tester and refiner" (6:27), a sentinel (6:17), "full of the wrath of the LORD . . . weary of holding it in" (6:11), "my heart is beating wildly" (4:19), suggesting the total emotional involvement of the prophet is clearly seen.

Structurally, the drama is expressed through the conflict among God, the prophet, and the people. Jeremiah argues with God (4:10), suggesting God has deceived the people. He and God speak in a dialogue in 5:1–5, where God challenges the prophet to find someone righteous. The complacency of the people is given direct speech in 5:12–13, a tone in stark contrast to that of the judgment coming to them. The priests and (false) prophets are given a voice: "saying 'Peace, peace' when there is no peace" (6:14). God directly addresses them: "O foolish and senseless people, who have eyes, but do not see, who have ears, but do not hear?" (5:20–22), a parallelism that becomes a prophetic formula, echoed by Jesus (John 12:40, quoting Isaiah 6:9–10).

So far, we have barely noted the parallelism that is such a central feature of all Hebrew poetry, including prophetic poetry. This section gives us some fine examples of it, such as the analogy of natural borders in 5:22:

I placed the sand as a boundary for the sea,
a perpetual barrier that it cannot pass;
though the waves toss, they cannot prevail,
though they roar, they cannot pass over it.

This is the simplest form of Jeremiah's parallelism, a simple repetition of clause structure and idea. Usually, it is more climactic, each parallel unfolding a new step, as in 4:23–26, where each "I looked" ushers in some worse devastation, starting from a chaos reminiscent of that before God's creation of the world (Genesis 1:1) and climaxing in "and all its cities were laid in ruins," finishing up with the extra line with its own inner parallelism: "before the LORD, before his fierce anger." Other examples in this first section are 5:3, 6, 17; 6:24–25.

The first prophecy in the next group (chapters 7–10) is generally supposed to be the "temple sermon," 7:1–15, which is summarized later in chapter 26 and nearly led to a prison sentence for Jeremiah. If so, then this can be dated from the first year of Jehoiakim's reign in 609 B.C.E. The point of offense seems to have been the likening of the temple to the former shrine at Shiloh that was destroyed (1 Samuel 4). The temple's presence does *not* necessarily mean God's presence, especially when injustice and idolatry thrive.

In fact, dramatically, God tells Jeremiah to stop praying for the Israelites (7:16), an injunction repeated in 11:14 and 14:11–12, even though interceding for the people was seen as a prophetic duty. They will not listen. In Greek mythology, Cassandra is a prophetess whose predictions are fated not to be believed. Jeremiah is the Hebrew equivalent (7:27). Nevertheless, he is compelled to utter. Just as there is a tension within Jeremiah over this (8:18–21), so there is a tension in the language. One language construction is the conditional: "If my people . . . then . . . ," holding out the promise of blessing if there is return. The other construction is the judicial: "Because . . . therefore . . ." (as in 7:17–20). These constructions are held in tension, conditional time versus judgment time. When we read of child sacrifice in 7:30–33, we can perhaps see God's point quite clearly: Such crimes demand the utmost penalty.

Some of the other prophecies in this group take on other genre forms. Jeremiah 8:18–9:2 is a lamentation; 10:1–5 echoes the wisdom literature; 10:6–10, 23–25 could be part of a psalm; while 7:34 echoes Ecclesiastes 12:1–8. The Authorized (King James) Version translation of 10:16 echoes Job, though not more modern ones.

Finally, a number of images call for our attention. The image of *circumcision*, a symbolic one, is picked up from 4:4 and enlarged on in 9:25–26. Paul employs this symbolic meaning in Romans 2:25 (just as he uses 9:24 in 1 Corinthians 1:31). True circumcision is of the heart, not the flesh. The Negro spiritual "There is a Balm in Gilead" is, of course, taken from 8:22, except here it is a rhetorical question, part of Jeremiah's lament. Such images of *wounding and healing* run through the book. The simile of the people's idols' being "like a scarecrow in a melon patch" (10:5 New International Version) has a satiric solidity to it, which, unusually, the Authorized (King James) Version misses.

Section II: Jeremiah's Inner and Outer Conflicts (Chapters 11–20)

Although the covenant made at Mount Sinai in Moses' time has been hinted at before as the defining agreement between God and his people Israel, 11:3 constitutes the first actual mention of it. A further brief mention is made in 22:8–9 before the vitally significant prophecy about the new covenant that now needs to be made in chapter 31. The language of the covenant is in terms of "do this . . . then . . ." (11:1–8) and "because . . . therefore . . ." (11:9–12). God is no longer bound by it since the people have broken its terms so comprehensively.

Jeremiah quotes the covenant passages in Deuteronomy so exactly because it was that book in particular that was rediscovered in Josiah's reign and produced a brief revival. The vivid phrase "Egypt, the land of the iron-smelter" (11:4) echoes exactly Deuteronomy 4:20, and the phrase "a land flowing with milk and honey" (11:5) occurs frequently in the PENTATEUCH. Another extended METAPHOR, that of the *olive tree* (11:16), similar to the vineyard image used earlier, finds echoes in other prophetic literature Hosea (14:6), as well as in Psalms (52:8), and is then used by Paul in Romans 11:17–24 to explain the place of Israel in the new covenant.

Another way to see 11:1–17 is as God's complaint against his people. The "complaint" is a very old genre in literature, often by lovers against their mistresses. In the book of Jeremiah, there is a set of "complaints" by Jeremiah. Another similar form is the lament, already discussed. Some commentators collapse complaint with lamentation, but traditionally the two genres are quite separate. The complaint represents a cause that can be argued; the lament, a grief that cannot be assuaged.

The next part of this first group (11:18–12:6) contains a complaint by Jeremiah: The villagers of Anathoth have conspired against him. An actual event is reconstructed through prophecy. The complaint is against God for allowing this to happen. The English poet Gerard Manley Hopkins uses 12:1 to begin his famous poem "Thou Art Indeed Just, LORD," where he complains to God that his life is futile despite being totally committed to God's service. Jeremiah, too, is asking for an explanation, or at least some action. God's answer is in a series of rhetorical questions (12:5–6) centered on the image of an athlete. Job was similarly answered (Job 39).

Action against not just Jeremiah's neighbors but Israel's is promised in 12:14–17, though tempered with mercy and hope of restoration. The remaining passage, 12:7–13, could be seen as God's lament at having to abandon his covenant. Images of bride and wilderness, lion and hyena, and vineyard and harvesting continue through from the first section.

Chapter 13 contains the first of the enacted prophecies. Jeremiah is told to take a linen cloth, bury it at a place called Parah, and then dig it up. It was, of course, ruined. Jeremiah plays with the similar Hebrew words *Parah/Perath*, the latter meaning the Euphrates. The interpretation is found in 13:8–11: Judah will be ruined as the loincloth was, presumably by Euphrates, i.e., Babylon. The loincloth is a metonymy of an intimate garment, just as God had meant Judah to be intimate with him. The recurrent sexual imagery is barely hidden.

The second analogy is more violent. Full wine jars should symbolize celebration, but now they mean drunkenness, which will lead to God's violence, manifesting itself in the massacres of battle. Another play of words is here: *Nebel* means "a jar"; *nabal*, "a fool." In 25:15, similar imagery is expressed as "this cup of the wine of wrath" in an extended apocalyptic vision, not dissimilar to one in Ezekiel 23:31–34. Images of *drunkenness* run through the book, especially in the last section.

In fact, 13:19 suggests some punishment has already taken place, seemingly the first deportation referred to in 52:28, which occurred in 598 B.C.E. (see 2 Kings 24:8, 11). The last part of the chapter is a woe and denunciation, marked by a series of parallel rhetorical questions, including the proverbial "Can Ethiopians change their skin or leopards their spots?" The sexual imagery becomes explicit in 13:26: Their sexual humiliation shall be akin to their spiritual and physical promiscuity.

Chapters 14 and 15 represent the emotional center of the book, though not the theological one. We start with a lament over the drought conditions, described in a marvelous little set of parallel cameos (14:3–6). There appears to be a drama of repentance (14:7–9, 19–22), but God sees it as false, just like the false prophecies being given (14:13–16). Jeremiah is caught in the middle. He is told by God not to pray for the people (14:11), yet the "we" of the confession (see SIN) seems to include Jeremiah.

Chapter 15 increases Jeremiah's conflict. God in his most emphatic language yet says it is useless to intercede (see PRAYER): "Though Samuel and Moses stood before me." Both prophets had done so, of course, with good results: Exodus 32:11–14 and Numbers 14:13–25 in Moses' case; 1 Samuel 12:23 in the other. This all makes Jeremiah feel terrible: a useless mouthpiece. His impassioned complaint (15:10, 15–18) testifies to the joy he had at his calling (15:16), but now all is grief and insult. God reassures him of his own personal salvation (15:21), but that is all. In the face of evil, what is required is faithfulness, not success. The violent language God uses (15:3–4) matches that of the last chapter. This is the reality of war and rebellion.

In the next group of prophecies (chapters 16–17), the enacted prophecy of 16:1–4 is rather the reverse: a command not to act. Hosea had been told to marry and enact God's message. Here, Jeremiah is to remain single. Paul had the same feeling in 1 Corinthians 7:25–31 but does not claim any prophetic authority in his advice. The lament that follows (16:5–8) is equally ironic: It is prefaced by a command not to lament.

The continuing dialogue among God, Jeremiah, and the people is well exemplified in 16:10–15, where the translators have to put quotation marks within quotation marks. The language remains violent, "I will hurl you out of this land," yet there is still hope of return, a second exile with a second exodus, leading eventually to a second covenant. The simple but dramatically expressed lesson of 16:16–21 is, If you do not learn from history, you repeat it. Chapter 17 has strong echoes of the Psalms. Jeremiah 17:7–9 echoes Psalm 1; 17:10

echoes Psalm 139:23–24, showing the more lyrical side of Jeremiah's poetry. Jeremiah 17:9 is often quoted on its own, especially the Authorized (King James) Version—"The heart is deceitful above all things, and desperately wicked: who can know it?"—one of those aphorisms (plus rhetorical question) that brilliantly sum up the human condition. The last section of this chapter, praising Sabbath keeping, seems to predate much of the rest, being much more hopeful in tone, and in structure, an open condition.

The last group, chapters 18–20, contain the two famous pottery reenactments, which eventually lead to public rebuke and attack. The passage 18:1–12 is crucial in its succinct summary of covenant theology and the ongoing debate over God's purposes. The analogy of clay and potter is fully worked out. The potter's work can be spoiled, but it can also be redone. In any case, the potter has the legal and moral right to do with the clay what he wishes. The second enactment, 19:1–13, is equally fully worked out in its analogical form. In the place the people have offered their children as sacrifice, there will be the place of slaughter and the collection of bones.

In between is the equally violent complaint (18:19–23) made by Jeremiah to God on hearing of yet further plots against him. He wishes for vengeance, just as the Psalmist did in Psalm 109. Such righteous anger troubles modern readers, influenced by the Christian teaching on forgiving enemies. There is a depth of passion that we have to accept in reading the Prophets.

The most deeply felt complaint, however, is that in the next chapter, after Pashhur, chief of the temple police, had struck him publicly. Verses 20:7–18 challenge God as to his whole calling. The prebirth calling (1:5) is countered by the existential question

Why did I come forth from the womb
to see toil and sorrow,
and spend my days in shame?

The transparency of Jeremiah's emotions, the portrayal of the heavy burden of his calling, give reality and solidity to the presentation of man and message. The image of the message "like a burning fire" (20:9) is particularly memorable. It is a worse pain not to speak, even though, as his mother (20:14), he wishes there could be a failure to bear.

Section III: Denunciation of Faithless Kings and False Prophets (Chapters 21–29)

The first 20 chapters had a certain sort of three-way drama, which gave it cohesion and drive. This next section continues some of the same themes, but the dynamics of the drama changes, as do the language and literary forms. The drama is now between God and the prophet on one side; on the other, various kings and "shepherds," worked out as a two-way dialogue but set within certain specific narratives. The language changes from mainly poetry to mainly prose, as if to emphasize the more narrative setting. Laments, soliloquies, and rhetorical questions give way to WOES AND DENUNCIATIONS, taunts, antilaments, dreams and burdens (nearly always false), as the language of prophecy is extended. The enacted prophecy clashes with its counterfeit.

There is for us a strange anomaly, though. While nearly every chapter is carefully dated, and a specific narrative established, there seems no effort to arrange the chapters chronologically. Though they range over a 20-year span, from 609 B.C.E. (the Egyptian victory over Josiah) to 587 B.C.E. (the siege of Jerusalem), the chapters move backward and forward. Clearly neither Jeremiah nor his editors were interested in cause and effect in our modern historical sense, when it is important to have events in their right time sequence. Jeremiah's readers (as distinct from the immediate listeners to his individual prophecies) knew what had happened: Jerusalem had been smashed to smithereens and God's people had been taken into exile. What they wanted to understand were, Who was responsible? Why had God done this to them? Was there any future left? The arrangement of the chapters leaves us with no doubt as to the answers to those two questions. The first 20 chapters have shown us the failure to practice true religion and uphold a just society; these next nine chapters tell us of disastrous secular and spiritual leadership.

Chapters 21–23 begin with a hopeful little scenario. Pashhur is sent from King Zedekiah to Jeremiah, even as the city is besieged. The last time we saw Pashhur he was striking Jeremiah and humiliating him by putting him in the stocks (20:2). Is this a change of heart? He reminds Jeremiah of past rescues. Perhaps he was thinking of the last siege of Jerusalem, in 701 B.C.E., when King Hezekiah withstood the Assyrians under Sennacherib (2 Kings 19). Jeremiah quickly reverses their expectations of an optimistic response. The LORD is indeed a fighter, but *against* them (21:5, 10, 13). The repeated preposition is significant. There is a way forward—to surrender!—there is always a choice! always "the way of life and the way of death" (21:8). Their position is not invulnerable, whatever they may think (21:13, best in the New International Version).

The next chapter begins with the question of "who is responsible for this mess?" He has withering comments on all three previous kings: Shallum (Jehoiakim I, 22:11–12); Jeohoiakim II (22:18–19), and Coniah (Jehoiachin, 22:24–30). The latter he will not even call a king: "This man," he says (verses 22:18f.), could be seen as an antilament, though the term *taunt* would be better. This again is a very old literary form, even if somewhat relegated to the playground now. Another literary form is the "woe!" of 22:13 and 23:1. The word *woe* can introduce two distinct literary forms: the lament, as we have already seen (as in "Woe is me!"), and the denunciation (as in "Woe to . . .").

Chapter 23 is the second sort. A sudden denunciation bursts out against the "shepherds," that is to say, the spiritual leaders, be they priests or prophets. Much of the imagery in this chapter we have seen already (e.g., 23:7–8 = 16:14–15). But two images are new to Jeremiah; the first is "the council of the LORD" (23:18, 22). Most kings had councils to advise them, sometimes with executive powers. God's government is seen in this way. Only true prophets have stood in this council. It is a significant biblical image, occurring, for example, in Job 15:8; 1 Kings 22:19–23; and Psalm 89:7.

The other image is of the "burden" (23:33), where Jeremiah makes a play on words. The true prophet has a burden; the false prophet is a burden. A burden is an oracle, a message from God. It runs parallel here to "dreams" (23:25). Dreams were a traditional way of receiving a message from God, as with Joseph the dreamer in Genesis. But for every true means of spiritual communication, there is a false (see REVELATION, GOD'S). That is why, in 1 Corinthians 12, Paul has to list "discerning of spirits" as a necessary ministry for a church. Jeremiah certainly had this gift: Our hindsight shows just how realistic and accurate his prophecies were and how false the others.

The next chapter moves backward in time from the actual siege to just after King Jehoiachin's surrender 10 years before, when he and many of the noble and professional classes were deported to Babylon, known as the first deportation. Jeremiah is given another picture, presumably some mental image that impressed itself strongly on him, of two fig baskets, one of good fruit, the other of bad. Those who were taken into the first deportation are the good figs; those remaining are *not* chosen by God at all as a righteous remnant—far from it. They will be disposed of. Some future is offered the good figs (24:7), anticipating 31:31–34.

We now move to a very significant chapter, where the book moves into the style of APOCALYPTIC WRITING. This was a genre that developed from Jeremiah's time onward, through Ezekiel, Daniel, and Zechariah, and then into the New Testament, culminating in the book of Revelation. This is an early example. It deals with future events in terms of conflict and violence, till evil is thrown down and a reign of righteousness established. It is visionary and cosmic rather than prophetic and local, and its imagery develops its own TYPES and tropes.

Here, Jeremiah moves from a prophetic understanding that Nebuchadnezzar is God's instrument to a prediction of a 70-year exile, repeated again in 29:10 and taken up several times by the writer of the Chronicles (2 Chronicles 36:21). The language is dramatic here: 25:10 echoing 7:34. But in 25:13, the text states: "everything written in this book which Jeremiah prophesied against all the nations." There is a first mention of a book but also a wider perspective that moves us into the cosmic perspective typical of the apocalyptic. This general perspective is different from specific prophecies against other nations in chapters 46–51.

The central image is the "cup of the wine of wrath" (25:15, 28), an image taken up in other

apocalyptic writings, such as Revelation 14:10, from which it enters secular literature, as in John Steinbeck's *The Grapes of Wrath*. Jeremiah himself "took the cup from the LORD's hand"; then follows a long list of some of the nations, then their drunkenness from it, their vomiting, and final destruction—a readily visualized dramatic extended image. Piles of corpses and lands laid waste are also part of the apocalyptic scenario, as in 25:33–38. God's loud voice of judgment, however, rises above all the din of battle and confusion (25:30) in this doomsday scenario.

The remaining chapters of this section deal with the false prophets, and four in particular are named. The encounter with Hananiah is particularly dramatic. Jeremiah's prophetic enactment of wearing a yoke (27:2) is challenged by Hananiah (28:1–11), who reinterprets the prophecy by breaking the yoke and predicting freedom. Jeremiah utters a counterprophecy against Hananiah, including his quick demise, which is recorded in a terse endnote (28:17). The dialogue is between true and false prophecies and is fully recorded either as straight narrative or as dialogue embedded within the prophecy.

Chapter 26 presents us the temple sermon mentioned earlier in 7:1–15 and fills out the physical threats to Jeremiah's life. Fortunately, he does have some friends at court (26:17–19). Chapter 29 is another literary form, the letter or EPISTLE, developed later in the New Testament as a standard vehicle for theological discourse. There are at least three letters mentioned in the chapter. The first is Jeremiah's letter to the exiles of the first deportation, telling them to settle in for a long stay (29:1–23). It contains the much quoted verse "For I know the plans I have for you," declares the Lord, "plans to prosper you and not to harm you, plans to give you hope and a future" (29:11 New International Version), where the antithetical parallelism "not to harm" blends in with rhythms of the positive parallels. Out of sight does not mean out of mind.

Then there is a letter from one of the prophets in exile already back in Jerusalem, which is paraphrased by Jeremiah (29:24–28). The unflattering letter is a protest concerning his prediction of a long stay. It is sent to Zedekiah the priest, who, fortunately, is sympathetic to Jeremiah, as are a few others (26:16–19), and reads him the letter. Thereupon Jeremiah pens his second letter to the three false prophets in Babylon, again refuting them and prophesying a bad end for them (29:30–31).

Section IV: The Promise of Restoration (Chapters 30–33)

Chapters 30 and 31, which return to poetry, are "consolations," the opposite of laments. They look forward with hope over a present fraught with suffering. Parts may originally have been said or written somewhat earlier, even in the reign of Josiah, as it seems to refer to the northern kingdom. So in 30:18 "the city" is not named, so that it could include SAMARIA, the northern capital, as well as Jerusalem, the capital of the southern kingdom, Judah. Whatever the chronology, Jeremiah is binding both nations into their original unity as recipients of God's covenant.

The theme is stated in 31:2,3: finding "grace in the wilderness." This is where the false prophets were wrong. They wanted to avoid the wilderness of punishment or trial, but as we have seen, wilderness imagery runs throughout Jeremiah, as it does throughout the Hebrew Bible. This is a profound theological truth, which needs to be allied to the next line, "I have loved you with an everlasting love." Many critics claim that God is portrayed as a harsh judge with little love. Jeremiah's depiction of him undermines such claims. The proverb "For the LORD reproves the one he loves, as a father the son in whom he delights" (Proverbs 3:11–12) that is taken up in the New Testament (Hebrews 12:5–6) is exactly Jeremiah's language too. There is a continuity in the depiction of God's love from the Hebrew Bible to the New Testament, not a disjunction.

If Jeremiah 20 was the nadir and emotional focus of the book, then Jeremiah 31 is its theological focus and climax. It is a compilation of several prophecies given at different times, one of which may have been as a dream (31:26), but Jeremiah's inspiration has melded the constituent parts together into one powerful statement of hope and consolation, grounded not on human aspirations but on the very nature of God himself. The climax

is in 31:31–34, where the old and the new are contrasted. In the New Testament of the Christian Bible, Jeremiah's contrast of old and new covenant becomes a central theological feature, and Hebrews 8:8–12 quotes it in full. The old covenant at Sinai was cut in stone; the new cut in hearts; the first had to be taught and learned; the new shall be immediate knowledge, as much like knowing a person as knowing a thing. The old had little room for forgiveness; the new will have no memory of sin forgiven. And just as the old was given in the wilderness, so the new will be forged out of the wilderness experience of exile.

Natural and PASTORAL imagery surrounds this, rather than the legal language of the old covenant. Thus the "land of milk and honey" is located in dancing and vineyards (31:4–5), brooks of water (31:9), the shepherd gathering a scattered flock (31:10), a watered garden (31:12), and so on. In places the language is psalmlike (31:7). At the end of the chapter, the imagery becomes grander and more cosmic (31:35–37): The covenant God is also the Creator God. We move in the genre of consolation in 31:9, 21. When Rachel "refuses to be comforted" (31:15, quoted by Matthew 2:18), the LORD says, "Your children shall come back to their own country" (31:17).

Chapters 32–33 return to prose and a more specific narrative scenario. The siege of Jerusalem was briefly lifted in 588 B.C.E. The moment is seized by Jeremiah for yet another enacted prophecy: He is to buy a field and go through all the legal formalities. Again, it enacts hope for the future, that law and order will be restored. The field can symbolically be seen as Israel, Jeremiah as God. Then follows a wonderful prayer by Jeremiah. Such prayers are rare in the prophetic books. It is a very specific prayer too: all about purchasing the field at the time "the siege-ramps have been cast up against the city to take it" (32:24).

God's answer is immediate. It reiterates much of what has been said in the previous chapter, concluding with the reaffirmation of Jeremiah's action: "Fields shall be bought in this land of which you are saying, It is a desolation" (32:43). In chapter 33, Jeremiah is back in detention after his brief freedom to buy the field. The message of restoration is not muted, however. A dialogue is set up between what the people say, "It is a waste" (33:10), and what God says. Jeremiah 33:10–11 echoes the formula image of 7:34 and 16:9, adding a Psalm echo. Verses 33:14–26 are not in the Septuagint version, leading some to think it is a later addition. But the references to restoration of a Davidic kingship only repeat 23:5–6. All that is new is the reference to the "levitical" priesthood, i.e., those who traditionally served in the temple rituals. More significant is the language of God's covenant with "the day and the night" (33:20, 25), as well as with a specifically Davidic covenant (33:21), which widens the scope of the new covenant language away from strict parallels with the Sinai covenant to wider concepts of God's faithfulness.

We need to see here the fundamental difference between the Hebrew view of the future and the Greek concept of tragedy. In Greek tragedy, the future is ordained and prophesied by fairly impersonal forces. Whatever the protagonist does to prevent his fate, he only hastens it. In Jeremiah's theology, "fate" is conditional, contained within a laid-down covenant. Even when the covenant is broken, there is always the possibility of renewal because of the loving and forgiving nature of God, who is personal and who communicates, not enigmatically, but in plain language. Thus there is no need of tragedy, whereas for the Greeks, tragedy was an innate universal law.

Section V: The Last Days of Jerusalem (Chapters 34–45; 52)

The section is entirely in prose and so lacks many of the poetic features of the earlier sections. There are the central images of *planting and building* (42:10) and a scathing image of the pharaoh being defeated as "a shepherd picks his cloak clean of vermin" (43:12). The drama lies in the arguments that take place between Jeremiah and the Judean leaders (for example: 38:24f.; 37:17f.; 43:2f; 44:16f.) and the chaotic events that followed (chapters 40–41).

It might seem the narrative's purpose is to prove that Jeremiah's prophecies were accurate, thus validating the first half of the book. This would be too limited a view: Jeremiah takes no pleasure in being proved right. For him, there is no need of proof. Is then Jeremiah a Cassandra-like prophet? Even in Egypt, with Judah and Jerusalem laid waste, no one will believe him (44:20–30). Has his whole ministry been a waste of time?

So what is this section meant to show? First, just how intransigent the people of God were in their religious delusion, how being out of sync religiously meant they became out of sync politically too. Zedekiah's blinding is symbolic as well as actual. Second, it shows Jeremiah was the only realist amongst them. He could see the Babylonians were being used by God and, therefore, people did not need to fear them (38:2, 20; 42:11–12). In fact, his depiction of the Baylonian officials (39:11–40:6) is very even-handed. To everyone else, this seemed treachery. God had to start again, as he did with THE EXODUS under Moses. And the EXILE in Babylon was the only way to this.

That is why the book finishes in Babylon. This is where the new hope will arise: There is still a Davidic king; there are remnants of the people, just as there are remnants of the temple. Jeremiah's personal fate, whatever that might have been, is unimportant compared to that—and it is Jeremiah who has already given them hope of restoration before he died.

His ministry, then, must be seen as heroic. A strange little incident prefigures this sort of heroic faithfulness. In chapter 35 we meet the Rechabites, a nomadic group driven into the city by the Babylonian army. Though tested by Jeremiah himself, they remain true to their vows. This is yet another sort of enacted prophecy—and one that applies to Jeremiah himself. Despite every pressure, he has remained true.

Section VI: Judgments against Surrounding Nations (Chapters 46–51)

In Jeremiah 1:5, Jeremiah is told that he is to be "a prophet to the nations." In this section, we see extensive evidence of this for the first time. Each of Israel's neighbors is addressed. At times, Israel had been at war with almost all the nations mentioned, the exception being Elam, which was located on the other side of Babylon. Jeremiah, however, does not drag up historical grievances against these nations.

There is a much greater sense of God's being a sovereign over all the nations, and his dealing with them is related to what they now are. Certainly, in some cases, they are still against Israel, perhaps hoping to profit from its defeat, but their main attribute is pride.

Most of the passages are in poetry and rich in imagery and rhetorical devices. On the whole, the imagery is formula imagery, but in each case, there is some local detail to specify the nation, sometimes through mentioning main towns and cities, the name of its gods, or some geographical or local feature. For example, stock images are of need of healing, women in childbirth, locusts, savage animals, floods, and wine and drunkenness. The genres are of denunciation ("woe to!") and taunt songs; references abound to passers-by astonished at the destruction; of hissing.

As for specific images and references, the floods in Egypt are those of the RIVER NILE (46:7–8); local names are Migdol, Memphis, Tahpanhes, and Thebes; local gods are Apis and Amon. The image of a snake (46:22) is a specific reference to Egyptian mythology. Or for Moab, local names are Nebo, Heshbon, Horonaim, Luhith; the local deity is Chemosh; local references are to salt (48:9) and wine (48:11) in an extended simile describing the local wineries. In a sense, the cities and towns are synecdochic: The part stands for the whole. Parallelism demands similar terms, and the devices of synecdoche and metonymy (see IMAGERY, BIBLICAL) generate such terms.

The major section on Babylon is more complex. The language itself is no more complex: Various images are repeated, usually in parallelisms, in variations, rather like a symphony, building up to a climax. But in the light of Jeremiah's previous attitude to the Babylonians, accepting their inevitable victory, trusting them for favor, and showing various Babylonian officials as sensible men, such an attack might seem contradictory. Yet there are modern parallels: War stories exist of humane Germans and wise generals; yet the total destruction of Nazi Germany is nevertheless seen as deserved, a result of the arrogance and cruelty of the regime. More specifically, Jeremiah attacks certain false prophets already in exile in Babylon for predicting a quick end to the exile and a quick return home (chapter 29). And yet he, too, predicts an end and a return. However, Jeremiah puts no time frame in his predictions; only the utter certainty of Babylon's downfall at the hands of some power from the north, which came to pass, sure enough, in 539 B.C.E., when the Persians suddenly invaded the country (Daniel 5:30). But this was nearly 60 years after the first deportation and long after Jeremiah had died. His enacted prophecy recorded at the end of the section (51:63–64), done by proxy this time, dates from 594 B.C.E.

Chapter 51 is the longest in the book. It contains examples of highly charged parallelisms (51:20–23)—the hammer hammered (cf. 50:23); a psalmlike passage transcribed from 10:12–16 (51:15–19)—Psalm 104 would be a good comparison; a dramatic dialogue (51:34–37) between a personified Jerusalem and God; and one between the prophet and the exiles (51:50–51); as well as the enacted prophecy mentioned. Images of *wild animals* abound, as do *battle images* and images of *wilderness and waste places*. Images specific to Babylon would include the "destroying mountain" (51:25), referring to the ziggurats, and wordplay on placenames: *Merathaim*, which means "double rebellion" and "Land of the Lagoons"; and *Pekod* (50:21), which means "punishment" and is the name of a tribe adjacent to Persia.

For the exiles, the strongest image, however, would not have been the fate of its oppressor but the image of God as their Redeemer, "pleading their cause" (50:33–34) as a righteous remnant (50:20), a remnant that includes both the present exiles from Judah and the previous ones from the northern kingdom, Israel (50:17), previously devoured and "gnawed" by Nebuchadnezzar but now to be restored to its pasture (50:19). This whole last section completes Jeremiah's message: not on a note of compromise with an all-powerful enemy but seeing that enemy now under judgment, and God's redemption to be manifested by restoration and "an everlasting covenant that will never be forgotten" (50:5).

CHARACTERS

Baruch   Jeremiah's scribe and personal assistant, first mentioned in 32:12–16 and most famously in writing down Jeremiah's early prophecies and then taking them into the temple to read to the religious leadership (chapter 36). Baruch's fear for his own life is described in chapter 45, where he is promised his life "as a prize of war." He accompanied Jeremiah to Egypt (43:6–7). Other helpers of Jeremiah are Ahikam (26:24) and Ebed-melech (38:7–13; 39:15–18).

Gedaliah   Appointed by Nebuchadnezzar to be governor of Judah after the fall of Jerusalem (40:5). He sets up his headquarters at Mizpah but is assassinated there by Ishmael, though he had been warned of the danger.

Hananiah   A prophet, and Jeremiah's leading opponent among the "false prophets." He, too, enacts a prophecy to contradict Jeremiah's (chapter 28). Jeremiah denounces him, and he dies later that year. Other false prophets are Shemaiah (29:24–32) and Ahab and Zedekiah (29:21–23).

Jehoiachin   At 18 years old, he was king for three months in 597 B.C.E., the victim of the rebellion by his father, Jehoiakim, against the Babylonians. He was taken in the first deportation to Babylon and stayed in prison till Nebuchadnezzar's death in 561 B.C.E., when he was released.

Jehoiakim (Eliakim)   Eliakim was an older son of King Josiah and chosen by the Egyptians to take the throne in 609 B.C.E. under the name of *Jehoiakim*. He had little sympathy for Jeremiah, burning the book of prophecies given to him and killing another prophet, Uriah (26:20–23). After the Egyptian defeat by the Babylonians in 605 B.C.E., he became a vassal to them, then rebelled against them in 602 B.C.E. and again in 598 B.C.E. He died during the first Babylonian siege of the capital, Jerusalem, and was briefly succeeded by his 18-year-old son, Jehoiachin. Jeremiah's judgment of him is recorded in 22:18–19.

Jeremiah   Often referred to as the "weeping prophet" (9:1). The prophet whose prophecies are preserved in the book of Jeremiah. At God's command, he remained unmarried. He is shown as a complex character, uncompromising and consistent, realistic yet visionary, pessimistic yet hopeful of the future. He is worn down by constant opposition and rejection and laments his calling. Yet heroically he continues at great danger to himself, suffering beatings, imprisonment, and near-death and finally being carried off against his will to Egypt, where, presumably, he dies. In the end, he becomes the only spiritual leader left to the remnant in Egypt. As a true prophet, he wishes to intercede for the people but is forbidden. As a "prophet to the nations" (1:5) he also speaks against surrounding nations and Babylon itself

Johanan   A rebel leader after the fall of Jerusalem. He kills Ishmael, then abducts Jeremiah and takes him to Egypt but refuses to listen to his advice.

Judah, people of   After the division of Israel into northern and southern kingdoms, the southern kingdom became known as Judah. However, there was no generally accepted term for its people. The term *Jew* was not really used till after the Exile, though the King James Version sometimes uses the term in Jeremiah. Other translations use *Judeans* or *people of Judah*. Jeremiah attacks them as being religious only as idolators, with little concept of monotheism, or of Deuteronomic worship and covenant. As such, they will suffer judgment. However, there is a promise of restoration, when they will be given "a new heart" to worship and love God.

Nebuchadnezzar (Nebuchedrezzar)   Rose to the Babylonian throne in 605 B.C.E. and immediately consolidated and extended the Babylonian Empire throughout the Middle East. His policy was to deport defeated people, or at least their leaders, and resettle them in Babylonia. This is what he did in 597 B.C.E. and 586 B.C.E. to the southern kingdom. The second time, however, his patience seems to have run out, and he assassinated most of the rebellious leaders of Judah, including the king's sons, though sparing Zedekiah himself. He died in 561 B.C.E.

Pashhur   Priest and chief officer in the temple, an inveterate opponent of Jeremiah. He puts him in the stocks (20:2) and then into a mud-filled cistern (38:6). Jeremiah predicts he will go into exile and die there. King Zedekiah uses him as an intermediary with Jeremiah (21:1), though this leads nowhere. Other priests mentioned are Zephaniah (21:1), the second priest, and the chief priest, Seraiah. Zephaniah appears more sympathetic to Jeremiah (29:25–29). Both are put to death by Nebuchadnezzar (52:24–27).

Zedekiah   The last king of the southern kingdom. He was born Mattaniah, being Jehoiachin's uncle, but still only 21 years old when he ascended the throne as the Babylonian choice for king after Jehoiachin's deportation, given the name of *Zedekiah* by them. He is shown as a weak and vacillating king (ch. 37), who finally rebels, hoping for an Egyptian alliance. After trying to escape the city during the second Babylonian siege, he is captured by the Babylonians, blinded, and taken into captivity. We do not hear of his death.

Job

Why does a righteous God make righteous people suffer? This is the question the book of Job considers. Throughout the centuries, people have been wrestling with this question, believers as well as skeptics, philosophers, theologians, and, most of all, people who themselves have been challenged by suffering in their lives, following in the footsteps of Job.

The book of Job belongs to the genre of WISDOM LITERATURE. Other wisdom books of the Hebrew Bible are Proverbs, Ecclesiastes, and the Song of Solomon. Biblical wisdom starts with the assumption that the world is a wisely ordered divine creation. By observing these wise orders in nature and society, divine wisdom can be attained. Living according to the divine order helps one live a successful life. Wisdom also deals with the limits of knowledge and of life, especially in Ecclesiastes and in the book of Job. The "fear of the LORD," which

Job's testing and patience (Job 1:6–22), engraving by Julius Schnorr von Carolsfeld

means respect of and obedience to God, forms the basis of all wisdom and, at the same time, marks its limits.

The story of the book of Job is set in the patriarchal era depicted in Genesis. We know virtually nothing about its author and its time of writing, however. A famous person named Job is mentioned in the sixth-century B.C.E. text of Ezekiel 14:14, 20. In the caves of Qumran (see DEAD SEA SCROLLS), fragments of the book have been found, together with a commentary on Job from the first or second century B.C.E.

The suffering of the righteous is a theme found in extrabiblical literature of the ancient Near East as well. There is, for example, a work known as "I Will Praise the LORD of Wisdom" (*Ludlul bel nemeqi*). In it, a God-fearing man becomes gravely ill. His friends accuse him of being a wrongdoer, and his family becomes hostile to him. He himself believes that he must have committed some sin, even if he does not know what it is. He appeals for deliverance and in the end is restored to health. This text, in its Accadian version, was written around 1200 B.C.E. Other texts dealing with similar subjects are extant from Egypt, Canaan, and Sumer. Although the theme of Job was therefore not unique to Israel, the book itself can be seen as an independent creation giving a new answer to the question of suffering.

The book of Job has a narrative prologue (chapters 1–2) and epilogue (42:7–17), framing the poetic speeches that make up the main part of the book. The dialogue commences with a lament of Job (chapter 3), followed by three cycles of speeches of Job and his three friends, Eliphaz, Bildad, and Zophar (chapters 4–14; 15–21; 22–26). These speech cycles are closed by two more general speeches of Job (chapters 27–31). After that follow four speeches of Elihu (chapters 32–37). Finally, God himself enters the dialogue with two speeches, each followed by a short answer of Job (38:1–42:6).

There are some logical tensions among the individual blocks of the book, especially between the narrative framework and the poetic speeches. In the prologue, for example, Job is depicted as a very pious man. In his speeches, however, he goes quite far in accusing God. Furthermore, the prologue gives an explanation for Job's suffering, whereas the speeches deal with suffering that is unexplainable. Finally, a certain Elihu appears in the dialogue section but is neither introduced in the prologue nor assessed in the epilogue, as is the case with the other friends of Job. In the past, these tensions have been explained from a literary-critical point of view, assigning the narrative frame, the speech cycles, and the speeches of Elihu to different stages of the literary history of the book. It has to be said, however, that the book makes most sense in the form we have it. The tensions can be very well explained as different aspects of a complex overall topic. Hypothetically reconstructing the literary history of the book does not in fact help us to understand the intention of its final form.

The book is written in a distinctive dialect of the ancient Hebrew language that is not attested elsewhere but shows affinities to other languages of the Canaanite realm. The poetic speeches employ parallelism throughout. The book as a whole, as well as the individual speeches, prove themselves masterpieces of literary design. In particular, the numerous images and metaphors contribute to the distinctive character of the text.

SYNOPSIS

Job is a very righteous and upright man. He has seven sons and three daughters and a vast possession of livestock. Job is so devout that he even makes sacrifices for sins his children might have committed.

One day, a heavenly council takes place. Among the angels, SATAN also presents himself before the Lord. God points out to him the exemplary piety of Job. But Satan supposes that Job was worshipping God only because God had given him great wealth. If one could take away his possessions, he would turn away from God instantly. God allows Satan to test Job.

In a series of cruel strokes of fate, Job loses all of his property and all of his children. Although he is deeply dismayed, he keeps being faithful to God.

After some time, another heavenly council takes place. Again God points out to Satan the piety of Job. Satan supposes, however, that if one could only harm Job physically, he would surely renounce God. God allows Satan to test Job again.

Job's whole body is now inflicted with loathsome sores. He is suffering terribly. His wife mocks him because of his devoutness. But he still keeps faithful to God.

Three friends visit Job: Eliphaz, Bildad, and Zophar. When they see him, they weep, and they sit down with him for seven days in silence.

Then Job begins complaining about his suffering. A conversation develops, in which Job and his friends wrestle with the problem of Job's suffering. The friends are of the opinion that since God is just, there must be a dark secret in the life of Job for which his suffering is a punishment. Job, however, is not aware of having committed any major sin. He continues complaining, he criticizes his friends for what they say, and in the end he even accuses God of treating him unfairly. The parties cannot come close to each other, so after a long time of struggling the discussion remains at a standstill. Now a young person named Elihu asks to speak. But he is not able to solve the problem either. Finally, God himself enters the discussion. He turns the gaze of his discussion partners to his creation. He describes things like weather phenomena and different animals, pointing out that the creation is a witness to his majesty and wisdom and at the same time is incomprehensible and uncontrollable. When God finishes his speech, Job submits to him and repents.

God reprimands the three friends for what they said. They have to make a burnt offering as a sacrifice for their sins, and Job intercedes for them so that God will forgive them. Finally, God restores the fortunes of Job. He gives him twice as much as he had before. His family reunites with him. He gets seven sons and three daughters again. Job dies after a long and rich life.

COMMENTARY

The Prologue (1:1–2:13)

The background for the problem of the book of Job is the assumption of a just, divine world order. In ancient Near Eastern wisdom thinking, this is expressed particularly through the principle of retribution: that good deeds lead to good consequences, whereas evil deeds lead to evil consequences. This relationship is seen partly as a built-in mechanism of the rules of society. Believing in a righteous God, however, people also expect that God himself will guarantee the validity of that principle.

But this opinion is not always in agreement with the reality that is experienced. The counterexample par excellence is that of the suffering of the righteous. The prologue depicts Job as an extraordinarily pious and an extraordinarily wealthy man and, therefore, as a prime example of the positive side of the principle of retribution. But the situation changes radically when Job loses his family, his property, and his health in quick succession. On the basis of this experience of unearned suffering, the book of Job poses the question of the justice of the world order of God. In philosophy, the issue is dealt with under the heading of theodicy, "justice of God."

The book of Job does not deal with the problem of suffering in itself. According to the Hebrew Bible, which is the canonical context of the book of Job, suffering in general is a consequence of human renunciation of God, which causes the wrath of God to be visited on the world (see Genesis 3:14–19; Leviticus 26:14–39; Deuteronomy 28:15–68). Hence, the book of Job does not treat the suffering in the world in general but the disproportion that some individuals are much more affected than others.

A distinctive aspect of the prologue are the two descriptions of heavenly councils. The ultimate limits of knowledge, the border between heaven and earth, is lifted for a short moment, and the reader catches a glimpse of the divine rule over the world and receives an explanation for Job's suffering: The righteousness of Job is to be tested.

This explanation of suffering at the beginning of the book stands in a certain tension with the following text and especially with the speech of God that deals explicitly with unexplainable suffering (see below). In order to understand the book's message, it is important to note that the heavenly council is not meant to give the final solution to the book's subject. Otherwise, the book could have ended after chapter 2. Rather, the implications of the scenes in heaven are the following:

Through that glimpse of heaven the reader gains additional knowledge than do all the figures of the book. The reader becomes able to look at the following dialogues from a God-like perspective. The reader learns how fruitless human reasoning on the rule of God can be and is warned not to engage in such speculations.

Furthermore, from a pastoral point of view, the heavenly council scenes tell the reader, "I do not know why I have to suffer; I cannot look into heaven. But if I could, I would surely see that my suffering does make sense before God."

The wager between God and Satan should therefore not be understood as giving a universal explanation for the problem of suffering. However, its theme of testing the faith is more than just an arbitrarily chosen example of a reason for suffering. There is a certain dilemma within the principle of retribution. On the one hand, it is expected that a righteous God blesses those who are faithful to him, but, on the other hand, this same righteousness of God can lead human beings into a superficial kind of worship that is executed only for the purpose of personal wealth. In order to prove true human righteousness, paradoxically, God has to suspend his own divine righteousness. In any case, Job withstands all trials in a masterly manner: "In all this Job did not sin" (1:22; 2:10). His piety proves to be genuine, and the accusations of Satan cannot be substantiated. Satan disappears from the scene and does not play any further role in the book.

The Cycles of Speeches of Job and His Three Friends (Chapters 3–31)

The discussion of Job and his friends centers on the dogma of retribution throughout. From the suffering of Job, the three friends can only infer that he must have committed a grave sin.

Eliphaz, in particular, stresses the point that if somebody has to suffer misfortune, he necessarily must have committed a sin. But since Job is a reasonably righteous man, his suffering would not be long. Before God, no one could really claim to be without any sin.

Bildad's point is that the wisdom of the ancestors should not be thrown to the wind. They teach that sin is regularly followed by punishment. The sudden death of Job's children is a typical end for godless people. Job, however, was spared in order to get a second chance.

Zophar, too, argues that Job must have sinned. If God would speak, this would instantly become clear. Job could be lucky that God is merciful. Without God's mercy, the punishment of Job would have been even harder. In other words, in Job's punishment the mercy of God is already taken into account.

The reader knows that the friends are not right. There is no sin in Job's life that bears any relation to his suffering. Job was "blameless and upright, one who fears God and turns away from evil" (1:1, 1:8; 2:3).

Accordingly, Job defends his innocence. But he believes in the principle of retribution as well. The ultimate consequence for him is to challenge God. If the proportion of act and consequence is the first principle, either the integrity of Job or the integrity of God has to be put into question (see 32:2; 40:8).

Whereas the friends of Job mainly talk *about* God, Job wants to enter into dialogue *with* God, talking to him, lamenting before him, requesting explanation from him. In this respect, the speeches of Job stand out positively against the speeches of the three friends.

The closing speeches of Job in chapters 27–31 are of a more general kind. The speech in chapters 27–28 can be seen as a general refutation of the position of the three friends. In 27:1–10 Job rejects the words of the friends; in 27:11–23 he turns back

their own argument against them. The poem on the unattainability of wisdom in chapter 28, often marked out as an interlude, or even as a later insertion, logically belongs in its context: Despite the view of the friends, human beings cannot easily find explanations for what God is doing. Wisdom is God's concern; the concern of humans is to fear the Lord. The speech of chapters 29–31 forms a systematic defense of Job's position before God. First, Job describes his situation previously (chapter 29) and now (chapter 30). Then follows a detailed list of sins Job has not committed. The defense is closed with a signature (31:35), together with the expression of hope that his adversary would frame a detailed statement of claim as well, so that Job would be able to defeat it.

At the end of the book, God rebukes the three friends for what they have said. They wanted to protect God from being criticized, but they did wrong. Job, in contrast, is praised, for he spoke of (or to) God "what is right" (42:7). Therefore, according to the book of Job, God is not opposed to people who moan or complain about their suffering. Whatever bad feelings a person has, there is room for expressing them before God. On the contrary, God rebukes those who want to stop such a person from complaining by giving cold comfort and cheap "pious" explanations on the sense of suffering.

The Speeches of Elihu (Chapters 32–37)

Elihu plays a special role in the book. Unlike those of Job's other three friends, Elihu's name does not appear in the prologue or in the epilogue. Furthermore, the text does not record any reactions to his words, either by Job, or by God, or by the narrator. From this some people infer that the speeches of Elihu must be a secondary addition to the text. Through Elihu's speeches, someone else wanted to give his personal opinion on the subject under consideration. But if a later editor added four chapters of speeches into the book, he could, of course, easily have inserted a reference to Elihu at the prologue or at the epilogue as well. To assume a textual addition only moves the problem of Elihu's appearance from the author to a later editor but does not solve it. In any case, in the present form of the book, the sudden appearance of Elihu functions as a retarding moment withholding the expected answer of the Almighty (31:35, see 38:1) for some time.

Elihu also assumes that the teaching of retribution is valid. He points out, however, that this principle is not to be seen as a blind mechanism but rather as a channel through which God wants to communicate with a person. Through suffering, God requests human beings to confess their sins. On the whole, this position is only a slight variation on what the other three friends support.

The concluding passages of Elihu's speeches (36:22–37:24) contain descriptions of the creation that sound very similar to some elements of the speeches of God. In order to assess these descriptions, however, we must ask what purpose they serve. Elihu's final point is that God is great in power and justice (37:23–24) and all human beings have to submit to him. While this is a true statement, it does not help to explain Job's suffering any better than the arguments of the other friends do. From the information given in the prologue, the reader knows that Elihu, as the other friends, does not get to the heart of the matter.

The Speeches of God (38:1–42:6)

The reader naturally expects the final answer of the book from the speech of God and is therefore all the more surprised that God does not seem to speak about the suffering of the righteous at all. God neither explains to Job why he has to suffer, nor reacts to Job's claim to be innocent, nor comments on the principle of retribution. God does not, in fact, seem to give answers at all, but rather he asks a lot of questions himself. Moreover, the subjects of his speeches are things like the size of the earth, weather phenomena, and wild animals.

The key to understanding this speech in the context of the book is the indirect, empirical approach to knowledge that is typical of wisdom literature. In his speech, God turns the gaze of the wise to his creation. By observing God's creation, wise people can learn about who God is and how he rules his world.

The rhetorical questions and the descriptions of the speeches can be ordered into a sequence of three sections:

The first section is made up of rhetorical questions expressing that Job was not present when the world was being created. Not he, but God, was the Creator. Therefore Job simply does not know many things (38:4–11).

The second section deals with the daily maintenance of the natural world order. Again this is the business of God, not of Job (38:12–38).

In the third and longest section of his first speech, God speaks about the wild animals of his creation (38:39–39:30): It is not human beings who care for the *lion*, the *raven*, and the *mountain goat*—as a farmer breeds and raises livestock—but God. The *wild ass* and the *wild ox* are made to enjoy their freedom, not to be used by human beings. In a humorous way even the behavior of the *ostrich* is depicted. It functions according to its own rules, which are not comprehensible to human beings. Its wings flap wildly but it cannot fly. It leaves its eggs unguarded so that animals may trample on them. It has no share in understanding—but it can run faster than a horse. And this is something God created! The power and the pride of the *horse* are not given to it by human beings, but by God. Again, the way of living of the *hawk* and the *eagle* is not governed by human wisdom or power, but by God.

The second speech of God is almost entirely devoted to Behemoth and Leviathan (40:15–41:26), which are two mighty creatures of God that again cannot be controlled or exploited for human purposes. The Hebrew words *Behemoth* and *Leviathan* probably refer to the hippopotamus and crocodile, respectively, though scholars are not absolutely sure here. In any case, Leviathan is also the name of a chaos monster that appears in mythical texts. In Egyptian myth, the God Horus kills the hippopotamus and crocodile and therefore gains control over the chaos. According to Job, however, God is not the conqueror of those "chaos" animals but rather their creator! He created them and made them live among the other animals of his world.

The two speeches of God can be summarized by the following four statements: It was not human beings who created the world, but God. It is not human beings who run the world, but God. It is not human beings who have a full understanding of the world, but God. The creation of God is mighty and marvelous but at the same time incomprehensible to and uncontrollable by humans.

Applied to the theme of Job, this means many aspects of the divine world order, whether in the natural or the moral order, remain incomprehensible for human beings. Leviathan is living in this world as the suffering of the righteous is. The only sense both make, they make for God. Job has no right to an explanation for his suffering, any more than he has a right to have the purposes of wild animals explained to him. And neither does he have the competence to question God's rule. Instead, he can trust that the mighty God directs his world in wisdom and that in his plan even personal suffering makes sense.

Creation, therefore, in the book of Job has a dialectical function of revealing God and hiding him at the same time. What we learn to understand about God in this book is that we cannot fully understand him. This leads the faithful reader into fresh humility before God and even deeper "fear of the Lord."

The Epilogue (42:7–17)

The epilogue describes the restoration of Job's health and his former possessions. At first this seems to be just a happy ending. But there is more to it. That God doubles Job's former property means that he compensates him, according to the law of Exodus 22:3. God restores exactly the justice Job had to learn he could not call in from him. The epilogue corrects the wrong impression one might have received from the dialogue section that the principle of act and consequence was totally irrelevant. The readers who, informed by the heavenly scene, believed themselves to be on the safe side criticizing the position of the friends, are now set right. With David Clines, the conclusion can be drawn, "The problem with the dogma of retribution is not that it is wrong, but that it is a dogma" (David J. A. Clines, "Deconstructing the 'Book of Job', in 'What Does Eve Do to Help: And Other Readerly Questions to the Old Testament.'" In Journal for the Study of the Old Testament. Supplement Series 94. Sheffield, England: JSOT Press, 1990, 123).

To sum up the book's message: When someone is struck down by suffering, neither he nor his comforters should hastily try to give cheap, "pious"

explanations. Rather, the person should respect God's majesty and be aware of his or her own limitations in comprehending the work of God. However, the person can take all his complaints before God. He can trust that God rules his world in wisdom and that there is a purpose even for personal suffering.

Christian believers draw connections between the book of Job and the mission of Jesus Christ. Job suffers, though he is innocent, and he is finally justified. The servant of the Lord, Son of God, suffers and dies, though he is innocent, in order to justify all who believe in him, carrying away their sins. By this he makes way for a new life and a new world where there is no more suffering (see Isaiah 53; John 1:1–18; Mark 10:45; Galatians 4:4–5; Revelation 21:4).

CHARACTERS

Elihu   A companion of Job's three friends and an angry young man. He is annoyed about what Job and his friends say. His opinion is that through suffering, God wants to make Job confess his sins.

Eliphaz, Bildad, and Zophar   Friends of Job. When they hear about Job's misfortune, they visit him in order to comfort him. But they also wrongly believe that Job's suffering must be a punishment for a great sin Job had committed.

God   In his speech, God talks about his creation, demonstrating his majesty, wisdom, and incomprehensibility to human beings. Human beings do not have the competence to question God's rule. Instead, they should trust that God directs his world in wisdom, and that in his plan even personal suffering makes sense. At the end of the story, God restores Job's fortune and compensates him for his losses. This demonstrates God's justice, in spite of his incomprehensibility. Another aspect of God's justice is that he does not just refuse Satan's request but instead allows the case to be tried.

Job   Job is a very pious and righteous man, and he is very wealthy too. But suddenly he loses all his property and his children and is struck down by a severe illness. Job suffers heavily, and he feels he has been treated unjustly by God. In all his righteousness, however, he raises himself above God when he believes that he can even tell God what is right or wrong. In a fresh encounter with God, he arrives at a deeper understanding of what it means to fear the Lord. He learns to respect God's sovereignty and to trust him, even if he does not understand all that God is doing. In the end, God restores the former state of Job and compensates him for his losses.

Satan The Hebrew word *Satan* means "accuser" and in the Hebrew Bible is used for human prosecutors as well as for the divine opponent of God, who first appears as the snake in the Garden of Eden and whose character only slowly emerges in the course of the biblical history and literature. In no instance, however, is Satan an antagonist to God of equal power. No dualistic worldview, no cosmic struggle between good and evil, can be derived from the Bible. Rather, God is the final source of the blessing as well as of the curse. In the book of Job, Satan is subordinate to God. He cannot act without authorization from God. Also, the final responsibility for what Satan does is taken by God himself. Satan is a being on the surface very much concerned with justice. But his intention is surely a negative one. He is jealous of Job's faithfulness to God. He, therefore, wants to torture Job and/or make him turn away from God. And he knows how to accomplish this. By accusing Job, Satan gains for himself the right of inflicting Job with suffering. God allows him to act for some time. But then he restores Job's state and even compensates him. Satan has not succeeded.

Joel

The book of Joel stands second among the Lesser or Minor Prophets of the Hebrew Bible, where it consists of four chapters rather than three. We are told nothing of its writer or its time of writing. Internal evidence is sparse, and there are no references to Joel or the invasion of locusts anywhere else in the Hebrew Bible. For all that, the intertextuality with other prophets is strong. Verbal echoes

or references occur with Amos, Micah, Obadiah, Zechariah among the Minor Prophets, and Isaiah, Ezekiel, and Daniel with the other writing prophets. There are also similarities with Nahum.

The result has been that scholars have failed to agree in their dating of the book. At one extreme, it is placed in the minority of Joash, king of the southern kingdom of JUDAH 835–796 B.C.E., a date that would make Joel the earliest of the writing prophets. Other scholars place Joel as a contemporary of Amos and Hosea, where the compilers of the Hebrew Bible put him. Still others place the book at the time of Malachi (ca. 450 B.C.E.); the extreme dating is at the beginning of the fourth century B.C.E. Those who have placed him there have had the problem of explaining various turns of language that date from an earlier time, but religious writers do often employ archaic forms of language. No single line of argument can be sustained definitely, and all are open to objections.

What is incontrovertible is the dramatic and visionary nature of the prophet's imagination. He opens with a specific local catastrophe and within three chapters has reached the end of time and the great judgment. The book is structured in three huge steps, we might almost say leaps of the imagination. The midpoint of the book is also its fulcrum (2:18), where the LORD is no longer seen as adversary but as deliverer.

SYNOPSIS

The immediate catastrophe is a plague of locusts, not an uncommon feature of Middle Eastern life, exemplified by there being nine separate words for locusts in Hebrew. But this seems to have been greater than normal and accompanied by a drought (which may have borne them in the first place). In chapter 1, Joel urges the people, and the priests especially, to repent by fasting and wearing sackcloth. The plague is seen as a type of "the day of the LORD" (1:15).

In Chapter 2, the massive swarm of locusts is described more intensely, in terms of an invading army more devastating than any human army. They block out the light, and again, Joel is reminded of the day of the Lord (2:11). He calls priests and people to repent through a solemn assembly.

The reversal (2:18) occurs where God replies. He will "repay you for the years that the swarming locust has eaten" (2:25). He will pour his Spirit out on every one of his people; there will be apocalyptic signs and a much more far-reaching deliverance for all in JERUSALEM.

The final chapter or step builds on this "afterward" as he envisions the day of the Lord in terms of a great judgment in the Valley of Jehoshaphat, which literally means "the LORD judges." Again, apocalyptic signs herald this. The climax is a new blessing and forgiveness for Israel, and the presence of the Lord in a renewed Jerusalem forever.

COMMENTARY

Joel establishes the uniqueness of the catastrophe in the first chapter. He opens with a rhetorical question to the elders: "Has such a thing happened . . . in the days of your ancestors?" It is to be stored in their oral history and passed down to future generations. We are reminded of the plague of locusts that Moses drew on Pharaoh (Exodus 10:12–15; Psalm 78:46; 105:34), which contains much the same formula: "as has never been before, nor ever shall be again." Images of locusts are to be found in Nahum 3:15, 17. We wonder whether they can be literal or whether Joel is symbolizing an invading army? The similes in chapter 2 mean it is the locusts who are literal; the human army, figurative. But in his second imaginative step, the locust army certainly becomes a type or analogue of all devastating armies that have ever invaded Israel. Three of the terms Joel uses for locusts in the parallelisms of 1:4 are unique to him.

Ironically, Joel's first appeal is to the drunkards (1:5). The devastation of the vines, one of the metonymies of lost fertility, will affect them directly. He lists other features of lost fertility in 1:10–12, forming an extended parallelism, generating an urgency to "wail" and "mourn." The Israelites will no longer be able to offer grain offerings to God. Thus the priests have to be involved as much as the alcoholics! Drought and fire images crowd in (1:17, 20). The fire imagery may be derived from the reddish color of the locusts, but 1:19 suggests literal fire, adding to the overall devastation. The picture is bleak.

The second step is to raise this catastrophe to eschatological proportions (2:1–2). Apocalyptic language is employed: "The day of the LORD is coming," "a day of darkness and gloom," and so on. The army of locusts arrives in a blazing fire. Joel creates a dramatic antithesis of before and after in 2:3, setting Edenic fertility against desert waste. He is to renew this antithesis in his climax in 3:18–19. The scenario is generalized away from Israel to "nations" (2:6) and then to the whole cosmos (2:10). This is Joel building the apocalyptic feel—this is a cosmic catastrophe, just as the day of the Lord is cosmic in implication. By Joel 2:11, we have the vivid image of "The LORD utters his voice / at the head of his army" (as also 2:25, ironically standing against Proverbs 30:27). This is God's army—an army of vengeance against sinful humanity, his instrument just as the armies of ASSYRIA and BABYLON were seen as instruments of God's justice by Jeremiah and Isaiah. But even they did not have God leading the armies.

But God is also his people's protector (2:12). He tells them to fast, as long as it is genuine: "Rend your hearts and not your clothing" (2:13) is Joel's unique and much-quoted way of expressing it. Meaningful repentance was always a central concern for the prophets (e.g., Isaiah 1:17; Hosea 6:6; 12:6; Zechariah 7:5, 9). Joel appeals to God that Israel is God's people. If they are devastated, then God's good name is at stake (2:17).

The turning point is reached in 2:18–19 as Joel has the assurance of God's response. The anthropomorphism of God's jealousy is often used *against* Israel (as Exodus 20:5). Here it is *for* Israel, as Zechariah 1:14; 8:2. God turns right around in a quite dramatic reversal, such as we see in Hosea (Hosea 2:22). He will bless them with new fertility and "no more . . . make you / a mockery among the nations." The New International Version has "never again," a somewhat stronger declaration repeated in 2:26–27 and 3:17. The same metonymies of plenty are repeated, with rain replacing drought. The sense of repayment (2:25), rather than just restoration, is interesting.

The promise of the outpouring of the Spirit in 2:28–32 is startling. This takes us into a new realm, out of the material into the spiritual. Apart from

Moses' enigmatic statement in Numbers 11:29, no previous prophet had ever suggested a general gift of prophecy to everyone. On the contrary, Zechariah even suggested an end to the spirit of prophecy (Zechariah 13:3–5), replacing it with a "spirit of compassion and supplication" (Zechariah 12:10; cf. Ezekiel 39:29). It was left to the New Teastament writers to seize hold of this as a sign of a new era (Acts 2:17–21). The New Revised Standard Version (NRSV) inconsistently puts 2:30f. as prose, the rest of the book being in poetry, yet when this passage is quoted in Acts, it sets it out as poetry. For us, the promise of the coming of the Spirit sits strangely with language that is otherwise more typically APOCALYPTIC WRITING (2:30–32).

In fact, it becomes a bridge passage to the final step of universal judgment in the Valley of Jehoshaphat, a name only used by Joel. Later, the place of judgment was seen as the Valley of Kidron, lying just outside Jerusalem. Only a few nations are mentioned: Tyre and Sidon, Philistia, Egypt, Edom. Interestingly, Assyria and Babylonia are not mentioned, but the Greeks are. Only Daniel and Zechariah mention them elsewhere, suggesting perhaps a later date.

Joel 3:10 is startling in its deliberate reversal of Micah's and Isaiah's hope of beating swords into plowshares (Isaiah 2:4; Micah 4:3). This is an era of deliverance from enemies rather than universal peace. The winepress image for God's anger (3:13) reinforces this. Used also in Isaiah 63:3 and Lamentations 1:15, it became another New Testament apocalyptic feature (Revelation 14:18–20; 19:15). Elsewhere, winepresses are another metonomy for prosperity. Joel 3:16 is an echo of Amos 1:1 in its sacred geography.

The book climaxes with a final reversal. No longer under judgment, but its enemies judged on Mount Zion (as also Obadiah 16–17), Israel will enjoy a future prosperity, figured by new water sources (cf. Isaiah 30:25–26; Ezekiel 47:1–12; Amos 9:13) and the LORD'S presence permanently on Mount Zion (as also Zechariah 14:20–21). Joel's overall vision is not unique to him, but certain literary and theological features are: his construction of eschatology from a local catastrophe and his prediction of a universal outpouring of the prophetic gift.

John (Gospel)

Authorship

The four Gospels have similar titles, beginning, "The Gospel according to. . . ." This shows that the titles do not stem from the authors but were added at a later stage, when the early churches put the four Gospels (see GOSPEL [GENRE]) together in one collection. At that time, the tradition held that the author of this book was John, one of the TWELVE DISCIPLES of Jesus, who belonged to the inner circle of three (Mark 9:2; Galatians 2:9). The internal evidence regarding the authorship points to an anonymous character within the story who refers to himself as "the disciple whom Jesus loved." He appears only in the second half of the book (13:23; 19:26; 20:1–10; 21:7, 20–24) and is designated as the author in a kind of editorial note in 21:24 that says: "This is the disciple who testifies to these things and who wrote them down. We know that his testimony is true." This "Beloved Disciple" is also identified as the anonymous companion of Andrew in 1:35–42 and of Peter in 18:15–16, and as the anonymous eyewitness in 19:35–37.

The identification of the Beloved Disciple with the apostle John does not take place in the text, but it is the unanimous position of the early church, supported by several indications. First of all, many disciples are mentioned by name in the text (see 1:45; 6:5, 8; 11:16; 13:26; 14:22; 21:2), and the number of disciples is given as 12 (6:70), but John the brother of James and the son of Zebedee—who is well known from the other Gospels and Acts—is never mentioned. To be accurate, one should add that the name John is used frequently in the first chapters but always with reference to JOHN THE BAPTIST. A second argument that favors the identification is the undoubted closeness of the alleged author to Jesus. Of the three disciples in the inner circle around Jesus, Peter is mentioned by name and as partner of the Beloved Disciple, whereas James the son of Zebedee and brother of John was killed as a martyr as early as the year 44 C.E., so he cannot have been the author (Acts 12:2). The third argument is that the author clearly poses as an eyewitness and indeed has an excellent knowledge of times, places, events, and backgrounds.

Critical scholars agree in denying that the apostle John was the author of this gospel, but they offer a range of alternatives. Some refer to another John, an Elder John, who according to them is mentioned as author by Bishop Papias in the second century. It is likely, however, that this is based on a misunderstanding of what Papias actually wrote. Others argue that the "Beloved Disciple" is a veiled reference to the disciple Thomas or to a follower of Jesus who did not belong to the group of 12, such as Lazarus. Still others think that the "Beloved Disciple" was not a historical character at all but is the idealized, faithful, and understanding follower of Jesus. In the latter case, the real author of the gospel would be an unknown genius whose name has not been preserved.

Despite suggestions that the author must have used sources, linguistically the text is a unity; only the first (the prologue) and the last parts (chapter 21) differ slightly. So whatever sources the author may have had are now hidden beneath the surface.

Date and Readership

Although scholars in the 19th century suggested a very late date for John's gospel, even in the second half of the second century, the publication of a manuscript fragment in 1935 brought the scholarly world to its senses. This manuscript contains a fragment of John 18 and is commonly known as Papyrus 52; it stems from EGYPT and dates from the first half of the second century. However, John's gospel did not originate in Egypt, an indication that the original text must have been written earlier still.

The traditions of the church tell us that John was the last of the four evangelists to write his gospel, and that he lived to a ripe old age in the city of Ephesus in Asia Minor (modern-day Turkey). These traditions are increasingly being accepted as credible. This puts the writing of the gospel in the period between the years 70 and 100 C.E., with a tendency toward the later part of the period. Verses like 21:19–24 can only have been written after Peter's death in the sixties of the first century. There is much external evidence for the existence of the gospel in the second century, in fact more than for any other part of the New Testament.

John's gospel pays much attention to the dialogue between Jesus and the Jewish leaders. This emphasis probably reflects the gospel's target audience, which could consist of Christians who lived close to Jews as well as of Jews who so far had not accepted Jesus as the one he claims to be in this gospel, God's own Son and his definitive revelation. In the early church it was thought that John had also written to refute the heretical teaching that Jesus had not been a true human being but that probably reads back the focus of the letter 1 JOHN into the gospel.

The evangelist himself states his aim in writing in 20:30–31: "Jesus did many other miraculous signs in the presence of his disciples, which are not recorded in this book. But these are written that you may believe that Jesus is the Christ, the Son of God, and that by believing you may have life in his name."

John and the Synoptics

There is no space here for a full-scale comparison between John's gospel and the other three gospels, but the very fact that those three are known as the SYNOPTIC GOSPELS points to the different character of John. John situates Jesus' public ministry in Galilee as well as in Samaria and JERUSALEM. (To explain the difference with the Synoptics, it has been suggested that on several occasions only the brothers James and John went to Jerusalem with Jesus, rather than all disciples.) As to the style of Jesus' teaching, John does not use many parables (see GENRE) but rather long dialogues. For the content of Jesus' teaching, John does not focus on the KINGDOM OF GOD / (KINGDOM OF HEAVEN) but on Jesus himself and his relationship with God the Father. Whereas a reading of the Synoptics suggests that Jesus' entire public ministry lasted no longer than a year, John punctuates his narrative with indications that it was longer. He shows that Jesus initially worked side by side with John the Baptist for some time (3:2–24). John 7:1 and 3 suggest a longer period in Galilee than is actually described. More importantly, he tells of at least three PASSOVER festivals during Jesus' ministry (2:13; 6:4; 11:55; and possibly in 5:1). This provides evidence that the ministry lasted for three years or more.

(With this knowledge one can reread the Synoptics and also find indications of a ministry of more than one year in Mark 14:3, 14, 49; Matthew 23:37; and Luke 6:17.)

Luke and John have in common that they pay attention to personal interviews between Jesus and individuals.

Relationships and connections between people and churches in the EARLY CHURCH were closer than is often assumed. It is therefore likely that when John wrote this gospel half a century after the life of Jesus, he had access to at least one of the other gospels. The explanatory notes in 3:24 and 11:2 can be read as intended for readers who knew Mark's gospel. John may consciously have set out to include in his book things that the Synoptics had not included, to prevent unnecessary duplication. However that may be, it is best to read John first and foremost for its own sake and in its own right as a vital witness to Jesus Christ.

Literary Character

Although the fourth gospel can be seen as an ancient biography, John is closer to history proper than the other three gospels. Despite the absence of a prologue like Luke's, the original readers must have read this gospel as history. Several factors contribute to this verdict. First of all, the text clearly claims to be based on eyewitness testimony. Whereas Luke 1:1–4 suggests that the author knew eyewitnesses and used written sources, in John the implied author is himself one of the disciples and as such a primary eyewitness. Second, John pays much attention to topography; nearly every episode in the gospel is located, sometimes with great exactness. Although some locations may have a symbolic meaning, the evangelist's primary interest is in the actual topography. (Modern research and discoveries show the accuracy of his descriptions.)

Third, the fourth gospel offers a detailed chronological framework. John presumes that his readers know exactly which year he has in mind when he refers to the 46th year of the building of the temple in Jerusalem (2:20), although modern scholars struggle with this. His further points of reference are the Jewish festivals of Passover (2:13; 6:4; 11:55), Tabernacles (7:2), and Hanukkah (10:22).

In addition, two weeks are described in full detail, the first week of Jesus' ministry in 1:19–2:11 and the last week in chapters 12–20; consequently, most of the action is dated with great precision. In fact, following a convention among Greek historians, John also includes both the earliest and the latest possible points of reference, eternity (1:1) and Jesus' return (14:3; 21:23), in a metahistorical framework.

Fourth, John is more selective than the other evangelists, another virtue highly valued by classical historians. Whereas Matthew has 20 miracle stories, and Mark and Luke 18 each, John has just eight. While his book is similar in length to the other gospels, John has included fewer episodes, leaving him space for longer dialogues and more detailed descriptions of the miraculous signs.

Fifth, John has more than 100 narrative asides, i.e., inclusion of the narrator's voice to explain an element of a story. These asides are not only used to clarify the thoughts and feelings of the characters in the story but also to indicate time or space, to explain Hebrew or Aramaic words (see BIBLE, EARLY LANGUAGES OF), and to refer the reader to the Hebrew Bible. Finally, John includes the type of elaborate speeches that were regarded as essential in ancient historiography; in this respect his gospel resembles Matthew's, but his speeches are more unified. John presents extended conversations and discourses that are closer to real-life speech than the highly compressed rendering of Jesus' teaching of the Synoptics.

Most discourses have a rather stereotypical format. They start off as dialogues between Jesus and one or more other people, but gradually the other party (largely) fades away and the voice of Jesus takes over. In the end, the people Jesus meets only act as foils for his self-revelation. Scholars generally assume that toward the end of the discourses it is the evangelist who is speaking rather than the historical Jesus, elaborating the traditions available to him.

Jesus regularly introduces his words by the Greek words *Amen, amen,* rendered as "I tell you the truth" (New International Version) or "Very truly" (New Revised Standard Version), e.g., in 3:5 and 5:25. The sayings thus introduced are the key sayings in a particular discourse; in these the vocabulary and style of Jesus are best preserved.

Themes

In the *Dictionary of Jesus and the Gospels*, Edgar McKnight compares the fourth gospel to "a musical fugue, with a theme announced and developed to a point, after which other themes are introduced and interwoven with the earlier themes." Over and above the themes that occur in the prologue (see Commentary below), many other themes from the Hebrew Bible appear and are reinterpreted in terms of Jesus Christ. This is designed to show that Jesus Christ is the one about whom the Hebrew Bible speaks and who fulfills Scripture; in essence, his identity is what connects all separate themes. Among other things, Jesus is presented as the tabernacle (1:14), the new temple (chapter 2), the serpent lifted up in the desert (3:14), the true bread (6), the good shepherd (10), the true vine (15), and the king (18–19). Thus there is continuity in God's plan even amid the discontinuity of the arrival of the new age.

John and the Hebrew Bible

John is dependent on the Hebrew Bible, but his use of it differs from that of other New Testament writers. There are few direct quotations and "proof texts" by which the early church tried to show that Jesus was the Messiah. There are, however, numerous allusions to the Scriptures.

All the themes that have been mentioned earlier and in the Commentary on the Prologue below stem from the Hebrew Bible. John shows how all that God began to do in Israel has now been fulfilled in Jesus. Jesus is the one about whom Scripture speaks and who fulfills Scripture. This includes the religious festivals: Chapter 5 narrates how Jesus appears at the Festival of Weeks (Pentecost), which in that era focused on Moses and the Law. Chapter 6 (verse 4) shows Jesus as the fulfillment of the Jewish Passover and as superior to the manna given by Moses. In chapter 7 Jesus attends the Feast of Tabernacles, of which water and light were important elements; he presents himself as the living water and the light of the world. His appearance at the Festival of Dedication, which focused on the temple (10:22–39; cf. in the books from the INTERTESTAMENTAL PERIOD, 1 Maccabees 4:36–59), makes it clear that no more temple is needed now that God has come to his people in person.

John does not add much to what the Hebrew Bible already revealed about God. He is called "the only true God" (17:3). What is new compared to the previous era is that Jesus appears as the preeminent revealer of God (e.g., 1:18, 51; 3:13; 12:45; 14:9) as well as the Son of God. Hence in this gospel God is primarily called "Father" (some 125 times!) but only by Jesus.

Notably absent from the gospel is any discussion of the question of the role of the Law and the individual commandments in the life of the believers, which plays such a large role in Matthew, Paul, and James. In this gospel Jesus simply commands his followers to love one another (13:34; 14:15, 21; 15:10, 12, 17).

Misunderstandings and Double Meaning

John places much emphasis on the divinity of Jesus, and he shows that the disciples and others spectacularly fail to understand Jesus' identity during his lifetime. To bring this out sharply, John includes many examples of the misunderstandings that arose. Part of the problem for the disciples is that Jesus often uses terms and phrases that are open to misunderstanding (such as "again" or "from above" in 3:3–8), and that he uses familiar words and concepts in an unexpected way, such as "temple" in 2:19–22. What follows is just a selection of cases. The first misunderstanding occurs in 1:10–13, where it says that "his own" failed to believe in him. In 2:3–7 and again in 7:2–14 the disciples misunderstand the timing of Jesus' mission, and in 6:32–35 the same is true for the identity of the bread. In 8:21–22 Jesus' audience thinks he will commit suicide, and in 11:11–14 the word *sleep* is used ambiguously. In 11:23–27 the timing of the Resurrection is the subject of misunderstanding, and in 14:4–6, the simple concept "way." The final misunderstanding occurs in 21:20–23 and is explained at length by the narrator.

It could be suggested that these misunderstandings are John's equivalent to the Synoptic parables (see Mark 4:10–12). In both cases Jesus speaks at one level but should be understood at another.

Sacraments

Among the enigmatic aspects of the Gospel of John is the probably deliberate lack of clarity about the Christian institutions or sacraments, BAPTISM and the LORD'S SUPPER. Does the evangelist show any awareness of the practice of the church? On the one hand, John does not even mention Jesus' own baptism in 1:29–34 or his institution of the Lord's Supper in chapter 13—although both acts are implied. This silence is in line with the gospel's lack of explicit directions for the Church. On the other hand, water, bread, and wine are mentioned so often in the text and there is so much symbolism that it is hard to avoid the impression that John frequently alludes to these institutions. Thus the idea of being born of water and Spirit in 3:3–5 reminds the informed reader of Christian baptism, as does the discussion of washing in 13:1–17. But regarding 1:33, certainty is hard to obtain. The wine of the Lord's Supper is hinted at in 2:1–11, and bread and wine together appear in 6:51–58. However, the reference to blood and water flowing from the pierced side of Jesus in 19:34–35 is disputed: Why does the evangelist pay so much attention to this simple fact unless for him it has a deeper meaning?

SYNOPSIS

It is relatively easy to distinguish several parts in John's gospel. In addition to the prologue and the epilogue, there are two main sections, with chapter 13 marking the new beginning. For convenience, we have split the second main section into two so that the story of Jesus' death and Resurrection forms a section of its own.

Section I: The Prologue (1:1–18)

In sometimes elevated terms the Evangelist introduces his book with a hymnlike passage that presents the major themes. The main character is Jesus, the Word of God.

Section II: Public Ministry (1:19–12:50)

This part of the gospel shows a constant alternation of stories that report a miracle or sign performed by Jesus and discourses of various lengths; two elements of the one kind are often followed by two of the other kind. John 2:1–11 describes "the first of Jesus' miraculous signs" (2:11), namely, the changing of water into wine at a wedding in the Galilean town of Cana. This is followed by another symbolic act, which, however, is not miraculous, the cleansing of the temple in Jerusalem (2:12–17), and by a speech that draws out its significance (2:18–25). Chapter 3 contains a major discourse that starts off as a dialogue with the Jewish leader Nicodemus but that ends as a monologue with added comments from the evangelist. Chapter 4 forms a counterpart to this encounter, describing a meeting of Jesus with an outcast woman far away from Jerusalem. The final verses of this chapter are given to a sign story in which Jesus meets a court official in Galilee and heals his son. Chapter 5 opens with yet another meeting, this time with an invalid in Jerusalem, who is healed by Jesus. This sign is followed by a discourse about Jesus' relationship with God and his identity.

Chapter 6 has two miraculous signs back to back, Jesus' feeding of a large number of people on five loaves and two fish and his walking on the water of the SEA OF GALILEE in a storm. The subsequent discourse revolves around the theme of Jesus as the life-giving bread. At the end John reports major frictions among Jesus' followers and the departure of many. On behalf of the Twelve Disciples, however, Peter confesses Jesus as God's emissary.

Jesus' second visit to Jerusalem coincides with the Feast of Tabernacles and gives rise to another passionate discourse about his identity (chapter 7). On the last day of the feast, Jesus promises the coming of the Holy Spirit. A story about a woman who has committed adultery (7:53–8:11) is followed by a long and intense discourse on the theme of light of the world. Jesus performs the healing of a man born blind and becomes involved in an angry and prolonged exchange with the Jewish authorities over his authority to work miracles (9). This is followed immediately by a discourse in which Jesus sets himself up as the good shepherd of his people (10:1–21) and a final dialogue with the Jews during the Festival of Dedication. Jesus' last and greatest sign before his own resurrection is the raising from the dead of his friend Lazarus (chapter 11). Whereas this leads many Jews to put their trust in him, the Jewish leaders decide to eliminate

Jesus raises Lazarus from the dead (John 11:38–44), engraving by Julius Schnorr von Carolsfeld

him because he is perceived as a challenge to their position.

The section ends in chapter 12 with stories that mark the preparations for Jesus' death and his final move to Jerusalem. Jesus is anointed by a friend, and he enters Jerusalem in triumphal procession to public acclaim. During a meeting with Gentiles, Jesus announces that his time has come to die (12:20–36). The narrator adds a comment about the divided opinions among the population (12:37–43), and Jesus has the final say with a call to faith.

Section III: Private Ministry (Chapters 13–17)

This entire section is set in one place, the room where Jesus and the disciples celebrate the Passover meal. The references to eating stop after chapter 13. Although there is a suggestion that the company might leave the room in 14:31, this only actually happens in 18:1. After an initial action of Jesus, the washing of the disciples' feet, all attention is focused on the spoken word.

Jesus predicts that he will be betrayed, and Judas indeed leaves the place (13:18–30); Jesus continues by saying that Peter will deny knowing him. He promises that after his departure he will prepare a place for his followers with his Father and emphasizes that he is the only way to the Father (14:1–4, 5–14). This is followed by a series of sayings about

the Holy Spirit, who will come as Jesus' replacement, and about his departure (14:15–31). Jesus uses a metaphor of a vine and its branches for an extended discussion of the believers' relationship with him (15:1–16) and warns his followers against opposition from unbelievers (15:17–16:4). A second passage about the coming and the role of the Spirit (16:5–15) is followed by another one about the time after Jesus' departure. Chapter 17 is taken by a long prayer of Jesus in which he speaks about his own glorification and intercedes for his disciples and for the future believers.

Section IV: Jesus' Passion and Resurrection (Chapters 18–20)

John describes the arrest of Jesus by a group consisting of Jews and Romans, with the help of his disciple Judas. He is taken to the high priest for questioning. In a series of parallel scenes, Peter is challenged by several people about his relationship with Jesus and denies him three times. The report of Jesus' trial before the Roman governor Pilate takes more space than the Jewish hearing (18:28–19:16). The discussion centers on Jesus' identity as a king and on Pilate's desperate conviction of his innocence. The crowd presses for Jesus' crucifixion, and at long last the governor gives in. The description of the actual crucifixion and death is brief (19:17–30); the piercing of Jesus' side immediately afterward receives much attention. Jesus is quickly buried because the SABBATH is approaching (19:38–42).

The narration of the Resurrection focuses on Mary Magdalene's finding of the empty tomb; the story line is interrupted by a scene with two disciples, one of whom believes that Jesus is alive again, but subsequently Mary is the first person to see the risen Jesus. Only in the evening does Jesus appear to all his disciples, and then a week later to Thomas, who had missed the first meeting.

Section V: The Epilogue (Chapter 21)

It seemed as if 20:30–31 had brought the gospel to a close by stating the author's purpose in writing it, but a new scene is added in which Jesus meets some disciples in Galilee (21:1–14). He reinstates Peter and discusses with him the fate of the Beloved Disciple (21:15–23). Verse 21:24 is a comment on the trustworthiness of this disciple and verse 25 comments on Jesus' greatness.

COMMENTARY

Section I: The Prologue (1:1–18)

The prologue to John's gospel is one of the best-known parts of the Bible. It is admired by many, and it gained the evangelist John the symbol of majesty, the eagle. Parts of it are highly poetic, but it is interspersed with prose phrases (verses 6–9, 13, 15, and 17). This situation has led to much speculation about the prehistory of the text, which, e.g., may consist of a core that originated in Judaism, but no firm conclusion can be reached.

As it stands, the prologue fits the rest of the gospel exactly. Apart from the person of John the Baptist (see Characters below), all themes in the prologue are directly related to who Jesus is, but his name is only used for the first time with full effect in verse 17. He is described as preexistent (cf. 17:5), as life (cf. 5:26), as light (cf. 3:19; 8:12; 9:5), and as Son of God (cf. 3:16, 36). The prologue also sings about his divine glory (cf. 12:41) and contrasts the light of his coming with darkness (cf. 3:19). It anticipates Jesus' rejection by "his own" (cf. 4:44). The climax occurs when seeing Jesus is said to be equal to seeing God (cf. 6:46).

The one element that has no parallel later in the gospel is the description of Jesus as the Word. In the contemporary Hellenistic culture, especially among philosophers, the concept of the word (Greek *logos*) was very popular, whereas the Jews held the Word of God (God's revelation in speech and as contained in the books of the Hebrew Bible) in high regard. It is John's masterstroke of genius to apply all of these human concepts to Jesus as their culmination, and to say that the Word was a person who was from the beginning with God and was himself God.

The first words of the gospel are a repetition of the opening of the book of Genesis, the first book of the Hebrew Bible; the evocation of creation is reinforced by the references in verse 3. The rest of the prologue draws on the WISDOM LITERATURE (see also GENRE).

In verse 10 and more often in this gospel, "the world" is a negative concept, symbol of the humans who reject Jesus. Yet it can also be used positively, as in 3:16, which speaks of God's love for the world. That Jesus reveals God's glory (verse 14) again makes him God's equal (cf. Exodus 16:7, 10; 40:35). According to verse 17, Jesus surpasses God's previous good gifts to his people. Whereas Exodus 33:20 said that no one would see God and live, Jesus becomes the visualization of the God of Israel.

Section II: Public Ministry (1:19–12:50)

The passage 1:19–34 unpacks the brief reference to John the Baptist in verses 6–8. Essentially, what John the Baptist does is refer to Jesus as the one who is greater than he and as the Lamb of God (verses 29 and 36). The concept of the Lamb builds on the prophecy of the lamb carrying away sins in Isaiah 53:5–7 as well as on the Passover lamb (Exodus 12), and it is one of the few indications of the atoning effect of Jesus' suffering in the gospel. The term *the Jews* (verse 19 and often in the gospel) refers to Jesus' opponents from Jerusalem, not to all Jewish people. The Messiah, Elijah (Malachi 4:5), and the Prophet (see Deuteronomy 18:15), mentioned in verses 20–21, are the three characters expected in the end times (see LAST THINGS).

The elements of the narrative part of chapter 1 are strung together and connected with 2:1–11 by references to "the next day" and "the third day" in 1:29, 35, 40 (implied), 43, and 2:1, which together suggest a sequence of seven days. The narrative in 1:35–51 shows how people who were originally followers of John the Baptist shift allegiance and start following Jesus, and how Jesus calls others to follow him as well. The idea of open heaven (verse 51) is derived from the story about Jacob in Genesis 28; it probably marks Jesus out as the true Israelite.

The story of the wedding in Cana leaves much unstated, such as in what relationship the wedding pair stood to Mary and Jesus. In fact, Jesus is so central to the story that the bride is not mentioned at all and the groom only in passing. Weddings could last up to a week so that much food and drink needed to be provided; failure to do so was a major embarrassment, from which Jesus saves these people. The story is full of symbolism: The number of six jars of water for ritual purification refers to the incompleteness of the old covenant with its strict rules. The water itself also represents the old order of Judaism over against the wine, symbol of the days when God will act on behalf of humanity (Amos 9:13–14; Hosea 14:7). It is possible that the theme of the wedding invites us to see Jesus as the bridegroom (cf. Mark 2:19–20), for the Hebrew Bible sees the days of the Messiah as a wedding (Isaiah 54:4–8; 62:4–5). Water recurs as a theme in chapters 4, 5, 7, 9, and 19. Jesus' "hour" (verse 4, cf. 12:23; 13:1; and 17:1) is the time of his death and subsequent return to God.

John uses a different Greek word to refer to Jesus' saving acts (*sēmeion*) than the Synoptics (*dunamis*) in order to draw out their referential character: They are signs of God's saving grace in Jesus. It is remarkable that John numbers the first two miraculous signs of Jesus (2:11; 4:54) but not the subsequent ones. The high level of symbolism in the gospel leads the reader to expect a total of seven signs, the number of fullness, and indeed seven are described in the present section of the book: the two earlier plus the healing in 5:1–18, the feeding in 6:1–15, the walking on the water in 6:16–21, the healing in chapter 9, and the revivication in 11. However, Jesus' own resurrection in chapter 20 and the catch of fish in 21 are no less miraculous, so that in fact the gospel contains eight or nine signs. Does the author want to suggest that Jesus' new life opens up endless possibilities?

Jesus driving the moneychangers from the temple (John 2:15), etching by Rembrandt

The cleansing of the temple (2:13–22) fulfils Zechariah 14:21 and is a prophetic act of criticism of the formalistic way in which Judaism had developed. In verse 19 Jesus uses the word *temple* to refer to himself and, in fact, announces his death and resurrection. The Synoptic Gospels suggest that Jesus performed this powerful act toward the end of his life. As it is inherently unlikely that he did the same thing twice, one's opinion about when it actually happened depends very much on one's overall estimate of the texts. The work of extending and beautifying the temple (2:20) had been started by HEROD the Great in the year 20 or 19 B.C.E. so that this episode is set in 27 or 28 C.E.

The final verses of chapter 2 should be taken with the story about Nicodemus in chapter 3 so that the following structure becomes visible:

A	2:23–25	summary report
B	3:1–12	dialogue with Jesus
C	3:13–21	comment
A	3:22–24	summary report
B	3:25–30	dialogue with John
C	3:31–36	comment

The preceding implies that not all of 3:1–21 consists of words of Jesus but that at some stage the evangelist takes over and adds his own comments.

That Nicodemus arrives at night is literal as well as symbolic, and his lack of understanding is typical of the group he represents. The theme of the meeting between Jesus and him is the need for spiritual transformation, here called "being born again." The very word translated as "again" (NIV) is deliberately ambiguous and can also be taken as "from above" (cf. NRSV). Equally ambiguous is the Greek word *pneuma*, which means both "wind" and "spirit"; in verse 8 Jesus compares the powerful but invisible effects of both. Verse 14 reflects Numbers 21:4–9; the reference to Jesus' being "lifted up" includes both his death in the elevated position on the cross and his return to God, and it invites the reader to see his death as a form of glorification. Verse 16, the testimony to God's love in Christ, ranks among the best-known verses in the Bible.

The second half of chapter 3 basically repeats that John the Baptist is no more than a herald of Jesus, the Son of God, and the comments in verses

31–36 echo those in verses 13–21. Both passages redefine the idea of condemnation away from its being a divine act toward seeing it as an inherent part of the human act of disbelief. Basically, we condemn ourselves. The powerful imagery of light and darkness used here picks up the language of the prologue and returns later in the gospel. Only in 3:22, 3:26, and 4:2 in the entire New Testament are we told that Jesus baptized in the same way as John the Baptist.

The need to travel through SAMARIA (4:4) is not geographical, for Jews usually avoided the area altogether by traveling east of the River JORDAN. The introduction of a man, a woman, and a well reminds the reader of similar stories in the Hebrew Bible that resulted in a marriage and that involved Eliezer (Genesis 24), Jacob (Genesis 29:9–14), and Moses (Exodus 2:15–21). In this way the narrator does create expectations that are fulfilled in an unexpected way. The fact that the Samaritan woman is out in daytime ("the sixth hour," verse 6, is midday) shows that she is an outcast, for the normal time for getting water was early in the morning. In the Hebrew Bible "living water" symbolizes God's life-giving revelation (e.g., Jeremiah 2:13; Zechariah 14:8). Verse 20 refers to Mount Gerizim, where a Samaritan temple stood in the past; this verse is one of the several attempts by the woman to talk about "religion" rather than about herself, all of which Jesus turns around to attain his goal. He does indeed manage to instill a good measure of faith in her, which she is quick to share with others. It is remarkable that the gospel is positive about the faith of this woman and the many other Samaritans (verses 39–42), as well as about Jesus' reception back in Galilee (verse 45), whereas it is generally less positive about the response "the Jews" give to Jesus. The story of the healing of the boy in 4:46–54 is equally affirmative in its description of the faith of his father, probably a Jew who served at the court of Herod Antipas.

In clear contrast, in 5:1–18 Jesus heals a man who shows no sign of faith as he had given up all hope of ever being cured of his paralysis. This shows that Jesus is not dependent on the faith of the people he wants to help. Exceptionally, the Jewish feast in verse 1 is unspecified, presumably

Jesus and the woman of Samaria (John 4:5–26), etching by Rembrandt

because it plays no further role in the story. First, the healed man is accused of breaking the law for carrying an item on the Sabbath (verse 9), then Jesus himself, presumably for performing a healing (verse 18). The laws in the Hebrew Bible only forbid customary employment on the Sabbath, but the rules of Judaism were much stricter. In this passage, verses 3b–4 are a later addition, probably an explanatory marginal note that ended up in the main text of some manuscripts. The intention of the Jewish leaders to kill Jesus occurs for the first time in verse 18 and frequently afterward (e.g., 7:1, 30; 8:37; 10:31; 11:8). It marks a shift after the generally positive reception in the first four chapters.

The discussion about Jesus' authority in 5:1–18 is carried over into the rest of the chapter, with Jesus arguing that he is only acting on God's authority and is exercising God's judgment. The idea of judgment leads to the claim that obedience to Jesus grants a person acquittal in judgment, and that the eschatological judgment is already being exercised in the present by Jesus, so that believers already enter the life eternal. In the remainder of the chapter Jesus stresses his personal authority as God's emissary and as the one who was spoken of in the Scriptures.

Chapter 6 is the only chapter in John that deals with the ministry of Jesus in Galilee, which forms the core of the Synoptic Gospels. No wonder that the similarities between John and Mark are larger here than anywhere else, although Mark includes two feeding miracles (6:30–44 and 8:1–13) and John only one. In Mark the former miracle is followed by Jesus' walking on the sea (Mark 6:45–52; cf. John 6:16–21), the second by a dialogue on bread (Mark 8:14–21; cf. John 6:22–65), and by a confession of Peter (Mark 8:27–30; cf. John 6:66–71). Only John has preserved the names of the disciples in verse 5 and only John shows how after the feeding Jesus is trying to escape an attempt to make him king by force (verse 15). The latter information helps to explain the abruptness of Jesus' withdrawal in Mark 6:45. The number of 5,000 includes only the males present, hence the statement in verse 7 that even 200 pieces of silver, that is, 200 day's wages, would not buy enough food for the crowd.

The discourse about the life-giving bread is the longest in the gospel; it is conceived as a kind of sermon on Psalm 78:24 and Isaiah 55:1–2. The discourse mixes metaphorical and nonmetaphorical language in a bewildering manner. Jesus sets himself up as the fulfillment of the manna that the Israelites had received from Moses (verses 22–34), so as greater than Moses, and as the bread of life (35–51b). The saying "I am the bread of life" is the first of the "I am" sayings (see below under Characters). More than anywhere else in the gospel, in this chapter Jesus speaks about a hope for the future, in particular in the repeated promise to raise up believers at the last day (verses 39, 40, 44, 54). The realization of this hope depends on a person's close connection to him as the bringer of life and salvation. Verses 51c–58 depend entirely on the metaphor of eating and drinking Jesus, the Son of man. This is as close as John gets to describing the LORD'S SUPPER with its ceremonial use of bread and wine. (Mark 14:22 says that when instituting this ceremony, Jesus referred to the bread as his "body.") The giving of Jesus' life is a reference to his death on the cross.

In verses 60–66 the word *disciples* is used in a wider sense than usually to refer to all Jesus' followers, many of whom are offended by his words and turn their back on him. In verse 67, by contrast, "the Twelve" Disciples through Peter express their unchanged allegiance.

The Feast of Tabernacles forms the background to chapters 7 and 8; this autumn harvest festival is described in Leviticus 23:33–43. The uncertainty over who Jesus is dominates chapter 7. As in the Synoptics (Mark 3:21, 31–35), John shows that Jesus' own brothers did not believe in him during his lifetime. The theme of hatred (verse 7) is developed in 15:18–25 and 17:13–19. The chapter's structure resembles that of chapter 3:

A   Jesus teaches 14–24
B   Debate among the audience 25–31
C   Attempt to arrest him 32–36
A   Jesus teaches 37–39
B   Debate among the audience 40–44
C   Attempt to arrest him 45–52

Verses 14–24 combine the themes of Jesus as superior to Moses and of his attitude toward the Sabbath. Verse 15 refers to Jesus' lack of formal training to be a scribe. The temple guards (32) were a kind of Jewish police force with a wide brief. The words of Jesus in verses 37–39 are not a literal quote from the Hebrew Bible but a conflation of Psalm 78:16, 20 with Zechariah 14:8. Verse 42 combines elements from 2 Samuel 7:12–16; Isaiah 11:1, 10; Psalm 89:4–5, 36–37; and Micah 5:1.

The passage 7:53–8:11 is absent from the oldest manuscripts. In some manuscripts it appears after John 21:25, after John 7:36, or even after Luke 21:38. It has a different vocabulary and style from the rest of the gospel and must be a story about Jesus that originally circulated separately and was later included in the gospel. Nonetheless, it has the ring of being authentic as it shows Jesus' humane treatment of a person in need, without undermining the authority of the Law.

The rest of chapter 8 continues the report of Jesus' presence at the Feast of Tabernacles from chapter 7, with 8:12 picking up from 7:37–39, in particular. The light metaphor is common in the Hebrew Bible as well as in many other religions; Jesus makes an enormous claim in calling himself the light of the entire world. The law meant in verse 17 is Deuteronomy 19:15, which is also recalled in Matthew 18:16; 2 Corinthians 13:1; and 1 Timothy 5:19. In verses 21–30 the emphasis shifts to Jesus' authority, which is based on where he came from and where he will return.

The theme of 8:31–59 is "Who are the real children of Abraham?" Abraham is the well-respected progenitor of all who believe in God. Jesus argues that physical descent is not enough and that it is faith in him as God's Son that matters. Verse 31 shows that the dialogue addresses people who had stopped believing in Jesus (contrast verse 30, but cf. 6:60–66). The use of strong language against them is based on commitment, and it aims to shock in order to deter. The sharp tone of this passage culminates in verse 44 with Jesus' calling his adversaries children of the devil. Although in modern times such allegations are unacceptable, in ancient polemics this was quite common. Such "demonizing" language is used later for another apostate, Judas (13:18–30). It also occurs in the contemporary historian Josephus and in the Dead Sea Scrolls. Examples in the Hebrew Bible are Isaiah 1:2–4; Jeremiah 20:8; and Hosea 1:2; 2:2; 4:10–19; 11:2. Its use here is not a case of anti-Semitism, for it is an internal Jewish disagreement and John's gospel as a whole is an appeal by Jews to Jewish readers. In verse 48, *Samaritan* is a swearword for somebody with absurd ideas. Verse 57 is the source of the tradition of describing a person who turns 50 years old as Abraham or Sarah.

Chapter 9 revolves round the theme of blindness, with verse 5 establishing a link with the preceding discourse. Whereas a blind person is cured and enjoys sight, it turns out that the Jewish leaders are spiritually blind because they refuse to acknowledge Jesus. In verses 1–12 the (unsolicited) miraculous sign is described, whereas 13–34 focus on the response by the Pharisees, who here represent the Jews who do not accept Jesus as the person who has the power and the authority to perform this miracle. They interview the healed man, his parents, and then him once more. Only in 35–41 does Jesus reappear on the stage, in order to instill true faith in the healed man. The description of the Pharisees' investigation and several of Jesus' words are highly ironic.

In chapter 10, verses 19–21 refer to the healing of the blind man. In the intervening verses Jesus describes himself as the good shepherd of his people, in outright opposition to the Pharisees and other leaders who had treated the healed man so badly. The metaphor of the shepherd stems from Psalm 23 and Ezekiel 34; sheep were common in Israel at the time. In verse 6 the metaphor is described as a "figure of speech" as distinct from a parable; because it is not a parable, Jesus can shift the imagery and go on to describe himself as the door of the sheepfold. The sheep in verses 1–5 are the Jews; the other ones in verse 16 are the Gentiles who will believe in Jesus at a later date. Verse 10 contains a glorious promise of full life for those who follow Jesus. The metaphor allows Jesus to raise again the theme of his suffering and death in verses 11–18, this time with emphasis on the fact that he dies of his free will. In 10:22–30 the setting changes but the theme of sheep and shepherd recurs, this time with emphasis on Jesus' identity as the Messiah expected by the Jews (see JESUS CHRIST). In verses 31–39 it shifts to his identity as the Son of God. For the Festival of Dedication or Hanukkah, see 1, 2, and 3 Maccabees. The laws in the Hebrew Bible prescribed capital punishment for blasphemers—for example, people who declare themselves to be God—so in a sense the Jews who do not believe in Jesus are correct in their desire to kill him. In verse 34, Jesus proves from Psalm 82:6 that others than God can legitimately be called "god," so that his own claim is not necessarily sacrilegious.

Verses 10:40–42 provide a typical transition to the next long episode, which tells about the resuscitation of Jesus' friend Lazarus. After the episode, John repeats several times that Jesus' following among the ordinary people was enormous (11:45; 12:9, 12). This is the only resurrection John includes. If Jesus had traveled to Bethany immediately, he might have healed Lazarus, but he deliberately planned to perform this resuscitation as his final miraculous sign in public. Moreover, in the introductory dialogue he focuses attention on himself rather than on the miracle. In calling himself "the Resurrection and the life," he claims that there is no (eternal) life apart from him. The entire chapter uses ironies of delay. For example, if Jesus loved Lazarus so much, why did he not do the thing we would have done—rushed straight to Lazarus's home, not wait till he was dead and buried? The very personal dialogue gives us interesting insights into Jesus' own emotional life.

In 11:45–54 the division of opinions about Jesus reaches its climax, with the Jewish leaders declaring him state enemy number one. They fear he or his followers will begin a revolt against the Roman occupation, which will be disastrous for the country. Caiaphas was high priest between 18 and 36 C.E., so not just during that year. John 11:50–52 is the clearest expression of the aim of the death of Jesus in this gospel, and John uses to the full the ironic situation that it is the unbelieving high priest who speaks these words as a prophecy: Jesus will die "for the people." The same pregnant use of *for* also occurs in 6:51 and 17:19.

Verses 11:55–57 belong to chapter 12 as the prelude to the final PASSOVER festival in Jesus' life. From here to chapter 20 the events in the narrative all occur within one week. The final preparation for Jesus' death is his anointing by Mary of Bethany. This action has just as much double meaning as the words of the high priest. On the personal level this woman expresses her great devotion to her Lord; on a wider scale it marks Jesus' identity as the Messiah, that is; the anointed one, of Israel. Mary's expense was considerable, for 300 denarii (silver coins, verse 5) was a year's wages for a laborer.

The story about Jesus' entry into Jerusalem reflects the continuing division among the Jews over him: Some are ecstatic, others totally negative; Lazarus is even included in the plan to kill Jesus. The texts quoted by the crowd as Jesus enters his capital city as king of the Jews are from Psalm 118:25 and 26 and from Zechariah 9:9. But his choice of a donkey to carry him reflects his intentions: Donkeys symbolized humility and are by nature unfit for war.

Jesus' dialogue with the Greeks, probably Greek-speaking Jews (see DIASPORA), is arranged by two disciples with Greek names. To explain the merit of his death, and to call the audience to follow him, Jesus uses imagery from nature that requires no knowledge of the Hebrew Bible. The number of references to Jesus' approaching death increases even more (12:24, 27, 32). Verse 27 is one of the few places that reveal that Jesus struggles with the idea

of death. He goes on, however, to point out that his death is beneficial for all. The ruler of this world (verse 31) is the devil. John 12:34 is a remarkable saying because the title *Messiah* or *Christ* is not common in the Hebrew Bible (here called Law). The people may be thinking of Psalm 89:37 and Ezekiel 37:25. The verses quoted in 12:38–40 are Isaiah 53:1 and 6:10. Jesus' final words in public (12:44–50) contain so many of the themes he has touched on previously that they are rightly seen as a summary of his teaching.

Section III: Private Ministry (Chapters 13–17)

This section is conspicuous for what it does not state, that Jesus instituted the LORD'S SUPPER as a lasting ceremony for his followers. Instead John reports that Jesus washes the feet of the disciples. This is an act of self-humiliation as washing feet was a slave's job. At the same time it is an acted parable of Jesus' voluntary death and a symbol of its cleansing effect. That is why Jesus insists

Jesus washing the feet of Peter (John 13:8), woodcut by Albrecht Dürer

Jesus before Caiaphas (John 18:24), woodcut by Albrecht Dürer

the coming of the Holy Spirit as his replacement ("another *paraklētos*"—that is, advocate or counselor) and the ability to do greater things than he did. John 14:23 refers to the Spirit without mentioning him by name. Jesus calls the place where he will go after his glorification and where the believers will join him later "my Father's house"; this place is never called "heaven" in the Bible (cf. 17:24–26), although it is in popular parlance.

The parabolic speech about the vine in chapter 15:1–8 is followed by explanation in verses 9–17. The key words are *fruit* and *remain*. In the Hebrew Bible the vine is a symbol for the people of God (Psalm 80:9–19; Isaiah 5:1–7, 27:2–6; Jeremiah 2:21, Ezekiel 15:1–6, 17:5–10 19:10–14); it is also common in the New Testament (Matthew 20:1–16, 21:28–32, 33–41; Mark 12:1–9; Luke 13:6–9, 20:9–16). Here Jesus sets himself up as the vine. Bearing fruit can mean making other disciples or growth in Christian character. The words referred to in 15:20 can be found in 13:16; 15:25 refers to Psalm 35:19 and 69:4.

The suggestion that Jewish Christians will be banned from synagogues (16:2) also occurred in 9:22, 34 and 12:42; by the time John wrote his gospel this prediction was probably being fulfilled. From 16:3 themes from chapter 14 are repeated, and chapter 17 uses the persecution motif from 15:18–16:3. Verses 16:20–21 compare the transitory sadness of the disciples to that of a woman giving birth.

After the word *hour* had been used repeatedly to refer to Jesus' approaching death, in 17:1 he announces that his hour has come. This will raise the reader's attention! These words are part of his longest prayer by far, which has for centuries been known as the "high priestly prayer," possibly because Jesus intercedes so forcefully for others. Yet at the same time this prayer is very personal. He prays for himself (1–5), for his followers (6–19), and for the world (20–26). The name (17:11–12) expresses a person's identity.

Section IV: Jesus' Passion and Resurrection (Chapters 18–20)

John's narrative is remarkable for the minute historical details it retains, such as 18:28a (avoidance

that Peter, who fails to see its meaning, has to be included in the action just as the other disciples are. In verse 1 the narrator uses the ambiguous words *eis telos*, which mean both "to the end" and "to the fullest." The quote in verse 18 is derived from Psalm 41:10.

The second half of chapter 13 contains ominous words addressed to the treacherous Judas and the insensitive Peter. In between, however, are marvelous sayings of Jesus about his glorification and about the power of mutual love. The former recall Isaiah 49:3 and the use of the perfect tense indicates that Jesus considers his public ministry complete. The latter tell his followers that they must love one another and that, when their love is seen, the outside world will acknowledge them as followers of Jesus (verses 34–35).

Chapters 14–16 belong closely together as Jesus' instructions to his disciples on the eve of his departure. Connecting themes are the promise of of ritual defilement), 18:31b (legal status of the Jews), and 19:13 (location). The Kidron Valley (verse 1) with the brook of the same name was to the east of Jerusalem, between the city and the Mount of Olives. In the story of the arrest all initiative, remarkably, lies with Jesus, who gives himself up yet protects his disciples as a good shepherd. In particular, verses 5–6 show his majesty. John does not explain why the former high priest and power behind the throne Annas carries out the first hearing of Jesus. He pays more attention to the trial before PILATE, describing the many times Pilate enters and leaves his headquarters. Pilate makes many desperate attempts to please the Jewish leaders and yet to release the innocent Jesus: making Jesus confess something harmless, releasing him rather than a rebel, and making Jesus look pitiable by torturing him. His

hearing focuses on Jesus' status as a king, but he fails to understand the way Jesus is king of the world without the intention to overthrow the Roman rule. In 19:11 it is unclear whether the person who handed Jesus over is Judas or the high priest.

It was common for crucified people to have a note attached to the cross stating their conviction; in the case of Jesus, Pilate uses this note to take revenge on the Jewish leaders by stating that the convicted man is "the king of the Jews." The languages Latin, Greek, and Hebrew (Aramaic) cover the entire civilized world (see BIBLE, LANGUAGES OF).

Here as before John presents the crucifixion as a glorification rather than a humiliation. He includes three utterances from Jesus, whose final word, "It is finished" (verse 30), sounds more of a cry of triumph than of defeat. The way John uses proof texts from Scripture in chapter 19 (verse 24 uses Psalm 22:18; verse 28 uses Psalm 69:21; verse 36 is based on Psalm 34:20, Exodus 12:46, and Numbers 9:12; whereas verse 37 quotes Zechariah 12:10) is different from his usual procedure and resembles the way Matthew normally uses the Hebrew Bible. The breaking of bones (verse 31) was often done to crucified people who were still alive; it increased the suffering but also hastened their death. In 19:35 the author, the Beloved Disciple, gives his testimony. In 19:39 it would seem that Nicodemus is excessive in the amount of spices he brings.

In the Easter story the gospel does not hide the fact that initially all witnesses find it hard to believe that Jesus is alive again; only "the other disciple," probably John himself, believes when he sees the empty tomb. The Scriptures in mind in verse 9 may be Psalm 16:9–10 and Hosea 6:2. As in Matthew 16:19, Jesus grants the disciples the power to forgive the sins of the members of the community (verse 23).

The "first conclusion" (20:30–31) is the clearest expression of the author's aim in writing; the text is preserved in different versions, however, with one group of manuscripts suggesting the readers should come to faith and the other group that their faith should be strengthened.

The Crucifixion (John 19:17–30), woodcut by Albrecht Dürer

Section V: The Epilogue (Chapter 21)

After the Resurrection Jesus only "showed himself" (verse 1) occasionally, leaving the disciples waiting until his ascension and Pentecost (Acts 1–2). They make good use of the time, as they must eat, after all. The story of the miraculous catch of fish resembles Luke 5:1–11, which had taken place several years earlier; both stories point to the future task of the disciples as missionaries. It is remarkable that the number of fish, 153, is mentioned. Mathematically, this is a fascinating number, but it is uncertain whether John has a deeper meaning in mind, and if so, which one.

Just as Peter had three times denied that he knew Jesus (13:38, 18:17, 25–27), so after the meal he has to confess his love for him three times in order to be reinstated as a disciple.

CHARACTERS

disciples, the   John mentions the names of many individual disciples. They are usually with Jesus, and in chapters 13–17 they are the recipients of much private teaching. Prominent among them are the Beloved Disciple, Peter, Judas, and Thomas. The latter is shown as a man of courage (11:16) who finds it hard to believe in the resurrection of Jesus until he has seen Jesus for himself (20:24–29) and then makes the perfect confession of Jesus as Lord and God. He is intriguingly known as "the Twin," but this allusion is not developed.

Peter three times resists Jesus' intention to suffer on behalf of his people (see 13:2–11, 13:36–38; 18:8–11); yet he matures, and in 21:18–19 he is told that he, too, will suffer martyrdom. The disciple who betrayed Jesus, Judas, is singled out several times in narrator's comments before his very act.

See also 6:60–72 and the Commentary above.

Holy Spirit   During Jesus' ministry on earth, the Spirit empowers him; in this respect John is at one with the Synoptics. The Holy Spirit is a prominent object of teaching in chapters 14 and 16, the speech that prepares the disciples and the Church for the future after Jesus' departure. After Jesus is gone, the Spirit will take over as divine presence with the believers. The word

Paraclete that is used here is unique to John, and its translation is disputed: It literally means "the one called in," hence can be "comforter" (Authorized [King James] Version), "counselor" (New International Version), "advocate" (New Revised Standard Version), or "helper" (New American Standard Bible). The Paraclete is much like Jesus himself (14:16) and could be described as the abiding presence of Christ. At the end of the gospel John leaves no doubt that the Spirit came on the disciples as soon as Jesus' ministry on earth had ended (20:22).

Jesus Christ   In this gospel the emphasis is on the divinity of Jesus. He claims this for himself on numerous occasions, and his actions vindicate him. A key word used to express this is *glory* (Greek *doxa*; e.g., 1:14; 2:11; 17:5, 22, 24). Even the Passion and death of Jesus are seen in a remarkably positive light and described as a kind of glorification or exaltation (3:14; 12:23, 32–33).

Jesus is the Son of God (5:25–27), hence *Father* is the common word in the gospel to describe God. The word used for Jesus as Son of God (Greek *huios*) differs from that for the believers as children of God (*tekna*, 1:12; 11:52).

In the relationship of the Father and the Son (1:14, 18; 17:2) there seem to be both equality and subordination: Their equality comes out in 5:18; 10:38; and 14:7–10; the subordination of Jesus, in 5:19; 14:28; and 17:4.

Yet Jesus is also depicted as a human being, most clearly in 1:14; 6:42, 51; 10:33; 11:33; and 19:5. Much discussion in the gospel centers on the title *Christ* (Hebrew *Messiah*), which is not a proper name but a title; see, e.g., 1:19, 41, 45; 7:25–44; 9:22; and 20:31. John writes to provide evidence that Jesus is indeed the Messiah, who was promised in the Hebrew Bible. In the earlier commentary we saw that Jesus is also called the Word, the Son of God, and the Lamb of God.

Jesus reveals much of himself in the so-called "I am" sayings, which all claim that he is the fulfillment of an aspect of the Hebrew Bible. Note that the divine name in the Hebrew Bible, *Yahweh* or *the Lord*, means "I am," so that with these sayings Jesus once again claims identity with God.

Saying	Reference	Hebrew Bible model
I am the bread of life/the living bread	6:35, 48, 51	Exodus 16:13–31
I am the light of the world	8:12	Isaiah 60:1–5
I am the door [gate] of the sheep	10:7, 9	Ezekiel 34
I am the good shepherd	10:11, 14	Psalm 23
I am the resurrection and the life	11:25	Daniel 12:1–4
I am the way and the truth and the life	14:6	Proverbs 4:1–19
I am the (true) vine	15:1, 5	Psalm 80:8–18
I who speak to you am he	4:26	cf. John 18:5, 6
It is I; do not be afraid	6:20	
I am one who testifies for myself	8:18	cf. John 8:24, 28
Before Abraham was born, I am	8:58	Exodus 3:14
. . . you may believe that I am he	13:19	

John the Baptist   This gospel pays much attention to John's ministry of preaching and baptizing and rather explicitly puts him down as inferior to Jesus. This has led some to believe that at the time of writing there were people around who had more respect for John than for Jesus. The religion of the Mandeans that survives today worships John and rejects Jesus.

Moses   Moses is not a character in the story, but he is mentioned regularly in the first half of the gospel as the representative of the old dispensation. Through him God blessed Israel, but what Jesus bears is superior: The immediate revelation of God himself.

Nicodemus   Nicodemus, member of the Jewish Council, represents the old order of Judaism, which is in need of transformation as a response to Jesus. After his extended meeting with Jesus in chapter 3, he reappears in 7:50–51 and 19:39, still without making an explicit confession of faith in Jesus. The reader is left to wonder about his status.

1 John

Authorship and Reception

From the beginning of this letter the attentive reader is struck by the similarities between this letter and the Gospel of John. Although the present text is anonymous, there is little doubt that it must stem from the same person or circle who produced the fourth gospel. Following a strong tradition of the early church, traditionally both texts are ascribed to the apostle John, who allegedly wrote them toward the end of his life. This would put them after 70 C.E. but before the end of the first century. According to the same tradition, at that time John lived as a church leader in Ephesus in Asia Minor (present-day Turkey), where he may have moved before or during the Jewish war (66–73 C.E.). A more specific date cannot be given, and we cannot know whether the gospel had already been written when this letter was penned, although the way in which 1:1–4 seem to imitate the gospel's prologue would suggest so. This lack of clarity is no problem, though, for the readers will in any case have been familiar with John's preaching of the gospel that at some late stage was immortalized in the written gospel.

The addressees of this letter cannot be identified with any certainty. They will be a church or a group of churches in the region where John works, whom he loves, and about whom he is well informed. They must have been Christians for some time as a church split has already taken place in their midst. In line with the designation of this letter as "Catholic" (see James), many people think it was a kind of circular letter.

As with all the letters, the title did not originate with the author but was added later in order to distinguish it from the other letters that bear John's name. The inclusion of the letters in the canon is by order of length, which is not necessarily the order in which they were written.

This letter was known and accepted as early as Bishop Papias of Hierapolis early in the second century. With its unique blend of emotive and doctrinal emphases it has been a much-loved Christian Scripture ever since.

See also EPISTLE.

Occasion and Aim

Although it can very well be read as a timeless treatise on love, light, and forgiveness, the reason for writing this letter was rather grimmer: A split had taken place in the community to which it is addressed and quite a few members had left. John refers to those who had seceded as heretics and deceivers (2:18–19). As they are not given a name, they may not have had one notable leader. They are also called "false prophets" (4:1) in the same way that at the end of the first century all teachers were called prophets.

Those who had left had failed to acknowledge the true humanity of Jesus (2:21–23; 4:2–3), which was a hard doctrine for Christians from a non-Jewish background (see 2 John). John does not discuss the doctrinal issues in much detail here because he already looks back on the unfortunate split in the church; his aim now is not polemical but pastoral. He is writing to encourage the remaining members that they are safe in their faith (2:20–21; 5:11–13). Many times he uses the verb *to know* to strengthen his readers (e.g., 2:12–14). His writing has a deliberately conservative tone because the secessionists had been the "modernists" who wanted to add innovations to the doctrine of Christ and because rest is now of the essence.

Models Used

In the absence of the normal features of a letter such as greetings and personal notes, it is unclear whether this book can be called a letter at all. Some have called it a treatise, a tract, or a sermon, but we should not lose sight of its personal character, which would seem to justify the label *letter* after

all. It has no peers within the New Testament or outside.

As noted, in terms of theology, vocabulary, and other characteristics, this text is very close to the Gospel of John. There are also some similarities with the letter of James, which may have been known to John. Both authors make much of the unity of faith and lifestyle. Phrases such as "Jesus is the Christ" (2:22; 5:1) and "Jesus is the Son of God" (4:15; 5:5) were probably used as acclamations in the worship of the churches at the time.

Themes

The two main themes throughout are the person of Jesus, i.e., his true humanity and the inseparability of this confession from the obligation to imitate the lifestyle of Jesus Christ.

Because of the troubled position of his readers, John makes much of the certainty of faith in order to encourage them after the church split. As basis for the assurance that the readers are close to God, he refers to the earthly life of Christ (1:1), the apostolic teaching (1:2–3), his own credibility (5:13), their experience (2:5, 20–21, 27; 3:1, 24; 4:13–16; 5:20), and the testimonies of God, the HOLY SPIRIT, and others (3:24; 5:6–12).

A key term for the relationship between God and the believers is *love*, verb and noun together occur 46 times. Other core words are *fellowship* (1:3, 6, 7), *confidence* (New International Version 2:28; 3:21; 4:17; 5:14), *to know* (numerous times), *to abide in* (= to remain close to, 2:6, 24, 27–28; 3:6; in the Greek also 4:12), *to have the Father/the Son/the testimony* (2:23; 5:10, 12), and the frequent terms that evoke family relations such as *Father, children,* and *being born of God* (2:29; 3:8; 4:7; 5:1, 4, 18).

The Theme of Sin

It seems that on the topic of whether Christians commit sin, John contradicts himself. On the one hand, he writes that all humans are sinners who need God's forgiveness (1:6–2:2); on the other hand, he seems to suggest that Christians do not habitually sin (5:18) and that sinners are, in fact, not believers (3:4–10). The strongest anomaly occurs in 5:16–18, as verse 18 says that believers do not sin, whereas the previous verses talk about gross sin.

It will not do to distinguish different types of sin, as any such distinctions are postbiblical inventions. More helpful for solving this riddle is the insight that the word *lawlessness* in 3:4 is a technical term from the Hebrew Bible for insurrection against God, a state of fundamental estrangement. (See the use of *lawlessness* in 2 Thessalonians 2.) This enables us to see that John is saying that Christians do not live in such a state of fundamental enmity with God and that, consequently, they are basically right with him. John stipulates that whosoever lives in close connection with God cannot be called lawless or a sinner (chapters 3 and 5)—but this does not mean that they do not go wrong in actual life (chapter 1).

Style

This is the most repetitive of all New Testament books. It has a limited vocabulary, many parallelisms (see POETRY, BIBLICAL), and a marked preference for verbs over nouns. The letter's language is not bad Greek but quite earnest in tone. The style is simple but by no means always clear. A key problem is that John regularly uses the words *he* and *his* without explicating whether they refer to God the Father or to Jesus Christ (see, e.g., 2:3–8 and 3:2–3; some translations add the clarification).

The writer regularly uses *we*, which sometimes refers to him and the readers over against the world (1:6; 2:1; 4:7) but refers to him alone over against the readers when it comes to the experience of Jesus' earthly life (1:5; 4:14).

SYNOPSIS

No logical progress is clearly apparent in this letter. A certain alternation of doctrinal and ethical passages can be discovered but no real argument. Themes such as sin and love occur several times without any apparent rationale. Although some scholars suggest that there are two main parts (1:1–2:27 and 2:28–5:21, or 1:1–3:10 and 3:11–5:21), or three (1:1–2:28; 2:29–4:6; 4:7–5:21), in view of the lack of an overall argument it is better to distinguish the constituent smaller units without combining them, as follows:

The basis for fellowship (1:1–4)
Sin and forgiveness (1:5–2:2)

Knowing God is obeying (2:3–11)
Knowledge of the truth (2:12–14)
Warning against temptation (2:15–17)
The deceivers (2:18–27)
Two classes of people (2:28–3:10)
Love and confidence (3:11–24)
The Spirit (4:1–6)
More on love (4:7–21)
Transition from the focus on love to focus on faith (5:1–4)
Faith (5:5–12)
Salvation, prayer, and sin (5:13–21)

The words *eternal life* enclose the whole letter as they occur in 1:2 and 5:20.

COMMENTARY

Many Christians cherish this letter because it refers to God as light (1:5), as love (4:8, 16), and as the source of love (3:1; 4:7, 10, 16). He is also described as true (5:20), faithful (1:9), and righteous (3:7), and frequently designated as "the Father" (1:2; 2:1, 15, 16; 3:1). He has shown his love by sending his Son, Jesus, to this world (4:9) and by adopting the faithful as his children (3:1).

The letter begins with a remarkably abstract description of John's experience of the life of JESUS CHRIST, which nonetheless amounts to a claim to having been an eyewitness. John bases his relation with the addressees on their common faith in "the word of life," who is Jesus. In 1:5–2:2 we find the paradox that although all believers remain sinners, forgiveness is available through Jesus Christ. The words "If we say . . ." occur three times in this passage, and John is probably quoting his adversaries in order to correct what they taught.

In chapter 2 John emphasizes that all who want to remain in fellowship with God must obey the commandments given by Jesus. He uses the phrase "Whoever says . . ." three times to introduce ideas that are not in themselves wrong but should be matched by appropriate behavior. Numerous repetitions reinforce the message of this chapter, whereas "By this we may be sure" encloses 2:3–5.

Under the images of "children," "fathers," and "young people" the whole congregation is addressed in 2:12–14. They are encouraged on the grounds that they know the saving truth about Jesus. When reading 2:15–17 it is useful to keep in mind that according to Christianity, things such as beauty and riches are not bad in themselves but that they tend to draw believers' attention away from God.

Verses 2:18–27 are the key to the historical situation behind this letter. Some former members have left the churches because they denied the true humanity of Jesus. Such a view was unacceptable in early Christianity, and it earned them the label *Antichrists*. The antithetical passage 2:28–3:10 champions the idea that there are just two types of people, the children of God and the children of the devil. This passage is built with the help of the words *reveal* and *everyone who*, and it is enclosed by the repetition of words *doing what is right*. In 3:11–24 John describes hate and love in their outworking, whereas 4:1–6 revisit the issue of the deceivers who have left the church. Here the author argues that the Holy Spirit is the best weapon against the deception of these false teachers. The most profound passage on love (4:7–21) looks at it from the perspective of God the Father, whereas earlier in the letter the perspective had been that of Jesus.

Focusing on faith, John discusses the life and certainties of the believers in 5:5–12. In 5:7–8 the Authorized (King James) Version reads: "(7) There are three that testify *in heaven, the Father, the Word and the Holy Spirit, and these are one. (8) And there are three that testify on earth,* the Spirit, the water and the blood." The words in italic constitute a more explicit expression of the doctrine of the TRINITY than is normally found in the New Testament. These words are only found in a few late biblical manuscripts, and they are clearly a secondary addition that should not be included in modern Bibles.

The final passage (5:13–21) is steeped with words for knowledge that are meant to encourage the readers. The kind of knowledge in the author's mind is not intellectual but experiential knowledge. Formally speaking, this passage is a kind of appendix—much like John 21 in the author's gospel—but it is also an integral part of the letter's message. The mortal—that is, deadly—sin mentioned in 5:16–17 is the state of insurrection against God, the position of "lawlessness" described in 2:28–3:10. People who live in this state have never been Christians in the first place. We can paraphrase 5:18 as "We know that a Christian does not fall away from him."

CHARACTERS

The only proper name in the letter is that of Cain (3:12), a character in the Hebrew Bible (Genesis 4).

deceivers or Antichrists   These people are not mentioned by name, and it is difficult to know how numerous they were. John describes them as former members of the congregation who have now left, possibly of their own accord (2:18–19). Their fault was the denial of the human nature of Jesus Christ (2:20–23; 4:2–3). They are also called "false prophets" (4:1) in view of the fact that they taught the congregation the wrong doctrine.

Holy Spirit   Toward the end of the text the Holy Spirit is mentioned as the witness to and the custodian of the truth about the identity of Jesus Christ (3:24–4:6; 5:6–11). He is also referred to as the divine anointing that every believer has received (2:20, 27). Elsewhere in the Bible *anoint* refers to a literal activity, but here it is a metaphor for blessing.

Jesus Christ   By comparison there is less about Jesus in this letter than in many other texts. A possible reason might be that John had already written, or was in the process of writing, his gospel, which is all about Jesus. The main emphasis in this letter is on Jesus' true humanity, which is the result of his incarnation, i.e., his coming to earth as a real human being, not just as a phantom. For this event the term *flesh* is used (4:2–3; cf. 2:22–23). As at the beginning of the gospel, Jesus is initially called "the Word" (1:1). He is also the Savior (4:14), whose blood was shed (1:7) when he died as the atoning sacrifice (2:2; 4:10) on behalf of humankind (3:16). John alludes to the Resurrection of Jesus in 3:8 and 4:4 and to his return to earth (see LAST THINGS) in 2:28, 3:2, and 4:17.

John   Although it is written with unmistakable warmth, this letter is quite impersonal because

John does not tell the readers much about himself. He is clearly their spiritual leader and addresses them with phrases like "little children" (2:1, 12). The one thing about himself he does give away is that he was an eyewitness to the life and death of Jesus Christ (1:1–3).

2 John

Date and Authorship

The short letters 2 John and 3 John were written by "the elder" (2 John 1; 3 John 1). In the texts themselves this author never reveals more about his identity. Comparison with 1 John shows that that letter, which is totally anonymous, must stem from the same person. Because 1 John is close to the fourth gospel, it must have the same author again. This gospel is traditionally attributed to the apostle John. So by inference 2 John may also have been written by this apostle. No other names have been suggested by the tradition or by modern scholars, most of whom, however, think of an anonymous author.

It was not uncommon for apostles to refer to themselves as "elder" (1 Peter 5:1). John here certainly writes as somebody in a position of authority (verses 9–10) to people who know his identity. If it had not from the beginning been linked with a famous person like John, this small document would not have been preserved.

As with all the epistles, the letter's title did not originate with its author. It must have been added when the early churches started collecting the letters John had written in order to distinguish this one from the others.

2 John was one of the last parts of the New Testament to be written; exactness is hard to achieve, but it is safe to say that it stems from the period between 80 and 100 C.E. It treats with the same issue as the longer 1 John and was probably written before that letter. At the time of writing John must have been old, but he is still able to travel (verse 12).

On the term *Catholic* used to describe this letter, see James. See also EPISTLE.

Readers and Reception

The readers are addressed as "the elect lady," which must be a reference to a church. The sender is among the children of her "elect sister" (verse 13), a reference to another church. It is unclear why John uses these cryptic designations. (We cannot completely rule out the idea that he has an individual woman in mind, but the majority of interpreters argue for a church. The Greek word for "church" is feminine. The *you* in verses 6 to 10 is plural in the original Greek.)

We do not know which church is in meant. As the ecclesiastical tradition says that after 70 C.E. the apostle John lived in Asia Minor, in the region of Ephesus, it is probably a church in that area. The slightly formal tone of this letter might suggest that John was not the founder of this church but still felt responsible for it as an "elder." In 1 John the more informal addresses "children" and "my little children" are used so John probably wrote 1 John to a different group of people. The intended audience probably knew him but had not received a letter from him before. Verse 10 suggests they are a well-established group.

The short letter was probably known to Bishop Polycarp of Smyrna around 140 C.E. and later to Irenaeus around 180. A council in Carthage in the year 256 was the first to refer to this letter as "the epistle of John." It is no surprise that for a long time this letter was hardly known: Its content is not very spectacular, and it largely overlaps with the more explicit 1 John; the absence of the name of an apostolic author was no recommendation either.

SYNOPSIS

The letter, which is not divided into chapters, contains the usual elements of a Hellenistic letter. After a greeting (1–3) and thanksgiving (4), the author discusses issues of behavior (5–6) and of teaching (7–11). In comparison to Paul's letters, the order of teaching and behavioral issues has been reversed. At the end we find a concluding sentence (12) and greetings (13).

COMMENTARY

Although by New Testament standards this is a small letter, from the perspective of the first readers it was by no means short. At 245 words it would hardly have fitted on one side of the standard writing material, a piece of papyrus of some eight by ten inches. As the previous Synopsis showed, the letter follows the common format of a Hellenistic letter. Authors always began by stating their own name.

In verse 4 we find the kind of positive opening remark about the readership that was recommended by classical rhetoric. It served to enable an author or speaker to connect more smoothly with the audience.

Verse 4 indicates that the author has been in touch with some members of the church to which he writes and that he is favorably impressed with it. He is now addressing the problem that "many deceivers have gone out into the world, those who do not confess that Jesus Christ has come in the flesh" (verse 7). This heresy, the denial of the human nature of the divine Savior, is also the subject of 1 John and of much second-century sectarian literature. It seems that at the time of writing the persons who teach such ideas have not yet reached the letter's addressees. The threat is imminent, but John expects he will still have time to visit the church (12). His weapon against the heretics is refusal of admission to homes and churches (10–11). People should not believe the new teaching of the heretics but "abide in the teaching of Christ" (9).

Nobody in the first century, not even Christianity's opponents, ever disputed the *existence* of Jesus Christ. As to his *identity,* opinions were divided. For people with a Hellenistic (see CULTURES OF THE BIBLE) worldview, the alleged humanity of this divine person was quite a stumbling block as gods were not supposed to be truly human in any way.

The style of this letter is simple and straightforward. Interesting is the personification that sees the church addressed as "the elect lady" (verse 1) and "dear lady" (5), its members as its children (4), and another church as its sister (13). In antiquity cities, peoples, and areas were often personified. We also see this in the Hebrew Bible, e.g., in Isaiah 54, Ezekiel 16 and 23, and Hosea 1–3. In the New Testament the CHURCH as a whole can be represented using female language (e.g., 2 Corinthians 11:2–3; Galatians 4:26–31; Revelation 19:7–9).

The core of the letter revolves around two groups of concepts, which are introduced at the beginning (verses 1–4) and then discussed one at a time. They are on the one hand love and commandments (5–6) and on the other hand truth and teaching with their opposites, deceivers and antichrist (7–11). The first group is used to encourage the readers to continue leading good lives, the second to warn against the approaching heresy.

The radical stance taken here against heresy, i.e., a virtual boycott, has parallels in Matthew 18:6–9, 17; Acts 5:1–11; 1 Corinthians 5; 2 Thessalonians 3; 2 Timothy 4:14–15; and 1 Peter 2. From the way John writes it is clear that in those days there was no ecclesiastical structure to which he could appeal and that could help him combat heresy. The only weapons he has are his personal authority and his pen.

CHARACTERS

The letter is quite impersonal in that no human persons are mentioned by name. Previously we have discussed the identity of "the elder" (JOHN THE EVANGELIST) and "the elect lady" (the recipient church).

Antichrist Verse 7 is the first in world literature to use the word ANTICHRIST, which John later repeated in 1 John 2:18, 22; 4:3. Remarkably, unlike in later parlance, here it does not refer to one specific person in the future or to a world power. John rather uses it in the plural for his own adversaries who were already active in the world. What characterizes the antichrists is not their power or their use of violence, but their deception. They are people who deny key elements of the faith and who try to win others over to the same position. John uses strong words to warn the readers against them. In the later church only Bishop Polycarp of Smyrna (see above) used the word *Antichrist* in the same way; later it referred to a future enemy.

Jesus Christ On close reading it seems that the concept of "truth" is used more or less as a personification of Jesus Christ, so that John's expression "in truth" resembles the expression "in Christ," which is frequent in Paul's letters. "To know the truth" (verse 1) is virtually identical to knowing Jesus through faith. Otherwise the letter talks about Jesus in verse 7, emphasizing that his coming "in the flesh," called his incarnation, is a key element of the Christian faith that cannot be denied without vitally damaging its content. "Flesh" here is a morally neutral way of referring to human existence in its full sense. Denial of the coming of Jesus "in the flesh" automatically entails denial of his death and resurrection, which are key elements of the Christian faith.

3 John

Unlike 1 and 2 John, which are written to churches, this letter is written to a named individual, Gaius. Other persons occur in the letter as well, but we are unable to establish where they lived or where the author was at the time of writing. As has been said under 1 John, the author probably lived in Asia Minor, and so it is likely that the person he writes to also lives in that area.

2 John and 3 John were written by "the elder" (2 John 1; 3 John 1); for a discussion as to why this person is taken to be JOHN THE EVANGELIST, see 2 John. As with 2 John, the letter's title did not originate with its author but was added by those who collected the apostolic letters. For Gaius this was probably the only letter from the author he ever received.

3 John is one of the last parts of the New Testament to have been written; as does 2 John, it dates from the period between 80 and 100 C.E., but at the time of writing the old apostle John was still able to travel (verse 14). The impression this letter creates is that at the time of writing, despite the death of the other apostles, the missionary spirit of Christianity is still very much alive. The verses 5–8 allude to travels by Christian missionaries in a way that suggests that such traveling was common.

Verse 9 contains a reference to a letter the author previously wrote "to the church." It is just possible that this letter is either 1 John or 2 John, but not very likely. The letter in question was probably an exhortation to hospitality, which is not the topic of 1 or 2 John. As the addressee, Diotrephes, did not like its contents, he is likely to have destroyed this letter. 3 John was probably written before the other two letters. Its form is closer to that of classical letters than the form of 1 and 2 John, showing the least Christian appropriation of the letter genre. Moreover, at the time of writing of this letter there is as yet no fear of heresy, as there is in the other two letters.

The reception of 3 John was even slower than that of the other two Johannine letters, and its place in the canon of the New Testament was only secured in the fourth century. This is not surprising in view of its size and the lack of important theology.

On the term *Catholic* used to describe this letter, see James. See also EPISTLE.

SYNOPSIS

The letter, which is not divided into chapters, contains the usual elements of a Hellenistic (see CULTURES OF THE BIBLE) letter. After the introduction (1–2) and words of thanksgiving (3–4), there is a discussion of three named persons, Gaius (5–8), Diotrephes (9–10), and Demetrius (11–12). Concluding remarks (13–14) are followed by greetings (15).

COMMENTARY

With 219 words, this is the shortest New Testament document, yet it is not short in comparison with Hellenistic letters. The opening is of the conventional type: "X to Y, greetings"; at the end short greetings are extended.

Unlike the other two letters of John, this one was not written to address doctrinal issues but to resolve a power struggle. In fact, John has several intentions with this letter, such as to encourage Gaius, to voice disagreement with the behavior of Diotrephes, and to recommend Demetrius. For letters of commendations compare 2 Corinthians 3:1–3 and Colossians 4:7–9.

It is possible that Demetrius was himself the person who delivered the letter to Gaius, and that he was sent to prepare the way for a visit by the elder John himself. This hypothesis is based on the fact that PAUL occasionally recommends the person who carries a letter from him (Romans 16:1–2; Philippians 2:25–30; Colossians 4:7–9), and 3 John 12 might be a similar gesture.

The letter is written in simple, effective Greek. The term *beloved* functions as transition marker (verses 2, 5, and 11).

The main ethical issue at stake is that of a good lifestyle in the imitation of Christ. The key virtue of hospitality is under threat from people such as Diotrephes (10) but duly exercised by Gaius (5–6). It is remarkable that whereas John in 2 John basically disallows the offering of hospitality, in this letter he actively encourages it. The reason for this difference is that in 2 John he is combating heretical teachers, whereas in this letter no such adversaries are on the horizon. The people who need hospitality are Christian missionaries who were not supposed to have concerns about their livelihood, as it had been ordained by Christ in Matthew 10:8–10. In this way they could positively distinguish themselves from the traveling pagan philosophers, who emphatically asked for money in exchange for teaching.

No fewer than six times in this short letter (1, 3 [twice], 4, 8, 12) the word *truth* is used. In this letter it is roughly synonymous with the right confession of faith, but, as in 2 John, it also functions as a personification of JESUS CHRIST. So the opening verses say that the good relationship between John and Gaius is based on friendship as well as on common faith in Jesus.

CHARACTERS

Within the New Testament this is a remarkable text because it never mentions Jesus Christ directly, although in verse 7 there is a reference to "the name" (cf. 1 John 2:12; 3:23; 5:13), and as we just saw "the truth" also alludes to him. He is, of course, presupposed, but the text focuses on the human protagonists.

Demetrius   This person is only mentioned to us in one verse in this letter, as he is unlikely to be the same as Demetrius in Acts 19:24. Evidently John is sending him to deliver the present letter and to prepare his own coming, so that his success is vital to John. Praise is heaped upon his head in words that remind the reader of John 19:35 and 21:24.

Diotrephes   Known to us only from this short letter, this person appears as the opposite number to Gaius. The presenting issues are all about power and influence, not about doctrine. Verses 9–10 suggest that Diotrephes not only is after his own interest, but that he already has quite a position within his house church. The author has no fewer than six criticisms of him: Diotrephes puts himself first, he does not receive the elder, he spreads false charges against the elder, he lacks hospitality, he hinders others from being hospitable, and he puts good people out of the church. In short, Diotrephes is a dangerous person and John needs to act. The "calling attention to what he is doing" (10) is probably a euphemism for strong action. There is obviously no group of leaders in the church that could deal with Diotrephes, and it seems that, as PAUL had, despite being an apostle John finds himself in a hard situation without effective power.

Gaius   The name *Gaius* was extremely common in the Hellenistic world, and in the New Testament we meet several persons of this name:

- Gaius from Macedonia, who was a traveling companion of the apostle Paul and who visited Ephesus together with him (Acts 19:29)
- Gaius from Derbe, who also traveled with Paul (Acts 20:4)
- Gaius from Corinth, who had been baptised by Paul (Romans 16:23; 1 Corinthians 1:14)

It is unlikely that one of these three is the same as the Gaius who is being addressed in this letter. In a fourth-century text, the Apostolic Constitutions (7:46), a reference occurs to a person called Gaius whom the apostle John installed as the first bishop of Pergamum in Asia Minor, together with a Bishop Demetrius of Philadelphia. This is likely to be the same Gaius as in our letter, but the text is too late for the tradition to be historically reliable.

The name *Gaius* is Latin, indicating that his background may have been pagan, although at the time Jews could bear Greek names such as *Andrew* and *Philip*, and even Latin names such as *Priscilla* and *Aquila* (Acts 18:2).

The letter as a whole shows that John and Gaius know each other well, and verse 1 testifies to a warm relationship. The fact that John calls Gaius his child (4) suggests that he had been converted through him. Verse 2 might hint at some health problems Gaius had, whereas verse 11 suggests volatility. According to verse 9, he and Diotrephes have leading positions in different house churches in the same town. Gaius must be affluent as he owns a house that is large enough to receive guests and is able to supply whatever they need for further journeys (5–8). He leads an exemplary life, and John merely encourages him to continue in this way.

Jonah

The book of Jonah is placed fifth in the Minor or Lesser Prophets of the Hebrew Bible. There is no stated author, and debates over the date of composition have ranged from the eighth century B.C.E. to the fourth century B.C.E. The earliest date sees the book as the direct writing of the Jonah ben Amittai, mentioned once in 2 Kings 14:25 as delivering a message concerning the borders of the northern kingdom during the reign of Jeroboam II. The latter reigned 793–753 B.C.E., a period of great Assyrian weakness. The latest date takes into account references to Jonah in the Apocrypha, especially 3 Maccabees 6:8, though it is not mentioned in Tobit, which also has an Assyrian context and which mentions the prophecies of Nahum. A typical dating is before 612 B.C.E., the date of the eventual fall of Nineveh.

It is certainly an unusual book among the 12 Lesser Prophets, the only one that consists mainly of prose NARRATIVE. The only section of poetry (Jonah 2) is not a PROPHECY, either, but a psalm of deliverance. In fact, the narrative *is* the message. There is barely any record of Jonah's actual message apart from one verse (3:4). When we compare this to the prophecy of Nahum, who similarly preached against Nineveh, the contrast is stark.

This narrative form makes it the most accessible of all the minor prophets, and it is often, indeed, told as a children's story, as are some of the stories in Daniel. There is nothing obviously "difficult" about it, and yet the most tremendous debate has raged over the mode of interpretation that should be applied to it. Suggestions range from the mythological; through the allegorical, symbolic, and parabolic; to literalist readings. This commentary will suggest a reading based on its likeness to the romance genre, with deliberate ironies and ambiguities written in to the story to challenge the readers.

When considering it as literature, we concern ourselves primarily with the genre of narrative, which can be either fiction or nonfiction. A choice between these two terms is not the real issue, which is rather the nature of narrative truth. In his *Poetics*, the Greek philosopher Aristotle claims that mythic (or imaginative) truth is truer than historical, because it is more typical and more universal. Whether the story actually happened miraculously or is an imaginative construct is much less important than the truths of prophetic insight and inspiration the narrative seeks to convey to its readers, then and now.

SYNOPSIS

The book falls into two halves, which can then be subdivided into two again, neatly making up the four chapters of the book. The story begins abruptly with Jonah's call, not unusual in itself, but highly unusual in his refusal to obey the call, which is to go to Nineveh, the capital of Assyria, the traditional threat to Israel. There is no argument or debate with God at this stage, just flight. Jonah makes for the nearest port, Joppa, and boards ship for Tarshish, which may have been a Phoenician colony in Spain—as far west as he could go, and in absolutely the opposite direction from Nineveh.

A great storm springs up, but Jonah is so deeply asleep he is unaware of it. The captain wakes him to urge him to pray to his god. The superstitious sailors see the storm as divine punishment and cast lots quickly to find out whose fault it is. The lot falls to Jonah, who immediately confesses his fault and asks to be thrown overboard, as his due punishment. The sailors try hard not to have to do this, since they fear worse by drowning a prophet, but finally they must.

As soon as they do, two things happen: The storm ceases, and a huge fish swallows Jonah. In the fish's belly, Jonah is not annihilated but realizes

Jonah cast forth by the whale (Jonah 2:10), engraving by Gustave Doré

his life is being spared. He sings a song of deliverance and thanksgiving, whereupon the fish disgorges him on dry land.

The second part concerns this second chance. Jonah makes for Nineveh, where his succinct preaching that Nineveh will fall in 40 days has immediate results. The whole city repents, led by the king himself (3:6–9). God's heart is touched by this repentance, and he decides to spare the city.

It is at this point that Jonah chooses to argue with God. He now gives as his reason for his initial disobedience his fear that God would indeed change his mind if his preaching were successful. He feels in a no-win situation. He now wants to die. He sits outside the city, but God will not allow him death. Instead, a plant grows up giving him shade, protecting him from the sun. Then a worm attacks the plant, and it dies as quickly as it grew. Jonah is angry for the second time with God. Why destroy the plant?

The climax to the story takes the form of a rhetorical question: God asks Jonah whether he does well to be more concerned about the fate of the plant than the fate of the 120,000 inhabitants of Nineveh, let alone their domestic animals.

COMMENTARY

Although the actual interpretation of the story raises as many questions as it answers, the structure is quite clear-cut. Not only do the four chapters mark clear divisions in the story, but there is a clear pattern of descent and ascent, typical of the romance. After Jonah's initial calling, he descends, first to the port (1:3), then below the ship's deck (1:5), falling into a deep sleep (1:5). He is then thrown into the sea (1:15), and finally into the fish's belly (1:17). This is then a journey to the underworld, a sort of dying.

Then begins his ascent, first, through his prayer (chapter 2), then in his preaching, which yields stupendous results (3:6–10). Then begins a second descent, first into anger (4:1); then into the heat of the desert (4:5, 8); then further anger—an anger enough to die (4:9). But there is no final ascent, as we might expect. The pattern is left unfinished on a question. We know what the answer should be, but does Jonah? So there is no happy ending, only a challenge.

The interpretation hinges on the question of irony. Should we read the story at face value and take all of Jonah's utterances at face value? Or should we question, say, the sincerity of his psalm in the fish's belly, as some scholars do? There are some obvious ironies, or at least very strange features. For example, Jonah's calling is to go to the place, where he should prophetically utter WOES AND DENUNCIATIONS, as in the manner of Nahum—except that Nahum, and other prophets who utter similar woes, are not usually expected to go to the place. We might think, then, that Jonah is just terrified—but the text refuses to say this, any more than it says why God wants him to go to the place itself. In fact, the denunciation is undermined by God's mercy, raising the whole question of the nature of prophecy. Is it predictive and final, or is it provisional? Jonah clearly thinks it should be the former, but that is not what the story nor Jonah's actual preaching shows.

The second strange point is the presentation of Jonah as an antihero missionary. Romance heroes descend to the underworld on a quest, usually, not because they are running away. Other Bible characters who have run away, like Jacob from Isaac, have not directly disobeyed God. So how can Jonah be the model of a good prophet? But it becomes stranger. Jonah's disobedience leads to the sailors' acknowledging the Lord as true God. It has to be mediated through his willingness to be thrown overboard, but God works an extra salvation out of prophetic sin. Then there are other noteworthy features: the deep sleep, the sudden storm arising and abating, the great fish, the three days and nights in the fish, the sudden conversion of a whole city. A too-literalist reading becomes bogged down in details of veracity and possibility, which do not seem the point of these features. The fish is perhaps the most ambiguous feature. It is not necessarily a whale (the Hebrew means merely "huge fish"), but is it meant to be seen as death or salvation? Jonah's psalm suggests it is salvation, saving him from drowning. But saving him for what? Jonah hopes it is a revisit to the temple, safe in Israel. But God is saving him for a second chance at the original commission.

To establish patterns of irony fully, we need first to establish what the theme is. The structural pattern of ascent would suggest it is the width of God's salvation. The first half of the book has the sailors' salvation, both literally and in terms of their recognition of God, and Jonah's salvation from his self-perceived punishment. This prepares us for the greater salvation of the whole of Nineveh. The point about Nineveh is that it is the type of the evil persecuting city. As early as the eighth century it was *the* threat to Israel; it then consumed the northern kingdom and nearly did the southern. Its cruelty was notorious. If God can save Nineveh, he can save anyone.

Such a conclusion would have been a direct challenge to those first Jewish readers who still believed salvation was only for the Jews, and who wanted to ignore the bolder vision of universal salvation found in some of the prophets, particularly Isaiah and Jeremiah. Jonah may have been one of these reluctant Jews: He is happy enough to give woes but reluctant to see repentance. But why give woes? Is it not to lead to repentance? That is the

question Jonah never answers, but that we, as readers, must answer. Jonah's reluctance is inconsistent, of course, and this is one obvious irony. He has been given a second chance, but he wants to deny this to the Ninevites. This is perhaps why some scholars have seen Jonah's prayer in chapter 2 as insincere, a parody of similar psalms (e.g., Psalm 18:6; 31; 69:1–2, 13). In posing such questions, the book seeks to give its Jewish readers not only a worldview of salvation but also a sense of shame at their own narrow and self-centered righteousness.

The reception of the story is often linked to postexilic times, when the Jewish nation was struggling to find a sense of destiny. The book poses the possibility of their being a prophetic nation to the rest of the world. Only a generous attitude on their part would enable them to carry out this message.

It is interesting to study later reception, especially in the New Testament. In the Gospels, Jesus talks of the "sign" of Jonah. In Luke 11:29–32, the sign is that Nineveh repented when Jonah preached to them, whereas the Jews refuse to repent when a greater than Jonah (i.e., JESUS CHRIST) preaches to them. The irony is established here very directly. The sign becomes ironically a denunciation of the Jews themselves for their disbelief. In Matthew 12:39–41; 16:4, a second meaning of the sign is given: that just as Jonah was three days in the fish's belly, so Jesus will be three days in the grave. The symbolism of the Jonah sign is clearly established in terms of death and resurrection. In Islam, Jonah (under the name *Yunus*) is seen as one of the great prophets.

CHARACTER

Jonah In Hebrew the word means "dove," and *ben Amittai* means "son of truth." Scholars have struggled to find a dovelike meaning. He is clearly an angry man, experiencing such intensities of anger he would rather die (4:3, 8). It has been suggested he has a death wish. But clearly, when the anger is turned to preaching denunciation, there is a fearsome anointing on it. But his character is so narrow he cannot adjust easily to the idea of God's mercy. It would seem he wants God to be as inflexible and severe as he. Jonah thinks he knows everything about being righteous, but he has much to learn. His case shows how fallible God's messengers can be and yet the purposes of God still be brought about.

Joshua

Joshua is the book of Israel's holy war. It describes how the Israelites took possession of Canaan as fulfillment of the promise that God had given centuries before to the patriarchs Abraham, Isaac, and Jacob. The name of the book is derived from its main character, Joshua, the leader of Israel after Moses' death. The name *Joshua* means "The LORD is Savior." The book is part of the primary history of the Hebrew Bible comprising the Pentateuch, Joshua, Judges, Samuel, and Kings, narrating the history of Israel from the CREATION of the world until the Babylonian EXILE.

The book does not give its author. Regarding the dating, two different positions are held by scholars: The classical historical-critical position understands the book as being part of the "Deuteronomistic history" originating from the seventh century B.C.E. (see the introduction to Deuteronomy). The fact that it may be based on older sources is also taken into consideration. The second position assumes that, on the whole, the book originates from the time of the events reported (14th or 12th century B.C.E.), with a final REDACTION at a later time taken into consideration.

There are several hints that point to an old age of at least some of the material:

1. The description of the borders of Canaan in Joshua 1:4 corresponds to the Egyptian understanding of "Canaan" in second-millennium B.C.E. sources. In particular, some regions are included that were not understood as being part of Canaan in later times any more.
2. Joshua 3:10 lists the tribes that would have to be expelled from the country. Three of them are particularly connected with the Late Bronze Age (1550–1200 B.C.E.): the Hivites, the Perizzites (both Hurrian peoples), and the Girgashites. Moreover, the names of the Anakites Sheshai

and Talmai in Joshua 15:14 are of Hurrian origin. Again, some of the names of Canaanite kings given in Joshua 11 and 12 are typical of the second millennium, but not of the first.
3. Some other elements of the story have striking parallels in extrabiblical texts from the same time, for example, the motif of spies hiding in the house of a prostitute (2:1–2) or the list of Achan's haul (7:21), which is typical of that time.

For the exact dating of the conquest of Canaan, scholars propose two different dates: either around 1400 B.C.E., relying on a literal understanding of numbers given in the biblical text (especially 1 Kings 6:1), or the middle of the 13th century B.C.E.: Archaeological excavations showed that several cities in the central area of Canaan were destroyed in the middle or near to the end of the 13th century B.C.E., which could be brought into relationship with Joshua's campaigns. On closer view, however, the archaeological picture is more complex. Some sites seem to have been destroyed in the 15th century B.C.E., others in the 13th century B.C.E. What is more, the biblical text (Deuteronomy 6:10–11; Joshua 11:13; 24:13) states that many of the cities were deliberately not destroyed during the conquest (for a discussion of Jericho, Ai, and Hazor, cities that *were* destroyed, see the Commentary below). But it may be the case that some cities were destroyed later, during the time of the Judges, as military conflicts continued for a long time after the conquest. In Tell El Amarna (Egypt) an archive was found, containing many letters written by Canaanite city kings addressed to Pharaoh Akhenaton (about 1379–1362 B.C.E.). In several letters, these Canaanite kings find themselves being threatened by a group they call "Apiru," a word that can be etymologically related to the Hebrews (Hebrew *ibhri*). While it is not appropriate fully to identify the "Apiru" with the Israelites, there are still indications that the Amarna letters reflect a situation that originated in the Israelite conquest of the land—at least if the early dating of the conquest is assumed.

From its genre, the book is best seen as a historical-theological narrative. It claims to relate historical information but shapes it into a narrative emphasizing some theological means and ends. The structure of the book has been analyzed by the Dutch theologian H. Koorevaar (*De Opbouw van het boek Jozua* [Heverlee: Centrum voor Bijbelse Vorming België, 1990], as summarized by J. Robert Vannoy in W. A. Van Gemeren [ed.], *New International Dictionary of Old Testament Theology and Exegesis* 4 [Carlisle: Paternoster, 1996], 811–814). The main structure is determined by three major divine commissions, namely, to cross the Jordan (1:1–9), to take the land (5:13–6:5), and to distribute the land (13:1–7). Each of these divine commissions is paired by a summarizing conclusion reporting the success of the mission (5:1–12; 11:16–12:24; and 21:43–45). The fourth and last main part of the book is not introduced by a divine commission. It is rather determined by the human answer to God, namely, the covenant renewal. This part also has a concluding passage (24:29–33) also rounding off the whole book. To each of the main parts a key word is assigned: *abhar* "cross" the Jordan (1:1–5:12), *laqakh* "take" the land (5:13–12:24), *khalaq* "distribute" the land (13:1–21:45), and *abhad* "serve" the Lord (22:1–24:33).

SYNOPSIS

Crossing the Borders (1:1–5:12)

God commissions Joshua to prepare the people for crossing the Jordan, in order to move into the area west of the RIVER JORDAN. As a preparation, Joshua sends two spies. In Jericho, they find shelter with a prostitute named Rahab, who hides them from Jericho's soldiers. As a reward, they promise that she and her family will be spared when Jericho is captured (chapters 1–2).

On the day of crossing the Jordan, priests carrying the ark of the covenant go into the water first. That moment, the river dams up, forming a wall in the north and draining out toward the south. The priests remain in the middle of the dry riverbed while all the people cross the river. The tribes of Reuben, Gad, and a part of Manasseh have already settled in the eastern Jordan area. However, they also cross the Jordan with an army in order to support the other tribes conquering the land. After the crossing, Joshua takes 12 stones from the riverbed

and makes a memorial out of them. After that, all male members of the people are circumcised, and the Passover is held. For the first time, the Israelites eat from the crops of Canaan. The same day, the manna ceases (3:1–5:12).

Conquering the Land (5:13–12:24)

An angel appears to Joshua instructing him how to conquer Jericho. For six days, the army is to march around the city silently once a day, led by the priests carrying the ark of the covenant. On the seventh day, they march seven times around the city and then shout out war cries.

The Israelites do as they are commanded. When they start to shout out war cries, the walls of Jericho fall down, and from all sides the soldiers enter the fortress. As commissioned by God, the city is banned: All the people are killed and no plunder is taken except for materials that are useful for the tabernacle. However, Rahab and her family are spared (5:13–6:27).

Only Achan, one of the soldiers, takes some of the booty for himself. As a next step, Joshua wants to conquer the fortress of Ai. The spies' opinion is that a small army of 2,000–3,000 soldiers would be enough. However, the campaign is not successful, and 36 Israelites die. Joshua is dismayed and asks God about it. God tells him that an Israelite had taken some of the devoted things, and therefore God had not been with them in the battle. By drawing lots, Achan is found and confesses. He is stoned to death and afterward burned (chapter 7).

Now God instructs Joshua to lure Ai's soldiers into an ambush. As the first time, he attacks with a small troop from the east and takes flight very early, luring the enemy soldiers out of the city. Suddenly, a much larger army attacks the city from the west. The fortress is conquered, and 12,000 people are killed (chapter 8).

The city of Gibeon is not far away from Ai. When the Gibeonites hear of the campaign, they become frightened and resort to a trick. They dress up as nomads pretending to have arrived from a far country. Joshua makes a peace treaty with them. Three days later, he realizes that he has been deceived. However, he does not want to break the peace treaty, which he made in the name of

The walls of Jericho collapse (Joshua 6:1–27), engraving by Julius Schnorr von Carolsfeld

the Lord. So he makes the Gibeonites his vassals (chapter 9).

Now five city-states form an alliance under the leadership of Adoni-zedek, the king of Jerusalem. They attack Gibeon because of their pact with Israel. Joshua intervenes and defeats the coalition. Since Joshua needs more time, he asks God to let the sun stand still until the battle is won. Joshua continues conquering several other cities in the southern part of Canaan. Meanwhile, another Canaanite alliance is formed in the north, led by Jabin, king of Hazor. They attack with a vast army but are easily defeated by Joshua's troops. In the course of this campaign, the city of Hazor is com-

pletely destroyed. The other cities Joshua conquers he leaves intact. All the campaigns take a couple of years. But finally, the whole territory is under Israelite control. Altogether, 31 city-states have been conquered (chapters 10–12).

Distributing the Land (13:1–21:45)

Now the land has to be distributed and taken possession of by the individual tribes of Israel. Reuben, Gad, and half of the tribe of Manasseh have already settled in the area east of the River Jordan that was already conquered under the leadership of Moses (chapter 13).

The western Jordan territory is divided by means of casting lots. But first Caleb obtains his land.

Caleb had been one of the 12 spies Moses had sent 45 years earlier to reconnoiter the territory. Only two of the spies, namely, Joshua and Caleb, trusted God that he would give success to the conquest of the land (see Numbers 13). As a reward for his faithfulness, Caleb and his family receive a special piece of land (Joshua 14).

After that, the territories of the individual tribes are determined, first for the large tribes: Judah in the south, to the west of the DEAD SEA; Ephraim and the second half of Manasseh in the heartland of Canaan. After that, all the tribes gather in Shiloh. There, the tabernacle is erected. Again spies are sent to find territories for the remaining seven tribes. The territories are then assigned by casting lots. The tribe of Benjamin is allotted the area along the borderline between Judah and Ephraim; Simeon is allotted an area inside the Judean territory. The tribes of Zebulun, Issachar, Asher, and Naphtali settle to the north of Manasseh, in the plain of Jezreel and even farther north. Finally, the tribe of Dan receives a territory at the western coast. However, they do not manage to conquer that area. Instead, they move to the north and settle around the city of Laish, which is renamed Dan. After that, Joshua receives a special piece of land for himself (chapters 15–19).

Six cities of refuge are appointed. People who have unintentionally killed a person can flee to these cities: The avenger appointed by the killed person's family (an ancient tradition) would not be allowed to enter them (chapter 20).

The tribe of Levi will be occupied with ritual. Therefore, the Levites do not obtain their own territory but instead several cities in the territories of the other tribes. The cities are allotted by casting lots. With this, the distribution of the land is finalized, and the people enjoy rest. All the promises God made to Israel's ancestors are now fulfilled (chapter 21).

Serving the Lord (22:1–24:33)

The people of the eastern Jordan tribes Reuben, Gad, and half of Manasseh, who had helped conquer the territory in the west, now return to their own inheritance. On their way, they build a great altar at the Jordan River. The western tribes hear of it and suspect them of worshipping other gods. They gather in order to campaign against them. But first, the priest Phinehas is sent to inquire about the situation. The people of Reuben, Gad, and Manasseh explain that they built the altar with just the opposite intention: that it may be a reminder to the eastern Jordan tribes to continue to trust in God. When the western tribes hear this, they are relieved (chapter 22).

When Joshua becomes old, he gathers all tribes in the city of Shechem. He explains to them that God has fulfilled all the blessings promised in the covenant. And he warns them to remain faithful to the covenant, because otherwise the curses, too, would come true. He also gives a short summary of the history of Israel from Abraham until the conquest of the land. The people unanimously declare that they want to serve God. So Joshua renews the covenant between God and his people (chapters 23–24).

COMMENTARY

Crossing the Borders (1:1–5:12)

The book of Joshua mainly deals with wars. Especially problematic to modern readers seems the fact that God orders the Israelite army to attack a peaceful land. While readers may relatively easily sympathize with Israel's actions during the Exodus from Egypt, they may be less sympathetic toward the conquering of Canaan, where so many people are either killed or driven out of their homes.

According to the Bible's own understanding, the reason for events like this is to be found in the holiness and justice of God. God allows human beings and nations to act well or badly according to their own will for the time being. But because he is a God of justice and also the creator and owner of the world, he will not allow evil to go unpunished forever. Therefore, when the time has come, he sends punishment. This can be by means of a divine intervention, as in the case of THE FLOOD, but also through war. For example, the Babylonians who conquered Jerusalem are said to have been used by God as a means for judgment over Israel.

The expulsion of the Canaanites is interpreted along the same lines. Therefore, it is said to Abraham in Genesis 15:16 that his descendants would take possession of Canaan only several generations later, "for the iniquity of the Amorites is not yet complete." Deuteronomy 9:4–6 argues that Israel does not receive the land of the Canaanites because of Israel's righteousness but "because of the wickedness of these nations." Deuteronomy 18:9–12 is even more explicit about the "abhorrent practices" of the Canaanites: "who makes a son or daughter pass through fire, or who practices divination, or is a soothsayer, or an augur, or a sorcerer, or one who casts spells, or who consults ghosts or spirits, or who seeks oracles from the dead."

Altogether, three factors play a role: the promise of land to Abraham, the necessity for Israel to settle somewhere after having escaped from Egypt, and God's judgment on the Canaanites. Theologians emphasize that the conquest of Canaan was a unique event that cannot be compared to any other war in biblical or modern times. In this context, however, it is of particular relevance that the first Canaan inhabitant the Israelites meet is not killed but receives mercy. It is Rahab's merit not only to have protected the Israelite spies but to have given witness to the true God (2:11). Therefore, this Canaanite prostitute becomes a symbol of the fact that despite the judgment that is already determined, a return to God is still possible. However, the book makes clear that, apart from her, none of the Canaanites chose this way (11:20).

The crossing of the Jordan is described in detail in the first main section. It contains an important symbolism, marking the transition from promise to fulfillment. As God dried out the Red Sea for the Israelites when they left Egypt, he dries out the Jordan for the Israelites when they enter Canaan. By making a wonder similar to the parting of the Red Sea happen under the leadership of Joshua, God demonstrates that he is with Joshua as he had been with Moses.

The Passover celebrated after crossing the Jordan again stands in relationship with the first Passover the night before the Exodus of Egypt. Circumcision and Passover are also important religious preparations for the conquest of Canaan as a holy act.

Conquering the Land (5:13–12:24)

From the Sinai region, the shortest way would have been to enter Canaan from the south. However,

this would have been unwise from a military point of view: The city-states of the whole of Canaan could have formed an alliance and blocked Israel from the start. Therefore, Moses and Joshua choose to enter the land from the east. For this, first of all, the sparsely populated territory east of the Jordan is taken. This is done under the leadership of Moses (see Numbers 20–21). After that, the people cross the Jordan moving to the west, thus separating the heartland of Canaan into a northern and a southern part. The two parts are then taken one after the other, with the Canaanites of the north and the south unable to form alliances with each other.

The first obstacle after the crossing of the Jordan is the strategically important fortress of Jericho (chapter 6). Interestingly, the conquest of Jericho is described in religious rather than military terms. An angel appears to Joshua to give instructions on how to take the city. Joshua has to remove his sandals, because he is said to stand on holy ground. This is reminiscent of Moses' doing the same when he first meets God in the burning bush (Exodus 3:5). The city of Jericho is then fully dedicated to God. He himself causes the city walls to collapse. Therefore, all the people and the booty in the city belong to him alone. The biblical word for this is the *ban*. However, the concept is not a specific biblical one but was widely known in the ancient Near East, as texts from Mari, Egypt, Assyria, and Moab (from 18th to the ninth century B.C.E.) show. It is about the concept of "total warfare" and about dedicating a city fully to the god who has made its conquest possible. The specific biblical viewpoint on this concept is that it is an act of divine punishment on the sins of the Canaanites, as stated earlier. The whole campaign is a religious enterprise more than a political one.

The archaeological evidence for the conquest of Jericho raises controversy. The British archaeologist John Garstang excavated the site in the years 1930–36. He found that the city had been destroyed by fire and part of the city walls had collapsed. However, the dating of this event is disputed. John Garstang dated the event to 1400 B.C.E., which would be compatible with the biblical presentation. However, later excavations by the archaeologist Kathleen Kenyon rather points to a destruction around 1550 B.C.E. Between 1550 and 1200 Jericho was even said to be unpopulated. But this position has again been challenged by newer research. Unfortunately, the site of Jericho has first suffered from unscientific excavation methods and later from destruction by the weather, so it will probably be impossible to get more reliable results.

The Hebrew name of the city of Ai (literally "the Ai") means "the ruin." According to archaeological insights, the city was uninhabited between 2400 and 1200 B.C.E. Nevertheless, Joshua 7–8 reports the conquering of Ai. A plausible explanation of this is that although Ai was not populated in Joshua's time, the people of the surrounding towns used it as a fortress when an enemy approached. Even today, the walls of Ai are up to 23 feet high. Joshua had to resort to subterfuge to lure the Canaanite army out of Ai in order to be able to attack them.

The third town to be burned and destroyed according to the biblical narrative was Hazor (Joshua 11). Hazor was an often-populated city. The archaeologist Yigael Yadin identified altogether 21 periods of population from the 29th until the second century B.C.E. One of them had ended by a fire. Again the exact dating of this event is disputed, 1400 B.C.E., the time of Joshua, is one possibility.

In all three cases, Jericho, Ai, and Hazor, one can see that archaeological interpretations are open to debate and we should not apply archaeology too readily either to prove or to disprove the authenticity of the biblical narrative.

Distributing the Land (13:1–21:45)

In the book of Joshua, there is a tension about the conquest of the land. Texts that imply a fast and complete conquest stand next to texts speaking of a lengthy and incomplete conquest. The reason for this is twofold. First, we have to distinguish between the first and second phases of the conquest. The first phase had the aim of breaking the power of the Canaanite city-states. The Israelite army moved from place to place but did not occupy the defeated cities permanently. This phase probably took about seven years. In this time, 31 city-states were defeated (see chapter 12). The aim of the second phase was the permanent settling of the Israelite tribes. Some of the tribes managed quite well; others did not. In some places, conflicts arose lasting for decades or even for centuries, as the book of Judges and probably the El Amarna letters (see introduction above) show. The second reason for the apparent contradictions is a theological one: One aim of the text is to show that God completely fulfilled his promise to Abraham. Therefore, it is said that the whole land was conquered (21:43–45). At the same time, the text wants to show that when disobedience to God leads to an incomplete conquest, the remaining Canaanites are set by God as a test to Israel not to be enticed to follow their gods (23:12–13). This means that one and the same event is described from two different perspectives: from the perspective of the divine blessing as well as from the perspective of human sinfulness. Joshua emphasizes the blessing but already prepares for the curse that is elaborated on in the book of Judges. The opposition of blessing and curse, together with the hope for a new beginning after the curse, is the basic pattern according to which Israel's history is interpreted in the Hebrew Bible.

Joshua 13–21 is shaped as a concentric structure (see STRUCTURES, LITERARY). The outer frame consists of texts that deal with special kinds of land distribution: Verses 13:8–33 are about the eastern Jordan area; chapters 20–21 are about the cities for the Levites. The next inner frame deals with the distribution of land to two individuals, namely, Caleb (14:6–15) and Joshua (19:49–51). Caleb and Joshua had been the two spies out of 12 who remained confident of the Lord's promise (see Numbers 13–14). Therefore, they receive extra treatment in the literary structure.

The text in between reports the distribution of the western Jordan area to the Israelite tribes. It begins with the three large tribes Judah, Ephraim, and Manasseh (chapters 15–17); after that follow the other seven tribes (18:11–19:48).

The section 18:1–10 forms the center of the structure. It relates the erection of the tabernacle in Shiloh and gives a summarizing report on the distribution of the land, naming all tribes again and referring to the eastern Jordan tribes and to the Levitical cities, therefore summarizing the whole content of Joshua 13–21.

Only one verse is devoted to the tabernacle (18:1), but its central position in the literary structure points to its overarching theological meaning: In the list of future blessings given in Leviticus 26:1–13, the promise of God, "I will place my dwelling in your midst," forms the climax. This promise is now fulfilled. More than about conquering and distributing the land, the book of Joshua is about the relationship between God and his people, visibly expressed in the erection of the tabernacle.

Serving the Lord (22:1–24:33)

The conflict between the tribes at the western and the eastern side of the Jordan shows that a unifying center is needed for Israel to stay together as a nation. This center is found in faith in God. The altar at the Jordan is erected as a witness that "Yahweh is God" (22:34). The retelling of this historical event also has a paradigmatic function for the continuing life of the community of Israel.

The topic of remaining faithful to the covenant is further developed in the last two chapters of the book. Joshua's farewell speech and his covenant renewal resemble the farewell speech and covenant renewal in Deuteronomy.

Joshua gives also a short summary of the history of Israel, beginning with Israel's ancestors, stating that they "served other gods" (see Genesis 35:2–4). Then he describes the further developments, emphasizing God's mighty and graceful acts, ending with the present situation calling the people not to serve other gods, but the Lord. The key "to serve" occurs several times within his speech (24:14–24, see also 24:31). Joshua warns the people not to become disobedient, because then the curses given in the covenant would follow. A hint that this would really happen is 24:31, saying, "Israel served the LORD all the days of Joshua, and all the days of the elders." What happened afterward is left unsaid here but will be described in the Book of Judges.

CHARACTERS

Achan   An Israelite taking part in the conquest of Jericho. Although it is strictly forbidden, he takes a mantle, silver, and gold for himself and hides them in his tent. However, the truth emerges, and Achan is stoned to death.

Caleb   One of the 12 spies who were sent by Moses to reconnoiter the territory. Because he remained confident in the promise of God, Moses promised him that he would obtain the particular area of Canaan he had spied out. This promise is fulfilled by Joshua.

Joshua   Leader of the people of Israel, successor of Moses. His main task is to conquer the land of Canaan and distribute it to the people. Joshua demonstrates that he is an able military leader. Moreover, he is fully committed to God. Therefore, God makes his military campaigns successful. As Moses does, Joshua urges the people to remain faithful to God. After the land is distributed, Joshua calls them together and renews the divine covenant with them.

Rahab   A prostitute in Jericho. She hides the Israelite spies in her house and helps them later to get out of the city. She also gives witness to the God of Israel. She and her family are therefore spared when Jericho is taken.

Jude

The tradition of the church accepts the content of verse 1, which says that this letter was written by Jude, "the brother of James," and, consequently, attributes this letter to Jude (Greek *Ioudas*). He is the same as the half brother of Jesus called Judas in Matthew 13:55 = Mark 6:3, and the James mentioned in verse 1 is the half brother of Jesus, who was the leader of the church in Jerusalem and who wrote a letter himself. Both James and Jude were sons of Joseph and Mary. Those who do not accept the letter's claim must regard it as a pseudepigraph.

It is difficult to ascertain the time of writing because the text contains very little specific information, e.g., about the adversaries Jude has encountered. The reference to "the apostles of our Lord Jesus Christ" in verse 17 suggests on the one hand that most apostles are people of the past but on the other hand that the addressees had been taught by them personally. This letter can have been written at any time between 60 and 90 C.E.

The readership is identified in theological rather than geographic terms (verse 1); we can define it as the worldwide church of Jesus Christ so that this is a truly catholic letter (see James). The use of the Hebrew Bible and of other Jewish traditions suggests that Jewish Christians in particular are in his mind.

The document's title in the Greek is simply *From Jude*. As the form of the title resembles that of the titles of the other New Testament letters, it probably stems from those who collected these letters.

In the second century this letter was very popular; later there were some doubts, probably due to its use of apocryphal traditions (see below), but it easily won its place in the New Testament canon in the fourth century. Because of its brevity and the negative tone of the middle part, in the 20th century it was the most neglected writing of the New Testament.

See also EPISTLE.

SYNOPSIS

Jude's letter is not divided into chapters. It follows a clear plan that reflects the way the ancients constructed deliberative speeches. After an opening greeting and a blessing (1–2), Jude says that the occasion and theme of his writing is the arrival of false teachers (3–4). He then discusses the false teachers, their bad personalities, and their coming judgment, with the help of many paradigms (5–16). The theological core of the letter is at the end, in the practical passage (17–23). The conclusion takes the form of a blessing (24–25).

In Jude, in comparison with Paul's letters, we lack thanksgiving at the beginning and greetings, personal notices, and prayer requests at the end. Much of this is in line with the very broad audience Jude is addressing.

COMMENTARY

The letter was written out of a concern that the church was being invaded by false teachers (on whom see below). Jude states that he gave up his original intention of writing and instead writes to remind his readers that they need to hold on to the gospel as it had been preached to them (verse 3). Verses 20–23 contain Jude's practical advice that will help the readers. He emphasizes staying close to God as well as showing love and mercy to those affected by the heresies in order to reclaim and restore them, so as to save them from perdition.

Jude follows the model of a Hellenistic (see CULTURES OF THE BIBLE) letter. There are close resemblances between this letter and 2 Peter, especially chapter 2 of that letter. It is usually thought that Peter made use of Jude's letter, but it is equally possible that the dependence occurred the other way around or that both used a common source. A difference between the two letters is that Jude does not mention the eschatological skepticism (the denial of the return of Jesus) that is the hallmark of Peter's adversaries. The blessing at the close of the letter resembles that in Paul's letter to the Romans.

In his description of the adversaries, Jude makes ample use of imagery from the Hebrew Bible and some apocryphal books (see also APOCRYPHA AND PSEUDEPIGRAPHA):

Source	Verse in Jude
The Exodus	5
The fallen angels (Genesis 6:1–4)	6
The cities of Sodom and Gomorrah (Genesis 19)	7
Michael and the devil (see below)	8–9
Cain (Genesis 4)	11
Balaam (Numbers 22–24)	11
Korah (Numbers 16)	11
Proverbs 25:14	12
Isaiah 57:20	13
Enoch (Genesis 5; see below)	14–15
Zechariah 3:2, 4	22–23

In verse 14 Jude refers to Enoch and then quotes from the book of Enoch (1:9). This book of Enoch is a composite Jewish book that dates from the period between 250 and 50 B.C.E. Large parts of it were lost for centuries and rediscovered in the 20th century. Moreover, in verse 9 Jude alludes to apocryphal traditions about an encounter between the angel Michael and the devil; according to some church fathers he is here using the apocryphal book Assumption of Moses. The fact that Jude can make use of these extracanonical writings suggests that both he and his readers accepted them as authoritative although not necessarily at the same level as the canonical Scriptures. A century after Jude, the important church father Tertullian shared his respect for the book of Enoch.

The large number of references is meant to encourage the readers through the conviction that nothing unexpected is happening: The coming of the adversaries had been foreseen, and it is merely a repetition of problems that have been solved in the past.

This letter is written in good and forceful Greek. Although we know little about Jude's personal situation, it is possible that a secretary (amanuensis) helped him in writing such a good letter in a language that may not have been his own.

Characteristic of this letter, in addition to the many allusions to previous texts, is the use of groups of three, for example, in the self-designations (verse 1), the attributes of the audience (1), the elements of the greeting (2), the actions of the opponents (8), the examples in verse 11, and the commands in verses 22–23.

CHARACTERS

adversaries   The adversaries are described as libertines. Jude refers more than once to their lifestyle as unholy, sexually immoral, and licentious (4, 6–8, 10, 16, 18). He emphasizes that their motivation is wrong and that they are entirely self-centered (8). The accusation in verse 4 probably means that they had other gods in addition to God the Father and Jesus Christ, or that they taught wrong ideas about God and Jesus. In contrast to these people, Jude and the examples he mentions from the Hebrew Bible are humble characters who act unselfishly.

God, Jesus Christ, the Holy Spirit   As a reading of verses 1 and 21–25 shows, the same activities are ascribed to God and to Jesus: showing mercy and keeping believers. There is no reference to the death and resurrection of Jesus.

Jude argues that a key difference between the believers and the false teachers is that the latter do not have the Holy Spirit living in them (19–20). This shows that possession of the Spirit is seen as a mark of Christians (cf. Romans 8:9–14). In Jude's practical advice the Father, the Son, and the Holy Spirit are each mentioned (20–21).

Judges

A sword that completely disappears in the paunch of a fat king, a woman cut up into 12 pieces, a man whose supernatural strength is broken by a prostitute—colorful characters and dramatic events are the hallmarks of the narrative contained in the book of Judges. It is a book set in a dark period of Israel's history.

Who were the "judges"? In times of peace, they probably had the task of judging the people. In the narrative, however, this receives only one passing mention (Judges 4:4–5). Much more important was the judges' role in times of crisis. When an enemy oppressed one of the Israelite tribes, a "judge," a charismatic hero who motivated the people and raised troops in order to fight the enemy, was appointed. When the war was over, the person remained a judge until his or her death.

The period of the judges was from about 1380 to 1030 B.C.E. The Al Amarna letters, correspondence between Canaanite city kings and Pharaoh Akhenaton (about 1379–1362 B.C.E.), confirm the overall picture of the book that the situation in Canaan was unsettled. According to the narrative, the PHILISTINES become an increasing threat to Israel toward the end of the time of the judges. This corresponds to extrabiblical sources according to which the "sea people" arrived at the coast of the HOLY LAND around 1200 B.C.E. Apart from this, the historical contents of the book cannot be backed up by extrabiblical sources. A firm chronology of the judges is difficult to establish. Some of the judges mentioned in the book were probably contemporaries working in different regions of Israel. It is not therefore possible simply to add up the years given in the text.

From its literary genre, the book is to be seen as a historical-theological narrative (see Part I).

The stories about the individual judges are put into an overall literary-theological structure. The book begins with a double introduction (chapter 1; 2:1–3:6), which discusses the problem of the incomplete conquest of the land and introduces the "cycles of disobedience" as the main literary-theological pattern of the book: The people are disobedient to God—God sends a punishment in the form of a military threat—the people cry out to God—God appoints a judge who delivers the people—after the death of the judge, the people again become disobedient. In the main part of the book, this pattern is carried out six times, in connection with the stories of the six "great" judges Othniel, Ehud, Deborah (with Barak), Gideon, Jephthah, and Samson. In between these stories, six "small" judges are mentioned in only one or two verses each: Shamgar, Tola, Jair, Ibzan, Elon, and Abdon. In addition to the 12 judges, Abimelech appears as a bad king in the Gideon cycle.

The book has a double conclusion, consisting of two stories that demonstrate the chaotic circumstances of this time, calling for an even stronger leader than the judges could be.

SYNOPSIS

A Double Introduction: Obedience and Disobedience (1:1–3:6)

After the death of Joshua, the tribes try to settle in the regions that were allotted to them. The tribe of Judah, together with the Simeonites, is the most successful of them. The whole mountain range is occupied. Only the three Philistine cities Gaza, Ashkelon, and Ekron at the coastal plain cannot be conquered. The tribe of Benjamin settles in its area but is unable to capture Jerusalem. So the Jebusites stay with them. The other tribes conquer their territories only partially and let the Canaanites continue to live among them. The angel of the Lord appears to the people. He is critical that the instructions to conquer the land have not been executed properly. Therefore, the remaining Canaanite peoples would become an ongoing temptation and punishment for Israel (1:1–2:5).

After the death of Joshua and the elders of his generation, the Israelites begin to turn away from God. Every time this happens, God gives the people into the hands of their enemies. When they cry out to him for help, he sends them a judge, delivering them from their oppression. But as soon as the judge has died, the people again turn to other gods.

These are the nations that are a continuing threat for Israel: the Philistines, Canaanites, Sidonians, Hivites, Hittites, Amorites, Perizzites, and Jebusites (2:6–3:6).

First Cycle of Disobedience: Othniel (3:7–11)

The Israelites turn away from God and serve other gods. Therefore, God lets the king Cushan-rishathaim from Aram-naharaim oppress the people for eight years. When they cry out to him for help, God appoints Othniel. Under Othniel's leadership, Cushan-rishataim is defeated. Afterward, the land has peace for 40 years, until Othniel's death.

Second Cycle of Disobedience: Ehud; Shamgar (3:12–30)

Again, the Israelites turn away from God. Therefore, God lets King Eglon from Moab attack Israel, in an alliance with the Ammonites and Amalekites. They oppress Israel for 18 years. When the Israelites cry out to God for help, God appoints Ehud as their judge. Ehud is a left-handed man. He is ordered to deliver a tribute to King Eglon. He takes a little sword, hiding it at his right side under the mantle. He pretends to have a secret message for the king. When all the servants have left the room, he stabs the king to death. Since Eglon is a very fat man, the sword completely disappears in his paunch. Ehud manages to leave the king's house without arousing suspicion. Back in Israel, he raises troops and conquers Moab. After that, the land enjoys peace for 80 years. After Ehud, Shamgar becomes judge. He kills 600 Philistines with an ox goad.

Third Cycle of Disobedience: Deborah (Chapters 4–5)

Again the Israelites are disobedient to God. God gives them into the hand of King Jabin of Canaan from Hazor, having Sisera as the commander of his army. Again, Israel cries out to God for help. At this time, Deborah, a prophetess, is judging Israel. Deborah sends to Barak, instructing him to recruit an army from the tribes of Naphtali and Zebulun and to attack Sisera. Barak, however, is afraid. He does not want to go without Deborah. Deborah agrees, but she prophesies that a woman will eventually kill Sisera, so it would not increase Barak's fame.

The Israelites attack and defeat Sisera's army. Sisera flees, pursued by Barak. On his way, Jael, a Kenite woman, offers Sisera shelter. When he is asleep in her tent, she takes a tent peg and hammers it through his temple so that he dies. When Barak arrives, she presents his dead body to him. After that, the land has rest for 40 years.

Fourth Cycle of Disobedience: Gideon and Abimelech; Tola; Jair (6:1–10:5)

Again, the Israelites turn to other gods. Midian conquers Israel and oppresses them. When the people cry out to God for help, God sends an angel to Gideon in order to appoint him. His first order is to destroy the altar of Baal that his family possesses and to erect an altar for God instead.

After that, Gideon recruits an army of 32,000 men in order to attack the Midianites. But God does not want the Israelites to trust in their own strength. He therefore requests that Gideon reduce the size of the army. Gideon sends back all those who are afraid; 22,000 men return to their homes. But still the army is too large. Gideon lets all the people drink from a creek. Anyone who takes the water with his hand to the mouth is sent home. Only those are left who lap the water with their tongue like dogs—300 men.

In the night, the men are posted in three groups around the valley where the huge Midianite army camps. Each of the men has a trumpet and a torch, hidden under a jug. When the signal is given, they smash the jugs, sound the trumpets, and make war cries. God confuses the Midianites so that they fight against each other and then flee.

Gideon's army pursues the fleeing troops. On their way, they are exhausted and stop off at the Ephraimite city of Succoth. However, the Ephraimites are offended that Gideon had not asked them for help during the fight. Now they do not want to support his army. Gideon marches on and captures the Midianite kings, Zebah and Zalmunna. On their way back, Gideon destroys Succoth.

The Israelites ask Gideon to become their king and to found a dynasty. However, Gideon refuses. But he makes an idol out of the golden earrings of

the Midianites. Gideon has many wives and fathers 70 sons altogether. With his maid, he also fathers a son and calls him Abimelech, "My father is king." After Gideon's death, his 70 sons reign over Israel.

Abimelech wants to become king. Since his mother's family lives in Shechem, he wins Shechem over to his plan. With a troop of mercenaries, he kills the 70 sons of Gideon. Only one, named Jotham, can flee. Jotham tells a fable, mocking Abimelech's kingship and prophetically announcing the destruction of Shechem.

After a short time, the inhabitants of Shechem secretly rebel against Abimelech, led by a certain Gaal. However, one of the city's elders betrays them to Abimelech. Abimelech destroys Shechem. After that he plans to conquer Tebez as well. However, a woman throws a large millstone out of the city tower's window and kills him.

After Abimelech, Tola and Jair are appointed to be judges in Israel.

Fifth Cycle of Disobedience: Jephthah; Ibzan; Elon; Abdon (10:6–12:13)

The Israelites continue to be disobedient to God. Therefore, God lets them be oppressed by the Philistines and by the Ammonites. They cry out to God for help. The people appoint Jephthah to free them. Jephthah first enters into negotiations with the Ammonites, but they fail. Now Jephthah decides to attack them. Before that, however, he makes a vow: He promises that when he is victorious and returns to his house, he will sacrifice the first to leave the house as a burnt offering to God. In fact, Jephthah is able to defeat the Ammonites. When he returns to his home, his daughter, his only child, walks out to meet him. Jephthah feels obliged to fulfill his vow. Jephthah judges Israel for six more years, then dies. The judges Ibzan, Elon, and Abdon follow him.

Sixth Cycle of Disobedience: Samson (Chapters 13–16)

The Israelites continue to be disobedient to God. Therefore, God gives them into the hands of the Philistines, oppressing them for 40 years.

In Zorah live Manoah and his wife. They do not have any children. An angel appears to Manoah's wife and announces to her that she will become pregnant and give birth to a son who will deliver the people from the Philistines. The son will be a Nazirite (a person consecrated to God in a special way); therefore she should not drink alcohol or eat any unclean food during her pregnancy. Samson is born and is blessed by God.

Samson seeks an occasion to make war against the Philistines. He meets a Philistine woman and sends his father to ask her parents for her hand in marriage. On the seven-day wedding, Samson poses a riddle to the 30 companions given to him and bets 30 robes that they will not solve it. At first, the companions cannot solve the riddle, but finally they obtain the answer from Samson's bride. Samson is very angry. He kills 30 people and gives their garments to the companions. After that, he leaves the bride's house, and the bride is given to one of the companions.

Some time later, Samson wants to visit his bride, but her father refuses. Samson takes revenge: He catches 300 foxes, binds torches to their tails, and drives them into the Philistines' fields so that the crops catch on fire.

After that, Samson hides in a cleft of a rock. The Philistines ask the Israelites to hand Samson over to them. Samson lets himself be bound voluntarily. Having arrived at the Philistines' place, however, he tears his fetters and kills 1,000 Philistines with the jawbone of a donkey. After that, he becomes a judge over Israel for 20 years.

Samson falls in love with a woman called Delilah. The Philistines bribe her to inquire from him the secret of his supernatural power. He lies to her and tells her that he only had to be bound with seven fresh bowstrings. The Philistines prepare the bowstrings and give them to Delilah, who binds Samson when he has fallen asleep in Delilah's chamber. But when the Philistines attack, he easily tears the strings. Twice more Delilah asks Samson for his secret, but he keeps lying, and every time the Philistines attack, he frees himself easily. But finally, he tells her the true secret of his strength: Since he is a Nazirite, his hair has never been cut. When Samson has fallen asleep in Delilah's arms, the Philistines cut his hair. Divine power leaves him. He is blinded and taken to prison. In prison, his hair starts growing again.

The death of Samson (Judges 16: 23–31), engraving by Julius Schnorr von Carolsfeld

The Philistines make a great feast in the temple of their god Dagon. They take Samson, in order to ridicule him. Samson is placed between the two large pillars of the temple. For a last time, Samson prays to God for strength. With his hands, he pushes the pillars apart, and the ceiling caves in on the celebrating Philistines.

A Double Conclusion: "There Was No King in Israel" (Chapters 17–21)

The section consists of two separate stories. The first begins with a man named Micah who lives in the Ephraim mountain range. Micah has some money that has been consecrated to God. He takes it in order to make a sanctuary in his house. A traveling Levite arrives. Micah invites him to be the priest of his family and gives him a salary.

The tribe of Dan is still looking for a place to settle. So far, they have not been able to conquer a territory. Five spies from Dan go to Micah's house. Micah's priest prophesies that they are on the right route. The five spies move on and reconnoiter the city of Laish. After that, they return to their people.

Now the whole tribe of Dan moves northward. When they arrive at the house of Micah, they take his idol and the holy equipment with them. They invite Micah's priest to be priest for the whole tribe. Micah cannot do anything against it.

The men of Dan move farther north and attack the guileless city of Laish. They rename the city Dan and settle there with the whole tribe.

The second story deals with another Levite from the Ephraim area, who marries a woman from Bethlehem in Judah as his concubine. Eventually, she becomes angry at him and returns to her family. The Levite travels after her to win her back. They stay in the house of his father-in-law for a couple of days, and then they plan to return. On their way, they spend the night at an old man's place in the city of Gibea. However, malicious men from the city surround the house and threaten them. The Levite gives his concubine to them. They rape her the whole night. In the morning, she lies dead at the threshold.

The Levite travels home, cuts his dead concubine into 12 pieces, and sends them throughout the whole territory of Israel. The whole of Israel is filled with indignation. They decide to destroy Gibea. However, the tribe of Benjamin, in whose territory Gibea lies, disagrees. Therefore, it leads to a fratricidal war. In battles involving heavy losses, Benjamin is defeated and almost totally destroyed.

COMMENTARY

The book's message is controlled by two overarching themes. One is defined from its introduction, the other one from its conclusion. The introduction discusses the problem of the incomplete conquest of the land in terms of the divine curse that fell on Israel because of their disobedience. From this result the "cycles of disobedience" (see introduction) that are described in the main part of the book. This theme points back to the book of Joshua.

The second overarching theme is the question of political leadership. The conclusion of the book comments on the desperate situation with the words "In those days there was no king in Israel; everyone did what was right in his own eyes." In the main part of the book, the judges are described as leaders helping the people in a crisis. However, they do not achieve political and religious stability on a long-term basis. What is more, not a few of them are quite questionable with regard to their attitude as well as their achievements. These observations lead the readers to the conclusion that

there is a need for a different, more effective, and more faithful type of leadership. This second theme points forward to the answer given in the books of 1 and 2 Samuel.

A Double Introduction: Obedience and Disobedience (1:1–3:6)

The book of Joshua emphasizes that the whole land has been conquered by the Israelites. That there were problems is only hinted at in a few places. The book of Judges, on the other hand, puts the accent on the problem that the land was *not* fully conquered. In particular, the book of Judges opens with a list of the territories and cities that Israel failed to take.

This difference between Joshua and Judges is often seen as a historical contradiction. However, it is important to see that Joshua and Judges are historical-theological narratives; therefore, the historical events are presented from certain theological perspectives. The main emphasis of Joshua is that God made his promise to Abraham come completely true. Therefore, it is said that the whole land was conquered (Joshua 21:43–45). The book of Judges, in contrast, deals with the fact that the conquest was incomplete and relates it to the disobedience of Israel. That the Canaanite nations cannot be driven out completely, the book of Judges interprets from four different angles:

- as an act of disobedience: the Israelites disobeyed the divine command to drive the Canaanite people out when they conquered the land
- as a result of disobedience: because Israel sinned God did not make them victorious when they tried to conquer the land
- as a punishment for disobedience: since Israel sinned, God punishes them by way of the continuing presence of the nations
- as a cause of further disobedience and punishment: the Canaanite nations entice Israel to follow other gods

Altogether, these aspects describe the fateful entanglements that result from human sin.

The complementary function of the books of Joshua and Judges is underscored by a literal quote. The concluding sentence from Joshua 24:31, "Israel served the LORD all the days of Joshua," is repeated in Judges 2:7 but followed by the information that after the death of Joshua, the people turned away from God. As in other places of the Bible, one and the same event is described first from the perspective of the divine blessing and then from the perspective of the divine curse due to human failure (see especially on Genesis 1–11).

The theological background of the time of the judges is then further elaborated on in the form of "cycles of disobedience":

- the people are disobedient to God;
- God sends a punishment in the form of a military threat;
- the people cry out to God for help;
- God appoints a judge to deliver the people;
- after the death of the judge, the people become disobedient again.

First Cycle of Disobedience: Othniel (3:7–11)

The purpose of the Othniel story probably is to give a first example of a "cycle of disobedience." Apart from that, there is not much individuality to the narrative. The name of the enemy, *Cushan-rishataim*, means "Cushan of double-wickedness" and is probably an intended ridiculing of the original name. The origin of the people "Aram naharaim" is uncertain. The tribe affected is probably Judah, since Othniel is from there.

Second Cycle of Disobedience: Ehud; Shamgar (3:12–30)

The Ehud story is already slightly more elaborate. God makes Eglon, the Moabite king, the means by which he punishes Israel. The fact that God orders and controls the destinies of nations is a conviction of the writers throughout the Bible. After the people cry out to God, God appoints Ehud as their deliverer. The Ehud story is very vivid. The scene at King Eglon's house especially captures the reader's interest. The tribe affected in this story is Benjamin. The "city of palms" (3:13) is Jericho.

Third Cycle of Disobedience: Deborah (Chapters 4–5)

Now the Israelites face the first major threat. Altogether, six of the northern tribes are involved.

The oppressor is Jabin, king of Hazor. Hazor was a strong city. Its population in that time has been archaeologically estimated as 40,000. Joshua 11:1–11 already speaks about a Jabin, king of Hazor, who was killed when Joshua conquered the city about a century before. That Jabin appears again in Judges 4 is not necessarily a historical flaw. It may well be that after Joshua's army had left the place, the city was built up again, and a successor of Jabin took on his name as a hereditary title.

Deborah is the only female judge. In the Hebrew Bible there are a few examples of women in leading positions (Miriam, Huldah, Athaliah; see also WOMEN IN THE BIBLE). The theme of a woman saving Israel is further elaborated by Deborah's prophecy that a woman would kill general Sisera.

The Song of Deborah is surely one of the oldest textual portions in the book of Judges. Scholars agree that it is contemporary with the events it describes. The song is a prime example of old Hebrew poetry, savoring every emotion and every moment of the story, e.g., when Sisera is killed by Jael, the Kenite woman: "He sank, he fell, he lay still at her feet; at her feet he sank, he fell; where he sank, there he fell dead" (5:27). The poem is not yet confined to the more strict line of parallelism that dominates classical Hebrew poetry, for example, in the psalms.

Fourth Cycle of Disobedience: Gideon and Abimelech; Tola; Jair (6:1–10:5)

This time, the Israelites are oppressed by Midianite nomads, traveling across the country with their tents and their herds, taking any agricultural yields they can from the Israelites. The Israelites tried to hide themselves and their food in ravines and caves. Also Gideon, the story's protagonist, is introduced beating out wheat secretly in a wine press. Gideon is presented as a complex character. He is a rather fearful hero. Three times he needs a divine sign to be sure of his commission (fire in 6:21, a woolen fleece in 6:36–40, and a dream in 7:13–14). In the case of the fleece he even carries out a crosscheck. Today's believers discuss how far it is appropriate to ask God for signs of this kind. Gideon is very successful in mobilizing 32,000 men for the fight against Midian—even too successful.

God wants people to trust in him more than in their own strength. This topic is taken up by several of the Hebrew Bible prophets. Having 300 men left, Gideon can still win. The audio-visual effect of the 300 is boosted by God so that the vast Midianite camp are totally confused and they flee.

The narrative of the battle against Midian mentions God several times. However, when Gideon takes revenge on Succoth, God seems to be totally absent. Gideon acts completely on his own behalf.

Whereas the revenge against Succoth can at least partly be understood, Gideon's conduct afterward becomes even more problematic. On the one hand, he turns down the offer of the Israelites to become their king and assures them that God should reign. On the other hand, however, his later behavior points in a different direction: He makes a golden idol and entices the people to idolatry. He takes many wives, the prerogative of a king at that time. He even names one of his sons *Abimelech*, meaning "My father is king."

Therefore, Gideon is far from being a leader of the people according to God's will. The ambivalence of his character is used to demonstrate the ambivalence of human rule.

Gideon's mistakes have consequences even for the following generation. The narrative uses Abimelech to demonstrate that monarchy is not a simple remedy to answer the questions of true leadership. One of the few fables of the Hebrew Bible, the search of the trees for a king (9:8–15), illustrates the problem.

Fifth Cycle of Disobedience: Jephthah; Ibzan; Elon; Abdon (10:6–12:13)

Jephthah is again an ambivalent figure. On the one hand, he helps Israel out of the crisis. On the other hand, his great fear when he begins to carry out his task leads him to make a vow that he will sacrifice as a burnt offering whatever emerged from his house first when God made him defeat the enemy and return home alive.

Maybe Jephthah hopes to see one of his household servants first, but instead the worst possible thing happens: His young daughter, his only child, comes out, happy to meet her father again. The daughter has to die without being able to live on in her descendants. Therefore, she is allowed to take two months to mourn her virginity (11:37). But even more, her death means the termination of Jephthah's clan.

It was Jephthah's fault to make the vow—God never requested a human sacrifice. However, this practice was known among the Canaanite nations (2 Kings 3:26–27). One could ask whether Jephthah was also at fault when he fulfilled the vow. In any case, Jephthah's daughter is presented as being especially faithful since she accepts the consequences of her father's stupid behavior without hesitating.

The execution of the sacrifice is not described. Some hints suffice, in the face of the tragedy of the event.

Sixth Cycle of Disobedience: Samson (Chapters 13–16)

At the beginning of the Jephthah story, a simultaneous threat of the Philistines and the Ammonites was introduced. However, the Jephthah story only described the Ammonites. Now the narrative turns to the more difficult and longer-lasting oppression by the Philistines. This shows that Jephthah and Samson were probably contemporaries. Samson probably is the most flamboyant personality of the book. He is a Nazirite, a person who was consecrated to God in a special way, especially empowered by God. But still he fails. His achievements as Israel's one-man army are considerable but not effective in breaking the Philistines' power. His illicit relationships with prostitutes and loose-living women are especially troublesome. Despite the fact that he is a Nazirite, he lacks discipline and true dedication. The narrator of the Samson story stays remarkably in the background. He lets the events speak for themselves. As with the Gideon story, the Samson story indirectly poses the question as to how a successful leader of Israel had to be. One point is made: The true deliverer of Israel is yet to come.

The Samson narrative contains the only riddle saying contained in the Hebrew Bible: "Out of the eater came something to eat. Out of the strong came something sweet" (14:14). The solution is a lion's skeleton containing a beehive.

A Double Conclusion: "There Was No King in Israel" (Chapters 17–21)

The stories of chapters 17–21 are sometimes said to be an appendix to the book of Judges. In the Christian Old Testament, the book of Judges is followed by Ruth. Therefore, Judges 17–18; 19–21; and Ruth 1–4 are sometimes described as a "Bethlehem trilogy," because all three stories have to do with people who come from Bethlehem. However, in the Hebrew Bible, Ruth is not placed after Judges. Further, Judges 17–21 form an integral part of the book: As a double conclusion, the chapters match the double introduction of the book in chapter 1 and 2:1–3:6. Although the two stories told do not stand in direct relationship to the activity of the judges, they belong in this time. Even more, the interpretation given to them is best seen as a final evaluation of the period of the judges.

The stories are characterized by idolatry, injustice, and violence. However, no direct evaluation is given. Instead, the stories are framed by a sentence repeated four times giving an interpretative clue: "In those days there was no king in Israel; everyone did what was right in his own eyes" (17:6; 21:25, and in a shortened form 18:1; 19:1). Thereby, the question regarding the true leadership of Israel is vigorously posed again, and an answer is suggested.

David will be the true king for whom Israel is waiting. He will conquer the territory that has not yet been conquered, he will free Israel from the Philistine threat, and he will, at least from an overall point of view, stand out in his justice and faithfulness to the Lord (see 1 and 2 Samuel).

CHARACTERS

Abimelech   Son of Gideon. He wants to become king. He wins the inhabitants of Shechem over to his plan. However, he does not have the right attitude. The people soon laugh at him. His story ends in much bloodshed when he destroys Shechem and is himself killed when attacking another city.

Deborah   The Hebrew Bible's example of a faithful female leader. Barak, who should have been the leader, wants instead to follow her. Therefore, she prophesies that the honor of having killed the enemy general will again go to a woman.

Delilah   A lover of Samson. Delilah uncovers from Samson the secret of his supernatural strength and delivers him to the Philistines.

Gideon   At first a rather cautious hero, but successful with the help of God. However, his success leads him to behave as a king even if he officially refuses to be one. At the beginning of his mission, he destroys the altar of Baal; at the end, he erects a new golden idol.

Jephthah   A successful general in the defeat of the Ammonites. However, he makes a vow that costs the life of his daughter, his only child.

Samson   A man consecrated to God, who is given extraordinary physical strength. Unlike the other judges, he does not lead an army but tries to fight the Philistines on his own. He lacks faithfulness and discipline and is drawn astray by prostitutes.

Judith

The book of Judith is not part of the Hebrew Bible but was included in the Septuagint (see BIBLE, EARLY TRANSLATIONS OF). The Roman Catholic Church as well as the Orthodox Churches recognize it as "deuterocanonical" (being of secondary canonical rank). In the Protestant churches, however, it is not accepted but is included in the Apocrypha of the Old Testament (see APOCRYPHA AND PSEUDEPIGRAPHA).

The text is extant in three different Greek translations only. They are based on a Hebrew original, which has, however, become lost. The book was probably written in the middle of the second century B.C.E. in Palestine.

SYNOPSIS

Nebuchadnezzar, king of ASSYRIA, wants to put the whole region of Canaan (see HOLY LAND) under his control. So, Holofernes, his chief general, sets out with his vast army to fight the Jewish people. A certain Achior, however, a leader of the Ammonites, warns him, telling him that he would only be able to defeat the Jews if they had sinned against their God. Otherwise, their God would protect them, and the Assyrians would be destroyed. But Holofernes does not like to listen to what Achior tells him and gives the order to kill him. Achior, however, happens to be saved by some Jewish warriors from the small city of Bethulia.

Now Holofernes decides to destroy Bethulia, and he lays siege to the city. When the people run out of water, the elders plan to surrender. They decide to wait for five more days, hoping for a wonder of God.

Then Judith appears on the scene. She is a young widow, beautiful, intelligent, and god-fearing. Judith criticizes the elders for not trusting in God enough. After having spoken a long prayer, she seizes the initiative: She takes a bath, dresses herself up, and puts on all her jewelry. Then she leaves Bethulia and freely lets herself be taken before Holofernes in the Assyrian camp. She flatters him with many words. She tells him that Achior's prophecy was correct, but since the Jews had started eating unclean animals in the course of the siege of the city, God would not protect them anymore.

Judith stays at the Assyrian camp for three days. On the fourth day, Holofernes holds a small banquet and invites Judith to it. Late in the night of the banquet, it happens that she is alone with Holofernes, who is very drunk. She seizes the opportunity, takes his sword that is hanging at the bedpost, and cuts off his head. She is freely able to leave the Assyrians' camp, and she returns to Bethulia.

The next morning, the Assyrians find their general dead. They flee in panic. The Jews from all the cities attack the fleeing soldiers. The rest of the people of Bethulia plunder the Assyrian camp, and they find great riches there.

The people of Bethulia praise the courage of Judith. They move to JERUSALEM, singing psalms of praise on their way. In Jerusalem, they offer burnt offerings at the temple and worship God.

COMMENTARY

The book of Judith is formally made up as a historical-theological NARRATIVE. But it should rather be deemed a folktale, since the story contains several historical flaws. Nebuchadnezzar, for example, was not king of the Assyrians reigning in Nineveh (Judith 1:1) but king of Babylon. Nebuchadnezzar's father had already destroyed Nineveh in 612 B.C.E. At the same time, Judith 4:3 and 5:19 point to a postexilic setting (after 536 B.C.E.), a time when neither the Assyrians nor the Babylonians were ruling anymore.

Furthermore, the route of Holofernes' army in Judith 2:21–28 beggars description. The location of the city of Bethulia is not known to us; possibly it is a fictitious city. Scholars discuss whether the story is intended to be historically true and only fails to be so, or whether its intention is nonhistoric from the start.

As in the books of Ruth and Esther, the hero of the book of Judith is a woman. The book demonstrates that God is with those who fully commit themselves to him. The words of Achior are proven true, though in the opposite way to that in which Judith makes Holofernes believe them. In the case of Judith, her concern for religious purity is especially emphasized. For example, during her stay in the Assyrian camp, Judith takes a ritual bath every day (12:5–9).

The character of Achior is also interesting. He is depicted as a heathen witness of the work of Israel's God, who finally converts to him (5:5–21; 14:5–10). This gives the book a universalistic stamp, despite all the national tones also heard in the text.

CHARACTERS

Achior   A leader of the Ammonites, who witnesses the power of Israel's God and converts to him.

Holofernes   Chief general of Nebuchadnezzar's army fighting against the Jews. Holofernes ignores Achior's warning that God will protect the Jews. Eventually, he is killed by Judith.

Judith   A young widow from the city of Bethulia. Judith is beautiful, pious, and very courageous, as she walks into the Assyrian camp. She seduces Holofernes and kills him, thereby saving her city from the enemy.

1 and 2 Kings

The book 1 and 2 Kings deals with the glory and decline of the Israelite kingdom. It covers the history of Israel from the time of Solomon until the Babylonian EXILE, i.e., from about 971 to 561 B.C.E. (Jehoiachin's release).

Regarding its genre, the book is a historical-theological narrative: Its main interest is history. The text attaches importance to presenting each of the individual kings together with the most important information about his reign. The second main interest of the text is theology: The history of Israel and Judah is interpreted as seen from God's point of view; the kings are assessed on the basis not of their political talent but of their attitude toward God. In particular, the book demonstrates that in the end spiritual decline was the reason for political destruction. At the center of the narrative stand, besides the kings, two prophets, through whom God declares his will and through whom he also acts powerfully. The third interest of the text is a literary one: By way of narrative shaping, the historical and the theological levels are welded together.

The book of Kings was originally one single book and was only later divided into 1 and 2 Kings for practical reasons (scroll size). The book is part of a larger group of books: Joshua, Judges, Samuel, and Kings together consider the history of Israel from the conquest of the Promised Land (see CANAAN, CONQUEST OF) until the Exile, when the land had to be left again. The four books fit together from a chronological as well as a thematic point of view. Together with the Pentateuch, the books can be seen as forming one great story stretching from the creation of the world until the Babylonian Exile. Many of the contents of the book of Kings are repeated in 2 Chronicles. For the purpose of this, see there. The last two chapters of Kings are also repeated (with slight variations) in Jeremiah 52, as an appendix to this prophetic book; some other passages reappear in the book of Isaiah (see Isaiah 36–39). Both prophets were contemporaries of 2 Kings. The book is dated mainly on the basis of its content. The historical presentation ends in the Exile; therefore, a time of writing around 550 B.C.E. is seen as the most probable. The author, however, makes use of older sources, namely, royal annals. He regularly refers to them in his book. Many scholars hold the view that the book came into existence in two or more stages. In any case, the form we have gives it a strong impression of unity. The literary shape of the book follows the chronological order of the individual kings. After the split of the kingdom, the kings of the northern and the southern kingdoms are dealt with alternately. The sections on the individual kings begin and end according to a fixed scheme: At the beginning, the name of the king is given, together with a dating in relation to the other kingdom; then follow the years of reign and sometimes the name of the mother. An assessment is given as to whether a king reigned according to the will of God or not (see, for example, 1 Kings 15:1–3). At the end of each section, there is often a reference to the author's source, from which more information on the king could be obtained. Information on death and burial is given as well as the name of the king's successor (1 Kings 15:23–24).

Only one section of the book of Kings does not stand inside such a royal "frame." It is 2 Kings 2, dealing with the prophetic office. This points to the fact that the literary center of the book is not dominated by kings but by two prophets, namely, Elijah (1 Kings 16:29–2 Kings 1) and Elisha (2 Kings 3–13), standing up against the dynasty of Ahab and the Baal worship introduced by him.

SYNOPSIS

The United Kingdom of Judah/Israel under Solomon (1 Kings 1–11)

When David has become old, Adonijah, one of his sons, wants to make himself king. He acquires some warriors as a bodyguard and enlists several influential people to his side, among them a certain Joab and the priest Abiathar. Then he prepares a feast, at which he inaugurates himself as king. Bathsheba, the mother of Solomon, learns of it. She informs David and recalls to him his promise to make Solomon king after him. David reacts immediately. Solomon is caused to ride on David's royal mule, trumpets are blown, and Solomon is officially anointed as king over Israel. When the people at Adonijah's feast hear about it, they all slink home. Adonijah begs Solomon for mercy, and Solomon grants it to him.

David has been given a virgin to care for him in his old age. After David's death, Adonijah appears before Bathsheba asking her to give this woman to him. Solomon sees this as another attempt by Adonijah to become king. He kills Adonijah, as well as Joab, who was on his side; the priest Abiathar is removed from his office.

God appears to Solomon in a dream. Solomon has one wish. He asks God for wisdom to be able to rule his people wisely. God likes this request, and he promises him great wisdom as well as extraordinary wealth and fame.

Two women who are prostitutes go to Solomon with a legal dispute. Both have given birth to a son. One of them has inadvertently crushed her baby during the night and then exchanged the two babies—at least, this is what the other claims. Both want to have the living baby as their own. Solomon suggests splitting it into two parts so that each of the two women would get half of it. One of the harlots agrees to the suggestion, but the other says, "Please, my lord, give her the living boy; certainly do not kill him!" Now Solomon knows that she is in fact the mother, because she wants to prevent her son from dying.

Solomon's wise ruling (1 Kings 3:16–28), engraving by Julius Schnorr von Carolsfeld

Solomon organizes his kingdom and appoints many officials for it. He becomes very powerful, wealthy, and famous because of his wisdom.

Solomon decides to build a temple for God in Jerusalem, as God has instructed David (2 Samuel 7). He enters into negotiations with King Hiram of Tyre (see LEBANON) and orders wood from him. He appoints compulsory laborers to fell the wood and to cut stones. In the 480th year after the Exodus from Egypt, in the fourth year of Solomon (966 B.C.E.), the building of the temple starts. The temple proper is about 60 cubits long, 40 cubits wide, and 30 cubits high (about 90 feet by 60 feet by 45 feet; about 30 meters by 20 meters by 15 meters). A vestibule and several outbuildings with three stories are also erected. The inner temple is divided into the Holy and the Most Holy by a wooden wall. Inside, the walls are lined with cypress, covered with fine gold, and decorated with palms and chains. For the Most Holy Place, two carved cherubim are made and overlaid with gold. The extended wings are each five cubits (about 7.5 feet; about 2.5 meters) long, so that the two figures standing beside each other extend over the whole width of the hall. In front of the house, Solomon makes two pillars, each 18 cubits (about 27 feet; nine meters) high, covered with copper. Many temple vessels are also manufactured. After seven years, the building of the temple is completed.

In a ceremonial act, the ark of the covenant is borne into the temple and placed in the Most Holy Place between the two cherubim, under their wings. A cloud fills the temple, symbolizing the presence of God. In a solemn PRAYER, Solomon thanks God that the temple has been erected according to his promise. He asks God to fulfill his other promise as well, making the Davidic kingdom an everlasting dynasty. He knows that God would not live in a house made by human beings, but he asks God to make the temple a place where God would answer the prayers of the people and where God would forgive sin. Even for foreigners, the temple would become a place where they could get to know the Lord. At night, God appears to Solomon. He confirms the prayer of Solomon, but he also warns Solomon that he will reject the people and the temple if they turn away from him.

The visit of the queen of Sheba to Solomon (1 Kings), engraving by Gustave Doré

After the temple is finished, Solomon builds a royal palace. He also fortifies several cities. By trading, Solomon's wealth increases more and more. Solomon even has a fleet of ships for trading.

The queen of Sheba visits Solomon. She is very much impressed by his wisdom and his wealth.

However, Solomon also has many wives. Among them are heathen women from several neighboring nations. They make Solomon turn to foreign gods and construct temples for them. God becomes very angry with that. As a punishment, different political enemies arise against Solomon. In addition, God announces that after Solomon's death the kingdom will split into two parts. Solomon dies after a reign of 40 years.

The Kingdoms of Israel and Judah until Omri (1 Kings 12:1–16:28)

After the death of Solomon, his son, Rehoboam, travels to Shechem, because the people have gathered there to make him king. The northern tribes, however, make it a condition that he should reduce the amount of taxes and of compulsory labor. Rehoboam, however, refuses. Therefore, the northern tribes do not accept him, and Rehoboam becomes king only over the southern tribes of Judah and Benjamin (and partly Simeon), from then on called the kingdom of Judah.

Jeroboam has been administrator over the compulsory labor of the northern tribes under King Solomon. However, he has fallen out of favor with Solomon and has fled to Egypt. Now he returns and becomes king over the northern tribes, from then on called the kingdom of Israel. Rehoboam of Judah plans to make war against Jeroboam, but a prophet advises him not to do so.

Jeroboam wants to prevent his people from traveling into the south to the Jerusalem temple for the religious feasts. Therefore, he fashions two golden calves and puts them up at Bethel and Dan. A prophet warns him to turn back from his wrong path, but he does not obey him. Jeroboam's son, Abijah, becomes sick and dies. God announces further punishment to Jeroboam: His whole family will be exterminated. After 22 years of reign, Jeroboam dies. His son, Nadab, becomes king in his place.

Meanwhile, Rehoboam, the son of Solomon with an Ammonite woman, reigns in the southern kingdom of Judah. He is also disobedient to the Lord. The worship of idols spreads throughout the country. Pharaoh Shishak invades the country. In Jerusalem, he plunders the temple treasures and those of the royal palaces. The splendor of Solomon is gone and will never be reached again. Rehoboam and Jeroboam are in continuous conflict with each other.

In Judah, Rehoboam is succeeded by Abijah, who follows in the footsteps of his father. He, in turn, is succeeded by Asa. Asa removes many idols all over the country. He is wholly committed to the Lord. When Israel attacks Judah, he pays the Arameans (see SYRIA) to repel them.

In Israel, Nadab, the son of Rehoboam, reigns for two years. However, a certain Baasha conspires against him and lets him and the whole family of Jeroboam be killed. He makes himself king in the city of Tirzah. But he is also disobedient to God, so God announces the destruction of his family as well. Baasha is succeeded by his son, Elah. After only two years, Elah is killed by Zimri, one of his officials. Zimri also exterminates all male members of Baasha's family. He himself reigns for seven days only. Omri, Elah's military leader, attacks Tirzah with the army and conquers it. Zimri is killed, and Omri makes himself king over Israel. Omri buys the mountain of Samaria and founds the new capital of Israel, the city of Samaria. But he continues to worship other gods. He dies after 12 years of reign, and his son, Ahab, succeeds him.

Elijah and Ahab in Israel (1 Kings 16:29– 2 Kings 1)

Ahab fuels God's wrath more than all the other kings before him. He marries Jezebel, the daughter of Ethbaal ("Baal exists"), king of the Sidonians (see LEBANON), and he introduces the worship of Baal into Israel as the official religion.

The prophet Elijah appears. He prophesies a drought that will last as long as he says so. After Elijah has given this prophecy to Ahab, he has to flee. Initially, he hides near a creek, and God sends ravens that provide him with food. When the creek is dried up, God sends him to the village of Zarephath to a widow, in order to hide in her house. However, the widow and her son are just about starving. Elijah promises her that the jar of flour will not be emptied and the jug of oil will not fail until the end of the drought. So Elijah stays with the widow. Eventually, her son becomes ill and dies. Elijah prays for him, and God raises him from the dead. The woman realizes that Elijah is really a messenger of God.

After a couple of years, God commissions Elijah to appear before Ahab again and announce to him the end of the drought. Before that, a contest is held on Mount Carmel. For it, Elijah summons all the priests of Baal there. Two altars are erected, one for Baal and one for God. Firewood and a bull are placed on top of each. However, no fire is put to them. Now the priests of Baal pray to Baal from morning until noon, but nothing happens. Elijah has seawater poured over the wood of God's altar to make sure it does not accidentally catch fire and to rule out cheating. Then he prays to God, and God lets fire fall from heaven, consuming the bull, the wood, and even the altar down to the ground. Now the people recognize that the Lord is truly God. The priests of Baal are executed. A cloud appears on the horizon, and soon afterward the rain begins to fall. Jezebel is very angry about the execution of the Baal priests. Elijah has to flee again. In the desert, he has a breakdown. He lies under a juniper tree and wishes he was dead. But God gives him food and strengthens him. Elijah goes wandering to the south until he reaches Mount SINAI. There, God appears to him. First a strong wind arises, but God is not in the wind. It is followed by an earthquake, but God is not in the earthquake. Then there is a fire, but God is not in the fire. Next the sound of a gentle blowing arises. Elijah covers his face and appears before God. God gives him new instructions: He should anoint Hazael to be king over Aram (Syria), Jehu to be king over Israel, and Elisha to be prophet in his place.

First, Elijah meets Elisha, who is plowing a field. He throws his mantle over him. Elisha says goodbye to his family and becomes Elijah's disciple.

King Ben-Hadad from Aram attacks the city of Samaria. A prophet informs Ahab that Ahab will gain the victory because God wants to demonstrate his power. The Arameans are defeated. The Arameans suspect that Israel's gods are mountain gods. Therefore, a year later, they attack Israel in the plain. Again God demonstrates his power and Ahab gains the victory. Ben-Hadad begs Ahab for mercy to spare his life, and Ahab grants it to him. The prophet rebukes Ahab for that.

A certain Naboth owns a vineyard near the palace of King Ahab. Ahab wants to buy it in order to make it a vegetable garden. Naboth, however, does not want to sell it. Ahab becomes very angry and laments before his wife, Jezebel. Jezebel appoints two false witnesses and commissions them to accuse Naboth publicly of having cursed God and the king. Naboth is stoned to death, and Ahab takes his vineyard for himself. God sends Elijah to Ahab in order to proclaim God's judgment over him: The family of Ahab will be extinguished, and Jezebel's corpse will be eaten by dogs. When Ahab hears these words, he is very depressed, and he fasts in sackcloth and ashes. Therefore, God promises to delay the judgment, so that it will happen only in the time of his son.

Ahab forms an alliance with King Jehoshaphat from Judah. Together, they want to make war against the Arameans. But Jehoshaphat first wants to hear a word of God about it. Ahab summons 400 prophets, who all predict that he will have the victory. Jehoshaphat, however, is not satisfied. Another prophet, Micah, is asked. Ahab dislikes Micah because he has always announced judgment to him. And again, Micah announces that Israel will be scattered like a herd without a herdsman: That is, Ahab will fall during the campaign. In addition, Micah explains that a lying spirit has been sent to the other 400 prophets. Nevertheless, Ahab and Jehoshaphat go to war. Ahab dresses as a simple soldier. However, a random arrow strikes him, and he dies the same evening.

Jehoshaphat is a king according to the will of God. He reigns over the southern kingdom of Judah for 25 years in total. He is succeeded by his son, Jehoram.

In the northern kingdom of Israel, Ahab's son, Ahaziah, is made king. As his father, he worships Baal. Eventually, he falls through a lattice in his palace and is severely injured. He lets Baal-zebub be asked whether he will recover. God sends Elijah, who announces judgment to him because he has not asked God. Ahaziah dies, and Jehoram, another son of Ahab, becomes king.

Elijah and Elisha (2 Kings 2)

Elijah sets off for Jericho; from there God wants to take him into heaven. Elijah asks Elisha to stay where they are, but Elisha does not want to leave him. So they travel together. When they have to cross the Jordan River, Elijah strikes the water with his cloak. The water divides, and they can cross the river on dry ground. Elijah asks Elisha for a last wish. Elisha says that he wants to inherit a double share of Elijah's spirit (which means, to come into his inheritance, since it was a custom that the first-born received two shares; see Deuteronomy 21:17). A chariot of fire and horses of fire appear, and Elijah rises in a whirlwind into heaven. Elisha takes Elijah's mantle and strikes the water of the Jordan. The water divides, and Elisha crosses. Fifty prophet disciples see this from a distance and confirm that Elijah's spirit lies now upon Elisha.

Elijah is taken up to heaven (2 Kings 2:1–14), engraving by Julius Schnorr von Carolsfeld

Elisha and Jehu in Israel (2 Kings 3–13)

The Moabites rebel against the Israelite oppression. Jehoram, king of Israel, forms an alliance with Jehoshaphat from Judah and with the king of Edom. Together they want to attack the Moabites. On their way, the army lacks water. The prophet Elisha is called. He explains how the army can get water according to the will of God. He also predicts victory over Moab. The Moabites are overpowered by Israel. As a last resort, however, Mesha, king of the Moabites, sacrifices his son on the city wall. The Israelites are so shaken that they return home without having conquered the city.

Elisha performs many wonders. He increases the oil of a widow. To another woman he promises a son. When the son eventually dies, he raises him from the dead. He makes noxious food healthy, and he feeds many people with 20 loaves.

Naaman, a commander of the Aramean army, is a leper. He learns about Elisha from an Israelite slave girl. Naaman travels to him with a large entourage. When he arrives at Elisha's house, however, Elisha does not open the door. He tells him to wash himself seven times in the Jordan River. Naaman is annoyed, but he obeys the words of Elisha and is healed. Naaman wants to pay Elisha, but Elisha does not want to take anything from him. However, when he has already departed, Gehazi, Elisha's servant, hurries after him and asks him for a gift. As a punishment, Gehazi immediately becomes leprous.

Time and again Aramean troops try to attack the Israelites. However, God always tells Elisha their plans in advance, and Elisha informs the king. At first, the Arameans believe there is a spy among them. But then they understand that Elisha is responsible. They attack the city where Elisha lives. But God confuses them so that Elisha can trick them. After they are trapped, Elisha lets them go.

But then the Arameans attack again and besiege the city of Samaria. The people run out of food. A woman tells King Jehoram that she has had to eat her own son. The king is very angry with Elisha, whom he holds responsible for the situation. He wants to kill him. But Elisha promises him that the siege will be ended the next day. The king does not believe him. Four lepers living outside the city gate are in such a desperate state that they decide to walk into the army camp of the Arameans, for good or for bad. When they arrive, they are very surprised that no one is there anymore. God has caused the Arameans to hear the noise of a giant army so they became frightened and fled.

Ben-Hadad, king of Aram, is ill. He sends his son, Hazael, to Elisha. Elisha predicts that he will become king. Home again, Hazael kills his father and makes himself king over Aram.

The prophet Elisha sends one of his disciples to make Jehu king over Israel. He instructs Jehu to destroy the family of Ahab. Jehu conspires against Jehoram, Ahab's son, the reigning king, and executes him. He also kills Ahaziah, the king of Judah, who is with Jehoram at that time. Jezebel, the king's mother, is thrown out of a window of her palace. Her corpse is torn into pieces by wild dogs. After that, Jehu gives orders to kill all male members of Ahab's family. In this way, Jehu fulfills the judgment God had announced to Ahab. Jehu also kills all Baal priests and destroys the idols. However, he does not obey God in everything. He reigns for 28 years. His kingdom is becoming smaller step by step, as the Arameans take over more and more of the land.

Meanwhile, in Judah, Athaliah, the king's mother, seizes the kingdom for herself. She destroys all the royal family of the house of Judah. Only a small son, Joash, is saved. The priest Jehoiada

takes care of him and raises him secretly in one of the temple buildings. After seven years, Jehoiada instigates a putsch with the help of the royal household troops. Athaliah is put to death, and Joash is proclaimed legitimate king.

As long as Joash is counseled by the priest Jehoiada, he does what is right in the eyes of the Lord. He restores the temple. A few years later, however, when the Arameans attack Jerusalem, he takes all the holy vessels and treasures out of the temple and uses them to buy his and the city's freedom. His officials conspire against him and beat him to death. His son succeeds him on the throne.

Elisha becomes mortally ill. The king of Israel, Jehoash, visits him. Elisha predicts that God will have mercy and free the land from the Arameans. Elisha dies and is put into a grave. Another person is being buried that day. When robbers appear, they throw him into Elisha's grave. The moment he touches Elisha's body, he awakes from the dead and stands up. God has mercy over Israel, and Jehoash can fight the Arameans and restore many Israelite cities to his control again.

The Kingdoms of Israel and Judah until the End of Israel (2 Kings 14–17)

In the southern kingdom of Judah, Amaziah becomes king. After he has gained a victory over the Edomites, he believes he is strong enough to attack the northern kingdom of Israel. However, the Israelite army overcomes him. Jerusalem is partly destroyed and plundered.

In Israel, Jehoash is followed by Jeroboam II. In his reign, the northern kingdom blossoms for a last time. The kings who follow him are not very strong anymore. Several of them are executed as a result of conspiracies. They all fail to act according to the will of God.

The Assyrians gain power and oppress the land. High taxes have to be imposed on the people in order to pay the tributes the Assyrians request. This increases the political instability.

Hoshea, Israel's last king, wants to make an alliance with Egypt in order to fight against the Assyrians. However, King Shalmaneser learns of it and puts Hoshea into prison. He conquers many Israelite cities and finally also Samaria, the capital, which falls after three years of siege. Large parts of the population are deported into other regions of the Assyrian Empire.

The reason for the fall of Israel is the disobedience of the people and the king to God. They have not been faithful to the covenant but have turned to other gods and worshiped them. God has sent many prophets in order to warn them, but they have not listened to them.

Eventually, the king of Assyria deports many people from other peoples and tribes into the area of Israel. Therefore, a mixed population and a mixed religion emerge. Some priests are sent into the region to promulgate faith in God. At the same time, however, many idols are worshiped.

The Kingdom of Judah until Its End
(2 Kings 18–25)

In Judah, King Hezekiah gains power. He reigns according to the will of God, being faithful to the covenant. Hezekiah stops paying tribute to the Assyrians. Therefore, King Sennacherib of Assyria arrives with a great army against Jerusalem. A messenger of the Assyrians asks Hezekiah to go to the city wall. In Hebrew, so that the whole people can understand, he ridicules God and tries to demoralize the Judaic soldiers with many words. Hezekiah goes into the temple and despairingly asks God for help. The prophet Isaiah appears and tells him that the Assyrians will not be able to conquer the city. During the night, the angel of the Lord goes into the Assyrian army camp and kills 185,000 soldiers. The next morning, the whole camp is full of corpses. Sennacherib has to return home. Some time later, he is killed by his sons.

Hezekiah becomes mortally ill. Isaiah tells him that he will die. Hezekiah prays to God. God sends Isaiah a second time to him, telling him that he will live for 15 more years. Hezekiah asks for confirmation of that message by a sign. God lets the shadow of the sundial go backward 10 degrees.

The king of BABYLON sends an embassy to Jerusalem. Proudly, Hezekiah shows them all his royal treasure. After the Babylonians have departed, Isaiah appears before Hezekiah, predicting to him that all the treasures he showed to them would eventually be taken to Babylon.

Hezekiah is followed by Manasseh and Amon. Both are disobedient to God and promulgate all kinds of idolatry and superstition. In addition, Manasseh sheds much innocent blood. God therefore announces a coming judgment over Judah.

The next king, Josiah, is a king according to the will of God. He lets the temple be renovated. During the renovation, the book of the Law of Moses is found. It is read to the king. Josiah realizes that the wrath of God must be great, since his predecessors and the people have not obeyed what is written there. Huldah, a prophetess, informs him that the curses predicted in the book of the Law will come true. However, since Josiah was so faithful to God, the judgment will be postponed until after his death.

After that, Josiah renews the covenant. He lets the Law be read before the whole people. The people agree to be faithful to the covenant again. Josiah also removes all the priests of foreign gods, destroys the idols, and demolishes the holy places all over the land. The Passover is celebrated according to the Law.

Eventually, Pharaoh Neco crosses the country in order to fight against the Assyrians. Josiah wants to stop him but is killed. Neco imposes taxes on the land.

Shortly afterward, the Babylonians gain power, under their king, Nebuchadnezzar. Judah pays tribute to him, but after a while they decide to stop. Nebuchadnezzar conquers Jerusalem and imprisons King Jehoiachin. The royal family, the leading families, and all craftsmen are deported to Babylon. The Babylonians make Zedekiah king in Jerusalem.

After nine years, Zedekiah revolts against the Babylonians. Again the Babylonian army approaches and besieges Jerusalem. When the hunger becomes severe, the Israelite soldiers make a sally but they fail. The Babylonians blind the king and take him to Babylon, and they kill the king's sons. They destroy the temple as well as the palace and all other important buildings of Jerusalem, and they tear down the city walls. Large parts of the population are deported to Babylon, and the temple vessels and treasures are taken there too. As a symbolic act, 12 priests and officials as well as 60 of the people are herded together and killed.

Nebuchadnezzar appoints a certain Gedaliah as governor over Jerusalem. After a short time, however, Gedaliah is assassinated by some nationalists. Fearing the Babylonians' revenge, many of the remaining Jews flee to Egypt.

Thirty-seven years later, the king of Babel grants pardon to Jehoiachin, the former king of Jerusalem. Jehoiachin is allowed to eat at the king's table, and an annuity for life is granted to him.

COMMENTARY

The chart on page 229 presents an overview of the kings of all of Israel and Judah, together with their dates of office and the related Bible passages, adapted from Edwin Thiele, *The Mysterious Numbers of the Hebrew Kings,* 2d ed., Grand Rapids, Mich.: Zondervan, 1983.

The book of Kings gives the number of years for each of the kings. In addition, the periods of office of the northern and the southern kings are synchronized with each other, for example, "In the twenty-sixth year of Asa king of Judah, Elah son of Baasha began to reign over Israel in Tirzah; he reigned for two years" (1 Kings 16:8). From this information, a relative chronology of all kings can be established. However, the numbers often seem not to work out. The reason is that the chronological systems of the two kingdoms are somewhat different. In the so-called accession-year system, the calendar year in which the king rose to power is called the accession year, and the following calendar year is reckoned as the "first year" of the king. This system was used in Judah. However, when Judah started making alliances with Israel, it took over Israel's system, in which the year of the king's accession was already reckoned as the "first year." So in this system, all numbers are increased by one. If these features, and some others, such as coregencies, are taken into account, all the numbers fit together. These difficulties show that the numbers were not made up by the author or final redactor of the book (who would have produced a unified system) but stem from the sources, the royal annals, some of which were already centuries old at his time.

In order to move on from the relative chronology to an absolute chronology, some "synchronisms," in this case, Assyrian campaigns against Israel, can be used. The Assyrian chronology is very exact and can be anchored with the help of astronomical events like eclipses of the sun. Synchronisms with Assyria can therefore be used in order to establish absolute dates for the Israelite monarchy, as given in the table (see Edwin Thiele, *The Mysterious Numbers of the Hebrew Kings,* 1983).

The historical information given about the kings and their terms of reign in the book of Kings is seen as authentic by most scholars. There also exist a good amount of extrabiblical sources from this time that confirm the names and campaigns of some of the kings. These portrayals from the view of Israel's opponents enrich our knowledge of the political circumstances of the time.

The United Kingdom of Judah/Israel under Solomon (1 Kings 1–11)

The book begins stating, "King David was old and advanced in years." This statement not only is a historical bridge back to the events told in the books of Samuel but sets the scene for what the book of Kings is all about: The time of David, God's anointed king, is over. God has promised an everlasting dynasty to him (2 Samuel 7). How will the kings of the dynasty behave? Will they prove worthy of their vocation?

The answer the book gives to this question is generally no. It depicts an ongoing decay of the kingdom until its extinction. In the reign of Solomon, the first king after David, the first hints to this decline already appear.

The first two chapters of the book deal extensively with the handing over of the kingdom from David to Solomon. The narrative illustrates the difficult problem of making the right son, who is also the bearer of the divine promise, the king's successor. Solomon asks God for wisdom. God grants it to him and gives him what he had not asked for: riches and honor. With Solomon, the Israelite kingdom reaches its zenith in terms of power, material wealth, and peace.

The main part of the Solomon narrative deals with the building of the Jerusalem temple. God had already promised David that Solomon would build the temple (2 Samuel 7). The building is described in detail, because it has extraordinary meaning from

KINGS OF UNITED ISRAEL

Saul	1050–1010	1 Samuel 8–31; 1 Chronicles 10
David	1010–971	1 Samuel 16:1–1 Kings 2:12; 1 Chronicles 11–29
Solomon	971–931	1 Kings 1–11; 2 Chronicles 1–9

KINGS OF ISRAEL (NORTHERN KINGDOM)

Jeroboam I	931–909	1 Kings 12:25–14:20
Nadab	909–908	1 Kings 15:25–31
Baasha	908–886	1 Kings 15:32–16:7
Elah	886–885	1 Kings 16:8–14
Zimri	885	1 Kings 16:15–20
Tibni	885–880	1 Kings 16:21–22
Omri	885–874	1 Kings 16:21–28
Ahab	874–853	1 Kings 16:29–22:40
Ahaziah	853–852	1 Kings 22:51–2 Kings 1:18
Joram	852–841	2 Kings 3:1–8:15
Jehu	841–814	2 Kings 9:1–10:36
Jehoahaz	814–798	2 Kings 13:1–9
Jehoash	798–782	2 Kings 13:10–25
Jeroboam II	793–753	2 Kings 14:23–29
Zechariah	753	2 Kings 15:8–12
Shallum	752	2 Kings 15:13–15
Menahem	752–742	2 Kings 15:16–22
Pekahiah	742–740	2 Kings 15:23–26
Pekah	752–732	2 Kings 15:27–31
Hoshea	732–722	2 Kings 17:1–6

KINGS OF JUDAH (SOUTHERN KINGDOM)

Rehoboam	931–913	1 Kings 12:1–24; 14:21–31; 2 Chronicles 10–12
Abijah	913–910	1 Kings 15:1–8; 2 Chronicles 13:1–14:1
Asa	910–869	1 Kings 15:9–24; 2 Chronicles 14:2–16:14
Jehoshaphat	872–848	1 Kings 22:41–50; 2 Chronicles 17:1–21:1
Jehoram	853–841	2 Kings 8:16–24; 2 Chronicles 21:2–20
Ahaziah	841	2 Kings 8:25–29; 2 Chronicles 22:1–9
Queen Athaliah	841–835	2 Kings 11; 2 Chronicles 22:10–23:21
Joash	835–796	2 Kings 12; 2 Chronicles 24
Amaziah	796–767	2 Kings 14:1–22; 2 Chronicles 25:1–26:2
Uzziah/Azariah	792–740	2 Kings 15:1–7; 2 Chronicles 26:3–23
Jotham	750–732	2 Kings 15:32–38; 2 Chronicles 27
Ahaz	732–715	2 Kings 16; 2 Chronicles 28
Hezekiah	715–686	2 Kings 18:1–20:21; 2 Chronicles 29–32
Manasseh	696–642	2 Kings 21:1–18; 2 Chronicles 33:1–20
Amon	642–640	2 Kings 21:19–26; 2 Chronicles 33:21–25
Josiah	640–609	2 Kings 22:1–23:30; 2 Chronicles 34:1–36:1
Jehoahaz	609	2 Kings 23:31–34; 2 Chronicles 36:2–4
Jehoiakim	609–598	2 Kings 23:34–24:7; 2 Chronicles 36:5–8
Jehoiachin	598–597	2 Kings 24:8–17; 25:27–30; 2 Chronicles 36:9–10
Zedekiah	597–586	2 Kings 24:18–25:26; 2 Chronicles 36:11–20

a religious point of view. The beginning of the construction of the temple is dated to the 480th year after the EXODUS from Egypt. The number 480 can be interpreted as 40 times 12, and some scholars therefore treat it as a symbolic number only, meaning something like "the fullness of time" (see NUMBERS, SIGNIFICANCE OF). From its context, however, a literal meaning is much more probable. Possibly, the number was rounded to give it a symbolic meaning along with the historical. The interpretation of this number is important because it affects the dating of the earlier events in the history of Israel. In any case, the connection made between the Exodus and the construction of the temple has a theological significance: God's plan of salvation, begun with the Exodus, reaches fulfillment and conclusion with the erection of the temple, the place where God will live among his people (Leviticus 26:11). All promises of God are now fulfilled.

The layout of the temple resembles Phoenician architecture. This is probably a consequence of the fact that Solomon appointed Phoenician craftsmen. The one great difference between the Jerusalem temple and all other ancient temples consists in the fact that in the Jerusalem temple there was no divine image.

For Solomon's temple dedication prayer, see the Commentary to the parallel report in 2 Chronicles 6.

The end of the Solomon narrative introduces the theme of decay: Solomon is seduced into worshipping other gods. In those times, this was a part of international diplomacy. On the other hand, however, it was irreconcilable with the Israelite belief that Yahweh alone was to be worshipped. As a result of the disobedience to God the first enemies of Israel arise. In the following centuries, political enemies will increasingly threaten the kingdom.

As a literary technique, the kingdom is first presented positively, and only at the end is there a sudden turn into the negative. This technique is applied several times in the book. The message here is that you should never rely on human beings or human institutions: They will disappoint you in the end. For example, Jehu fulfills all divine instructions and extinguishes the Baal worship, but in the end he allows the golden calves to be worshipped (2 Kings 10:28ff). Joash from Judah concerns him-

self very much with the renovation of the temple but in the end gives all temple treasures away to the invaders (2 Kings 12). Hezekiah stops all worship of idols, and he becomes a witness to the saving power of God. Yet in the end, in his foolish pride, he shows all the Jerusalem treasures to the Babylonian spies (2 Kings 18–20). Josiah again renews the covenant of the people with God, yet in the end he dies in a completely unnecessary military campaign (23:29). The same is true of the other kings. Even when they are judged to be generally faithful to the Lord, they allow some kind of heathen religion to continue (for example, Jehoshaphat in 1 Kings 22:41–51). In all these cases the reader is first invited to identify with the character and then is disappointed. The reader learns not to trust in human beings, but in God alone.

This theological understanding of the character of humankind also has repercussions in the biblical presentation of history: It allows and obliges the biblical writers to present human actors as they are, with their strengths and weaknesses. This is unique among all history writing known to us from the ancient Near East, which is made for the primary and also obvious purpose of glorifying the prevailing ruler.

The Kingdoms of Israel and Judah until Omri (1 Kings 12:1–16:28)

The breakup of the kingdom into the two kingdoms of north and south has, according to the book of Kings, a political as well as a spiritual reason: From a political point of view, the northern tribes no longer accept the pressure of taxes and compulsory labor put on them by the king of the south. From a political point of view, the breakup is God's punishment for Solomon's apostasy.

This combination of spiritual and political viewpoints runs right through the whole book. For each king, even at the beginning of the section, the narrator gives a judgment: Was the king obedient to God or not? The obedience is mostly measured on how the king dealt with the worship of other gods: Did he tolerate it, did he even promulgate it, or did he fight it?

Jeroboam, the first king of the northern kingdom of Israel, wants to prevent the population from traveling south to the Jerusalem temple. His reason is surely a political one. Therefore, he has two calves made as images for Yahweh and has them placed in Dan and in Bethel. This syncretism is rebuked intensely. In the course of the book, it is time and again called the "sin of Jeroboam," followed by many of the succeeding kings.

In general, all kings of the northern kingdom (with the possible exception of Jehu) receive negative judgments from the narrator, whereas in the southern kingdom at least some of the kings are judged positively. This explains from a spiritual point of view why the southern kingdom existed some 130 years longer than the northern kingdom.

However, the first king of the southern kingdom, Rehoboam, does not behave any better than Jeroboam. Under his reign, the worship of heathen gods blossoms. One immediate act of punishment is the campaign of Pharaoh Shishak (Sheshonk) taking away most of the riches Solomon had gained for the temple and the palace. The era of material wealth in Jerusalem has ended after only one generation. The campaign of this pharaoh is also documented in an inscription at the Amun temple in Karnak. There, a long list of cities that Pharaoh Sheshonk is said to have conquered, many of them in Judah and in Israel, is given.

Rehoboam of Judah is followed by Abijah and Asa. Asa is the first king to receive a positive judgment. The reason is that he fights temple prostitution and destroys many idols.

In its first years, the northern kingdom is politically unstable. It lacks a capital and lacks a recognized sanctuary. King Omri is the one who buys Mount Samaria and founds the city of Samaria as the new capital of Israel. Interestingly, in at least two extrabiblical documents Israel is later called the "house of Omri." This shows the overarching political significance of this king—even if the Bible does not record much about him.

Elijah and Ahab in Israel (1 Kings 16:29–2 Kings 1)

The paramount theme of this section and the two following (until 2 Kings 13) is the conflict between the worship of God and the worship of Baal. The narrative demonstrates that God is truly God and that faith in God leads to life, whereas faith in Baal results in death.

The section opens with the beginning of the kingdom of Ahab, who, more than any of the kings before him, deviates from the way of the Lord. The height of the disobedience is the erection of a Baal temple in Samaria, with which Ahab officially introduces the Canaanite Baal cult into Israel. This decision is influenced by his wife, Jezebel, daughter of a certain Eth-baal ("Baal is there"). Just as David makes Jerusalem the capital of Judah, and his son, Solomon, builds the temple there, so, as a diabolic counterpart, Omri makes Samaria the capital of Israel, and his son, Ahab, erects the temple of Baal there.

King Ahab is also mentioned in an extrabiblical source. In the year 853 B.C.E., the Assyrian king, Shalmaneser III, initiates a campaign against some kings of the western territories and names, among others, King Ahab of Israel.

When Ahab turns to Baal, God appoints Elijah as a prophet to be his voice. What is significant for Elijah, in contrast with the later prophets, is that not only is his task to proclaim the word of God but in him the power of God also becomes manifest. Several signs and wonders happen, such as the multiplying of food or even raising of the dead. Elijah personifies the fight for God and against Baal. From Elijah are derived life and death: Life for those who are obedient to God and death for the worshippers of Baal. Since Baal is a god of fertility and rain, it is of special significance that Elijah's first task is to announce a drought, demonstrating that God, not Baal, controls the rain. A climax is reached in the contest on Mount Carmel, where Baal remains silent but God demonstrates that he is the living God.

The description of Elijah's total breakdown afterward is distinctive. Elijah then has to go to Mount Sinai (= Horeb), where God had appeared to Moses. God appears to Elijah as well. The forces of nature, storm, earthquake, and fire, are only to prepare for the revelation of God. God himself appears in a "sound of a gentle blowing" (1 Kings 19:12)—God is different from what people might expect him to be.

Ahab's and Jezebel's worship of false gods also has consequences in other areas. So, the narrative on Naboth's vineyard shows the unscrupulousness of Ahab and especially of Jezebel. She declares injustice for justice and takes what she wants from anyone, just because she has the power to do so.

Elijah and Elisha (2 Kings 2)

The chapter 2 Kings 2 is the only one in the whole book of Kings that is not built into the literary frame of a king's reign (see introduction above). It describes the transition of the prophetic office from Elijah to Elisha and forms a central hinge of the book's literary structure.

The chapter is formed as a concentric structure (see STRUCTURES, LITERARY). Its center deals with Elijah's being taken up to heaven in a chariot of fire. Since Elijah has exerted himself so much for God, who is life, and against Baal, who causes death, Elijah does not need to die but is directly taken into heaven.

For this reason, among others, Elijah becomes the archetype for a Spirit-filled prophet. The end of Malachi, the last prophet book of the Hebrew Bible, predicts that Elijah will return to prepare the people for the coming of God. From the Christian point of view, this prediction has been fulfilled with JOHN THE BAPTIST, who, although he was not Elijah the person (John 1:21), appears "in the spirit and power of Elijah" (Luke 1:17).

Several connections drawn between Elijah and Moses are also remarkable: Elijah encounters God on Mount Sinai, as Moses did. The earthly life of Elijah ends in a distinctive way, as the life of Moses did. Elijah divides the water, as Moses did. It is therefore not accidental that at the end of Malachi there is a reference to Elijah as well as to Moses. In the New Testament, Moses and Elijah appear on the Mount of Transfiguration (Matthew 17).

These and many other references to Elijah in the New Testament and in Jewish literature show his significance in later interpretation—reflecting, of course, the extraordinary character of the Elijah narrative in the book of Kings itself.

Before Elijah dies, Elisha asks to become the heir of his spirit. The request is granted to him. After Elijah has been taken up, Elisha can divide the Jordan as Elijah had. The two wonders reported at the end of chapter 2 demonstrate the power that Elisha now has over life and death, as Elijah had before (see 2 Kings 1). Both instances display an excess of violence that is barely comprehensible to modern readers. The background to it is that even a small attack on God's holiness, here in the form of lacking respect for God's representative, is a sin that leads to death. In almost every case, however, the punishment is delayed because of God's grace. Overall, the stories point to the fact that Elisha now has the same power that Elijah had.

Why is the subject of prophetic succession emphasized here? It is possible that the prophetic succession is to be seen as a counterpart to the royal succession dealt with in the book. While the opening of the book asks how the kingdom can be maintained over the generations, the center of the book deals with the topic that prophetic authority cannot be inherited but is dependent only on the spirit of God. Another reason may be that Elisha executes some orders that God had given to Elijah. It is, therefore, important to show the continuation between the two.

Elisha and Jehu in Israel (2 Kings 3–13)

The rebellion of the Moabites against Israelite oppression after the death of Ahab (chapter 3) is also documented in an important extrabiblical source, the so-called Mesha-stele, from about 830 B.C.E. In it, King Mesha tells that he was able, with the help of the god Kemosh, to free his people from the power of the "house of Omri." What is more, the inscription contains the oldest extrabiblical evidence for the name *Yahweh*, the Lord, as the (main) God of Israel.

Chapter 4 totally leaves the realm of political history and depicts some wonders of Elisha, as he helps different poor and unhappy individuals with supranatural power. The wonders demonstrate the mercy of God. These stories especially sound unbelievable and implausible to many modern readers. However, wonders are by definition not accessible from a rational point of view. Therefore, they cannot easily be judged by such criteria. Faith presuppositions determine whether one accepts these stories as historical or not.

The healing narrative of Naaman in chapter 5 has an even deeper level of meaning. It demonstrates that non-Israelites can take part in God's grace. The expectation of spectacular supranatural experiences is not satisfied. Instead the story shows that simply obeying God leads to healing. Even more, for Naaman it is not about healing alone but about salvation: He not only has been healed by God but has also turned to God with all his heart.

Elijah has been instructed to make Hazael king over Aram and Jehu king over Israel. When the instruction is given, God points out that this will prepare God's judgment (1 Kings 19:15–17). Both orders, however, are not executed by Elijah but by Elisha. Elisha does not need to go to Hazael, but Hazael goes to him, sent by his father, who is ill. Elisha predicts to Hazael that he will be king, and he must weep because he sees in his spirit the sorrow Hazael will bring on Israel. The story also demonstrates that God is the Lord over the other nations as well as over Judah and Israel.

Jehu is anointed in order to make an end of the dynasty of Omri through Ahab and thereby fulfill the judgment announced by God. Jehu therefore stands at the end of a development that has begun with Ahab and that comprises the ministry of Elijah and Elisha, historical as well as literary. Indeed, Jehu proves an avenger of the righteous. He kills Jehoram, son of Ahab and king over Israel, and all male members of his family. Jezebel dies a shameful death. The Baal worship inaugurated by Ahab is stopped, and all Baal priests are killed.

King Jehu reigns for 28 years altogether. The biblical text remains silent regarding most of this time. An Assyrian source from 841 B.C.E. informs us that King Jehu from Israel paid tribute to the Assyrian king, Shalmaneser III.

The Kingdoms of Israel and Judah until the End of Israel (2 Kings 14–17)

This section describes first the ups and downs of both kingdoms. Again there is a fratricide: Amaziah from Judah gains a victory over Edom and therefore feels strong enough to attack Israel. David had also defeated the Edomites. Perhaps Amaziah felt like a second David, hoping to rule over all Israel. The text, however, says that Amaziah was *not* like his

father, David (14:3). Accordingly, the campaign does not succeed, and Judah is defeated by Israel.

The last decades of the northern kingdom of Israel are determined by the Assyrians' gaining power. The name *Assyria* is derived from one of their capitals, Ashur, located in upper Mesopotamia. The Assyrians were a belligerent people. Assyrian kings boasted about their cruelty. Eventually, the Assyrians spread their reign of terror over the whole ancient Near East.

In 745 B.C.E., Tiglath-Pileser rises to power in Ashur. Many small city-states in Palestine, including the kingdom of Israel under King Menahem (2 Kings 15:19f.), become obliged to pay tribute. After a few years, these states make an alliance against the Assyrians. They want the southern kingdom of Judah to join the alliance. King Ahaz of Judah, however, refuses. Therefore, the coalition decides to attack Judah first in order to remove Ahaz and install a king who will join the alliance. King Ahaz is afraid of the coalition, and he calls none other than the Assyrians to help him. The Assyrian army goes to Palestine and destroys many of the city-states. The kingdom of Israel is not destroyed but has to pay large tributes to Assyria. When Tiglath-Pileser dies, Israel wants to expel the Assyrian overlords. However, Tiglath-Pileser's successor, Shalmaneser V, conquers many Israelite cities. Samaria falls after three years of siege, in the year 722 B.C.E. The same year, Sargon II gains to power in Assyria. He makes Israel an Assyrian province, calling it Samerina. He lets many of the inhabitants be deported to different cities in Media and northern Mesopotamia (2 Kings 17:6). Eventually, the Assyrians deport people from Babylon and from Hamat in Syria into the region of Israel (1 Kings 17:24ff.). This is the end of the northern kingdom of Israel, and at the same time the beginning of the Samaritans, who later reappear in the books of Ezra and Nehemiah and again in the New Testament.

From a political perspective, the destruction of Israel happened because of the Assyrians and as a result of some dangerous political decisions of Israel's last kings. From a spiritual point of view, however, according to the book of Kings, the Assyrians were God's instrument, with which he executed his judgment over the disloyal Israel and let the curses of the Mosaic covenant be fulfilled.

The Kingdom of Judah until Its End (2 Kings 18–25)

The Assyrians are endangering the existence of Judah as well. King Hezekiah is one who fully relies on God. He gains military power and decides to refrain from paying tribute to the Assyrians. In order to prepare for an attack, he further fortifies Jerusalem. The text mentions a tunnel conducting the water of a well into the inner part of the city (2 Kings 20:20). In an archaeological excavation, the tunnel has been found, having an inscription confirming the biblical text. The inscription is one of the few extrabiblical texts in classical Hebrew.

The Assyrian army, led by King Sennacherib, approaches and besieges Jerusalem in 701 B.C.E., without success, however. The biblical report presents this as a wonder of God: The angel of the Lord kills 185,000 soldiers in the enemy's camp at night. A possible rational explanation could be the plague. Sennacherib's campaign is also documented in an Assyrian record. There it reads, "I locked Hezekiah up in Jerusalem like a bird in a cage." One has to read between the lines in order to understand that the siege against Jerusalem failed. The story demonstrates that history is not a question of military power alone but rather of one's relationship to God, who controls everything.

The reform of Josiah in 2 Kings 22f. is also important from a theological point of view. There are endless discussions over what exactly was the content of the book found in the temple during the renovations. Many critical scholars assume that the book was Deuteronomy or a predecessor of it. The relationship to Deuteronomy is established by the fact that Josiah's reforms reflect several sections of that book in wording and in content. What is more, however, critical scholarship often assumes that the book found was not, in fact, an ancient book but had been written in the time of Josiah himself. The "finding," therefore, was a trick in order to make it appear old and authoritative. In this case, the text would describe the beginnings of the biblical canon. However, that a religion of a God of truth could be based on a lie, is, of course, a far-reaching presupposition. There are no historical data supporting this position. More conservative scholars trust the biblical witness in that the book was, in fact, an old book, really the "Law of Moses," not necessarily, however, in its final form as we have it today. The narrator praises Josiah for his reforms. However, they do not seem to have had an effect beyond his own reign. The destruction of the kingdom of Judah is, from a historical point of view, the result of Babylonian campaigns in Palestine and Judah's attempts to free themselves from them. From a theological point of view, however, the destruction of the kingdom is interpreted as showing that God terminates all the covenants he has made with Israel. So the covenant with David (2 Samuel 7) contains the promise of an everlasting Davidic dynasty and the erection of the temple as a place where God will be near to his people. But now, the Davidic king is captured, and all his sons are killed. The temple is destroyed, and the temple vessels are taken to Babylon. The covenant with Abraham (Genesis 12) contains the promise to be a large people and to possess a land. Now the land has to be left: The people are deported to Babylon. And the people are destroyed in a symbolic sense: A representative group of 72 persons is killed (compare the 70 members of Jacob's family at the end of Genesis).

Regarding the Sinai covenant, all the curses announced there have come true (see Leviticus 26; Deuteronomy 28–30). The climax of the curses is reached, in that in the end the people are again in Egypt, from which they departed a long time ago (Deuteronomy 28:68). The fulfillment of this last curse is reported in the Gedaliah episode in 2 Kings 25:22–26. The whole salvation history is undone.

However, both passages in the Pentateuch dealing with blessing and curse (Leviticus 26; Deuteronomy 28–30) end with the announcement of a new hope: When the people return to God, God will again have mercy on them (Leviticus 26:40–45; Deuteronomy 30:1–10). This hope is expressed through the concluding section of the book of Kings (2 Kings 25:27–30): There still is a Davidic king, and even in the midst of all the distress, there are the first hints that God's history with his people has not yet ended.

CHARACTERS

Elijah   A prophet of God and King Ahab's opponent. Elijah not only proclaims the word of God but also performs several signs and wonders on God's behalf. Elijah personifies the fight for God and against Baal. In his words and actions he expresses that trusting God means life and trusting Baal means death. Therefore, at the end of his life he does not have to die but ascends to heaven instead. Malachi 4:5 predicts that he will return, preparing the people for the coming of the Lord. In the New Testament, John the Baptist is said to have spoken "with the spirit and power of Elijah" (Luke 1:17).

Solomon   Son of David, king over Israel. At the beginning of his reign, God asks him what he would like to receive from him. Solomon demonstrates his uprightness by not making a selfish request. Instead, he asks God for wisdom in order to be able to rule the people. God is pleased, and he blesses Solomon with exceptional wisdom as well as exceptional wealth. Solomon engages in extensive building projects, the most important of which is the temple in Jerusalem. However, Solomon also has many wives and is enticed into idolatry toward the end of his reign.

Lamentations

Lamentations is unique. It is the only example of a biblical book given over to the LAMENT and consolation subgenre, though there are many other laments throughout the Bible, 2 Samuel 1:19–27; Psalms 38; 79; 88; or Amos 5:2, for example. Because of this, the canons of the various versions of the Bible have not been sure where to place it or what to call it. In the Hebrew Bible it is in the Writings, along with the Wisdom Literature, following on from Song of Songs, a logical place to put it, since it is not a prophetic book. Its name is usually given as *Echah*, which is the first word of the book, simply meaning "how," repeated at the beginning of chapters 2 and 4. But sometimes the Hebrew word for elegy is used, *Qinoth*. However, in the ancient Greek translation of the Hebrew Bible,

the Septuagint (see BIBLE, EARLY TRANSLATIONS OF), it is placed after Jeremiah, on the assumption it was actually by Jeremiah, called *thrēnoi*, meaning "wailings" or "dirges." The Latin version, the Vulgate, follows this; the Latin word is *lamentationes*. All English versions of the Christian Old Testament have followed this.

The genre follows actual cultural practice of lengthy mourning rituals and practice. It is only in certain cultures, including the modern Western one, that outward shows of grieving are discouraged and restraint is urged. We need to enter the mind-set of the day to appreciate this book fully.

The book is a series of five poems over the fall of JERUSALEM around 587 B.C.E. The last lament is written a little later, as the realities of the aftermath are described. In JUDAISM, it is read on the ninth of the month Ab, the day set aside for mourning the destruction of the temple in Jerusalem. Though the book does not say so, many scholars see Jeremiah as the author: He was certainly on the scene; his thinking is very similar; and a great many of his prophecies are picked up in the book (e.g., Jeremiah 4:27–31; 6; 9; 13:18–27; 14:13–16; 16:16–21; 18:13–23; 23:9–40). Although other prophetic writings often have similar images and insights, those from Jeremiah are very pronounced, as practically every verse includes an echo from Jeremiah. Many of the ironies of the book are lost without having read Jeremiah first. And Jeremiah had clearly written laments (2 Chronicles 35:25; cf. Jeremiah 9:10f.; 14:17f.).

From a literary point of view, its acrostic structure (see STRUCTURES, LITERARY) is interesting. An acrostic is where each first letter of a line follows through the alphabet. In the Hebrew alphabet, there are 22 letters, so each chapter has 22 (or $22 \times 3 = 66$) verses, though the order of the letters is very slightly different in chapter 1. The Bible uses acrostics occasionally; the most elaborate example is Psalm 119, where each section has its verses starting with a particular letter of the alphabet. Strong emotions need strong literary structures to be expressed, and this acrostic form does just that. By using every letter of the alphabet, the completeness of the devastation is also symbolized. In chapters 1 and 2 each letter has three lines, though most modern translations break each line into two half-lines, while chapter 4 has two lines to each letter. Chapter 3 has three whole verses to each letter of one line each, though, again, modern translations split this into two half-lines. Chapter 5 is not an acrostic at all, though it still has 22 verses.

SYNOPSIS

Each lament takes a different perspective, leading to a cumulative understanding of the catastrophe. Chapter 1 is from the perspective of Jerusalem. In verses 1–11a, 17, the city is spoken of as "she," but in verses 11b–22, she speaks directly in her own voice. We see the physical desolation of the city and hear some acknowledgment of the city's guilt.

In chapter 2, the viewpoint is more toward God. Verses 1–10 tell what God ("he") has done. In verses 11–19, the writer acts as prophet, speaking as "I" to Jerusalem ("you"), reminding her of her false prophets and of God's bringing about the punishment prophesied. Finally, in verses 20–22 the prophetic voice merges into the voice of Jerusalem herself, pleading with God ("you"), as she does at the end of the first chapter.

In the long central chapter 3, the writer continues to speak of God's enmity in verses 1–20 as "I" speaking about "him." But in a dramatic turn in verse 21, the mercy of God is remembered, and "I" becomes "we" as the writer gives a word of consolation. This leads to a call to confession (verses 40–48) wherein God is addressed directly. After the confession, the call goes out for God to punish Jerusalem's enemies, as the writer's voice again blends with the city's.

Chapter 4 gives a brilliant series of cameos of the destroyed city, with woes against the allies of the invader. Interestingly, the invader is never named, though his allies are. The last chapter gives a sense of a dispossessed second generation (verses 1–18) speaking as "we." The "why?" question is again posed, and a plea for restoration joins earlier pleas. There is a question of theodicy, though in quite different terms from the book of Job. The book ends in a very open way: Nothing is resolved.

The only certainty is that God has acted in the way he said he would.

The book is thus structured carefully. The theological climax is reached halfway through, with a ray of hope bursting through the gloom of the earlier chapters. It is this climax that helps universalize the book. Then the book sinks back into its opening mood of desolation. Chapters 1 and 5 are close in tone, as are chapters 2 and 4. Chapter 3 rises to consolation, only to fall away from it again at the end. Such movements are not untypical of the grieving process.

COMMENTARY

It is not possible in a small space to do justice to the dense poetic texture of the writing. It contains all the major forms of poetry (see POETRY, BIBLICAL), especially parallelism. There are countless examples of straightforward parallelism (AB: A1B1), as in 1:1, 3, 14; 2:4, 6; 4:5. Sometimes the parallels become a list accumulating to a climax, as in 1:4; 2:5; 3:34–36; 5:13–14; or are otherwise expanded, as 2:15–16; 2:18–19. Typically the second part of the coda adds some unfolding, as in 1:2, where the first B coda of "tears on her cheeks" moves to "no one to comfort her," expanded into "all her friends have dealt / treacherously with her," which is again expanded into "they have become her enemies."

The figurative language (see IMAGERY, BIBLICAL) is similar to that of other poetic books, and even more dramatic. At times, the language is very similar to the psalms, especially Psalm 79, which could be seen as a mini-Lamentations, but also to Psalms 38, 44, 80, 88, 89:38–52. Metaphors abound: "Waters closed over my head" (3:54); similes even more so: "Our pursuers were swifter than the eagles in the heavens" (4:19). Most are natural or everyday images: "eagles," "pots of clay" (4:2); "ostriches in the desert" (4:3); "jackals" (4:3); "bears, lions" (3:10). Some things may seem figurative to us but may have been literal, such as "He has made my teeth grind on gravel" (3:16)—the water supply could have broken down quite literally.

What is most striking is the PERSONIFICATION. Jerusalem, as often in the Bible, is personified as a female figure, as in chapter 1. Again, typically of biblical language, the phrase "daughter of" (2:1), or even "virgin daughter of" (2:13), means the same. But much else is personified: "the roads to Zion mourn" (1:4); "the sword bereaves" (1:20). In fact, the latter is strictly metonymic, the sword standing as an instrument of the whole process of killing. And with God, the anthropomorphism is equally typical: "He has besieged and enveloped me with bitterness and tribulation" (3:5), an appropriate figure as literally the writer and the city have been besieged. God is seen as doing this directly, as first cause. The language echoes that of the book of Job at this point: God actively brings disaster on the individual (cf. 2:3–4, 8; 3:10, 43–44).

However, the language of lament is more specific. One of its main features are the little cameos imaging the absolute gut-wrenching destruction, as in chapter 4 or 5, echoing those of Jeremiah 14. Another feature is the constant contrasting of then and now: e.g., 1:1, 5, 17; 4:2, 12; 5:14–16. Another contrast is equally ironic: between the way animals normally behave and the way humans are now behaving in their degraded life: The jackals give milk to their young; the humans cannot (4:3). But worse still, in one of the cameos, mothers are even eating their children (2:20; 4:10), especially ironic because in their previous degraded idolatry, which has caused God's anger, they did actually sacrifice children (Jeremiah 19:5).

As we would expect, the vocabulary of tears features prominently: Even in chapter 1, we have "weeps," "tears," "no-one to comfort," "distress," "mourn," "desolate," "groan," "grieve," "bitter." The main difference between a lament and a woe is that the latter typically employs the language of anger, as in Psalm 35. We do get a glimpse of that in 3:61–66; 4:21–22. Even in the "Woe is me!" there is complaint rather than grieving, as in the book of Job. However, the tears of Lamentations are only ambiguously those of repentance. The prophetic voice certainly embraces repentance, as in 3:49–51, but Jerusalem's own voice is as much complaint as godly sorrow (1:16).

There are certain formulaic utterances, too, in the lament. We have mentioned the opening "How!" of chapters 1; 2; 4. Another is the appeal to passers-by: 1:12 and 2:15 echoing Jeremiah 18:16 and Ezekiel 5:14. But the deeper formula is theological: that this destruction is God's anger at the nation's apostasy, especially seen in the false priests and prophets (4:13). The formula is expressed as God's being the direct enemy, hence the anonymity of the human enemy, the second cause. Ultimately, it does not matter whom God raised up as an instrument of punishment (e.g., 1:5, 9, 14, 18).

But because God is the first cause, then there can be a source of consolation, the final feature of a lament, since God has entered into a covenant relationship and within that will remain faithful, as a redeemer (3:22–23, 58). However, the writer, quite honestly and humanly, cannot quite believe that God's covenant is still intact, given the outward evidence of devastation. He tries to balance the overwhelming feeling that the punishment is greater than the sin, or, at least, greater than they can bear, in chapter 2, with the faith that God's justice is maintained in chapter 3. But it is a difficult balance. His last cry is "unless you have utterly rejected us" (5:22). It is only in hindsight that we can see 3:25 to be truer than this final doubt.

Letter of Jeremiah, The

As with Baruch, the Letter of Jeremiah is part of the Apocrypha, i.e., recognized as deuterocanonical (belonging to the secondary canon by the Catholic and Orthodox Churches; see APOCRYPHA AND PSEUDEPIGRAPHA), and no Hebrew original exists. In the Septuagint, it is placed after Lamentations, while in the Vulgate (see BIBLE, EARLY TRANSLATIONS OF), it is attached to Baruch as chapter 6, as in the Authorized (King James) Version. The style, however, is quite different from that of Baruch, though the time frame is similar, covering the EXILE in BABYLON. The book purports to be by Jeremiah. Jeremiah did indeed send a scroll to the exiles (Jeremiah 51:60–64), but it was about the fate that would befall Babylon, whereas this is to warn against Babylonian idolatry. Certainly,

Jeremiah was strongly opposed to idolatry (Jeremiah 10), but it was the home-grown idolatry of Judah he spoke against. 2 Maccabees 2:1 suggests Jeremiah ranged wider in his letter, but far wider than is mentioned anywhere else.

The book is clearly written by someone with a firsthand knowledge of Babylonian ritual and practice. The details are far too precise for someone writing at a distance, in time or place, to know. And it does suggest someone who has experienced the fear that results from seeing thousands engaged in a ritual that threatens one's very belief system, as we also find in Daniel. While Jeremiah speaks specifically about a 70-year exile (Jeremiah 25:11), confirmed in 2 Chronicles 36:21 and 1 Esdras 1:58, the writer of this book talks of "seven generations" (verse 3), which could be as long as 280 years.

SYNOPSIS

The main thrust of the book is to encourage its readers not to be afraid of the power of idols. In fact, the book can be structured into sections each ending with the repeating phrase "so do not fear them" (verses 16, 23, 29, 65, 69), or "Why must anyone . . . call them gods?" (verses 40, 44, 52, 56). Their worthlessness is expressed in vivid imagery in terms of their powerlessness as mere inert blocks of wood covered by metal and of their moral bankruptcy. They can achieve no good purpose (verses 38–39, 59, 64). At the end, he reminds his readers of the one true God, who created the elements (verses 60–63), and the moral stature of anyone who refuses to bow to idols (verse 73).

COMMENTARY

Although titled a letter (see EPISTLE), the book is more a SERMON, with a few basic points repeated, and a good many examples, expressed as vivid similes (verses 9, 55, 59) or detailed images (verses 13, 18, 21–22, 26–27) that effectively trivialize the whole practice of idol worship. Examples of the priests' dishonesty (verses 10–11, 28–29, 33), the absurdity of their rituals (verses 30–32), and the illogicality of it all (verses 55, 57–58) move to a rhetorical climax as the failure of the idols to command the created universe (verses 60–69). An absurd image of "a scarecrow in a cucumber bed" (verse 70), used also by Jeremiah (Jeremiah 10:5), is an effective bathos, leading to the conclusion that "someone upright who has no idols . . . will be far above reproach" (verse 73).

Leviticus

The title *Leviticus* means "relating to the Levites" and points to the fact that the book mainly consists of ritual regulations concerning the priests, who were from the tribe of Levi. However, the book contains also some narrative passages. From a literary point of view, Exodus, Leviticus, and Numbers form a unified work (for introductory information, see the book of Exodus).

SYNOPSIS

Ritual Regulations for the Tabernacle (Chapters 1–10)

After the tabernacle has been erected (Exodus 35–40), the priestly service has to be installed. First of all, regulations are given on the different kinds of sacrifices: the burnt offering (chapter 1), the cereal offering (chapter 2), the peace offering (chapter 3), the sin offering (4:1–5:13), and the guilt offering (5:14–19). For each of the offerings, the detailed procedure is described. After that are additional details concerning each of the five types (chapters 6–7).

These regulations are first applied during the ceremonial act in which the tabernacle is inaugurated and in which Aaron and his sons are consecrated for the priestly office. Moses himself carries out the inauguration and makes the sacrifices. One week later, Moses announces that God will appear to the people. Aaron and his sons therefore make offerings in order to prepare themselves for the presence of God. Finally, the glory of God appears. A flame arises and consumes the prepared burnt offering (chapters 8–9).

After that, however, two of Aaron's sons, Nadab and Abihu, make a mistake. They prepare incense in a way that neglects the cultic regulations. Fire rises from God's glory and kills them.

The other priests are warned that they bear a lot of responsibility, since they act on behalf of the holy God. Because of the shock after two people have been killed, another violation of priestly law takes place. This time, however, God responds mercifully (chapter 10).

The Purity Code, the Day of Atonement, and the Holiness Code (Chapters 11–24)

Leviticus 11–15 deals with several regulations concerning the distinction between clean and unclean. First of all, clean and unclean animals are distinguished—only the clean animals are to be eaten. After that follows prescriptions for purification after childbirth (chapters 11–12).

A lengthy section deals with the subject of "leprosy": Under this heading fall different kinds of skin rash and abscesses as well as mold on clothes and on walls. The cases have to be examined by a priest, respectively, and corresponding measures have to be taken. After that the text deals with various kinds of bodily emissions that cause uncleanness (chapters 13–15).

Leviticus 16 contains prescriptions for the Day of Atonement. Once a year, the people have to give two male goats to the high priest. One of them is sacrificed as a sin offering. On the head of the other, the high priest has to lay both his hands, confessing all the sins of the people, thus putting them (symbolically) on the head of the goat. After that, the scapegoat is sent out into the wilderness. Only during this ceremony the high priest is allowed to enter the most holy place of the tabernacle once a year.

Leviticus 17–24 deals with regulations and laws concerning the distinction between clean and unclean and between holy and unholy. First of all, the text gives instructions for the handling of animal blood (chapter 17). After that are laws about sexual lapses (chapter 18). A collection of laws on different topics describes what it means to live a holy everyday life (chapter 19). Then some capital offenses are listed (chapter 20). The following chapters address themselves especially to the priests. They describe regulations concerning the holiness of the priests (chapter 21); the holy handling of sacrifices (chapter 22); the holy times, i.e., the Sabbath and the yearly feasts (chapter 23); as well as the holy objects in the tabernacle (24:1–9).

The section closes with a short narrative on a blasphemer who is punished by death (24:10–23).

Laws about the Land: Blessings and Curses (Chapters 25–27)

Leviticus 25 deals with the HOLY LAND, which the people are going to enter. Every seventh year is to be a sabbatical year, in which the fields have to lie fallow. Every seventh sabbatical year is to be a jubilee. In this year, all lands are returned to their original owners, and all people who have sold themselves as slaves become free again.

In Leviticus 26, God announces blessings and curses to the Israelites. If the people are obedient to God, God will bless them with a rich harvest, with peace, and with his presence among them. If, however, the people are disobedient, God will curse them with diseases, enemies, poor harvest, and more, and finally take them out of their land again. But even after the hardest curses, God will turn back to his people and make a new beginning with them.

Leviticus 27 determines the amount of money that has to be paid for redeeming people, property, and land. The chapter forms a counterpart to chapter 25.

COMMENTARY

Ritual Regulations for the Tabernacle (Chapters 1–10)

In Exodus 25–31, God commissions Moses on Mount Sinai to erect the tabernacle, to consecrate priests, and to inaugurate a regular priestly service. The first part of the order, the erection of the tent of meeting, is reported in Exodus 35–40. However, the tabernacle cannot be entered yet, because of the lack of priests. Only after the consecration of the priests in Leviticus 8–9 is the tabernacle ready for becoming a place of meeting between humanity and God (Leviticus 9:24).

Within the context of the consecration, several sacrifices are made. In order for readers to understand, the corresponding regulations about the sacrifices are placed before the narrative in Leviticus 1–7. Again (as in the book of Exodus), the juxtaposition of legal and narrative material is deliberate.

The significance of the sacrifices lies on several levels: First, they show that sin is a severe problem, if one wants to face the holy God, and one's sin has to be paid for. At least some of the sacrifices mean a financial burden for those making them, in the sense of paying a penalty. What is more, blood has to be shed in order to pay for sins. There the principle of representation is employed: Animal blood is shed on behalf of human sin.

The sudden deaths of Nadab and Abihu may seem harsh and unjustified. In order to understand the situation, however, one has to acquaint oneself with the world of the text. First of all, the ritual procedure is not seen just as a ceremony but as an effective way of making contact with the holy God according to the rules God himself has given. A careless handling of the ritual means a disregard of God's holiness, and, therefore, a sacrilege. Second, Nadab's and Abihu's disobedience is striking: They take something unholy into the realm of the holy, and what is more, they do something that only the high priest is allowed to do once a year on the Day of Atonement. Probably, Nadab and Abihu were driven by pride and arrogance rather than by devout enthusiasm. And, third, they did so at a crucial moment in history, at the very inauguration of the Israelite priesthood.

The problem of the refused sacrifice is typologically prepared in the story of Cain and Abel in Genesis 4, where God accepts Abel's sacrifice but rejects Cain's. A New Testament counterpart to Nadab and Abihu are Ananias and Sapphira, who likewise behave inappropriately at a crucial moment in church history and are punished by death (Acts 5).

Literarily, the narrative on Nadab and Abihu underscores the importance of the priestly regulations in Leviticus 1–7 and the distinction between holy and unholy that is further explained in the following chapters.

The Purity Code, the Day of Atonement, and the Holiness Code (Chapters 11–24)

The people of Israel are called to be a "kingdom of priests" and a "holy people" (Exodus 19:6). The purpose of the laws given in Leviticus 11–15 and 17–24 is to make this ideal become practical in terms of everyday living.

Why some species should be considered clean and others unclean (chapter 11) has been the subject of much dispute. Probably it is due to a mixture of different factors. First of all, certain dietary rules can constitute a mark of distinctiveness of a religious group. Therefore, the call to be a holy, separated people is matched by particular dietary rules. Second, hygienic considerations can be brought forward. Some of the species declared unclean are known as possible transmitters of infection, even by eating their flesh, e.g., pigs. Third, a notion of wholeness and integrity may be the reason. Only the species that correspond to a typical, normative pattern are considered clean. And, fourth, at least some of the regulations seem to be given in order to prevent resemblance with pagan sacrificial rites (e.g., Exodus 23:19).

For the topic of leprosy (chapters 13–14), a combination of ritual and hygienic aspects can be seen. Therefore, in some cases of rash, a sacrifice has to be made; in other cases, practical measures are taken, e.g., breaking stones out of the wall that have dangerous mold on them.

Animal blood (chapter 17) is of particular significance. It is seen as the carrier of the God-given life (see Genesis 9:4–6), and it also assumes a specific role in ritual contexts (see Leviticus 1–7, 16). Therefore, it is neither to be eaten nor to be poured out arbitrarily. Even today in Judaism animals are only allowed to be eaten if they have been slaughtered by letting the blood flow out from the body.

The short narrative on the blasphemer at the end of the section (chapter 24) shows the application of the laws given before and demonstrates the taking effect of the death penalty. Furthermore, it points to the fact that there should be no distinction made in applying the laws between an Israelite and a foreigner living among the people.

The section on the Day of Atonement (chapter 16) is placed in the middle between all the laws on purity and holiness. It therefore becomes a key of how to understand the laws. The Day of Atonement is given by God because of the fact that his standard of a holy living can never fully be met by human beings and that therefore a kind of purification is needed that does not originate inside, but outside, human beings. This act of cleansing, or forgiving of sin, is done by God himself, symbolized by the scapegoat's carrying away the sins of the people.

The New Testament takes up this concept and applies it to the mission of Jesus Christ (e.g., John 1:29; 2 Corinthians 5:21).

Laws about the Land: Blessings and Curses (Chapters 25–27)

The section Leviticus 25–27 is said to consist of regulations that are given to Moses on Mount Sinai (see 25:1; 26:46; 27:34). This is peculiar because at this point of the story Moses is no longer on the mountain: He had left the mountain in Exodus 34:29; accordingly, the laws of Leviticus 1–7 are given in the tabernacle, not at the mountain (see 1:1), and there is no hint in the narrative that Moses went up the mountain another time. The best explanation is that the narrator wants to point to the fact that the laws of chapters 25–27 originally belong to the Sinai revelation but were displaced for some literary reason, probably to prevent a break in the tabernacle cycle of Exodus 25 to Leviticus 10. After chapter 27, the insertion ends, and in Numbers 1:1 God speaks to Moses in the tabernacle again.

Leviticus 25 may at first glance give the impression of continuing the topic of Israelite feasts that began in chapter 23. A closer look, however, reveals that the chapter deals particularly with regulations concerning the PROMISED LAND. Given the background that the old Israelite culture was mainly agricultural, the allotment of the land obviously played a crucial role. The fact that all land had to be given back to the original owners after 50 years is a unique social component of the old Israelite law, which inhibited land speculation and ensured that every family could make a living.

The announcement of blessings and curses in Leviticus 26 is an element common to ancient Near East vassal treaties. The announcement consists of three parts: blessings, curses, hope for a new beginning. This pattern is also presented in Deuteronomy 28–30. It is the key for understanding the theological presentation of Israel's history in the books of Joshua, Judges, Samuel, and Kings. The pattern is already prefigured in the primeval history (see on the book of Genesis).

CHARACTERS

Aaron   Brother of Moses, from the tribe of Levi, consecrated to be the first high priest in Israel. Aaron has four sons, Nadab, Abihu, Eleazar, and Ithamar, who all are made priests together with their father.

Moses   In the book of Leviticus, the main task of Moses is to receive laws and regulations from God and pass them on to the priests and the people. Furthermore, Moses consecrates the first priests. He himself makes the first sacrifices in the newly made tabernacle.

Nadab and Abihu   Two sons of Aaron, who are ordained priests. They prepare incense for a sacrifice. However, in doing so they arrogantly disobey several ritual laws, thus acting sacrilegious. God kills them immediately.

Luke

Authorship

The four Gospels (see GOSPEL, GENRE) have similar titles, beginning "The Gospel according to . . ." This shows that the titles do not stem from the authors but were added at a later stage, when the early churches gathered the Gospels into one collection of Christian books. At that time the tradition was that Luke had been the author of the present book. In fact, this gospel is the first volume of a two-volume work; the second volume is Acts of the Apostles. The gospel and Acts have many features in common, such as ideas, linguistic character, and the person they are dedicated to, and they clearly stem from the same author.

The author introduces himself in the first-person singular in Luke 1:1–4 and Acts 1:1, as well as in the first-person plural in the so-called we-passages in Acts (see there), without ever mentioning his name. In the "we-passages" he presents himself as a traveling companion of Paul. The tradition of the church identifies him as Luke who is mentioned in Colossians 4:14; 2 Timothy 4:11, and Philemon 24. The verse in Colossians refers to Luke as a medical doctor, but attempts to find his profession reflected in his literary style or vocabulary are unconvincing. In the preface to the gospel the author does not claim to have been an eyewitness to the gospel story, but he shows he is a second-generation Christian; this would match his identification as Luke. If this identification is correct, the author was probably a Gentile, but in both his books he nonetheless displays a great knowledge of and love for the Hebrew Bible.

Scholars who date the publication of the gospel and Acts late in the first century have for that reason doubted Luke's authorship. Their alternative is to think of this gospel as an anonymous text.

Date and Readership

None of the four Gospels was written immediately after the lifetime of Jesus. Initially the people who followed his teaching had plenty of oral traditions available. The writing of the traditions only began when the Christian movement matured. The suggested date for Luke's gospel is closely tied to that of Acts, which narrates events up to the year 62 C.E., and to the publication of Mark, one of Luke's sources, which itself is of an unknown date. If we take the ascription to Paul's companion Luke seriously, the date can hardly be after 80 C.E., and there is nothing in Luke's gospel or Acts that forces us to go beyond that year. A date in the sixties of the first century C.E. is, in fact, even more likely.

Luke dedicates both books to a certain Theophilus (1:1–4), about whom we know next to nothing. Beyond him, Luke may be addressing a specific community of readers, but nothing is known for certain. A non-Jewish readership is most likely, but one that also had access to the Hebrew Bible. Traces of the use of the gospel only appear from the moment at which it had become part of the collection of four Gospels, about 150 C.E.

Literary Character

Luke has an excellent command of the Greek language, and he knows how to write a good narrative. Of the four evangelists, he has the richest vocabulary. More on his literary style can be found in the commentary on the first three sections that follow. As a narrator he is external to the story he tells. (Note that this is different in Acts.) At certain moments, however, notably in chapter 1, the perspective is that of the characters in the story.

All four Gospels belong to the genre of ancient biographies (see Matthew). Luke's gospel is the longest of the four and the only one with a sequel, Acts. Luke is one of the three so-called SYNOPTIC GOSPELS, which present a similar picture of Jesus. In comparison to the other two, Luke stands out as a well-ordered piece of literature with the long travel story (see Section V below) as its prominent characteristic. Luke pays much attention to events before the beginning of Jesus' public ministry, with "birth stories" that occupy the first two long chapters. As do the other gospels, he offers much direct speech, the style of which does not differ much from its context. This is probably the result of the fact that all spoken word was translated into Greek from the Aramaic (see BIBLE, LANGUAGES OF).

Themes

Among the themes that Luke has in common with the other Synoptic Gospels are the identity of Jesus Christ and the KINGDOM OF GOD (KINGDOM OF HEAVEN.) Of the Synoptic Gospels, Luke has most interest in the diverse humans whom Jesus meets. He pays particular attention to the role of women at all stages of Jesus' life. In comparison, Jesus' opponents receive less attention.

Luke has preserved several PARABLES of Jesus that are absent from the other gospels and are among the best known of all, such as the parables of the good Samaritan, the two sons, the lost sheep, and the rich man and Lazarus.

The message Jesus came to proclaim according to Luke could be summarized as a message of salvation (Greek *sōtēria*; see JESUS CHRIST) and of the arrival of the kingdom of God.

Sources

It is likely that much of the gospel material was transmitted orally for some time before being committed to writing; see at Matthew. Luke was in Israel with Paul in the late fifties of the first century C.E. (Acts 21:17–18; 27:1–2), and at that time he may well have spoken to eyewitnesses to the life of Jesus who were still alive. Information he acquired in this way may have fed into, e.g., the contents of chapters 1 and 2.

In addition to oral information, Luke, as did Matthew, made use of the gospel according to Mark. This verdict is based on the fact that the basic outlines of both books are very similar and that much of Mark can also be found in Luke, with the curious and enigmatic exception of Mark 6:45–8:26. Moreover, Matthew and Luke never agree on anything against Mark: Whenever the three disagree on anything, Mark's version is always supported by either Matthew or Luke. Also, had Mark been written last, the omission of much of Jesus' teaching in Mark would be inexplicable.

Some 35 percent of the material in the much longer Luke stems from Mark. Luke largely left Mark's order of episodes intact, but he made improvements to its vocabulary, word order, and other characteristics: Mark's long stories were abbreviated, its style was enhanced, and much teaching was added. Markan material for the most part occurs in blocks in Luke 3–6; 8–9; and 18–24.

Luke also has numerous words of Jesus in common with the Gospel of Matthew that do not occur in Mark. The best explanation for this remarkable and often verbal similarity is that both evangelists drew on a common source, usually called Q (see Matthew).

The work of the Jewish historian Josephus, who wrote at the end of the first century, resembles that of Luke, but literary dependence either way has not been found.

Luke and the Hebrew Bible

Luke does not often refer to the fulfillment of prophecies from the Hebrew Bible, so his use of the Scriptures is less conspicuous than that of Matthew. However, the Greek translation of the Hebrew Bible, the Septuagint, did exert influence on this gospel in several respects. Quotations are frequent, e.g., in 3:4–6 (Isaiah 40:3–5); 4:18–19 (Isaiah 61:1–2); 7:27 (Malachi 3:1); 22:37 (Isaiah 53:12); and 23:46 (Psalm 31:5). Explicit references to the Scriptures occur in particular in the first and the last chapter, as well as in Jesus' inaugural speech in Nazareth (4:16–22, see Commentary).

Less obvious but equally important are the echoes of Scripture, in particular in chapters 1–2, and the fact that stories and characters of the Hebrew Bible serve as models for Luke. For example, the temptation of Jesus (Luke 4:1–13) mirrors Israel's experiences in the desert (Exodus, Numbers), and Jesus' Sermon on the Plain (6:17–49) is probably inspired by Joshua 8:30–35. Even structurally the Scriptures shine through as Jesus' journey to Jerusalem (Luke 9–19) mirrors Israel's journey through the desert as recorded in Deuteronomy. The totality of the evidence shows that Luke saw the story of Jesus prefigured in the story of Israel. When his style (see below) is also taken into account, it appears that Luke was conscious of writing another volume of Scripture.

SYNOPSIS

Section I: The Prologue (1:1–4)

In the prologue, Luke announces his purpose and his approach for writing the present text. See Commentary below.

Section II: Birth Stories (1:5–2:52)

Luke begins the story proper by narrating the births of JOHN THE BAPTIST and of Jesus himself. Both births have something miraculous about them, and even before they happen they already give rise to songs of praise to God. John is the son of the elderly priestly couple Zechariah and Elizabeth (1:5–25). The reader learns that Jesus was not born in the hometown of his parents as they had to travel to Bethlehem by order of the Roman emperor (2:1–7). Angels announce Jesus' birth to shepherds, who are the first to worship the newborn child (2:8–20). Luke completes the birth stories by reporting on two visits of Jesus to the temple in Jerusalem, one as a newborn child (2:21–40) and one as a precocious 12-year-old (2:41–51). On the first occasion Jesus is greeted by two people who had expected his birth, Simeon and Anna; Simeon, too, sings the praises of God.

Section III: Preparations (3:1–4:13)

We are given the exact year in which John the Baptist began his ministry among the Jewish people, followed by a lengthy narrative about his activity of preaching and baptizing (3:3–20). As many are baptized, Jesus, too, goes forward; immediately after the event God declares from heaven that Jesus is his Son. This leads to a note on Jesus' age at the

Jesus is born (Luke 2:1–19), engraving by Julius Schnorr von Carolsfeld

time and the insertion of a genealogy (3:23–38). As in the other Synoptics, Jesus is then tempted in the desert by SATAN.

Section IV: Jesus in Galilee (4:14–9:50)

A brief note about Jesus' work in general is followed by the report of his programmatic speech in the synagogue of his hometown of Nazareth (4:16–21) and the lack of faith of the audience, which nearly leads to an untimely death for Jesus (4:22–30). After this striking beginning there follows the same mixture of stories, miracle stories, and teaching as in the other gospels: Jesus heals the sick (4:31–44; 5:12–26) and calls some followers (5:1–11, 27–32). His adversaries, the Pharisees, challenge his behavior with regard to fasting and to the SABBATH (5:33–6:11). Luke tells how Jesus prayerfully selects 12 close followers (6:12–16; see TWELVE DISCIPLES).

The extended block of teaching in 6:17–49 has been given the label Sermon on the Plain because it has clear resemblances with the longer Sermon on the Mount in Matthew 5–7. Afterward, meetings with individuals enable Jesus to perform miracles (7:1–17). A long section is devoted to Jesus' relationship to John the Baptist. A story in which a Pharisee and a woman play the leading roles focuses on the importance of forgiveness (7:36–50).

Chapter 8 presents the first great PARABLE, that of the sower, and its interpretation, as well as the first nature miracle, the stilling of a storm on the SEA OF GALILEE. Across the sea Jesus heals a demon-possessed man, and back home he heals a sick woman while he is on his way to raising a young girl from the dead. Jesus sends his twelve disciples out to do the same work as he does (9:1–6) so that his ministry attracts the attention of King HEROD. On the return of the disciples, Jesus feeds a group of 5,000 men (9:10–17).

The section culminates in the confession of Peter that Jesus is the Messiah (9:18–21). It is followed by the anticlimax of the first announcement of Jesus' early death and then by another climax, a revelation of his glory to the three core disciples, which affirms Peter's confession (9:28–36). Two more negative stories conclude the section, one on lack of faith and one on infighting among the disciples.

Section V: The Journey to Jerusalem (9:51–19:28)
No sooner has Jesus started his journey than he is confronted by people who struggle to be as radical as he in following their calling (9:57–62). He sends out 72 followers for a ministry similar to his own, which they accomplish with good results (10:1–24). He tells one of his most famous parables, which has become known as "the good Samaritan" (10:25–37); stays in the house of his friends Mary and Martha; and teaches his disciples about prayer and God's willingness to give (11:1–13). The rest of chapter 11 is taken up by teaching on diverse subjects that involve elements of controversy, such as demons. Jesus has strong words for the Pharisees in 11:37–53.

The teachings in chapter 12 largely revolve around the idea of discipleship and the demands it puts on Jesus' followers. Parables that occur here are those of the rich fool (verses 16–21) and a couple of parables without titles on readiness and stewardship (verses 35–40, 42–46). Jesus tells the disciples that their lives will not be easy (verses 49–53). In chapter 13 Jesus criticizes the Jewish nation for being unrepentant, telling the parable about the fig tree (verses 6–9). A healing on the Sabbath causes indignant responses (verses 10–17). Two brief parables follow, about the mustard seed and the yeast in the dough, and, subsequently, Jesus uses the image

of the narrow door to describe entrance into the kingdom of God. A death threat from King Herod causes Jesus to reflect on his approaching fate, that of dying as prophet in Jerusalem (13:31–35).

Verses 14:1–24 constitute one long scene set on a sabbath. The next scene sees Jesus on the road again, talking about the costs of discipleship (14:25–35). Chapter 15 contains three parables on the theme of how God in his love seeks to save humankind at all costs, the parables of the lost sheep, the lost coin, and the lost son.

Chapter 16 largely focuses on the theme of money and possessions. It opens with a difficult parable on a shrewd manager who uses money to make friends (verses 1–9) and concludes with the parable about the rich man and the poor Lazarus (verses 19–31). Mixed teaching follows (17:1–10) before we hear how of 10 people healed by Jesus only one, and a Samaritan at that, shows thankfulness (17:11–19). In the second half of chapter 17, Jesus discusses the definitive coming of God's kingdom. Chapter 18 opens with the parables of the persistent widow (verses 1–8) and of the Pharisee and the tax collector (verses 9–14), both of which are about prayer. Luke then describes meetings with young children and with a rich man who clings to his possessions. Another prediction of Jesus' death (18:31–34) is followed by his arrival at Jericho, the last city on his way to Jerusalem. Here he heals a blind beggar (18:35–43), meets the tax collector Zacchaeus (19:1–10), and tells what is known as the parable of the pounds (19:11–27). Luke concludes the long journey section with the remark that Jesus moved on to JERUSALEM.

Section VI: Jesus in Jerusalem (19:29–21:38)
Jesus enters Israel's capital city on a donkey in the company of an enthusiastic crowd, but his adversaries are unmoved. He himself weeps because he knows about the city's coming destruction (19:41–44). A brief account of the cleansing of the temple (19:45–46) is followed by a summary statement about Jesus' activities during his week in Jerusalem and the threat the Jewish leaders now pose to his life (19:47–48). Chapter 20 is filled with stories that illustrate the controversies between Jesus and the leaders: They question his authority, upon which he

tells a warning parable about the tenants of a vineyard who kill the son of the owner. Challenged again, Jesus explains that paying tax to the authorities is not necessarily bad, and he also handles a question about marriage in the afterlife. He then goes on the offensive with a question of his own (20:21–47). In the temple Jesus comments on the generosity of a poor widow (21:1–4) before pronouncing a long discourse about the future of the temple, the city, and the world. Included in this speech is a final short parable, that of the fig tree (21:29–31).

Section VII: Death and Resurrection (Chapters 22–24)

Just as the Jewish leaders grow more serious in their attempts to kill Jesus, one of his disciples, Judas, approaches them to offer his help (22:1–6); nonetheless, he is present at the Passover meal (22:7–21). Whereas during the meal the disciples quarrel about who is the most important, Jesus tries to prepare them for what is to follow (22:24–38). After the meal, he withdraws to pray; although he feels the temptation to escape his approaching suffering, he subjects himself to what he sees as the will of God (22:39–46).

With the help of Judas, Jesus is captured and taken to the house of the high priest. Peter follows him, but, when confronted, in his fear he denies that he knows him. The Jewish council quickly condemns Jesus to death (22:66–71), but the Romans take much longer to confirm the sentence. The Judean governor Pilate refers Jesus to the Galilean King Herod, and both regard him as innocent (23:14–15). However, in the end Pilate submits to pressure by the Jewish leaders and allows the crucifixion of Jesus (23:24–25), which immediately takes place just outside Jerusalem (23:32–43). Jesus dies and is buried by a few faithful friends (23:44–56).

The account of the empty tomb (24:1–12) does not contain an appearance of Jesus. He first appears to two of his followers on the road to Emmaus, and when the two have returned to Jerusalem, he appears to his assembled followers (24:13–36), teaching them that by his suffering and Resurrection the Hebrew Scriptures have been fulfilled (24:37–47). The gospel ends with a brief account of Jesus' ascension.

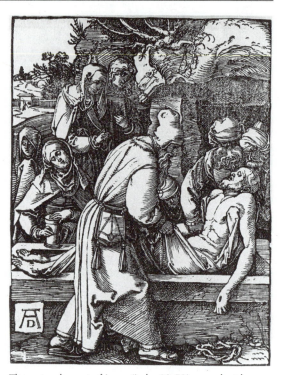

The entombment of Jesus (Luke 23:53), woodcut by Albrecht Dürer

COMMENTARY

Section I: The Prologue (1:1–4)

In the style of the best Greek literature, Luke opens his gospel with a display of his skills. In the original Greek this section consists of one long, well-built phrase that aims to inspire confidence in the author's talent and reliability as a historian. The fact that Luke writes a prologue at all shows that he sets out to write literature. This is the best Greek in the New Testament, so in the eyes of the first readers Luke must have been entirely successful.

Luke tells us that he is not the first to present a gospel, a life story of Jesus. The words *orderly account* in verse 1 can refer to oral and to written materials. Without criticizing his many anonymous predecessors, he suggests that there was room for improvement, and that he is well placed to offer a better gospel because he has done proper research. Note that Luke does not claim to have been an eyewitness to the events he is going to recount, and that the claim to offer an "orderly account" does not imply a chronological arrangement.

In the Hellenistic world it was common to dedicate a book to a noble person, who would in return sponsor the production of a good number of copies. Theophilus is not addressed as a fellow Christian, so he may be a person who is considering a transition to Christianity and who was probably not yet baptized. The book of Acts is also dedicated to him. It has been suggested that the meaning of the name *Theophilus*, "Friend of God," is symbolic and does not refer to an actual person.

Section II: Birth Stories (1:5–2:52)

There is a dramatic change in style at the beginning of this section, which is entirely written in the style of the Septuagint (see BIBLE, EARLY TRANSLATIONS OF). This can be seen in the use of phrases such as "and it came to pass," "in the days of," and "the house of," which occur in the Authorized (King James) Version (see BIBLE, ENGLISH EDITIONS OF) but are obscured in most modern translations. By using this Semitic style, Luke suggests that his story, the story of John and Jesus, is a sequel to and the culmination of the Hebrew Bible. He pays much attention to prophetic and angelic voices (see ANGELS) that proclaim that God is about to intervene once more in the affairs of his people Israel. Thus this section creates great anticipations in the reader—not all of which are fulfilled in the rest of the gospel because of the unbelief of Israel.

The first chapter skillfully intertwines the stories of John and Jesus in a concentric structure:

As can be seen, in the inner parts of the chapter the perspective is that of the women Elizabeth and MARY (MOTHER OF JESUS). The three central parts focus on Jesus, the outer parts on John the Baptist. It is possible that the extensive attention to John's status here and in 3:15–17 was necessary in order to confront followers of his who had wrong ideas about him; the same background is inferred for the fourth gospel's attention to John the Baptist (John 1:8, 26–34; 3:27–31; see also Acts 19:1–5).

Mary's song (1:46–55) leans on Hannah's in 1 Samuel 2:1–11. Much later it became part of the church liturgy as the *Magnificat*, whereas Zechariah's song (1:68–79) is in the liturgy as the *Benedictus*. Both closely resemble psalms from the Hebrew Bible. The initial infertility of Zechariah and Elizabeth reminds the reader of Abraham and Sarah in Genesis, whereas 1:37 is a quote from that story (Genesis 18:14 in the Septuagint version). The emphasis on the low social position of Mary reminds the reader of God's preference and care for the poor (e.g., Psalm 146; see Characters on page 255).

The circumstances of Zechariah, who is chosen by lot to officiate in the temple (1:8–9), reflect the situation that there were so many priests in Israel that they were on a rota. Zechariah's rather negative response to the angel's delightful message is in stark contrast to Mary's open and faithful reaction to the much harder message she receives, which entails the social disgrace of becoming a mother outside wedlock. The Latin translation of the angel's first word to her, *greetings*, "Ave (Maria)"

		Theme:	Perspective:
A	1:5–7	John's parents	narrator
B	1:8–20	annunciation of John's birth	Zechariah
C	1:21–23	Zechariah dumb	people and Zechariah
D	1:24–25	Elizabeth pregnant	Elizabeth
E	1:26–38	annunciation of Jesus' birth	Mary
F	1:39–45	Elizabeth blesses Mary	Elizabeth and Mary
E'	1:46–56	celebration of Jesus' birth	Mary
D'	1:57–61	Elizabeth gives birth	Elizabeth
C'	1:62–66	Zechariah speaks again	people and Zechariah
B'	1:67–79	celebration of John's birth	Zechariah
A'	1:80	John's youth	narrator

(1:28), has become part of the Western musical culture. Mary's virgin status recalls Isaiah 7:14 but also that entire chapter in Isaiah with its focus on saving trust in God.

Jesus' birth story in 2:1–7 is remarkable for its restraint and brevity; nothing is said about the exact birthplace, about any attending animals, or even about the time of year. (As the shepherds with their flocks were out at night, 2:8, it cannot have been winter.) The Greek word used in 2:7 is *katalyma,* which is a guest room (cf. 22:11) or a living room rather than an inn. (For "inn" Luke 10:34 uses another Greek word, *pandocheion.*) Nearly every house had an area where the animals lived, so the presence of a manger is unsurprising.

There is more social reversal to follow, for shepherds were social outcasts much like robbers and tax collectors. It is striking that such people were the first to hear the good news about Jesus—and to respond so positively (contrast King Herod in Matthew 2:3–12).

In the episodes about Jesus' circumcision and his presentation in the temple, Luke takes care to show how his parents act in accordance with the regulations of Genesis 17:12 (Luke 2:21), Exodus 13 (Luke 2:23), and Leviticus 5:11 (Luke 2:24). The story of the boy Jesus in the temple at 12 is again marked by the narrator's restraint. Later (second- and third-century) gospels abound in fanciful detail about Jesus' youth, but Luke's story is factual and merely emphasizes his wisdom and knowledge,

Jesus discussing with the teachers (Luke 2:46), etching by Rembrandt

including his awareness of belonging to God, his Father (2:49).

Section III: Preparations (3:1–4:13)

Again Luke's style of writing changes, and from here on the gospel is written in good but not difficult Greek that is not entirely free of influences of the Hebrew. In this section the attention on the role of the HOLY SPIRIT (see Characters on page 255) continues.

The synchronism in 3:1–2 contains the names of two high priests. While Caiaphas was the official high priest between 18 and 36 C.E., his father-in-law, Annas (John 18:13), was the power behind the throne. Luke continues (3:4–6) by quoting from Isaiah 40, which for Jews was a classic passage about God's coming comfort and salvation, which might even include those presently outside (verse 6). Verse 3:8 is based on an Aramaic wordplay, for in that language "stones" is *abanim;* "children," *banim.* It is John's role to prepare God's people for his intervention and to look for the fruit that would result from a life with God (verses 8–9). As do the prophets of old, John emphasizes the importance of justice and mercy. The combination of "Holy Spirit and fire" contains the positive and the negative, for fire is here used as a stronger means of purification than water. (See also BAPTISM.)

Following a typical summary statement in 3:18, in 3:19–20 Luke narrates events that actually happened much later, in the middle of Jesus' ministry (see at 9:7–9). Thus he completes the story of John before he embarks on that of Jesus. The Herod mentioned here is Herod Antipas, and the fact that John does not spare him shows that he is a true prophet. The baptism of Jesus (3:21–22) gains him God's recognition and approval in words based on the Hebrew Bible (Genesis 22:2, 12, 16; Psalm 2:7; Isaiah 41:8; 42:1; Jeremiah 31:20).

Luke's genealogy differs from Matthew's as it follows a different line from David than the royal line via Solomon; this is consistent with his emphasis on Jesus' lowly birth in the previous chapters. The genealogy presents Jesus as the culmination of the history of Israel and of all humankind; the genealogy and the subsequent temptation indicate that Jesus succeeds in what the first human, Adam

(3:38), failed to achieve: to obey God in the face of temptations.

Forty (the number of days Jesus spends in the desert) is the number that symbolizes preparation. At the moment when Jesus stands ready to begin his ministry, Satan tries to throw him off course with a triple enticement to obey him and gain an easy life (4:1–13). The order of the temptations differs from that in Matthew 4:1–11, but the evangelists agree on the fact that Deuteronomy is used to counter Satan. The passage also forms a telling contrast with 4:16–30: Jesus will not use his powers to serve himself but others, in particular the poor.

Section IV: Jesus in Galilee (4:14–9:50)

The first part of this section is enclosed by the summary verses 4:14–15 and 44, which form an INCLUSIO around it. This part contains the important "manifesto" that Jesus presents in his hometown of Nazareth. In this programmatic speech Jesus applies Isaiah 61:1–2a and 58:6 to his own person and ministry. He is the Spirit-filled prophet of the kingdom of God, the bringer of salvation who announces the release of the jubilee year. This "year of the Lord's favor" (4:19) was an old institution (Leviticus 25), which the Jews expected to be reinstated in the end times by the Messiah. In 4:24–27 Jesus himself refers to Elijah and Elisha, whom Luke will use as models in chapter 7.

In 4:31–44 and 5:12–26 Luke presents samples of Jesus' ministry of teaching and healing that derive from Mark 1–2. Luke hardly distinguishes illness and demonic possession, in that he uses the same Greek verb (Greek *epitimaō*, "to rebuke, call into submission") in both cases: Compare 4:35 and 9:42 with 4:39 and 8:24. In the same vein, 13:10–16 describes illness as the work of Satan. Jesus had a ministry as an exorcist (7:21; 13:32; Acts 10:38) that demonstrated the power of the kingdom of God (11:20) and in which his followers shared (9:1, 6, 49; 10:17). Luke has more references to demons than the other evangelists, but three important stories about demons are common to the Synoptic Gospels (Luke 4:31–37; 8:26–39; 9:37–43). Luke portrays a victorious Jesus who—apparently without prayer—simply commands the demons to leave people.

Much of 5:1–6:16 is devoted to Jesus' gathering of disciples. He first gains his four best-known disciples as a result of joining them in their professional activity as fishermen and enabling them to have a miraculous catch, showing that he knows more about fishing than the professionals. Fishing becomes a metaphor for salvation (5:1–11). Peter, the future leader of the disciples, is won over by Jesus' goodness rather than by his miracle and receives most attention.

Forgiving sins (5:21) is God's prerogative (Isaiah 1:18; 43:25; 44:22), so by explicitly doing this Jesus is making quite a claim (5:17–26). The calling of Levi enables Jesus to show that he wants to seek and to serve all social classes, including the tax collectors, who are outcasts (5:27–32). The sarcastic 5:31 is probably an existing proverb. A controversy over fasting enables Jesus to explain the joyfulness and the newness of his ministry, which preclude fasting (5:33–39). His first pair of parables (verses 36–38) deals with the new "containers" needed for the new dispensation. Verse 39 is an ironic comment on misplaced conservatism.

In the controversies in 6:1–11 Jesus claims authority over the interpretation and application of the Scriptures. Only now does Luke give the list of close disciples who have been chosen from a large number of followers. This brief scene leads straight into a long sermon, the Sermon on the Plain (see Synopsis), so called after the location mentioned in verse 17, a level place in the hills. The sermon consists of an introduction that gives the setting (17–19), blessings and woes (20–26), commands regarding love and judgment (27–38), and concluding parables in a setting full of questions and polarities (39–49). The so-called golden rule (verse 31) in some form or another was known among Jews, Greeks, and Romans.

Faith and the question of who Jesus is are the issues that hold together chapter 7, in which Luke depicts Jesus in parallel to Elijah and Elisha. Verses 7:1–10 can be seen as a miracle story or a quest story in which most attention goes to the faith of the foreign officer. This faith reflects the faith of Naaman, who was healed by Elisha (2 Kings 5), but whereas Naaman was proud, this man is very humble. The story of the widow at Nain and her revived son (7:11–17), which occurs only in Luke, reminds of that about Elijah, the widow, and her son (1 Kings 17:7–24), although here it is Jesus who takes the initiative to act. Widows were included in the category of the poor (see Characters below).

As John the Baptist looks at his bad circumstances, he questions Jesus' identity, but Jesus points out how he is fulfilling his manifesto of 4:16–20. He interprets John's role in words derived from Malachi 3:1 (7:27), and at the end of the scene he rebukes his contemporaries with a parable that explains why, though John and he differ much, they are both rejected. The moving mealtime episode in 7:36–50 has two contrasting lead characters, a socially respected but rigid and unbelieving Pharisee and a marginalized, desperate woman who shows great love; its complicated structure contains a parable (verses 41–42). Some interpreters identify the anonymous woman as Mary Magdalene (see 8:2; 24:10), but that is unwarranted. Neither is it correct to think that the incident is identical to the one in Matthew 26:6–13, Mark 14:3–9, and John 12:1–8, which took place in a different context later in Jesus' life.

In chapters 8 and 9 Jesus is constantly on the road. The summary 8:1–3 sheds important light on the makeup of his following—Jewish leaders would not be accompanied by women!—and on the way in which they sustained themselves. For the parable of the sower and its interpretation (8:4–15), see at Matthew 13. Luke 8:10 is a quote from Isaiah 6:9. The stilling of the storm in 8:22–25 is the second nature miracle; the first was in 5:1–11. For 8:26–39, see at Mark 5:1–20, which is the longer version of this miracle story, and for 8:40–56, where Luke faithfully retains Mark's sandwich structure, see at Mark 5:21–43. In both cases Luke has abbreviated Mark but faithfully preserved the elements of the stories. As in 8:42 and 43, the number 12 occurs in 9:1 and 17; that may explain the grouping together of the episodes here.

The first part of chapter 9 contains a sandwich structure of the type often found in Mark (see Mark under LITERARY STRUCTURE): The two parts of the episode about the sending out and the return of the disciples (9:1–6, 10–11) enclose one about King Herod. The wording of 9:1–6 shows that the disciples are sent out with the same task, powers, and results as Jesus himself; they can be seen as extra sowers of the seed, the gospel about the kingdom of God. They specifically visit villages (verse 6) while Jesus apparently focuses on the towns of Israel (5:12; 7:1, 11; 8:4; 9:10). Jesus' willingness to be disturbed by people who need him is striking; he allows the reporting back of the disciples to be cut short (9:10–11). As a result of the crowd's demanding behavior, Jesus is more or less compelled to provide them with food (9:12–17), and he does abundantly. (In the Hebrew Bible Moses—Exodus 16; Numbers 11—and Elisha—2 Kings 4:42–44—had similarly provided the hungry with food.)

The passage in the middle of the sandwich shows how the increased preaching attracts the attention of King Herod Antipas. Luke here mentions the death of John the Baptist, whose capture he had reported at 3:19–20. In reality, the cruel king would only meet Jesus as a prisoner (23:6–11), so the reader can conclude that his interest was not overly serious. The idea that prophets return (9:8) was common in Judaism. Between 9:17 and 9:18 Luke, who so far has followed Mark quite closely, has omitted all of Mark 6:45–8:26; see Sources above.

Jesus' Galilean ministry culminates in two important moments, Peter's confession (9:18–20) and the transfiguration (9:28–36), both of which are immediately followed by disappointments. Peter's insight that Jesus is the Messiah, the deliverer sent by God and long expected by the Jews (the Christ, verse 20), is correct (cf. 2:11, 26). Yet Jesus wants to keep this confidential because of the political overtones of the messianic expectations among the Jews (see JESUS CHRIST). Instead of planning a takeover of power, Jesus talks about his imminent suffering and death. (Here Luke, who is more positive about the disciples than Mark, has omitted Peter's opposition as found in Mark 8:32–33.) Jesus extends his warning about future suffering, which sharply contrasts to the triumphant notes of the preceding passages, to his disciples (9:23–27). The cryptic saying in 9:27 must refer both to the transfiguration that immediately follows and a preview of the kingdom of God, and to Jesus' resurrection as a further manifestation of the kingdom to which the disciples would be witnesses. The transfiguration

(9:28–36) has yet more facets: It is also a divine confirmation of Jesus' majesty and glory, given by the two main prophets of old as well as God himself, and a confirmation of his approaching death. After this marvelous event the lack of faith in the disciples (9:37–43a) is all the more disappointing, as are their lack of understanding of his destiny (9:43b–45) and their infighting (9:46–48).

Section V: The Journey to Jerusalem (9:51–19:28)

Jesus' journey to Jerusalem is a literary motif that appears from time to time in this long section (10:38; 13:22; 14:25; 17:11; 18:31, 35; 19:11). It is, however, impossible to trace his geographical progress, and according to 17:11 he still has not made much progress. There are no chronological records in the passage. Moreover, this section resembles the preceding one (and much of Mark) in that it consists of loosely connected narratives, parables, and other teaching, although it stands out as containing few miracle stories. Luke is less dependent on his sources Mark and Q here than anywhere else.

As can be seen in Mark, the tradition regarding Jesus already contained the journey. Luke has moved the beginning of the journey far forward, and he has given it much more emphasis. This section thus emphasizes Jesus' personal destiny as well as the importance of Jerusalem. Jesus' journey has parallels with Israel's journey in Deuteronomy, showing him to be the true representative of the people.

The section opens with a reference to Jesus' "departure" (9:51). The Greek word used (analēmpsis) occurs only here in the New Testament and means "taking up." It is a reference to the whole sequence of Jesus' suffering, dying, resurrection, and ascension. (The New International Version and New Living Translation add "to heaven" without basis in the original text.) The word is apparently intended to focus the whole of the section (cf. "to take up," Mark 16:19; Acts 1:2, 11): Jesus' future suffering and glorification are placed center stage. In 9:52–53 we find a reflection from the Samaritan side on the split between them and the Jews (see SAMARIA): A person traveling from Galilee to Jerusalem should not travel through Samaria.

The three short exchanges in 9:57–62 highlight different aspects of following Jesus on his journey: The first person is too greedy and is reminded of the real cost; the other two have valid reasons for not following but are nonetheless reminded that the kingdom of God supersedes normal conditions.

The sending out of the 70 or 72 followers (10:1–24) intensifies the campaign of the Twelve Disciples in the previous chapter. All Israel must know that its Savior has come. The manuscripts are divided as to whether 70 or 72 is the correct number. In verse 4b the idea is not that the messengers should be impolite but that they avoid the time-consuming ritual greetings of the East. In 10:21–22 Jesus speaks in the way he normally does in John's gospel.

Jesus tells the parable of the good Samaritan (10:25–37) in response to the question of a scribe as to who his neighbor is. Earlier the scribe had quoted the summary of the Israelite law from Deuteronomy 6:5 and Leviticus 19:18, whence the word *neighbor* comes, but he now looks for depth. In fact, Jesus turns the question around, telling the audience that they must be good neighbors—that is, show selfless love—to everybody, including outcasts and foreigners (10:25–37). The behavior of the priest and the Levite is in part based on the fact that touching a corpse would make one ritually unclean, so unfit to officiate. We are not supposed to attribute independent meaning in the elements of the story (the donkey, the inn, the two coins), for this is not an allegory but a story with just one point. The reluctant response of the scribe is striking: He cannot make himself utter the word *Samaritan!* The short narrative that follows again shows Jesus' unconventional attitude toward cultural norms: A woman is accepted as a pupil (disciple), not just as a servant of the men (10:38–42). Martha's domestic service is valued, but listening to Jesus' words is more important. Martha and Mary also occur in John's gospel, but Luke does not mention their brother, Lazarus (John 11; 12:1–6).

After teaching the disciples a model prayer (see LORD'S PRAYER), Jesus emphasizes God's willingness to answer prayers (11:1–13). From here numerous stories focus on the resistance Jesus meets. The allegation that he is aligned with the devil (11:14–15) is particularly malevolent. In countering it Jesus uses a vivid picture that to modern readers evokes the Middle Ages. For an explanation of the sign of Jonah (11:29–30), see JONAH. In the confrontation story 11:37–54, Jesus argues that outward cleansing and piety are only valid as symbols of what happens inwardly.

Jesus' warnings against the Pharisees reveal his great confidence in God but also his awareness of the increasing animosity he is facing (12:1–7). The blasphemy against the Spirit (12:10) is best explained as persistent opposition to God's calling. The parable about the rich fool (12:13–21) derives its title from the way God himself is made to address the rich person in the story: "You fool." It is a timeless story about the difference between "to have" and "to be," followed by explicit teaching on the same theme that has a parallel in Matthew's Sermon on the Mount and makes ample use of rural imagery (Luke 12:22–32 = Matthew 6:25–34).

The parable of the master who serves his slaves (12:35–38) combines the theme of watchfulness and readiness that dominates 12:32–48 with that of social reversal. The person expected is the returning Jesus (see LAST THINGS), who can be referred to as thief (verse 39), Son of Man (40), and master (43). In words directed at the crowd, Jesus more enigmatically challenges them to understand "the present time."

The theme of most of chapter 13 would seem to be the call to timely repentance, occasioned by some bad news (verses 1–3). The parable of the fig tree (6–9) is a strong warning to God's people to change their behavior, similar in tendency to the teaching in verses 22–30. The healing of the woman on the Sabbath (10–17) interrupts the flow of thought in the chapter. The mustard plant was common in Israel and grows from a tiny seed into a tall shrub. The wording in verse 19 stems from Psalm 104:12 in the Septuagint, verse 28 derives from Psalm 6:8, whereas the promise in 13:29 picks up the promises made in Isaiah 2:2–4 and 25:6–9; compare also Psalm 107:3. King Herod Antipas appears in chapter 9 as the murderer of John the Baptist so Jesus and the readers know what he is capable of doing.

Chapter 14 opens with the fifth and final healing on the Sabbath (cf. 4:31–37; 4:38–39; 6:6–11;

13:10–17), which once more establishes Jesus as "Lord of the Sabbath" (6:5). The subsequent teaching is also set in the house of the leading Pharisee, who is hosting Jesus. The Lord happily violates the social conventions by criticizing the tendency to seek places of honor at the table, telling a parable on the issue (verses 7–11), to which he adds teaching on not expecting to be reciprocated in giving banquets (12–14). The next parable also focuses on a meal, the festive meal God is preparing and to which all of humanity is invited (15–24). The excuses in verse 18–19 are false as oxen were not bought untried and fields not bought unseen. In the end, those who partake of the great dinner are the lower classes, and, consequently, the whole chapter sheds light on God's new social order, of which Jesus is the bringer. The theme of dynamic relationships is also the starting point for the teaching in verses 25–35, which then progresses by association. "Hate" (26) is not to be taken in the strong sense (Genesis 29:31–33; Luke 16:13). At the end of the chapter it has become clear that God invites everybody, but that the invitation is not unconditional.

The parables in chapter 15 are among the best-known parts of the whole Bible. Jesus tells them to distance himself from the Pharisees, who do not care for other people, so they have as common theme losing and finding, being happy and celebrating. The last of the three, the parable of the lost or "prodigal" son, should be called that of "the two sons," as the older turns out to be just as "lost" as the younger. It has an element of allegory in that the father is unmistakably God, whereas the older son represents the Jewish nation and the younger son the Gentiles. Both err, but God's love remains. The main character in the parable in 16:1–9 has variously been called "the shrewd manager," "the enterprising steward," and much more. The point of this parable is a recommendation of the prudent use of material possessions; cf. verses 10–13. A further parable on stewardship occurs in 19:11–27.

What is commonly called "the parable about the rich man and the poor Lazarus" is not in fact labeled a parable by Jesus or Luke, and it contains a third important character, Abraham (16:19–31). The fictional story would seem to have at least two distinct aims: to criticize rich people who did not use their money to assist those in need and to warn those who are counting on receiving a special revelation that they need to make do with God's general revelation in the Scriptures (called Moses and the Prophets). The interpretation should avoid drawing conclusions about the afterlife and any intermediate state as those things are not Jesus' topic here.

Chapter 17 begins with a series of unrelated sayings, leading to another note on Jesus' progress, which geographically is quite incomprehensible as there is no "region between Samaria and Galilee." In the ensuing episode the one healed Samaritan performs better than the others, who must be Jews. The discourse that ends the chapter is a preparation for the more elaborate teaching on the last things and Jesus' second coming in chapter 21. The parable of the dishonest judge (18:1–8) is an instruction to pray that will help Jesus' followers through the hard times. As in 16:1–9, the main character of the story is morally reprehensible—but to focus on that aspect is to miss the point of the parable.

Two passages now highlight the difference between professed and true religion: The parable of the Pharisee and the tax collector (18:9–14) points to the difference between the boasting of the religious professional and the humble faith of the outcast, whereas the narrative about the rich ruler (18:18–27) focuses on someone who outwardly fulfils all commandments of the law but inwardly clings to his material possessions so that they effectively prevent him from following Jesus. These two passages sandwich a short episode in which Jesus commends the worldview of little children as the requisite for entering the kingdom of God (18:15–17).

The well-known story about the tax collector Zacchaeus (19:1–10), unique to Luke, is well written, with its own exposition (verses 1–3), complication (4), crisis (5–7), and resolution (8–10). Thematically, it sums up perfectly what Luke wants to say about Jesus: He "came to seek out and save the lost"; he is concerned about individuals, in particular outcasts; and he offers the type of "salvation" that also affects people's lifestyles here and now.

The parable in 19:11–26 is probably the longest and most complicated of all parables; it combines the idea of the parable of the talents (Matthew 25:14–30), that Jesus' absence is not time to be wasted but to be used productively, with criticism of "a nobleman" who "went to a distant country" to be made king but who was hated by his subjects. In this person the audience was bound to recognize King Archelaus (see HEROD), who had made such a journey to Rome. Archelaus's character is reflected in the cruel response in verse 27.

It is not easy to determine where this section of the gospel ends. Some translations begin a new paragraph at 19:28, but that verse is rather the conclusion of the preceding passage if not of the whole section. Other interpreters prefer to take 19:28–44 with this section of the gospel but that seems less logical.

Section VI: Jesus in Jerusalem (19:29–21:38)

The parallel verses 19:47–48 and 21:37–38 form an inclusio around most of this section; they testify to the very public presence of Jesus in the capital city during the final week of his life as well as to his popularity.

The account of his arrival in Jerusalem emphasizes the fact that Jesus is indeed the king. The idea of spreading cloaks on the road for the king is that from 2 Kings 9:13 and the crowd adds the word *king* to their quote from Psalm 118:26 in verse 38. The thought that the stones will cry comes from Habakkuk 2:11. The crowd is ecstatic, but Jesus weeps because he already knows that the city will soon reject him, and, therefore, it will be rejected by God (verses 41–44).

Most of the section is composed of reports on controversies with the leaders in Jerusalem. Already when Jesus entered the city, the Pharisees had shown their annoyance at the crowd's enthusiasm (19:39), but Jesus challenges them by throwing the businessmen out of the temple, the bulwark of the establishment (19:45–46). In his statement in 19:46 he quotes from both Isaiah 56:7 and Jeremiah 7:11. Those who subsequently confront Jesus are the chief priests, the scribes (teachers of the law), and the elders (20:1, 19), spies sent by the same (20:20–21), and the Sadducees (20:27). The latter ask a question about something they do not believe in themselves, that is, the Resurrection.

In the long speech on the future of the temple, the city, and the world (21:5–38), Luke distinguishes more clearly than Matthew 24 and Mark 13 between what refers to the period leading up to the year 70 C.E. (verses 8–19), to the fall of Jerusalem in that year (verses 20–24), and to the second coming of Jesus (verses 25–28); see APOCALYPTIC WRITING.

Section VII: Death and Resurrection (Chapters 22–24)

Unlike what the reader would expect, in this final section Luke is quite independent of Mark's story line, and, in particular, much in chapter 24 is unique to him. A notable example of this independence is that Luke tells us about the involvement in Jesus' trial (23:7–12) of Herod Antipas, whom—ironically—the Romans had denied the title "king of the Jews" (cf. 23:3). In this gospel Jerusalem remains center stage, as Luke does not include any reference to a return of Jesus to Galilee. The disciples' return to the temple (24:53) rounds off the narrative that had begun there (1:9). In many passages we can again see the influence of the Hebrew Bible; 23:30, for example, contains a quote from Hosea 10:8.

As in the other Synoptic Gospels, the end of Jesus' stay in Jerusalem is precipitated by the decision of his disciple Judas to betray him to his enemies (22:1–6). As Judas had been with Jesus during his entire ministry, his human motives are hard to fathom, and this is not the place to discuss the speculations, but Luke blames SATAN above all (verse 3). After extensive preparations, Jesus and his disciples celebrate the Passover meal on the set day, but Jesus changes the meaning of its key elements, bread and wine, so that from then on the meal will be a reference to him (22:7–20). Instead of God's salvation of Israel from Egypt, Jesus' followers will remember his death, and the meal was given the name the LORD'S SUPPER. Paul will later refer to this event in words that are close to Luke's (1 Corinthians 11:23–25).

While still at the table, Jesus delivers a kind of farewell discourse (22:24–38; cf. the much longer discourse in John 14–16); at its heart is a quote from Isaiah 53 in verse 37, introduced simply as "It

is written." After the meal Jesus goes to his usual place for the night (22:39; cf. 21:37), making it easy for Judas to find him. But first the omniscient narrator presents the reader with a kind of internal debate by the praying Jesus over whether or not to agree to his suffering (22:41–45). He does accept it as God's will—an extraordinary decision as he could clearly have refused.

In the story of Jesus' arrest, Luke omits the detail that the disciples fled; this is implied in the fact that only Peter follows the captors (22:54). And Peter soon regrets his courage when humble servants of the high priest identify him as a follower of Jesus. He betrays him, as Jesus had known he would (22:55–62; cf. 22:34).

At several stages in the story Luke includes details about the way Jesus was tortured even before his condemnation (22:63–65; 23:11), although he omits the final flogging (Mark 15:15). This maltreatment explains why at the end of the trial Jesus

The Last Supper (Luke 22:14–21), woodcut by Albrecht Dürer

is unable to carry the crossbeam, as criminals were normally made to do, so that a bystander is called in to do it (23:26).

Luke records three sayings from the cross (23:34, 43, and 46), in contrast to one in Matthew and Mark (Matthew 27:46 = Mark 15:34) and three in John. The first two focus on other people, and none shows any bitterness (cf. Isaiah 53:7). Thus Jesus' attitude is in sharp contrast with that of those in control, who still hurl insults at him when he hangs on the cross (23:35–36). On the other hand, Luke records positive words from people not expected to speak thus (23:40–41, 47).

In the same way that the details of the crucifixion story in the four Gospels differ, so the accounts of what exactly happened on the morning of the Resurrection differ on details, in particular regarding the number and names of the women who were witnesses to the empty tomb. These differences, together with agreement on the main elements, testify to the diversity of the eyewitnesses and the traditions available to the gospel writers and suggest the Resurrection story was not invented by the humans involved.

The Resurrection itself had no eyewitnesses. On the Sunday morning some women go to the tomb to care for the body of Jesus, but on arrival they find the tomb open and Jesus gone (24:1–3). Angels tell them that Jesus is risen (24:4–8). The disciples do not believe the women's story, but Peter cannot solve the riddle of what happened as the body of Jesus is clearly gone (24:9–12).

In the final chapter as in the first, the abiding value and relevance of the Hebrew Bible are underlined as Jesus Christ himself twice shows his followers how what happened to him had been prophesied in the Scriptures (verses 25–27 and 44–47). The Judean town of Emmaus, seven or eight miles from Jerusalem, resembles the Galilean Nazareth as a town of no importance that acts as a foil for a great revelation. The story of the walk to Emmaus contains the ironic element that the two disciples tell Jesus what happened to him without recognizing him. To the reader, Luke had given his identity away in verse 15. The breaking of bread by Jesus, the guest, has high symbolic value as a reference to the sacrament of the Lord's Supper.

Jesus at Emmaus (Luke 24:30), etching by Rembrandt

A longer version of the ascension story (24:50–53) is found in the sequel to the gospel, Acts 1:1–12. Such overlap between two consecutive books was not uncommon.

CHARACTERS

children   Of the four evangelists, Luke pays most attention to children (1:41, 44; 2:40–52; 9:46–48; 15:11–32; 18:15–17); 9:47 would suggest that there was a child around wherever Jesus was. The "little ones" (17:2) can refer to new (immature) believers as well as to children, again showing how valuable they are. This attitude stands in sharp contrast to that of Jesus' contemporaries. A child was little valued indeed in antiquity. Greeks and Romans even controlled the size of their families by abandoning children to die of exposure.

Holy Spirit   The first half of Luke's gospel says more about the role of the Spirit in the ministries of John the Baptist and Jesus than the other gospels. At the outset there is the promise that John will be filled with the Spirit (1:15), and both his father and his mother (1:41, 67) act through the power of the Spirit. Jesus surpasses John in that he is even born through the power of the Spirit (1:35). Later it is the Spirit who sends him too on his way (3:22; 4:1, 14, 18). After this the references largely stop, but the point that Jesus is led by the Spirit has been made. As so often in the Hebrew Bible, the Spirit has prepared the people for God's active intervention. As in the other Synoptic Gospels, the Spirit is largely seen as a divine power, but in 10:21 he is the source of Jesus' ecstatic joy.

Jesus Christ   Luke uses diverse narrative methods to show the reader who Jesus is: He is revealed by his actions, his own words, and the words of others. Together these elements create the picture of a passionate human being who is at the same time more than a human, who actually is on God's side. He is called "a prophet" (7:16; 24:19) and claims the title for himself by association (4:24; 13:33). Other favorite characterizations of Luke include "Savior," "Servant of the Lord," and "Son of Man." See JESUS CHRIST.

John the Baptist   By presenting John's relative Mary (1:46–55) and his father, Zechariah (1:68–79), as singing songs that remind the reader of Hannah's words (1 Samuel 2:1–10), Luke effectively presents the young John the Baptist as a second young Samuel, a mighty prophet of the Lord who will initiate a revival in Israel. Other elements in the portrayal of John remind the reader of Samson (1:15 = Judges 13:5, 7, 14) and of the messenger prophesied by Malachi (2:6–7; 3:1, 18; 4:5–6).

rich and poor   In Judaism and in the New Testament, *poor* is not merely an economic term; it also includes those who are low, humble, and dependent on God. More than the other evangelists, Luke brings out Jesus' concern for them, and the theme of social reversal figures several times in the Commentary above. Large parts of chapters 12, 14, and 16 are devoted to teaching on the subject of wealth and possessions, and stories illustrate the desired behavior (18:18–27; 19:1–10; 21:1–4).

Jesus' mother, Mary, sings her hymn about God's choice for the poor (1:52–53), and Jesus is indeed born into a poor family who bring the sacrifice of the poor (2:24). Isaiah 61, a chapter with "good news for the poor," is quoted as being fulfilled in Jesus' "manifesto" (4:18; cf. 7:22). In his version of the beatitudes, Luke (6:20) includes a blessing for "the poor," where Matthew (5:3) has "the poor in spirit."

On the other hand, there are warnings and woes for the rich (6:24–26), who are pictured unfavorably (12:13–21; 16:19–31). But rich is essentially "self-satisfied." The role reversal initiated by God includes the revelation to shepherds who were outcasts (2:8–20) and Jesus' attention to "tax collectors and sinners" (5:30; cf. 15:2). Luke's positive references to Samaritans can also be included here (10:33; 17:16; cf. 9:52–56).

Yet Jesus depends on the generosity of wealthy women (8:3) and takes part in apparently lavish meals (7:34, 36; 11:37). The conclusion is that the gospel contains no simple code of behavior. A key term for Luke is *steward* (Greek *oikonomos*, "manager"), which basically denotes a slave who as such could not own property but just administer his master's (12:42; 16:1, 3, 8). All Jesus' followers can be considered "stewards" of whatever God gives them.

women   The general cultural climate, both among the Jews and in Hellenism (see CULTURES OF THE BIBLE), was negative about women. In such a context it is remarkable that many of the stories that Luke adds to Mark's gospel focus on women: He names Elizabeth, Anna, Martha, and Mary and includes many anonymous women as well. Jesus generally groups of both men and women, and Luke even depicts Mary as a disciple (10:38–42).

Luke shows how Jesus accepts women as people in their own right and uses them as positive examples (4:26; 17:35; 21:1–4) and characters in his parables (15:8–10). He healed women just as he healed men, and the raising of the boy in Nain (7:11–17) happened on behalf of his widowed mother. Women followed Jesus and supported him: That is, they acted as his patrons (8:1–3; cf. Acts 1:14). See also WOMEN IN THE BIBLE.

1, 2, 3, and 4 Maccabees

There are four books called Maccabees, all of which appear in the New Revised Standard Version edition with Apocrypha. None of them is part of the Hebrew Bible, and they are considered apocryphal by the Protestant churches. However, the Roman Catholic Church and the Orthodox Churches recognize 1 and 2 Maccabees as deuterocanonical (being of secondary canonical rank). 3 Maccabees is in the Greek and Slavonic Bibles but not in the Roman Catholic canon, whereas 4 Maccabees only appears in an appendix to the Greek Bible. The titles are derived from the nickname *Maccabee*, or hammer, given to Judas of the family of the Hasmoneans, who reigned over Judea from 164 B.C.E. until the Roman conquest in 63 B.C.E. The family's father, Mattathias, had died too early in the revolt he had started to play a large role (1 Maccabees 2:1, 49, 69–70). The titles are appropriate for 1 and 2 Maccabees only, as 3 and 4 Maccabees have nothing to do with the fortunes of the family.

All four books narrate events that took place in the INTERTESTAMENTAL PERIOD, but only the first two are historical. 1 Maccabees was originally in Hebrew, but only the Greek text survives. 2 Maccabees presents itself as the summary of a five-volume history by Jason of Cyrene (2:19–26), which is now lost; both the original and the excerpt were written in Greek. These two books date from around 125 B.C.E. 3 Maccabees is a romance not unlike the books of Judith and Tobit; it probably originated in Alexandria in the first century B.C.E. 4 Maccabees dwells on the martyrdom of a Jewish family—which is also described in 2 Maccabees 7—and was probably written in the first half of the first century C.E.

SYNOPSIS

1 and 2 Maccabees focus on the revolt of the Maccabees against the suppression of the Jewish religion by King Antiochus IV Epiphanes in the year 167 B.C.E. and the subsequent war of liberation. Unlike 1 and 2 Samuel or 1 and 2 Kings, the two books are not sequential but independent writings that cover largely the same ground. They describe the religious persecution by Antiochus, which culminated in the abolition of the sacrifices and the defile-

ment of the temple (see HEBREW BIBLE, WORSHIP AND RITUAL; 1 Maccabees 1; 2 Maccabees 3–6) and the insurrection and victory of the Jews (1 Maccabees 2–8; 2 Maccabees 8–15). Judas Maccabeus died in battle in 161 (1 Maccabees 9:1–19), but 2 Maccabees breaks off before this event. 1 Maccabees 9:20–16:24 additionally covers the careers of the brothers of Judas, Jonathan and Simon, who succeeded him. 2 Maccabees begins with a long prologue (1–2), which includes letters written ca. 125 B.C.E. by the Jews in Judea to those in EGYPT (see DIASPORA), calling them to celebrate Hanukkah, the festival of the rededication of the temple. Other letters appear in chapters 9 and 11.

3 Maccabees is set during the reign of King Philopator of Egypt (Ptolemy IV, 221–205 B.C.E.). The brief first episode describes his victory over his enemy Antiochus III of SYRIA at Raphia (217). In the second scene Philopator wants to enter the temple in JERUSALEM (1:9–15). The priests, the Jewish people, and divine intervention narrowly prevent him from doing so (1:16–2:24). The longest and final episode narrates how, on his return to Alexandria, Philopator seeks revenge on the Jews there and how this, too, is prevented by accidents and divine interventions.

4 Maccabees describes the martyrdom of the priest Eleazar, seven brothers, and their mother. The book begins with an introduction and provides illustrations from the lives of Moses and David (2:15–3:18). In 3:19–4:26 the scene is set; chapters 5–7 tell about the trial and execution of Eleazar; 8–12 describe the martyrdoms of the brothers and their mother; chapters 13–18 contain a long and eloquent epilogue.

COMMENTARY

As source texts for the revolt of the Maccabees, a key moment in the history of the Jewish people, 1 and 2 Maccabees are of great importance, especially as they were written soon after the events. The two regularly contradict each other on detail, however, and historians use an eclectic approach as to which version of each event is correct. As there existed two calendars, one with New Year in the spring, one in the fall, chronological details are hard to work out. Both books follow an era that starts in the year 311 B.C.E. (see, e.g., 1 Maccabees 1:10, 20).

In 1 Maccabees God is referred to indirectly as "Heaven" (e.g., 3:18; 4:10). The story is told without much reflection from a squarely pro-Maccabean viewpoint. In its second part the book quotes many documents and letters, which are presumed to be genuine.

2 Maccabees contains legendary stories and spectacular events, but on the other hand it is sometimes more exact than 1 Maccabees. It has Judas Maccabeus as its hero, to the detriment of his father, Mattathias, and his brothers. Chapters 6 and 7 present gruesome details of the martyrdom of some Jews, assuming that their blood contributes to the reconciliation of God (7:38). Divine intervention plays a large role, and there is an explicit belief in life after death (12:43–45).

The historical value of 3 and 4 Maccabees is limited. In fact, the third book has nothing to do with the Maccabees as the action is set in an earlier period. Yet in style, order of events, and theology, 3 Maccabees resembles 2 Maccabees, which the author will have used as a model. Its value is in the insights it provides into the tensions between Jews and Gentiles: the segregated position of the Jews in a pagan society (e.g., 3:3–7), the inability of the king to understand the Jewish laws (1:11–13; 3:17–23), and the Jewish view of "pagans," which can be compared to Paul's description in Romans 1.

4 Maccabees is loosely connected to 1 and 2 Maccabees in that the evil king who kills the Jews is Antiochus Epiphanes (5:1). In terms of genre it is a philosophical tract with rhetorical qualities that at times resembles a SERMON, rather than history (cf. 1:1). It is addressed to fellow Jews (7:19; 18:1–2). The author sets out to show that reason can and should rule over emotions (e.g., 3:5; 16:1–4), and the story line is interspersed with his comments. The ideas proclaimed resemble those of contemporary Stoicism, a philosophical school, whose four virtues are adopted (1:18), but the book has a very Jewish coloring nonetheless. It testifies to a great love for the Laws of Moses and a strong belief in the immortality of the soul. Its message of vicarious suffering that yield atonement of sins (6:27–29; 17:21–22) resembles that of Isaiah 53 and the New Testament, in which Jesus Christ is the one who effects atonement (Romans 3:25; Hebrews 9:11–15; 10:4–10).

CHARACTERS

Antiochus IV Epiphanes This king of Syria and Asia Minor ruled 175–163 B.C.E., encouraging the Hellenization of his kingdom including Judea (2 Maccabees 3–4; see CULTURES OF THE BIBLE). This policy was evidently popular with the Jewish upper class, and modern scholars argue that Antiochus acted largely on the invitation of the group of Jason and Menelaus, who are mentioned in 2 Maccabees 4. In 170/169 Antiochus plundered the temple treasury (Daniel 11:28; 1 Maccabees 1:20–23), and in 167 he banned the practicing of the Jewish faith. The temple sacrifices were suspended and replaced by sacrifices of unclean animals to the Greek god Zeus. Scriptures were to be destroyed; sabbaths, festivals, circumcision, and food laws were no longer to be observed. This triggered the Maccabean uprising, which led to the purification of Jerusalem and the rededication of the temple in 164. As archenemy of the people of God, he became a type of the ANTICHRIST. (See Daniel.)

Jonathan and Simon Maccabeus The brothers and successors of Judas. Jonathan ruled over Judea from 161 until 143 B.C.E., when he was captured and killed. After 152 B.C.E. he was also high priest. He was succeeded by Simon, who in 140 B.C.E. was recognized as "high priest and leader forever" (1 Maccabees 14:41–43). Simon secured freedom from paying tribute to the Syrians and dated public documents according to the years of his rule. When he was murdered, he was succeeded by his son, John Hyrcanus (134–104 B.C.E.).

Judas Maccabeus Son of Mattathias, brother of John, Simon, Eleazar, and Jonathan (1 Maccabees 2:1–5). He is the hero of the Maccabean revolt, who achieved the liberation of his country in 164 and died on the battlefield in 161 B.C.E. (1 Maccabees 9:19). The composer Handel devoted an opera to him, which includes the aria "See the conquering hero comes." In the books discussed here he remains a shallow character.

Malachi

The book of Malachi is the 12th and last of the Minor Prophets, and the very last book of all in the Protestant versions of the Christian Old Testament. The compilers of the Hebrew Bible held that genuine prophecy ceased after that, and not till the Messiah came would there be further revelation. In fact, historically, Ezra-Nehemiah and probably the book of Esther postdate Malachi, but they are not, of course, prophetic books. Numerous scholars hold that parts of the books of Daniel and Zechariah also postdate Malachi. Typical of the later prophets, the language used is prose.

The dating of Malachi is not a matter of great debate. Internal evidence suggests a postexilic time (see RETURN FROM EXILE) when there was a governor (1:8) rather than a king and when the temple had been rebuilt and its ritual resumed (1:10). This would date it after 520 B.C.E. The Ezra-Nehemiah narrative suggests a time before the coming of Ezra (Ezra 7), when religious life had become impoverished in the small province of Judah, which matches exactly what Malachi is describing. The date could be set between Ezra chapters 6 and 7, therefore. Ezra returned from exile in 458 B.C.E., so there is a 60-year gap into which this book can be fitted. Some earlier scholars, however, equated Malachi with Ezra.

This could be done because the name *Malachi* literally means "my messenger," so it could be a pen-name rather than a real one. Verse 3:1 is translated in this way. Certainly, the message of the book is about messages and the messenger, carrying a promise of a true messenger before the "day of the LORD" arrives. Though there is this eschatological note (see LAST THINGS), it is not APOCALYPTIC WRITING, as later writing was. Its tenor is much more akin to that of the preexilic prophets, who stressed covenant faithfulness and righteousness in God's people.

However, the style is unlike earlier prophetic style. It takes on the literary form of a courtroom drama, where God makes out a case against his people and quotes their words back to them as evidence of their unfaithfulness. The prophet speaks occasionally in his own voice but mainly reports God's cross-questioning and verdict. The concerns are ritual and practical. But unlike in the book of earlier prophets, there are no accusations over idolatry or threats of foreign invasion. The concern is that worship has become routine and second-rate, far less than God is going to accept.

SYNOPSIS

The book consists of no more than 55 verses, divided into seven sections with a brief prologue and epilogue. The first section (1:2–5) deals with God's elective love and is addressed to the people, variously called Israel, Judah, and Jerusalem in the book. The next two sections are addressed only to the priests (1:6–14; 2:1–9), accusing them of offering substandard sacrifices in the temple rituals and of failing to be true messengers. A description of the ideal priest-messenger is given.

The audience then returns to the people. In 2:10–16 the prophet directly addresses the people over the question of divorce as a type of covenant breaking. God intrudes at the end by saying, "I hate divorce." The next section (2:17–3:4) now speaks fully of "the Messenger" who will come before the day of the Lord to act as refiner and purifier. Chapter 3, verse 5 acts as a bridge passage leading into the next section (3:6–12), which addresses the failure to tithe, that is, giving of one-tenth of one's income back to God. Nehemiah 13:10–14 attests that the problem was still widespread later. The final passage (3:13–4:3) returns to "the day when I act," when the righteous and unrighteous will be separated in terms of final judgment.

A short epilogue (4:4–6) urges the hearers to be aware of message and messenger: the message of Moses and the true messenger, Elijah himself, the greatest of the prophets. He will usher in "the great and terrible day of the LORD" by restoring right relationships, thus presenting a curse on the land.

COMMENTARY

The introductory verse calls the book "a burden" (Authorized [King James] Version), the same term used in Zechariah 9:1 and 12:1. The term is more specific than the generic word for a prophecy, which is *oracle*. *Burden* suggests both the difficulty of giving such a word and the sense of a judgment being included in it. It is to Israel, here meaning all the returned exiles living around Jerusalem, all that is left of original Israel, and the original recipients of the covenant given under Moses. But there is no sense of a limited god; 1:5, 14; 2:11 all suggest a knowledge and worship of God among all the nations. The books of Daniel and Isaiah particularly portray this universal acknowledgment of God.

The first section (1:2–5) illustrates well the courtroom drama structure of much of the book. An opening statement is made. It is then queried by the people ("you"). God then provides evidence to support the statement. Here, a statement of God's love is evidenced and defined in terms of the experience of twins. One twin (Jacob/Israel) is "chosen" to receive God's love, while the other (Esau/Edom) does not. It is an old story, going back to Genesis (Genesis 25:24–26; 27:36; 28:6; 36:43). The whole concept of election is that it is unmerited, a sheer act of God's love. Edom is not punished because it is not elected, however, but as a result of deliberate unbrotherly acts of the one nation against the other, well described in the book of Obadiah but also prophesied in Isaiah 34; 63:1–6; Jeremiah 49:7–22; Ezekiel 25:12–14; Amos 1:11–12. Such well-documented prophecy has not actually been fulfilled (Malachi 1:3). We know from other historical records that the Edomites were invaded by the Nabateans (who built Petra in Jordan) and forced to remove to country south of Judah called Idumea. Thus there is living evidence of God's election.

In the dialectic that goes forward, hypothetical speech is given to the Edomites: "We will rebuild the ruins." So God replies to this as well. Finally, a further hypothetical speech is given to the people, "Great is the LORD . . ." when they see the frustration of the Edomites, unable to prosper again without God's favor.

The second section (1:6–14) uses this structure, but more elaborately. An opening statement is then questioned immediately, but this time not by the people but by God himself in a series of rhetorical questions: "If then I am a father . . . ?" Only then do the priests, here addressed, further question the rhetorical question, to which God immediately replies with the main accusation: Polluted food has been offered in the temple rituals. Again, the

questioning and answering continue till the exact nature of the sin is established. This is quite a different procedure from WOES AND DENUNCIATIONS, which entail a straightforward condemnation by the prophet or by God, with perhaps a few rhetorical questions. There is also some effective sarcasm: "Try presenting that to your governor." The structure is rounded off by the judgment "Cursed be the cheat. . . ."

The importance given to the priests here is significant. They are the agents of teaching and instruction of God's truth, rather than instruments of ritual. There is no obvious place for a regular prophetic ministry, aside from the corrective one being employed here. This is a somewhat different scenario from that of preexilic times. The picture of the ideal priest as messenger in 2:1–9 and "my covenant with Levi" is a concept not articulated before in those terms (see Numbers 18:21–24), as Levi is the tribe from which the priests are appointed (see Numbers). In fact, this section does not fall into the courtroom structure at all but is more of a denunciation with very strong language "Spread dung on your faces" (2:3). This strong language is repeated later when the failure to tithe is seen as robbery (3:8), in a question-answer sequence this time preceded by a strong denunciation (3:5–7).

In fact, this third chapter strikes a new and dramatic note as God announces the coming of a final messenger who will precede the Lord's coming. There is a certain ambiguity about whether it is the messenger's coming or God's coming that provokes the rhetorical questions "But who can endure the day of his coming, and who can stand when he appears?" (3:2). The messenger clearly does more than bear messages, however. Images of refining precious metals are used. In the epilogue, the messenger is actually named as the prophet Elijah (4:5). The mentioning of Moses (4:4) as representing the Law and Elijah as representing the prophets effectively concludes this section of the Bible. The New Testament writers picked up on this, referring it to John the Baptist (Matthew 11:7–15; 17:10–13; Mark 6:14–16) as the fulfillment of certain messianic expectations, and placing Moses and Elijah with Jesus at his transfiguration (Matthew 17:1–8).

One of the few passages spoken by Malachi (3:16) contains the image of "a book of remembrance." Messages are not only about being given, but also about being remembered (see 4:4). Those who remain faithful to the covenant become their own remembered message. The image becomes magnified in the later eschatological language of Revelation 20:12; 21:27, though the reference in Exodus 32:32 shows how old the image is.

CHARACTER

Malachi   Either the real name or the pen-name of the prophet who more than most prophets stands aside to let God argue his case with people and priests. He is almost anonymous in the lack of references here or elsewhere in the Bible, but he has a strong sense of the messenger, as both transparent transmitter of message and yet one able to command reverence as a truth teller and announcer of the truth.

Mark

Authorship

The four Gospels all have similar titles, beginning with "The Gospel according to. . . ." This standardization shows that the titles do not stem from the authors but were added at a later stage, when the early churches collected the four Gospels (see GOSPEL [GENRE]) in one collection. At that time the tradition held that Mark had been the author of the present book.

A person called John Mark appears several times in Acts as a traveling companion of Barnabas and Paul (Acts 12:25; 13:5, 13; 15:36–39). Paul mentions him in Colossians 4:10, 2 Timothy 4:11, and Philemon 24, and Peter in 1 Peter 5:13. The latter reference suggests that Mark had joined Peter in Rome. John Mark's mother owned a house in Jerusalem where the disciples met (Acts 12:12). The fact that Mark probably lived in Jerusalem led some to think that the anonymous young man in Mark 14:51–52 is Mark himself, but there is no evidence to support this idea.

The early church unanimously said that this gospel had been written by Mark. Although he was not one of the 12 close pupils of Jesus, as first Paul's traveling companion and later a member of Peter's group he was certainly in a good position to tell the story of Jesus. Early in the second century Papias says that Mark wrote down Peter's preaching. Although there is no hard evidence for the traditional attribution, there are no convincing arguments against it. The alternative is to think of this gospel as an anonymous text. Even those who deny Mark's role in writing the text continue to use his name in order to distinguish this gospel from the other three.

Date and Readership

None of the four Gospels was written immediately after the lifetime of Jesus. Initially the people who believed in him had plenty of oral traditions available. Only when the movement Jesus had started became more mature did some early Christians seriously start to record the tradition in writing. The suggested dates for Mark's gospel range from 40 to 70 C.E. There is nothing in the text that requires a dating beyond that year. As Mark's book was probably used by Matthew and Luke, a relatively early date is likely. This use is also the earliest evidence for its existence.

Literary Style

Although Mark probably expected that his book would be used by many churches, the tradition says that he wrote it in Rome. This is confirmed by the presence of several Latinisms in his language and by the relative lack of attention to the Hebrew Bible. The use of Latinisms also reveals another characteristic of this book, its colloquial, even simple, language.

In terms of structure, Mark's favorite device is to interrupt a short story with another story line, which is only apparently unrelated to the first story. The good reader is supposed to understand the connections between the two. The resulting A B A' form is known under such names as *sandwich*, *framing*, and *interpolation*.

Mark was probably the first person who wrote a gospel. In time, his book was used by the other evangelists as well as by the later church. Evidence for the use of Mark by Matthew and Luke is, for example, the fact that the latter two never both deviate from Mark's order of events. Also, in the frequent cases in which a narrative in Mark is longer than the parallel in the other two, it is more natural to explain the shorter versions of Matthew and Luke as abbreviations of Mark's story than the opposite (cf. Mark 5:1–20 with Matthew 8:28–34 and Luke 8:26–39).

Mark is the one evangelist to use the word *gospel* ("good news") in the first line of his text. Hence the title came to be used for all four descriptions of the life of Jesus and developed into the designation of the genre.

Unlike the other evangelists, Mark has not tried to arrange the teaching of Jesus in any recognizable way. The gospel rather gives the impression of a chronological report of his ministry. As in the other gospels, there is much dialogue, the style of which does not differ much from its contexts. This is probably the result of the fact that the spoken word was translated into Greek from the Aramaic.

Themes

Among the themes in this gospel, perhaps the main one, is the issue of Jesus' identity. Throughout the author suggests that Jesus is a human being but also more (see JESUS CHRIST). He gives insights into the struggles of Jesus' contemporaries as they had to make up their minds regarding him. It is no exaggeration to say that this gospel is a drama of mistaken identity. A subtheme is the negative reception of Jesus by both friend (see TWELVE DISCIPLES) and foe.

SYNOPSIS

Section I: Jesus in Galilee (1:1–8:21)

The opening scene (1:1–13) consists of four elements, the first of which is a quote from Scripture, followed by brief reports on the ministry of JOHN THE BAPTIST, the baptism of Jesus, and the temptation of Jesus in the desert. When John disappears from the scene after his arrest, Jesus begins his public life by announcing the arrival of the KINGDOM OF GOD (KINGDOM OF HEAVEN) (1:14–15). Having called four Galilean fishermen to be his followers, he speaks in the SYNAGOGUE of Capernaum. This is followed by a series of miracle stories that take place in and around the city of Capernaum, relating to a possessed person, Simon Peter's mother-in-law, a multitude of people, a person with leprosy, and a paralytic who is lowered through the roof of the house where Jesus is teaching (2:1–12). In summary notes the evangelist tells that Jesus did not want demons to make his identity known (1:34) and that he traveled through all of Galilee (1:39).

The call of Levi is followed by stories about Jesus' attitude toward the Jewish institutions of fasting and the day of SABBATH (2:18–3:6). The innovative and provocative character of his ideas causes Jewish leaders to seek his death, whereas on the other hand a large group of people follow Jesus, from whom he selects 12 core pupils. The rest of chapter 3 consists of stories about more opposition to Jesus, while chapter 4 is largely devoted to a diversity of PARABLES. The stories in chapter 5, about the stilling of a storm, the healing of a demoniac, and more miraculous healings, focus on the issue of Jesus' authority, and all take place around the SEA OF GALILEE (4:35–5:43). Despite the good things Jesus does, chapter 6 reports resistance against him as well as against his herald John the Baptist, who is even beheaded. The rest of the chapter tells about more miracles performed on and around the Sea of Galilee.

The theme of ritual purity unites the confrontation stories in 7:1–23. Following these, Jesus spends some time outside the land of Israel doing much the same things there as in his own land (7:24–8:10). The first section concludes with two short scenes that show how Jesus' opponents, the Pharisees, as well as his own pupils, fail to understand him and his God-given ministry.

Section II: Between Galilee and Jerusalem (8:22–10:52)

The middle section opens (8:22–26) and concludes (10:46–52) with the healing of a blind person. Only one more miracle story occurs in this section (9:14–29). Other key elements of this section are Jesus' repeated predictions of his approaching suffering, death, and resurrection (8:31–33; 9:1, 30–32; 10:32–34, 45), and the repeated notes that indicate his journey from Galilee in the north of

Israel to JERUSALEM in the south (8:27; 9:30, 33; 10:1, 17, 32, 46). Important scenes draw attention to Jesus' true identity, which is now recognized by some (8:27–30 and 9:2–13).

The second half of the section focuses on the countercultural values of the kingdom of God. A radical attitude toward sin is encouraged (9:42–49), a radical condemnation of divorce and adultery follows suit (10:1–12), and the danger of richness is exposed (10:17–31). The desire to be served rather than to serve is the subject of radical criticism (10:35–45) that culminates in Jesus' saying (verse 45) that he came to serve and to die. Several scenes in this section refer to children: Jesus sets them up as examples of good treatment of all people (9:33–37) and as persons not to be tempted to sin, before he blesses a group of children in 10:13–16.

Section III: Jesus in Jerusalem (Chapters 11–16)
In this section the flow of events is more coherent than previously. Jesus finally enters Jerusalem

Jesus's entry into Jerusalem (Mark 11:11), woodcut by Albrecht Dürer

about a week before the important Jewish festival of PASSOVER, and his arrival is one of triumph. The next day he throws all commercial activity out of the temple of God (11:15–19). Moments earlier he had cursed a fig tree for not bearing fruit, and the next morning the tree has already died. Jesus' adversaries are offended by his words and deeds (verse 18), and this leads to a series of hostile confrontations in the temple area: His authority to act as he does is disputed (11:27–33), and he tells a final parable to expose their wickedness, but he is attacked by the Pharisees (12:13–17), the Sadducees (12:18–27), and one of the scribes (12:28–34). This sequence of exchanges ends with the editorial comment that "no one dared to ask him any question" anymore (34), and Jesus regains the initiative with more confrontational sayings (12:35–44). Verses 13:1–2 act as a transitional passage in which the confrontations in the temple area come to a close and the attention shifts to future events. The rest of chapter 13 is one long teaching session on events to come (see LAST THINGS).

With 14:1–2 events start to accelerate because Jesus' main enemies decide that he has to die. An anonymous woman is one of the few people to be aware that Jesus is under threat, and she anoints him as an act of symbolic preparation for his burial. In contrast, one of the TWELVE DISCIPLES, Judas, decides to help Jesus' enemies and offers to betray him at a suitable moment. Jesus is still able to celebrate the Passover festival with his close followers, and he changes the meaning of the ritual so that from that time on it refers to his death and becomes an institution for his later followers (14:22–25). He foretells that all his present followers, including the passionate Peter, will forsake him. The first fulfillment of this prediction soon takes place when Jesus prays in a lonely garden at night while his close friends cannot even stay awake to pray with him (14:32–42). But worse, when a band of adversaries arrives to capture him, all his friends flee and leave Jesus alone.

The trial against Jesus fails to find an accusation against him that would warrant the death penalty. However, Jesus helps his judges by frankly claiming that he is God's long expected representative (14:61–62), something that so far in this gospel had

Agony in the garden (Mark 13:32–42), woodcut by
Albrecht Dürer

not been said with quite such openness and solic-
its the charge of blasphemy. The Roman governor
PILATE reluctantly agrees with the death penalty
pronounced by the court. Even on the cross Jesus
is still pestered by his adversaries as well as by two
criminals who are crucified with him, but he dies
relatively soon (15:25–37).

Because the Jewish day of rest is approaching,
Jesus is quickly buried in the presence of some
women. But when women revisit the tomb on the
morning after the day of rest, they find it open and
empty. An angel tells them that Jesus has been
raised from the dead (16:1–8).

COMMENTARY

Mark tells the story of Jesus in direct, forceful language. He includes relatively long stories and a limited quantity of teaching by Jesus. The gospel is
action-packed and often uses the word *immediately*
("at once") to connect scenes. Another indication
of rapid movement is the fact that many phrases

begin with the conjunction *and,* which is not normally translated into English. Likewise invisible in
most translations is the frequent use of the historic
present, i.e., the telling of the ancient story in the
present tense, which also adds to the vivid character. The colloquial character of language and style
matches the types of people who join Jesus in this
story: They are mainly ordinary persons such as
fishermen, women (who in those days were seen as
inferior to men), and outcasts such as lepers, tax
collectors, and other sinners.

The narrator in this story is omniscient. He is
external to the events and never appears in the
story itself. At the outset he reveals who Jesus is
in his opinion, the Christ (Messiah) and the Son
of God (1:1, 11). The book's leading question is
whether the characters in the story will agree with
the narrator. As presented by Mark, Jesus' public
life is characterized by conflicts with his relatives
and fellow inhabitants of NAZARETH (3:21, 30–35;
6:1–5), his followers (8:14–21), the Jewish authorities (e.g., 3:1–6; 8:11–13; chapter 12) and the powers of evil (1:12–13, 21–27; 5:1–13; 9:14–29). They
all somehow fail to recognize or to acknowledge
Jesus for who he is. The powers of evil do recognize
Jesus as "the Holy one of God" (1:24, cf. 1:34; 5:7),
but the value of that recognition is limited because
they do not submit to him voluntarily. However,
that acknowledgment does point the reader to the
fact that true insight is supernaturally given.

The second half of chapter 1 contains exact
indications of time that suggest that the short episodes that we find here may already have belonged
together in the oral tradition that Mark inherited.
Only in the final chapters does the evangelist again
indicate days and hours. The absence of exact data
in the rest of the text means that it is impossible to
determine how long Jesus' ministry lasted. The text
creates the suggestion that it was no more than a
year, but see at John (gospel).

Section I: Jesus in Galilee (1:1–8:21)
The powerful opening scene is sandwiched between
two occurrences (verses 1 and 15) of the word *gospel,* which is often translated as "good news." The
word is deliberately used in many different ways; it
can refer to the message preached by Jesus, to the

message about him as preached by the church, and to the rest of the gospel book that follows.

Mark says he is quoting the prophet Isaiah (1:2), but he combines the words of that prophet with those of the minor prophet Malachi, which was a usual practice at the time. He then describes in brief strokes the career of John the Baptist, Jesus' forerunner, who baptizes large numbers of Jews. These Jews all go through the water of the RIVER JORDAN, which reminds the reader of the passing of the Jews through the Jordan into the promised country under the leadership of Joshua. Thus the biblically literate reader knows that something new is about to take place. The expectation is heightened by the frequent mentioning of the wilderness (verses 3, 4, 12, 13), which in the Hebrew Bible stands for a place of preparation (e.g., for Moses and for the people of Israel).

At the BAPTISM of Jesus, God declares aloud what the readers will have to discover for themselves: Jesus is his beloved Son. The words spoken are based on Genesis 22:2, Psalm 2, and Isaiah 42:1, and at the end of the story they are echoed by those of the Roman officer (15:39). Another inclusion is formed by the tearing of heaven (1:10) and that of the temple curtain (15:38) to symbolize the new, direct relationship between God and humanity.

In contrast to Mark's style later on, the description of Jesus' stay in the desert is very brief. The number (see NUMBERS, SIGNIFICANCE OF) of 40 days recalls the period that Israel spent in the desert, suggesting that Jesus is tested as the people of Israel were (Deuteronomy 8:2, 16). The note about John's imprisonment (1:14) is proleptic and serves to clear the way for the sole ministry of Jesus. His message focuses on the KINGDOM OF GOD (KINGDOM OF HEAVEN), which can be defined as the fact that God controls the whole world. The power of this message is confirmed by the fact that people are willing to give up their ordered lives and to follow Jesus as he travels round.

The rest of this section has few explicit structural markers and in all kinds of ways emphasizes the radical newness of what Jesus does and represents in comparison to the prevalent religion. The responses to Jesus' first miracle—amazement, fear, unbelief, and rumors—are typical of the gospel as

a whole (1:21–28). Whereas the dark power that lives in the man who is healed (see SATAN) recognizes who Jesus is, most humans typically fail to do so. Summaries in 1:32–34 and 38–39 serve to suggest that Jesus performed many similar miracles throughout Galilee. These two summaries sandwich a passage that indicates that Jesus derived his special power from intense PRAYER.

Miracle stories such as 1:40–45 highlight the enormous publicity Jesus generated. He is, nonetheless, unhappy with this attention as the people go to him for the wrong reason: They do not want to hear his message about God but only to see his spectacular acts. But the miracles were not meant as aims in themselves! Jesus' touching the leper opposes the letter of the Law (Leviticus 13, esp. 45–46; this theme will be developed in Mark 7:1–23). But whereas a normal human would become unclean by touching a leper, with Jesus it is the other way around: His holiness is contagious! He does, however, instruct the man to obey the command that a cleaned leper should report to a priest (Leviticus 14).

The miracle story in 2:1–12 emphasizes the close connection between Jesus' words and his deeds: He does not just speak about a new beginning but actually makes it possible. Village houses at the time (verse 4) were small so that they soon filled with people, and they had flat roofs. In the biblical worldview there is not always a link between sin and illness as there seems to be in the case of this particular person; see also John 9. The story of the call of Levi continues the theme of sin and forgiveness; in both stories Jewish leaders publicly disagree with Jesus' open approach. The saying in 2:17 that the sick, not the healthy, are in need of a doctor is probably based on a generally known proverb.

More hostile confrontations are found in the subsequent stories. In the Hebrew Bible a few days of fasting—abstention from food for religious reasons—were ordained (Zechariah 8:19), but in the time of Jesus their number had been increased to twice a week by zealous Jews (Luke 18:12). In a few pithy sayings Jesus claims that he in his own person constitutes a true new beginning for the Jewish religion (2:19–22), as he subsequently claims to be Lord over the SABBATH, the most important of all religious institutions and a matter of national pride. The logic of Jesus' answer in 2:25–28 is that if King David was forgiven for disobeying the law, Jesus with his even greater authority can surely afford to do so.

In 3:1–6 the focus of interest is on the fact that the miraculous healing takes place on the Sabbath, and on the Pharisees' decision to kill Jesus out of anger. The Herodians were supporters of HEROD Antipas (6:14) and his dynasty. In striking contrast to the hatred of the leaders is the devotion to Jesus of large crowds, even from outside Israel's borders, and, in particular, of the 12 people whom he selects as his special followers and pupils (3:7–19).

Mark 3:20–35 is another sandwich: Teaching on Satan is enclosed by the story of the encounter between Jesus and his close family. His family is as critical of Jesus (verse 21) as are his enemies (verse 22)—but he dissociates himself from them all. The author underlines this by designating Jesus' family as "those outside," in contrast to the crowd inside.

The block of teaching in chapter 4 is placed at the heart of the first section of the gospel. The parables that Jesus tells focus on the mystery of the kingdom of God, first mentioned in 1:14–15, which with Jesus is both present and future, to be grasped with hands and yet far away (4:11–12). Despite the special teaching they receive (4:10, 33), the disciples completely fail to understand that Jesus is more than an ordinary human being and can be trusted in every situation (4:40–41).

The story of the healing of the possessed man (5:1–20) is an immediate answer to the question who Jesus is (4:41), God's powerful representative. This long story is full of vivid details. Jews do not eat pork, and so it has been suggested that the large herd of pigs that is destroyed was bred as food provision for the Romans; seen in this light Jesus' destruction of the herd was an act of patriotism. The next episode continues the theme of Jesus' power. It takes the form of another interpolation, the most obvious of Mark's framings: the story about the raising of the dead upper-class girl encloses that of the giving of new life to an older lower-class woman (5:21–24—5:25–34—5:35–43). The affectionate description *daughter* (34) is meant to reassure to the fearful woman.

The cycle of apparent success stories comes to an end in chapter 6, which tells that in his parental town of Nazareth Jesus cannot work miracles through the unbelief of the inhabitants. However, Mark's words in verse 5 that Jesus was powerless and performed "only a few miracles" are mildly ironic. The saying in verse 4 is a variation on a popular maxim.

The next paragraph reports events in reverse order: from the idea that John the Baptist is alive again via the story of his violent death to that of his imprisonment (6:14–29). By placing the story about the murder of Jesus' fellow prophet by the king (see HEROD) here, Mark suggests that the message of Jesus is being heard and resisted in much the same way as that of John had been. The logical conclusion is that Jesus, too, is at risk from enemies so that the story points forward to his death. The moving story of the beheading itself shows what a good narrator Mark is. It evokes the story about the prophet Elijah, the strong wife Jezebel, and the weak husband Ahab in the Hebrew Bible (1 Kings 21). Yet however demonic the queen is, the king is personally responsible for what happened at his banquet, says verse 17.

The next story, about another meal (6:30–44), may have been placed here for the sake of deliberate contrast. In a pastoral setting Jesus cares for a large number of people. The reference to green grass (verse 39) suggests springtime. Mark offers no explanation of what Jesus actually did to multiply the food. The sequence of the verbs in verse 41 (*take, bless, break, give*) makes the story a pre-echo of the Lord's Supper (14:22). Some interpreters also find a deeper meaning in the numbers (5, 2, 12 and 5,000), but to others they are just historical figures that occur in the other three gospels as well. The Greek text of verse 44 makes it clear that all 5,000 people were males; this ties in with their sitting "in groups" (39), which has military overtones. The story about Jesus' walking on the water takes place in the same area and combines the two themes of his identity and the disciples' inadequate reactions. In contrast, the inhabitants of Gennesaret and surroundings respond with faith and openness to Jesus (6:53–56). In this episode healing and salvation are near equivalents.

The confrontations in 7:1–23 are sparked off by Jewish authorities who have traveled north from Jerusalem, an ominous portent of Jesus' fate. Whereas in verses 1–13 it is the scribes who undermine the Law, in the rest of the passage the roles are reversed.

It seems that Jesus wanted his trip north of the border (7:24–8:10; cf. earlier trips abroad in 3:8 and 5:1–20) to be unnoticed (verse 24), but he was recognized and subsequently did similar things there as in Israel. The second feeding miracle (8:1–10) is not a mere repetition of the first but differs from it in many details. Its meaning is picked up in 8:20–21, sandwiching some reports about exchanges with the Jewish leaders. The first section of the gospel ends with a hurl of questions, most of them rhetorical, which symbolize the gross deficiency of the disciples' understanding up to this point. It seems that Jesus' career is going to end in total failure.

Section II: Between Galilee and Jerusalem (8:22–10:52)

As we saw in the Synopsis, this section as a whole is sandwiched between two stories of healing blind men. These two men act as foils for Jesus' disciples and for all other characters in the story: Whereas the former regain their sight and see, the latter are blind to who Jesus really is.

Two important scenes, both set in the far north of the country (8:27–30 and 9:2–13), draw attention to Jesus' identity. For the first time Peter realizes that Jesus is the Messiah (8:29), but he cannot accept Jesus' announcement of his suffering (8:30–32). The word *Messiah* stood for everything the Jews expected God to do for them in his future, but they expected a human to take this role, and Jesus refuses to fit this mold. In the second scene Jesus reveals his glory to three of the disciples in order to make clear that the Messiah is a divine rather than a human being, but they cannot accept this either (cf. 9:10, 19, 32).

The episode sandwiched between these two scenes offers another corrective to popular messianic expectations. It argues that, at least initially, the Messiah will not be successful and triumphant; he will suffer and even die. These corrections to

the popular picture obviously made it much harder for the majority of the people to see Jesus as the fulfillment of their expectations.

It cannot be a coincidence that the last miracle story in the gospel—with the exception of that of the second blind man—occurs immediately after these scenes (9:14–29). A new phase in Jesus' life has begun, and from now on the gospel will concentrate on his teaching, often given only to the disciples. Thus the remainder of chapter 9 is a loose collection of Jesus' teaching about discipleship. Verses 44 and 46 are missing in the best manuscripts and thus probably not original. The imagery in verse 49 is that of sacrifices in the temple, but with the worshippers in the role of sacrifices; it means that total dedication to Jesus will cause suffering. In verse 50, however, salt is used in a different way, in its conserving role. This shows that Mark has gathered originally distinct sayings of Jesus together.

The geographical note in 10:1 is unclear to modern readers, but it implies that Jesus is still on his way to Jerusalem. His teaching on divorce is much stricter than that of his contemporaries and stricter even than that of the Hebrew Bible (Deuteronomy 24:1–4). As before, the disciples receive private explanation of Jesus' words (10:10–12, 23–27). This part of chapter 10 makes much use of the idea of the kingdom of God. Whereas the Gospel of Luke has much to say about money and possessions, Mark's only contribution to the topic is found in 10:17–31.

As the previous two predictions are, Jesus' third prediction of his suffering is followed by a contrasting story about failing disciples (10:32–34, 35–45). Verse 45 draws on Isaiah 53:10–12, which speaks about the vicarious suffering of God's servant; Jesus clearly identifies himself as this servant and declares that he will die in order to pay for the sins of humanity (see SALVATION). This profound declaration completes his teaching of the disciples.

In all likelihood Jesus and the disciples now join the crowds of pilgrims on their way to the Passover festival in Jerusalem. Jericho was the final town on the route; from there they had to climb up to Jerusalem. The previously blind Bartimaeus (10:46) was probably well known to Mark and his readers, so that his name was preserved; usually those healed in the Gospels are anonymous.

Section III: Jesus in Jerusalem (Chapters 11–16)

Readers then and now would expect that as God's long-awaited Messiah, Jesus would be received with open arms in the capital city of Israel. And indeed the multitude that arrives with him treats him as a king by spreading their cloaks and palm branches on the road (11:7–8), and they hail him as "the one who comes in the name of the Lord" to restore the kingdom of his ancestor, David (11:9–10). Their exclamation *Hosanna* is an expression of praise, which Luke has rendered with "glory" (Luke 19:38).

But as the story of the last week of Jesus' life unfolds, we hear little more about these people. They are still around to protect Jesus (11:32; 12:12, 37), but they do not actively take his case forward. On the other hand, the Jewish leaders still hate Jesus, and it is they who move first by arresting him at night (chapter 14). Once Jesus has thus been shown powerless, the crowd can easily be convinced to choose against him and in favor of the release of the criminal Barabbas (15:6–11). The best explanation for this change of opinion is that they had expected Jesus to be a political king who would somehow bring the Roman occupation to an end. His failure to do this was such a disappointment to them that they were easily turned against him. Yet from the fact that Jesus entered the city not on a camel or on horseback but on a donkey (11:7; cf. Zechariah 9:9), they could have known that he never had any political or military intentions in the first place: Donkeys were symbolic of humility and are unsuitable for warfare. Other passages from the Hebrew Bible that influenced the story about Jesus' entry are Psalms 24; 118:25–26.

The two episodes about the cursing of the fig tree and its stunning effect (11:12–14, 20–25) are intertwined with the three-part narrative about Jesus' presence in the temple (verses 11, 15–19, 27). In the middle part Jesus attacks the traders in the temple and throws them out in order to reclaim it for a purer worship of God. In doing this he enacts prophetic texts such as Zechariah 14:21b, Malachi 3:1–5, and Ezekiel 37:26–28. The curs-

ing of the fig tree is unique among the signs Jesus performed as being purely negative; it is an acted parable to illustrate God's coming judgment. In the books of the prophets and in popular thinking the fig tree is a metaphor of Israel (Jeremiah 8:13; 24; Hosea 9:10, 16). In his explanatory words Jesus encourages his followers to expect great things from God (11:22–24).

The subsequent episodes apparently also take place in the temple (see 13:1), and they focus on confrontations with the Jewish leaders. In 12:10–11 we once more meet with usage of Psalm 118, this time of verses 22–23. In the language Jesus spoke, Aramaic, these words may have included a wordplay on *eben* (stone) and *ben* (son). Some of the topics discussed in the temple are political, as in 12:13–17; others are entirely religious, as in 12:18–27, which shows Jesus' attitude toward life after death. The Jewish belief in life after death had increased since the time of the Hebrew Bible, but the Sadducees, mentioned only here in Mark, had not embraced it. In his parable about the vineyard and in his other teaching, Jesus openly attacks the lack of faith of the Jewish leaders and announces God's judgment on them.

The summary of God's commandments that Jesus gives in 12:28–34 is not unlike what contemporary Jewish teachers said, according to Jewish writings (the Mishna). Chapter 13:1–2 is a transitional passage that equally brings the preceding exchanges in the temple to a conclusion as it prepares the way for the rest of chapter 13, which takes its cue from the destruction of the temple.

As in section I, this discourse of Jesus (chapter 13) occurs in the middle of the present section (cf. chapter 4). It is one long speech about the future in apocalyptic terms (see LAST THINGS), delivered in answer to comments from a pupil about the beauty of the temple. The tone of the speech is one of warning against persecution, idleness, and temptations. What is less clear, however, is which part of the discourse refers to the events leading up to and including the destruction of Jerusalem and the temple by the Romans in the year 70 C.E., and which part relates to events that mark the end of time. Although interpreters are divided, we would think that verse 24 marks the transition from the one topic to the other, as verses 24–27 must refer to the second coming of Christ. The enthronement of the Son of Man that is described here stems from Daniel 7:13. The "desolating sacrilege" (verse 14) is also from Daniel (9:27 and 11:31) and refers to the institution of pagan sacrifices on the altar in the temple. This kind of defilement of the temple happened in 70 C.E. Later historians tell that the Christians fled the destruction of Jerusalem by virtue of heeding Jesus' warning in verses 15–19.

It is quite likely that Jesus' prediction of the destruction of the temple in this discourse was the major factor in the decision of the Jewish leaders finally to get rid of him, which Mark reports immediately afterward (14:1–2). They may have misunderstood him—willfully or not—as saying that he was personally going to destroy the temple (cf. 14:58).

Amid the darkness and gloom of this last week of Jesus' life, the story of a woman's devoted love for him stands out as a bright spot. John 12:1–8 identifies the woman as Mary from Bethany. What she does is in sharpest contrast with Judas' betrayal of his friend and master, which follows immediately.

Despite the circumstances Jesus and his disciples celebrate the Passover meal for which they had traveled to Jerusalem; this was a long-standing Jewish custom (Exodus 12; Deuteronomy 16:1–8). Jesus probably celebrated a day earlier than most other people, on Thursday night, probably because he was aware of events to come. His institution of the sacrament of the meal (14:22–25; see LORD'S SUPPER) in remembrance of him at this moment is the counterpart of the sacrament of baptism at the beginning of his public career. Both ceremonies are meant to involve his followers physically in his achievement.

Jesus' blunt prediction at the table that all disciples will desert him meets with Peter's usual boldness (14:26–31), which makes his actual denial of Jesus all the more tragic. The story of the actual denial (14:66–72), even sealed by Peter with an oath, is sandwiched between the two trials before the Jewish and Roman authorities.

Mark does not explain why after the meal Jesus went to the lonely Garden of Gethsemane to pray, but Luke 21:37 shows that during his ministry in Jerusalem, Jesus always left the city at night. It appears that he did this in full consciousness that the garden would provide his enemies with the best possible opportunity to catch him out of sight of the multitudes, who could have protected him (verses 41–42), and during the night before the official Passover festival. The story of his prayer in the garden provides insight into his relationship with God, whom he addresses as *Abba*, "Father." It also shows that Jesus voluntarily sacrificed his life.

Mark's description of Jesus' double trial emphasizes his innocence: He is killed for merely religious reasons. As the hearing by the Jewish council (Sanhedrin) during the night had no legal status, the Roman governor had to pronounce the death penalty. The connection between the questions about the temple and Jesus' role as Messiah is that the Jews expected the Messiah to build a new temple. Thus, in reply to the unnamed high priest, Jesus declares for the first time in this gospel that he is the Messiah. Although claiming to be the Messiah (verse 62a) was not an offense in the Jewish religion, claiming to be seated at the right hand of God ("the Power," verse 62b) was. Jesus' words are based on Daniel 7:13 and Psalm 110:1. During the rest of the proceedings Jesus is remarkably silent (15:4–5).

Chapter 15 contains a string of timings: daybreak (verse 1), nine o'clock (25), noon (33), three o'clock (34), and evening (42). The Roman governor PILATE (26–36 C.E.) has Jesus flogged (verse 15), a severe physical punishment in its own right and unwarranted in the situation. He may have done this to elicit pity for Jesus. Purple (verse 17) was the imperial color. The fact that Jesus is described as "king of the Jews" by Pilate (verse 12), the Roman soldiers (verse 18), the inscription over his head on the cross (verse 26), and the mocking bystanders (verse 32) is full of irony: Without realizing it, from the perspective of the narrator, these people all speak the truth that Jesus is the king, crucified by his own people. In 15:24, 29 and 34 there are allusions to Psalm 22.

Mark's description of Jesus' suffering on the cross is very restrained. Most attention goes to Jesus' interaction with the two men crucified with him and to the verbal abuse Jesus suffers. The centurion, a Roman commanding officer, on the other hand, is given the correct knowledge of Jesus' identity: He is the Son of God! His confession forms an INCLUSIO around the narrative with the words of God in 1:11. It also forms a striking contrast with the preceding verse, which tells about the tearing of the curtain in the temple in such a direction—from top to bottom—that human hands could not have done it. The exclusive character of the Jewish religion is ended when God himself tears the temple open and a Roman officer understands better than the other characters who Jesus actually is (15:38–39).

The introduction of the women in 15:40–41 serves as a preparation for their role in the final passage of the gospel. Only now Mark tells the readers about the important role they had played earlier in Jesus' life. The story of Jesus' burial serves to show that he was really dead.

As can be seen in the earliest manuscripts, Mark's text ends in a very abrupt way: "and they said nothing to anyone, for they were afraid" (16:8). No wonder devout scribes missed a convincing statement of the Resurrection such as occurs in the other gospels. As a result, several additions to the text were composed that bring the story to a more "acceptable" end in the form of post-Resurrection appearances of Jesus. Thus we have a so-called longer ending and a shorter ending, as well as a few others. The longer ending won the day and was incorporated into the many medieval manuscripts of the gospel. From there it made its way into translations such as the Authorized (King James) Version, with verse numbers 16:9–20. This ending, however, is probably a compilation of the final parts of the other three gospels, Matthew, Luke, and John, written after the Church had accepted all four Gospels as authoritative.

For a long time scholars thought that 16:8 was not the original closure of the gospel and that a piece of text had been lost, however unlikely that would be for a text that was soon highly regarded and used by Matthew and Luke. Both grammatically and theologically verse 8 seemed unacceptable as a conclusion. More recently, however, opinions have changed, and it is now believed that the original author did mean 16:8 to be his final word.

Parallels have been found for the unusual grammar of the verse, and increased understanding of Mark's literary strategy suggests that this is just a last touch of irony. Throughout the gospel the TWELVE DISCIPLES (see below) had failed to understand the deeper meaning of events. At the same time, the earliest readers knew that the message of the Resurrection had been spread by the same women and disciples regardless.

CHARACTERS

crowd, the   From the beginning Jesus attracts a large following (1:33, 37, 45; 2:4, 13; 3:7–9), and we can speak about a mass movement. But their behavior is totally unpredictable, in part because their expectations of Jesus are not fulfilled. They threaten to overrun him (3:9; 4:1; 5:24) and prevent him from eating (3:20). They do become very excited by his powerful miracles (7:37). Jesus' attitude is one of compassion (6:34), but he does keep his distance (1:35, 45; 3:7; 4:36; 6:31). Their behavior in the final week of his life is particularly volatile: On the Sunday they hail him as the king of Israel (11:7–10) and accept his message (11:18; 12:37). The Jewish leaders cannot arrest Jesus for fear of the crowd (12:12), but by the end of the week they desert him and let themselves be stirred by their leaders to prefer the murderer Barabbas to him (15:11).

Some minor characters are presented as particular examples of faith, such as the leper (1:40–45), Jairus (5:22–23), the bleeding woman (5:25–34), Bartimaeus (10:46–52), and the Roman officer (15:39).

disciples, the   On the positive side, it is to the disciples' credit that they follow Jesus early on and with much enthusiasm and dedication (1:18, 20; 2:14). They also accomplish a mission in accordance with Jesus' instructions (6:7–13). On the whole, however, Mark's description of them is quite negative. He repeatedly shows their lack of understanding and faith (4:35–41; 6:45–51; 8:14–21; 14:50), and this is, in fact, a theme that holds the whole book together. Who Jesus was only became clear when his life culminated on Calvary and in his resurrection from the tomb three days later. Yet the disciples were with Jesus early (1:16–20; 2:13; 3:13–19), and they had often been taught by him (4:10, 34; 7:17–23; 8:27–30), so they should have understood him much sooner. Mark indicates that three of them, Peter, John, and James, formed a kind of inner circle (5:37; 9:2; 14:33; cf. 13:3)— but they also receive the severest criticism (8:33; 9:5–6; 10:35–41; 14:26–31, 66–72).

From a literary perspective, the disciples serve as a foil for the readers who live after the key events of cross and Resurrection, and their stumbling helps the readers to consider the right interpretation of Jesus for themselves. The reader could be like a member of the crowd who recognizes Jesus immediately just moments after his disciples have failed to do so (6:49, 54).

Jesus Christ   After the explicit opening phrase of his gospel, Mark emphasizes what Jesus does rather than who he is: He is a traveling teacher who heals and performs other miracles, proclaims the coming of the kingdom of God, and is admired by nearly everybody. Jesus is also an example of servant-shaped leadership. Much emphasis falls on the miracles Jesus performs, as they show his special power and as such point to his divine authority. They serve as signs that the kingdom of God has come.

Most people in this gospel fail to recognize that Jesus is not only the expected Messiah of the Jews but also the Son of God. And it is indeed a paradox that the Son of God appears in humility, weakness, and suffering. The confession of his divinity is only made by the demonic forces that confront him (3:11; 5:7) and by the Roman officer at the cross (15:39); in addition, God (1:11) and Jesus himself (14:61–62) make this claim. See also JESUS CHRIST.

Mark   As noted, the name *Mark* was attached to this anonymous text by the later church. See further Authorship and Literary Style above.

opponents, Jesus'   Although Mark mentions Herodians and Sadducees as adversaries of Jesus, the most frequently mentioned are "teachers of the law" and the Pharisees. They remain flat characters in the story, typified by their legalism and their use of trick questions in their attacks on Jesus, which he evades in a sophisticated way (especially chapter 12). In a subtle way Mark shows that while Jesus teaches the crowds in parables, when talking with his opponents he engages in theological ideas and quotations from the Hebrew Bible, seeking to undermine their legalism.

Matthew

Authorship
The four Gospels have similar titles that begin with "The Gospel according to. . . ." This shows that the titles do not stem from the authors but were added at a later stage, when the early churches compiled the four Gospels (see GOSPEL [GENRE]) together in one collection. At that time the tradition held that Matthew had been the author of the present book.

The book itself never mentions its author; nor does it contain many clues about his identity. From the choice of subjects, the way they are dealt with, and the organization of the material in five "books" (see the Synopsis) it is likely that the author was so familiar with the Hebrew Bible that he must have been a Jew. This impression is strengthened by stylistic phenomena such as the frequent use of repetitions and of sequences of two and three, which are drawn from the Hebrew Bible.

The early church unanimously said that this gospel had been written by Matthew, one of the 12 close pupils of JESUS CHRIST. He is himself a character in one passage within the narrative (9:9–13), and he is mentioned in the list of disciples (10:3; see also Acts 1:13). Later generations have doubted Matthew's authorship, basically because they think they need to date the publication of the text after the lifetime of Jesus' close followers. Although there is no hard evidence for the traditional date, there are no convincing arguments against it. The alternative is to think of this gospel as an anonymous text. Even those who deny Matthew's role in writing it continue to use his name in order to distinguish this gospel from the other three.

Date and Readership

None of the four Gospels was written immediately after the lifetime of Jesus. Initially the people who believed in him had plenty of oral traditions available. Only when the movement Jesus had started became more mature did some early Christians seriously begin to write down the tradition. The suggested dates for Matthew's gospel range from 60 to 90 C.E. If we take the ascription to the disciple Matthew seriously, the date can hardly be after 70 C.E., and there is nothing in the text that forces us to go beyond that year.

Although some scholars argue that Matthew wrote for a specific community in Israel or Syria, concrete facts are unavailable, and it is safer to assume that the author expected that his book would be used by many churches. What is clear, though, is that this book was written for Christian believers and not primarily for people who had never heard about God and Jesus Christ. The book also presupposes knowledge of and a great respect for the Hebrew Bible; in fact, it seems to aim at Jewish Christians first and foremost.

In the early church this gospel was the most popular of the four, probably because it is eminently suitable for systematic teaching. Traces of its use are apparent from the early second century onward. As soon as lists of gospels that are accepted by the church appear, Matthew is one of the four, emphatically so in the work of the church father Irenaeus (late second century). It is probably because of its close connections with the Hebrew Bible that Matthew always appears at the head of the four Gospels.

Literary Character

This gospel is a well-ordered piece of literature in which blocks of narrative and teaching alternate. Characteristic of Matthew are the five blocks of teaching interspersed in the life story of Jesus. This number 5 will remind Jewish readers of the five books attributed to Moses, the Pentateuch. Each of these five blocks concludes with a phrase like "When Jesus had finished saying [all] these things" (7:28; 11:1; 13:53; 19:1; 26:1).

All four Gospels belong to the genre of ancient biographies, which described the lives of great men for the benefit of later generations. Ancient biographies were highly selective and were not concerned to report what were seen as irrelevant parts of their heroes' lives. That is why in this gospel after the birth narratives the story moves straight to the beginning of Jesus' public ministry without paying any attention to his childhood and adolescence. As the other gospels do, Matthew offers much dialogue, the style of which does not differ much from its contexts. This is probably the result of the fact that the spoken word was translated from the Aramaic.

This gospel is written in simple but correct Greek. There is a tradition from Bishop Papias of Hierapolis (who lived in the first half of the second century C.E.) that Matthew originally wrote in Hebrew, but the present text hardly has the hallmarks of a translated text. As can be seen in the Synopsis, Matthew often makes use of groups of three as a basic literary structure. For example, there are three cycles of 14 names in his genealogy (1:1–17) and three tableaux in his story about the birth and childhood of Jesus (1:18–25; 2:1–12; 2:13–23).

Themes

Among the themes in this gospel, perhaps the main one is the issue of the identity of Jesus. Throughout, the author suggests that Jesus is a human being but also more (see JESUS CHRIST). He gives insights into the struggles of Jesus' contemporaries as they had to make up their minds regarding him. Second, there is the kingdom of heaven; whereas the other gospels use the term *kingdom of God*, Matthew prefers this term, which avoids the use of God's name and is thus less offensive to Jews who were reluctant to pronounce God's name. In comparison to the other gospels, Matthew stands out as a book with relatively little human interest, much teaching, and detailed attention to the lifestyle of followers of Jesus.

Sources

As the Synopsis below shows, this gospel, like all gospels, is a composite text that consists of numerous short narrative units that belong to various genres such as historical stories, miracle stories (healings, exorcisms, provisions, rescues, and epiphany), pronouncement stories, independent words, parables, teaching, and personal contacts. It is likely that much of this material was transmitted orally for some time before being committed to writing. The disciplines of study form history and tradition history look at the prehistory of these units in their oral and written forms, respectively, but they do not often lead to agreed results. Redaction criticism is the discipline that studies the editorial activity of the evangelists in weaving together the small units and putting their own marks on the material.

There is basic agreement about the fact that "Matthew" must have made use of the shorter Gospel according to Mark. This verdict is based on the fact that the basic outline is very similar in both books and that nearly all of Mark can also be found in Matthew (the exceptions are Mark 1:23–28, 35–39; 4:26–29; 7:32–37; 8:22–26; 9:38–40; and 12:41–44). Put the other way around, nearly half of the material in the much longer Matthew stems from Mark. Many of the changes in vocabulary, word order, and so on that Matthew made can be explained as improvements. Mark's long stories were abbreviated, its style was enhanced, and much teaching was added.

Matthew also has numerous words of Jesus in common with the Gospel of Luke. The best explanation for this remarkable similarity is that both evangelists drew on a common source, usually called Q, which may have circulated in oral or written form. Though this source has never been recovered, many scholars are convinced that it existed. In places the similarities between Matthew and Luke are indeed impressive; for example, compare the identical passages Matthew 3:7b–10 and Luke 3:7b–9, or the near identical passages Matthew 7:3–5 and Luke 6:41–42. Q may have been a collection of words of Jesus in the style of the Hebrew Bible prophetic books, but its real extent is, of course, unknown.

Whereas in Mark and Luke Jesus' teaching is found scattered throughout the text, redaction criticism shows that Matthew has collected large bits of teaching together in his five blocks of teaching. The usefulness of redaction criticism, however, is reduced by the observation that Jesus as an itinerant teacher will have repeated the same stories and teachings at regular intervals. Conse-

quently, differences in order, setting, and phraseology among the four Gospels suggest that different versions of his words have been preserved rather than that the evangelists have tweaked the traditions available to them.

Matthew and the Hebrew Bible

Matthew often refers to the Hebrew Bible and quotes elaborately from it in order to show that in Jesus and his ministry Hebrew Bible prophecies were fulfilled. In the Hebrew Bible he has discovered many announcements of Jesus' ministry, and he pays much attention to pointing out how Jesus fulfills them all in his person and work. In certain passages even the later church comes in sight, as in 4:15–17 (quoting Isaiah 9:1–2) and 12:18–21 (quoting Isaiah 42:1–4).

A problem for modern readers is that Matthew sometimes detects prophecies where others would not see them, even in places where it seems likely that the authors of the Hebrew Bible themselves did not realize that their words were prophetic. It is important to realize that in Matthew's view prophecy is much more than seeing propositional predictions come true. His interpretation of the Scriptures is similar to that of Jewish scribes at the time as well as to that of the authors of the DEAD SEA SCROLLS, i.e., much more associative than modern approaches. In Jewish interpretation the common presence of a name or a single word can cause entire passages to be seen as closely related. Matthew sometimes understands fulfillment as finding an additional level of meaning for a Hebrew text, a technique that will have been convincing for his original audience.

Throughout his gospel Matthew emphasizes both the continuity with Israel's past and the new elements that Jesus introduced. It is one of the author's aims to show how Jesus brings the previous revelation of God to its fulfillment. This is to say, Matthew argues that the Law is not abolished but fulfilled, as the thematic passage 5:17–20 explains. Although the detailed commandments are no longer binding, the intentions of the Law are confirmed and reach to full fruition in Jesus' ministry. Christians are supposed not to ignore the Hebrew Scriptures but to read them through the lens of Jesus Christ.

SYNOPSIS

Section I: Introduction (Chapters 1–4)

Matthew begins with some introductory stories that relate Jesus' background and his miraculous birth. He then presents the person and mission of Jesus' forerunner, JOHN THE BAPTIST. Jesus himself is baptized by John before he begins his own ministry. Initially Jesus largely ministers in the north of Israel (mainly Galilee), where he concentrates on the area of the SEA OF GALILEE.

The gospel begins with a GENEALOGY of Jesus. The story of the birth of Jesus is told from the perspective of Joseph, the man who adopts Jesus as his son so that he becomes a descendant of DAVID, the great king of Israel. As representatives of the peoples of the earth, magi visit the newborn Jesus (2:1–12). These magi alert the ruthless king HEROD to his birth, and he decides to kill all young boys in the town of Bethlehem where Jesus was born, but Jesus and his parents escape to Egypt thanks to a divinely sent warning. After the death of Herod, the family of three returns to Israel and settles in NAZARETH.

Jesus' public appearance is prepared by the preaching ministry in Judea of John the Baptist, who calls on the nation of Israel to repent before the arrival of the Savior (3:1–12). Jesus himself is among those who are baptized in the RIVER JORDAN, at which occasion a voice from heaven marks him out as a very special person. He is now ready to start his own ministry, and SATAN makes an attempt to prevent him (4:1–11). Jesus returns to Galilee and moves from Nazareth to Capernaum. He begins to preach about the kingdom of heaven (4:12–17), calling his first disciples (see TWELVE DISCIPLES); men who had so far been fishers now travel the country with him (4:18–22). Matthew concludes the first part of his story with a programmatic summary of Jesus' mission: He preaches and performs MIRACLES, gaining a large following from all over the country of Israel (4:23–25).

Section II: First Block of Teaching: The Sermon on the Mount (Chapters 5–7)

The first block of teaching, presented as a sermon by Jesus, is known as the Sermon on the Mount. Jesus begins this sermon with the so-called beatitudes, in which he blesses certain types of people. He then discusses his people's task in the world, which metaphorically is to be salt, light, and a city on a hill (5:13–16), and he clarifies that the Hebrew Bible LAW is not abrogated but reaches its full purpose in him (5:17–20).

In the heart of the sermon Jesus discusses the three main elements of the Jewish religion: obedience (5:21–48), prayer and other rituals (6:1–18), and love (6:19–7:12). Under the heading of obedience he spells out what this means with respect to several specific commandments. The passage on rituals consists of three carefully structured elements, alms (6:2–4), prayer (6:5–15), and fasting (6:16–18). The core element here—which is also the core of the entire sermon—is that Jesus offers his audience a model prayer, which has become known as the LORD'S PRAYER (6:9–15).

The final part of the sermon (7:13–27) emphasizes the authority of Jesus, as claimed by him and as recognized by the world. The message of Jesus is not being successful but about following him unconditionally. Verses 7:28–29 are a comment on the impact of the sermon as a whole.

Section III: Narratives about Healings and Other Miracles (Chapters 8–9)

The Sermon on the Mount is followed by a section filled with narratives about healings and other miracles that is made up of three units (8:1–22; 8:23–

Jesus is baptized (Matthew 3:13–17), engraving by Julius Schnorr von Carolsfeld

9:17; 9:18–38) of three elements each. In total 10 miracles are recorded, most of them healings.

An interim summary (8:16–17) quotes words from the prophet Isaiah to show that Jesus was also fulfilling Scriptures when he performed miracles. In contrast to the story of a person who finds it hard to follow Jesus unconditionally (8:18–22), there is the story of Matthew, whose positive response to Jesus' call takes only moments (9:9). Well known is the story of the stilling of a storm (8:23–27), which has parallels in all other gospels, including John. The section concludes with a summary (9:35–38), which looks back to 4:23–25.

Section IV: Second Block of Teaching: The Mission Discourse (Chapter 10)

This block of teaching consists of words addressed to Jesus' followers and hinges on his and their missions in the world. It begins with a short narrative that introduces the Twelve Disciples whom Jesus selected from the larger group of his followers; they basically perform the same acts as he does so that there are more workers in the harvest (10:1–4; cf. 9:38). The structure of this section is concentric:

A Instructions for itinerant missionaries
(10:5–15)
B Troubles and family division (10:16–23)
C Jesus and disciples are called Beelzebub
(10:24–25)
D Encouragement (10:26–31)
C′ Jesus and disciples confess one another
(10:32–33)
B′ Troubles and family division (10:34–39)
A′ Reception of the missionaries (10:40–42)

Section V: Jesus the Messiah Brings Radical Change (Chapters 11–12)

As does the previous narrative section, this one consists of three groups of three paragraphs (11:2–30; 12:1–21; 12:22–50); in each the first two elements are negative in outlook, but they are followed by a positive element. The first deals with the lack of belief of John the Baptist and of the Galilean cities where Jesus ministered. The second group of three paragraphs focuses on the regulations regarding the Jewish Sabbath, and in the third the Jewish leaders again appear as Jesus' opponents.

Section VI: Third Block of Teaching: Parables of the Kingdom (Chapter 13)

The third block of teaching consists largely of PARABLES, including well-known ones such as the parable of the sower, the parable of the weeds among the grain, and the parable of the pearl. The public storytelling is interspersed with private explanations Jesus gives to his followers of the parables of the sower and of the weeds. There are also no fewer than three discussions of parables in general (13:10–17, 34, 51–52). In conclusion, Matthew tells that Jesus was rejected in his hometown of Nazareth.

Section VII: Culmination of Jesus' Galilean Ministry (Chapters 14–17)

This variegated selection of narratives does not have a strong thematic bond. The organizing principle sometimes is that of action and reaction. Jesus' ministry reaches some high points, and it can now be seen to have a clear direction: He will soon be heading toward his end in JERUSALEM and the foundation of the church afterward. Chapter 14 starts with the narrative of the death of John the Baptist. Two well-known miracles follow, the feeding of 5,000 people and Jesus' walking on water. In chapters 15 and 16 Jesus meets many people; the focus is on clashes with the Pharisees, but after 16:21 he is mostly alone with his disciples, teaching them. Peter's confession of faith (16:13–20) and the transfiguration (17:1–8) are the high points here.

Section VIII: Fourth Block of Teaching: Sin and Forgiveness (Chapter 18)

This section focuses entirely on the subjects of sin and forgiveness. It consists of two groups of three paragraphs, the first about the theme of "little ones" (18:1–14) and the second about the way in which followers of Jesus must forgive others as they are themselves forgiven (18:15–35). The parable of the unforgiving servant is a very memorable story.

Section IX: On the Way to Jerusalem (Chapters 19–22)

A summary statement (19:1–2) brings the previous section to a close and forms the transition to the narrative section in which Jesus travels to Jerusalem and, subsequently, has several exchanges with the Jewish leaders.

Jesus preaching (Matthew 19), *(The Hundred Guilder Print)* etching by Rembrandt

Jesus' teaching on divorce and marriage (19:3–12) is followed by the short episode of his blessing of the children. The moving story about the young person who cannot bring himself to follow Jesus because of his affluence is followed by related teaching on money and reward that includes the striking parable of the laborers (20:1–16).

Jesus then makes a triumphal entry into Jerusalem (21:1–11) and shows his authority by cleansing the temple. This major act of provocation leads into teaching about his authority and human obedience that includes the parable of the two sons (21:28–32), that of the tenants of the vineyard (21:33–46), and that of the wedding banquet (22:1–14). In answer to critical questioning, Jesus formulates the greatest commandment (22:34–40).

Section X: Fifth Block of Teaching: On the Future (Chapters 23–25)

Chapter 23 can be seen as concluding the confrontation of chapters 21–22 and at the same time beginning the discourse of 24–25. It is a long invective by Jesus against the Jewish leaders, especially the Pharisees, followed by a short lament over the city of Jerusalem.

Chapter 24 is one long speech that deals with the future (see LAST THINGS), delivered in answer to comments from the pupils about the beauty of the temple. The tone of the speech is one of warning, and its intention is underlined by no fewer than five subsequent parables: two short ones at the end of chapter 24 and three in chapter 25.

These three, the parable of the 10 bridesmaids, the parable of the talents, and the parable of the sheep and the goats, are among the best-known stories Jesus told.

Section XI: The Story of Jesus' Suffering, Death, and Resurrection (Chapters 26–28)

The story tells how Jesus' adversaries and his own pupil Judas play roles in the drama of Jesus' arrest, but between these two episodes it highlights how a woman shows her devotion to Jesus by preparing him for burial (26:6–13). Jesus celebrates the Passover meal with his close pupils and announces that when he is arrested, they will all desert him, including Peter, who strongly denies that possibility. After the meal Jesus goes to the Garden of

The betrayal of Jesus (Matthew 26:47–50), woodcut by Albrecht Dürer

Gethsemane, where he prays fervently that he will not have to suffer; already at this point the followers desert him by falling asleep (26:36–46). When a horde arrives sent by the Jewish leadership and arrests Jesus in the garden with the help of Judas, the other disciples flee for their lives.

Jesus is first tried before the high priest and sentenced on the accusation of blasphemy because he speaks about himself as equal to God (26:57–68). Asides report how Peter three times denies any affiliation with Jesus and how Judas commits suicide. Under strong pressure from the mob the Roman governor agrees to order the crucifixion of Jesus. All the while Jesus has been tormented (26:67; 27:26, 27–31) so that he is now too weak to carry his own cross to the place of execution (27:32). Not many details are given about Jesus' suffering on the cross, other than that he is taunted by the bystanders as well as by two criminals who are crucified at the same time. After three hours of miraculous darkness, Jesus dies (27:50).

The final episodes of the gospel are ordered concentrically:

Jesus' death and burial (27:57–61)
   The guard (27:62–66)
      The empty tomb (28:1–10)
   The guard (28:11–15)
Jesus alive and sovereign (28:16–20)

This arrangement makes the Resurrection of Jesus central in the final part of the story. Jesus is restored to life by the power of God. Fittingly, the final words of the text are spoken by him as he commissions his followers to continue his ministry in the entire world.

COMMENTARY

Section I: Introduction (Chapters 1–4)

For modern readers the beginning of this gospel is not very attractive: It is a dull genealogy. Yet from the point of view of his first readers, this was an important and clever move: Matthew shows that the life story of Jesus continues the story line of the Hebrew Bible. The very first word of the book in the original Greek, "genealogy" or "birth," is *genesis*, which is a clear allusion to the opening of the Hebrew Bible as well as to Genesis 5:1, which can

Jesus bearing the cross, woodcut by Albrecht Dürer

be translated as "the book of the genesis of Adam." The opening also cements the connection to Abraham, who would be a blessing to all nations, and to King David.

This signifies that God makes a new beginning that nevertheless is in continuity with his former revelation. At the same time the genealogy is not narrowly Jewish because four foreign women (Tamar, Rahab, Ruth, and "the wife of Uriah") are mentioned to show the inclusiveness of the community of faith even under the old dispensation.

Chapters 1 and 2 highlight Jesus' royal claims. His legal father, Joseph, is shown to be a descendant of the royal house of Israel and in particular of King David. Jesus is hailed as a king by the magi, who have followed a star of royal quality. The Roman puppet King Herod realizes that even as an infant Jesus is a serious rival, and he mercilessly tries to kill him. In these first chapters several angel appearances and dreams or nightly visions propel the story. Later on such elements are much less frequent. Between the events in chapters 1–2 and the beginning of chapter 3, many years have passed as Jesus is now an adult man.

Straight fulfillment formulas appear in 1:23 and 2:5–6, 15, 18, 23. Once the prophet quoted is identified as Jeremiah, the other cases are left to the readers. John the Baptist refers to the prophet Isaiah and quotes his words to explain his own mission as forerunner of Jesus (3:3), and the author himself includes a lengthy quote from that same prophet to justify Jesus' Galilean background. But the use of the Hebrew Bible also includes an implicit deliberate parallelism between King Herod and the pharaoh of the exodus (Exodus 1–6): Both fear for their throne, both consult magicians, and both indiscriminately kill young boys.

The relationship between Mary and Joseph is such that although they are not formally married, they have been promised to each other. In JUDAISM this type of relationship was just as binding as legal wedlock but did not involve sexual contact.

Compared to Mark, the narrative of the temptation in the desert in Matthew 4:1–11 (and in Luke) is much longer. It is a moot point whether the dialogue (see STRUCTURES, LITERARY) is internal or external. For Matthew this episode shows that Jesus is the obedient Son of God and Israel's true king. Three times (see NUMBERS, SIGNIFICANCE OF) Satan invites Jesus to do something that would diminish his reliance on God alone, but Jesus refuses. As a real human being Jesus could have fallen under these temptations, as Adam did, so they are not just an idle game. The authority of the Hebrew Bible in his life is seen in the fact that all three times he quotes it. The baptism of Jesus does not show that he, too, was sinful and needed to repent. It rather shows his total obedience to all that the Father asked him to do.

At key moments Matthew tells his audience that Jesus' teaching centered on his proclamation of the KINGDOM OF GOD (KINGDOM OF HEAVEN.) It is the last word in the passage 4:12–17, which is more or less programmatic for Jesus' ministry. The short episode 4:18–22 shows how the circle of Jesus' followers grew gradually until he selected 12 of them to be his core pupils (10:1–4; cf. Mark 3:13–15).

Section II: First Block of Teaching: The Sermon on the Mount (Chapters 5–7)

The title usually given to this section, The Sermon on the Mount, is derived from the narrative frame in which Matthew presents this speech of Jesus, which refers to his being on a mountain. Obviously, a level place on a hilltop must be in mind. Although tradition claims to know the identity of the mountain, Matthew gives no information that could help us in this regard.

Many Christians see this sermon as a kind of constitution of the kingdom of God or of the church, although others claim that national governments should also take this message to heart. Many of Jesus' requirements are strikingly radical. "If your right eye causes you to sin, tear it out and throw it away" (5:29) and "Be perfect, as your heavenly Father is perfect" (5:48) are cases in point. In that light it is hard to see how governments could be expected to abide by the entire Sermon on the Mount.

The transition from the previous section is eased by preparatory words in 4:23. In this extended sermon Jesus largely addresses those who—possibly having been followers of John the Baptist before—are already his supporters. Much of the material that is found together here appears all over Luke's gospel. It is thus often said that Matthew artificially collected together many bits and pieces of Jesus tradition. Indeed, Matthew has the clear tendency to systematize the tradition. It is also likely, though, that during his prolonged career as a teacher, Jesus frequently repeated the same ideas to different audiences, and that Matthew and Luke have recorded versions of the same teaching given at different moments.

The literary structure of the so-called beatitudes is unparalleled in the New Testament. The repetitions and parallelisms work powerfully on many readers. The word *blessed* here means "fortunate," "to be congratulated." Jesus commends a lifestyle that puts the kingship of God center stage. It is also said that the personal characteristics recommended here are those of Jesus himself.

It is no accident that the first block of Jesus' teaching contains a long passage on how his teaching relates to that of the Hebrew Bible (5:17–48).

As stated previously, Matthew is careful to show both the continuity (the same God, the same ethics) and the discontinuity (a new mediator, Jesus) between Jesus and what went before. In several ways parallels between Jesus and Moses are suggested (see Characters on page 283).

As to the details, Jesus discusses the laws against murder (5:21–26), against adultery (5:27–30), against divorce (5:31–32), about the proper use of God's name (5:33–37), and about retaliation (5:38–42) and the law of love (5:43–48). Some of his ideas are stricter than those of contemporary Judaism, such as those that relate to the absolute prohibition of adultery and divorce, and to murder. In other areas he is more lenient, to such an extent that the law of retaliation is more or less abolished.

The text of the Lord's Prayer (6:9–13) is somewhat problematic. Some older manuscripts and the Authorized (King James) Version offer a longer text that includes the words "For the kingdom and the power and the glory are yours forever. Amen." This longer version is still generally used in most churches, although the words were probably added by an early scribe.

The use of the appellation *Father* for God does not stem from the Hebrew Bible but was introduced by Jesus and adopted by the Christians (Galatians 4:6–7; Romans 8:15), as was the Lord's Prayer as a whole, which has been used in many churches around the world through the ages.

It is not easy to find a connecting theme for the passage on love (6:19–7:12). Initially Jesus talks about material possessions in what appears to be a commentary on "Your kingdom come. Your will be done" (6:19–34). He follows this with what look like commentaries on "Forgive us our debts" (7:1–6) and on "Give us this day our daily bread" (7:7–11). The concluding sentence in 7:12 is known as the "golden rule," and it harks back to 5:17 in referring to the Law and the Prophets.

An example of a chiastic structure (see POETRY, BIBLICAL) is found in chapter 7:

A   two ways of walking (13–14)
B   false prophets (15–20)
B′ false claims (21–23)
A′ two ways of building (24–27)

Section III: Narratives about Healings and Other Miracles (Chapters 8–9)

In 4:23 Matthew had told his readers that Jesus both taught and proclaimed the kingdom and performed miracles. After a section devoted to the teaching, we arrive at a section that details these miracles. The present section is at the same time the most focused of all on the deeds of Jesus. Having *spoken* with authority, Jesus now *acts* with authority in healing people of disorders such as leprosy, paralysis, and blindness.

In quick succession many healings and other miracles are reported. Matthew has shortened stories that also occur in Mark and in Luke, and he has only left skeleton versions. His aim is to show that Jesus controls the forces of nature and the dark, and that with apparently divine authority he forgives sins. It should be noted, however, that not all those who witness these displays of divine power believe in Jesus as a special person but rather remain unconvinced that he is somebody special. Themes in this section are the identity of Jesus, following him, and the necessity of faith. In addition to his unconditional helping of everybody, there is his unconditional demand that all follow him.

The pagan context of the story of the healing of two demon-possessed persons (8:28–34) is illustrated by the presence of swine in the land; to the Jews pigs were unclean. Jesus' prioritizing of human well-being over anything else is vividly illustrated by the demise of the swine. The healing of an older woman is sandwiched in the narrative of the raising up of a young girl (9:18–26). As this is also the case in Mark, tradition must have remembered that these events were related.

The final summary in the section (9:35–38) draws it all together and forms a bracket around chapters 5–9 (4:23 = 9:35); at the same time these verses introduce chapter 10 by indicating the need for more workers to spread the word of God.

Section IV: Second Block of Teaching: The Mission Discourse (Chapter 10)

The four Gospels are not very specific about when exactly Jesus called 12 of his followers to be his closest friends and allies. In the present passage Matthew assumes that the 12 are already a distinct group, but this is the only time they are listed by him. The New Testament often refers to these people as Jesus' *disciples,* meaning pupils. After they began a ministry of their own at the end of Jesus' ministry, they became known as the *apostles* ("sent ones").

Appropriately, after the listing of the disciples, the themes of the subsequent teaching are the missionary role and the authority of the disciples, both in parallel with the ministry of Jesus and at a later stage, even after Jesus had left this world. Jesus does not hide the fact that—both for the disciples and for his later followers—suffering can result from associating with him.

The structure of the section demonstrates that its main message is that there is no need to fear. It is possible that at the time when this gospel was written, the Christians were being persecuted and needed some encouragement; note that 10:26–31 resemble 6:25–34 and 7:7–11, which also fit loosely in their contexts.

Section V: Jesus the Messiah Brings Radical Change (Chapters 11–12)

After a typical transitional verse (11:1) this section contains narratives that show how radical Jesus' message was and how mixed the response of his own people. No wonder both John the Baptist and Jesus are confronted with misunderstandings and rejection. All the more shocking is it that even his precursor John the Baptist fails to understand who Jesus is. The passage consists of John's doubtful question and Jesus' answer to him, which sparks off further comments on John, the last and greatest prophet of the old dispensation. In conclusion, Jesus laments "this generation's" response to John and him (11:2–19).

A theological summit is reached at the end of chapter 11, when Jesus explicitly invites people to him (11:25–30). The way he several times addresses God as his father in this passage reminds many readers of the style of the Gospel of John. Jesus' actual invitation (11:28–30) is extended not so much to the strong as to the weak in life. A similar passage is found a little later in 12:15–21 (cf. also 9:12–13). In contrast to the legalistic Jewish leaders, Jesus, God's servant, is meek and mild, and

he cares for the weak. Likewise the end of this section contains a kind of invitation to join Jesus' true family, God's new family (12:46–50).

Section VI: Third Block of Teaching: Parables of the Kingdom (Chapter 13)

Again, the particular form of Jesus' ministry in this section is illuminated by references to the Jewish Scriptures, this time to Isaiah 6 and to Psalm 78, which is called the work of a prophet (13:35). Note that so far Matthew had not included any parables. Because of the prevailing unbelief of his people, Jesus concludes that he should teach in parabolic form rather than in straightforward terms. Thus the use of parables is Jesus' attempt to respond to the mixed reception he is receiving. He refers to his parables as "secrets" or "mysteries" (verse 11); the Greek word usually indicates an insight into the will of God that was denied to most people but granted to an elect group. Jesus justifies his mixed results and shifts his attention to the new people of God, which is forming in the midst of Israel.

The so-called parable of the sower should rather be called the parable of the seeds as it focuses on the results of the seeds sown in different places (13:1–9). Little attention is paid to the sower, who might first of all represent Jesus and then anybody who tells the world about "the kingdom" (13:18).

The parable of the weed explains why in the present time the world and even the church are mixed bodies full of "good and bad": Only "at harvest time," that is, at his return, will Jesus separate the two (see LAST THINGS).

Section VII: Culmination of Jesus' Galilean Ministry (Chapters 14–17)

So far the narrative could be said to be somewhat static, but from now on it has more direction. This section opens with the dramatic story of the murder of John the Baptist. Its shocking cruelty and injustice prefigure the drama of Jesus' own crucifixion. But for now John's death only leads to Jesus' withdrawal (14:13). The narrator interestingly does not comment further, whereas a modern writer would have considered Jesus' inner feelings.

Sometimes minor themes hold the narrative together. For example, in 15:1–16:12 the theme of "bread" occurs regularly: Verses 15:1–20 are about eating and defilement, 15:22–28 mention the Gentile woman who receives the children's bread, in 15:32–39 a Gentile crowd is fed with bread, and in 16:5–12 bread and yeast (leaven) are used as metaphors. Later on the connecting themes are faith and discipleship in the new people of God.

The second half of chapter 15 is probably entirely set outside the borders of Israel. Matthew tells how a Gentile woman shows faith in Jesus and how he heals and feeds a crowd that apparently also consists of non-Jews.

Peter's confession of faith occurs after another disappointment over the lack of faith in the Pharisees. The leader of the band of followers confesses Jesus as the Son of God (16:13–20). As if immediately to quell any premature enthusiasm, Jesus answers by predicting his Passion and by emphasizing the costs of discipleship. But then the story of the transfiguration forms the divine confirmation of Peter's confession. It gives the witnesses and the readers a view of Jesus' divinity that compensates for the apparent hopelessness of his fate on earth.

The story about Jesus and the payment of temple tax (17:24–27) could be misread as a somewhat naive miracle story: The great miracle worker helps himself to money to pay the tax by making a fish provide the correct coin. But it contains the profound claim that Jesus is exempt from the temple tax because he is on the side of the one to whom the tax is paid, who in the end is God. As Son of God, Jesus is in a different league.

Section VIII: Fourth Block of Teaching: Sin and Forgiveness (Chapter 18)
Twice Matthew has Jesus refer explicitly to the church that would come into being after his period on earth (16:17–20 and 18:17–18). It is clear that he foresaw the continuation of the group of his followers beyond his own mission. As 16:16 makes clear, the basic confession of the church is the identity of Jesus. In 16:18 Jesus points to Peter, one of the Twelve Disciples, and promises him an important role as first leader of the church. Jesus institutes a meal (26:26–27) and baptism (28:19) for his disciples.

In addition, all five blocks of teaching contain much that is directly relevant to the time after Jesus. The church will consist of those who give heed to Jesus' call to radical discipleship (chapters 5–7; 8:19–22; 16:24–25; 19:21–22), and Matthew's favorite term for its members is *disciple,* which basically means "pupil," one who follows a teacher to be shaped by him. Rather than create regulations for rituals and leadership structures, Jesus focuses on obedience to his teaching as the mark of the church. Many other passages make it clear that Jesus did not expect the church to be perfect (7:15–20; 13:24–30, 36–43, 49–50; 22:1–14; 25:31–46).

The famous parable of the lost sheep (18:10–14) is a clear illustration of the love of God for all of humankind, including those who have strayed. The well-known parable of the unforgiving servant (18:23–35) is a great example of hyperbole (see IMAGERY, BIBLICAL), shedding light on an everyday reality. If followers of Jesus claim that they live through divine forgiveness, they surely must forgive each other as well.

Section IX: Chapters 19–22: On the Way to Jerusalem
In chapters 19 and 20 the unifying idea is greatness, humility, and reversal; this is made explicit in 19:30 and 20:16. The parable of the laborers in the vineyard shows God's freedom to accept whoever comes to him, regardless of his past. The subject of chapters 21–22 is Jesus' person and authority, and Israel's response to him.

Whereas Matthew had organized the middle part of his gospel thematically, from here on the historical order to the events returns. Jesus goes on his way to the capital city, Jerusalem, to meet his end, as he repeats once more (20:17–19).

The account of Jesus' arrival in Jerusalem (21:1–11) is deeply moving. The identity and authority of Jesus pervade the section: He is both a royal person and a very meek ruler. At this moment he is widely accepted as Messiah and apparently in control of the situation, but he already knows that he will soon be rejected. It looks as if his entry into Jerusalem is a resounding success, but the Jewish nation is increasingly divided over him and his authority. To the spectators the outcome is in the balance, but the readers know that Jesus will not survive. The passage employs several verses from the Hebrew Bible, such as Zechariah 9:9, which is quoted by Matthew; Psalm 118, which is quoted by the crowd; and Isaiah 62:11.

Once Jesus is in Jerusalem, nearly every episode focuses on a confrontation with the Jewish leaders. In the parables he now tells, such as about the wicked tenants and about the wedding banquet, Jesus openly contrasts the unfaithfulness and unwillingness of some (the majority of the Jews) with the faith of others (his followers from Israel and the other nations).

Section X: Fifth Block of Teaching: On the Future (Chapters 23–25)

Jesus' speech in chapter 24 is known as the Synoptic Apocalypse because it is about future events. It is the hardest passage in the gospel. Probably verses 1–28 deal with the events leading up to and including the fall of Jerusalem to the Romans in 70 C.E., whereas the remainder of the chapter (24:29–42) is about the last things and the return of Jesus. In more detail the following can be said:

The disciples ask about the destruction of the temple, mistakenly supposing this will only happen at his return (24:1–3)

The present age: a long delay marked by suffering and witness (24:4–14)

The Jewish War of 67–73 C.E. (24:15–21)

Jesus reverts to the subject of 4–14 and refers to the whole period between his two comings (24:22–28)

The return of Jesus (24:29–31)

Impression of the whole of HISTORY since Jesus (24:32–42)

Use of the Hebrew Bible is less prominent in this section, but 24:30 must be noted as an allusion to passages about the Son of Man in Daniel 7:13–14.

Section XI: The Story of Jesus' Suffering, Death, and Resurrection (Chapters 26–28)

The final chapters of the gospel are the only place where the narrative is more or less linear and leaves little space for speeches. To the attentive reader Jesus' death is not a surprise: Several times he had made it plain that he expected to meet a violent end at the hands of Israel's leaders (16:21–28; 17:22–23; 20:17–19). The last of this series of pre-dictions (26:1–2) opens the final part of the gospel, and its prominent position sets the tone for what follows. Matthew sees the death of Jesus in the light of the prophecy of Isaiah about the servant of the Lord (Isaiah 53). In 20:28 Jesus says that he came "to give his life a ransom for many." In the light of the legal and sacrificial systems of ancient Israel (see HEBREW BIBLE, WORSHIP AND RITUAL) this means that he died in lieu of humankind so that their relationship with God could be restored. Otherwise the gospel does not say very much about the meaning of Jesus' death, but there was a traditional conviction among the Jews (seen in Isaiah 53 and in the apocryphal 2 Maccabees 7) that the death of the righteous would atone for the sins of the nation. The development of this theology was left to thinkers like the apostle Paul.

There is an explicit quote from the prophet Jeremiah in 27:9–10 that in fact also makes use of Zechariah 11:12–13. The Hebrew Bible is referred to in 26:24, 31, 54, whereas 26:11, 15, 23, 28, 53, 60, 64, 67 and 27:24, 29, 34, 35, 39, 43, 46 have been identified as allusions to it. In many places Psalm 22 shimmers through the account. This psalm about betrayal and suffering must have been in the mind of Matthew if not in that of Jesus himself.

The reason the Jewish authorities have to take Jesus before the Roman officials after condemning him to death is that under the Roman occupation they had no right to execute capital punishment. The Roman governor Pilate normally resided in Caesarea, but he was in Jerusalem to supervise the celebrations of the Passover festival. Matthew tells that the governor cannot see any reason why the innocent Jesus should be killed but that he nonetheless accedes to public pressure and then washes his hands "in innocence" (27:24). This action might be a deliberate parody of what is prescribed in Deuteronomy 21:1–9. The expression itself also occurs in Psalm 26:6, but it became proverbial as a result of this incident.

The next verse, 27:25, is one of the most abused verses in Scripture. The Jewish people cry that the blood of Jesus may come "on us and on our children." Anti-Semites have taken this utterance as an excuse to call Jews the murderers of Jesus Christ.

Pilate washing his hands (Matthew 27:24), woodcut by Albrecht Dürer

This is not so. The teaching of the New Testament makes it clear that it is not the Jews who are to blame for Jesus' crucifixion, though some of the local people and the Romans were instrumental in it, but that Jesus died because this was the will of God and that all humans are equally guilty of it because of their sin.

In the descriptions both of the death of Jesus and of his resurrection the restraint of the writer is striking. No gory details are included, because it is more important to know *that* and why Jesus died than how. In the same way, the Resurrection has already taken place when the women arrive at the tomb of Jesus so that there are no eyewitnesses to it. The earthquake and the angels are not the event itself, but they are subsequent signs that only serve to focus attention on the emptiness of the tomb and to interpret the event.

Matthew alone supplies many details that show his Jewish background, such as the earthquake at the moment of Jesus' death; the highly symbolic rending of the veil in the temple, which illustrates that humankind can now freely approach God; and the guard at the tomb.

CHARACTERS

disciples, the Whereas Mark's picture of the disciples is quite negative, Matthew shows more diversity and indicates that they did reach some positive understanding of Jesus' message (13:51; 16:12; 17:13) and identity (16:15–17). In this way they can become models for the readers and the later church, but Matthew also alludes to the effectiveness of the teaching of Jesus. As pointed out, much of Jesus' blocks of teaching focuses on them.

While the Jewish leaders (see below) are Jesus' adversaries and the disciples are "with" him (12:30), the crowds are the undecided group who are called to join Jesus as well.

Among the disciples Peter stands out as their impulsive leader and spokesperson (14:28; 15:15; 16:16; 17:4; 18:21; 19:27). In several episodes three disciples, Peter, James, and John, receive special treatment (17:1–8; 26:36–46). The latter two, the sons of Zebedee (4:21), were apparently so highly regarded that their mother mistakenly thought them to be Jesus' own favorites (20:20–23).

Herod, King The Herod who threatens the baby Jesus in chapter 2 is Herod the Great (died ca. 4 B.C.E.); the Herod in chapter 14 who has John the Baptist beheaded is Herod Antipas, one of his sons who ruled over Galilee. The brief reference in 2:22 is to another son, Herod Archelaus, who ruled Judea after the death of his father.

Jesus Christ Matthew uses a wide array of titles to refer to Jesus, such as Son of Man (30 times), King, Lord, Son of God, Messiah (English: Christ), Son of David, Servant of the Lord (based on the prophet Isaiah), and Immanuel. This last title means "God is with us," and its occurrences form a bracket around the whole gospel (1:23 and

28:20; see also 17:17; 18:20; 26:29). Matthew uses it to suggest that the man Jesus is at the same time God himself. Only in a parable told toward the end of his life does Jesus claim to be God's Son for the first time in the ears of the general public (21:33–45).

The reader needs to be aware that when Jesus uses the title *Son of Man,* he is referring to himself, and that in such passages it is the equivalent of *I.*

But more than through the titles, Jesus' identity is presented through the stories about what he says and does; hence it is said that Matthew's Christology is a narrative Christology. The narrative about the cleansing of the temple (21:12–17) is a case in point. This event is of huge significance for the ministry of Jesus. In Malachi 3:1–3 and in the apocryphal Psalms of Solomon 17:30, it is prophesied that the Son of David will "purge Jerusalem and make it holy as it was even in the beginning." Consequently, Jesus' radical action is not merely an attack on commercial malpractice, still less an attack on the sacrificial ceremony as such, but it establishes a claim to being the long-awaited Son of David, that is, a claim to divine authority.

In several ways Jesus is presented in comparison with Moses, the greatest character of the people of Israel so far. The overall structure of the book, with its five blocks of teaching as discussed previously, sets Jesus up as the new Moses, the new lawgiver. Chapters 1 and 2, in particular, show Jesus as the new Moses in that both are threatened by a murderous king (cf. Exodus 1), go into exile, and return to their country. Early on both emerge from the water (3:16 cf. Exodus 2:10), and both pass through a period of testing of 40 units of time (4:1–2, cf. Acts 7:30) (see NUMBERS, SIGNIFICANCE OF on 40 as a period of testing). As Moses does from Mount Sinai, Jesus teaches on a mountain (5:1; 8:1; 28:16–20).

Jewish leaders, the As we have seen, in Matthew the Pharisees are severely criticized by Jesus. Hypocrisy is one of the main accusations. Just as Jesus does, they emphasize radical obedience to God—but they do not put into practice what they preach, says Jesus.

Jesus' polemic as quoted by Matthew is so forceful that it has been called anti-Semitic. However, such criticism overlooks that in the Hebrew Bible such harsh stances including the use of strong language are common (see, e.g., Isaiah 1:2–4 and Hosea 1:2; 2:2; 4:10–19; 11:2) and that both Jesus and Matthew are themselves Jews taking part in internal Jewish polemics. Moreover, in contemporary Jewish sources the same tone and the same types of accusations can be found used in internal polemics. Although modern readers may not like this style, contemporary readers would not have been unduly offended by the words of Jesus and Matthew.

John the Baptist Matthew leaves his readers in the dark regarding the origins of John the Baptist. (The Gospels of Luke and John have more information about him.) Before Jesus' ministry begins, John as his forerunner announces the coming of the kingdom of heaven and challenges the Jews to prepare for it. He makes it clear that belonging to the nation of Israel in itself is not enough to please God and that repentance is required. He particularly addresses the religious establishment of PHARISEES AND SADDUCEES and scribes. As a sign of their repentance, the people are invited to be baptized. Although contemporary Judaism knew periodic ritual immersion, BAPTISM as a one-time act was an innovation.

When Jesus begins his ministry, John disappears from view, only to reappear briefly in 11:2–15 and 14:1–12. His execution by Herod has little impact on Jesus' activities.

Joseph and Mary In this gospel the story of Jesus' birth is told from the perspective of the man who adopted him as his son but who was not involved in his conception, Joseph the carpenter from Nazareth. Matthew emphasizes Joseph's readiness to obey God in a series of hard decisions, as well as the fact that he and Mary had not participated in any sexual activity. Unlike Mary (in 12:46–50 and 13:55), Joseph is not mentioned in the story of Jesus' adult life, so it is usually presumed that he had already died at that time. Jesus' mother, Mary, appears several times, but she plays no major role in the story.

Micah

The PROPHECY of Micah stands sixth among the Minor Prophets in the Hebrew Bible. The prophet himself lived during the reigns of the southern kingdom's rulers Jotham (742–735 B.C.E.), Ahaz (735–716 B.C.E.), and Hezekiah (716–687 B.C.E.).

The dates make Micah a slightly younger contemporary of the prophet Isaiah. Isaiah was probably from JERUSALEM, the capital, and from a higher social class, but there are distinct similarities in their messages. Scholars often group these two prophets with the older prophets Hosea and Amos, as prophets who emphasized God's standards of right living and right relationships. Micah's mes-sage was to both northern and southern kingdoms (1:1); the northern kingdom is called variously SAMARIA (its capital) or Jacob, and the southern kingdom Judah, Zion, or Jerusalem. The term *Israel* is ambiguously used to refer to either kingdom or to the undivided nation.

The book contains no narrative, consisting of a series of poetic prophecies or oracles that take on a number of literary forms, including WOES AND DENUNCIATIONS, laments, taunt songs, and complaints. Traditionally, the book has been considered a unity, the words of the one prophet. More recently, some scholars have suggested that, unusually for the Minor Prophets, some additional material (chapters 4, 5, 7) was incorporated later. They

Micah exhorting the Israelites to repentance (Micah 4:3), engraving by Gustave Doré

base this assertion on the more universal outlook and a reference to BABYLON (4:10) rather than to ASSYRIA, the empire that was threatening the two kingdoms in Micah's day.

This debate throws up a consideration of how prophecy came to be written down. Only in the case of Jeremiah do we have a clear account of how spoken prophecy was recorded by a secretary close to the prophet. In Micah's case, we presumably have a selection of his spoken prophecies, written and arranged because they seemed especially memorable and by a scribe or other literate person. The prophecies were certainly still very much remembered in Jeremiah's day, more than 100 years later, since there was a lively debate about them (Jeremiah 26:17–19, quoting Micah 3:12).

SYNOPSIS

Chapters 1–3 and 6 deal with deep failures within the societies of the northern and southern kingdoms. Particularly singled out for repeated mention are social injustices, maladministration by corrupt leaders, idolatry, and false prophets and priests (1:3–7; 2:1–11; 3:1–3, 8–11; 6:9–12). Such failures will have dire consequences, which God will either bring about or allow to happen, namely, lack of prosperity, military defeat, destruction of towns, and finally exile (1:8–16; 2:3–4; 3:4–7, 12; 6:13–16). But even in the prediction of destruction, there is given a promise of hope in a restored remnant (2:12–13).

This latter promise is then expanded in the other chapters (4–5; 7). Restoration (4:6–8; 5:7–9; 7:18–20) will be accompanied by power over other nations (4:11–13; 5:10–15; 7:11–17). But the power will be primarily spiritual. In his most exalted vision, in the book's midpoint, Micah sees a restored Jerusalem as the center of worldwide worship of God (4:1–5). These chapters also contain references to the same failures as the other set of chapters (4:9–12; 5:3; 7:1–10). The first and last chapters book-end the prophecy, in that they summarize its main themes and emphases.

COMMENTARY

The first and last chapters take the form of a complaint, as might be presented in a law court. Verse 1:2 opens with "let the LORD GOD be a witness against you," and 7:9 concludes with "until he takes my side and executes judgement for me," where the *my* is Israel rather than the prophet. The main courtroom device occurs in 6:1–5, however, where God asks the nation, "What have I done to you?" at the same time reminding them of what he has done *for* them: "For I brought you up from the land of Egypt." The questions are rhetorical: There can be no valid answer by way of complaint of the nation—the complaint is God's alone. The courtroom device is typical of the prophets (cf. Isaiah 5:3f.; Hosea 4:1; Zephaniah 3:8).

The "I" voice varies between God and the prophet, as he is both God's spokesman and a human being, appalled by the corruption in society around him. Verse 1:8 suggests the grieving prophet, and yet "the gate of my people"(1:9) suggests God as much as the prophet, though literally the reference must be to the southern kingdom's being infected by the sins of the northern. In 7:8–10 the "I" voice seems most likely to be the nation as a whole, though it could refer again to just the suffering prophet. The "I" of 6:6 is a rhetorical voice, asking how to make atonement for sins, with the answer given in 6:8, which becomes the core of the moral message of the book: "To do justice, and to love kindness, / and to walk humbly with your God" (cf. Hosea 6:6; Amos 5:21–24).

The rhetorical devices mentioned in the last paragraph show the literary sophistication of the prophet. We can further exemplify this by looking at 1:8–16, which consists of a series of elaborate puns and plays on words over the places mentioned. For example, in 1:10 *Beth Ophrah* in the Hebrew means "house of dust," hence the "roll yourselves in the dust." All the names are bent to mean some form of mourning in this strange lament. It opens with "Tell it not in Gath," the same phrase used in David's lament in 2 Samuel 1:20f. A more conventional lament occurs in 7:1–9, beginning with the formulaic "Woe is me!" As with the writer of Lamentations, he waits for God to hear his cry (7:7). The lament then rises to faith as he addresses the enemy: "Do not rejoice over me, O my enemy" (7:8), a psalmlike turn of phrase, which eventually rises, as do many of the Psalms, to a triumphant conclusion: "Who is a God like you . . ." (7:18–20), where he asserts the fundamentally merciful nature of God. The phrase is possibly a wordplay on Micah's own name (see below). The passage must be one of the most beautiful Bible passages on the forgiveness of sin.

Other rhetorical devices include brief taunt songs (2:4; 7:10), where the sarcastic tone echoes the prophet's own (2:11). The attack on the false prophets, as we might expect, is the most sarcastic of all the denunciations. 2:6 has a convoluted sentence mimicking the false prophets attacking Micah—"The prophets say, 'Don't prophesy, "Don't prophesy."'" He then denounces them for the consequences of their falsehoods. He stands in antithesis to them (3:8, echoing 3:5), and his powerful rhetoric "I am filled with power" conveys exactly that.

Equally powerful is his vision of "the last days." There has been an apocalyptic hint in 1:3–4, but the tone of 4:1–5 is of restoration after judgment. The verses are interesting because they are the same as in Isaiah 2:2–4, except that Micah has two extra verses (4:4–5). The use of one prophet's words by another is not unique—Obadiah and Jeremiah use the same phrases in their denunciations of Edom. But it does suggest contemporaneity. There are other similarities to Isaiah in this chapter: 4:8 echoes Isaiah 21:8 in the use of the watchtower image (a common metaphor for the prophet); 4:10 echoes Isaiah 21:9 in the reference to Babylon (rather than Assyria); and 4:12 echoes Isaiah 21:10 in the image of the threshing floor. There are other powerfully rhetorical passages, including 5:7–9, with its elaborate parallelisms, and the messianic 5:2, quoted in Matthew 2:6: Bethlehem was David's birthplace, thus a metonymy for a restored Davidic monarchy.

The structures of the opening chapters have parallel features: denunciations of social injustices, followed by an announcement of the punishment, followed by a promise of a restoration. In chapter 3 this promise is delayed and extended into 4:1–8, where the promise is structured antithetically to the denunciation: Destruction of the city and temple is matched by their restoration (4:1); the failure of the priests to teach is matched by God's teaching (4:2); and the failure of the leaders to rule justly

will be matched by God's judging in righteousness (4:3).

CHARACTER

Micah   The name is a shortened form of *Micaiah*, meaning, "Who is like the LORD?" He was born in a village in Judah, Moresheth (1:1), presumably the same as the Moresheth-Gath of 1:14, lying in the foothills toward the coastal plain. He was preaching to the northern kingdom before its fall in 721 B.C.E. (1:6–7) and experienced the siege of Jerusalem by the Assyrians in 701 B.C.E. (5:1). His main prophetic concern was God's anger at the rampant social injustice, as was Amos's before him and Jeremiah's after. Also he denounces the false religion of both priests and prophets, but especially the latter. Jeremiah 26:17–19 suggests his prophecies were taken to heart in Hezekiah's reign.

Nahum

The book of Nahum stands seventh in the Minor Prophets in the Hebrew Bible. Nothing is known of its writer, except that he was from the village of Elkosh, which may or may not have been in the southern kingdom of Judah. His message is directed almost solely against the city of Nineveh, which here is representative of the whole oppressive Assyrian Empire. The prophecy is given at the point of its demise, which occurred in 612 B.C.E., after successive attacks by the Medes from the north and the Babylonians (also known as the Chaldeans) from the south and east. This would be during the reign of Josiah in Judah.

Such a date would make Nahum contemporary with the young Jeremiah, and prophesying just after Zephaniah and just before Habakkuk. But the obvious point of comparison is with the book of Jonah. Both prophets are almost solely concerned with Nineveh. In Jonah's case, he takes a message of salvation to the wicked city, a message that appears to have been received. In Nahum's case, however, the message is of judgment and destruction, with no mercy given. Theologically, one could say the two books together represent "the goodness and the severity of God" (Romans 11:22 King James Version).

The two books differ in a literary sense too. Jonah's is largely a prose narrative; Nahum's, a highly poetic series of prophetic utterances. Both, however, do contain an extended psalmlike passage. The book of Jonah can be taken allegorically or symbolically, and not historically. Nineveh then becomes a type of the evil empire, but no one is ever so evil as to be outside God's mercy if he responds to his message. In Nahum, the setting has to be taken historically. Only after this is acknowledged can Nineveh be seen as a type of evil empire. The joy and relief at its downfall could then be likened to, say, the downfall of the Nazi regime.

SYNOPSIS

The book's opening section (1:2–14) is an extended HYMN or PSALM to God as the divine warrior. It thus sets the theme of warfare and victory. Both Judah and ASSYRIA are addressed. Judah is given hope for the future; Assyria is given the judgment of total annihilation. Verses 1:15 and 2:2 form a bridge passage, again reassuring Judah of divine protection. The rest of chapter 2 (2:1, 3–13) is a vivid description of the battle of Nineveh and the enemy marching against it. Nineveh's defeat is pictured, leading into a taunt song and a final word from God on its destruction. The third chapter is addressed to the city itself, again a vivid impressionistic picture of the chaos and humiliation of defeat. Another taunt song likens Assyria's defeat to that of EGYPT. A third taunt song mocks its attempts to defend itself. Finally the king of Assyria is addressed: No one will shed any tears at all over his defeat. He is a hated and cruel enemy.

COMMENTARY

The opening verse classifies the prophecy as "a burden" (Authorized [King James] Version, following the Hebrew), a term used in Zechariah 9:1; 12:1 and Malachi 1:1, among other prophetic writings. The term usually implies a message either difficult to give or full of judgment. Here the latter would be true—Nahum is only too happy to deliver it! It is described as a "vision": The highly imaginative

descriptions of battle scenes suggest the vividness of a vision, since there is no evidence that Nahum was ever present at a battle.

The Divine Warrior hymn is seen elsewhere in the Hebrew Bible as well as in other Near Eastern literatures. For example, Zechariah 9:1–15; 14:1, 3, 5 form two such hymns, including references to a theophany and the cosmic disturbances of the Lord in battle fighting for his people. Psalm 98 contains passing references to similar divine activity, in a tradition that goes back to Exodus 15:3 and Joshua 5:13–15, and then extends forward into later APOCALYPTIC WRITING (e.g., Revelation 19:15). The very term *Lord of Hosts* (Nahum 2:13) also suggests this divine activity.

The portrayal of the divine warrior is both fearsome and yet reassuring. The cosmic disturbances of storm, whirlwind, drought, earthquake, and fire are profoundly fearsome, but to his people "The LORD is good" (1:7), a stronghold and refuge, as also the Psalms portray him (e.g., Psalm 31). By contrast, the imagery used in speaking of his enemies is ludicrously weak: "dry straw," "thorns." 1:14 is the real object of this attack: The Assyrian idols and temples are weak and worthless, in the face of God's true greatness and power, as are the "plots" of the enemies (1:9, 11).

As poetry, the rhythms and contrasts work powerfully. There is careful crafting. There is some evidence that chapter 1 was conceived as an acrostic psalm. And the parallelisms used (see POETRY, BIBLICAL) are as sophisticated as anywhere in the Hebrew Bible. 1:12 is a good example of contrasting parallelism. The first and third lines begin "Though . . ." but their subject matter is in complete contrast—the enemy's full strength versus Judah's affliction. The second and fourth lines contrast in the opposite way: Strength leads to annihilation; affliction leads to promise of a future. 1:10 illustrates a triplet parallelism based on a set of three similes of pitiful weakness ("thorns," "drunks," and "dry straw"), with the third line chiastic (that is, set the opposite way around). There is also some hyperbole ("rebukes the sea and makes it dry," possibly an allusion to the crossing of the Red Sea), continued into 1:15, "never again shall the wicked invade you." This has to be taken as what God would wish or as meaning "never again will Assyria invade you."

The description in chapter 2 of the army marching against Assyria is very vivid, as are the later descriptions of 3:1–3. It is called the "shatterer's" army (2:1) (an alternative reading is "the scatterer's"). It is ambiguous whether the army is the Lord's or the Chaldeans'. In a sense, it is both, as Babylon's army became an instrument of God's judgment. The image of plunder becomes central—the Assyrians had plundered all the surrounding nations, including the northern kingdom of Israel (in 722 B.C.E.). Now they are going to be completely plundered (2:9, echoed in 2:11; 3:1). It is almost as if the prophet is present, giving the commands. This is retributive justice: eye for eye. As the Assyrians led conquered nations into exile, so they, too, will now be exiled (2:7).

All this climaxes into a taunt song (2:10–13), where the taunting is centered around the lion, an Assyrian emblem. Taunts typically carry rhetorical questions, as "What became of . . . ?" as here (2:11). Lions also are a metonymy of military prowess and strength just as messengers are a metonymy for authority (2:13). The mocking alliteration of 2:10 in the Hebrews is kept in many English versions.

Nahum 3:1–3 dramatically convey the chaos of battle. The city is addressed as "city of bloodshed," appropriately as the Assyrians were renowned for their cruelty (3:19), a cruelty that shall be reciprocated (3:10). The Assyrians were also renowned for their use of magic and sorcery. The prostitutes of 3:4 were sorceresses. The sexual connotations are continued (3:5) in imagery of exposure and nakedness (compare Isaiah 47:2–3 in talking of the Babylonians). Prisoners were routinely stripped naked at the time, but the stripping is metonymic also of the idolatrous power of magic and divination being exposed for what it is. No lament will be possible (3:7) as it *was* possible for Jerusalem when that later was to be devastated (as in the book of Lamentations). Only further taunt songs are possible, as 3:8f. Again is the rhetorical question "Are you better than . . . ?" Further humiliating similes are used, as in chapter 2: figs dropping into the mouths of the eaters—the eaters do not even have to work

for the fruit, so easily do they obtain it (3:12)—and soldiers likened to women (3:13).

Whatever the Assyrians do, the taunt song continues, nothing will prevent defeat. A double simile of locusts is used: They are plentiful and they strip everything destructively. The Assyrians can be as plentiful as locusts, but their number will not prevent their devastation as locusts devastate a land (3:15–17). The insect imagery is in ludicrous contrast to the warhorses of 3:2 or the stars of heaven (3:16). Nahum is enjoying himself in all this ridicule—not something most prophets were allowed to do for very long—as he extends the simile into an image of the locusts sitting on a fence on a cold day. What effective bathos! Assyria's earlier taunting of Jerusalem (Isaiah 37:10–13, 17) is now fully turned back on itself.

CHARACTER

Nahum The prophet reveals himself as an accomplished poet who can write in sophisticated literary structures. At the same time he can portray vividly the reality of battle and evoke mockery, and contempt for the enemy. But even in the midst of militaristic language, he can comfort and promise peace to Judah.

Nehemiah

See Ezra.

Numbers

The title of the book Numbers derives from the fact that it contains many numbers: census lists, lists of gifts for the tabernacle, and others. As a whole, however, the book is the third part of the story of Israel that began in the book of Exodus and is continued in Leviticus, dealing with Israel's deliverance from Egypt, the giving of the Law at Mount Sinai, and the wilderness wandering to the HOLY LAND. From a literary point of view, Exodus, Leviticus, and Numbers are best seen to form a unified work. One distinctive feature of Numbers that it shares with Exodus is that they combine several different genres, including narrative, lists, prophecy, and legal material, into one single text. Although this seems strange to modern readers, it has an inner logic. The legal material and the lists are introduced at the points of the story where the information is needed to understand the preceding or following narrative, respectively. (For more introductory information, see the book of Exodus.)

SYNOPSIS

The Purification of Israel (Chapters 1–6)

A census is taken recording all men who are able to go out to war, tribe for tribe. The total number of men enrolled, without the tribe of Levi, is 603,550 (chapter 1). After that, the order of encampment and marching is determined. The Israelites are to camp around the tabernacle, tribe by tribe: on the eastern side the tribes of Judah, Issachar, and Zebulun; on the south side Reuben, Simeon, and Gad; on the west side Ephraim, Manasseh, and Benjamin; and on the north side Dan, Asher, and Naphtali. The tribe of Levi is to camp directly around the tabernacle. While marching, the tribes are to follow one another, beginning with Judah and ending with Naphtali; the Levites are to travel at the center of the procession (chapter 2).

Levi is the tribe that God has elected for the service of the tabernacle. Therefore, the Levites are counted separately. The total number of male Levites, from the age of one month onward, is 22,000. One of the Levites' most important duties is to transport the tabernacle on the journey. The text gives detailed instructions for this (chapters 3–4). After that are legal stipulations concerning the purification of the people: the placement of unclean people outside the camp, regulations for uncovering hidden faults, and regulations for the correct conduct of the voluntary self-commitment as a Nazirite. Finally, the people receive the priestly blessing (chapters 5–6).

Information Relating to the Journey (7:1–10:10)

This section consists mainly of chronological flashbacks. First, the text lists all the gifts the tribes have given for the inauguration of the tabernacle: about six ox wagons and a great amount of silver and golden vessels for use in the ritual service. Then follow stipulations on the consecration of Levites and on an alternative date for the Passover feast in case it cannot be kept at the appointed time. After that, the movement of the pillar of cloud and of fire over the tabernacle is described, through which God tells the people when to travel and when to camp. Finally, trumpet signals are agreed for assembling the congregation and for setting out on the journey.

The Journey from Sinai to the Borders of Canaan (10:11–26:65)

Now the nation sets out according to the prescribed marching order. But the journey has hardly begun before the people start complaining again (see Exodus). The manna is too dull for the people; they want to have meat. Moses addresses himself to God, complaining that the people are too much of a burden for him. God answers him by appointing 70 elders to support Moses in his work. After that, God sends a great quantity of quails so that the people have meat to eat. But God is also very angry with the people and sends a plague as well. Some time later, Miriam and Aaron become jealous of Moses and question his authority. God calls them to go to the tabernacle and takes them to task. As a punishment, Miriam becomes leprous for seven days (chapters 10–12). The people reach the southern border of Canaan. Twelve spies are sent out to reconnoiter the territory. After 40 days they return. They describe the agricultural abundance, but they also tell the people of the military strength of Canaan's inhabitants. They even start a rumor that they met giants there. Only two of the spies, Joshua and Caleb, are still confident that the people will occupy the land with the help of the Lord (chapter 13).

The Israelites are in great distress at the spies' report. Moses' attempt at appeasement fails. The people rise in revolt against him and want to stone him. At that moment, the glory of God appears on top of the tabernacle. God is very angry and states that he wants to destroy Israel and found a new nation with Moses' family. But Moses intercedes on behalf of the people. Therefore, God mitigates

Spies explore Canaan (Numbers 13:1–27), engraving by Julius Schnorr von Carolsfeld

the sentence: The people have to stay in the desert for 40 years, until all adult members of the current generation have died. Only the next generation will be allowed to enter the Promised Land. The people then mourn. They decide, nevertheless, to start conquering the land. But God is not with them, and they are severely defeated by its inhabitants (chapter 14). The text continues with a block of legal material: regulations on voluntary grain offerings that will be given from the yields of the land of Canaan in the future, regulations concerning unintentional sins, and the command to make special fringes on the corners of the garments reminding the people of the divine laws (chapter 15).

A group of Levites and some other leading people rebel against Moses and Aaron. In particular, the Levites ask for priestly rights. An assembly is summoned, where God is asked to give a sign about whom he wants to be leader. God announces the annihilation of the whole group of rebels. However, Moses intercedes with God, and God decides to kill only the leading families of the rebellion: The ground under them splits apart, and they fall into the crevice. The next day, the whole people start rebelling against Moses and Aaron because of what happened. God sends a plague among the people. Aaron intercedes on behalf of the people and stops the plague. After that, God confirms the role of Aaron as high priest through a sign (chapters 16–17).

Another block of legal material follows, dealing with the duties of the priests and Levites, respectively, and the tithes that have to be given to them. After that, the ceremony of the red heifer, which is needed for purification of people who have become unclean, is described (chapters 18–19).

The people run out of water. Again they start complaining against Moses and Aaron. God instructs Moses and Aaron to talk to a rock in front of all the people so that it will give water. However, instead of speaking to the rock, Moses, in his anger, beats it with a stick. The rock then cracks and becomes a water source. But God punishes Moses and Aaron for their disrespect, announcing that they will not enter the Promised Land. The Israelites plan to conquer the land starting from east of the Jordan. For that, they have to cross the country of the Edomites, their sister people (see Genesis 25:23–26). The Edomites, however, refuse. They approach Israel with an army. The Israelites evade them and take the long way around the Edomites' territory.

After that, Aaron dies. The people weep over him for 30 days. His son, Eleazar, is appointed as his successor (chapter 20).

In the wilderness on their long way around Edom, the people again become impatient, speaking against God and Moses. As a punishment, God sends poisonous snakes among them. The people ask Moses for forgiveness. God instructs Moses to make a serpent of bronze and put it upon a pole. Anyone who looks at that serpent is immediately healed of the snakes' poison.

Israel enters the eastern Jordan part of Canaan, moving northward. The Amorites who live there attack them but are easily defeated. After a short time, Israel is in control of the whole east Jordan territory (chapter 21).

Now Israel camps in the plains of Moab (to the northeast of the DEAD SEA) and prepares to conquer the west Jordan territory. The Moabites are in great dread of them. Balak, king of the Moabites, sends to Balaam, a famous Midianite seer, that he may put a curse on Israel. Although God appears to Balaam telling him not to go, Balak's messengers

put such pressure on him that he finally decides to go. On his way, the angel of the Lord bars his way three times, but only Balaam's she-ass can see him. When Balaam beats her heavily, she suddenly begins to speak, asking, "What have I done to you that you have struck me so hard?" That moment Balaam's eyes are opened and he can see the angel. God takes Balaam to task, and he asks for mercy. God sends Balaam to continue his mission but instructs him to speak over Israel only what God tells him to say. Balaam reaches Balak, and they go up a mountain, from which they can see out over the whole Israelite encampment. The spirit of God descends upon Balaam, and instead of cursing he utters a blessing over Israel. Balak is very angry, but Balaam even prophesies to him that the Moabites will eventually be defeated by Israel (chapters 22–24).

Now the Moabites and Midianites try to weaken Israel another way. They send women to seduce the Israelites to have sexual relations with them and take part in the sacrifices of the Moabite gods. God answers, commanding that all apostate Israelites have to be killed. Phinehas, son of Eleazar, son of Aaron, is exemplarily zealous carrying out God's command and making atonement for the Israelites. Therefore, God honors him and promises him and his family a perpetual priesthood. God also instructs Moses to attack the Midianites, punishing them for what they did (chapter 25).

The section ends with another census. As in Numbers 1–3, first the 12 tribes are enrolled, in total 601,730 men from the age of 20 years onward. Then the male Levites are counted, in total 23,000 from the age of one month onward.

Preparations for the Conquering of Canaan (Chapters 27–36)

The section starts by giving some laws on the inheritance in cases when there is no son who can inherit the land—as in the case of Zelophehad, who has only daughters. In this case the daughters are to inherit the land; if there are no daughters, other relatives of the family inherit the land.

Moses is concerned about his succession. God appoints Joshua, son of Nun, as Moses' successor (chapter 27).

Next are laws on regular offerings that have to be made at the tabernacle daily, weekly, and at the great feasts in the course of the festal year. Another law is on vows made by women (chapters 28–30).

As commanded by God (25:16–18), the Israelites now attack the Midianites, taking revenge for what they have done to Israel. The campaign is very successful, and the Israelites gain great plunder in animals and women (chapter 31).

The tribes of Reuben, Gad, and a part of Manasseh want to settle down in the eastern Jordan territory that is already conquered. Initially, Moses refuses, but he gives way after the tribal leaders have promised to help the other tribes conquer their territory and only afterward return to their possession (chapter 32).

Now follows a list of all the stages of Israel's journey from Egypt until the plains of Moab. Then God commands Israel to conquer the land. Its present inhabitants are to be driven out; after that the land is to be justly divided between the individual tribes and families. From each of the tribes a person is entrusted with the task of dividing the land among the tribal families. After that, the text describes the outer boundaries of the territory to be conquered (chapters 33–34).

The people of Levi do not get their own tribal territory. Rather, they are assigned 48 cities throughout the territory of the other tribes. Six of these cities become cities of refuge. People who have unintentionally killed a person can flee to these cities: The avenger appointed by the killed person's family (an ancient tradition) will not be allowed to enter them. An associated legal section follows, defining the difference between murder and unintentional killing (chapter 35).

For a second time, the daughters of Zelophehad give an occasion for a legal regulation. It says that women who have inherited a piece of land are allowed to marry only men of their own tribe. The regulation safeguards the land so that it is not lost to another tribe (chapter 36).

COMMENTARY

The Purification of Israel (Chapters 1–6)

The section contains lists and legal sections compiled in order to demonstrate how the people of Israel are finally made ready as people of God to begin their journey to the Promised Land.

The section begins with the census list of the 12 tribes. The point of the list is not just to give the numbers. Rather, the census serves as a kind of military inspection or mobilization, making the people ready for their mission. The Levites, however, are not counted from a military perspective. Their duty will be to take care of the tabernacle (chapters 1–4).

The legal material that follows deals with some specific issues concerning ceremonial impurity. More regulations of this kind have already been given in the book of Leviticus. The function of the passage here is to give the notion of completeness of cleansing. The people are now finally prepared to be God's holy people.

The priestly blessing in 6:22–27 serves as conclusion, not only for the section of Numbers 1–6, but for the whole stay of Israel at Mount Sinai. This has begun in Exodus 19, where God has announced the making of a covenant with Israel and making Israel a "kingdom of priests" and a "holy nation" (Exodus 19:5–6). This covenant is now finalized, and the people finally receive the blessing of God.

The priestly blessing of 6:22–27 is a text used even today on a regular basis for concluding Christian church services. From the placement of the passage in the context of Exodus-Leviticus-Numbers, it has to be noted, however, that the blessing does not just mean a hope that God may give something good. Rather, the text implies that God wants to guard those who are sent by him to fulfill his mission.

Information Relating to the Journey (7:1–10:10)

At first sight, the material presented in this section is very diverse. Moreover, nearly all the passages are out of their chronological order and date back to the time of the consecration of the tabernacle (see Leviticus 8–10). The key to the logic of presentation is that the text calls to mind different events and circumstances that are necessary for imagining the beginning of the journey.

Reading through the list of ritual vessels given by the 12 tribes, the reader will be able to imagine the task of transporting the tabernacle and all the related accessories. Six ox wagons are provided for the transport (chapter 7). Many people are needed for this task, hence the description of the Levites' consecration in chapter 8.

One reason to keep the Passover feast on an alternate date is a long journey (9:10). The law is probably recorded here since Israel is about to begin a long journey. Also, the description of the pillar of cloud and of fire connects to the upcoming departure (chapter 9). The trumpets are used on different occasions. One of them, again, is to signal the setting off of the people (chapter 10).

Many scholars see the section of 7:1 to 10:10 as belonging to the Sinai block, which would then extend from Exodus 19 to Numbers 10. This division is based mainly on geographic considerations. From a literary and theological point of view, however, the blessing in Numbers 6 forms an appropriate conclusion for the spiritual preparation of the people of Israel at Mount Sinai, while the flashbacks of chapter 7–10 very much relate to the following journey.

The Journey from Sinai to the Borders of Canaan (10:11–26:65)
The setting out of the people is described is great detail here, taking up much of the information of the preceding chapters, for example, the movement of the pillar of cloud explained in 9:15ff., the marching order of chapter 2, and the regulations concerning the transportation of the tabernacle in chapters 4 and 7. This underscores the idea that the people are now beginning to put divine order into practice (see PILGRIMS AND WANDERERS).

However, as on the first part of the journey (see Exodus), the people are again depicted as being often dissatisfied and disobedient. The divine plan of salvation is boldly questioned when they long for the food they have been given during their slavery in Egypt—they would rather be in slavery than taken by God into the Promised Land. The revolt against the leadership of Moses reaches even as far as Aaron and Miriam, Moses' brother and sister. The peak, however, is reached when the Israelites despair because of the spies' report, indirectly denying that God has the ability to make his promise of the land come true.

What follows is a pattern that occurs several times in the books of Exodus and Numbers: After Israel has sinned, God announces or begins a punishment. Then Moses intercedes with God on behalf of the people, and God mitigates the punishment or even refrains from it. The pattern depicts God as a God of holiness and of grace as well. These two divine qualities stand in a certain tension to each other, which enables Moses even to negotiate with God to some extent. The pattern shows that Israel cannot truly meet the requirements of God's holiness. But God tempers justice with mercy, to achieve which, however, Moses is needed as a mediator. In the New Testament, this relationship is typologically applied to Jesus Christ, who is described as the mediator between God and humanity (1 Timothy 2:5–6; Hebrews 9:15). Also, the 40 years of wilderness wandering are typologically interpreted in the sense of a time of purification and/or trial (Luke 4:1–2; Hebrews 3).

The narrative is again interrupted by a block of legal material. The overarching subject here is enduring 40 years of wilderness wandering without giving up. The two sections on cereal offerings (15:1–16 and 15:17–21) both begin with the explanation "when you come into the land . . .": Although a time of 40 years of wilderness wandering lies before the people, they should not give up the hope of finally reaching the land and eating from its rich yields, from which they will love to give some offerings to God. The remaining regulations deal with the problem that people may forget some of God's commandments in the course of the journey. Therefore, a reduced compensation is stipulated for unintentional sins (15:22–29). These mitigations, however, do not apply to intentional violations of the law—this point is underscored by the narrative about the man gathering sticks on the Sabbath who is stoned to death (15:30–36). In any case, the people should try to remember all the laws, even by making certain fringes on their garments (15:37–41).

Another revolt against Moses and Aaron is incited. A large number of Levites are among the rebels, claiming for themselves priestly rights. This time not only Moses but also Aaron intercede with God. In particular, Aaron makes atonement for the people putting on incense (16:47). Corresponding laws follow in chapter 18, namely, making atonement for offenses connected with the sanctuary and other laws defining the responsibilities of priests and Levites, respectively. The ceremony of ritual purification in chapter 19 falls in the same category. It answers the fear of the people expressed in 17:12–13 that they may all die because they are unclean. The ritual purification as described in that chapter should not be understood as an alleged act of magic by which purity is achieved by itself, but as a symbolic act conducted very consciously as an outer expression of an inner conviction.

The episode of the Waters of Meribah (chapter 20) very much resembles an incident from Exodus 17:1–7. Then, too, the people complained about their lack of water. God instructed Moses to strike a rock, from which a water source erupted. In the second episode in Numbers 20, however, Moses is not to strike the rock but to speak to it—and he fails to do so. God answers Moses' disobedience by announcing to him that he will not enter the Promised Land. For modern readers, this sentence seems very harsh in view of the relatively small offense. From the point of view of the story itself, however, Moses committed a great sin in dealing very laxly with a divine instruction in the presence of the whole congregation of Israel. Here, he was disrespectful of the holiness of God (20:12; see Psalm 106:32–33).

Another occasion on which the Israelites complain concerns the bronze serpent in 21:4–9. The serpent forming a rod is a symbol also found in Greek mythology (staff of Aesculapius). The New Testament takes it as a symbol for Jesus Christ, who took upon himself the sins of humanity on the cross (John 3:14–16; 2 Corinthians 5:21).

The Israelite campaigns in the east of the Jordan valley show the strategy they chose to conquer the land: First, the sparsely populated territory east of the Jordan is taken. After that, the people camp at the plains of Moab, northeast of the Dead Sea. They will cross the Jordan moving to the west, thus separating the heartland of Canaan into a northern and a southern part. The two parts will then be taken one after the other, with the Canaanites of the north and the south inable to form alliances with each other. The strategy is described in detail in the book of Joshua.

The wars against the native population of Canaan are described as commanded by God. From a modern point of view, this poses a moral problem. For a discussion, see the book of Joshua.

A remarkable individual described in these chapters is the seer Balaam. We have the distinctive story of his donkey's suddenly starting to speak. Interestingly, Balaam is known to us also from an extrabiblical source. In Tell Deir Alla (biblical Succoth), north of the plains of Moab, an Aramaic inscription has been found containing "prophecies of Balaam son of Beor, seer of the gods." The inscription is dated to around 800 B.C.E.; its content may stem from an even earlier time. In any case the inscription is evidence that Balaam was a well-known character not only in Israel and in the book of Numbers.

The section closes with a census list, resembling the one standing at the beginning of Numbers. After the generation enrolled there was rejected and had died in the wilderness, the second generation is enrolled and thereby prepared for entering the Promised Land.

Preparations for the Conquering of Canaan (Chapters 27–36)

The last 10 chapters again contain very diverse material (narratives, lists, and legal texts). The overarching theme here is the preparation for conquering the Holy Land. The daughters of Zelophehad appear at the beginning and at the end of the block and therefore form a frame around the remaining material. In both places, special cases of the law of inheritance are discussed. The focus is on ensuring that the inherited land will stay with the family and the tribe for whom it was originally allocated. Only after even the problematic cases of the distribution of the land are fixed are the people ready to conquer the land.

The description of daily, weekly, and yearly sacrifices (chapters 28–29) overlaps with some other texts concerning sacrifices and feasts (Exodus 29:38–41; Leviticus 1–7, 23; Numbers 15). Here a special emphasis is put on the species and numbers of animals the priests have to sacrifice on a given day of the year. The regulations are probably given here since the priests did not have the necessary resources at their disposal for making all these sacrifices up to that time but are about to obtain them—since the campaign against the Midianites (chapter 31) will yield a great number of animals. Also notable is the fact that the story of the Midianites lists the booty and its portion given to the priests in a very detailed manner (31:32–47). The legal text of chapter 30 discusses cases in which a father or husband can invalidate a vow made by his daughter or wife. The law is probably recorded here because the Israelites also capture 32,000 young women from the Midianites. Many of them have probably made vows to their gods, which have to be invalidated before Israelites could marry them.

The three remaining chapters are related to the conquering of the land again. Chapter 34 describes the borders of the land to be conquered. The area of Canaan is described exactly the way it is also documented in Egyptian sources from the 14th and 13th centuries B.C.E. At no point in history, however, did Israel possess the whole land. Numbers 34 therefore stands as an ideal of divine promise that can never be realized—because of human failure, as the book of Judges explains.

The tribe of Levi will be occupied with the ritual ceremonies. Therefore, the Levites do not obtain their own territory but instead several cities throughout the country. The land around the cities or villages up to a distance of 1,000 cubits (about 450 m) also belongs to them. From this regulation, based on a rather complicated argument, a rabbinic rule developed that it is not allowed on Sabbath to go more than 1,000 paces from one's house.

The book of Numbers ends rather abruptly, but not unintentionally, at the moment Israel has to cross the Jordan in order to enter the land of Canaan. All preparations are made; all divine standards are given. The reader is waiting for the holy nation to enter the Promised Land.

CHARACTERS

Aaron Brother of Moses, installed as Moses' spokesperson by God, and first high priest of Israel. In the book of Numbers, Aaron appears most of the time as Moses' companion, not playing an individual role.

Balaam A Midianite seer who is sent by the Moabites to put a curse on Israel. However, the spirit of God descends upon him, and instead of cursing he utters blessings over Israel. Balaam is referred to also in an Aramaic inscription found in the region from around 800 B.C.E., containing "prophecies of Balaam son of Beor, seer of the gods."

Moses In the book of Numbers, Moses is depicted as the mediator between God and the people. First, Moses receives laws and regulations from God and passes them on to the people. Moses also has the highest authority as political and military leader of the people. At the same time, he is very humble (12:3) so God himself supports Moses' authority. Moses also feels with the people: On several occasions, he intercedes with God on their behalf, asking God to refrain from punishment, and God regularly answers Moses' prayers. On a few occasions, however, Moses is shown as being tired of leading such an obstinate people.

Obadiah

The book of Obadiah is the shortest of the Twelve, or Minor, Prophets, consisting of just one chapter of 21 verses. It occurs between Amos and Jonah in the Hebrew and Christian Bibles, being the fourth book, but in Septuagint (see BIBLE, EARLY TRANSLATIONS OF) versions, it usually lies fifth, after Joel, though still before Jonah. The order gives no clue as to its date or who Obadiah was. References to a total disaster befalling JERUSALEM (verses 11–12) suggest the fall of Jerusalem in 586 B.C.E., when the Babylonians besieged, captured, and burned the city. One of the major prophets to witness this was Jeremiah, and five of the verses here are almost identical to verses in Jeremiah (verses 1–6 = Jeremiah 49:14–16, 9), again suggesting some proximity in time. Other earlier or later less likely dates have been suggested.

The Hebrew (see BIBLE, LANGUAGES OF) word for the author is *Obadyah*, meaning "worshipper of, or servant of, Yahweh" (see GOD), so this may not have been his real name, but a pseudonym suitable for a prophet. Nothing more is known about him, but a reading of the book of Jeremiah suggests there were independent prophets, such as Uriah (Jeremiah 26:20–23), whose messages were never recorded, or only briefly so. The whole period after the fall of Jerusalem must have been totally confused, so it is amazing anything written survived at all, let alone biographical notes.

The main object of the message is the principality of Edom, which lay in what is today the southern part of Jordan, with the Dead Sea and the Negev forming its western border. There was a long history of enmity between the two nations of Edom and Israel (see HOLY LAND). Edom was descended from Esau, Jacob's twin brother (Genesis 25:24–26). Between the two brothers enmity existed and they went their separate ways. In Numbers 20:18–21 this enmity reemerges when the Edomites refuse passage to the Israelites on their trek (see EXODUS) to the Promised Land under MOSES. Then in 2 Samuel 8:12–14 we read of David's conquest of the principality and suzerainty under Solomon (1 Kings 11:14–22 = 1 Chronicles 18:12–13). The Edomites revolted against Judean control (2 Kings 8:20–21 = 2 Chronicles 21:8–10) and maintained independence through the Babylonian invasion.

SYNOPSIS

God utters a judgment against Edom. The inhabitants are proud of their apparent invulnerability to attack, but they will be overrun unexpectedly (verses 1–8). The main reason for God's judgment is that they aided the enemy in its destruction of Jerusalem and refused to give shelter to the refugees (verses 9–16). The prophet then turns to the future restoration of Israel (see RETURN FROM EXILE), both northern and southern kingdoms (see MONARCHY). After the massive dispersal after the Babylonian invasion, exiles will return and reclaim the Promised Land (verses 17–21).

COMMENTARY

The PROPHECY is technically a "vision," a picture that imprints itself sharply on the prophet's mind or imagination (see REVELATION, GOD'S). Certainly, the descriptions of the events, past and present, are dramatically visualized. He addresses Edom directly

for the first two-thirds of the chapter, though a heavenly messenger's (see ANGELS) words are embedded in the prophecy with a separate message to the surrounding nations, urging them to attack Edom (verse 1). The Edomites' words are heard, too, in an apparently rhetorical question: "Who will bring me down to the ground?" (verse 3). The irony is that it is not a rhetorical question at all; there is a real answer, which is "God." But this is part of their impercipience (verse 7). Mountain imagery is strong, as Edom was a hilly country, and their trust, even pride and arrogance, seem to have been in their geography (verse 3). But being high, even as high as the eagle's "nest set among the stars" (verse 4)—a wonderful hyperbole (see IMAGERY, BIBLICAL)—means, as in Greek tragedy, the farther to fall (verse 2).

The fact these verses are to be found in Jeremiah suggests a widespread enmity toward Edom. Maybe Obadiah quoted them from Jeremiah or vice versa. But other writers of the time felt similar enmity. Lamentations 4:21; Psalms 137:7; Isaiah 34:5–7; and Ezekiel 25:12–14; 36:5–7 all build up a picture of Edomite duplicity and arrogance, which will be met by total devastation. The prophet here cries out in an aside, "How you have been destroyed" (verse 5), seeing in his vision the event as having happened. He asks rhetorically, would not thieves and harvesters have left something behind. But not Edom.

The most dramatic section is from verses 8–15, held together by the recurring phrase "On that day. . . ." In the Bible, the phrase nearly always connotes some sort of judgment or catastrophic happening. Ten times "on that day" (when Edom appears to triumph) is repeated, climaxing on the 11th occasion with "the Day of the LORD" (verse 15), which, with its metaphor of drinking, refers to a final judgment by God over not only the Edomites but all oppressive nations (verse 16) (see LAST THINGS). Other repeating phrases and parallel constructions (see POETRY, BIBLICAL) give the passage an amazing resonance. "But you should not have" occurs seven times, a litany of betrayal of Judah committed by the Edomites. Words of boasting (the Hebrew word means "make great with your mouth") and gloating, of calamity and disaster, interweave dramatically with specific acts: "looting his goods," "to cut off fugitives . . . at the crossings," and so on.

Jeremiah (27:1–11) mentions an anti-Babylonian alliance, including Edom, so Edom's double betrayal of trust and brotherhood (verse 12) is a particular source of anger. The skill of the word painting and tone of controlled anger are reinforced by an amazing confidence, when we consider that the picture on the ground would have seemed quite the opposite.

As we move on to the wider perspectives of the final section, such confidence seems even more an act of faith, which could only have been inspired by the concreteness of the vision. The center of restoration will be Mount Zion (verses 17, 21), which shall "rule Mount Esau," consummating the mountain imagery. The fire of a burning JERUSALEM is replaced by the fire of judgment burning up Edom "as stubble" (verse 18). The returning exiles are named—"house of Jacob," "of Joseph," "Israelites"—to show a united kingdom possessing the land, whose regions are spelled out in a roll call and where the towns are often synechdochal (see IMAGERY, BIBLICAL) of countries. The climax, "and the kingdom shall be the LORD's," reaffirms God's sovereignty in the midst of chaos and betrayal in this striking little prophecy.

CHARACTER

Obadiah   The prophet speaks with the same passionate and literate intensity as Jeremiah, whose message against the Edomites he repeats and enlarges. As a prophet, he sees himself as God's spokesman, refusing even to identify himself.

1 Peter

A French scholar (C. Spicq) once appropriately described 1 Peter as "the most condensed New Testament résumé of the Christian faith and of the conduct it inspires—a model of a 'pastoral letter.'" The main theme of this letter is the suffering of Christians in society and their response to it. It is a general letter of encouragement to

people following Christ who live in an extensive area in Asia Minor (modern Turkey). There are no indications that Peter knew the addressees personally. The churches to which they belong may have been founded by Jews who had been banned from Rome in 49 C.E. and had settled in Asia. As the letter's title resembles that of the other New Testament letters, it probably stems from those who collected these letters. The letter was already known to Clement of Rome (ca. 95 C.E.) and to Irenaeus. Its place in the canon of the New Testament has never been in doubt. On the term *Catholic* or "General" used to describe this letter, see James. See also EPISTLE.

In form and style Peter leans heavily on Paul's letters, and the Greek (see BIBLE, LANGUAGES OF) is correct so that his secretary probably deserves credit for it (see comment on 5:12 below). The situation he writes about is one of social discrimination and threat of local persecutions, not of worldwide organized persecution, which fits well in the sixties of the first century C.E., the final years of Peter's life. As place of dispatch Peter mentions Babylon (5:13), which is usually taken as a covert reference to Rome; it is unlikely to be the real BABYLON in Mesopotamia. Later Church traditions have it that Peter was martyred for his faith in Rome ca. 67 C.E.

1 Peter and the Hebrew Bible

The letter has a particularly Hebrew flavor, and it is clear that Peter regards the Church as the continuation of biblical Israel. This is most evident in 2:1–10, which use "holy priesthood" and Zion language (see JERUSALEM). Yet verses such as 1:14 and 1:18 show that the readers have a non-Jewish background.

For its limited length, 1 Peter has more quotes and allusions from the Hebrew Bible than any other book in the New Testament. These are used to support the argument rather than as teaching in their own right. Peter is aware that an important similarity between his readers and the people of Israel is that both live in hostile environments and struggle to behave as God's people. Here is a list of important connections with the Hebrew Bible:

1 Peter	Hebrew Bible	Subject
1:2	Exodus 24:8	sprinkling of blood
1:16	Leviticus 11:44–45; 19:2	holiness
1:24–25	Isaiah 40:6–8	temporariness
2:4–8	Isaiah 8:14; 28:16; Psalm 118:22	the cornerstone
2:5, 9	Exodus 19:5–6	nation of priests
2:10	Hosea 1:10; 2:23	people of God
2:22–25	Isaiah 53:4–12	the suffering of Jesus
2:25; 5:4	Psalm 23; Ezekiel 34	Jesus the good shepherd
3:6	Genesis 18:12	Sarah's example
3:10–12	Psalm 34:12–16	lifestyle
3:20	Genesis 6; 7:13	Noah
4:14	Isaiah 11:2	the Spirit of the Lord
4:17	Ezekiel 9:6	judgment begins at the house of God
4:8, 18; 5:5	Proverbs 10:12; 11:31; 3:34	wise sayings
5:8	Psalm 22:13; Ezekiel 22:25	lions

As to the effective history of the letter, more than any other New Testament document 1 Peter contributed to the wording of the second-century so-called Apostles' Creed, which contains tenets such as "suffered," "descended into hell," "raised," "ascended into heaven," and "seated at the right hand of God" that are directly from this letter.

SYNOPSIS

The letter contains four main parts, two of which begin with the address "Dear friends" (2:11; 4:12). After the opening greeting (1:1–2) Peter discusses the identity of the people of God as a holy nation (1:3–2:10). He pays attention to the readers' new birth and consequent hope of salvation, which are based on the Resurrection of Jesus Christ from the dead.

The second and longest part is about the responsibilities of the people of God to lead exemplary lives (2:11–4:11). Initially several walks of life are discussed, such as society, the slave–master relationship, and marriage. From 3:8 the possibility of oppression is faced and Jesus Christ is set up as an example of how to behave in adversity. Part 3 is devoted to coping with suffering (4:12–19). In the final part of the letter the responsibilities of the leaders and the members of the churches are addressed (5:1–11). The closing words are personal but brief (5:12–14).

COMMENTARY

Peter's intention in writing is to help his readers to live under the threat of persecution; his answer to the challenges is that they should live in a holy manner, that is, that they should appropriate the moral goodness of God (1:15; see HOLINESS). So the response to bad treatment must be good behavior, love, and charity. Throughout the letter Peter shows how holiness has implications for day-to-day life. The believers' role in society is not merely that of passive victims of injustice; they can have a transformational effect by showing the love of God and by following the example of Jesus. Peter includes pieces of conventional teaching (see ETHICS) in 2:13–3:7 and sets Jesus up as an example (3:18; 4:12–14).

Peter addresses the readers as elect and strangers (exiles) in the world (1:1; cf. 1:17), meaning they are resident aliens on earth as their true citizenship is in the KINGDOM OF GOD (KINGDOM OF HEAVEN). This status already indicates the theme of the letter, which is Christian responsibility in a society in which the believers are no longer truly at home. Peter's insight is that the readers should, nonetheless, remain within the existing social structures and exercise beneficial influence wherever possible. Because in 1:2 the Father, the Son, and the Spirit are all mentioned in one phrase, it is an implicitly trinitarian clause (see TRINITY). Apart from 1 Corinthians 15, few passages in the New Testament have so much to say on the Resurrection of Jesus Christ as the first chapter of 1 Peter. Christian BAPTISM is mentioned and alluded to in 1:21–22 and 3:21, but earlier suggestions that this letter is a baptismal liturgy are now rejected, as baptism is by no means the overarching theme of this letter.

Important in this letter is the imagery of rocks and stones, which signify strength and reliability. In the Hebrew Bible God is often called a rock (Psalm 28:1) and Jesus had given the name *Peter* (= rock) to his disciple Simon (Matthew 16:16–18). Employing Psalm 118:22 and Isaiah 8:14; 28:16, Peter now uses the image in 2:4–8 with reference to Jesus Christ as well as the believers.

In one of the most difficult passages in the New Testament (3:18–22), Peter argues that the readers may well have to die for their faith, following the example of Jesus. Yet for Jesus death was the way to victory, and in that vein he preached to the fallen angels. Peter then moves quickly from this to the time of Noah (see FLOOD, THE), when faithful people were also ostracized by society. He compares the waters of that time to the water of baptism and argues that baptism makes certain of salvation and is a real cleansing of sins. The phrase that Jesus "preached to the spirits in prison" (3:19) is clarified by the comment that he "preached to those now dead" in 4:6.

It appears that 4:11 is a closing sentence. Did the author receive new information during the process of dictating and writing, or did he think of more points to discuss? The rest of the letter does not differ much from the preceding part. In 4:12–19 Peter shows that suffering is a part of the Christian experience. He helps the readers not just to endure but actually to rejoice in suffering (cf. 3:17). It can prove the reality of their faith, and it is a sharing in Christ's sufferings.

The use of the word *Christian* in 4:16 is remarkable, for it occurs in only two other places in the New Testament (Acts 11:26; 26:28). As the word was probably coined by Romans, Peter's use is possibly influenced by his stay in Rome.

In 5:12 Peter gives credit to Silvanus for helping him with this letter. Although some think Silvanus was the letter bearer, it is more likely that he acted as secretary. As such, he will have converted Peter's (Hebrew) dictation into good Greek.

CHARACTERS

Jesus Christ   Within the New Testament, this letter contains the clearest application of Isaiah 53 to the suffering of Jesus Christ. Peter has much to say about Jesus' suffering as his readers also suffer. But Jesus is more than an example; he is the one who bore the sins of humanity so that they can receive forgiveness and healing (2:24), and he is risen from the dead.

Mark   This person also occurs in Acts as John Mark (12:25; 15:37, 39) and is the alleged author of the second gospel. In 5:13 Peter hints at an intimate relationship with him, which explains why many see Peter is the inspiration behind Mark's gospel.

Peter   The letter adds little to what we know about this important disciple from the four Gospels. It is possible that the letter is not very personal in character because Peter does not know the readers personally. Reminiscences of Peter occur in 1:8 (Jesus' appearance to Thomas), 2:23 (Jesus' torture), and 5:5 (the washing of the disciples' feet, John 13).

Silvanus   At the end of the letter the Silvanus is mentioned is Peter's helper. He is also known as Silas and was Paul's traveling companion on his second journey (Acts 15–17). With Paul he wrote 1 and 2 Thessalonians, and he now acts as Peter's secretary.

2 Peter

This letter is the spiritual testament of the apostle Peter, who in 1:13–15 openly writes about his approaching death. It is a general wake-up call, which is, in particular, concerned about false teaching (chapter 2) and questions raised by the alleged delay of the return of Jesus Christ (chapter 3). As the form of the title resembles those of the other New Testament letters, it probably stems from the Christians who collected these letters. The title is entirely correct, because 3:1 refers to the present letter as the second the author has written. Peter is mentioned as the author of the letter in 1:1, and there are several personal elements. In 1:16–18 he claims to have been an eyewitness to Jesus and in particular to the transfiguration (Matthew 17:1–8).

Nonetheless, many interpreters think the letter is not from Peter but a later forgery. One argument for that theory is the nature of its language: This letter is written in good, elevated Greek and differs radically from the rather simple Greek of 1 Peter. In order to accept that Peter, a simple Aramaic-speaking fisherman from Israel (see BIBLE, LANGUAGES OF; TWELVE DISCIPLES), is responsible for it, we must at least assume that he had ample help from a secretary. This, however, is an entirely reasonable assumption, which finds ample support in our knowledge of writing practices in the Hellenistic world (see CULTURES OF THE BIBLE). Even literate people employed secretaries, who would have more or less freedom. The differences between 1 and 2 Peter can be explained by the assumption that Peter relied on two different secretaries (*amanuenses*).

Another argument against Peter's authorship is the strong resemblance between chapter 2 of this letter and the letter of Jude, which is also included in the New Testament. The usual explanation of the similarities is that the present author borrowed from Jude's letter. It is equally possible, however, that both authors drew from a common source. This is the more likely as the form of 1 Peter also is not particularly original, drawing heavily on the general model of Paul's letters.

The letter is included among the Catholic or general epistles (see at James) for a good reason, for the address in 1:1 is very general. The text contains no further indications of the identity of the intended readers. Assuming that Peter was the author, writing toward the end of his life, and that the Church traditions that say that he was crucified by Emperor Nero are reliable, the letter was written around the year 67 C.E. Those who deny its authenticity usually date it sometime in the second century, making it the last of the New Testament documents to have been written. At the time of writing some epistles of Paul had probably already been accepted as part of Holy Scripture, as this letter suggests in 3:15–16. Yet the reference to Paul and his writings could also stem from an earlier date, even from the lifetime of the apostle Peter, for by 67 C.E. all of Paul's letters had been written

and there was regular contact among the different Christian groups.

SYNOPSIS

The letter is in four main parts with introduction and conclusion. The short introduction mentions author and addressees and conveys a wish. The first part is a call to a good lifestyle such as usually occurs toward the end in other New Testament letters (1:3–11), but the exhortation is on Christian terms in that it first mentions the divine enablement and then the requirement. The second part is a discussion of the authority of Jesus and the prophets that serves to authenticate Peter's own writing (1:12–21). Chapter 2 is concerned the false teachers who threaten the Church, and chapter 3, with the return of Jesus Christ and its alleged delay. This final chapter begins with a repetition of Peter's reason for writing (3:1–2), it refers to people who deny the return of Jesus (3:3–7; see LAST THINGS), and it discusses its certainty (3:8–10), before taking the letter full circle with another call to holy living (3:11–18). The conclusion arrives quite suddenly and is very brief.

COMMENTARY

In formal terms the beginning of the letter is like that of most other New Testament letters, but the closure is more abrupt as there are no personal notes or greetings, just a brief phrase in praise of God.

Although 2 Peter contains no actual quotes from the Hebrew Bible such as are characteristic of 1 Peter, there are nonetheless references to Noah (who also appears in 1 Peter 3:20), to Sodom and Gomorrah (2:6), and to Lot (2:5–8) as well as Balaam and his donkey (2:15–16). As in the first letter, here, too, we find a personal reminiscence, this time of the transfiguration of Jesus (1:16–18).

Evangelical Christians often refer to 1:19–21 to support their high view of the inspiration and authority of the Hebrew Bible, and by implication also of the New Testament. In this passage Peter argues that the prophets, and hence all authors of the Hebrew Bible, only transmitted what God gave them to transmit so that the Scriptures are the Word of God.

As explained, chapter 2 closely parallels the letter of Jude. There are two notable differences between the two letters. The first is that eschatological skepticism (the denial of the return of Jesus) characterizes Peter's adversaries but not Jude's, the second that Peter does not include the numerous references to apocryphal literature (see APOCRYPHA AND PSEUDEPIGRAPHA) that we find in Jude. We do not have a clear picture of the people Peter has in mind.

The best-known line in the letter is derived from Psalm 90:4 and found in 3:8: "With God a day is like 1000 years, and 1000 years like a day." This is a great saying to counter eschatological frustration. In Peter's days as in ours, people thought that the delay of Jesus' return made it implausible. Peter's saying indicates that God's understanding of time differs from that of humans, presumably because he exists beyond time. Peter's explanation for the fact that Jesus has not yet returned is entirely positive: God is patient and he wants as many people as possible to repent (3:9; cf. Ezekiel 18:23). Equally positive is his advice about what Christians should do in the meantime: lead a holy and exemplary life (3:11). The image of the thief in the night occurs often in the New Testament (Matthew 24:43; 1 Thessalonians 5:2, 4; Revelation 3:3; 16:15).

The general Jewish-Christian expectation is that at the end of time God will create "a new heaven and a new earth" (Isaiah 65:17; Revelation 21:1). Yet most people assume that there will be some continuity between this world and the next, on the authority of texts such as Romans 8:18–23 and Revelation 21:24–26. It seems difficult to fit 2 Peter 3:10 into this picture of purified continuity as the text seems to suggest wholesale destruction. Yet this is largely due to a textual problem. Whereas older translations follow an inferior Greek text that translates "the earth also and the works that are therein shall be burned up," the best Greek text translates as "the earth and everything that is done on it will be disclosed" (New Revised Standard Version). Consequently, Peter does not say that at the end of time the earth will be completely destroyed but that it will be thoroughly purified by fire. Whereas the origin of the world (Genesis 1; see CREATION) and its first purification (THE FLOOD) came through water, the final cleansing will be with fire.

CHARACTERS

adversaries   The adversaries are described as libertines. Their lifestyle is unholy, sexually immoral, and licentious. Peter says that they are driven by greed (2:3). So both their motivation and their ideas are wrong, although we learn more about the former than about the latter.

Peter   The full name Simeon Peter (1:1) also occurs in Acts 15:14. When he writes this letter, the apostle feels that his life is coming to an end. To express this he uses the metaphor of living in a tent and then discarding it (1:13–14). Otherwise we know nothing about his circumstances at the time of writing. The tradition of the Church says that he was executed by the Romans around the year 67 C.E. The letter has a pastoral tone and is the attempt of an older leader to help the next generation of believers.

Philemon

At some 335 words Philemon is the shortest of the preserved letters of PAUL and close in length to the usual letter (see EPISTLE) in the Greco-Roman world. Because of its brevity there is no division in chapters, just in verses.

This letter is related to Paul's letter to the Colossians. In Colossians 4:9 Paul announces that Onesimus, "one of you," will accompany the letter that he is writing to the Colossians. The same Onesimus is the bearer of the letter to Philemon. Epaphras, a person from Colosse (Colossians 4:12), is also mentioned as Paul's coworker in both letters. These data have led scholars to the conclusion that the addressee, Philemon, lived in Colosse, and that Paul wrote and dispatched both letters at the same time. The other two people mentioned as addressees in Philemon verse 2 are unknown to us and play no role in the argument; they are probably Philemon's wife and son. Timothy's role as coauthor is equally indistinct.

Paul is in prison as he writes but does not say where. The place is likely to be either Rome or Ephesus, although that Paul was ever imprisoned in Ephesus is a well-founded hypothesis rather than a confirmed fact. The date of writing would be in the mid-fifties of the first century C.E. if Paul was imprisoned in Ephesus or between 60 and 62 if he was in Rome. Paul's expectation to be released and his intention to visit Philemon in Colosse, which is not far from Ephesus, would favor the former imprisonment.

Onesimus, who according to verse 12 is the deliverer of the letter, is also its main subject, and he may have asked Paul to write this letter on his behalf. What happened to Philemon and Onesimus after the letter was written and received is unknown, but the fact that the letter has been preserved suggests a positive outcome. Early in the second century Bishop Ignatius of Antioch refers to one Onesimus as bishop of Ephesus. The reference could be to another person, but the age matches if Onesimus was a young man at the time Philemon was written.

Despite its brevity, this letter readily found a place in the canon of the New Testament.

SYNOPSIS

This letter contains the following elements, which are common to most Pauline letters:

Greeting and address (verses 1–2)
Salutation (verse 3)
Thanksgiving (verses 4–6)
Discussion of issues (verses 7–22)
Greetings (verse 23)
Benediction (verse 24)

In the body of the letter Paul addresses the situation of Onesimus with an introductory courtesy (verses 8–9), an appeal (verse 10), background information (verses 11–14), a string of arguments (verses 15–16, 17, 18–19, 20), and closing remarks (verses 21, 22).

COMMENTARY

The historical situation that gave rise to this letter is that the slave Onesimus has run away from his master, Philemon, and has sought refuge with Paul. In this situation he has become a Christian, for that is how Paul's comment that he had become Onesimus's father during his imprisonment (verse 10) must be interpreted. Yet Paul has now convinced Onesimus that he must go back to his master. With this letter Paul requests, however, that Philemon allow Onesimus to return to Paul as an assistant, a veiled way of saying that Onesimus should be released from slavery.

It is remarkable that Paul writes to Philemon with an authority like that of a bishop, yet in a very courteous way. He takes time before he moves to his point in verse 8. It is only by referring to Onesimus's usefulness and to his desire to keep him as an assistant that Paul suggests that Philemon should set the young man free. Release of prisoners was a common practice in the Roman Empire.

Neither in this letter nor anywhere else does Paul directly attack human slavery. The small groups of Christians at the time were not in a position to do this anyway, and the imminent expectation of the return of Jesus Christ (see LAST THINGS) did not encourage attempts at social reform. However, by treating Onesimus and Philemon as equals (verse 16), Paul fundamentally undermines the institution of slavery. From the beginning there was neither male nor female, neither slave nor freeman in the Christian community (Galatians 3:28).

Verse 9 contains a word that can be translated as "old man" or as "ambassador"; translators and interpreters are uncertain what Paul meant. In verse 10 he declares that he has become Onesimus's father, a reference to the latter's conversion to faith in Jesus. Paul is thus his spiritual father (cf. 1 Corinthians 4:15). Verse 11 contains a pun on Onesimus's name, which means "useful": Paul says that he was once "useless" to Philemon but is now useful: i.e., he lives up to his name.

The entire letter is a successful piece of rhetoric, with Paul using a carefully dosed array of arguments to convince Philemon. Already in the thanksgiving section he refers to "all the good" that the addressee "may do for Christ" (verse 6). The latter's personal debt to Paul is only brought to bear toward the end (verse 19) and is followed by Paul's mentioning of his intention to pay a visit to Philemon (22). Is this intention an expression of the unconditionality of the friendship or a thinly veiled attempt to determine how his letter will be received?

CHARACTERS

Jesus Christ It is characteristic of Paul that even in this pragmatic letter he refers frequently to faith in JESUS CHRIST. The introduction (verses 4–6) lays the foundation for the requests that follow, in the form of the common faith of sender and addressee, but no specifics about Jesus are mentioned.

Onesimus An otherwise unknown slave, on whose behalf the apostle Paul writes this letter in an attempt to placate his master, Philemon. Onesimus had run away from Philemon and had become a Christian while with Paul. How and why he had gone to Paul is not stated. Although verses 18–19 are rather unclear to later readers, it seems that he had also stolen items from Philemon; if so, that was a capital offense.

Paul This letter confirms the portrait of the apostle Paul in Acts by showing that he had connections among the upper classes. It also shows his courage in providing hospitality to Onesimus, for it was a criminal offense to accommodate a runaway slave. Equally brave is Paul's attempt to secure his new friend's release from slavery.

Philemon Philemon is an otherwise unknown slave owner in Colosse, a town in Asia Minor, in whose house a Christian house church meets. Paul addresses him as friend and knows about his activities (verse 7), although he has never visited Colosse, so it is likely that the two had met somewhere else. The reference to his personal indebtedness in verse 19 suggests that Philemon, too, was a convert of Paul.

Philippians

Of the many letters in the New Testament that we have from the hand of the apostle PAUL, Philippians is the most joyful and cheerful. Paul has received help from the church in Philippi and is writing this letter to express his gratitude. This church had been the first he founded on traveling to Europe (Acts 16:11–40) in difficult circumstances (1:30; 1 Thessalonians 2:2). The apostle had revisited it later (Acts 20:6), and it had obviously flourished since then. Paul's reference to "overseers [= bishops] and deacons" in the opening greeting suggests a well-established community, although we should not read later developments into the earliest churches. The city of Philippi was a Roman colony, a settlement of former soldiers, situated in Macedonia (northern Greece). For such Roman readers Paul's words "our citizenship is in heaven" (3:20) are very loaded, and for them he refrains from making much use of the Hebrew Bible.

Philippians is one of the letters written by Paul while in prison. He was imprisoned in Caesarea in 58–60 and in Rome in 60–62 C.E., and probably in Ephesus in the mid-fifties of the first century. We cannot be entirely certain during which imprisonment the present letter originated, and the references to the imperial guard (1:13) and to the emperor's household (4:22) are inconclusive. The period in Rome is the most likely, as Paul's words in 1:20–25 suggest that he is now of advanced age and in grave danger. The letter was probably carried to Philippi by Epaphroditus, who had also delivered the gifts of the church to Paul (2:25; 4:18). See also EPISTLE.

SYNOPSIS

After the usual greetings, Paul begins with a cordial thanksgiving to God for the Church and its faith, which leads to a prayer that their love will increase even further (1:1–11). He then pays ample attention to his personal circumstances, obviously by way of account to his sponsors (1:12–26). It is unclear to him whether he will be released or convicted, but he is open to both possibilities. Paul next encourages the readers to lead worthy lives, despite the fact that they also have to cope with some form of persecution (1:30). His exhortation becomes more specific when he sets up Jesus Christ as an example of humility and readiness to serve (2:1–18). The letter seems to be coming to a close with Paul's announcement that he will send Timothy to Philippi and hopes to go there himself (2:19–24). First, however, Paul will send Epaphroditus back to his hometown, presumably with the letter (2:25–30). Both missionaries are warmly commended.

The phrase beginning with *Finally* could be the letter's final line, but for some reason Paul continues with some warnings against unspecified troublemakers intermixed with testimonies about his own faith (3:1–4:1). Whereas they are proud of their achievements, Paul refuses to boast; he puts all his trust in Jesus Christ. A few specific exhortations follow (4:2–9) before Paul discusses the relation between the Church and himself (4:10–20) and concludes the letter with warm greetings.

COMMENTARY

The central message of Philippians is that the church should try to be like Jesus Christ in its lifestyle. The author focuses his readers' attention on Jesus and life in imitation of him, frequently using phrases like "in Jesus" and "in the Lord." As in some other letters, for the encouragement of the readers Paul also employs imagery derived from athletics (1:27; 2:16; 3:12–14; 4:1, 3) that highlights perseverance. The expressions "the day of Jesus Christ" (1:6) and "day of Christ" (2:16) refer to his return, which is also mentioned in 3:20 (see LAST THINGS).

The best-known and most influential part of the letter has the form of a hymn about JESUS CHRIST (2:6–11). This profound text praises his voluntary humiliation on behalf of humanity, which Paul also mentions in 2 Corinthians 8:9. Jesus was equal to God in heaven, but he became human and died by crucifixion, yet was subsequently exalted in heaven. The name "above every other name" is the divine name JHWH (Yahweh), rendered as "Lord" in English translations (also in 2:11; see GOD); this means that Paul calls Jesus God. Verse 2:10 reflects

ancient cosmology. The verses that precede and those that follow the hymn draw out the consequences of living as a follower of Jesus. In other letters, Paul also occasionally uses hymns (Colossians 1:15–20; 1 Timothy 3:16).

The dominant note of the letter is *joy and rejoicing*; the word group occurs 16 times throughout the letter. Despite his extreme hardship and uncertain future, even in the face of death, Paul is very grateful to the Philippians for their support and full of confidence that God will bless them and him even more. Yet there are also several calls to unity (2:2–3, 5, 14; 3:15; 4:2), although Paul does not spell out why these are necessary. A specific call occurs in 4:2–3, where two otherwise unknown women in the church are mentioned by name. The word for "companion" or "yoke fellow," *syzygos* (4:3), has sometimes been taken as a proper name because nobody can work out who is meant here.

The beginning of chapter 3 differs in tone from the rest of the letter, and this difference has led critical scholars to suggest it is not original to the letter, but this idea is surely overcritical. It is hard to see where the interpolation would have ended in the first place. Verse 2 suggests that some Jews want the Philippians to be circumcised; *dogs* was often used by Jews against Gentiles, but here Paul uses it against these legalistic Jews. Verses 18–19, on the other hand, evoke pictures of libertines: quite the opposite position. Moreover, in 1:15–18 Paul had already criticized another group, people in Rome who preach the gospel with wrong motives, and in 1:28 he had hinted at adversaries of the church. After his angry outburst Paul soon passes to the positive topics of how Jesus had changed his life (3:4–6) and how he enjoys mystical communion with Jesus (3:7–11; see for similar tones Romans 6:5).

Paul did not normally allow churches to support him because he wished to support himself by making tents (Acts 18:3). Verse 4:10 indicates that even the Philippians had not always assisted him regularly, but 4:15 shows that this had been the case at the outset; the latter verse uses a technical business term. That the Philippians have this privilege once more points to the special relationship between Paul and them but probably also to his needy situation as a prisoner. He does not specify the kind of help he had received; Epaphroditus may have taken money with him from Philippi to buy him clothing and food.

The positive encouragements in 4:4–7 are remarkable in the mouth of a prisoner on death row. The secret of his trust is no doubt the prayer that he commends to his readers. Throughout the letter there are hints at the reality of suffering for the faith for both Paul and the readers.

CHARACTERS

Epaphroditus   A coworker of Paul, who is mentioned three times in Philippians. He was the messenger of the church in Philippi, and he is therefore not to be confused with the Epaphras who is mentioned in Colossians and Philemon. The Philippians had heard that Epaphroditus had been gravely ill, and Paul confirms that this was "for the work of Christ," probably referring to his hazardous journey to Paul in Rome. He had been restored to good health by the time Paul wrote this letter and would return home with it (2:25–30).

Paul   In this letter Paul sets himself up as an example of Christian behavior with more emphasis than in most of his letters. Faced with his impending sentencing, he is torn between a desire to be with Jesus Christ and one to continue his earthly ministry, to which he refers seven times as "the gospel." This dilemma is beautifully summed up in "For me, living is Christ and dying is gain" (1:21). Paul also gives some insight into his Jewish background, characterizing himself as a former Pharisee (3:5–6).

Timothy   Timothy was Paul's younger coworker (Acts 16:1–3) and sometimes envoy who is mentioned as coauthor in several letters (2 Corinthians, Colossians, 1 and 2 Thessalonians, Philemon). Paul also wrote two letters to him (1 and 2 Timothy). In Philippians Paul refers to him in the third person (2:19–23), suggesting that his role in conceiving the letter was limited. This passage is a warm commendation of the young man.

Prayer of Azariah

See Daniel.

Prayer of Manasseh

Manasseh was king over Judah from 696 to 642 B.C.E., reigning for 55 years. The biblical reports in 2 Kings 21:1–18 and 2 Chronicles 33:1–20 are very negative about him because he reintroduced idolatry and syncretism in the land. However, 2 Chronicles adds that when he was taken captive to Babylon, he confessed his sins before God and God forgave him. 2 Chronicles 33:18–19 also hints that this prayer was written.

The Greek text that came to us as the Prayer of Manasseh, however, is probably not this original prayer. It may be of second-century B.C.E. Jewish or even Christian origin. The text belongs to the deuterocanonical books (i.e., being of secondary canonical rank) of the Orthodox Churches. The Roman Catholic as well as the Protestant churches reckon it among the Apocrypha (see APOCRYPHA AND PSEUDEPIGRAPHA).

The psalmlike text consists of only 15 verses. In verses 1–8, Manasseh praises the power and the mercy of God, in 9–10 he confesses his sins, and in 11–15 he asks for pardon and promises God to praise him all his life.

Proverbs

The book of Proverbs is the Hebrew Bible's introduction to old Israelite wisdom. The genre of the biblical WISDOM LITERATURE is, in the first instance, not defined by the topics dealt with but rather by its specific approach to knowledge. While the priests base themselves on the Law of Moses and the Prophets on the visions God gives them, the wise learn the will of God by observing their environment. Since God created the world in wisdom, the one who observes nature can acquire divine wisdom. If you see through the mechanisms of human interaction and learn to behave accordingly, your life will be successful. A prerequisite for such a wise way of living, however, is respect for God: "The fear of the LORD is the beginning of knowledge" (Proverbs 1:7).

Other wisdom books of the Hebrew Bible are Ecclesiastes and Job, and, in a wider sense, the Song of Solomon. However, the wisdom books stand in a certain tension to each other: While the book of Proverbs is quite optimistic regarding the possibilities of human knowledge and successful living, Job and Ecclesiastes mainly consider the limits of such an approach. Therefore, the book of Proverbs often is said to be "traditional" wisdom (old, "naive"), while Job and Ecclesiastes are called "critical wisdom," or even "crisis of wisdom." But the fact has to be recorded that Proverbs is specifically designed as an introductory work. It addresses itself to the "simple" and "young" (1:4) and schematizes reality for didactical purposes. The book of Job, in contrast, has as its main emphasis learning respect before God, and Ecclesiastes surely is a book for "advanced" readers. Interestingly, in the old Jewish tradition (in the Babylonian Talmud, Tractate Baba Bathra 14b) the wisdom books appear as a group in the order Job, Proverbs, Ecclesiastes, Song of Solomon—which would mean, first the "fear of the LORD" has to be learned; then follows Proverbs as the "basic course" of wisdom; after it Ecclesiastes, the "advanced course"; and finally the Song of Solomon as highlight on successful living. In the Apocrypha related to the Hebrew Bible, the book Sira and the so-called Wisdom of Solomon also belong to the wisdom genre (these books are discussed elsewhere in this volume). See also APOCRYPHA AND PSEUDEPIGRAPHA.

The book of Proverbs is divided into seven parts by way of subtitling. The first main part, chapters 1–9, serves as a theological foundation. Here, in a more systematic way the principles of biblical wisdom are explained. The other six parts mainly consist of collections of individual proverbs.

According to the subtitles, Proverbs 10–22 and 25–29 stem from King Solomon (period of office 971–931 B.C.E.). In the biblical tradition, Solomon is depicted as an extraordinarily wise man. In addition, in the time of Solomon, the court opened itself for international diplomatic relations—as can be seen from many non-Israelite names in the lists of Solomon's court officials. This is probably the context in which wisdom thinking, widespread in the ancient Near East, found its way to Israel and was restructured to gain its specific Israelite distinctness. This is another reason for connecting the Israelite wisdom literature to the name of Solomon.

Other authors of Proverbs named in the text are Agur and Lemuel (or, his mother; see 30:1; 31:1). We do not know anything about these people. The collections in Proverbs 22–24 originate from an anonymous group of "wise men" (22:17; 24:23). In the subtitle of 25:1 we find the note that these proverbs of Solomon were collected by the "officials of King Hezekiah of Judah" (period of office 715–686 B.C.E.). This points to the fact that the book of Proverbs developed step by step. The title of 1:1, The proverbs of Solomon son of David, king of Israel, can therefore be understood in different ways. Some scholars relate the title to the first main part, chapters 1–9. Others see the statement as the main title relating to the whole book, in the sense that the largest parts of the book stem from Solomon, or in the sense that Solomon is the canonical "father of wisdom," even if he did not write down every wisdom saying. According to the second interpretation, Proverbs 1–9 are not necessarily from Solomon but from the final redactors of Proverbs, who wanted a theological foundation to precede the proverb collections.

The date of the final editing of Proverbs cannot be fixed with certainty. A possibility is the time of Hezekiah (seventh century B.C.E.).

SYNOPSIS

Introduction to Wisdom (Chapters 1–9)

The first part of the book can be divided into a series of sections. Ten so-called Instructions have been detected. In each of the instructions, the wisdom teacher, or "father," gives some teaching to his disciple, or "son." Next to the instructions there are two speeches of wisdom and two poems about wisdom.

The second instruction (chapter 2) contains the "teaching program" of Proverbs 1–9. It asks the reader to turn to wisdom, and it describes its consequences with two positive and two negative statements. The four topics thereby defined are treated in more detail in the remaining "instructions" of Proverbs 1–9.

2:1–4	Introduction: Call to accept wisdom
2:5–8	"then you will understand . . ."
	Wisdom leads to a proper relationship with God
	(expounded in instruction 3 [3:1–12])
2:9–11	"then you will understand . . ."
	Wisdom leads to a proper way of life
	(expounded in instruction 4 [3:21–35])
2:12–15	"it will save you from . . ."
	Wisdom protects against evil men
	(expounded in instructions 1, 6, and 7 [1:8–19; 4:10–19; and 4:20–27])
2:16–19	"you will be saved from . . ."
	Wisdom protects against dangerous women
	(expounded in instructions 8, 9, and 10 [5:1–23; 6:20–35; and 7:1–27])
2:20–22	Conclusion

The first and the second topic are therefore treated in instructions following the "teaching program." For the third and the fourth topic, three instructions are devoted to each. As an irregularity to the scheme, one of the instructions warning of evil men is placed in position 1 rather than in position 5. The reason for that probably is a rhetorical one: The reader should not be immediately confronted with a system (instruction 2) but be introduced to the subject via an example. For this reason, instruction 5 was placed at the beginning of the text. The "empty" fifth place was afterward filled with a more general call to wisdom (4:1–9).

Nine of the 10 instructions (except instruction 4) begin with a call to obedience to the parental instruction. Wisdom, therefore, is something learned by education and is passed on from generation to generation.

The first speech of wisdom (1:20–33) warns those ignoring her that there will be a "too late."

The speech belongs to the introductory motivational part and leads on to the "teaching program" in chapter 2.

The first poem on wisdom (3:13–20) emphasizes especially the priceless worth of wisdom.

The second speech of wisdom (8:1–36) is the theological highlight and conclusion of the first main part. The speech describes personified "Lady Wisdom" (see PERSONIFICATION) as the first of God's works of creation and as his muse while he created the earth (8:22–31; see 3:19–20). The point made is that the divine world order is founded on wisdom. To be wise therefore means to observe the divine orders and live accordingly.

The second poem on wisdom and folly (9:1–18) consists of three parts: The first and third parts are shaped in parallel. Lady Wisdom (9:1–6) and Lady Folly (9:13–18) invite the passers-by to a meal in their houses, respectively. Therefore, the reader is called to make his or her decision between wisdom and folly. The middle part of the poem (9:7–12) contains proverbs about the relationship between the wise and the fool. It also repeats the statement of the beginning of the book, "The fear of the LORD is the beginning of wisdom," which therefore forms a frame around the first main part.

The first main part of Proverbs 1–9 is the theological foundation of old Israelite wisdom. The explanations given here form the background on which to understand the following proverbial collections.

Words of Solomon (10:1–22:16)

Proverbs 10:1–22:16 is a collection of 375 proverbs. This number equates to the numerical value of the name *Solomon*. (Each letter of the Hebrew Bible also has a numerical value: Shelomoh = $Sh + L + M + H = 300 + 30 + 40 + 5 = 375$). The proverbs follow each other in a rather arbitrary sequence, although some kind of thematic grouping has been detected.

The basic principle the proverbs are based on is the relation of act and consequence, or the principle of retribution. This is expressed in an antithetic manner: The one who does good will receive good; the one who does bad will receive bad. The collection involves two contrasting groups of people: the righteous versus the wicked on a moral and religious level, and the wise versus the fool on an intellectual level. The groups are equated to each other: The wise is also the righteous, and the fool is also the wicked. The groups of people are characterized by their actions: diligence versus laziness, honesty versus lying, faithfulness versus wickedness, and so on. The acts have their corresponding consequences: blessing versus curse, life versus death, and so forth. Act and consequence often relate concretely: The person who gives will be given to; the one who deceives will be deceived.

On the one hand, the principle of act and consequence is a mechanism built into society. On the other hand, it is also based on the will of God, because it is an aspect of the way he achieves justice. Further, in spite of all human planning and reckoning, the sovereignty of God has to be respected and the limits of human knowledge have to be recognized.

These principles are expounded in the individual proverbs, or thematic clusters of proverbs, and applied to different topics, for example, acting wisely in the economic area; using one's tongue wisely, particularly in the setting of a court; wisely respecting God and the instruction of the parents.

Words of the Wise (22:17–24:22)

What is distinctive in this section is its proximity to the Egyptian Teaching of Amenemope (12th century B.C.E.). Especially in the section 22:17–23:11, virtually every verse has a parallel to Amenemope. In addition, there is an analogy in form: The Teaching of Amenemope is divided into 30 chapters; Proverbs 22:20 announces that "thirty sayings" will be given (some versions render "excellent sayings" instead), as is indeed the case.

A direct literary dependence of the Proverbs section to Amenemope is, however, improbable. It is rather assumed that the Proverbs section was written as a free association to the Egyptian Teaching. Possibly, the text stems from an Egyptian scribe who had to learn the Teaching of Amenemope at school (we know that the text was used for educational purposes) and later went to Solomon's court as an official.

Typically, the references to Egyptian religion in Amenemope are not taken over in the biblical text. Rather, the sayings are made to fit into the biblical frame of the "fear of the LORD."

The 30 sayings can be divided into three groups of 10 sayings. The groups can be summarized as follows:

Sayings 1–10: If an official has risen through the ranks, he should not use his power to do injustice, he should not set as his highest goal to gain riches, and he should behave very carefully when invited by the rich and powerful.

Sayings 11–20: Wisdom means living in an upright way and avoiding dissoluteness. Wisdom is passed on in the family and results in blessing for the family.

Sayings 21–30: Wisdom means to honor God and the king and, whether dealing with friends or with enemies, always to keep in mind that God will establish justice and that he expects human beings to do the same. To live according to this wisdom is like eating honey for the soul.

More Words of the Wise (24:23–34)

This short section deals with the topics of justice and work. It is formed as two rows: the judge (23b–25), the right reaction (26), and diligence (27), and the witness (28), the wrong reaction (29), and laziness (30–34).

More Words of Solomon (Chapters 25–29)

The second collection of Solomon's proverbs is much more structured than the first. It consists of several groups of proverbs connected to each other thematically.

The first section, 25:2–7a, consists of three blocks of two proverbs each dealing with the king. The second section, 25:7b–10, gives instruction to act wisely in trial.

Proverbs 25:11–28 is about good and false talking. This section uses many images and comparisons. Moving on from the outer to the inner rings: Verses 11f. and 27f. are about fitting and unfitting words; in 13f. and 25f. different forms of water (snow, clouds without water, fresh water, dirty water) are compared to different kinds of words. Verses 15 and 23f. describe the subversive power of the tongue. Verses 16f. and 21f. are about hospitality; the verses are connected via the words *hate* and *eat*. At the center, verses 18–20, three comparisons demonstrate inappropriate behavior.

Chapter 26 describes bad characters: the fool (26:1–12), the lazy (26:13–16), the quarrelsome (26:17–21), and the devious flatterer (26:22–28).

Chapter 27 contains different proverbs, mainly around the topic "the human character matures when accepting criticism and admonition."

In chapters 28–29, six proverbs stand out, giving the section an overall structure. These structuring proverbs consist of alternating statements about the wicked and the righteous, and the second line of each proverb fits to the first line of the next structuring proverb, as dominoes do:

28:1   The *wicked* flee when no one pursues,
          but the *righteous* are as bold as a lion.

28:12   When the *righteous* triumph, there is
             great glory,
          but when the *wicked* prevail, people go
             into hiding.

28:28 When the *wicked* prevail, people go
             into hiding,
             but when they perish, the *righteous*
             become great.

29:2   When the *righteous* are great, the
             people rejoice,
          but when the *wicked* rule, the people
             groan.

29:16 When the *wicked* are in authority,
             transgression increases,
             but the *righteous* will look upon their
             downfall.

29:27   The unjust are an abomination to
             the *righteous*,
          but the upright are an abomination to
             the *wicked*.

These verses form the framework for chapters 28–29. They define the topic of the section, namely, the rule of the righteous versus the rule of the wicked. In the sections between the structuring verses, the topic is developed. To sum up, chapters 28–29 warn the powerful not to become greedy and suppress the poor but to do the opposite, obey the Torah, fear God, and reign in honesty, wisdom, and justice.

Words of Agur (*Chapter 30*)

The chapter of the proverbs of Agur shows a preference for enumerations and numerical sayings. From its content, the section is about small and great, humility and pride, modesty and arrogance. There is no clear development of thought, yet the proverbs are arranged by topic. In some places there are motifs bridging from one to the next proverb ("ravens" in verse 17 and "eagle" in verse 19, "way" in verses 19 and 20, etc). The verses 1–9 concentrate on the relationship to God, while verses 10–32 deal with observations the wise man has made in his environment.

Agur calls to a modest, levelheaded style of life, not making too many words. The "small" should honor the "great" (man-God, child-parents), but also the "great" should deal respectfully with the "small" (master-slave, rich-poor, example of small animals that deserve respect).

Words of Lemuel (*Chapter 31*)

The instruction given to the king is a literary genre often found in the ancient Near East. In verses 1–9, Lemuel is admonished not to spend his life with amorous adventures and drinking sessions but to fulfill his duties and give justice to those who cannot help themselves.

The verses 4–5 and 6–9 are arranged in parallel:

1. negative	2. positive
wine, strong drink (4)	strong drink, wine (6)
drink, forget (5a)	drink, forget (7)
rights of the afflicted (5b)	rights of the afflicted (8–9)

The section in verses 10–31 is a poem about the virtuous woman. It has the form of an alphabetic acrostichon, which means, each verse begins with a successive letter of the Hebrew alphabet. The form expresses order and completeness.

The noble woman is depicted with "typical" traditional female character traits like solicitude and carefulness. On the other hand, she is also a manager, leading a staff of servants, having a wide range of duties and possibilities for self-fulfillment. The text paints an image of a successful way of life according to wisdom standards; the noble woman becomes a metaphor for "Lady Wisdom" (see

Proverbs 8–9) and therefore legitimately serves as a conclusion to the whole book. It has to be noted, however, that the poem is not directed toward telling women how they have to behave but to men who can be happy if they find such a woman. See also WOMEN OF THE BIBLE.

Psalms

The Psalter (book of Psalms) is the Hebrew Bible's book of hymns and PRAYERS. It contains prayers from all kinds of real-life situations, from the personal as well as from the religious realm. All kinds of emotions are expressed openly before God: joy and sadness, fear and security, doubt and confidence. As the church reformer Martin Luther said: "Here you can look into the saints' heart." Therefore, many of the psalms directly appeal even to modern readers. The book of Psalms surely is one of the most popular books of the Bible.

However, the Hebrew Psalter is more than a collection of prayers: It is also a textbook on prayer and on the relationship of the individual believer to God. At the same time it is a reflection on the history of the people of Israel, beginning with the Davidic kingdom and ending with the restoration after the Babylonian Exile (see RETURN FROM EXILE) and the everlasting kingdom of God.

Authors and Dates of the Psalms

From the 150 psalms, about 100 are assigned to different authors. Most of them, 73, have King David as their author. Some other psalms stem from the Levites, who were responsible for the music at the temple (see 1 Chronicles 15:16–19): Asaph (Psalms 50 and 73–83), Heman (88), Ethan (89), and the Korahites (42; 44–49; 84; 87–88). Two psalms are assigned to Solomon (72 and 127) and one to Moses (90). For many of the psalms, however, it is disputed whether the names given in the psalm titles were part of the original text and whether they are historical or not. Generally speaking, conservative scholars tend to accept the names as historical, while liberal scholars are more skeptical about them. In any case, the author names and also the situational information given in some of the

psalm titles point to an interpretive context for the psalm that should be considered for interpretation.

The book of Psalms came into existence over a long period. According to the psalm titles, one first focal point of psalm writing was the time of David (period of office 1010–971 B.C.E.). The last psalms were written after the Babylonian Exile. It is assumed that there had been several earlier collections of psalms that were later integrated into the present form of the book. Possibly, the final redaction of the Psalter was done by those responsible for the closing of the whole canon of the Hebrew Bible (see FORMATION OF THE CANON: THE HEBREW BIBLE).

The Poetry of the Psalms

The psalms are the best example of Hebrew poetry. Its main feature is the so-called line parallelism. One and the same thought is expressed twice in two lines using different words. Instead of a rhyme of words as in much Western poetry, the Israelites employed a "rhyme of thoughts." To be more detailed, three different kinds of parallelism can be found: The synonymous parallelism,

> . . . but their delight is in the law of the LORD,
> and on his law they meditate day and night.
>   (Psalm 1:2)
> His line shall continue forever,
> and his throne endure before me like the sun.
>   (Psalm 89:36)

the emblematic parallelism, where one line serves as an illustration of the other,

> As a father has compassion for his children,
> so the LORD has compassion for those who fear
>   him. (Psalm 103:13)

and the antithetic parallelism, where the two lines contrast with each other:

> for the LORD watches over the way of the
>   righteous,
> but the way of the wicked will perish. (Psalm
>   1:6)

There are variations on these basic forms, e.g., parallelisms consisting of three or more lines. Important for interpretation of parallelism generally is that the two lines should not be interpreted separately. Rather, the second line fills out the meaning of the first, and the message derives from both lines read together as a single thought.

The second main feature of the Hebrew poetry is the extensive use of images and metaphors (see IMAGERY, BIBLICAL). The modern reader will feel especially unfamiliar with the frequent use of *metonymy*, which means that a word is replaced by another word standing in a certain relationship to it. For example, in the prayer "Let me hear joy and gladness" (Psalm 51:8), the psalmist does not literally want to "hear joy" but rather to hear something that makes him happy, which is, in this case, forgiveness of sin. So in this metonymy, the cause is replaced by its effect. More examples: "How majestic is your name in all the earth" (Psalm 8:1, 9)—here the name stands metonymically for God's revealing his glory to the human beings. "Let us burst their bonds asunder, and cast their cords from us" (Psalm 2:3)—the foreign kings were not literally fettered, but they had to pay tribute. So in this metonymy, the concrete replaces the abstract.

A variation of this is the *merism*, where two opposing elements are given in order to express a complex whole: "The Lord will keep your going out and your coming in" (Psalm 121:8)—going out and coming in refer to going out of the city gates in the morning in order to work in the fields and returning in the evening. Therefore, the statement can be translated "The LORD will keep your daily work." Another example is "You know when I sit down and when I rise up" (Psalm 139:2), which again points to everyday life, day (rising up) and night (sitting down).

Frequently, images are used as comparisons. An example of a *simile* (a comparison using the word *like* or *as . . . as*) is "I am poured out like water" (Psalm 22:14). The point of comparison is that there is no stability, and the feeling expressed is losing control. An example for a *metaphor* (a comparison equating the two elements without using the word *like* or *as*) is "For the LORD God is a sun and shield" (Psalm 84:11). The points of comparison are power and protection; the feeling expressed is security and safety.

Sometimes, only the comparing element is given (*hypocatastasis*): "dogs are all around me" (Psalm 22:16). This sentence is really about bad people. The point of comparison is that both are shady (dogs were considered unclean animals), life-threatening aggressors, and the associated feeling is panic and fear of death.

The language of the psalms is also highly conventional. The "righteous" frequently mentioned, for example, are people who live their lives with God (not those who believe they do not make any mistakes); when the text speaks about believers in trouble, they are often described as "the poor" or "the needy." This is conventional and does not mean that poverty is seen as a virtue per se. On the opposite side stands the "wicked" or the "fool." These words do not refer to criminals or idiots alone but rather to all who trust in themselves instead of trusting in God. Another word used conventionally is *enemy*. It can denote the hostile army but also a neighbor whom the psalmist is in conflict with, or even a nonpersonal threat or obstacle.

All these poetic features contribute to the density of the text; in very few Hebrew words (often only three or four per line) a lot can be said. To analyze these features, however, some expertise is needed. Modern Bible translations often help the reader by resolving some of the figures of speech. But then, however, the immediate contact to the Hebrew poetry is lost.

Many of the psalms are written as songs. Often, the psalm titles give the name of a melody, a musical instrument, or another instruction referring to music. The word *Selah* occurring in the text of several of the older psalms is probably an instruction regarding the musical accompaniment of the psalm. In the Hebrew temple worship, music played an important role, as lists of temple musicians show (e.g., 1 Chronicles 25). At the same time, however, many of the psalms are made for prayer and meditation of the individual.

Psalm Genres

Many of the psalms use recurring elements. This enables us to group the psalms into different genres. The genre "LAMENT of the individual," for example, typically consists of the following elements: address of God, lament, request, expression of confidence, promise to praise God (see Psalms 3, 7, 12, 13, etc.). Other genres are praise of the individual (Psalms 30, 32, 34, etc.), lament of the people (44, 60, 74), and praise of the people, also called hymn (8, 29, 33, 104, 105). Not all psalms, however, fit into one of these classes. Rather, there are many mixed forms.

More specialized psalm genres are the royal psalms that deal with the history of the Davidic kingdom (Psalms 2, 45, 72, 89, 110, etc.); the kingship of Yahweh, psalms that praise God as king (Psalms 47, 93, 95–99); the wisdom psalms that reflect on the justice of God and on the relationship of act and consequence (Psalms 37, 73, 78, 127, 128, etc.; see Proverbs, Job, Ecclesiastes); psalms of Torah wisdom that combine wisdom thinking and the study of the word of God (Psalms 1, 19, and 119).

Besides all genre classifications and conventions, the reader has to bear in mind that each psalm is also a work of art in itself.

Themes of the Book of Psalms

The scholar Dietrich Bonhoeffer has identified the following important topics in the Psalms:

- creation: Psalms 8, 19, 29, 104
- the Torah (the Law/word of God): 1, 19, 119
- the history of salvation: 78, 105, 106
- the Messiah: 2, 22, 69, 72, 89, 110, 132
- feasts, temple, worship: 27, 42, 48, 81, 84, 87, 122, etc.
- the blessings of life: 37, 103, etc.
- suffering, temptation, consolation: 13, 31, 35, 41, 44, 54, 55, 56, 61, 74, 79, 86, 88, 102, 105, etc.
- confidence: 23, 37, 63, 73, 91, 121
- sin—the seven traditional confession prayers: 6, 32, 38, 51, 102, 130, 143; but see also 14, 15, 25, 31, 39, 40, 41, etc.
- innocence: 5, 7, 9, 16, 17, 26, 35, 41, 44, 59, 66, 68, 69, 73, 86, etc.
- the enemies: 5, 7, 9, 10, 13, 17, 21, 23, 28, 31, 35, 36, 40, 41, 44, 52, etc., especially 137
- the end: 39, 90, 102; the hope for eternal life; 16:9ff.; 49:15; 56:13; 73:24; 118:15ff.; the final victory of God and his Messiah: 2, 96, 97, 98, 110, 148–150

The Psalms as a Book

For a long time, the Psalter has been seen as a collection of individual psalms. The sequence of the psalms was not considered to be of any meaning. Only since the 1970s onward has scholarship begun to examine the criteria according to which the psalms are ordered. Today we can say that the book of Psalms is not an anthology but rather a unified literary work.

The main feature of its structure is its organization in five so-called books: Psalms 1–41; 42–72; 73–89; 90–106; and 107–150. The seams between the books are marked by certain formulas of praise, which appear at the end of the last psalms of Book I to IV, respectively. For example, Psalm 41:13 reads:

> Blessed be the LORD, the God of Israel, from everlasting to everlasting. Amen and Amen.

Similar formulas are found in 72:18–19; 89:52; and 106:48.

The inner structure of the books varies from book to book. For the first three books, an interpretative framework has been found, consisting of specific psalms placed at the beginning and ending of each of the books (Gerald Wilson, *The Editing of the Hebrew Psalter* [Chico, Calif.: Scholars Press, 1985]). In particular, there is a series of royal psalms 2–72–89 (at the beginning of Book I and at the end of Books II and III) that describe the history of the Davidic kingdom from the enthronement of David (2) along the installment of his successors (72) until the destruction of the kingdom due to the Babylonian Exile (89). To be more exact, characteristic *pairs* of psalms frame the first three books, where an individual and a communal (national, royal) psalm are placed together in each of the instances (Psalms 1 + 2, 42f. + 44, 71 + 72, 73 + 74, and 88 + 89). The order of the psalms in the bodies especially of Books II and III is a subject still disputed among scholars. In Book IV, on the other hand, the holistic message is already well understood. The book draws theological conclusions from the Babylonian Exile and the loss of the kingdom. Book V is structured using formal features like repetitions of the phrase "Give thanks to the Lord" and "Praise the Lord (Hallelujah)." It deals with the time of the restoration after the EXILE.

Scholars assume that the final redactors gave the Psalter its shape by selecting and ordering psalms that were already present and by writing more psalms in order to complete the structure. For Books I to III they probably took over a lot of older psalms, so they did not have as many redactional possibilities as with Books IV and V. Signs of redactional activity are, for example, that Psalms 1 and 2 are untitled (and therefore probably editorial), whereas the rest of the psalms of Book I are ascribed to David. We find a similar situation in Psalm 71 and 72 at the end of Book II—here the block of Davidic psalms ends in Psalm 70. However, not all of the framing psalms are untitled—in some places the editors were probably able to make use of already existing psalms.

More details concerning the holistic reading of the book of Psalms can be found below.

BOOK I: PSALMS 1–41

The first book of Psalms is introduced by Psalms 1 and 2. Here an individual and a communal (royal) psalm are combined. Psalm 1 starts with a blessing; Psalm 2 ends with one. After the introduction, the first book is probably divided into four blocks of psalms; 3–14, 15–24, 25–34, and 35–41, the interpretation of the second block being the surest. Most of the Psalms 3–41 are assigned to David as their author. In the following, space allows us to comment on only a selection of psalms.

Psalm 1

Psalm 1 is a wisdom psalm, more strictly, a psalm of Torah wisdom, as Psalm 19 and 119 are. It deals with two opposite ways of life and illustrates them by using an image for each. The believer is compared to a tree, planted at the water, prospering and yielding its fruits. The godless person, however, is compared to chaff that the wind blows away. The way of the believer is further defined by being joyful about the word of God. The word *meditate* in verse 2 originally means "to mutter"—at that time people never read silently but muttered while reading.

The fact that the book of Psalms opens with a reference to the study of the Torah is significant in more than one respect. First, it is stated that the way of the individual in relation to God starts with the decision to take seriously and to study the word of God. Second, the word *Torah*, "(divine) instruction," can be applied to the Psalter itself. In this way Psalm 1 is an invitation to study the Psalter intensively. This also implies that the psalms are not to be seen as prayers of human beings directed to God only but turn into being the word of God as well.

Third, seen from a canonical point of view, "Torah" is to be understood as the Pentateuch, the first and foundational canon part of the Hebrew Bible. As the second canon part, the "Prophets," refers to the Torah (see Joshua 1:8), also the third canon part, the "Writings," refers to the Torah, by way of Psalm 1. In both instances, very similar expressions are used, for example, "meditate on the Law day and night" and the metaphor of the successful way (for more information on the structure of the Hebrew canon, see in Part I).

Psalm 2

Psalm 2 is a royal psalm, dealing with the enthronement of David as king over Israel (see 2 Samuel 7:8–16). Into the midst of the storm of nations God installs his king on Mount Zion and gives him great power.

The psalm is part of the row of royal psalms 2–72–89. Together these psalms summarize the history of the Davidic kingdom.

The promises given to David reach beyond his historical context. Therefore, the psalm has also a messianic layer of interpretation. Especially the statement of 2:7, "You are my son; today I have begotten you," is quoted several times in the New Testament, applying it to Jesus Christ (Acts 13:33; Hebrews 1:5; 5:5). The two following verses of promise are also used in the New Testament (Hebrews 1:2; Revelation 2:27; 12:5; 19:15). Psalm 1 opens up the individual point of view from which the book of Psalms can and should be read; Psalm 2 opens up the national-historic and royal perspectives. Both perspectives are developed throughout the book. Psalm 1 is opened by a word of blessing; Psalm 2 is closed by one. By this the two psalms are bound together. There are hints that in some parts of the Jewish as well as the Christian tradition, Psalms 1 and 2 were even seen as a unified psalm.

The introductory Psalms 1 and 2 are without a title. From Psalm 3 until the end of Book I there follows a large block of (mostly) Davidic psalms.

Psalm 3
The first Davidic psalter (Psalms 3–41) opens with a series of psalms of lament (3–7). The kingdom of David is presented as a kingdom in conflict. In Psalm 3, a contextual note is given in the title, A Psalm of David, when he fled from his son Absalom, hinting at a related historical background (see 2 Samuel 15). In his distress, David turns to God, begging for help; in spite of the threat, however, he knows that he is always secure in God (3:5–6).

Psalm 8
Psalm 8 is a praise of God for his creation and especially for the position he assigned to humanity. Though human beings seem to be small and insignificant compared to the Moon and the stars, God still gave them a place of honor. "Yet you have made them a little lower than God, and crowned them with glory and honor" (verse 5). With these statements the psalm refers to the CREATION account, especially to the commission given to humans to rule the earth in Genesis 1:28.

Psalm 14 and the Psalm Group 3–14
According to the scholar G. Barbiero (*Das erste Psalmenbuch als Einheit: Eine synchrone Analyse von Psalm 1–41* [Frankfurt a. M.: Lang, 1999]), this group can be compared to Genesis 1–11: Psalm 8, at the center, describes humanity as being installed by God in order to rule the earth. The psalms around it, however, deal with the negative impact of the rule of human beings, who have separated themselves from God. Humanity is fallen and now harasses the anointed king, David. It is significant that Psalms 9–14 often speak about "man" as the enemy of God's kingdom: So David prays that mortals should not prevail (9:19); the nations should recognize "that they are only human" (9:20), "so that those from earth may strike terror no more" (10:18; see 11:4; 12:1, 8). According to this interpretation, Psalm 8 with its positive statement about the rule of humanity is sharply contrasted by the surrounding psalms.

Psalm 14 concludes the group. It is less personal than the preceding psalms but rather uses a more general, third-person style. While human beings ignore God and draw ruin upon the earth, God looks down from heaven upon the "children of men" and concludes, "There is no one who does good, no, not one" (14:3). Such is the condition of fallen humanity.

Psalm 19
Psalm 19 is a psalm of Torah wisdom. It deals with the glory of God in his creation and in his Law. The first part, verses 1–6, praises the majesty of God as it can be recognized in nature. It is a revelation without words and still universally understandable. The sun is singled out as one of the mightiest works of God.

Without any transition, the psalm continues in verses 7–10 with a praise of the Torah, the (written) word of God. So the revelation without words in creation is compared to the revelation through words in the Bible; the heat of the sun penetrating everything is compared to the clearness of the Law scrutinizing every human act, word, and thought.

The third part of the psalm, verses 11–14, moves on into the personal realm. The light of the Torah has unveiled the secret sins of the psalmist. He asks God for forgiveness and for guidance. Finally, the psalmist joins in the praise of creation with his own words.

Psalm 22
"My God, my God, why have you forsaken me?" It is not by chance that Jesus Christ quoted the beginning of Psalm 22 when he was near to death on the cross. From a Christian point of view, Psalm 22 is the "psalm of the suffering of Jesus." Several of the psalm's statements find a typological fulfillment in the New Testament (see NEW TESTAMENT, RELATIONSHIP WITH THE HEBREW BIBLE): "All who see me mock at me; they make mouths at me, they shake their heads; 'Commit your cause to the LORD; let him deliver—let him rescue the one in whom he delights!'" (22:7–8; see Matthew 27:39, 43); "my tongue sticks to my jaws" (22:15; see John 19:28) "my hands and feet have shriveled" (22:16); "they divide my clothes among themselves, and for my clothing they cast lots" (22:18; see John 19:24).

Also the statements about the worldwide act of salvation after the rescuing of the suffering (22:26–29) are interpreted as pointing to the salvation through Jesus Christ.

In itself, the psalm is tied to the suffering of King David (1:1), but it is also applicable to anyone in a certain desperate situation. Its imagery is very dense, involving worms, bulls, lions, dogs, and other animals and using metaphors like "I am poured out like water" and "my heart is like wax" (22:14).

Psalm 23

This Davidic psalm of confidence is probably the most popular psalm of the Bible. The psalmist uses the widespread shepherd motif for illustrating his relationship to God. The psalmist feels secure with God as a sheep with a good shepherd would. The herdsman leads the sheep to green grass and fresh water. But even if he has to walk through dark valleys, in difficult times, God the shepherd is there, and he leads and keeps the believer. The shepherd image is also used by the prophets and in the New Testament Gospels (esp. John 10:11).

In the last two verses the shepherd metaphor is abandoned, and the blessing of God is illustrated with a table set for a rich meal. The psalm closes turning to the "house of the LORD," the temple, which is the place of perfect communion between God and human beings. The reference to the temple is best explained when seeing the psalm in the context of the group 15–24 (see below).

Psalm 24

Psalm 24 is a hymn to the king of glory. The psalm begins in verses 1–2 with a hymnal praise of God, the creator and Lord over the whole earth. The verses 3–6 give conditions to be fulfilled in order that one can approach the temple and have communion with God.

This section is very similar to Psalm 15. The third part of the psalm, verses 7–10, describe the coming of the king of glory, the LORD of Hosts, into his temple.

The original life setting of this psalm is unknown. At least some parts of the psalm may be of ceremonial origin. The repetition of material from Psalm 15 is probably done for literary purposes (see

below). In the Christian context, songs based on Psalm 24 are sung in Advent, referring to the coming of Christ.

Psalms 15–24 as a Group

The psalm group 15–24 is formed as a concentric structure (see STRUCTURES, LITERARY). Proceeding from the outer to the inner rings: Psalms 15 and 24 deal with being at the temple; the righteous may approach God at the temple. Thereby, Psalm 24 repeats some of the statements of Psalm 15. Psalms 16 and 23 are psalms of confidence; Psalms 17 and 22 are psalms of lament. Psalms 18 and 20–21 deal with the king. At the center stands Psalm 19, a praise of the word of God. The message of the group can be summarized as follows: He who is obedient to the Law is allowed to be near God and is secure with God. On this basis the Davidic kingdom stands firmly.

BOOK II: PSALMS 42–72

Book II contains of a group of Korahite psalms, 42–49; a single Asaph psalm, 50; the second group of Davidic psalms, 51–70; and two editorial psalms, the latter of which is assigned to Solomon. Regarding a holistic reading, Book II of the Hebrew Psalter is the one least understood so far. Clearly recognizable, however, are two pairs of psalms framing the book at its beginning and its ending. In both cases, an individual and a communal psalm are put together as an interpretive clue to the book.

Psalms 42–43 and 44

According to the Hebrew Bible, Psalms 42 and 43 are originally one single psalm. That this is correct with regard to content can be seen, for example, in the refrain occurring three times, in 42:5; 42:11; and 43:5. The theme of the psalm is "rejected by God." The psalmist longs for reunion with God, but he feels that God has forgotten him.

The rejection of the individual in Psalms 42–43 is paired by the rejection of the people in Psalm 44. In this psalm, verses 1–8 relate the signs and wonders God had shown his people in the past. This is contrasted in verses 9–16 with the current powerlessness of the people, its suppression and ridiculing by the neighbor peoples. In verses 17–26 Israel prays to God, asking for restoration.

The psalmic pair 42–43 and 44 therefore opens Book II with the theme of rejection. The original historical circumstances of the rejection mentioned in 44:11–14 are not easy to reconstruct. From the retrospective view of the postexilic redactors of the book of Psalms, however, the Babylonian EXILE would be the most plausible interpretation. This would assign Book II to an exilic setting. On the other hand, some times of distress during the reign of David also play a role in Book II.

With Psalm 42, the so-called Elohistic Psalter commences, reaching until Psalm 83. In this part of the Psalter, the name of God, *Yahweh*, is used very seldom. Instead the more general term *elohim*, "God," is used. In the rest of the book, the ratio between the usages of these two words is the opposite. One possible explanation is that the group of Psalms 42–83 had been an early collection of psalms stemming from a slightly different tradition than the other psalms. But a synchronic interpretation is also possible: The name *Yahweh* is in the Hebrew Bible mostly used in relation to the covenant between God and Israel. When Israel is distanced from God because they are rejected, accordingly, the name is not used. Psalms 42–44 introduce a time of rejection, which fits in with the beginning of the Elohistic Psalter. Likewise, the ending of the Elohistic Psalter can be explained: From Psalm 84 on the hope for restoration moves to the front in Book III, and so the name of *Yahweh* can be used again.

Psalm 51

Psalm 51 is traditionally seen as the fourth of the seven psalms of repentance (6, 32, 38, 51, 102, 130, 143). The title names David's adultery with Bathsheba and his arranging of her husband's death as the historical background (2 Samuel 11–12).

The psalm is divided into two parts. Verses 1–9 can be titled "from repentance to forgiveness": The psalmist recognizes his sinfulness; he confesses his sins before God and asks for forgiveness. Sin affects the relationship of the individual to God (verse 4). The second part, verses 10–17, can be titled "from renewing to praise." The psalmist asks God to accept him anew and to renew his heart, so that he can again walk on his way with God, and he praises God for the grace received from him. While God is described as holy and as judge in the first part of the psalm (verse 4), the second part describes him as merciful savior (verse 14).

The last two verses, 18 and 19, especially the request to "rebuild the walls of Jerusalem," most probably do not stem from the time of David but from the Babylonian exile. Possibly, these verses are editorial and function in transferring the message of the psalm into the context of the exile (see also above, Psalm 44).

Psalms 71 and 72

The second group of Davidic psalms ends with Psalm 70. After it follows a pair of editorial psalms. Again an individual and a communal (royal) psalm are combined. Psalm 72, a royal psalm, is titled From Solomon. In this case, however, the translation for Solomon might be more fitting (the Hebrew allows both). The psalm describes the kingdom's being handed over to the successor. The time of David has ended; all hopes now lie with his son, Solomon. The psalmist asks all kinds of blessings for the new king, so that he may reign in peace, justice, and power. The handing over of the kingdom is of special importance because God had promised an everlasting dynasty to David and he also promised that David's son would build the temple (see 2 Samuel 7). The psalm is the second in the row of royal psalms 2–72–98.

Psalm 71 is a prayer of an old person. It reads as an individual application of the event described in Psalm 72. The old individual prays along with the old David. In Psalm 72:18–19, there is the formula of praise that separates the individual psalm books from each other. After it follows 72:20: "The prayers of David son of Jesse are ended." This editorial statement underscores the interpretation of Psalm 72 given earlier. The kingdom is handed over to Solomon, and the time of David has ended.

BOOK III: PSALMS 73–89

As is Book II, Book III is framed by two pairs of psalms, which are meant to aid as interpretive clues to reading the whole. However, the holistic interpretation of the body of the third book is still disputed in scholarship.

Psalms 73 and 74

Psalm 73 is a wisdom psalm. It deals with the problem of act and consequence typical of the wisdom literature (see especially Job), touching also the theodicy question. The psalmist relates that he nearly stumbled in his faith when he saw that the godless people seemed to have such a happy life. On the other hand, he, as a believer, had to face so many difficulties. He broods over it a long time, until one day in the temple he suddenly gains understanding about it (through a vision?): The end is what matters. God will scorn the godless people like a dream rapidly being forgotten after waking; however, God will receive believers with honor. So, faith in God is not senseless, and God establishes justice in the end.

Psalm 74 is a lament about the destruction of the sanctuary. The historical background can be reliably reconstructed: It is the destruction of the Jerusalem temple by the Babylonians in 587 B.C.E.

The two psalms are connected through the mention of the temple. Moreover, Psalm 73, from the viewpoint of the individual, gives an interpretation for the situation depicted in Psalm 74, namely, that godless people seem to gain the upper hand over the people of God.

With the destruction of the temple, the opening psalms give the larger context, on which the following psalms of Book III are to be interpreted.

Psalms 88 and 89

Psalm 89 concludes the series of royal psalms 2–72–89. In its first half, till verse 37, it recounts in detail the promise that God had given to David and his successors (see 2 Samuel 7). It repeatedly points to the fact that God had given this covenant as irrevocable, unconditioned, and eternal. The second part, from verse 38 on, in contrast deals with the actual painful situation, namely, the destruction of the kingdom. Has God violated his oath? Despairingly, the psalmist asks, "Lord, where is your steadfast love of old, which by your faithfulness you swore to David?" (verse 49).

Again in the companion psalm, the same theme is translated onto the personal level. Psalm 88 is a prayer in great despair and desertion. The current distress is brusquely described, without any statement of confidence or of hope.

With Psalms 88 and 89, Book III ends in great despair and with a difficult unresolved issue.

BOOK IV: PSALMS 90–106

Seen as a whole, Book IV is a theological reflection on the Babylonian Exile and especially on the destruction of the Davidic kingdom. Therefore, the book can be seen as an answer to the series of royal psalms 2–72–89. The group of Psalms 90–92 starts with a recollection of God, who, beyond all transitory human institutions, is the true refuge for the believer. As a consequence, Psalms 93–100 bear witness to God as the real king of Israel and of all people.

In Psalms 101–103, the people take a new vow of loyalty to God and ask for restoration; all hope is placed in the forgiving grace of God. Psalms 104–106 finally are an extensive retrospective view of the history of Israel, from the creation until THE EXILE, demonstrating the power and grace of God but also the repeated disobedience of the people that finally led to destruction. The book ends with the request that God might lead his people back from Exile.

Psalm 90

Psalm 90 contrasts the eternity of God with the transience of human beings. God is from eternity to eternity, but human beings are like grass that flourishes in the morning but withers the same evening. The reason God exposes humanity to transitoriness is his wrath for their sin (see Genesis 3). The psalm closes with the request that God have mercy on the people.

The psalm has a meaning for the life of the individual, but it can also be interpreted with regard to the Babylonian Exile. The infirmity of all human institutions, especially the Davidic kingdom, is contrasted with the eternity of God. People should not trust in human institutions, even religious institutions, but only in God. In this context also the psalm title "of Moses" is of special significance: After the destruction of the kingdom, Israel has to return to its roots. Moses appears seven times in Book IV of the Psalter. Outside Book IV, in the rest of the Psalter, he is referred to only once (77:20).

Psalm 91

Psalm 91 is a psalm of confidence. The psalm emphasizes that true refuge can only be found in God, and that refuge in God means total security. The psalm, however, should not be understood as saying that people who trust in God never experience adversity.

Psalm 92

Psalm 92 reads as a second part and response to Psalm 90. True, human beings are transitory, but for those who are under God's refuge and in community with him, life still has a lasting quality. The godless are really short-lived, like grass (92:7; see 90:5–6), but the believer is rather like a palm tree or a cedar, strong even in old age (92:14; see 91:16). The prayer for grace of Psalm 90:14 is answered in Psalm 92:2.

Psalms 93–100

Now the perspective changes from the role of human beings to God himself, whose qualities are described, or rather praised, in Psalms 93–100. Psalms 93 and 95–99 belong, together with Psalm 47, to the genre of kingship of Yahweh psalms. In each of the psalms there is the proclamation "The LORD is king!" In Psalms 94 and 100 this statement is missing. From the rest of their content, however, the psalms fit very well into this group.

The qualities of God praised in these psalms are God's power, his justice, his role as avenger and judge, his holiness, and his grace. The sequence of addressees of these psalms is also interesting: First the psalmist himself praises God's power (93); then he addresses, one after the other, God (94), the people (95), and the whole earth, including all peoples, nature, and all gods (96–99). He asks for obedience and praise to God, who is king and judge of the whole world.

Psalm 100 forms an appropriate ending for the group. The statement "Know that Yahweh is God" (100:3) sums up all that was said about Yahweh before. While the name *God* was qualified in all other occurrences ("God of revenge," "God of Jacob," "my God," "our God," "a great God," "forgiving God"), in 100:3 it simply says, "God." No further definition is needed.

Furthermore, in Psalm 100 all people are described not only as creatures of God but even as part of the universal people of God. This is deemed to be one of the most spectacular theological statements of the Hebrew Bible, because it expands the national covenant between God and Israel to encompass all nations.

Psalms 101–103

Psalm 101 is a vow of loyalty to God that David takes. In its present location, it functions as a renewal of Israel's loyalty to God taken in the Exile, as a precondition for God's forgiving his people and returning them from exile. Psalm 102 is a prayer for the restoration of Zion. A clear historical context can be discerned: Jerusalem lies in ruins. Regarding its content and its motifs, the psalm is very close to Psalms 90 and 92 (motifs of transience of human beings, grass, and eternity of God).

Psalm 103 is the Hebrew Psalter's most beautiful song of grace. In many images the mercy of God and his will to forgive are illustrated. Again the grass motif from Psalm 90 is used (103:15). The transience of humanity is overcome by God's eternal grace. The psalm ends turning to the kingdom of God. The angels in heaven are asked to join in the praise of the merciful God.

Psalms 104–106

These three psalms each end with the word *Hallelujah*, "Praise the LORD." They present an outline

David praises the Lord (Psalm 103), engraving by Julius Schnorr von Carolsfeld

of the salvation history from the creation of the world until the Babylonian Exile. The psalms build on one another chronologically, but each has also a different emphasis.

Psalm 104 sings about the Creation and about God's rule over creation. Several elements of the Creation account (Genesis 1) are taken up: light, sky, water, soil, irrigation, plants, Sun, Moon. Verses 27–30 show that creation is not a single, past act, but instead refer to its daily maintenance. The psalm closes with praise of God.

Psalm 105 describes the wonderful guidance of God in history, from Abraham until the entry into Canaan, the Promised Land. The covenant with Abraham is the legal basis for Israel's claim to the land and therefore also forms the basis for the return from exile. But it is also important for Israel to keep the commandments of God.

Psalm 106 continues these thoughts. As a new aspect of the presentation of history, the repeated disobedience of the people is introduced. With a certain chronological overlap, the psalm starts with the slavery of the people in Egypt and moves on until the Babylonian Exile. The wonderful deeds of God are each contrasted with the disobedience of the people. The psalm, therefore, is a confession of sin of the people. It closes asking God to take his people home to their land.

BOOK V: PSALMS 107–150

While Book IV ends with a prayer for returning from exile, Book V begins with giving thanks for the return that has taken place (Psalm 107:1–3). So the transition from Book IV to Book V resembles the transition from exile to restoration. Therefore, Book V is the book of return and of new beginnings. Praise and joy are the characteristics predominant in this book.

Book V is divided into three parts by means of formal features. Each part begins with a psalm containing the phraseology "O give thanks to the LORD, for he is good; for his steadfast love endures forever"; each of the parts ends with psalms having *Hallelujah* "Praise the LORD":

107	"O give thanks to the LORD . . ."
108–110	Psalms of David
111–117	"Praise the LORD . . ."
118	"O give thanks to the LORD . . ."
119	(without title)
120–134	Songs of Ascent
135	"Praise the LORD . . ."
136	"O give thanks to the LORD . . ."
137	(without title)
138–145	Psalms of David
146–150	"Praise the LORD . . ."

The intensity of the use of the phrases increases from part to part. So in Psalm 107 the phrase "O give thanks to the LORD . . ." stands at the beginning, in Psalm 118 it stands at the beginning and ending, and in Psalm 136 it appears (in shortened form) even at the end of each verse. The same is true for "Praise the LORD," which occurs one time in each of the Psalms 111–117 (the second "Praise the LORD" at the end of Psalm 113 should be moved to the beginning of Psalm 114), two times in Psalm 135, and even 12 times in Psalm 150.

The core of the structure is made up of Davidic psalms in the first and third parts, and the large Torah psalm 119 together with the psalms of pilgrimage in the second part of the book.

Psalm 107

Psalm 107 begins with the expression of thankfulness by those who returned from exile (verses 1–3). Then follow four episodes structured in parallel, each describing an act of deliverance by God (verses 4–9, 10–16, 17–22, 23–32). The psalm concludes with a reflection seeing God's blessing and curse in relationship to the acting of human beings (relationship of act and consequence). The psalm connects the return from exile to the wider theme of returning to God. This is the perspective from which the whole Book V should be read.

Psalm 110

This Davidic psalm presents some problems in understanding. Some parts of it are difficult to translate, and there are also some uncertainties in the textual transmission of the psalm. On the other hand, the psalm has been a great stimulus for readers and has had a long history of interpretation in the Jewish as well as in the Christian realm. It talks about an eternal priest and king sitting at the right hand of God. So it is surely a messianic psalm, an interpretation that suits well its placement in Book V (where the original Davidic kingdom is long ago).

The New Testament sees the psalm fulfilled in Jesus Christ. The first verse, for example, is quoted in Matthew 22:44; Acts 2:34–35; Hebrews 1:13; 10:12–13; 1 Corinthians 15:25; and Philippians 2:8–11. The connection to the priesthood of Melchizedek (verse 4; see Genesis 14:18–20) is discussed in detail in Hebrews 5–7, applying it to Jesus Christ, the true high priest.

Psalm 119

Next to Psalms 1 and 19, Psalm 119 is the third psalm of Torah wisdom. It is placed at the center of Book V, thus emphasizing the importance of its subject.

Psalm 119 is by far the longest psalm (and chapter) of the Bible. It is a meditation on the word of God. The psalm is formed as an alphabetic acrostichon: Each group of eight verses begins with the same letter of the Hebrew alphabet. The first eight verses begin with the letter *aleph*, the second eight verses begin with the letter *beth*, and so on, so that from the 22 letters of the alphabet, 22 × 8 = 176 verses are derived. Eight is also the number of important terms used for describing the written and spoken word of God: *torah* "law, instruction"; *davar*, "word"; *imrah*, "word"; *edah*, "testimony, decree"; *mishpat*, "ordinance, judgment"; *chok*, "statute"; *mitswah*, "commandment"; and *piqqudim*, "precepts." Each of the terms appears in (nearly) all of the eight verse blocks. The psalmist is joyful about the law, he strives to keep God's commandments, he laments over the wicked people who despise God's ordinance, and, in times of trouble, he longs to hear God's graceful words.

A succession of thought cannot be seen in the psalm; rather, the same basic statements are repeated with variation time and again. Therefore, a meditative approach in reading fits the character of the psalm best.

Psalms 120–134

The psalms 120–134 all have the same title, Song of Ascents, i.e., Songs of Pilgrimage to Jerusalem (which lies on top of a mountain). Their historical background is that, according to the Law of Moses, the Israelites from all over the country had to join together in Jerusalem three times a year: for the Feast of the Passover, at Pentecost, and for the Feast of Tabernacles. That this journey to Jerusalem was not only an outward pilgrimage, but could also be a journey of a person's heart back to God, can be seen from the Psalms 120–134 (see PILGRIMS AND WANDERERS).

The 15 psalms 120–124 can be divided into three groups of five psalms each. The first psalm, 120, is not yet about the pilgrimage but about the situation before the pilgrimage starts. The psalmist is living abroad (the nations of Meshesh and Kedar in verse 5 could be rendered as "heathens and barbarians"), surrounded by lie and malice. "From where will my help come?" is the question asked by the psalmist in Psalm 121. The gaze to the mountains, where people believed the gods to live, does not help him. He turns to the only living God, who made heaven and earth (and those mountains). This God, he is confident, will keep him. In almost every sentence of this psalm the word *keep* or *keeper* occurs.

In Psalm 122, people decide to travel to Jerusalem, a decision about which our psalmist is very happy, and they finally arrive at its gates. Jerusalem is the place where the house of God (122:1, 9) and the house of David (122:5) stand. Three times the psalm wishes piece (Hebrew *shalom*) to Jerusalem.

The Psalms 123 and 124 round off the message of the first group. They relate themselves back, especially to Psalm 121. The question of Psalm 121 "I lift up my eyes to the hills—from where will my help come?" is answered in Psalm 123: "To you I lift up my eyes, O you who are enthroned in the heavens!" The second statement of Psalm 121 "My help comes from the LORD, who made heaven and earth" is echoed at the end of Psalm 124: "Our help is in the name of the LORD, who made heaven and earth." So the group is bound together by theme and motifs.

The second group 125–129 is about what the meaning of the pilgrimage is: All is about the blessing of God.

The framing Psalms 125 and 129 mark the border between the person who turns to God and the person who does not. Psalm 126 seems to have a totally different subject, namely, the return from the Babylonian Exile. But the point is that the psalm draws a connection between the return from exile and the pilgrimage to Jerusalem that also can be understood as a kind of return from exile (see Psalm 120). Verses 1–3 describe the past situation of exile; verses 4–6 apply this to the present situation.

Psalms 127 and 128 form the center of the group. Both psalms are about the fact that the reason for well-being is not diligence and hard work but God's blessing. Or, to put it the other way around: All work leads to nothing if God does not give his blessing to it. Psalm 128 asks the reader to "fear God," i.e., to believe him and obey him, and he will give his blessing. The blessing is very concretely described as successful work, many children, and old age.

The third group 130–134 of the pilgrimage psalms deals with the arrival at the temple. When human beings encounter the living God, they first realize their own sinfulness. Only the forgiving grace of God makes communion possible (130). After having received forgiveness, the believer can be as near to God as a small child in the arms of its mother (131).

The middle psalm of the third group, Psalm 132, is about the house of David and the house of God, as the middle psalm of the first group is (122). The psalm is about the Davidic covenant, namely, that God will build a "house" for David, i.e., an everlasting dynasty, and that David's son will build a house for God, i.e., the temple. After the travelers have arrived at the sanctuary, they receive God's blessing. Psalm 133 uses three images describing the blessing. In Psalm 134, the believers bless God in the temple, and God blesses the believers.

Psalm 137

Indignation is the reaction of many people when they read Psalm 137. The last verse is especially shocking: "O daughter Babylon, you devastator! Happy shall they be who pay you back what you have done to us! Happy shall they be who take your little ones and dash them against the rock!"—Is one allowed to pray to God in this manner? Many believers would answer "No!"

However, some points have to be taken into consideration: First of all, the Babylonians had done the Israelites great injustice, even comparable to that of the statement quoted. Therefore, the emotion of hate and revenge is authentic and understandable as a typical human reaction. An authentic emotion, in turn, can and should be taken to God. As Psalm 139:1–4 says, God already knows the inner thoughts and feelings of human beings. And who could handle such feelings better than he? Only a bad pastoral counselor would forbid his or her client to talk openly about emotions. These things have to be spoken out before further steps can be taken.

That there are, in fact, further steps in coming to terms with the issue has been shown by the holistic interpretation of the book of Psalms. According to the structure of Book V (see above), Psalm 137 is placed together with the group of Davidic psalms 138–145. So the old psalms of David are reused in order to give help in assimilating the distress of the exile.

After the lament in Psalm 137 is a change of perspective in Psalm 138. The psalmist concentrates on God and on his power, receiving new strength from him. In Psalm 139 (see also below), the psalmist lets his inner motifs be scrutinized by the God who knows him fully. Verses 19–24 can especially be best understood in relation to Psalm 137: "Do I not hate those who hate you, O LORD?" and "Search me, O God, and know my heart; test me and know my thoughts. See if there is any wicked way in me, and lead me in the way everlasting." God will remove all destructive emotions from him. In Psalms 140–143 the psalmist asks God to help him, and in Psalm 144 the trouble is finally overcome with the help of the Lord.

Psalms 138 and 145 can also be seen as forming a frame around the group. The question of Psalm 137:4 "How could we sing the LORD's song in a foreign land?" is answered in these two psalms: Not only the psalmist but the kings of all heathen nations (including Israel's enemies) and finally all flesh shall join in the praise of God.

Psalm 139

Verses 1–18, especially, of this psalm are very popular, as a remarkable description of God's omniscience, omnipresence, and omnipotence. God knows the believer through and through his or her deeds, words, and thoughts (verses 1–6). There is no place to which one can flee from God (verses 7–12). God holds the whole of a person's life in his hands, from his forming that person inside the mother's womb; all the days of his life God knows beforehand (verses 13–16). For the human being who has recognized this, there are only wonder and praise (verses 17–18).

However, the psalm is not a theological reflection per se. Suddenly, the psalmist reveals himself as a person threatened by enemies and being full of hate. The statement of verse 1, "You have searched me and know me," turns into a request in verse 23: "Search me, O God, and know my heart." The reaction to the threat here is a critical self-analysis as well as a prayer that God may search him and guide him on the right way.

Read in context, this last part of the psalm can be seen in the background of Psalm 137.

Psalm 150

The book closes with a hymn of praise. Twelve times in six verses, the psalmist issues a call to praise the Lord. The psalm is part of the final "Hallelujah" group 146–150, a fitting conclusion to the whole Hebrew Psalter. Having arrived at Psalm 150, the reader has pursued a long war, starting with obedience (Psalm 1) and ending in joy.

As Reinhard Kratz writes: "Going through the five books the reader meditates about the individual stages of the history of Israel applying them, in remembrance and confirmation, to stages of his own, individual life. He experiences them as a way from trouble already suffered to experienced or still expected blessing, and as a way from the political condition of the kingdom and its destruction to the eternal kingdom of God. This kingdom has already become real—by way of the individual experience of deliverance, obedience to Torah and ceremony and preservation and provision of the life—but is at the same time still outstanding" ("Die Tora Davids," *Zeitschrift fuer Theologie und Kirche* 93 [1996], p. 27, translated by Julius Steinberg and Martin Manser).

Psalm 151

The Septuagint (see BIBLE, EARLY TRANSLATIONS OF) translation of the Psalter contains an additional psalm, which is, however, said to be "outside the number," thus not belonging to the canonical psalms. The psalm is recognized as deuterocanonical (i.e., being of secondary canonical rank) by the Greek and Russian Orthodox Churches and in the Slavonic Bible. Among the DEAD SEA SCROLLS, a Hebrew version of it has been found. The psalm is assigned to David. In it, David tells that he was small among his brothers and the youngest of his family; he was a shepherd and a musician. Yet God called him to be king over Israel. He went into action against Goliath and killed him, cutting his head off with his own sword.

The psalm is said to be written after his fight against Goliath. It draws on the events reported in 1 Samuel 16 and 17. In its style, it is quite different from the canonical psalms of David. Whether it is original or not cannot be decided. In the old Syrian translation, Psalm 151 is the first of a series of psalms (151–155) about the deeds of David in 1 Samuel 16–17.

Revelation

Revelation is the last book of the Bible and one of the hardest to understand, partly because it is among the most literary of all. Although it is popular in certain circles, many other people conveniently avoid it. Only the most accessible parts of the book, chapters 2–3, 13, and 20–22, enjoy general attention.

Initially, however, Revelation was well received in the Christian communities, and it left many traces in the second century. In the third century some influential theologians criticized the book because of its teaching on the millennium (see below). One of them, Dionysius of Alexandria, also launched an argument about the authorship of the book. Moreover, the elevation of the church to state church of the Roman Empire in the fourth century turned the book's strong criticism of the empire into an embarrassing relict. As a result, for a long time Revelation lived on the margins of the canon.

The book's title is taken from the very first word of the text, which in Greek is *apokalupsis* and in Latin *revelatio*. Hence many English speakers use the title *Apocalypse* as a synonym or as an alternative for *Revelation*. The use of this word implies a claim to divine inspiration (see REVELATION, GOD'S). The author uses *prophecy* (1:3) and *testimony* (22:16) as synonyms for the word *revelation*. The scope of the revelation that John received is indicated in 1:1–11 and 19, which together suggest that he was shown visions that span the whole of history. (Note that the title is in the singular as the book is presented as the result of only one revelation.)

Authorship

The author's name, John, was added to the book's title from 1:1, 4, and 9, where the author emphatically refers to himself by this name. The addition was necessary for the sake of distinction as in the early church other written revelations circulated as well, for example, revelations attributed to Paul and to heroes of the Hebrew Bible (see APOCRYPHA AND PSEUDEPIGRAPHA). John (Greek *Iōannēs*, Hebrew *Iochanan*) was a common name among Jews at the time.

There are four other writings in the New Testament whose authorship is attributed to a person called John, the Gospel of John and the letters 1, 2, and 3 John. These four are usually thought to have been written by the apostle John, the son of Zebedee, although in none of these does the name of the author appear. On the other hand, the present book does claim to have been authored by a "John," but he styles himself as a Christian prophet rather than as an apostle (1:3; 19:10; 22:7, 9, 18, 19). Nonetheless, according to the tradition of the church Revelation was also written by the same apostle John while he lived in Ephesus in Asia Minor. Geographically this tradition is in harmony with the connection between the author of Revelation and the island of Patmos (1:9; see Commentary).

Although John saw his visions on Patmos, he was commissioned to send the written account of his experiences as letters to seven churches on the mainland of Asia Minor, the first of which was Ephesus (1:11; cf. chapters 2–3). This state of affairs suggests that the author of Revelation had a position of authority in western Asia Minor, that fits with his being the apostle John.

Several arguments count against the common authorship of Revelation, the fourth gospel, and the three letters. The most important is the different type of Greek used in Revelation (see below). This difference was already noticed by Dionysius of Alexandria, mentioned earlier, who concluded that no one author could write such different types of Greek. Theologically there are both important similarities and differences among these writings. For a proper understanding of Revelation, however, the issue of authorship is not very important.

Readership

As already indicated, the intended readership of the book primarily consists of the members of the seven churches mentioned in 1:11, which are addressed individually in chapters 2 and 3: Ephesus, Smyrna, Pergamum, Thyatira, Sardis, Philadelphia, and Laodicea. No doubt copies of the whole book were originally sent to each of the churches. These churches lie more or less in a circle; a messenger who followed the Roman road system, starting out from Ephesus, could easily travel around the other churches delivering the copies and return from Laodicea to Ephesus. John expressly orders the recipients not to seal the book (22:10), meaning that its contents are meant for general release. The concluding passage, 22:8–21, gives the distinct impression that the book is in fact intended for reading in the whole worldwide church.

Time of Writing

The time of writing was traditionally put at the far end of the first century, in or just after the reign of the Roman emperor Domitian (81–96 C.E.). This tradition stems from the authoritative church father Irenaeus. Yet recently many scholars are arguing for a date immediately after the disastrous reign of the emperor Nero (54–68 C.E.) and before 70 C.E., the year of the destruction of the city of JERUSALEM and the temple.

Both dates have their pros and cons. Both Nero and Domitian persecuted the Christians. The reference to seven kings in 17:9–11 has often been taken as a reference to Roman emperors, and as suggesting that Revelation was written during the rule of "the sixth emperor." However, it has proved impossible to work out with certainty who is meant by the sixth emperor.

Genre

Revelation shows the characteristics of several types of literature.

Initially it appears as a *letter* (see EPISTLE), not to one person or church but to seven specific churches in Asia Minor. Chapter 1 contains greetings, a doxology, and personal notes, while chapter 22:8–21 resembles the closure of a letter. And, of course, chapters 2 and 3 contain seven short letters to churches in Asia Minor. As a letter Revelation must have constituted meaningful and relevant communication for its first readers, although they may not have understood every single element of it.

More clearly than in the other New Testament letters we have to do with a form of dual authorship. On the one hand, John is the author, who emphatically focuses attention on himself in chapters 1, 10, and 22, using the first-person singular. On the other hand, it is the risen Lord Jesus who commands him to write down the visions he has seen (1:17–20). Each of the seven letters is introduced with a formula in which Christ dictates to John the content of the letter (2:1, etc.), so that in the letters the first-person singular pertains to Christ.

From the beginning the book also presents itself as PROPHECY (1:3; 19:10; 22:7, 10, 18–19), and as such it stands in the tradition of the prophetic books in the Hebrew Bible. John claims prophetic authority for the visions he received as well as for the way he has recorded them. The unique wording of 22:18–19 suggests that he is aware that he is writing Christian Scripture, which will be canonical at the moment the ink is dry. Nowhere else in the Bible is the claim of inspiration so clear. There are two descriptions of John's call to be a prophet (chapters 1 and 10), both of which resemble the call stories of Isaiah (Isaiah 6), Jeremiah (1), and Ezekiel (1–3) from the Hebrew Bible. What distinguishes John from the previous prophets, however, is the fact that his message was not delivered orally but committed to writing straight away. This points to the fact that the book is also an apocalypse.

In the third place, Revelation is an apocalyptic book (see APOCALYPTIC WRITING), that is to say, it contains insights into another world and another time that were revealed by supernatural means. As all Jewish and Christian apocalypses do, Revelation expresses the conviction that God is in control of history and that in the end he will make all things well. Another characteristic of the apocalyptic genre is the use of much poetic language. Thus Revelation is full of imagery (see IMAGERY, BIBLICAL).

Finally it is worth mentioning that Revelation also contains liturgical materials such as hymns, lamentations, acclamations, doxologies, and beatitudes (see GENRES, BIBLICAL).

Approaches

Traditionally, it was thought that the "events" described in a later chapter simply followed those in the earlier chapters, but it is now suggested that Revelation contains much repetition. In this view, the cycles of seals, trumpets, and bowls in fact describe the same "events" from different points of view, whereas chapters 2–14 and 17–18 also cover the same material from yet another perspective. The close similarities among chapters 6, 8, and 16 would suggest that some form of repetition or recapitulation is clearly intended. The cyclical way of reading is, therefore, also known as the *recapitulation* approach.

In terms of what the book refers to, there have always basically been two main views, the *idealistic* and the *historical* interpretation. The first sees Revelation as a symbolic text that provides images of world history seen as a battle between God's kingdom and the powers of evil. This interpretation does not read the text for references to specific future events or to a future millennial kingdom, but it argues that the message of the book is that Jesus Christ reigns as king at the present time and that he and the believers are involved in a cosmic conflict with his adversaries. This approach allows the reader to focus on the motif in all of history and to hear the book's call to side with God. Thus Revelation warns the believers effectively against the powers of this world. This approach tends to ignore the prophetic and the apocalyptic character of the book.

The alternative approach is that of the *historical* interpretations. These have in common that they do detect references to specific historical events in the book, although often couched in symbolic terms. Within this general approach further distinctions can be made. Some interpreters hold that Revelation basically relates to contemporary history; this interpretation is also called the preteristic approach. The main person alluded to, according to this view, is the Roman emperor at the time of writing, whether he be Nero or Domitian. Adherents of this approach argue that John addresses issues in the churches in Asia Minor, and the advantage of this approach is that it does justice to such allusions to first-century situations and to the presumed relevance of the text for its first hearers. As does the previous one, this approach ignores the prophetic-predictive character of the book (1:19).

Another version of the historical interpretation assumes that Revelation forms a prediction of history as a whole, a description of church history and world history. In this view the Muslim threat to the church in the seventh and 16th centuries is described in Revelation, as are anti-Christian characters like Hitler and Stalin. The early church generally approached the book is this way. In later periods one Protestant interpretation was that the seven seals represented the era of the church under the Roman Empire and that the seven trumpets stood for the subsequent period of suffering under the ANTICHRIST, who was none other than the pope of Rome. Later on, the French emperor Napoleon and Adolf Hitler were also discovered on the pages of Revelation. This approach focuses almost entirely on Western Europe to the exclusion of the rest of the world, so that it stands guilty as a one-sided interpretation.

Yet another form of historical interpretation argues that Revelation is a prediction of events that even now are still in the future, "the end times," as they are called. According to some, all of chapters 4–22 are still future; others assume that many elements of the book have a double fulfillment, one in world history as a whole and one in the future.

The school of interpretation called *dispensationalism* adds some extra elements to this futuristic interpretation. From Daniel it draws the idea that all of Revelation 4–20 speaks about only a future seven-year period called "the Great Tribulation." It also assumes that the Christian believers will be taken away from the earth just before those seven years in what is called "the Rapture." Much of the ensuing persecution will befall Jews who fail to accept Jesus as their Messiah. In this approach much is made of the millennium (see LAST THINGS) as predicted in 20:1–6. This approach struggles to show the relevance of Revelation for the church and by denying the poetic character of the book tends to overly literal interpretations.

The final type of historical interpretation, the *salvation historical* approach, combines elements from the preceding approaches: It sees chapters 4–7 as relating to history as a whole, and chapters 8–22 as a mix of references to history and to the future. This approach is close to the idealistic one in that it recognizes repetitions of patterns in history. Thus it is argued that the anti-Christian power manifested itself initially both in Antiochus IV Epiphanes (168 B.C.E.; see Daniel) and in the Roman Empire. But anti-Christian forces are also seen at work in the present time in general and expected in the future "Babylon." The beast from chapter 13 is interpreted as the Roman Empire *and* as SATAN's threat to the church now *and* as the eschatological Antichrist.

As does the dispensationalist approach, this one assumes that Christ will inaugurate the millennium on his return to earth. It agrees with Christian interpretations of the prophetic books of the Hebrew Bible in assuming that many prophecies have two foci, one within the period a prophet could oversee and one beyond his personal horizon.

Models Used

As is to be expected in an apocalyptic book, John makes use of mythic symbols and images that we also find in previous apocalyptic books. It should be added, however, that Revelation can be understood without much knowledge of the origins of its elements because John has thoroughly christianized his materials. Comparison of Revelation with Jewish apocalypses is useful for an appreciation of its genre and general characteristics, but hardly for insight into its composition, details, and message.

Much more relevant for the modern reader is John's use of the Hebrew Scriptures. He never quotes the Hebrew Bible, but he includes countless echoes of its themes and vocabulary. It is said that at least two of every three verses in Revelation have words from the Hebrew Bible echoing in the background! Whole passages are also modeled on passages from the Scriptures as will to some extent be shown in the Commentary. Throughout the book the influence of Isaiah, in particular chapters 6, 54, 60, and 65, is felt.

Occasion and Aim

It is usually assumed that Revelation was written from a situation of persecution to Christians in a similar situation. Traditionally, the Roman Empire had been religiously tolerant. The emperor cult was a first-century C.E. innovation, which required everybody to give sacrifices to the living emperor. For Christians (and Jews) this form of worship was of course impossible, giving the Romans a weapon against them if they so wanted. In Asia Minor this cult of the living emperor was enthusiastically accepted by the populace rather than imposed by the authorities.

The seven churches that are addressed in chapters 2–3 have in common with each other and with the rest of contemporary Christianity that they all live in the Roman Empire and have to find their way vis-à-vis the empire's claims to absolute loyalty and allegiance. But the letters written to these churches strongly suggest that the situations of the churches differ widely (see Commentary) and that at least some of the churches were in fact not under any threat. It is likely that at the time of writing the emperor did not persecute Christians systematically and that the pressure from the emperor cult was not heavy. We do well to distinguish between persecution on the one hand and oppression and repression on the other.

Revelation basically deals with the internal affairs of the churches and with their relationship to Jesus Christ rather than with their social and religious context. But where glimpses of that context can be seen, the impression is that there are trouble, oppression, and poverty (2:9–11, 13; 3:8–10; 6:9–11; 12:14–17; 13:7–8; 17:6). John himself is on Patmos (1:9) in what is probably exile for religious reasons.

It appears that John is aiming to achieve several objectives at the same time. Those who have compromised with the lifestyle of the world around them, he tries to rally; they are shown that the Roman Empire is a dangerous whore who lures people with her charms (17–18). Those afraid of persecution and of the future he encourages by pointing to the sovereignty of God and Jesus, which can inspire confidence in their own fate as well as in that of the world as a whole. All readers are being warned that in a hostile world, suffering cannot be avoided and has to be borne in order to be victorious (1:9; 2:2–3; 13:10; 21:7). The Greek root meaning "conquer" appears at the end of all seven letters (2–3) as well as in 5:5; 12:11; 15:2.

SYNOPSIS

It soon becomes obvious that the number 7 is important in this book: Explicitly there are seven letters (2–3), seven seals (6:1–8:5), seven trumpets (8:6–11:19), seven thunders (10:3–4), and seven bowls (16), whereas several other groups of 7s can be detected. It thus seems logical that the book as a whole would also consist of seven parts; and several suggestions to this effect do exist, for example, 1–3; 4–5; 6–7; 8–11; 12–14; 15–19; 20–22. Yet it appears that such structures, attractive as they may be at first sight, are a tour de force that does not really fit the actual contents of Revelation.

A more natural reading shows that 1:1–8 is the introduction to the prophecy and contains an opening in letter style. The rest of the first chapter is taken by a majestic vision of the risen Jesus Christ as he appears to John and charges him to write to the seven named churches in Asia Minor. Chapters 2–3 contain these seven messages to the churches in the form of letters in which Christ addresses their particular situations. The conceptual core of the book is formed by chapters 4–5, which show that—whatever goes on in the world—God is seated on his throne, receiving the worship of all creation, and reigning unperturbed. He passes sovereignty to Jesus Christ, who is depicted as a lamb that had been slaughtered—that is, that had died—and is now alive again.

The next main part of the book begins with scenes describing the opening of the seals of the book and giving the reader insight into history (chapter 6). The first four scenes are short and general; the fifth and the sixth seem to allude to end times. The sequence of seals is interrupted by two other scenes, which tell about groups of people saved from disasters and from persecution (chapter 7). Subsequently, the delayed opening of the seventh seal (8:1–5) forms an anticlimax because it merely leads into a silence, which is followed by another sequence of seven, that of the seven trumpets (8:6–9:21 and 11:15–19), which again result in massive judgments. As is the previous cycle, this one is interrupted by two apparently unrelated scenes, chapter 10 recording what can be seen as a second calling of John, and 11:1–14 telling the story of two witnesses who are killed but in the end vindicated by God. It seems that the blowing of the seventh trumpet, 11:15–19 describes a scene of final judgment.

Chapters 12–14 form a new beginning, possibly even the beginning of the second half of the book, and describe the relationship between the people of God and the powers of this world. The first episode tells the story of a woman and the birth and career of her son, the divine Savior, whose adversary is a dragon. Chapter 13 describes two beasts that persecute the believers; one beast receives worship as if it were God and the other enforces this worship. Chapter 15 is a kind of prelude to chapter 16, the last cycle of judgments, executed by means of seven bowls that are poured out without interruptions. At the end a battle erupts at Harmagedon.

The last part of the book has a sandwich structure. On the one hand there is a lengthy description of the city of this world, BABYLON, and its overthrow (17:1–19:10). The city is depicted as a whore riding on a scarlet beast with seven heads and 10 horns; in the end the beast attacks and kills the woman. This picture is balanced by the concluding description of the city of God, the New Jerusalem (21:9–22:9), and the way the new world comes about (21:1–8). Sandwiched between the descriptions of these squarely opposed cities there are two scenes of final judgment (19:11–21 and 20:11–15), which in turn sandwich the description of the millennium, the interim messianic reign (20:1–10). Revelation closes with an epilogue that strongly recommends the book as a reliable and relevant prophecy (22:10–21).

COMMENTARY

Throughout the book there are beautiful HYMNS that represent the faithful response of the audience (4:8, 11; 5:9–10, 12, 13; 7:10, 12; 11:16–18; 15:3–4; 19:1–3, 6–8). They are among the most explicitly Christian elements of the book, and many have been used by later Christian hymn writers.

Throughout the book it strikes the reader that despite harrowing descriptions of suffering from increasingly severe judgments, humankind does not convert to God. They may call for help, but there is no repentance (6:16–17; 9:20–21; 16:9, 11).

Pride of place among the book's images is that of the one that says that the faithful "have washed their robes and made them white in the blood of the Lamb" (7:14). Other striking images say that a two-edged sword emerges from the mouth of Christ (1:16) and that "the whore of Babylon" was "drunk with the blood of the saints and the blood of the witnesses to Jesus" (17:6).

In what follows we could not possibly mention all occasions when the text alludes to the Hebrew Scriptures. To give an example, Psalm 2, which speaks about the coming reign of God and about the Messiah as his Son, is alluded to in Revelation 2:26–27; 6:15; 11:15, 18; 12:5; 14:1; 19:15.

Chapter 1

This breathtaking vision of John is recorded in partial dependence on Isaiah 6 and Ezekiel 1. The body of the chapter is characterized by the frequent use of *as* to indicate that the ascended and glorified Christ is in fact beyond John's comprehension. The vision is said to be so impressive that John falls down as if dead (1:17). The imagery used here is that of both royalty and priesthood, and it reflects beauty (verses 13, 15, 16), light (verse 16), and power (verse 16).

John's vision of Christ (Revelation 1:9–20), engraving by Julius Schnorr von Carolsfeld

In verse 9 John declares that he stayed on the isle of Patmos "because of the word of God and the testimony of Jesus" (1:9). Patmos, an island off the coast of present-day Turkey, is not far from the city of Ephesus, to which the first of the seven letters is sent. This suggests that John may have been in exile on the island as a measure by the Roman authorities to obstruct his Christian ministry. As islands to the southwest of Turkey were used by the Romans to exile adversaries, this suggestion is more likely than that John was on Patmos to preach the gospel.

The lamp stands (verses 12, 20) represent the churches, as 7 is the number of representative fullness. The image stems from Zechariah 4:2 but has been changed from one seven-branched lamp stand into seven separate ones, suggesting the self-sufficiency of each church.

Verse 19 is often seen as an indication of the contents of the book, which describes both "what is" and "what is to take place after this."

Chapters 2–3

The letters that John writes to the seven churches do not simply repeat the same message seven times—they reflect a diversity of local situations. Some of the churches are praised for their vibrant faith (2:2–3; 3:10–11) by Jesus, the true author of the letters, while others are criticized as spiri-

tually dead or dying (3:2, 15). In one church a believer, Antipas (2:14), has died as a martyr, and some other churches also face persecution (2:10). Several churches are troubled by Jews who have not accepted Jesus as the Messiah (2:9; 3:9). False teachers and deceivers are trying to win a foothold (2:2, 14–15, 21–24). The letters are full of allusions to local details: Pergamum, for example, had a large pagan temple on a mighty rock that would be called "the throne of Satan" (2:13), and Laodicea was known for its lukewarm water, gold, clothing, and eye salve (3:16–18).

Although they convey different messages, the seven letters are very similar in structure: The angel of the church is addressed with "These are the words of . . ." and a description of Jesus Christ. Jesus then says that he "knows" the church's situation and delivers praise or rebuke. In conclusion, the stereotypical "anyone who has an ear" is called to listen to "what the Spirit is saying to the churches" suggesting that the letter should be read out in the meeting of the congregation—and a promise is held out to "everyone who conquers." It is unclear what exactly is meant by "the angel of the church."

The two references to "food sacrificed to idols" and the reference to Balaam (2:14, 20) remind the readers that they are not to compromise with paganism. In Jewish tradition Balaam (Numbers 22–24) was the prototype of the false teacher who tried to mix good and bad convictions. He advised the people of Israel to eat unclean food and to fornicate with foreign women. John thinks that similar dangers threaten the churches in Pergamum and Thyatira. According to Acts 15:20, 29, although Christian believers were not bound by the Jewish law, they were not supposed to eat food sacrificed to idols. As the local trade guilds of the time were dominated by religious rituals and practices, consequently Christians could not remain members of them, the text suggests. So by alerting the readers to the danger of false compromise, the text is effectively *creating* dissatisfaction with their situation.

Dispensationalism takes the seven letters as predictions of seven periods in the history of the Christian Church. The final two churches addressed, Philadelphia and Laodicea, are seen as images of the split church of the end times, of which some parts will be faithful to God and some parts lapse into heresy and compromise with paganism.

Chapters 4–5

These chapters lay down the basic position of the book. All emphasis is on the sovereignty of God and the serene worship he receives in heaven, regardless of what happens on earth. Read in this way, Revelation is a book with a bright and hopeful core.

In the descriptions of heavenly affairs John depends on Ezekiel 1–3. The scroll Jesus receives from God represents the book of history, and the opening of its seals illustrates his authority to direct history. It is striking that according to 5:3–5 nobody else in the universe is worthy or fit to do so. The narrative about the tense silence and John's passionate weeping is very effective, and the same is true of the event that follows: The arrival of Jesus is announced as that of the mighty lion, symbol of conquering power—but a tiny humble lamb appears instead! Moreover, that lamb has recently been slaughtered and its wounds are still visible.

This powerful imagery points to the tension in the identity of Jesus as the divine person who died the shameful death on a cross. The author's intention is not that the reader play off the identities of lion and lamb but that they are kept in balance. True Christian victory occurs neither by violence nor by force but through the way of self-sacrifice.

Chapter 6

The identity of the first of the four horsemen is hotly disputed. While some see the white color of his horse as a symbol of the triumphant spread of the gospel over the earth, others want to align him with the negativity of the riders who follow and see him as a symbol of military power. The subsequent riders represent war, famine, and deadly diseases. The four pictures as a whole would paint an ominous picture of history.

The fifth seal contains a call for vengeance from Christian martyrs; the response they receive tells them to be patient as history has not ended. The sixth seal contains a description of a final judgment in terms derived from the Hebrew Bible and Mat-

thew 24, but it is followed by an intermezzo in the next chapter.

Chapter 7

The two pictures here show the continuity between Israel and the Christian Church, and they again call for patience and faithful endurance. The expression "the blood of the Lamb" (7:14; 12:11; cf. 1 Peter 1:19) is an allusion to the sacrificial system of the Jewish religion, in which the blood of an animal atoned for the sins of the one who sacrificed it. The imagery means that Jesus, the Lamb of God (cf. John 1:29), has offered the atoning sacrifice for humankind (cf. 1 John 2:2).

The Opening of the Seventh Seal (8:1)

As this is the final seal on the scroll, the readers' expectations are at a high: Now the end will be revealed! However, in a masterly stroke John describes nothing of the kind and keeps the readers

Four horsemen of the apocalypse (Revelation 6:1–8), woodcut by Albrecht Dürer

The opening of the fifth and sixth seals (Revelation 6:9–12), woodcut by Albrecht Dürer

in suspense. He just reports a long silence during which even the heavenly singing (4:8; 7:10–12) has died down. In real life even a two-minute silence is long. No explanation of this anticlimax is given, and no parallel texts exist to help the reader interpret its meaning. Is it a silence before the storms of judgment that will follow? Or is this a return to the silence of eternity before the creation of heaven and earth, or just a sign of reverence for God Almighty? In contrast, later the blowing of the seventh trumpet is also postponed, but that event does lead to a positive statement that God's kingdom has arrived (11:15–19).

Chapters 8–9

Chapters 8 and 9 are among the gloomiest parts of Scripture. Trumpets symbolize the announcement of the next set of judgments over the earth, whereas in the Hebrew Bible locusts (9:3) represent devastation. The name *Apollyon* (9:11) means

"destroyer" and is also an allusion to the Greek god Apollo, whose symbol was the locust. Much of the other imagery in these dark chapters is derived from Exodus 7–10, the story of the plagues on Egypt before the Exodus.

Chapter 10

Once more the book of Ezekiel, in particular the stories about the calling of that prophet, has influenced John's choice of words. The eating of the book symbolizes appropriating its message. It is unclear whether the book mentioned here is the same as that in chapter 5, as the Greek words chosen are not identical. The reference to seven thunders (verses 3–4) is a clever suggestion that there is more to history than is recorded in this book.

Chapter 11

Verses 1–2 reflect Ezekiel 40–42 and Zechariah 2:1–5. This suggests that the act of measuring symbolizes the divine protection of the core parts of "the temple," which probably symbolizes the faithful believers. A period of 42 months is indicative of a limited time span.

It is likely that verses 3–14 deal with the ministry of the Church and the suffering that this entails. "The two witnesses" have the traits of Moses and Elijah, the two major prophets of the Hebrew Bible. Interpreters are strongly divided over whether to take the references to the city in which they operate (8, 13) as references to the literal Jerusalem, to the Roman Empire, or to the world in general.

In verses 15–19 the blowing of the trumpets (chapters 8–9) is resumed, and it seems that history reaches its climax, although the tone of the description is quite muted.

Chapter 12

As chapters 4–5 do, this chapter offers a look behind the scenes of what happens on earth. It sheds light on the supernatural background to the conflict between God and the Church, on the one hand, and the adversary, on the other hand. It is likely that this chapter is based on religious myths and symbols from several ancient religions (Greek, Egyptian, and Mesopotamian) that John has appropriated. On the other hand the Jews often depicted their nation as a woman, and a close parallel is found in Isaiah 26:16–27:1. The story of the woman continues in verses 13–17, whose eagle symbolism stems form Exodus 19:4 and Deuteronomy 32:10–11. In the interposed verses 7–12, Michael (verse 7) is the protector of the people of God (Daniel 10:21; 12:1), and the defeat of Satan in verses 8–9 reflects the triumph of Jesus Christ over death at Easter.

Chapter 13

This chapter belongs to the best-known parts of the Revelation. The imagery used here depends in part on Daniel 7–8.

Numerous interpretations have been given of the number of the beast, the number 666 (verse 18). In addition to much nonsense there are at least four explanations that scholars have examined:

- The number 666 is the number below the divine level of 777, the symbol of perfection.
- The three Greek letters used to write this number (*chi, xi,* and *sigma*) are the abbreviation of the name *Christ* (*chi-sigma*) with the symbol of the snake in between.
- The triple 6 is connected with the sixth seal, the sixth trumpet, and the sixth bowl, which allude to the day of God's wrath, so that it points to imperfection and to evil destruction.
- Using Gematria, the ancient habit of giving numerical value to each letter in the way that $a = 1$, $b = 2$, etc., we get the letter value of "Emperor Nero" (*nrwn qsr*). The variant reading of 616 that is found in several manuscripts points in this same direction: The Hebrew spelling is $nrwn\ qsr = (50 + 200 + 6 + 50) + (100 + 60 + 200) = 666$. The Latin spelling is $nrw\ qsr = (50 + 200 + 6) + (100 + 60 + 200) = 616$.

This last explanation in perhaps the most interesting, as several other elements in Revelation also point to Nero as the anti-Christian beast, such as allusions to myths concerning his return from Parthia or from the dead (13:3, 12, 14).

Chapter 14

This chapter contains seven small units. In sharp contrast to the previous chapter, the first unit (1–5) points forward to the final victory of Christ as described in chapters 19–20. The number 144,000, 12 times 12 times 1,000, is a symbol of great fullness. The second to the fifth units (5–7, 8, 9–12, 13) consist of brief proclamations. Units six and seven (14–16, 17–20) are closely parallel and depict the judgment of the world, with the grain harvest representing the gathering of the faithful believers and the grape harvest the condemnation of the unbelievers. The exaggerated numbers in verse 20 evoke the severity of the judgment.

Chapter 15–16

The judgments described here resemble those of the trumpets, but the emphasis is shifted to their harmful effects on humanity. As in chapters 8–9, here again John depends on Exodus 7–10 for his images. This means that the whole earth will now experience afflictions similar to those that once befell Egypt—and will be similarly unrepentant.

Chapters 17–18

In picturesque language John describes the world powers that oppose God as a heady mixture of military might, finance, and sex. Among his models are Jeremiah 50–51 and Daniel 2, 7, and 8. It is clear that the believers are not immune to the temptations from the powers of the world, as they have to be called upon to "come out of her" (18:4). The fact that in the long list of merchandise in 18:11–13 humans are mentioned last is a powerful criticism of slavery, which was overlooked for centuries.

Those who object to the fact that female images are used to represent evil can be reminded of the fact that the New Jerusalem is likewise represented as female; in fact, the two cities Babylon and Jerusalem form antipodes (see Synopsis).

There is an intriguing reference to seven kings in 17:9–11 that has been used in attempts to determine the year in which Revelation was written. John tells us that five of the kings have fallen, one is alive, and one is still to come. Not unreasonably, many think that this could be a reference to Roman emperors and believe that Revelation was written during the rule of "the sixth emperor," but it has proved impossible to work out who is meant. Part of the problem is that in 68–69 C.E. no fewer than three emperors ruled, each for a very short period without being properly recognized.

Chapter 19

This chapter uses the traditional images of the wedding banquet and the rider on horseback to convey its message. Some of its vocabulary depends on Isaiah 24–27. The joys of heaven are described in terms of a festive meal as in, e.g., Isaiah and Matthew 22, reflecting the fact that the people of Israel could truly enjoy the good fruits of the earth. A common meal implies belonging as children of God. The difference between the Hebrew Bible and the New Testament is the central role given to Christ, who prepares and presides over the table.

Chapter 20

The idea of a millennium before the end of the world can be found in Jewish texts as well: 1 Enoch, 4 Ezra, the Sibylline Oracles, and 2 Baruch. This chapter also alludes to Isaiah 24–27, whereas Ezekiel 38–39 supplied the names *Gog* and *Magog* (verse 8). The differences between those who interpret Revelation literally and those who largely see images come to a head here: Is the millennium an actual future period or a symbol of God's present or future sovereignty? What is clear, however, is that at the end all powers of evil are defeated by God and Jesus Christ so that the future is bright, and "all is well that ends well."

Chapters 21–22

This part of Revelation owes much of its imagery to Genesis 2–3 so that these passages form an INCLUSION around the whole of the Bible. Other sources of inspiration were Isaiah 65 and Ezekiel 40–48.

In 21:1–8 the new city descends from heaven to earth and its description is full of symbols of perfection. What characterizes the glorious future life are not things or situations but first and foremost the presence of God with humankind, as it was in Genesis 2. In this respect Revelation is entirely theocentric. No longer will there be a clear separation between heaven and earth; God will be everywhere (21:22–23; 22:5). Otherwise the descriptions of the future state are almost entirely symbolic. The cubic form of the New Jerusalem, for example (21:16), is simply the perfect form in the eyes of the ancients. Many phrases are also in the negative form, describing the absence of all evil things and people (21:4, 8, 25; 22:3, 5).

CHARACTERS

angels   There are probably more ANGELS on the pages of Revelation than in any other book of the Bible. Despite their number and their roles, they remain clearly subject to God Almighty, and they act as instructed by him. None is given a personal name as was usual in contemporary Jewish literature, and as we also see in Daniel and in Luke 1–2; this, too, underlines their servant position.

The most important angel from the narrative point of view is the one who is sent to John to convey the revelation (1:1; 22:6, 10, 11, 16). Also important are the seven who blow the seven trumpets that inaugurate key events (8–9 and 11:15) and the seven who pour out the seven bowls of the wrath of God (15–16).

Each of the seven churches in chapters 2–3 has its own angel; but their identities remain unclear. In 12:7, nine angels appear who have sided with God's adversaries and could be called fallen angels.

God   Throughout the book it is clear that God is firmly in control of events on earth, and this omnipotence is the theme of chapters 4–5. God's sovereignty means there is no blind fate. In good Jewish fashion John carefully avoids describing God in human form; he is often referred to as "the throne" (7:9; 8:3; 14:3; 16:17; 19:5; 20:12; 21:3) or "a voice" (9:13; 10:4, 8; 11:12; 14:13; 16:1, 17) in order to preclude a direct reference, using imagery that symbolizes his authority and activity. Much attention is paid to the worship that God receives in heaven, possibly in contrast to the resistance to his reign on earth. His holiness is emphasized (4:8; 6:10; 15:4; 16:5).

Revelation describes not only God's final judgment but also his punishments throughout history (16:2), which aim at the conversion of humans but are generally unsuccessful (9:20–21; 16:9, 11). The terrible events that take place on the earth are partly due to the devil (most clearly in 12) and partly to judgments by God, who acts in just wrath (6:16–17; 11:18; 15:7).

Jesus Christ   Interpreters such as Martin Luther have complained about the lack of Christian content in Revelation, but this is the result of a misreading of the book. Immediately in chapter 1 there is an impressive presentation of Jesus Christ—not of God, as would be the case in the Hebrew Bible. In 1:5 Jesus is called "the firstborn of the dead, and the ruler of the kings of the earth." In the final chapter it is again Jesus who dominates the scene (22:12–16, 20–21). In many respects Christ is shown to be equal to God: in name (1:17 and 2:23 = 1:8), in title (1:8 = 22:13), in activity (22:6 = 22:16), and in occupancy of the throne (22:1, 3). In 11:15 the word *he* (singular) is used to refer to "our Lord and his Messiah." By equating Jesus and God, Revelation attempts to preserve Jewish monotheism.

There are not many references to Jesus' life and work (1:5, 18; 5:9; 7:14), but chapters 12–14 are based on the facts of his birth, life, and glorification. From these elements as well as from chapter 5 it can be seen that Revelation shares the New Testament perspective that "the last days" have already begun.

Chapter 5 contains the strikingly paradoxical description of Jesus as Lion and Lamb, which refers to his power and his temporary humiliation in becoming human. The message of the book is that Jesus is, and will be, victorious not in a militaristic way, but because he died a sacrificial death. Thus Revelation opposes both the contemporary Jewish ideology of violence and the Roman Empire, which was based on superior military power. Christ's first coming was like that of a Lamb, but his second coming will be like that of a Lion. Overall the title *lamb* occurs 28 (= 4 times 7) times, another symbolic number.

Satan   The most elaborate description of God's adversary occurs in 12:9: "The great dragon . . . that ancient serpent, who is called the Devil and Satan, the deceiver of the whole world." He is here depicted in personal terms but the power of evil is also embodied in systems such as the totalitarian state (chapter 13; cf. the fourth beast in Daniel 7) and the totalitarian economy of perversion (chapters 17–18). In addition, other characters in the story (Jezebel in chapter 2; the beasts in 13) seem to be his incarnations.

He is active throughout history (12) but increasingly so toward the end (13). With his allies he

openly opposes Jesus Christ on earth. After these allies have been locked away (19:19–20) Satan will be bound for a limited period (20:1–3). This interlude will not lead him to repentance, and on his release he will resume his old habits, only to be defeated again and to be condemned to eternal damnation (20:7–10). Satan requires absolute surrender from humankind (13:3–4, 8), but he also attacks his own followers (9:4). He acts on his own account, but paradoxically it is God who allows him to act (12:9; 13:5).

Remarkably, the word *Antichrist* is not used in this book (only in 1 John and 2 John), although 17:8 is close, but the fact that the word *beast* has the article the first time it is used (11:7) does point to the fact that John is using an existing concept of the eschatological adversary.

Spirit; Trinity   Revelation refers to the Holy Spirit at the end of each of the seven letters (2–3); otherwise he is consistently described as "the seven spirits" (1:4; 3:1; 4:5; 5:6), possibly alluding to the fullness of his activity in the seven churches, which are representative of the church universal (cf. the description of the Lamb in 5:6).

One of the few places in the New Testament to form a building stone for a doctrine of the TRINITY, together with Matthew 28:19 and 2 Corinthians 13:13, is Revelation 1:4–5 which mentions God as "the one who is and who was and who is to come" and "Jesus Christ, the faithful witness, the firstborn of the dead, and the ruler of the kings of the earth."

Romans

Ancient letters always opened with the identity of both the addressees and the sender. PAUL often had coauthors, but the opening of this particular letter mentions only him as its writer. Whereas the authorship of some of his letters has been disputed, Romans is the norm against which Paul's other letters are measured. See also EPISTLE.

As with all letters, the title did not originate with Paul or the scribe. It must have been added when the early churches started exchanging the letters Paul had written to several of them, in order to distinguish the letters from each other.

In all likelihood the church in Rome consisted of several house churches that were made up of Christians from a pagan (1:5–6; 11:13) as well as from a Jewish (2:17, 25; 4:1; 7:1) background. The church had not been founded by Paul, and its origins are unknown. It is possible that Roman Jews had come to faith in Jesus Christ elsewhere, for example, in Jerusalem, and had taken the gospel message home with them.

The letter was written during Paul's third missionary journey, around the year 57 C.E., while the apostle was staying in Corinth. Apparently, he writes entirely on or from his own initiative and not in response to any issue that the addressees had called to his attention. In chapter 1 Paul states as his reason for writing that he is hoping to visit the readers and that in preparation he wants to share his understanding of the gospel with them. The word *gospel* (Greek *eu-angelion*) is here used in its original meaning of "good news," the good news that in Jesus Christ God has made peace with humankind. (The use of the word *gospel* to refer to a written account of the life of Jesus is secondary.) The final chapters (15–16) show that Paul is trying to involve the Roman Christians in his apostolic ministry, including a collection for Jerusalem. More particularly, he is networking so that he will be enabled to visit Rome, and from there to proceed to Spain. Specifically, 15:24 implies a request for financial, logistic, and even linguistic support.

In addition, the middle chapters of the letter (9–11) suggest that Paul may have been aware of problems between church members from a Jewish and from a pagan background, which were possibly due to the return of Jewish Christians from the exile imposed on them by the emperor in the year 49 C.E. (Acts 18:2). Paul tries to show how both groups belong to the one worldwide church.

SYNOPSIS

Although this letter has certain characteristics of an essay written for a wider audience, it also has the unmistakable marks of a letter. At the beginning there are greetings (1:1–7) and a thanksgiving

(1:8–10); at the end we find plans for the future (15:14–33), many greetings (16:1–16, 21–23), and final prayers (16:25–27).

At the transition to the body of the letter Paul announces his plans for a visit (1:11–15) and states as his theme the gospel that reveals the righteousness and the power of God (1:16–17 New Revised Standard Version; New International Version "from God" is less correct). He continues by showing how all humanity is in need of this gospel because they are all separated from God through their sins, whether they are from a Gentile background (1:18–2:16) or Jews (2:17–3:20). Paul repeats in more detail what the gospel is (3:21–31). Abraham, the father of the Jewish people, is used as a model of faith, the only correct response to the gospel (chapter 4). Other ramifications of the gospel message are laid down in much detail (chapters 5–8), and particular attention is paid to the place of Jews and Gentiles within the community of those who believe the gospel (chapters 9–11). In places Paul betrays his personal involvement with the subject by referring to "my Gospel" (2:16; 16:25).

In the second part of the letter Paul discusses the practical demands that the gospel makes on the lifestyle of the believers. The general principle is laid down in 12:1–3, which is followed by instructions on gifts, love, attitude toward the government, openness to the future, and the relationships of groups with different opinions on contested issues (12:4–15:13). As explained, the final part (15:14–16:27) is the most personal element of the letter.

COMMENTARY

Paul is not the founder of the church in Rome, and he has never been there, but he wants to share with Romans the gospel as he preaches it. Consequently, this letter is the most systematic exposition of his thought that we have, and it rightly takes the first place in the collection of his letters. It has clear similarities with Galatians, in which Paul also expounds his key thoughts but in a troubled situation. It is striking that the position of Israel receives much attention at the heart of the letter. Most of what Paul says relates to the Church as a whole, but it can also be read at a personal level.

To make the exposition livelier, in the first part Paul uses the rhetorical device of the *diatribe* (fictional classroom discussion): He introduces an imaginary dialogue partner, who contradicts him and asks questions that enable him to move to the next step in his argument. This device can be seen in 3:1, 5, 9, 27; 4:1; 6:1, 15; 7:7, 13; 9:19, 30; and 10:14. Another stylistic device is the frequent use of pairs of antithetical words, such as *Jew—Gentile; law—faith; works—faith; Adam—Christ; unrighteousness—righteousness; slave—free; under the law—apart from the law; sinful nature* (New International Version; literally "flesh")—*the Spirit*. Nearly every passage in chapters 1–11 is built on some such antithesis.

What readers consider the theme of the letter depends largely on which part of it they see as the most important. In 1:16–17 Paul announces that he will discuss the gospel, that is, the message about Jesus Christ and the righteousness he brings to those who believe. He had already mentioned the gospel in 1:1–2, 9, and 15. This gospel entails the acceptance of humans by faith in God alone (chapters 1–4), peace with God (chapter 5), the spiritual union of faith of the believers with Christ (chapters 6–7), the spiritual life (chapter 8), and the close relationship between the Church and Israel (chapters 9–11). Each of these subthemes could be elevated to the main theme of the letter, but it is better to see them as aspects of the gospel as the main theme.

A key element of Paul's presentation of the gospel is his use of the Hebrew Bible to back up or illustrate his words. In many places he quotes the Scriptures directly, normally without mentioning the exact source, but the prophet Isaiah is mentioned by name several times in chapters 9, 10, and 15. Even the letter's theme (1:16–17) is based on a quote, in this case from the prophet Habakkuk. Throughout Paul shows that the gospel confirms and fulfills rather than contradicts the Scriptures. In this context it should be commented that the best translation of 10:4 is that Christ is the "goal, real meaning, substance"—not the "end"—of the Scriptures (the Greek word is the versatile *telos*).

In sharp contrast to the positive message of the gospel in 1:16–17, Paul presents a bleak description of the condition of humankind. All humans are under the wrath of God because of their sins; God allows humanity's sins to have disastrous effects on individuals and society. In chapter 2 Paul adds the thesis that it makes no difference whether people know and respect God's law as revealed in the Hebrew Bible or not: Despite such knowledge all humans are equally sinful and in need of salvation. Admittedly, the Jews had been given several privileges such as the Law of Moses and circumcision (2:17–29), but these things do not put them beyond recrimination as they were unable to change their hearts. A series of quotes form the Hebrew Scriptures sums up and seals the accusation: "There is no one righteous, not even one" (3:10).

With an emphatic "but now" Paul turns to an expanded presentation of the gospel: "The righteousness of God has been disclosed" through Jesus Christ (3:21 NRSV). This righteousness implies that on the basis of Christ's atoning sacrifice God is able to forgive all sins, past, present, and future, of all who believe, Jews and non-Jews alike. Yet the idea that God's justification extends to Jews and Gentiles alike was revolutionary, and at times it had been hotly disputed, as can be seen in Acts 15 and in Galatians. Therefore, Paul takes time to show that it already occurs in the Hebrew Bible in the story of ABRAHAM, who was justified by faith and not by works (chapter 4). The fact that Abraham was later circumcised, that is to say, bore the physical sign of Jewishness, was irrelevant in this respect.

Romans 5:1–11 and 8:1–30 expound the great results of the accomplishment of Jesus Christ, such as peace and freedom, in jubilant tones. In between these two passages Paul provides further explorations of the gospel and its ramifications. In 5:12–21 he contrasts Jesus as the new man with Adam, the first man: Adam brought sin into the world; Jesus brought forgiveness; both Adam's sin and Christ's righteousness have wide implications, making their perpetrators heads of humanity. Christ's resurrection shows that by his obedience unto death he has undone the consequences of Adam's failure.

After summarizing the whole argument up to that point in 5:20–21, Paul's theme in chapters 6 and 7 is the question whether morality is not undermined as God's grace makes observance of the Jewish Law obsolete. His answer to this no doubt real-life objection is threefold: You have died to sin (6:1–14), you must now live to God (6:15–7:6), and the Law was not so effective anyway (7:7–26). Paul uses a series of metaphors: of death and resurrection (6:1–14), change of ownership of slaves (6:15–23), and change of husband (7:1–6). Romans 6:1–7 is one of the few passages in the New Testament to discuss the meaning of Christian BAPTISM, which is a symbolic enactment of the death and burial of the old life of the believers and of their rising to a new form of life. The background to Paul's words is the fact that baptism was performed in the open air by full immersion. The interpretation of 7:7–26, which argues that the law is ineffective because human nature is inexorably sinful, is hotly disputed. The major difficulty is the use of the first person: Is Paul referring to his present personal experience, which he sees as typical of all Christians, or is he referring to his Jewish experience under the Law—one of constant failure to live ethically—thus picking up points made in chapter 2, or saying something else? The prevailing answer is that Paul is referring to the experience of the people of Israel and identifying with it.

Chapter 8 is the chapter about the role of the Holy Spirit in the Christian life, arguing that the Spirit lives in all believers (verses 9, 14–15). The Spirit is the believers' help in dark times and their hope for the future (verses 18–27). The conclusion of the chapter is a well-known expression of the absolute certainty that nothing can separate believers from God.

Chapters 9–11 contain the core New Testament discussion of the relationship between the Church and the Jews. Paul argues that the Jewish element in the Church forms the factor of continuity with the previous period of history. The community of believers is represented as an olive tree. Through unbelief several branches were cut off, whereas through faith in Jesus Christ new branches, formerly Gentiles, have been grafted in. But these obviously do not have a place above the older branches, and even less do they form the entire tree. Paul deeply regrets the failure of many of his fellow Jews to accept Jesus as the promised Messiah, but he upholds God's love for them and (according to some commentators) in veiled terms hints at a future conversion of the Jews (11:25–26). Previous generations have read these chapters as a discussion of the election of individuals to salvation, but Paul clearly writes about the collective. Likewise in 8:18–25 his focus is on the cosmic effects of the gospel, and in chapters 12–15 all ethical guidance is aimed at the well-being of the church and society as a whole. Any conclusions as to the individual believer are secondary.

Chapter 13:1–7 is a well-known passage about the believers' attitude toward the government, in which Paul expresses a remarkably positive view of its beneficial effects on individuals and society. These words were written in the early years of the reign of the emperor Nero, who toward the end of his life showed signs of mental illness, became a bad ruler, and persecuted the Christians in Rome after accusing them of starting the great fire in the city (64 C.E.). According to the later legend Paul was even martyred at Nero's instruction.

The discussion of the relation between "strong" and "weak" believers in 14:1–15:13 recalls what Paul had written in 1 Corinthians 8–10 not long before. Similarly, the brief discussion of the gifts of the believers in Romans 12:4–8, with reference to the body metaphor, comes across as an abbreviation of Paul's longer treatment of the topic in 1 Corinthians 12. Otherwise Paul's two longest letters have little in common.

In 13:11–14 we find a reflection of Paul's lively expectation of the return of Jesus Christ (see LAST THINGS). The recommendation of Phoebe in 16:1–2 suggests that she is the leading person among those who will carry the letter to Rome. In 16:22 the scribe (*amanuensis*) whom Paul used to pen the letter relinquishes his anonymity to make himself known as Tertius and to convey Christian greetings. The words of blessing of God in 11:33–36 and 16:25–27 are known as doxologies; in some important ancient manuscripts the latter doxology appears not at the far end of the letter but after chapter 14 or chapter 15, or in two places. This suggests that at some moment versions of Romans circulated without chapter 16 and without 15 and 16, possibly as a result of attempts to give the letter a more general character by omitting the personal details.

The letter to the Romans has played an important role at key moments in the history of the Christian Church. The most important father of the church, Augustine, was converted to Christianity after reading 13:13–14. The 16th-century reformer Martin Luther took his cue from the phrase on justification by faith in 1:17. And at the beginning of the 20th century the Swiss theologian Karl Barth started an influential renewal movement after studying and writing on this letter.

CHARACTERS

Holy Spirit The whole of chapter 8 focuses on the role of the Spirit in the believers. Paul makes it clear that the Spirit is an integral part of the Christians' experience (verse 9). The Spirit is at work in the renewal of the believers, with them he longs for the last things, and he mediates their prayers (verses 26–27).

Jesus Christ Paul does not tell the life story of Jesus, but it is presupposed everywhere in this letter. In particular Jesus' death on the cross and his resurrection are the foundation for Paul's exposition of the gospel. The key passage about the transition of humanity from despair to liberty refers to God's intervention in Jesus and to his atoning sacrifice on the cross (3:21, 25).

Romans 1:3–4 alludes to the two aspects of the person of Jesus, his humanity as son of David and his divinity as seen in his power, whereas 9:5 is unique in Paul's letters in that he calls Jesus "God" without any qualification such as "Son of."

Paul Despite the sometimes abstract contents of the letter, it is also highly personal. Paul warmly announces his plan to visit the readers and in the final chapter shows his personal involvement with them through the inclusion of a long list of names. Moreover, in chapters 9–11 he shows his heartfelt concern about the unbelief of so many of the Jews, his own people, introduced by a deeply moving self-effacing utterance in 9:1–5.

In the past the passage 7:13–25 was often read as autobiographical, but that reading has been abandoned. The use of the first-person singular here is a rhetorical device to drive home the seriousness of sin, not a reflection of Paul's personal situation.

Roman Christians The greetings in chapter 16 provide a fascinating insight into the diversity of the Church in Rome at the time of writing. Several members are identified as relatives of Paul; that at the very least means that they were Jews, and quite a few of those included are women. In verse 7 a (married) couple of disciples is mentioned, Andronicus and Junia. *Junia* may be the Latin name of the woman who is called by the Hebrew name *Joanna* in Luke 8:3. The name and role of Erastus (verse 23) are attested in a secular Corinthian source.

Ruth

The book of Ruth is a historical-theological narrative. It depicts some exemplary actions taken by people who eventually became ancestors of the famous King David. At first sight it is a simple family story. On closer examination, however, the book turns out to be a most artistically designed piece of literature.

In today's bibles, the book of Ruth is placed between Judges and Samuel and so becomes part of the large history work reaching from Genesis to Kings. Originally, however, it was designed as an independent booklet. In the Jewish liturgical calendar, the book is read out every year at Shavuot (Pentecost), the concluding festival of grain harvest.

The author of the book is anonymous. The story is written from the perspective of an omniscient narrator standing outside the story. The narrator does not describe any thoughts or inner feelings of the characters; nor does he himself give any comments or other direct evaluation of the events reported. He simply lets the events speak for themselves. This points to a claim for objectivity and reliability. Evaluations and theological statements, however, are indirectly given through the literary shaping of the story.

It is difficult to give an exact date when the book was written. Most scholars have decided approximately 950–600 B.C.E. The oldest extant manuscripts have been found at Qumran (see DEAD SEA SCROLLS). The story takes place in the time of King David's great-grandparents, about 1100 B.C.E.

The book contains four verses of poetry, 1:16–17 and 1:20–21, which are marvelous examples of parallelism (see POETRY, BIBLICAL). Verses 16 and 17 express Ruth's extraordinary loyalty to her mother-in-law and are sometimes used in wedding contexts today.

SYNOPSIS

The story begins with a famine in the land of Israel. Elimelech, a man from Bethlehem, decides to leave his country. Together with his wife, Naomi, and his two sons, Mahlon and Chilion, he travels to the country of Moab and settles there. But after some time, Elimelech dies. Mahlon and Chilion marry two Moabite women, named Orpah and Ruth. Both couples, however, remain childless. This was a great shame in the culture of that time. After 10 years, Mahlon and Chilion also die, so Naomi is left alone with her two daughters-in-law.

When Naomi hears that the famine in Israel has ended, she decides to return home. Both her daughters-in-law want to go with her, but she advises them to stay back in Moab, because there would be hardly any future for them in Israel. Orpah finally gives way, but Ruth does not change her mind. Her loyalty to Naomi, to Israel, and to the God of Israel is so strong that she does not want to depart from her mother-in-law. So they reach Bethlehem together, but without much hope for their future. In the ancient Near Eastern culture, women without a husband or family would have a very low standard of living.

In order not to die of hunger, Ruth makes use of an old Israelite law. It permitted poor people to glean in a field behind the pickers, taking what they left. In the field she happens to meet Boaz, the owner of the field. Boaz, who has already heard about Ruth's story, praises her for her exemplary loyalty to Naomi. He offers her protection, allows her to take from the pickers' food for herself, and invites her to continue gleaning behind the pickers

Ruth gleans in the grain field of Boaz (Ruth 2:1–23), engraving by Julius Schnorr von Carolsfeld

in his own fields until the end of the barley harvest. He orders the pickers to leave more grain for her.

At night, Ruth tells her mother-in-law what has happened. Naomi is very happy about it. She explains to Ruth that Boaz is a near-relative of the family and, therefore, a so-called kinsman-redeemer. A kinsman-redeemer was needed when a husband died without having fathered a son. In the culture of that time, the continuation of the family line through male descendants was very important, and its breaking off was seen as a great shame and a curse. In the biblical wording it is "His name was blotted out of Israel." In order to prevent such a disaster, the brother or another near-relative of the dead was to father a son with the dead man's wife. This was called "levirate marriage." The son born was regarded as the son of the dead person. The relative also had to take financial responsibility for the family. In this way, a broken family line could be reinstated, or, to use the biblical wording, "The dead man's name will be maintained on his inheritance" (see Deuteronomy 25:5–10). Therefore, Naomi advises Ruth to remain with Boaz, her possible kinsman-redeemer, until the end of barley harvest.

In order to woo Boaz to enter into levirate marriage with Ruth, Naomi develops an original but also somewhat audacious plan. At night, Ruth is to creep to the threshing floor, the place where Boaz is sleeping, and lie down at his feet. The plan is carried out. In the middle of the night Boaz wakes up and is aware of Ruth. They talk, and Boaz agrees to help. But he also explains that there is another relative of Elimelech who is nearer to him and, as regards kinsman redeeming, he has to be asked first. Under cover of darkness Ruth returns to her home.

The next morning, Boaz convenes the other kinsman-redeemer and 10 of the elders at the city gate, the usual place for dealing with legal matters. He tells them about Naomi and Ruth. The other kinsman-redeemer initially agrees to buy the field that belongs to Elimelech and from that provide Naomi with food. But when he hears that he would also have to enter into levirate marriage with Ruth and so take financial responsibility for a prospective son, he refuses.

Therefore Boaz, the second nearest kinsman, takes responsibility and enters into levirate marriage with Ruth. The story has a happy ending: A son is born, the family line of Elimelech and Mahlon is reinstated, Ruth and Naomi have found a new home. The short genealogy at the end of the book shows that the reinstated family line further continues to David, the great king of Israel.

COMMENTARY

Parts of the book of Ruth appear to be organized along concentric patterns (see STRUCTURES, LITERARY). In other words, the first paragraph of a textual section corresponds to the last, the second to the second last, the third to the third last, etc. The paragraph that is placed in the center of such a structure is thereby given prominence.

For example, the second chapter of the book describes the first encounter between Ruth and Boaz, one day at the beginning of barley harvest. The events are told in a natural, flowing manner, but at the same time consistently following such a concentric pattern.

Verse 1	introducing information
2	dialogue Naomi—Ruth
3	Ruth gleans in the field
4–7	dialogue Boaz—harvester
8–9	Boaz invites Ruth to drink
10	Ruth as foreigner has found favor
11–12	Boaz: "May the LORD reward you ... under whose wings you have come for refuge!"
13	Ruth as foreigner has found favor
14	Boaz invites Ruth to eat
15–16	dialogue Boaz—harvester
17	Ruth gleans in the field
18–22	dialogue Naomi—Ruth
23	summarizing comment

The blessing that Boaz speaks to Ruth (2:11–12) stands at the center of the literary structure and is therefore given prominence.

The third chapter of the book describes a second encounter between Ruth and Boaz, one night at the end of barley harvest. This chapter again is built around a dialogue between Boaz and Ruth, its center having the words of Ruth (verse 9): "I am Ruth, your servant; spread your wing over your servant, for you are next-of-kin." In 3:9, Bible translations use the word *cloak* or *covering* of Boaz, which is correct in terms of meaning. In the original Hebrew, however, the word *wing* is used, as in 2:12. That means that there is a word connection between the literary centers of chapters 2 and 3. Through literary shaping, the "wings of God" and the "wing of Boaz" are set into relationship to each other. Ruth's hope to find refuge under the "wings" of God is fulfilled by Boaz's taking Ruth under the "wing" of his cloak and marrying her. Or, in other words, God's kindness becomes visible when human beings act courageously on his behalf. The text asks the reader to follow this example and not just let things happen but decide to act on behalf of God.

Another example of showing initiative on behalf of God is given by Ruth the Moabite. According to biblical law, the Moabites were not admitted to Israel. The reason for this was that the Moabites had not agreed to sell bread to the Israelites at the time the Israelites were crossing their country (see Deuteronomy 23:3–6). The idea that Naomi took a Moabite women of all people back to Israel must have been embarrassing for the faithful Israelites.

But Ruth uses her initiative and does what her ancestors refused to do: She provides food for her Israelite mother-in-law. By that she abolishes the anti-Moabite law for herself.

The book of Ruth shows not only how individuals act courageously on behalf of God, but also how God uses those individuals to make them part of his overarching purposes.

When Ruth starts providing food for Naomi, the text says, "As it happened," she went to a field of Boaz. Behind this seeming coincidence, Naomi instantly recognizes an act of God. God has taken up Ruth's initiative for food and transformed it into a plan for redeeming the whole family of Elimelech (2:20).

But there is an even wider perspective on God's redeeming acts. This can be seen by comparing the beginning and the ending of the book of Ruth. At the beginning of the book, we are told that the story takes place during the time of the Judges. This statement is not only meant historically; it also has theological implications: According to the book of Judges, this was a dark era, characterized by disobedience of the people and by failure, and by the Philistines' constant military threat. One reason for this is seen in the lack of an appropriate Israelite monarchy (see Judges 17:6; 18:1; 19:1; 21:25). The famine mentioned in Ruth 1:1 fits very well into that picture. The cause of the famine should not just be seen in difficult weather but rather in the absence of God's blessing (see 1:6b). After all, Israel is the Promised Land, the land that should be "flowing with milk and honey" (Exodus 3:8).

The wrong decision of Elimelech to move outside the land of the covenant of God, the death of Elimelech in Moab, 10 years of barrenness of his sons' marriages, and, finally, the death of Mahlon and Chilion complete the image of absence of God's blessing.

The book ends with a genealogy that describes an intact family line of 10 generations. With regard to literary structure and to content, it stands in opposition to the 10 years of barrenness at the beginning of the book. The family line culminates in DAVID, one of the most famous individuals of old Israel. After the first kingdom of Saul had failed, David was God's chosen king, who once and for all defeated the Philistines and who was promised an everlasting kingdom. That the family line of David is intact is the result of the initiatives of Ruth and Boaz. Through their actions resulted a redemption not only of one family but also of the whole nation. With that the book of Ruth shows, if people act courageously on behalf of God, he, in turn, will make them part of his greater plan of salvation.

From a canonical point of view, this line can be extended even more: In the New Testament, Jesus of Nazareth is said to be the definitive fulfillment of the promise given to David. In the genealogy of Jesus in Matthew 1, Boaz and Ruth are again mentioned. Through their faithful actions, they have become part of God's plan of salvation on a family level, on a national level, and even on a worldwide level.

The book of Ruth not only demonstrates positive human behavior but also gives counterexamples. In order to do so, pairs of characters are put into contrast. Orpah and Ruth at first both decide to accompany Naomi to Israel. But then Orpah allows herself to be made to stay back in Moab. Her decision does not necessarily need to be judged negatively. Orpah does what people normally would do. However, because of her decision she drops out of the story and does not play any further role in God's history. With this background, the exemplary loyalty of Ruth to Naomi becomes even more evident.

Another pair of characters placed in opposition with each other are Boaz and the other kinsman-redeemer. As does Orpah, the other redeemer at first agrees to act according to the will of God. However, as Orpah, he changes his mind after some further discussion. Interestingly, the name of the other redeemer is not given in the book. Instead, he is called "a certain one." He refuses to "maintain the dead man's name on his inheritance," in fear of losing his own name (i.e., not being able to provide sufficient farmland for his own son to continue the family line). But eventually, the opposite happens. He loses his name because he was *not* willing to maintain Elimelech's name. In other words, concentrating on one's own interests will not make a person suitable for being part of God's greater story. Rather, it will lead to total insignificance (cf. Psalm 1:4; Proverbs 10:24). Boaz's name, however, because he took responsibility, is maintained and even replaces the name of Elimelech in the concluding genealogy.

A third pair of characters standing in contrast to each other can be seen in Elimelech and Boaz. Whereas Elimelech's actions lead to barrenness and death, Boaz's actions lead from emptiness to fullness, from sadness to happiness, from barrenness to the birth of a son, of a family redeemer and ancestor of a king redeeming the whole nation. It is obvious which of these models should be followed.

All the elements of the narrative are carefully arranged so that an overall symmetric structure emerges. Chapters 2 and 3, the two encounters between Ruth and Boaz connected by the "wing" theme, are framed by chapters 1 and 4, which are shaped very much in parallel and contrast to each other. In chapter 1, there is complaining before the women of Bethlehem, and Naomi gives herself a name expressing her bitterness; in chapter 4, there is praise of the women of Bethlehem, and the child is given a name expressing new hope. The comparison between Ruth and Orpah in chapter 1 stands in parallel to the comparison between Boaz and the other kinsman-redeemer in chapter 4. Finally, 10 years of barrenness and hopelessness in Moab at the beginning contrast with 10 generations leading to David, the redeemer of Israel, at the end.

CHARACTERS

Boaz   Boaz is prominent and rich. He takes responsibility for the family of his dead relative Elimelech by entering into levirate marriage with Ruth. Through this faithful act he becomes part of God's greater salvation history. His name is mentioned not only in the genealogy of David but even that of Jesus Christ.

Elimelech   Elimelech is the husband of Naomi and father of Mahlon and Chilion. He decides to leave the land of Israel and to settle in Moab, together with his family. But then he dies. The marriages of his two sons are childless for 10 years, and finally his sons also die. Elimelech is a countercharacter to Boaz. While his actions lead into emptiness and death, Boaz' actions lead into fullness and new life.

God   At only one place in the story is God's acting explicitly stated by the narrator: "The LORD made her conceive" in 4:13. However, God is often mentioned in the reported speech of the characters. The book of Ruth is about God's acting behind the scenes, of human and divine deeds' being intertwined with each other.

kinsman-redeemer   The other kinsman-redeemer refuses to assume financial responsibility for the family of Elimelech. If he maintains the name of his dead relative, so he fears, he will lose his own name. But his plans do not work out. It is just *because* he only cares for himself that in God's history he becomes totally insignificant and literally loses his name. This other kinsman-redeemer is a countercharacter to Boaz.

Mahlon and Chilion   Mahlon and Chilion are sons of Elimelech and Naomi, and husbands of Ruth and Orpah. After 10 years of marriage they both die without having fathered a child.

Naomi   Naomi has to suffer a cruel fate. Her husband, Elimelech, and her two sons, Mahlon and Chilion, die in the land of Moab. Only Ruth, one of her daughters-in-law, stays with her when she returns to Israel. She does not want to be called *Naomi*, "Pleasant," anymore, but *Mara*, "Bitter." But when Ruth becomes proactive and provides food for Naomi, Naomi finds fresh hope. Behind what is happening she recognizes God at work for her. Now she decides and prepares for a levirate marriage between Ruth and Boaz. In the end her life turns from emptiness to fullness, from the experience of death to new life.

Orpah   Orpah is a Moabite and Naomi's daughter-in-law. After the death of her husband, she decides to leave Naomi and stay in Moab. Therefore, she does not play any further role in God's history. Orpah is a countercharacter to Ruth.

Ruth   Ruth is a Moabite and Naomi's daughter-in-law. In all her words and deeds, she shows a loving commitment and extraordinary loyalty to Naomi, her family, her people, and her God. After the death of her husband, Ruth decides to stay with her mother-in-law; she helps her by providing food for her and maintaining Elimelech's family line by entering into levirate marriage with Boaz.

1 and 2 Samuel

Can a human being rule the holy people of God? This is the question behind the historical presentation of the three main characters in the book of 1 and 2 Samuel: *Samuel,* the last "judge," personifies the direct rule of God, not by way of political structures, but by God's spirit. Samuel's task is to constitute the Israelite monarchy, even against his own will. *Saul* is the first king of the developing monarchy. Because he is disrespectful to God, God rejects him even while he still reigns. *David,* finally, is the king "after God's own heart." He has to fight many struggles and is not free of personal failure. Nevertheless, God blesses him and promises him an everlasting dynasty.

The two books of Samuel originally form one single book. At the same time, the book is part of a larger group, consisting of the Pentateuch and the books Joshua, Judges, Samuel, and Kings, narrating the history from the CREATION of the world until the Babylonian EXILE.

The book of Samuel was written by an anonymous author or group of authors. The dating of its final editing is disputed, as it is dependent also on the dating of the books that precede and follow it. However, the abundance of events, figures, and locations in the book demonstrates that the author is historically well informed. Therefore, the first written sources must have originated not long after the events occurred.

The oldest surviving manuscripts were found in the caves of Qumran (see DEAD SEA SCROLLS), one of them dating to the third century B.C.E. Regarding the transmission of the text, there are several divergences between the standardized Hebrew text, the old Greek translation (the Septuagint; see BIBLE, EARLY TRANSLATIONS OF), and the Dead Sea findings. Sometimes, parts of sentences or even whole sentences are added or omitted. However, these divergences do not mean deviations in terms of content or message. The English translations are mainly based on the Hebrew text; footnotes indicate where the Greek tradition is preferred.

The events reported in the book cannot be confirmed in detail by archaeology. However, the basic parameters regarding Israel's neighboring nations can be confirmed. The most prominent of Israel's enemies at that time are the PHILISTINES, who arrived at the coast of the HOLY LAND around 1200 B.C.E. The Philistines did not leave any written records; therefore, the biblical texts of Judges and Samuel remain important sources of information about their history. The Philistines are described as the first who make use of iron on a larger scale, hence their military strength (e.g., 1 Samuel 13:19–22).

There are no direct clues for dating the events reported in the book. However, starting with some points of contact between Israel and the Assyrians in the ninth century B.C.E., the years given in the book of Kings can be used to calculate David's reign to 1010–971 B.C.E. The information given on Saul's reign in 1 Samuel 13:1 is corrupted. A New Testament passage (Acts 13:21) reckons 40 years. This can be inferred indirectly from 2 Samuel 2:10: Ishbosheth, son of Saul, probably born after Saul's enthronement, becomes his successor at the age of 40 years. Other scholars opt for a 20-year reign of Saul, 1030–1010 B.C.E.

Regarding its genre, the book is a historical-theological narrative. On the one hand, the book narrates historical events, even down to the details. On the other hand, the selection as well as the arrangement of the material were done for certain theological purposes. The inner literary structure of the book is the subject of discussion. Some of the structures presented are taken from H. Klement, *II Samuel 21–24: Context, Structure and Meaning of the Samuel Conclusion* (Frankfurt am Main: Peter Lang, 2000).

SYNOPSIS

Samuel, the Last Judge of Israel (1 Samuel 1–8)
Hannah is very sad that she does not have any children. In the temple at Shiloh, she makes a vow to God: If God gives her a son, she will make him

available to God. God answers her prayers, and she becomes pregnant, giving birth to a son named Samuel. When he is weaned, she gives him to the temple, where Eli, the priest, raises him. After that, Hannah gives birth to more sons and daughters.

At the temple of Shiloh, Eli serves, together with his two sons, Hophni and Phinehas. However, the sons do not handle the sacrifices with care and cheat the people who want to give offerings at the temple. A prophet appears announcing that Eli and his family will die (chapters 1–2).

At night, God calls Samuel. Since revelations of God are rare at this time, he first thinks Eli had called him. God announces to Samuel that he will bring judgment on Eli's family.

A battle follows between Israel and the Philistines, in which the Philistines seem to be stronger. The Israelites hurry to take the ark of the covenant from Shiloh, accompanied by Eli's sons. The Philistines are afraid, but they fight even harder. They defeat the Israelite army and win the ark of the covenant. Eli's sons die. A messenger arrives at Shiloh and reports the disaster. Eli falls from his chair and is dead (chapters 3–4).

The Philistines place the ark of the covenant in their temple of Dagon in Ashdod. But the next morning, Dagon lies in front of the ark with his face toward the ground. Also, a mysterious power originates from the ark, bearing the bubonic plague to the Philistines. (The Septuagint adds that rats appeared—probably the carrier of the disease.) The Philistines decide to take the ark back to Israel. For 20 years, the ark stays in the house of a certain Abinadab. His son, Eleazar, is consecrated to keep it (chapters 5–6). Samuel calls the people to repent and turn back to God, promising that God will give them victory over the Philistines. The people agree and remove all foreign gods. When the Philistine army approaches, the Israelites attack, led by Samuel, and defeat them. As long as Samuel lives, there is peace (chapter 7).

When Samuel is old, he installs his two sons as judges. However, the sons are not righteous but accept bribes. The people ask God to appoint a king over them instead. Samuel is furious about it and asks God. God gives a negative assessment too. The installment of a king means not only a rejection of Samuel and his family but also a rejection of God as king over Israel. Nevertheless, God instructs Samuel to do according to the will of the people. Samuel tells the people about the rights a king would have over them. But the people stand by their request (chapter 8).

Saul: From His Coronation to His Rejection (1 Samuel 9–15)

Saul, a young farmer from the tribe of Benjamin, searches in vain for his father's lost donkeys, together with some servants. When they are about to return home, they arrive at a city where Samuel is staying. Since he is a seer, they want to ask him about the donkeys.

God has already instructed Samuel about Saul. When Samuel is alone with Saul, he anoints him to be king over Israel. Later, he gathers the people at Mizpah and publicly appoints Saul as king. Many of the people are on Saul's side, but some doubt his abilities (chapters 9–10).

The Ammonites besiege Jabesh-gilead. Saul is informed of this. He rallies troops from all over Israel, 300,000 people from the northern tribes and 30,000 from Judah. He defeats the Ammonites. Now the people want to execute Saul's critics, but Saul is lenient. In Gilgal, Saul's kingship is affirmed. Samuel hands over his responsibilities as a leader to Saul. Now Samuel speaks positively about the kingdom; however, he urges the people to remain faithful to God (chapters 11–12).

Jonathan, Saul's son, provokes the Philistines. Therefore, Saul musters his troops again. Samuel had given the instruction that Saul had to wait seven days for him to arrive and make offerings before the army would go to war. When the seven days are over and Samuel does not appear, Saul decides to make the offering himself. Shortly afterward, Samuel arrives. He is very angry. Through his disobedience, Saul has squandered his chance to be the founder of a lasting dynasty. Now God has appointed someone else as Saul's successor (chapter 13).

Nevertheless, God makes Saul victorious over the Philistines. However, in a critical situation during the battle, Saul makes a vow that no one must eat anything until revenge is carried out. But his son, Jonathan, has not heard about the vow and eats honey he finds on the battlefield. When the Philistines start to flee, Saul asks God whether he should pursue them, but God does not answer. Saul inquires the reason for God's silence and threatens to kill the one responsible. The lot falls on Jonathan. The people intercede on Jonathan's behalf, so that he is not killed. However, Saul does not pursue the Philistines further on that day (chapter 14).

Samuel commissions Saul to attack the Amalekites and kill every person and every animal that belong to them. Saul, however, does not fully obey the commandment. He spares Agag, the Amalekite king, and all valuable animals. Samuel appears and takes Saul to task. He announces to him that God has rejected him because of his disobedience (chapter 15).

David in Saul's Service (1 Samuel 16–20)

God commissions Samuel to go to Jesse in Bethlehem and anoint his youngest son, David, to be king over Israel. The spirit of God comes on David. At the same time, the spirit departs from Saul, and an evil spirit begins to frighten him. Saul's servants look for a musician in order to soften his mood. It happens that David is chosen. Every time the evil spirit pesters Saul, David plays the harp, and Saul feels better (chapter 16).

The army of the Philistines and the army of the Israelites take up positions against each other. Goliath, a very large and strong champion of the Philistines, appears. He mocks the Israelites and challenges them to send a man for a duel. David hears about it and decides to accept the challenge. However, the armor they give him is too heavy for him. He therefore puts it off and appears before Goliath with only a slingshot and five stones. Goliath ridicules him. David hurls a stone, hitting Goliath on his forehead and breaking his skull, at which Goliath falls. David takes his sword and chops off his head. The Israelites are encouraged. They shout war cries and attack the Philistines, who flee (chapter 17).

Saul takes David to his royal court. David forms a friendship with Jonathan, Saul's son. Saul makes David a general, and he is very successful in defeating the Philistines. A song is composed:

David kills Goliath (1 Samuel 17:45–51), engraving by Julius Schnorr von Carolsfeld

"Saul has killed his thousands, and David his ten thousands." Saul becomes jealous of David. In a situation when David plays the harp for him, Saul throws his spear, but David eludes him. Saul then changes his tactics. He offers him his daughter, Michal, as a wife but requests 100 foreskins of the Philistines as the dowry. He hopes David will die at the Philistines' hands. However, David kills 200 Philistines and takes the foreskins to Saul. He then marries Michal. David becomes increasingly famous, but Saul hates him more and more (chapter 18).

Jonathan intercedes with his father on behalf of David. As a consequence, Saul receives David at the court again. But in another fit of jealousy, he again throws his spear at him. Now David leaves the court and returns to his home for a short time. He narrowly manages to escape Saul's soldiers and finds shelter in Samuel's place. He contacts Jonathan. When Jonathan intercedes with Saul on behalf of David, Saul throws his spear after his son. Now Jonathan knows that Saul will not change his mind about David again. Jonathan gives David the sign they had agreed. The two then say good-bye to each other (chapters 19–20).

Saul Persecutes David (1 Samuel 21–26)

David goes to the priest Ahimelech in the city of Nob and receives food and a sword from him. He then hides in the cave of Adullam. He gathers a group of people around him, about 400 men. Saul tracks down David. He finds out that the priest Ahimelech has helped him. Saul kills all the priests of Nob (chapters 21–22).

The Philistines fight against the city of Keilah. David hears about this and goes with his troops to their assistance. They repel the Philistines. Saul hears about this and approaches Keilah. David leaves the region and moves to the wilderness of Ziph, but the people who are living there betray him. Saul begins to chase David. When both armies are separated only by a mountaintop, the message reaches Saul that the Philistines have invaded the country again (chapter 23).

Saul pursues the Philistines but soon returns, following David into the wilderness of En-gedi. In one of the caves, Saul wants to relieve himself, not knowing that David and his warriors are hiding at the back of the cave. David manages to cut off a piece of Saul's mantle without his realizing it. When Saul has left the cave, David appears behind him and presents the cloth to him. Saul is ashamed, and he returns home (chapter 24). Samuel dies and is buried in Rama, his hometown. All Israel mourns for him. David needs some food for himself and for his warriors, probably in order to hold a funeral service. He asks a certain Nabal, a rich cattle breeder, for support. David's men had been protecting his herds for some time. But Nabal refuses. David becomes angry and wants to attack him with his warriors. Abigail, Nabal's wife, hears of it. She sends her servants carrying a lot of food. She goes to him to make peace, apologizing for her husband's foolish behavior. When Nabal hears of it, he suffers a stroke and dies 10 days later. Abigail becomes David's wife (chapter 25).

Again, people tell Saul where David is hiding. Saul approaches with an army. David hears about it. David and his scouts approach Saul's camp at night. David still does not want to kill Saul since he is God's anointed one. Instead, he creeps up on the sleeping Saul and takes his spear and his mug. They leave the camp and begin shouting so that Saul and his troops wake up. They present the spear and the mug to Saul. Again, Saul is ashamed and returns to his place (chapter 26).

Saul, David, and the Philistines (1 Samuel 27–31)

However, David does not trust Saul. In order to be safe from him, he decides to go over to the Philistines. Achish, king of Gath, allows him and his 600 men to settle down in the city of Ziklag. David makes several raids, telling the Philistines that he will attack Judah. In fact, he fights against the Amalekites and other non-Israelite people groups. The Philistines muster their army in order to attack Israel. Achish requests that David and his warriors join the army.

Saul also musters his troops. He is very afraid and asks God what to do, but God does not answer him. Therefore, Saul decides to go to a medium, asking the dead Samuel through her. Samuel appears and announces Saul's downfall.

The other Philistine kings do not agree with David's joining their army. Although Achish intercedes on his behalf, they send David and his warriors back to Ziklag. Arriving home they find out that Ziklag has been plundered by the Amalekites in the meantime. Moreover, David's wives have been captured. David chases the Amalekites and defeats them. They free all who have been captured and take great plunder. They then return to Ziklag.

The battle of the Philistines against Israel begins. The Philistines are superior. Jonathan and two other sons of Saul are killed. When Saul realizes that the situation is hopeless, he kills himself with his sword.

The Two Kings: David and Ishbosheth (2 Samuel 1–3)

In Ziklag, David hears of Saul's and Jonathan's death, and he is very sad. He returns to Judah. In the city of Hebron, he is made king over Judah. In the meantime, Abner, Saul's general, makes Ishbosheth (= Ishbaal) king over the other tribes of Israel. The followers of the two kings meet at the pool of Gibeon. They enter into battle. David's troops are victorious. However, Ishbosheth continues to reign for two years.

Ishbosheth and Abner then begin to argue. Abner deserts to David. David receives him in a friendly manner. But Joab, David's general, does not trust him and kills him without David's knowledge.

When David hears about it, he mourns Abner and speaks a curse on Joab.

David King over All Israel (2 Samuel 4–9)

Ishbosheth is deeply dismayed about having lost Abner, his most important man. Shortly afterward, he is killed by two of his own soldiers. Now all male descendants of Saul are dead, with the exception of Mephibosheth, who is paralyzed in both feet. All Israelites go over to David. In Hebron, David is made king over whole Israel (4:1–5:5).

David conquers Jerusalem from the Jebusites and makes it Israel's capital. The Philistines attack twice, but David easily repels them with the help of God. In an act of celebration, David takes the ark of the covenant to Jerusalem and places it in a holy tent (5:6–6:23).

David plans to build a temple in Jerusalem. However, Nathan, a prophet, appears to him. He tells him that God does not want David, but a son of David, to build the house of God. But in turn, God promises to build the house of David, i.e., to strengthen his dynasty so that it will last forever. David is very moved by this and answers God in a long prayer of thanksgiving (chapter 7).

David continues to be a victorious general. He defeats the Philistines and breaks their power once and for all. He also subjugates the Moabites, the Arameans, the Ammonites, the Amalekites, the king of Zobah, and the Edomites and obliges them to pay tribute (chapter 8).

David wants to do a favor to Saul's family on behalf of Jonathan. He finds Jonathan's paralyzed son, Mephibosheth. He grants him pardon and allows him to live at the court for the rest of his life (chapter 9).

David's Personal Crisis (2 Samuel 10–12)

The Ammonites gain a new king. David sends messengers as a sign of friendship. But the Ammonites do not trust them and suspect that they are spies. They humiliate them and send them back. The Ammonites realize that they have provoked David. They muster troops supported by the Arameans. David hears about it. He attacks and defeats them. The next war season, he again sends his troops against the Ammonites. But he himself remains in Jerusalem. From the flat roof of his palace he observes a beautiful woman bathing. Her name is Bathsheba. She is the wife of Uriah, a soldier participating in the campaign against the Ammonites. David calls for Bathsheba and sleeps with her.

Bathsheba becomes pregnant and informs David of it through a messenger. The army temporarily returns to Jerusalem. David tries to make Uriah sleep with his wife, but he refuses and stays with the other soldiers. When the army leaves again, David commissions Joab, his general, to post Uriah at the front, where the battle is most dangerous, and then let the troops withdraw from him. What David intends happens soon: Uriah is killed when the army attacks a city. Now David takes Bathsheba as his wife, and she gives birth to a son.

God sends Nathan, the prophet, to David. Nathan tells him a story of a rich man who steals the only lamb of a poor man. David is upset but soon realizes that he is the one being described. David repents. Therefore, he does not have to die. However, the adulterous son dies, and a curse is put on David's further time of reign. Then David and Bathsheba have a second son, named Solomon.

Joab, David's general, conquers other Ammonite cities. In order for him not to receive all the honor, he calls David to join and lead the army when they attack the Ammonite capital Rabbah (2 Samuel 10–12).

Absalom's Rebellion (2 Samuel 13–20)

Amnon, David's firstborn, falls in love with his half sister, Tamar. He pretends to be ill and rapes her when she gives him food. After that, he pushes her away from him again. Absalom, Tamar's brother, is very angry. He waits for an opportune moment and lets Amnon be killed. After that he flees, fearing the revenge of his father, David. Joab intercedes on behalf of Absalom, so that he can return to Jerusalem. However, David does not receive him. After two years of waiting, Absalom forces Joab to make an arrangement. Father and son meet again (chapters 13–14).

Absalom wants to become king instead of David. With cunning, he enlists many people on his side. After some time of preparation, he lets himself be made king in Hebron. David hears about it and leaves Jerusalem in order to put himself in a safe position on the east side of the Jordan. Only his concubines stay at the palace. David also sends Hushai to Jerusalem as a secret ally.

Absalom and his followers march into Jerusalem. Absalom sleeps with David's concubines. Ahithophel, Absalom's counselor, advises him to pursue David immediately. But Absalom also wants to hear Hushai. Hushai contradicts Ahithophel. He gives the advice to wait for a few days raising troops and then attack David (chapters 15–17).

Absalom follows Hushai's advice. Therefore, David has the opportunity to raise his own troops. Before the battle begins, David requests that the soldiers spare Absalom. The battle begins, and David's army is stronger. Absalom becomes caught in a tree with his long hair. When Joab sees him, he kills him. David is informed of the victory. But he is very sad about his son. All his warriors are ashamed. Joab takes David to task and warns him not to offend his troops in that way.

David plans to return to Jerusalem. At the Jordan, mainly the people of the tribes of Judah and Benjamin welcome him and confirm his kingship.

The northern tribes and Judah argue. Sheba, a Benjaminite, persuades the northern tribes to reject David. Many people follow him. Sheba barricades himself in a city named Abel of Beth-maacah. Joab prepares to destroy the city, but the inhabitants throw Sheba's head over the wall. Then the warriors return home (chapters 18–20).

Yahweh for David, Not Saul (2 Samuel 21–24)

There is a famine. David inquires of God about the reason for it and hears that Saul had destroyed the city of Gibeon in spite of an existing peace treaty. David apologizes and offers compensation. The Gibeonites request seven male descendants of Saul in order to hang them. David wants to spare Mephibosheth; therefore he chooses seven male descendants of Saul's daughters and hands them over to the Gibeonites, who hang them (21:1–14).

David has at his disposal a group of mighty warriors, who have killed the Philistine giants and have protected David in dangerous situations (21:15–22; 23:8–39).

In a psalm, David praises the power of God and the blessing that he has given to David. In his last

words, he praises the king who rules justly and in the fear of God (22:1–23:7). God becomes angry with the Israelites. He incites David to make a national census. The results are 800,000 men fit for military service, and in Judah, 500,000. But God sends a punishment in the form of a plague that kills 70,000 people. When the angel of death reaches Jerusalem, God stops him. The threshing floor of a certain Araunah is the place where the angel stops. David buys the estate. He erects an altar on it and makes offerings. God answers David's request and stops the plague (chapter 24).

COMMENTARY

Samuel, the Last Judge of Israel (1 Samuel 1–8)

The section is structured according to a concentric pattern (see STRUCTURES, LITERARY):

1:1–2:10	A	wish for a child
2:11–36	B	two corrupt sons of Eli
3–4	C	Samuel announces judgment: battle against Philistines lost
5	D	ark of the covenant with the Philistines
6	D′	ark of the covenant back in Israel
7	C′	Samuel brings deliverance: battle against Philistines won
8:1–3	B′	two corrupt sons of Samuel
8:4–22	A′	wish for a king

A new age of God's salvation history begins with the prayer of a faithful woman for a son (A). The paramount importance of this event is signaled by the psalm celebrating God's justice and mercy leading into a prophetic announcement of a king. Thereby, the main theme of the book is introduced. Hannah's song of praise later becomes a model for Mary's praise in Luke 1:46–55.

The king theme appears again in chapter 8 (A′), although in a negative context. The wish of the people for a king is seen as rejection of God as king over Israel. In other words, a political structure cannot replace the vision of being God's people. Throughout the Hebrew Bible, the monarchy and human rule in general evoke mixed feelings. The prophets criticize the people's reliance on kings and armies instead of trusting God (e.g., Jeremiah 17:5–7); many of the human rulers are depicted negatively, beginning with Abimelech (Judges 9) and Saul (1 Samuel 13–31) and continuing with the later Israelite kings who turn away from God and lead Israel into destruction (see the book of Kings).

At the same time, however, throughout the Bible is the notion of a savior king appointed by God in order to help Israel out of distress. It begins with the promise of Genesis 49:10 that the "scepter shall not depart from Judah." The book of Judges demonstrates that Israel is not well off without a king; especially the closing chapters of the book express the hope that the monarchy may be a way out of the crisis (see Judges 17:6; 18:1; 19:1; 21:25). In the book of Samuel, apart from the positive statement in 1 Samuel 2:10, there is a more positive speech of Samuel in 12:13–15. But most of all, King David is presented as a king "after God's own heart" (1 Samuel 13:14; see Psalm 2).

The tension between positive and negative statements on the monarchy has led scholars to the idea that the antimonarchial passages of Samuel must have been written by a different author or redactor from the one who wrote the promonarchial passages. However, it has to be stated that the reason for the inner tension in the book is not a literary one but lies in the factual situation of the monarchy. It is not far-fetched to say that the book of Samuel has been written exactly for the purpose of exploring the inner tensions of the monarchy theme, personified in Saul and David. Samuel appoints two kings: Saul, an example of failure, and David, an example of a successful monarch. In the ring structure of 1 Samuel 1–8, two corrupt sons each appear at the beginning and at the ending. The bad behavior of Eli's sons (B) leads to the destruction of Eli's family and to the loss of the ark of the covenant to the Philistines. The bad attitude of Samuel's sons is the reason the people ask for a king.

The next inner ring deals with the activities of Samuel and with wars against the Philistines. Samuel is presented as being faithful to God, so that God is with him. In chapter 3 (section C), Samuel is called by God. The way in which God calls people is described very differently throughout the Bible (see REVELATION, GOD's). In the case of Samuel, it takes the form of an audible voice—so that Samuel first thinks it is Eli who called him. The message Samuel receives is judgment. Therefore, the following battle against the Philistines is lost. The people believed that having the ark of the covenant with them would make God be with them, but they were mistaken. In chapter 7 (C′), Samuel calls the people to return to God. This time God really is with the Israelite army; therefore, the second battle against the Philistines is victorious.

Interestingly, the two central chapters do not deal with any human initiative. Rather, God himself is at work. The Philistines may have won the ark of the covenant. But such a sinister power originates from it that they soon decide to return it to the Israel. Therefore, the turning point of the narrative in chapters 1–8 is brought about by God himself. He is in control of everything.

Saul: From His Coronation to His Rejection (1 Samuel 9–15)

The events that lead to Saul's anointing are described in detail. That Samuel can foresee the future proves his divine authorization. The beginnings of the monarchy are humble. Some of the Israelites are not convinced that Saul will be a help for them. It is also striking that after his coronation, Saul works as a farmer in the fields (1 Samuel 11:5).

The Ammonites' siege of Jabesh-gilead is the first chance for Saul to show himself as a king. The offering of the Ammonites to make a covenant that allows them to gouge out the right eyes of all inhabitants of the city is an open provocation. The Ammonites are so self-assured that they even allow the city to send messengers throughout the country calling for help. However, Saul is able to raise a vast army of 330,000 warriors in one week and totally defeats the Ammonites. Thereby the skeptics are silenced.

At this point, Samuel officially hands over his role as a leader to Saul. But Samuel remains as a prophet critically accompanying the monarchy. With this he becomes the model for the prophetic office in general: Most of the biblical prophets have the task of being a critical counterpart to the kings. At the same time, Samuel seems to have been the founder of a school of prophets (1 Samuel 19–20).

However, the decline of Saul begins quickly. Two events reported in chapters 13 and 15 especially demonstrate his disobedience to God: In Gilgal, after Samuel does not appear at the agreed time, he makes the burnt offering himself. From a psychological point of view, his decision is quite comprehensible: He is under pressure because the Philistines are approaching and his own troops are already dispersing in fear. However, Saul thinks in human categories only, forgetting that the blessing of God is the deciding factor in successful warfare.

In the second case of disobedience, Saul does not fully execute the ban on the Amalekites as he was instructed. Again, his decision is understandable: From a human perspective, it does not make sense to kill all the animals. But again, Saul disregards the spiritual aspects. The ban is an ancient Near Eastern concept meaning that the defeated people and all their property were fully devoted to the deity who made the victory possible. Therefore, the ban was seen as a ritual act. Therefore, Saul's disobedience in this case meant that he dealt carelessly with the holy, and that is blasphemy (see also the comment on Leviticus 10:1–2).

The story in chapter 14 shows another problematic aspect of Saul: His rash vow almost costs the life of his son and heir to the throne. Saul's impulsive and irrational character is revealed more and more in the course of the narrative.

David in Saul's Service (1 Samuel 16–20)

This section is marked by an exceptional tension and tragedy, especially when seen from Saul's perspective. While Saul is still king, Samuel secretly anoints David to be king. It happens that David travels to Saul's court in order to serve him. David seems to be a great blessing for Saul, helping him personally and militarily. So everyone wonders why Saul is not happy about him. Saul, on the other hand, realizes more and more that David is the one Samuel told him would be king in his own place. Any attempt of Saul to push David back results in David's increasing his status even more. This results in extreme jealousy.

What is irritating in the narrative from a historical point of view is that in 16:21 David becomes Saul's personal armor bearer, but in 17:55–58, after the killing of Goliath, Saul does not even seem to know David. A possible solution is that the chronological order of presentation is left for a thematic reason. In fact, a concentric structure emerges:

16:1–13	A	Samuel anoints David to be king
16:14–23	B	Evil spirit influences Saul; David goes to Saul's court
17:1–18:4	C	David kills Goliath—covenant with Jonathan
18:5–16	D	David as military leader—Saul's fear
18:17–30	D′	David as the king's son-in-law—Saul's fear
19:1–7	C′	Jonathan defends David because of his killing of Goliath
19:8–17	B′	Evil spirit influences Saul: David flees Saul's court
19:18–24	A′	Samuel protects David, prophetically divesting Saul of his office

The block is framed by the two encounters between Samuel and David. Enclosed in the frame is the time when David was in Saul's service, bracketed by two scenes where David plays the harp for Saul in order to soothe his spirit. The inner part is determined by the heroic deeds of David and Saul's jealousy. The first striking event is David's fight against Goliath, which may actually have happened before David was called to be at Saul's court. This would explain, as stated, why Saul did not know David in 17:55–58. Goliath is said to be six cubits and a span of height, which is a little over nine feet. The fight of David and Goliath has become a model indelibly planted into the cultural memory of the Christian world.

The middle part of the structure shows that any measure Saul takes to put David under his control has the opposite result. When Saul removes David from the court, David increases his glory as a warrior; when Saul asks for 100 foreskins of Philistines as a dowry for marrying his daughter, hoping that David will die trying, David returns 200, again increasing his fame. Whatever Saul does, he cannot oppose the divine destiny. In the end, there is only pure hatred.

The friendship between David and Jonathan, Saul's firstborn son, is also remarkable (1 Samuel 18:1–4). Their friendship is even stronger than the love of a woman could be (2 Samuel 1:26). Sometimes it is alleged that this friendship was in fact a homosexual relationship. However, since the Mosaic LAW condemns homosexuality, it cannot have been the intention of the writer to give this impression.

The reasons the friendship became so deep are not explicitly given. Probably Jonathan, himself the heir to the throne, intuitively realizes that David is the chosen one to become Saul's successor. This may be the reason that he hands his clothes, the signs of a prince, over to David. On another occasion, Jonathan expresses the wish to be the second man in a coming kingdom of David (1 Samuel 23:17). Jonathan continually tries to help David. Therefore, his father, Saul, becomes very angry with him (1 Samuel 20:30–33).

Saul Persecutes David (1 Samuel 21–26)

Here, David becomes an outlaw. He gathers some dubious people around him. He travels from place to place with them, constantly on the run from Saul and his troops. The narrative demonstrates that David is always the moral winner. It is Saul who kills all the priests of Nob because they helped David, but it is David who drops his guard in order to help the city of Keilah against the Philistines. It is Saul who wants to kill David, but it is David who spares Saul twice. Each time Saul is ashamed and withdraws, but he does not change his basic plan to kill David. The one rejected by God seems to retain the upper hand, whereas the chosen one in all situations, as difficult as they may be, proves that he is worth his election.

The encounter of David, Nabal, and Abigail (chapter 25) is also an example of what wisdom and folly mean. In some respect, Nabal symbolizes Saul. In his folly, he wants to be king (25:36) and rejects God's chosen one, and doing so can only lead to his destruction. Marrying Abigail, David inherits also a large piece of land in the region of the Calebites. Possibly, this is a preparation for his becoming king in Hebron in the same region later.

Saul, David, and the Philistines (1 Samuel 27–31)

What is especially intriguing about this section from a narrative point of view is that there are two narrative threads, that of David and that of Saul, which are intertwined with each other by the movement of the Philistine army, leaving behind the one of them and approaching the other.

The section begins with David's pretending to change over to the Philistines' side, living among them with his warriors. As a consequence, however, the Philistine king, Achish of Gath, requests that he join the army that is mobilized against Israel. It is divine providence that the other Philistine kings do not trust David and send him back home to their territory—where he finds out that the Amalekites had launched a raid in the time of their absence. Because of his early return, he is able to catch up with the Amalekites and recapture the prey.

On the other hand, the battle of the Philistines against Israel forms the final destruction of Saul's kingdom. Most of his lifetime, Saul had tried to continue to reign, painfully aware of the fact that God had already rejected him a long time before. It may well be that he always hoped for a chance to reaffirm his former election. When the Philistines approach, he even tries to contact the dead Samuel through a medium, hoping for any kind of support or confirmation from the authority of his better days, but in vain. On the battlefield, when three of his sons are already killed and the Philistines press the Israelite army, the moment has arrived when he finally gives up and kills himself.

The Two Kings: David and Ishbosheth (2 Samuel 1–3)

When a messenger reaches David in Ziklag reporting the death of Saul and Jonathan, the narrative again demonstrates David's faithfulness to Saul as God's anointed king. The messenger wrongly asserts that he was the one to kill Saul. But instead of receiving honors, as he intended to, David lets him be killed.

David moves back into the territory of Judah. In the city of Hebron he is made king over Judah. However, Abner, Saul's general, does not accept him. Abner makes Ishbosheth (= Ishbaal), a son of Saul, king over the other tribes of Israel. Probably this did not happen at once, but only five years after Saul's death: Ishbosheth reigned two years in total (2:10), whereas David was king over Judah for seven years (5:5). Abner seems to have been more important than Ishbosheth: When Abner goes over to David, the power of Ishbosheth is gone.

David King over All Israel (2 Samuel 4–9)

To a certain extent, the narrative on the kingdom of David over all Israel forms a counterpart to the narrative on Saul in 1 Samuel 9–15. Both kings begin their reign with successful military campaigns. However, in the case of Saul, a certain disrespect of God and ritual matters soon becomes visible. David, in contrast, is especially faithful to God and concerned with correct worship. Therefore, the kingdom of Saul is rejected while the kingdom of David is affirmed.

Interestingly, David expresses respect to Saul and his family. He kills the murderers of Ishbosheth and provides an honorable burial (chapter 4), and he grants pardon to the only direct male descendant of Saul who is still alive—since he is Jonathan's son (chapter 9). Mephibosheth does not have any function in chapter 4. But he is mentioned there in order to form the INCLUSIO to chapter 9.

Chapters 5 and 8 report David's military victories, so confirming that David is successful as king and receiving God's blessing. Chapter 5 focuses on the conquest of Jerusalem and the defeat of the Philistines; chapter 8 again mentions the Philistines and gives a summary on the other nations David defeats and makes Israelite vassals. These reports can be seen as the last step of Israel's conquest of Canaan (see CANAAN, CONQUEST OF). Whereas Joshua 21:43–45 already affirms that God has fulfilled his promise of giving the whole land of Canaan to Israel, the book of Judges begins with a list of territories that have not yet been conquered. In particular, within Judah and Benjamin, it is the Philistine territory and Jerusalem (Judges 1:18–19, 21). It is especially these two regions David conquers at the beginning of his reign over all Israel.

Chapter 6 reports the transport of the ark of the covenant to Jerusalem. The narrative demonstrates

that David respects ceremonial ritual and, therefore, God himself. Saul lacks this kind of respect and squanders the promise of an everlasting dynasty (1 Samuel 13:13). David, in contrast, is respectful and receives the promise.

The section of 2 Samuel 4–9 forms the high point of the David narrative. Only in this section is David unqualifiedly successful. Before and after the section, other people challenge David's throne. Therefore, the dynastic oracle occupies the central place in the whole David narrative.

David's Personal Crisis (2 Samuel 10–12)

Royal annals of the ancient Near East were written with the purpose of giving the most positive picture of the king possible. For example, only victories are recorded in Egyptian inscriptions. From the point of view of such a chronicle, a report like 2 Samuel 10–12 would be totally beside the point. However, the biblical history writing allows, or even demands, a perspective that takes into consideration the dark sides of the human character as well. In the biblical narrative, there is only one true hero, namely, God.

The setting of 2 Samuel 10–12 is a war against the Ammonites. However, they are not the real subject of the section. With psychological cleverness, the story narrates that David does not participate in the campaign but leads an idle life in Jerusalem. Walking around on the flat roof of his palace, he lets his gaze wander over his city and sees beautiful Bathsheba bathing. Now one step follows the other: adultery, pregnancy, and attempts of concealment, ending with a contract killing of Bathsheba's husband.

When the prophet Nathan confronts David with his offense, he shows true repentance. Here, he is different from Saul, who wants to ignore his mistakes. It is particularly striking how many words Saul uses in 1 Samuel 13:11–12 and 15:15, 20–21, 24–25, 30 to explain his disobedience, whereas 2 Samuel 12:13 reports only one sentence of David: "I have sinned against the LORD." (However, the inner feelings of David are expressed with more words in Psalm 51, which is his prayer of repentance.)

Since David repents, he does not have to die—as was the penalty for adultery. However, the adulterous child has to die. The second son of David with Bathsheba, Solomon, is especially loved by God (12:25–26); David promises Bathsheba to make him the heir to his throne (see 1 Kings 1:13, 30).

Finally, David's general Joab makes him compensate for having stayed at home while the army was fighting. He calls him to lead the army personally in the last strike against the Ammonites.

Although God has forgiven David, David has to bear the consequences of the curse Nathan has spoken out (12:10–12). In this sense, chapters 10–12 form a bridge from the heyday of chapters 4–9 to the new times of trouble in chapters 13–20.

Absalom's Rebellion (2 Samuel 13–20)

Absalom's rebellion is described as being a consequence of David's adultery with Bathsheba. This can be seen from a psychological point of view: Amnon, David's oldest son, follows in David's footprints when he rapes Tamar; Absalom himself is probably indignant at David's making Bathsheba his favorite wife and her son, Solomon, his heir to the throne. He feels neglected and therefore rebels. But besides these psychological reasons, the text describes the disaster also in terms of divine providence. By means of these mechanisms, God makes Nathan's curse come true, particularly that Absalom sleeps with David's concubines in a tent put up on the roof of David's palace so that all the people can see them (16:22, see 12:11).

Amnon (chapter 13) obviously lacks personality. This is revealed not only by the way he tries to be closer to Tamar, but also in the way he pushes her away afterward. He seems to be incapable of contact.

Absalom's relationship with his father is distorted, at least from the time he has killed Amnon, in the course of which he has to flee from David. When Joab helps him to return to Jerusalem, Absalom waits for his father, calling him for two years in vain. Finally, he wrings the concession to be received by his father. However, the reconciliation seems to have been only on the surface. By continually neglecting Absalom, David provokes sheer hatred, leading almost to the destruction of the kingdom.

Yahweh for David, Not Saul (2 Samuel 21–24)

The ending of the book seems odd: After the customary farewell speech, we have a report of another great failure of David. The first narrative in this section deals with an event of Saul's reign that is not mentioned earlier in the book. Saul conquers Gibeon, so violating an old peace treaty. He thinks that his power as the king stands above the old tribal laws, but he is mistaken. When David has become king, the Gibeonites request that seven male descendants of Saul be hanged as compensation. David grants their request. But afterward, he also ensures an honorable burial. With that, David demonstrates his respect for the tribal law as well as the family of Saul.

At the end of this section stands a corresponding narrative about the severe guilt of David: David takes a national census of Israel. The text does not say why this is seen as so negative. The point is probably not related to the statistics per se, but what is David's purpose behind it: By counting the people, David expresses the attitude of being Israel's owner. He counts them for his own glory, so overstepping the glory of God. In terms of failure, David does not seem to be any better than Saul. Going by the punishment, David's guilt is even greater than that of Saul. However, the difference between the two is that David repents and remains faithful to God. He accepts God as the greater king while Saul does not. Saul is therefore rejected, but David remains as God's anointed one.

Included in this frame of comparison are texts that celebrate David. The names of David's heroes are given to emphasize David's military power as a sign that God blesses his kingdom. A contrast with Saul can also be seen: Although Saul "stood head and shoulders above everyone else" (1 Samuel 9:2), it is not he who fights Goliath and the other Philistine giants, but David and his warriors. One more time Saul is mentioned: In David's song of thanksgiving, he is one of David's enemies (2 Samuel 22:1). David's song is a typical example of a psalm and is also found as Psalm 18 in the book of Psalms. With this, a connection is established to the many Davidic psalms, some of which are explicitly related to situations of his life (Psalms 3, 7, 18, 34, 52, 54, 56, 57, 59, 63, and 142).

In his lasts words in 23:1–7, David points out the difference between the one who is ruling justly and in the fear of God and the worthless one who is thrown away like thorns.

CHARACTERS

Abner   Saul's military leader. After Saul's death, Abner makes Ishbosheth king over Israel and serves him. But after a quarrel, Abner goes over to David. David welcomes Abner, but Joab, his military leader, distrusts him and kills him.

Absalom   Son of David who wants to become king in place of David. In the decisive battle, he is caught with his long hair in a tree. Joab, David's military leader, stabs him to death.

David   The youngest of eight sons of Jesse from Bethlehem. Samuel anoints him to be king while Saul is still ruling. First, David serves Saul, but later Saul wants to kill him, so he flees and lives as an outlaw. He even stays with the Philistines for some time. When Saul falls, David becomes king over Judah and, after seven years, king over all Israel. David is faithful and obedient to God. God makes him victorious over his enemies and promises an everlasting dynasty to him. However, there is also failure in his life. He commits adultery with Bathsheba and afterward lets her husband be killed. But after he repents, God shows him mercy. David becomes an example of a just and God-fearing ruler.

Goliath   A Philistine of extraordinary physical height (over nine feet) mocking the Israelites and challenging them to a duel. David accepts and kills him with his slingshot.

Hannah   A faithful woman. Hannah is barren and prays for a child for a long time. Finally, she gets a son, whom she names Samuel. She gives him to the temple of Shiloh, consecrating him fully to God.

Ishbosheth   Son of Jonathan, grandson of Saul, king over the northern tribes of Israel. His name can be translated as "man of shame" and is probably a conscious ridiculing of *Esh-baal* (so in 1

Chronicles 8:33; 9:39), meaning "man of the Lord" or "man of the god Baal." Abner, Saul's military leader, installed him. He does not seem to have been very powerful. When Abner leaves him after two years, he is killed by two of his own soldiers.

Joab   Military leader of David and a great support to him. Joab is a man who knows what he has to do, even if David does not like some of his decisions. When David allows himself some leisure in Jerusalem and goes astray, Joab calls him to join the battle and lead the army personally. When David's son, Absalom, eventually revolts against David, Joab kills him. With this Joab achieves political stability; however, he disobeys a direct order of David and deeply hurts his feelings as a father.

Jonathan   Firstborn son of Saul and close friend of David. Jonathan intercedes with Saul on behalf of David and informs David of Saul's plans. Jonathan hopes to become the second man in a kingdom of David, but he is killed in a battle against the Philistines together with his father and his two brothers.

Mephibosheth   Son of Jonathan, brother of Ishbosheth. After an accident, both his feet are paralyzed. He is the last male descendant of Saul. David grants him pardon.

Michal   Second daughter of Saul. Michal falls in love with David, and they marry. As a dowry, Saul asks David to give him 100 foreskins of Philistines, but he gives him 200. Eventually, Michal saves David's life when Saul's soldiers want to capture him. After David has to flee from Saul, Saul gives Michal to another man. However, after Saul's death, David asks Mephibosheth to take her back to David. On one occasion, when David is dancing in front of the ark of the covenant, Michal despises him and mocks him. God therefore makes her barren.

Samuel   The last judge to rule Israel. He is faithful to God, and God therefore reveals himself to him. He leads the Israelite army into battle against the Philistines and defeats them. Samuel anoints the first two Israelite kings, Saul and David. With the beginning of the monarchy, Samuel refrains from his role as a leader but remains as a prophet instructing the kings about the will of God.

Saul   The first king of Israel. He is disobedient to God in several instances. God therefore rejects him. Nevertheless, Saul tries to continue to reign and to fight David, who he knows is the chosen one of God. Saul has an impulsive and sometimes irrational character and is troubled by moods of depression caused by an evil spirit. During a battle against the Philistines, he gives up and kills himself.

Sirach

The wisdom book of Jesus Ben Sirach is not part of the Hebrew Bible. The Roman Catholic Church as well as the Orthodox Churches recognize the book as "deuterocanonical" (being of secondary canonical rank). In the Protestant churches, however, it is not accepted but is included in the Apocrypha of the Old Testament (see APOCRYPHA AND PSEUDEPIGRAPHA).

The book as a whole is extant only in a Greek translation. Of the original Hebrew text, about two-thirds is preserved. However, the manuscripts differ significantly. This points to the fact that already in early times different versions of the text were used.

Verse 50:27 (and 51:30, according to some versions) tells that the author of the book is "Jesus, son of Eleazar, son of Sirach," a wisdom teacher from Jerusalem. *Sirach* is the Greek version of the name; its Hebrew form is *Ben Sira.* In the Latin Bible the superscription reads, *Liber Ecclesiasticus,* "Book of the Church." This title probably points to the fact that Christians used the book officially, whereas it was not recognized by the Jews. Ecclesiasticus can easily be confused with Ecclesiastes, the Greek name of the book of Qohelet.

The Greek translation of the book of Sirach contains a foreword, in which Ben Sirach's grandson claims to have translated the book. The dating given there (the 38th year of King Euergetes) can be calculated to 132 B.C.E. Jesus Ben Sirach himself

had probably written his book some 60 years earlier, around 190 B.C.E. This date is confirmed by a passage in chapter 50 that strongly suggests that Jesus Ben Sirach was a contemporary of the high priest Simon II, who died some time after 200 B.C.E.

SYNOPSIS

The book consists of three parts:

1. A collection of proverbial sayings (1:1–42:14): This part very much resembles the book of Proverbs. A large number of PROVERBS and similar types of sayings are put together giving wisdom advice on all kinds of subjects. In most instances, the proverbs are forming little thematic blocks. Examples are the "Fear of the Lord" (1:11–20), the dangers of being seduced by women (9:1–9), and the advice even for the pious man to see the doctor in case of illness (38:1–15).

2. God's glory in nature and in the history of Israel (42:15–50:29): The first section of this part praises the magnificent works of God in nature (chapters 42–43). The second section is called Hymn in Honor of Our Ancestors. It is a summary of the important and famous personalities of the Hebrew Bible (chapters 44–49). It leads to a eulogy of the high priest Simon, a contemporary of Jesus Ben Sirach (chapter 50).

3. Two appendixes (chapter 51): The book is closed by a psalm of thanksgiving and a poem on Ben Sirach's search for wisdom.

COMMENTARY

In its literary genre, the book belongs to the WISDOM LITERATURE of the Hebrew Bible, especially the book of Proverbs. The wisdom admonitions of the book call for obedience to the Lord and give advice for living a successful life. The principle behind many of the sayings is the relationship between act and consequence, saying that good acts lead to good consequences, whereas bad acts lead to bad consequences. More than in the book of Proverbs, there is a moralizing and legalistic imprint on these sayings. The book also contains quotations of and allusions to the books of Job (see 2:1–5; 40:1–10; 1:1–10) and Ecclesiastes (see 14:11–17; 18:4–6). However, the depth of existential drama of these two books is not reached. Rather, the statements are reinterpreted and put into the frame of the principle of retribution. Some images of the Song of Solomon are also used (see 24:13–17), allegorically transferred to describe "Lady Wisdom."

A new aspect of Sirach compared to the wisdom books of the Hebrew Bible is that it integrates other streams of tradition into wisdom. First of all, Ben Sirach's wisdom is Torah wisdom. Wisdom is gained, not by observing nature (see Proverbs), in the first respect, but by observing the Torah, the Law of Moses (24:23–34). Love of wisdom and love of the Torah are, according to Ben Sirach, identical. The idea of a fusion of the perspectives of wisdom teacher and scribe can first be seen in Psalm 19. In its advanced stage, it is found in the postbiblical books of Ben Sirach and Baruch (3:9–4:4).

Furthermore, for Ben Sirach, observing the Law also means observing the ceremonial ritual (35:1–10). In addition, he integrates reflections on Israel's *history* in his book (chapters 44–49). So it can be said that virtually all aspects of biblical tradition—with the exception of the prophetic messianic hopes—are molded into an overall Torah wisdom perspective controlled by the principle of retribution.

That the book of Ben Sirach was not included into the canon of the Hebrew Bible can be argued for from three perspectives: (1) From its content, the strong retributional imprint on all the biblical tradition does not correspond to the intention of the Hebrew Bible. Also, the greatly exaggerated praise especially of the high priest Simon (chapter 50) does not correspond to the Hebrew Bible's much more ambivalent presentation of human character. Only God can receive unconditional praise. (2) From a historical perspective, Sirach was written after the closure of the Hebrew canon. This argument, however, only proves true if the conservative dating of the closure of the canon is accepted. (3) Sirach himself did not intend to write a book of Holy Scripture, but a book that *interprets* holy Scripture. This can be seen from Sirach's own words as well as from the foreword of the Greek translation.

Nevertheless, the book is a valuable historical witness not only for a form of faith of 190 B.C.E. but also for the shape of the Hebrew Bible at that time. Especially from the section on the biblical history (chapters 44–49) we can see that the "bible" of Ben Sirach must have been (roughly) the same as today's Hebrew Bible.

In addition, the Greek foreword to the book (132 B.C.E.) refers to the Hebrew Bible three times, using the tripartite formula "the Law of Moses, the Prophets, and the other books of the fathers" in each of the instances. This is a strong suggestion that the canon was a clearly defined entity by that time. This tripartite formula is a common designation for the Hebrew Bible even today.

Song of Solomon

The Hebrew Bible would not be complete without a text dealing with the greatest gift of God in creation, namely, the love between man and woman. The Song of Solomon, also called the Song of Songs, is a masterpiece of the ancient Near Eastern love lyric.

However, believers of the past and the present have had many struggles with the Song. Sexuality was often considered a theme not appropriate for Holy Scripture. In the Jewish as well as in the Christian tradition, allegorical approaches have therefore been developed. In those approaches, the male, for example, stands in a figurative sense for God or Jesus Christ, whereas the female lover stands for the people of Israel or the Christian Church. In fact, several biblical texts use the image of marriage for describing the relationship between God and his people. But in the Song of Solomon, this approach leads to absurd interpretations, for instance, when people try to explain the spiritual meaning of the female body parts depicted in the Song.

Rather, the Song of Solomon has to be understood as part of the Hebrew Bible WISDOM LITERATURE, along with Job, Proverbs, and Ecclesiastes. Biblical wisdom starts with the assumption that the world is a wisely ordered divine creation. The wise try to fathom this order, e.g., to reveal mechanisms of human interaction, in order to help people live a successful life. Not least, therefore, human love falls within their area of responsibility (see Proverbs 30:18–19). The Song of Solomon also falls in with the invitation of Ecclesiastes 9:9 to enjoy marriage. The wisdom character of the Song is underscored by the attributed Solomonic authorship, since Solomon is regarded as the patron of the Israelite wisdom. Furthermore, a wisdom saying is found at the concluding climax of the book in 8:6b–7. All this contributes to a literal or "natural" understanding of the Song.

According to 1:1, the author of the book is King Solomon, who reigned 971–931 B.C.E. The text of the Song contains some further allusions to Solomon, although partly in a negative, distancing manner (8:11–12). Some take this fact as a hint that the information from 1:1 is not original. In any case, there are archaic grammatical and linguistic forms in the Song that fit well into the time of Solomon. From Egypt, we have several texts of this sort from the late second millennium B.C.E. Other scholars, however, date the book much later, even into the third century B.C.E. The oldest extant manuscript fragments are from the caves of Qumran (see DEAD SEA SCROLLS).

IMAGES AND SYMBOLS

For today's readers, many of the images and metaphors of the Song sound very strange. For example, the statement "Your hair is like a flock of goats" (4:1) would surely not be accepted as a compliment today. In order to understand the meaning of such comparisons, two aspects have to be taken into account.

First, many of the comparisons are not based on visual appearance alone but rather include inner aspects. Concerning body parts, for instance, the arms symbolize power, the neck stands for pride, and the hair for strength. So, the hair of the woman does not look like a flock of goats. The point rather is that a flock of wild black goats racing down a slope in great leaps expresses exuberant vigor. This is the same vigor the lover finds in the long black curly hair of the woman when she is turning her head (4:1). Again, the neck of the woman does not look like a tower. Rather, the lover sees in her the same kind of pride and independence as in a strong fortress (4:4). Again, the man does not look like a forest. Rather, his body is strong and healthy as a strong cedar, and he exudes majesty as the tall Lebanon mountains do (5:15).

Second, the key to many of the images is the conventions of ancient Near Eastern art. Not nature, but culture, gives the meaning to the images. On many paintings, for instance, lovers are marked by a dove placed between them. The dove is thus a cultural symbol for the wish for love. The statement "Your eyes are doves" (1:15; 4:1; 5:12), therefore, can be rendered as "You are giving me a tender look."

Another example is the gazelles and hinds that are mentioned often in the Song (e.g., in 2:7). In the graphic art of that time, they are often depicted in connection with goddesses of love. So they reveal themselves as cultural symbols of love and of new life. In more than one respect it therefore makes sense to compare the breasts of the woman to "two fawns, twins of a gazelle" (4:5).

Very often in the Song, a flower named *Shoshannah* appears (from which the name *Susan* is derived). Traditionally, it is rendered as *lily*. Investigations have shown, however, that the flower under consideration is rather the lotus. In ancient Near Eastern artwork, the lotus is an important symbol for regeneration and new life.

Many of the images employed belong to a rural setting. A PASTORAL genre can therefore be defined for the Song.

STRUCTURE

In critical scholarship, there is no consensus as to the literary shape of the Song. Over time, three different approaches have been developed. The first, traditional approach interprets the Song as a drama, constructing an overall plot. However, this attempt is deemed a failure by most scholars today. The second approach, starting from a historical-critical point of view, assumes that the Song is not really a single song but rather an anthology of little independent poems. A problem with this approach is the considerable repetition of motifs and phrases throughout the text, which are marks of literary organization rather than diversity. The third approach is that of recent scholarship working from a literary perspective. Here, an overall poetic structure of the Song is assumed. However, different scholars give various suggestions as to the overall structure. We must admit that our understanding of the structure of this ancient poetry is developing only slowly.

In the following structure, it will be assumed that the logic of the Song does not derive from a narrative plot but rather from the emotions expressed. There is an interplay of mutual expressions of increasing desire for each other. More precisely, the structure can be described as a cyclic progression consisting of four characteristic sections:

A "She longs for him": The lover is not present; the woman expresses her feelings for him to the daughters of Jerusalem.

B "She sees him arriving; she praises him": The woman describes the arrival of the lover and praises his positive features, talking about him, not to him.

C "He praises her beauty and longs for her": Now he speaks, describing her beauty and expressing his feelings for her. In most of the instances, he talks directly to her.

D "She invites him/she gives herself to him": As an answer to his words, she expresses her devotion and invites him to come. Since her wish is not yet fulfilled, again her longing pours out.

From 2:5 on, this sequence is covered four times in total (2:5–17; 3:1–5:1; 5:2–7:12; 7:13–8:14). The introductory section 1:2–2:4 differs in some respects but nevertheless fits into the scheme roughly.

There are also formal elements that are repeated in each cycle in a characteristic way. For instance, the A sections of all cycles except the first end with the statement "I adjure you, O daughters of Jerusalem" (2:7; 3:5; 5:8; 8:4). Additionally, the phrase "I am faint with love" stands in 2:5 and 5:8; the phrase "O that his left hand were under my head" is found in 2:6 and 8:3. The sections 3:1–4 and 5:2–7 are formed as nocturnal dreams. The theme of finding the beloved man is expressed both in dreams and 8:1–2. The wish of bringing

the beloved one into the house of the mother is expressed in 3:4 and 8:2. All these motives and phrases are common for the A sections only. In an analogous way, formal correspondences of the B, C, and D sections can each be given. For example, in the C sections only the man is speaking. The individual poems in which the beauty of the woman is praised have many images in common. All four D sections contain a request to the beloved man to come. These examples are enough to demonstrate the rationale of the structure.

The structure seems to be quite strict. But at the same time, there is a lot of freedom of design. In fact, the structure functions as the backbone of the Song, binding together a lot of different images, stories, and metaphors, which are virtually floating over the structure, giving the whole Song a dream-like, even intoxicating impression.

From this interpretation it also follows that there should be only one male and one female main person identified in the Song. King (1:4) and shepherd (1:7) are not different figures but merely roles in which the lovers appear. Even today, according to some Syrian traditions, wedding couples are dressed up as king and queen.

COMMENTARY

The First Cycle of Longing (1:2–2:4)

The first cycle serves as a double introduction. The reader is introduced to the theme and to the male and female protagonists. At the same time, the lovers begin to know each other. As the opening of the Song, the woman praises the love of the man and expresses her longing for him (1:2–4). After that follows an episode on the "keeper of the vineyard and her brothers" in 1:5–6. This is the first half of a little story, the second part of which is found in 8:8–12 (for a comment, see below).

The core of the first cycle is made of a row of dialogues between the lovers (1:7–2:3a), paying each other compliments. The characteristic feature here is a frequent change of speakers. The cycle ends with expressions of her longing and of fulfillment (2:3b–4). By this, a thematic INCLUSIO to the beginning is established; it is intensified by the motif of him taking her into his house (1:4; 2:4). The inclusio corresponds to the A and D sections of the cyclic structure. The dialogues, in turn, contain elements that appear again in the B and C sections of the following cycles. However, the cyclic structure is not yet fully maintained.

The Second Cycle of Longing (2:5–17)

The second cycle describes an encounter between the lovers in springtime. The man initially goes to the house of his beloved. The following events are set in nature or rather in the vineyard the young woman has to guard (2:15; see 1:6). But at the end, the man again seems to be absent and is invited by the woman. The motifs, therefore, are connected to each other rather loosely. The text consists of a chain of allusions, giving the Song a dreamlike character. But the elements are held together by the basic "emotional" structure described: She longs for him (A, 2:5–7), she sees him approaching and praises his assets (B, 2:8–10a), he praises her beauty and longs to meet her (C, 2:10b–15), she invites him (D, 2:16–17).

The invitation of the lover is arranged in two sections marked by the repeated occurrence of the phrase "Arise, my love, my fair one, and come away" in verses 10 and 13. The whole section 2:8–17 is bound together by the inclusio of verses 9 and 17 using the phrase "like a gazelle or a young stag."

The Third Cycle of Longing (3:1–5:1)

In the third cycle, the elements are again bound by the four-part emotional structure.

The nocturnal dream expresses the wish of the woman to bring her lover into the house of the mother, which means to marry him (A, 3:1–5). The arrival of the lover is then expressed using an image of a royal wedding, Solomon's arriving at the bride's house in his litter (B, 3:6–11). The C section of the third cycle consists of three parts (4:1–7; 4:8–11; 4:12–5:1). They are carefully structured using a characteristic way of addressing the girl in the form A-Address-A'. So the praise of her beauty begins in 4:1 with the words "How beautiful you are, my love, how very beautiful!" A corresponding statement is found in 4:7. The next part, the Lebanon Song of 4:8–11, is framed by addressing the woman as "bride" in verses 8 and 11. Inside that frame, there is another pair of addresses, "my sister, my bride," in verses 9 and 10. The third part,

the Garden Song, is again framed addressing the woman as "my sister, my bride" in 4:12 and 5:1.

The images and metaphors used in this section have to be understood against the background of ancient Near Eastern cultural conventions, as explained earlier. The Lebanon and the individual mountains mentioned symbolize majesty and original, unspoiled vitality. The garden can be called the paradise of love. The image expresses a symbolic return to the Garden of Eden.

The third cycle contains some allusions to the theme of wedding. Verse 3:11 explicitly speaks about the "wedding day." In 4:1, a veil is mentioned, again alluding to a wedding context. Furthermore, the women is called "bride" in several instances. Since the marriage ceremony was carried out in the "house of the mother," 3:4 can also be understood in this way. The Garden Song in 4:12–16 forms an appropriate climax in that context. Only here of all D sections, her invitation is answered by him (5:1). That the wedding theme occurs at the central circle of the Song is surely of some significance.

The Fourth Cycle of Longing (5:2–7:12)

The third cycle is several verses longer than the second. This increase is continued in the fourth cycle. Elements of the cyclical structure are here combined into a larger, dramalike section comprising 5:2 to 6:3.

The A section is formed as a nocturnal dream (5:2–8), as has been the case in the third cycle. The two dreams, however, stand in contrast to each other. An explanation of that is that the first dream is about "bringing the beloved into the house of the mother," which expresses the wish to have the marriage arranged, whereas the second dream expresses sexual desire outside any marriage context. So in the second dream, the watchmen, symbolizing the moral order, are intervening. The beloved man is not found.

The formula "I adjure you," which is a characteristic of the A sections, is adapted in the fourth cycle for dramatic reasons and now expresses the request to the daughters of Jerusalem to find the lover. Before the daughters of Jerusalem start searching, however, they want to know whether the lover is really worth the effort. This, in turn, stimulates the women to praise the lover's beauty (B, 5:9–16). The dramatic plot of the fourth cycle explains why the B section does not include the element of the arrival of the lover, as is the case in the other cycles.

Now the daughters of Jerusalem agree to help. They ask the woman where to start searching. The woman answers, "My beloved has gone down to his garden." Understood literally, the women now know where to go, so the dialogue is finished. At the same time, however, the answer alludes to the Garden Song of 4:12–16, where the garden symbolizes the woman herself. The lover, therefore, is present and immediately starts speaking in the C section. Again, the dramatic elements are bound together by the underlying emotional structure.

In the C section, the passage 6:4–10 is marked as a unity by the inclusio of verses 4 and 10, repeating the phrase "awesome as an army with banners." Again, the passage 6:11–7:12 is bound together by the phrases "whether the vines had budded . . . whether the pomegranates were in bloom" in 6:11 and 7:12, and, additionally, by the motif of his desire in 6:12 and 7:11.

The Fifth Cycle of Longing (7:13–8:14)
The fifth cycle begins with the A section in 7:13–8:4 expressing the tension between the desire of the woman and the moral values of the society.

The B section comprises verses 8:5–7. This series of parallelisms can be understood as promises of marriage. At the same time, some fundamental statements about the power of love are made. These words are the final focal point of the Song.

The cycle ends with two short passages that form the sections C and D (8:13–14), respectively. By this the last cycle is completed.

The Girl's Own Vineyard (1:5–6; 8:8–12)
One sentence is repeated three times in the Song and thus can be seen as its motto: "I adjure you, O daughters of Jerusalem, by the gazelles or the wild does: do not stir up or awaken love until it is ready" (2:7; 3:5; 8:4). The question is when is the right time for love. This question is also taken up by a little story, which is inserted into the structure of the Song in 1:5–6 and 8:8–12.

In 1:5–6, the young woman complains that she has been made keeper of the vineyards by her brothers, who had been angry with her. The sun has tanned her deeply, and she is unhappy about that. By keeping the vineyard, she is not able to keep her own vineyard, which means, she is not able to act in her own interest.

The intention of the brothers becomes clear when looking back from 8:8–9. They believe their sister to be still too young for meeting a lover. If she acted as a wall, which means not opening herself to a potential lover, then they would support her, but if she acted as a door, they would intervene. Making her keep a vineyard was probably just a means of achieving the latter.

The young woman, however, believes that she is already mature enough for love. Probably, it is in the vineyard of all places, where she gets to know a young man (see 2:9–15). In any case, she takes up the image of the brothers, turning it upside down and describing herself as a proud city that opens its doors to the conqueror (8:10). She does not keep the vineyards of others anymore but instead acts in her own interest (8:11–12). So the story deals with the difficult phase of the growing up of a girl into a young woman. It also speaks about the responsibility of the family to accompany and guard her in the process, so that her leaving home occurs at the right time and in the right way.

Therefore, the Song of Solomon also deals with moral aspects of sexuality, although in a very discreet way. The watchmen in the two nocturnal dreams (3:3; 5:7), for instance, stand for the opinion that love can be enjoyed best when handled according to the divine moral order.

Sexual desire and moral orders obviously sometimes are into conflict with each other. However, in the Song of Solomon, the resulting tension is not just endured or even depicted as a problem, but on the contrary: Tension is the principle from which the emotional structure of the text lives. Immediate sexual satisfaction is not what the Song would define as the art of love. Rather, it celebrates the tension; it enjoys and savors every single moment of expectation, awaiting what is coming with great suspense.

CHARACTERS

bride, the The bride is the main speaker of the Song. She is in love with a man and expresses her longing for him. In one place, she is called the Shulammite (6:13), which may be the place where she is from, or a female form of *Shelomoh* with the meaning of "Solomon's lady." This should, however, not be understood as historical information but rather as a poetic symbol.

daughters of Jerusalem, the A group of young women accompanying the bride. They listen to the bride when she goes into raptures about her lover, and they help her look for him. For the pastoral GENRE it is typical to have such a background group of people.

groom, the In the past, the groom has often been seen to be Solomon. Solomon is mentioned positively in 3:7 but negatively in 8:11–12. Alternatively, two different lovers have been identified in the Song: Solomon and a country lover (see 1:7). However, the most probable explanation is that the Song plays with Solomon motifs among others, using elements of a royal wedding in order to add to the color of the Song, without intending a historical identification.

Susanna and the Elders

See Daniel.

1 Thessalonians

Date
This letter is possibly the oldest extant Christian document. Two other Christian documents—both also part of the New Testament—might be older, but their dating is uncertain; they are the EPISTLE attributed to James the brother of Jesus and PAUL's letter to the Galatians.

1 Thessalonians was written in the year 50 C.E. from the city of Corinth, where the authors were staying and where they had been in touch with the addressees. In the passage 2:17–3:13 the authors give a detailed account of these recent contacts with the Thessalonians. Prior to this they had spent some time in Thessalonica and had founded the church, as is described in Acts 17:1–10. Although from ACTS OF THE APOSTLES alone it may seem that their stay in the city was short, there are indications in the letter (2:9) as well as in Philippians 4:16 that they stayed long enough to engage in their normal occupations (Paul was a tent maker, Acts 18:3) and to have contacts with the city of Philippi some 100 miles away. The fact remains that Paul's departure had been sudden and forced (Acts 17:10).

The letter provides no details about the city of Thessalonica other than that it shows the presence of a small group of Christians there at the time of writing. See also EPISTLE.

Literary Character
Ancient letters always opened with the identity of both the addressees and the senders. The opening of this letter mentions three people as the senders, Paul, Silvanus (also known as Silas), and Timothy. All three are known to us from other Pauline epistles and from the New Testament book of Acts of the Apostles. The actual writing would not have been done by either of them but by a paid secretary, with the three senders dictating the letter together. The secretary's style makes it impossible to identify parts contributed by the individual authors.

Nonetheless, in several places (very openly in 2:18; 3:5; and in 3:1–2; 3:6; 5:27) the letter is clearly written from the perspective of the apostle Paul alone. That need not surprise us as it is clear that Paul was the central person in the movement to preach the gospel in Greece in the middle of the first century C.E. Although he was usually surrounded by coworkers, he remained at the helm. The tradition that largely refers only to Paul as the author is basically correct.

As with all the epistles, the letter's title did not originate with the authors of the letter. It must have been added when the early churches started collecting the letters Paul had written to several of them, in order to distinguish these letters from each other.

Reception

The first sign of the existence of this letter could have been found in the other letter that the three authors sent to the same church, the letter now known as 2 Thessalonians. However, despite the fact that this letter discusses the same theme of the future and the return of Christ Jesus, in it no reference is made to 1 Thessalonians. This has led some scholars to think that 2 Thessalonians was in fact written before 1 Thessalonians, a suggestion that is not impossible because the order in which Paul's letters appear in the New Testament is largely based on their relative length and not on the date of writing. However, the revised order faces up to the fact that 1 Thessalonians also does not refer to a previous letter. The order of writing of 1 and 2 Thessalonians remains disputed.

As soon as we find evidence for the existence of a collection of Paul's letters in the early church, 1 Thessalonians is an undisputed part of it. As far as we know, it later made its way into the canon of Scripture without any discussion.

SYNOPSIS

The letter has two main parts, chapters 1–3, which deal with the relationship between the authors and the addressees, and chapters 4–5, which discuss the return of Jesus Christ. It is remarkable that the theme of the second part also appears at the end of each chapter: 1:9–10; 2:19–20; 3:13; 4:13–18; and 5:23–24. The phrase "brothers (and sisters)" is a frequent transition marker (2:1, 9, 17; 4:1, 13; 5:1, 12).

Paul's letters usually contain the following elements (in parentheses the verses in 1 Thessalonians):

Greeting (1:1)
Thanksgiving and prayer (here much extended, 1:2–2:16)
Apostolic travel (2:17–3:13)—an element not found in all letters
Discussion of issues (4:1–5:22)
Closure with greetings (5:23–28)

After the usual greetings Paul gives thanks to God for the change in the readers from pagans to followers of Jesus Christ. The example of their con-

version and Christian lifestyle has become known in other places, and they eagerly await Christ's return (chapter 1). Paul then rehearses his time in the city, emphasizes his friendly relationship with the readers, and lays out his personal behavior as an example (2:1–16). He tells how, unable to travel himself (2:18), he sent his coworker Timothy back to Thessalonica and how he rejoiced when Timothy returned with positive information about the faith of the congregation (2:17–3:13). A section with mixed practical instructions introduces the second half of the letter (4:1–12). Subsequently, Paul addresses a particular concern of the congregation about the death of some of their members (4:13–18) and adds more general instructions about how to prepare for the return of Jesus (5:1–11). The final teaching is again more general (5:12–22). Good wishes and a blessing bring the letter to a close (5:23–28).

COMMENTARY

Paul and his fellow authors follow the common model of a Hellenistic letter. However, the letter is far longer than letters usually were at that time, and its length can be considered a deliberate innovation. The style of this letter is simple and direct, but it is also marked by repetitions of several kinds; a few features stand out, the first of which is that Paul regularly says something by first denying its opposite ("not A but B"). Examples of this emphatic style are 1:5a; 2:1–2, 3–4, 5–7, 13b; 4:7, 8, 15–17; 5:4–5, 6, 9, 15, 20–21. This way of expressing himself is less frequent in his later letters. The passage 5:1–11 makes clever use of contrasts, with concepts relating to day and light put over against such relating to night and darkness.

Paul had several reasons for writing this letter, which he clearly indicates in the text. In the first place he congratulates the readers with the way they live as Christians. The readers are new to the faith, and Paul had had to leave them prematurely, as we can see in Acts 17:5–10. The letter is a mixture of praise for how well they are doing and exhortation to do even more. Chapters 1–2 focus on the praise, chapter 4:1–12 on the instruction. In the second place Paul attempts to explain why he had not yet returned in person but had merely sent his coworker Timothy. In the third place Paul comforts the readers regarding the death of some members and its consequences. These untimely deaths had given rise to questions about the return of Jesus Christ, which the congregation had expected prior to any deaths. Paul basically says that the dead will not be worse off than the living because both groups will be united with Jesus on his return.

The relationship between author(s) and addressees is very good (3:6), and the tone of the letter is upbeat. It is remarkable that Paul's self-presentation in this letter is totally unpretentious as he begins without mentioning the title *apostle,* which he cherished. The title does occur in an almost apologetic way, in 2:7, where it also denotes his fellow authors. This fact testifies to the relationship of mutual respect that he has with the addressees.

Several times Paul points to the problems of persecution that both parties face and intimates that this is not unexpected for a follower of Christ (1:6; 2:2, 14–16; 3:3–5, 7).

One passage, however, forms an exception to the positive tone of the writing, 2:14–16, in which Paul lashes out against those who make life hard on the readers, the Jews who do not accept Jesus as the Messiah.

The overarching theme of this letter is that of the return of Jesus Christ, which is the subject of the teaching section 4:13–5:11. On the one hand, Paul conveys information about it; on the other hand, he exhorts the readers to adjust their lifestyles to their expectations. Specifically, they are called to be holy, that is, to show behavior that is pleasing to God and their fellow humans.

Another theme is that of Paul's example, which should be followed by the readers. In the first half of the letter he unequivocally sets himself up as a model for their behavior; see in particular 2:10. His faith, hope, and love should be mirrored by them, as well as his diligence in working with his own hands to earn his living. The theme of work recurs in 2 Thessalonians. The present letter is the first text ever to use the now famous triad of faith, hope, and love (in 1:3) to refer to the readers' lifestyle.

Called to follow Paul's example, the Thessalonians are also imitators of the churches in Judea in the way in which they cope with persecution (2:14). Yet they are not merely described as passive imitators of the apostles and other churches: They for their part have already become examples to others (1:8–9) so that a kind of chain effect develops. Moreover, while Paul wanted to encourage them by visiting them (3:2), he in return is encouraged on hearing Timothy's report about them (3:7–9).

In recent use of the letter, pride of place goes to the passage 4:13–18, which speaks in a very specific and concrete way about the future of individual believers and the return of Jesus Christ. Since the 19th century some interpreters have read this passage as saying that the faithful among the Christians will suddenly be taken away from the earth while the unbelieving part of humankind will be left behind. This sudden disappearance is called the rapture, and it is seen as the beginning of the end times. This interpretation was popularized in the 1990s by the best-selling Left Behind series (Tim LaHaye with Jerry Jenkins) and prior to that by Hal Lindsey.

The traditional interpretation of this passage does not support the idea of a rapture. The text refers to "being caught up in the clouds together . . . to meet the Lord in the air" so that the believers will be with him forever. The Greek word used points to a going out to meet a dignitary in order to accompany him to the place he will visit. This suggests Paul means that the destination of the returning Lord and his human attendants is the earth.

CHARACTERS

Holy Spirit In 1:5–6 Paul refers to the power and the joy that are given by God's Holy Spirit. It is likely that he alludes to enthusiastic utterances that were experienced in the church and contributed to the assurance of faith. At the end of the letter he returns to the work of the Spirit when he urges the congregation not to inhibit inspired words (5:19–22). The suggestion "test everything" is thus not a general saying but pertains to what the Spirit is doing (or not) in the congregation.

Jesus Christ All emphasis in this letter is on his future, which, as indicated, is mentioned at the end of each chapter. When he returns to earth from heaven he will rescue the believers (1:10) and make sure that the living are not privileged over those who have already died (4:13–18). Although his coming is expected, it will nonetheless be like that of a thief in the night (5:2). This combination of expectedness and surprise is an interesting paradox that has parallels elsewhere in the New Testament (Matthew 25:1–13). The expression "like a thief in the night" likewise has parallels in 2 Peter 3:10 and Revelation 3:3.

Paul   In addition to what has already been said, we note that Paul refers to himself in relation to the church both as a father (2:11–12) and as a mother (2:7). In his loving care he is like a mother; in his efforts to educate the church he is a father. In similar vein in 2:17 he writes that being separated from the readers made him and his follow authors feel like orphans.

Satan   Paul attributes the fact that he was unable to travel to Thessalonica to the actions of the devil (2:18). He intimates he was afraid that the same enemy would have attacked the church (3:5), but his fears were unwarranted.

2 Thessalonians

This letter was written between Paul's visit to Thessalonica in the year 49 C.E. and the next visit he paid to Macedonia, the region of which Thessalonica was the capital city (Acts 20:1; 1 Corinthians 16:5), in 55 C.E. It presumably originated shortly after 1 Thessalonians, so in the period 50–51 C.E., the only period when the three authors were together, and it was dispatched from Corinth. This makes the letter one of the oldest extant Christian documents.

The same three people present themselves as authors as in 1 Thessalonians, Paul, Silvanus, and Timothy. Critical scholars often do not accept this ascription and claim that the letter is pseudonymous, mainly because it resembles 1 Thessalonians too closely to be authentic.

As with all the New Testament epistles, the title did not originate with the authors of the letter but was added when the early churches started collecting the letters Paul had written, in order to distinguish these letters from each other.

This letter has always lived in the shadow of 1 Thessalonians, which is larger and richer in content. Yet from the first collection of letters of Paul it is always present.

SYNOPSIS

Paul's letters usually contain the following elements (in parentheses the verses in 2 Thessalonians):

> Greeting (1:1–2)
> Thanksgiving and prayer (1:3–12)
> Discussion of issues (2:1–3:15)
> Closure with greetings (3:16–18)

After the formal opening words (1:1–2), Paul adds what is formally a prayer for the church. There is thanksgiving in 1:3–4, but only in verses 11–12 is it specified what Paul is praying for; in between he assures them of God's judgment over their enemies, which is a comfort to them. The main topic is the return of Jesus Christ, and Paul emphatically explains that this has not yet happened (2:1–2); on the contrary, before it takes place "the lawless one" (verses 3, 8, and 9) must arrive and draw people away from God (2:3–12). However, despite the prospect of hard times, the readers are safe in the protection of the God they are worshipping (2:13–15) and Paul blesses them (2:16–17).

The practical section begins with a request for prayer for Paul and assurances of God's faithfulness (3:1–5). Paul then addresses those in the church who have left their occupations in eager anticipation of the return of Jesus Christ and urges them to resume normal life (3:6–13). Some notes on disobedient members are appended (3:14–15) before Paul closes the letter with a prayer for peace in his own hand (3:16–18).

As in 1 Thessalonians, the phrase "brothers and sisters" functions as a transition marker (1:3; 2:1, 13; 3:1); in 3:6 its role is taken by the synonymous *beloved.*

COMMENTARY

Paul and his fellow authors follow the common model of a Hellenistic letter. However, the letter is longer than was usual at that time, and its length can be considered a deliberate innovation. The style of writing is simple and straightforward.

From 2:2 and 3:17 it seems that the church in Thessalonica had received a letter allegedly from Paul, which has not come down to us. It claimed that "the Day of the Lord"—that is, the day of Christ's return—had already come (2:2) and Paul denies that this is the case. Paul is writing quickly to counteract the effects of the spurious letter, among which were idleness and living at the expense of others.

A real frenzy must have gripped part of the church as many had left their jobs and were idly awaiting the return of Jesus. Paul's own expectation of his return was no less vivid than theirs, but in chapter 3 he nonetheless urges the church members to return to normality.

The letter also contains references to persecution from outside (1:4–8; 3:3), but later readers are left unaware of the details. As no mention is made of martyrs, it might just be social pressures that threaten the addressees. Yet it is possible that these hardships were so severe that they caused them to long more for the deliverance that the return of Jesus would produce.

As in 1 Thessalonians, Paul encourages a community of new believers in their lifestyle. He expresses much satisfaction about their progress (1:3–4; 3:4). He makes the congregation jointly responsible with him for the good behavior of all members (3:6–15). Much of the letter is devoted to prayers and exhortations to pray (1:3–4, 11–12; 2:16–17; 3:1–5, 16).

As in the earlier letter, the return of JESUS CHRIST is the subject of the teaching section. Apparently, the first letter had not worked out as Paul had hoped, a spurious letter has been received by the readers, and Paul is compelled to write again to correct misunderstandings regarding the timing and circumstances of Jesus' return. In comparison with the first letter, the new element is the information that before Jesus returns, another character must come onto the scene, "the lawless one."

CHARACTERS

Jesus Christ Although he never reflects upon this openly, it is natural for Paul to refer to Jesus as very close to God (1:1, 2, 12; 2:16; 3:5). Jesus is the one whose return to earth is eagerly awaited by author and readers alike.

lawless person and his restrainer, the The designation *the lawless one* is only used in the second chapter of this letter and nowhere else in the Bible. It refers to a human being who will rise against God and even declare himself god (2:4). He will set himself up in the temple of God, which can either be the literal temple in JERUSALEM or a metaphor for the church of God. In 40 C.E. the Roman emperor Caligula had already ordered his statue to be erected in the temple in Jerusalem, but his death had prevented the execution of this decree. Paul is confident that Jesus Christ will defeat "the lawless one" on his return; therefore, the lawless person is an eschatological character. It is likely that this person is the same as the ANTICHRIST and the beast in Revelation 13:1–8, although quite different vocabulary is used in each description. The main reason for identifying them is that they are all said to deceive many humans by means of power given to them by Satan (2:9–12).

Still more enigmatic for modern readers is the fact that Paul refers to yet another character, the "one who restrains" "the lawless one" (2:6–7). Paul tells the first readers that he had taught them about these things (2:5–6), so for them this reference must have been clear enough, but later readers are not so privileged. Paul apparently assumes that the antichrist will only be able to break in after the removal of a restraining power. Numerous suggestions exist regarding the identity of this restraining power, such as the Holy Spirit, an angelic power, the stability of the Roman Empire, or Paul himself as the leading Christian missionary.

Paul The apostle sets himself up as an example to imitate for the readers (3:7, 9), as he had in his first letter.

Satan He is mentioned in this letter as the one who empowers "the lawless one" (2:9) and as "the evil one" who directly threatens the church members (3:3). It should be noted that the characters discussed earlier are not identified as Satan but as his human emissaries.

1 Timothy

The first letter to Timothy is one of a series of three PASTORAL epistles in the New Testament written by the apostle Paul; the other two are 2 Timothy and Titus. The term *pastoral* is derived from the Latin *pastor,* meaning a "shepherd," a figurative term often given to church leaders, then and today. The pastoral epistles, therefore, are instructions to these two church leaders, Timothy and Titus, as to how to lead their churches.

They are written by the apostle PAUL. Acts 16:1–5 is the first mention of Timothy and Paul's mentoring of him, beginning on his second missionary journey. From then on, Timothy is mentioned frequently in association with Paul, especially in greetings to letters Paul wrote to various churches (e.g., Romans 16:21; 2 Corinthians 1:1). In particular, Timothy was with Paul on some of his difficult third missionary journey, during which he spent over two years at Ephesus, one of the main cities of the province of Asia Minor, in modern-day western Turkey (Acts 19–20). In Acts 19:22 he sent Timothy off to Macedonia in Europe ahead of him, suggesting he was already entrusting Timothy with the task of evangelizing. On a subsequent leg of the trip, Paul's plans had to be changed on short notice, but Timothy and others managed to meet him at Troas (Acts 20:5). The remainder of that chapter shows us Paul's concern for the church at Ephesus, even though his plans did not allow him to revisit it. But he did meet with its elders (Acts 20:17). As we no longer hear of Timothy, we must presume he either returned home or, quite likely, was appointed then and there as church leader of the church at Ephesus, despite his youth and inexperience.

The young church at Ephesus quickly encountered problems typical even today of church planting, especially in pagan and third world countries, where church growth often mushrooms quickly from almost nothing. These could be summarized as problems of

- "wolves" or false teachers;
- finding reliable leaders;
- falling away of converts;
- church discipline;
- specific pastoral problems, often linked to the clash of the pagan culture and the Christian ethic. Such problems here include forms of worship; women, especially widows; and slaves.

It has been suggested that such problems take a long time to appear, and, therefore, this letter was written long afterward. Quite the contrary: Such problems appear quickly, and the letter has all the appearance of being a stopgap letter quickly written, suggesting some ground rules to contain the problems until Paul could intervene in the situation personally. Ironically, he never did. And these recorded ground rules actually became part of an ongoing accumulation of pastoral experience that helped give the early church a firm foundation.

Recent scholars have thought the language and style of the letters are not typically Pauline, in contrast to his more theological letters. They have therefore drawn the rather extreme conclusion that Paul did not write them at all, but they are pseudepigraphical, written in his name by someone else, probably some time later. In this case, this would amount not just to a claiming of Paul's authority but to a complete identity theft, as there really are many personal details that only real people would know of each other, for instance, Timothy's having given up drinking wine (1 Timothy 5:23). A less radical suggestion would be to realize that Paul dictated all his letters. If Paul was writing this letter in haste and on a troubled journey, he may well have left the scribe a good deal of latitude in making a final draft. For precise dating, see the discussion in 2 Timothy.

SYNOPSIS

Chapter 1 is an introduction, containing greetings typical of any letter of the time (1:1–2). The purpose of the letter is to establish ground rules for Timothy to use in the church at Ephesus. Such rules are a type of law that Timothy must use with authority against false teachers who also claim to be teaching the law.

The main body of the letter (2:1–6:2) sets out rules for dealing with the various pastoral problems outlined in the introduction. Thus, false teachers, mentioned in the first chapter, probably because that seemed the most urgent of the problems, are again spoken of in 4:1–4. Marks of good leaders are listed in 3:1–13 and more personally applied to Timothy himself in 4:6–5:3. The falling away of converts is addressed in 4:1 but more in the conclusion. Matters of church discipline are set out in 5:17–22 and elsewhere, as these various problems do not form neat boundaries but overlap. Other problems concern church prayer meetings (2:1–8), women (2:9–15), widows (5:3–16), and slaves (6:1–2).

The conclusion (6:3–20) is rather a jumble of last-minute advice about problems, especially the falling away of converts, personal exhortation to live a godly and exemplary life, doxology (praise to God), and a real farewell.

COMMENTARY

There are a number of interesting features about the letter. Though it is not particularly "literary" compared to some of Paul's other letters, it is interesting to note the number of literary sources he draws upon to give authority to what he is saying. As we would expect, some sources are drawn from the Hebrew Bible, as 5:18 (drawn from Deuteronomy 25:4) and 5:19 (Deuteronomy 19:15). Some sources are either early Christian credal statements or from early HYMNS, as 1:15; 2:5–6; and 3:16. Others are axioms or proverbs common to classical literature or just well-known cultural saws. Verse 6:7 may be based loosely on Job 1:21 but in fact was also stated by the Roman writer Cicero. The quotation "the laborer deserves to be paid" (5:18) was used by Jesus in Luke 10:7. It is loosely equivalent to Deuteronomy 24:15 but is not a direct quote. Terms like *old wives' tales* were typical in Greek debating to insult the opponent's ideas. Other verses sound as if they are proverbs, though they may well have been original to Paul, as 5:24 and 6:10. We have to remember the Ephesian church would be drawn from a mixture of quite different cultures; at the same time, the New Testament had not yet been written, so Paul is working hard to create a series of sources meaningful and relevant to these pastoral situations.

The same could be said for the imagery used. It is based more on culture than on traditional Jewish

figures. Thus he writes of "making shipwreck of one's faith" and "fighting a good fight"—a metaphor drawn from the athletics field rather than a military one; keeping spiritually fit and in good shape (4:7–8), drawn from the gymnasium that would be at the heart of every Greek town. The most significant imagery is like this. The image of the "household of God" (3:15) is based on family values held as firmly by the Greeks and Romans as the Jews and is seen again in the tests for church leaders.

Words are central to the problems being faced: "myths and endless genealogies" (1:4), "speculations" (1:4), "meaningless talk" (1:6; Authorized [King James] Version has "vain jangling"), too much chatter (5:13), "accusations" (5:19), "profane chatter and contradictions" (6:20). That is why Paul needs to construct some set of "sayings" (1:15) to set against them. New Revised Standard Version "sayings" is a poor translation for the Greek *logos*, "word." These "words" may be sound teaching (1:10; 4:6, 13), which becomes a central necessity for the Ephesian church; they may be prophetic words, such as Timothy received at his ordination (4:14); or they may be words derived from the literary sources we have examined.

As the letter is a specifying of ground rules, the language of instruction predominates. This contains obvious references to giving instructions (as 1:3, 18; 3:14; 4:6) and use of verbs as in *I urge you* (1:3; 2:1; 6:2) and "I charge you" (6:13). The repetition of "urge" actually suggests to us Paul's own urgency, just as his repeated insistence that Timothy remain pure (6:11, 14). There is all to play for; the situation is on a knife edge, and Paul's "care for all the churches" (2 Corinthians 11:28) obtrudes powerfully into his tonalities and diction. Similar uses of verbs are "I desire" (2:8), "I would have" (5:14), "I warn you" (5:21), "I permit" (2:12)—they are a mixture of exhortation and a sharing of what Paul has customarily done before. Imperatives predominate as verbal forms: especially *let* (2:11; 3:10, 12; 4:12; 5:9, 16, 17; 6:1, etc.), "do not/refuse to/never/no longer" (5:1, 11, 19, 22, 23, etc.), and "must" (3:2, 4, 6, 7, 8, 9, etc.).

The latter "musts" are an example of lists of qualifications for church leaders. Such lists were common in the general culture of the day; Paul applies them to two sets of leaders, "overseers" and "deacons." "Deacons" were an office set up in the first days of the Christian church (Acts 6:1–6), where certain qualifications were already set down, though they were not at that point called deacons. The term means "waiter" and so suggests people who did practical or administrative jobs in the church. The Greek word for "overseer" is here *episkopos* (3:2), from which the words *episcopal* and *episcopalian* are derived. The word was in general cultural use for someone in a leadership position. In this case, they would be under Timothy in the church. It is generally supposed that the term signifies pretty much the same as "elder" (Greek *presbuteros*), which is actually the word used in 5:17, when Paul returns to the topic of good leaders, here those who can teach and preach.

The language used about women seems harsh by modern Western standards, and it is not surprising that many people today find the letter difficult to read. Paul's alleged low opinion of women starts at Eve (2:14), as he uses a rabbinical rather than a scriptural exegesis, and continues through many widows (5:13) to women in general (2:9). In defense, it could be said that the cultural views on women at the time were equally low or even lower. At least Paul allows them instruction and presence in church gatherings. But Paul is not usually as demeaning; elsewhere he theologically disallows any barrier between male and female in terms of salvation (Galatians 3:28). This has caused some heart searching over the meaning of 2:15, regarding salvation through childbearing. Interpretations range from reading Mary into the fulfillment of Eve, so that salvation came through a woman, to trusting that women be safely delivered *in* childbearing. Most pagan women prayed to a suitable deity to be "saved" before giving birth. It could just mean that having children will "save" women from the vanity and silliness they would otherwise be prone to—the responsibilities of motherhood would mature them to the type of godly woman described in 2:9.

The need to help widows was again a cultural necessity and seen as a civic virtue by the general culture, as was the practice of hospitality. We have to guess why Paul spends so much time on the topic. There were clearly many widows in this church, and it may be that some relatives were hoping the church would take care of them and so relieve them of responsibility. Paul talks of another "list," of those entitled to financial help, but in return, those on the list have to be engaged in certain duties.

CHARACTERS

enemies and false teachers   See 2 Timothy.

Paul   See 2 Timothy.

Timothy   Born of a mixed marriage of a Jewish mother and Greek father in Lystra in the province of Galatia, he had been raised as a Jew and was well versed in the Hebrew Bible. However, he had not been circumcised. After his conversion and recommendation to Paul, he was then circumcised so as not to give offense to the Jews to whom they would be preaching. Paul took him with him on his second and third journeys and entrusted him with various commissions. With the agreement of local elders, he was ordained by the laying on of hands to the leadership of the Ephesian church, even though still a young man, probably meaning under 29. Various prophecies for him were given at this time, and a gift of teaching was recognized in him.

2 Timothy

Paul's second letter to Timothy is the second of three PASTORAL epistles, letters written to give specific help and encouragement to individuals being mentored by Paul (see the introduction to 1 Timothy for a fuller account). It is a very different letter from Paul's first one to Timothy, however. It is much more personal, with a much greater sense of personal danger. The state of the churches is only a secondary issue. How many letters and how many years had passed between the first and the second letter, we cannot know, since neither letter refers to the other. Paul is now in prison, and Timothy does not seem to be in sole charge of the church at Ephesus—he is certainly free to go to visit Paul in

Rome. It may well be that Timothy has taken up the role of an evangelist (4:5) or perhaps more of an itinerant teaching ministry (4:2).

The dating of these pastoral letters has been a matter of some debate. There is nothing in the two letters to Timothy that cannot be fitted into the details of the Acts of the Apostles. Maybe two years later is a long time to ask for a coat back (4:13), but longer waits have been known. The earliest dating for 1 Timothy would be thus toward the end of Paul's third missionary journey, and some time during Paul's imprisonment in Rome as recorded at the very end of Acts (Acts 28:30) for 2 Timothy. These give dates of 58 C.E. and 60–62 C.E., respectively. However, there are several details in the third pastoral, Titus, that do not fit well into Acts, though it is not impossible for them to do so. Titus 1:5 refers to Paul's leaving Titus behind in Crete, and Titus 3:12 talks of spending a winter at Nicopolis in Dalmatia (present day Croatia). Many scholars, therefore, propose a release for Paul from the Acts imprisonment, and a period of further travel of some 12–18 months, and then a second, deadly imprisonment under the emperor Nero around 64 C.E., which could then be the date of 2 Timothy. Yet other scholars suggest Paul did not actually write the letter at all, and it was written somewhat later. The letter is so personally detailed, and so full of Pauline expressions, however, that this idea is not easily tenable. And there is enough in common between the two letters to Timothy for this one to authenticate the former one.

SYNOPSIS

The letter begins with a standard greeting (1:1–2), which already sets the warm relational tone of the letter. Timothy is his child (Greek *teknon*), a word used both by masters to disciples and as a term of endearment to an adult (rather like "dear boy").

The main body of the letter can be divided into four heads, following the chapter divisions. Verses 1:3–18 ask Timothy not to distance himself from Paul's suffering in prison. Chapter 2 exhorts Timothy to teach others and warn them, suggesting a continuing public ministry for Timothy, but at the same time, he needs to teach and warn himself. The issue of sound teaching as opposed to false

is the one continuing concern from the first to the second letter. The third chapter sees this more in terms of a battle between truth and falsehood, teaching and deceiving, where practically, Timothy needs to live in the truth and resist falsehood. The final chapter (4:1–8) urges him to live in the light of Jesus Christ's second coming (see LAST THINGS).

The conclusion or farewell greetings paint a picture both of Paul's loneliness in prison and yet of the ability he still had to direct a number of people in the affairs of the young church. The bottom line of the letter is that he wants Timothy to travel to him and before winter, when all traveling by sea stops (4:9, 21). As in many of his other letters, he sends greetings to friends and forwards greetings from fellow Christians in Rome.

COMMENTARY

The language and style of the epistle are more obviously Pauline than those of the first letter. Phrases like "in Christ Jesus" (1:9) are typical, as are some of the images (races, contests) and analogies (household utensils). However, there is no solid mass of teaching or instruction. It is more a candid personal letter from a man who constantly has to come to terms with his suffering and the nearness of his death, to a much loved disciple who has not yet proved he has the fearlessness and courage to move out into his full ministry and pay its full price in terms of persecution and opposition. And this is set against a background of continuing error and deception in the church Paul has spent all his life to establish in truth. There are thus complicated tonalities, as various tensions run to and fro. There are moments of triumph and hope, moments of near-despair. In such conflicting emotions, we are not going to find an ordered sequence of instructions and wise words to pass on.

One example are Paul's references to his own suffering. They are scattered throughout the letter and range from his using them as an example to Timothy (3:10–12), to complaint of abandonment (1:15; 4:16), betrayal (4:10, 14), and isolation (4:10–11). In between he uses them as exhortation (1:8–9) and testimony narrative (1:16–17; 3:11; 4:17). Some of these uses stand in tension with one another, further highlighted by the somber prognostication of the evils of the "last days" (3:1f.) and of the necessary persecution of all Christians (3:12). Thus the complexities of Paul's sufferings are set against a wider background, which establishes it in history and theological significance. The "list of vices" of 3:1–5 is not dissimilar to that of 1 Timothy 1:9–10.

Other key areas are less complex. The continuance of false teaching (2:16–18, 23–26; 3:6–9) is now also set in the wider context of the last days (3:1–7, and compare Jude 17–19). And Timothy's need to show more courage is straightforwardly expressed: *shame/ashamed* in 1:8, 12, 16; 2:15 and the strong *spirit of cowardice* in 1:7. Images of the soldier (2:4) and the athlete (2:5) reinforce this idea. Together with this, he needs to proclaim the message "in season and out of season" (4:2 King James Version). The tension that does exist is typical of any father-son relationship: how to allow maturity and give praise while still very sensitive to moral inadequacies.

There is, as with the first letter, a good deal of the language of instruction: "avoid," "shun," "have nothing to do with," on the one hand; "proclaim," "convince, rebuke and encourage," on the other. Sometimes the imperative is expressed as a general principle, "The Lord's servant must not be. . . ." Unlike in the first letter, however, there is less attempt to support these instructions with outside sources of authority—there is no need to do that. A fragment from an early Christian hymn is quoted (2:11–13), interestingly antithetical, and some references to the Hebrew Bible (2:19 = Numbers 16:5, aptly quoting an earlier heresy). But other references are extrabiblical (as Jannes and Jambres, traditionally Pharaoh's magicians opposing Moses, 3:8). An important statement about the Scriptures is made, however (3:16).

What is also noticeable is the amount of imagery used to sharpen the instruction and exhortation: soldiers and athletes (2:3–5; 4:7–8), farmers (2:6), chains (2:9), gangrene (2:17), foundations with seals on them (2:19), utensils (2:20–21), libations (4:6), and lions' mouths (4:17). Very little of this is traditionally religious; the figures and analogies are everyday ones. Particularly noticeable is the exhortation to guard the "deposit" (Greek *parathēkē*)

(1:12, 14, which is also the closing exhortation of 1 Timothy 6:20). While Paul is being "guarded" in prison, so he guards the truth and so must Timothy. This is the letter's most telling moment of truth.

CHARACTERS

enemies and false teachers   Both letters mention a number of enemies. Some are generalized and are more the enemies of the church than personal ones, such as those referred to in 1 Timothy 1:4–7; 4:1–4; 6:3–5, 9; 2 Timothy 2:23; 3:13. Similar people occur in Titus (Titus 1:10–16). They are typified by wrong, self-serving teaching; stirring up of controversy; generation of empty words; money seeking, which then degrades into immoral behavior. However, there are some named enemies. Hymenaeus (1 Timothy 1:20; 2 Timothy 2:17) and Philetus (2 Timothy 2:17) are guilty of all the above. Alexander (1 Timothy 1:20; 2 Timothy 4:14) seems to have done Paul personal harm. Phygelus, Hermogenes (2 Timothy 1:15), and Demas (2 Timothy 4:10) have personally disappointed Paul by their desertion of him.

friends   These seem notable for their absence at crucial moments (4:16). Nevertheless, a large number are mentioned, some as visitors (Onesiphorus), some as helpers (Luke, Mark, Tychicus, Crescens, and Titus), and some as local Christians (Eubulus, Pudens, Linus, and Claudia). There is a tradition that Linus became second bishop of Rome. It may well be that Tychicus was the letter bearer, as he was destined for Ephesus. He is mentioned in Titus 3:12 and elsewhere.

Paul   In his first letter to Timothy and in that to Titus, Paul was clearly a free man, engaged in his apostolic mission. In this letter, however, Paul is now "chained like a criminal," having had a first hearing of the case against him, which remains unspecified. Nevertheless, his first concern is for Timothy to keep the church in the truth. However, he cannot help feeling his life's course is now nearly at an end (4:6). What concerns himself is that he will be rescued from "every evil attack" (4:18), so that his death will leave his reputation clear. He is basically sending the letter as a substitute for his presence: In the first letter he wanted to go to Timothy. In this second, Timothy has to go to him. Paul's need for companionship is very evident.

Timothy   See 1 Timothy.

Titus

Titus is the third of the PASTORAL epistles, written by PAUL to two church leaders, Timothy and Titus, giving them instructions for the new churches they are leading. There is no mention in this letter of the other letters or of Paul's circumstances, except that he has recently left Titus in Crete. For possible dating of the letter, see the introduction to 2 Timothy. The best supposition is that it was written at much the same time as 1 Timothy, as the material in it is so similar, that is, either about 58 or 63 C.E. It lacks the urgency of the other letter, either because Paul is more confident in Titus or because the problems the new church plants were facing were less pressing in Crete than in Ephesus. It is thus a shorter, calmer, more ordered letter, which contains a certain amount of doctrinal statement as well as instruction.

SYNOPSIS

The letter sets out typical greetings in 1:1–4. Titus, like Timothy, is Paul's child (Greek *teknon*), his faithful disciple. The first chapter deals with the appointing of elders, Titus's first priority in the new churches set up in Crete. The problem of "wolves," divisive people in the church, is addressed. They are mainly Jewish "converts," if they have truly been converted, but seem to be guilty of those vices the Cretans were renowned for, especially lying.

The second chapter deals with what Titus should say to whom: young and old, men and women, and slaves. There is a simple statement of the message of salvation that is to be delivered to all. The third chapter contains a list of the practical and behavioral virtues Titus should teach the church as a whole, and he touches briefly on church discipline. The final few verses (3:12–15) are the fare-

wells, personal and administrative instructions, and greetings.

COMMENTARY

As suggested, the material in the letter does not differ greatly from that in 1 Timothy, though it is more compact and more tightly ordered. One obvious similarity is the list of qualifications for elders: Greek *episkopos*, meaning "overseer" (1:7), is used alongside *presbuteros*, an "elder" (1:5). Quite often the same words are used in both lists; the New Revised Standard Version sometimes disguises this point. Thus they are to be *sōfrōn*, which the New Revised Standard Version translates variously as "sensible" (1 Timothy 3:2) and "prudent" (Titus 1:8). There are some 17 features in common. 1 Timothy adds "not a recent convert" and "well thought of by outsiders" (3:6, 7).

Another feature in common are personal instructions to the recipients. Both are told not to let themselves be looked down upon (2:15; 1 Timothy 4:12). But the tone is more measured in Titus. In Titus 2:7–8 Paul already seems assured that Titus *will* show gravity and integrity, whereas Timothy is constantly urged to be pure, to avoid and shun youthful lusts, and so on. In both letters, instructions to be given to the churches, especially about avoiding controversies and setting a high standard, and concerning slaves, are set out. Both letters also address specific groups within the church, but Timothy is told how he should behave toward them (young and old, men and women), while Titus is to tell them how to behave. There are no instructions in Titus for deacons, women in general and widows in particular, or church meetings.

The style and language are more obviously Pauline. But unlike in 1 Timothy, he is less concerned to create a body of "words" to support his instructions. He quotes a Cretan author, Epimenedes (ca. 600 B.C.E.), against them (1:12). Otherwise there is only one obvious "word" (again, unhelpfully translated "saying" by the New Revised Standard Version). This turns out to be a marvelous thumbnail presentation of the gospel (2:14; 3:3–7). The New Revised Standard Version translation "water" (3:5) should be "washing" (Greek *loutros*), which is a figure for regeneration, not a literal instrument of it, just as is the figure of "pouring out" used of the renewing of the Holy Spirit. The letter as a whole uses the term *Savior* frequently (1:3, 4; 2:13; 3:6) and *salvation* (2:11).

Two matters that Paul is more obviously concerned with here (or perhaps more clearly expresses) are the importance of good works by the church and their living a high moral life so as to present no opportunity for any slander against them. Thus good works are referred to in 1:16; 2:7, 14; 3:1, 8, though 3:5 stresses that these works cannot provide salvation—a typical Pauline distinction. Injunctions not to invite reproach occur in 1:5, 7; 2:5, 8, 10.

CHARACTERS

enemies and false teachers See 2 Timothy.

Paul See 2 Timothy.

Titus Titus is not mentioned in the Acts but is referred to in Galatians 2:1–3 as a companion of Paul and Barnabas at the Council of Jerusalem. He was a Greek and therefore uncircumcised. Paul points out that no one expected him to become circumcised, and thus with due consistency, no other Gentile should be. Paul's arguments won the day. Frequent mentions of Titus in 2 Corinthians show how useful he was in healing the rift between Paul and the Corinthian church. Now he is establishing churches in Crete. In 2 Timothy Paul is planning to send him to Dalmatia. He is thus an assistant apostle, it might be termed, one in whom Paul has full confidence.

Tobit

The book of Tobit is not part of the Hebrew Bible but was included in the Septuagint (see BIBLE, EARLY TRANSLATIONS OF). The Roman Catholic Church as well as the Orthodox Churches recognize it as deuterocanonical (being of secondary canonical rank). In the Protestant churches, however, it is not accepted but is included in the Apocrypha of the Old Testament (see APOCRYPHA AND PSEUDEPIGRAPHA).

The text of the book is extant in Greek, Syrian, and Latin translations. Fragments of the supposedly original Aramaic text have been found at Qumran (see DEAD SEA SCROLLS). The manuscripts differ in some details of the story. The book is to be dated roughly 200 B.C.E.

SYNOPSIS

Tobit is a Jew of the tribe of Naphtali whose family had been deported by the Assyrians. He is a pious and charitable man, very much committed to the Mosaic Law. His family, however, is very poor. One of his main tasks is to go out into the streets at night, looking for Jews who have been slain and secretly burying them according to the Law. On one of these occasions, fresh droppings of sparrows fall into his eyes, and he becomes blind. He loses all his hope and asks God to let him die.

Sarah, the daughter of one of Tobit's relatives, Raguel from Ecbatana, also prays for death. She had been engaged to seven men one after the other. But each of them was killed on the wedding night by a demon called Asmodeus.

Tobit had once lent some money to a person named Gabael. Since he needs the money urgently, he sends his son, Tobias, to take it back from him. As Tobias leaves the house, he meets the angel Raphael, who has been sent by God as an answer to both of the prayers. But Tobias does not know that Raphael is an angel.

The angel Raphael accompanies Tobias on his way. When Tobias washes himself in a river, a big fish tries to swallow his foot. Raphael advises Tobias to catch the fish and take out his gall, heart, and liver. Raphael tells Tobias that burning the heart and the liver of the fish will drive any demon or evil spirit out of a person. And the gall can be used to heal a person's eyes.

They go to Raguel's house, and Tobias falls in love with Sarah. He asks her to marry him. Sarah as well as her parents are very much afraid of the demon. But on the wedding night, Tobias burns the heart and the liver of the fish, so casting out Sarah's demon. The demon flees to Egypt but is bound there by the angel Raphael.

Raguel helps Tobias to find Gabael, and he gets the money back from him. Together with his bride,

Tobias and the angel (Tobit 6:4), engraving by Gustave Doré

Tobias returns to his father's home. He takes the gall of the fish and puts it on Tobit's eyes so that they are healed.

So the prayers of two pious and committed people who had experienced sorrow and grief lead to joy and happiness.

COMMENTARY

The book of Tobit is a religious folk tale. Some historical statements made by the book prove to be mistaken. For example, Tobit is said to have been a young boy at the time of the schism between Judah and Israel in 931 B.C.E. But it is also said that he experienced the Assyrian captivity around 730 B.C.E. His son, Tobias, again, is said to have died after the fall of Nineveh in 612 B.C.E.

The message of the story is that God answers the prayers of those who fear him. However, the wonders God does are not easily recognized as such: The angel appears as a normal human being, and the casting out of a demon and the healing of a blind man are seemingly performed by simple medical means.

Some of the book's teachings have influenced medieval thinking but are not accepted in theology today: In several instances, the book points out the importance of giving to the poor, as giving alms purges away sin and even delivers from death (4:7–11; 12:9). This, however, can lead one to the medieval practice of selling indulgences. Further, the Latin version of Tobit, which was much used in the Middle Ages, has a particularly negative view of sexual desire (see 3:16; 6:22; and 8:9 in English translations that are based on the Vulgate).

CHARACTERS

Asmodeus An evil demon who kills seven of Sarah's husbands, each of them during the wedding night. But then he is driven out by Tobias. Asmodeus flees to Egypt, but the angel Raphael binds him there.

Gabael A man with whom Tobit once left 10 talents of silver. Tobit instructs his son, Tobias, to travel to Gabael and take the money back.

Raguel A relative of Tobit and father of Sarah. Raguel helps Tobias to find Gabael.

Raphael An angel who accompanies Tobias on his journey. Raphael tells Tobias how to use the innards of the fish for driving out Sarah's demon and for restoring Tobit's eyesight.

Sarah A very pious young woman. Sarah suffers heavily through the demon Asmodeus, who kills each of her fiancés during the wedding night. But God answers her prayers by sending Tobias and the angel Raphael to her. Tobias marries Sarah, and on the wedding night, he drives out the demon.

Tobias Son of Tobit, and the young hero of the story. Tobit sends Tobias on a journey to Gabael. On the journey, he meets Raguel, and he marries Raguel's daughter, Sarah. The journey becomes the means by which God answers the needs of Sarah as well as of Tobit.

Tobit Father of Tobias. Tobit is a pious and exemplary charitable man, who has helped many

Jews during the time of the Assyrian oppression. But he becomes very poor and eventually has an accident through which he becomes blind. He loses all his hopes and prays to God that he may let him die. But God has a better plan for him, which involves restoring his eyesight, his wealth, and his reputation and finding a wife for his son, Tobias.

Wisdom

The book of Wisdom is not part of the Hebrew Bible but was included in the Septuagint (see BIBLE, EARLY TRANSLATIONS OF). The Roman Catholic Church as well as the Orthodox Churches recognize it as deuterocanonical (being of secondary canonical rank). In the Protestant churches, however, it is included in the Apocrypha of the Old Testament (see APOCRYPHA AND PSEUDEPIGRAPHA).

The book presents itself as being written by King Solomon, famous for his power, wealth, and wisdom. Although the name of Solomon is not mentioned explicitly, chapters 6–9 very clearly resemble the biblical narrative on Solomon's prayer for wisdom (see 1 Kings 3; 2 Chronicles 1). However, strong arguments speak against a Solomonic authorship: (1) The work is written in Greek. There are no hints that the text is a translation of an original Hebrew text. (2) The pathos, rhetoric, and style of the book are truly Hellenistic. (3) The philosophy of the book centers on the concept of life after death, which does not fit within the Hebrew Bible wisdom thinking.

Therefore, attributing authorship to Solomon has to be seen as fictional. The author uses Solomon's name in order to give more weight to the thoughts he wants to promote. The real author surely was a pious Jew but one who lived in a Hellenistic context of the first century B.C.E. In his book, there is an emphasis on the relationship between Israel and EGYPT. From that, scholars follow that he possibly lived in Alexandria, a center of Jewish DIASPORA life in the north of Egypt.

SYNOPSIS

The book consists of three parts: The first part compares the fate of the righteous with the fate of the wicked. It argues that although life on earth often does not seem to be governed by the principle of retribution, there will be a final judgment after death, in which full justice will be achieved (1:1–6:24).

In the second part, we learn about Solomon's encounter with wisdom. Solomon explains the origin and nature of wisdom. He gives advice on how wisdom can be attained. He recounts the prayer in which he had asked God for wisdom (6:25–9:11).

The form of prayer is formally kept for the third part of the book. From its content, the text describes the work of wisdom in the history of Israel. It starts with some events from the beginning of the biblical history but then concentrates mainly on the Exodus from Egypt. It shows the distinction God makes in dealing with Egypt, on the one hand, and Israel, on the other hand (9:12–19:22).

In two lengthy digressions, the author discusses God's ways of punishing people, and he heavily criticizes Egyptian idolatry (11:15–12:22; 12:23–15:19).

COMMENTARY

From its literary genre, the book belongs to the WISDOM LITERATURE of the Hebrew Bible (especially Proverbs, Job, and Ecclesiastes). It agrees with the biblical wisdom literature in that wisdom is a gift of God that can be obtained by fearing the Lord and by prayer. Wisdom helps in leading a successful life.

Concerning the tension between belief in the justice of God and experienced injustice, which is expressed mainly in the books of Job and Ecclesiastes, the book of Wisdom makes a large step forward, offering a new explanation and solution. It argues that God originally created human beings to live in eternity and that there is a life after death including a judgment day, when everyone will be judged according to his or her way of living. People who are faithful to wisdom will be given eternal life in God's presence; the wicked people, however, will perish (see LAST THINGS).

In some respects, the book of Wisdom employs Greek philosophical thinking, for example, by making a strong distinction between body and soul (2:2–3; 8:19–20). The writer does not believe, however, in immortality of the substance of the soul, as the Greeks did. He rather builds on the rare statements on afterlife of the Hebrew Bible (Ecclesiastes 12:14; Daniel 12:2, 13; see Job 19:23–25), exploring them in full detail, thus forming a bridge between Hebrew Bible and New Testament thinking on an afterlife. Some Hellenistic influence can also be seen in the magnificent praise of wisdom in 7:15–8:8, where wisdom is described as "a breath of the power of God, and a pure emanation of the glory of the Almighty . . . a reflection of eternal light, a spotless mirror of the working of God, and an image of his goodness. Although she is but one, she can do all things, and while remaining in herself, she renews all things."

Some of this language is reused for describing the relationship of Jesus Christ to God in the New Testament (Colossians 1:15; Hebrews 1:3; John 1). Other New Testament allusions to the book of Wisdom are Matthew 27:40, 43 (see 2:17–19) and Romans 1:22–25 (see 12:23–27). These allusions do not mean that the book of Wisdom was seen as canonical but show that it was a well-known book in New Testament times.

CHARACTER

Solomon   The book presents itself as being written by Solomon. In the text, Solomon points out that despite his extraordinary fame, he is a mortal human being like everyone else. He describes wisdom as a most precious gift he longed for and he received from God after a prayer.

Zechariah

The prophet Zechariah lived in postexilic times (see RETURN FROM EXILE), and the first part of his prophecies can be internally dated to 520 B.C.E. He is mentioned in Ezra 5:1 as one of two prophets urging the governor, Zerubbabel; the high priest, Joshua (or Jeshua); and the Jewish people to complete the rebuilding of the temple. The other prophet is Haggai, whose prophecies precede the book of Zechariah in the Hebrew Bible. The historical background can be read in Ezra chapters 1–6.

The foundation of the temple had been laid around 536 B.C.E. (Zechariah 8:9 suggests Zechariah was not present, though other prophets were) but for various reasons had not progressed. While Haggai addressed Zerubbabel particularly, Zechariah takes a more general, less urgent approach, rather more mystical, addressing Joshua rather than Zerubbabel. The two prophets are thus complementary to each other.

In Zechariah's prophecies we are very aware of the "former prophets," whom he frequently refers to without naming any specifically. These prophecies form vibrant subtexts. It is quite possible that the second part of Isaiah was written at the end of the exilic period, even into the first few years of the return. There are in particular many echoes of those prophecies. Ezekiel was another prophet of the exile, and Jeremiah's prediction of 70 years of exile is constantly in Zechariah's mind (e.g., Jeremiah 25:11–12). But he seems aware of earlier prophets, too, and their oracles both of judgment and of restoration (e.g., Hosea 14:1–7).

The second part of the book of Zechariah (chapters 9–14) is somewhat different from the first. It is in verse as well as prose; the first-person account of Zechariah is replaced by an anonymous set of oracles, which have no named author or date. This has led many scholars to suppose they were not Zechariah's but those of some later disciple or disciples. The growth of APOCALYPTIC WRITING in the fourth and third centuries B.C.E. has suggested to such scholars a later date, as they see the second part as typical in this genre. A possible reference to GREECE (Hebrew *Jawan*) has suggested a date concurring with Alexander's conquest, perhaps his siege of Tyre (see LEBANON) in 332 B.C.E. However, the Hebrew word need not refer to a specific country. Others have put the final chapters as late as the Maccabean period (see INTERTESTAMENTAL PERIOD). In complete contrast, some earlier scholars date some of these chapters in preexilic times. A conservative approach would be to say that Zechariah was the author, but perhaps some 40 years later. By then Greece was establishing itself as a world power.

There is some unity between the two parts: The first part of Zechariah is also apocalyptic in certain aspects, and the parts are structured in a similar way. In other words, it could be held that there is not sufficient difference to posit a different author.

SYNOPSIS

Visions and Promises (Chapters 1–8)

The first part can be subdivided into eight visions (1:7–6:8) and a series of oracles and an enacted prophecy (1:1–6; 6:9–8:23). The eight visions are as follows:

- The four horsemen patrolling the earth (1:7–17)
- The four horns and the four blacksmiths (1:18–20)
- The man measuring Jerusalem (2:1–13)
- Satan accusing the high priest and the priest's reclothing (3:1–10)
- The lampstand and the two olive trees (4:1–14)
- The flying scroll (5:1–4)
- The removal of the woman of wickedness (5:5–11)
- The four patrolling chariots (6:1–8)

The main themes emerging from the visions are that the Lord will restore his blessing on his people as they renew their faith, rebuild the temple, and repopulate the city. Their enemies will be destroyed, and all nations will recognize God's presence in the holy city. There will be a joint rulership of prince and priest.

The other sections comprise an introduction (1:1–6), calling for God's people to return to him; an enacted prophecy (6:9–15), crowning the high priest; and a long oracle, springing from a query about the place of fasting (chapters 7–8). Basically, *fasting* has become an empty ritual (compare Isaiah 58:1–12; Jeremiah 14:12), and God's purposes are to replace it with *feasting* in a restored Jerusalem.

Prophecies of War and Peace (Chapters 9–14)

The six chapters can be divided into a long poetic prophecy (9:1–11:3), which promises both peace and restoration in the future, but peace only achieved through battle. Chapter 9 can be seen as one of the "divine warrior" HYMNS of a type to be found elsewhere (e.g., Nahum 1:2–14) and in other Middle Eastern literatures. It includes a theoph-

any and victory banquet (9:14–15). This is then repeated in 14:1, 3, 5, and taken up in 11:1–3 as a LAMENT over the fallen nations. This is followed by a prose section (11:4–16) around the extended image of sheep and shepherds, both true and false. This is summarized in a short poem split into two (11:17; 13:7–9). The final long section is a prose apocalyptic, dealing with the Lord's final victory as his enemies battle outside Jerusalem. The final scene is the nations' proceeding to the holy city to offer their sacrifices at the renewed temple, returning to the theme of the first part.

COMMENTARY

Visions and Promises (Chapters 1–8)

The prose of the first part is highly literary prose, in terms of both its subtextual allusions, imagery, and symbolism, and its structures, particularly of the visions. The internal structure of each vision is fairly similar, although no two are identical. The general pattern is:

i introduction as to time or place
ii what the prophet sees
iii the prophet asks the attending angel for an explanation
iv the interpretation is given
v the prophet is given a further oracle.

It can be seen these visions are somewhat different from those given to preexilic prophets. For example, when Jeremiah is shown a picture of an almond branch (Jeremiah 1:11–12), God speaks to him directly, and the interpretation is given directly to the prophet by God. What we have in Zechariah is an angelic intermediary to provide the interpretation. A dialogue is thus set up between prophet and angel. God does sometimes speak to the prophet directly if there is an oracle to give. The switch from active interpretation to spectator role with explanation given by an intermediary is best seen in the book of Daniel. In the first half of Daniel, he is the active interpreter of dreams; in the second half, he has to ask an angel for interpretation. The change is a shift of imaginative stance, which leads to the setting up of the apocalyptic genre.

It is not always clear in this how many angels are involved. In the first vision there are mysterious angelic horsemen, with a leader, but who is spoken of as a man (1:8); but there must also be another angel present, "who talked with me" (1:9). Then there is the "angel of the LORD" (1:11–12); then "the LORD" himself (1:13). Whether there are two or three angels involved, it is clear Zechariah is not addressed directly by the Lord.

The message is also more hidden by the symbols used. The horsemen, symbols used later in apocalyptic literature (e.g., Revelation 6:1–8), represent the patrolling eyes of God around the world. But we do not know whether we are to take their colors symbolically. No explanation of the colors is given at any time, a characteristic that has not prevented various commentators from offering their own. The horsemen in Revelation are different from the horsemen here. Even within the text, as here, where there are many references to horses (6:2–3; 9:10; 10:3, 5; 12:4; 14:15, 20), it cannot be assumed all references bear the same symbolic or metaphoric weight. In some cases, it is just the sheer mystery and otherness of the vision that is meant to impact us, as in Ezekiel's first vision (Ezekiel 1).

However, where allusions and echoes to *earlier* prophetic writing are made, then we can treat these as subtexts that help determine meaning. Thus in vision 2 "horns" echo their use in Daniel as world powers, and blacksmiths become symbols of God's anger as in Haggai 2:22 and more significantly Isaiah 54:16. In vision 3, the measuring line echoes Ezekiel's vision of the restored temple (see Ezekiel 43:2–5 especially, also Jeremiah 31:39; Revelation 21:15–17); and in vision 4, the image of filthy clothes echoes Isaiah 64:6 as well as ritual instructions for priestly apparel in Leviticus 21:10–15. Satan as accuser in the heavenly courts is not dissimilar to his appearance in the book of Job (Job 1:6–8; also 1 Chronicles 21:1).

However, not all the symbolism here alludes to previous subtexts. That of the lamp stand with its seven lamps and two olive trees seems original to Zechariah. The lamp stand is different from the ritual lamp stand of Exodus and enters the symbolic language of apocalypse, as is seen in Revelation 5:6, where the lamps become the eyes of God. The olive trees are not explained, interestingly, but clearly need an explanation in the way the horses' colors

do not. We can guess they refer to being a source of oil, and anointing oil to symbolize office, presumably the twin offices of priest and prince. In the New Testament, the book of Hebrews makes a great deal of this concept of priest-king in Melchizedek, seeing him as a type of Christ (Hebrews 7, quoting Psalm 110, and referring to Genesis 14:18).

Arising from this point, many commentators have seen messianic symbolism in the anointing and in the references to the "branch" (Zechariah 3:8; 6:12). This image picks up on Isaiah 4:2; 11:1; Jeremiah 23:5–6; 33:15–16. See Commentary on chapters 9–14 for other messianic references.

Prophecies of War and Peace (Chapters 9–14)

There are two cycles in this part, both marked by the term *burden* (King James Version), a better term than *oracle* (New Revised Standard Version) (9:1; 12:1):

Burden 1:

A: Attack on God's people by their enemies and defeat of enemies (9:1–8)
B: Victory for Ephraim, Judah, and Jerusalem (9:10–17)
C: Against false shepherds (10:1–3)
D: Deliverance and restoration (10:4–12)
E: Lament for the conquered nations (11:1–3)

Burden 2:

A: Defeat for the hostile nations (12:1–5)
B: Victory for Judah and Jerusalem (12:6–9)
C: Mourning for rejection of the true shepherd (12:10–14)
D: Cleansing and restoration (13:1–6)
E: Attack on God's people by their enemies (14:1–2)
F: Victory through the Lord's intervention (14:3–5)
G: Messianic reign (the true shepherd) (14:6–11)
H: Defeat of enemies (14:12–15)

The final verses (14:16–21) are a conclusion, returning us to the initial idea of the temple restored to its ideal holiness (compare Ezekiel 44:4–7).

Interrupting this scheme are two sections: first, 11:4–16, a prose narrative over certain false shepherds, told in an enigmatic *I*-voice, which may or may not be Zechariah's, and which seems an actual historical commentary on 10:1–3; second, 11:17 and 13:7–9, a parallel poem, which might be called Song of the Shepherds, again moving from the false to the true shepherd.

The writing is highly literary but difficult, especially if we are looking for historical counterparts. Some of it is reminiscent of Isaiah in particular. For example, Zechariah chapter 10 echoes Isaiah 41:17–24 and 43, while Zechariah 12:10–14 reflects the suffering servant of Isaiah 52:13–53:12. One of the main images is that of the shepherd, which has to be understood as a strong image, that of a powerful ruler rather than a gentle pastor. This would reflect typical Middle Eastern usage of the time (for example, Ezekiel 34:23–24). The true shepherd emerges as the Lord himself (14:3; compare Ezekiel 34:15) in the final chapter, where a full-blown apocalyptic emerges, with divine intervention and reshaping of the holy geography at the full appearance of the Messiah, as also in Ezekiel (Ezekiel 38; 47). In such a full presence of God, there will be no further need for prophecy (13:2–6; compare 1 Corinthians 13:8). In connection with the messianic, there is a growing emphasis on the Davidic line (12:7–13:1).

The New Testament writers also saw the messianic import of this second part with reference to Jesus Christ. Thus 9:9 is quoted in Matthew 21:5, which also quotes 11:12–13 in Matthew 27:10, though Matthew actually attributes the quotation to Jeremiah, presumably because it was Jeremiah who purchased a potter's field (Jeremiah 32:6–15), a connection more obvious in King James Version's "the potter" than the New Revised Standard Version's "treasury." Verse 12:10 is echoed in John 19:34 and quoted in Revelation 1:7. Jesus consciously refers to himself as "the good shepherd"(John 10:11), thinking of these passages as much as, if not more than, Psalm 23.

Besides imagery of sheep and shepherds, there is much warfare imagery, which includes plagues, panic, and fire and stands in tension with images of peace and fertility, including spring rains and living water. Political references abound in terms of a hoped-for national unity, the defeat of surrounding nations, and the establishment of the ideal national boundaries as set out in Genesis and Exodus. Whatever century these passages were written in, it would be true to say national boundaries dissolved frequently. No wonder the writer appeals no fewer than 17 times to a permanence to be established "in that day," when God's kingdom and worship will be established unchangeably.

CHARACTER

Zechariah   Mentioned in Ezra 5:1 and 6:14 as one of two prophets encouraging the completion of the temple. Nehemiah 12:16 suggests he was also a priest, so like Ezekiel he was probably a prophet-priest. His series of visions and oracles are apocalyptic in nature, though there are passages more typical of earlier prophecy, where the people's ethical behavior and heart attitudes are the focus. As Ezekiel does, he thus stands at the transition from preexilic to postexilic prophetic literature.

Zephaniah

The PROPHECY of Zephaniah is placed ninth in the Minor or Lesser Prophets in the Hebrew Bible. The Hebrew name is *Tsefanyah*, which means "the LORD conceals." The writer states he is writing in the reign of King Josiah (639–609 B.C.E.). Certain reforms were effected by the king after 622 B.C.E. (2 Kings 23), so perhaps the book was compiled before and just after that date, as the prophet presumes a very unreformed Jerusalem, only at the end seeing a bright future. Some scholars take the writing back to Josiah's grandfather, Manasseh, when there was rampant paganism, as there was also in the short reign of his son, Amon. A few take the book to be written much later, but the specific details given of Jerusalem suggest someone there at the time and before Assyria had fallen in 612 B.C.E. The date suggested would make him a contemporary of the prophets Nahum, Habakkuk, and the young Jeremiah.

Each of the minor prophets has some special emphasis, which makes him unique. Zephaniah's emphasis was on "the Day of the LORD" (see LAST THINGS). Although other prophets had used the term previously, none had emphasized it so much. Later on, the term came to be used in APOCALYPTIC WRITING, and Zephaniah may be taken as creating the foundation for this type of writing in this respect. He establishes the pattern of the "day" as cataclysmic, as a result of God's anger at human unfaithfulness, but not a final end, which is, rather, a restoration for a "remnant" who have remained faithful.

SYNOPSIS

The prophecy divides rather unequally into judgment (1:1–3:8) and restoration (3:9–20). Within the long first part, there is a careful chiastic structure, thus:

A   Judgment of the world (1:2–3)

B   Judgment on Judah (1:4–2:3)

C   Judgment on Judah's neighbors (2:4–15)

B1 Judgment of JERUSALEM (Judah's capital) (3:1–7)

A1 Judgment on the World ("all nations") (3:8)

Sections B, B1 are by far the most detailed, cataloging sins of idol worship, syncretism, religious indifference, and injustice. Section C has woes against the Canaanites of Philistia, the Edomites and Ammonites, the Cushites, and ASSYRIA.

Though the second section is much shorter, it is extremely powerful and is a fitting rhetorical climax to the prophecy. The poetry takes on a new power as the writer talks of a "gathering up" of the scattered faithful, a restoration of God's love, and a promise never again to inflict such punishment.

COMMENTARY

The Judgment (1:2–3:8)

The opening verses are dramatic in their hyperbole (see IMAGERY, BIBLICAL): "I will utterly sweep away everything from the face of the earth, says the LORD" (1:2) with "sweep away" repeated twice in 1:3, as the CREATION is undone completely. This universal picture is important: Though Zephaniah focuses on Jerusalem, his vision is worldwide. The Israelites may be the Lord's particular people, but he is still Lord of the world.

The judgment is soon focused on Judah, the southern kingdom of Israel; the northern kingdom

had fallen to the Assyrians long before, in 722 B.C.E. (see MONARCHY). There is a cumulative list of sins against which God is angry. Such accumulations, with their parallel structures, become a powerful rhetorical tool. Here each line begins "Those who . . . ," listing the pagan worship of the stars (1:5); the mixing of the worship of Yahweh and Molech, or Milcom; and the sheer indifference and apathy of many (1:6). These sins are common objects of attack by most of the prophets (e.g., Hosea 10:5; Jeremiah 19:13), based on prohibitions in the Law (e.g., Deuteronomy 4:19; 6:13).

The judgment will fall principally on the leaders (1:8), further suggesting Zephaniah's greater association with them as an upper-class person himself. The image used is ironic: There will be a sacrifice, as if for sin, but the Lord will provide the sacrifice and invite the guests (1:7). The sacrifice will be their destruction. His attack on them is detailed, mentioning their proclivity for foreign fashions, symbolizing a spiritual attitude, and even the superstition of jumping over the threshold of the temples of idols, first mentioned in 1 Samuel 5:5.

The most significant language, however, in this section is that concerning "the day of the LORD" (1:7) which recurs some 14 times in the following 15 verses, either in that form or as "that day," "the great day of the LORD," "a day," or "the day of the LORD's anger." The phrase is found in earlier prophets, such as Amos (Amos 5:18–20), Joel (Joel 1:15), and Isaiah (Isaiah 2:6–22), but it is Zephaniah who uses it most systematically, building up, through repetition, to a crescendo in 1:18. Repetition is one of the rhetorical devices most typical of WOES AND DENUNCIATIONS, a dramatic drumbeat of future disaster. Synecdoche (see IMAGERY, BIBLICAL) is also typical. Rather than generalizing the features of this "day," specific details are picked out: "a cry," "a wail," "the Fish Gate" (1:10), each individual item representing a total catastrophe for the whole city.

Basically, the "day of the LORD" means the day when God will intervene directly in some obvious way. Typically, it means a day of judgment, but as the final section shows, it can also be a day of mercy and salvation. The theological question is whether this day is preordained, no matter what happens, or whether it is provisional. Zephaniah 2:1–3 suggests its provisionality in human terms, as also in the book of Jonah. Jonah was annoyed, in fact, when Nineveh repented and the day of judgment was postponed. Zephaniah certainly suggests that repentance is the way to avoid its inevitability.

However, the feeling of inevitability is strong, just as it is in Jeremiah. There seems to be an anticipation by the prophet that any repentance will be incomplete. The tension is resolved theologically by positing the idea of "the remnant," another central prophetic trope. Verses 3:12–13 set out the nature of this remnant: "a people humble and lowly."

Interestingly, the remnant idea also appears in the next subsection (2:4–15). The woes against foreign nations posit remnants for three of the nations (2:7, 9b, 11b), though significantly not for Assyria. Assyria, the main enemy that had already obliterated the northern kingdom, will be left totally devastated forever (2:14–15), the imagery of owls in the ruins echoing Isaiah 13:21 and 34:11, though in Isaiah the woes are against Babylon and Edom. Interestingly, God himself has been proclaiming his judgments in the first person most of the time, the prophet acting as his voice. But with Assyria, the narrative reverts to the third person.

Woes against neighboring nations are another prophetic commonplace, their most worked-out expression being in Jeremiah 47–51. Obadiah's whole prophecy is a denunciation of Edom. Here, we can note that Philistia and Canaan have been conflated (2:4), whereas earlier in the Hebrew Bible, the two are seen as separate entities. There is a play on words in 2:4: *Gaza* and "deserted" or "abandoned" (New International Version) sound similar in Hebrew, as do *Ekron* and "uprooted." Moab and Ammon can be linked as they were both descended from Lot. Cush (Ethiopia) is only briefly mentioned, possibly a covert reference to Egypt. Zephaniah is the son of *Cushi*, which literally means "Ethiopian," so there may be some personal reference here, picked up in 3:10.

The third subsection (3:1–8) returns to Jerusalem. This time its injustice is stressed, as in Jeremiah (Jeremiah 6:13f.). There is a strong sense that the city will not repent (3:7). A law court image is used in 3:8. God himself will be witness to testify against Jerusalem as well as the surrounding nations. Zephaniah is concerned to establish God's justice (3:5, 7–8). He is not an arbitrary tyrant but a patient sovereign.

The Restoration (3:9–20)

We now move to the time when "that day" now becomes one of hope and restoration, both morally and geographically. The remnant will be purified, synecdochally represented by "pure speech" (3:9), by having had the proud removed in the destruction (3:11). They will be "gathered" from their exile or scattering, again a typically prophetic trope (e.g., Joel 3:1–2; Jeremiah 31). Their restoration will be permanent, just as after Noah's flood God promised never again to destroy (Genesis 8:21), of which this seems to be a conscious echo.

The book ends in a wonderfully dramatic climax of joy, as God's promises of restoration are piled up in parallelisms on each other, the very opposite rhetorical movement to the list of woes:

> he will rejoice over you with gladness,
> he will renew you in his love;
> he will exult over you with loud singing
> as on a day of festival. (3:17–18)

Such ecstatic statements, emerging from woes of total destruction, surely span the whole gamut of prophetic emotion to be found in Hebrew poetry.

CHARACTER

Zephaniah In Zephaniah 1:1 the writer traces his genealogy back four generations to Hezekiah, whom most scholars take to mean King Hezekiah (716–687 B.C.E.), thus making him part of the upper class in Jerusalem. He was presumably born in the reign of Manasseh, prophesying in the early part of the reign of Josiah. He is clearly an educated man. As a poet, he has a well-developed sense of the forms of Hebrew poetry, and as a prophet, he has the same dramatic intensity we see in the Major Prophets. His vision of the Day of the Lord is the earliest full formulation of that concept.

PART III

Related Entries

Aaron Brother of MOSES, from the tribe of Levi. Aaron is installed as Moses' spokesperson to negotiate with Pharaoh. Later, he is consecrated to be the first high priest in Israel and founder of the Israelite priesthood. He appears to be a rather weak character. See also Exodus and Leviticus in Part II.

Abraham Ancestor of the people of ISRAEL, married to Sarah. God calls Abraham to leave his homeland and move to the land of Canaan. God promises that he will become a great nation and that he and his family will be a blessing even for the whole world (Genesis 12:1–3). God changes his original name, *Abram,* to *Abraham,* meaning "father of a multitude." Abraham has to wait a long time for his heir to be born, his son ISAAC, who becomes the bearer of the divine blessing after him. The Genesis narrative shows us Abraham as a person who vacillated between faith and doubt, with faith triumphing. Hence in the New Testament he is seen as an example of faith in God (Romans 4; Galatians 3:6–9; Hebrews 11:8–19).

Abraham and Isaac (Genesis 22:5–6), etching by Rembrandt

acrostic A poem in which the first letters or words of each poetical line taken together form a new sentence. In the Hebrew Bible, only the subtype of alphabetic acrostic is employed, where the 22 verses of a poem each begin with the 22 letters of the Hebrew alphabet in succession. Examples are Psalm 145 and Lamentations 1, 2, and 4. In Lamentations 3, each letter is repeated three times, resulting in 66 verses; in Psalm 119, each letter is repeated even eight times, resulting in 176 verses in total. The notion carried by the alphabetic acrostic is that of completeness: It is "from A to Z." In the New Testament the acrostic does not occur.

Adam and Eve The first human beings, who were created directly by God, according to Genesis 1 and 2.

The name *Adam* is the Hebrew word for "human being." In the creation account, a connection is drawn to the "ground," Hebrew *adamah:* Man is taken from the ground, and he will return to the ground again. Adam symbolizes not only humanity as CREATION but also humanity as fallen (see FALL, THE). Adam's sin, his arrogance toward God, is at the same time the sin of all humanity. The consequence of this sin is death. The New Testament describes Jesus Christ as the "second Adam," the new humanity, who overcomes sin and overcomes death as the consequence of sin and opens up a new way to life for his followers (Romans 5:12–21).

Eve stands as a paradigm for the relationship of man and woman, in creation as well as in Fall. (The name *Eve* is derived from the Hebrew word for "to live," since from her all other human life arises.) She is introduced as the perfect person opposite to the man: "a man leaves his father and his mother and clings to his wife, and they become one flesh" (Genesis 2:24). After the Fall, however, in which Eve plays a larger role than Adam, the relationship between man and woman is distorted: Now the woman desires her husband but has to accept the fact that he rules over her.

Although the significance of Adam and Eve mostly lies on a paradigmatic level, the Bible presents them throughout as historical beings as well. For example, the genealogies of Genesis and of 1 Chronicles 1–9 draw a genealogical connection between Adam and the people of Israel. In Luke 3:23–38, the genealogical line of Jesus Christ is traced back to Adam (the purpose of this again a religious one).

allegory See TYPES; "The Age of Systematic Approaches" in Part I.

angels Supernatural created beings who live in the presence of God. Hebrews 1:14 provides the shortest definition: "Are not all angels ministering spirits sent to serve those who will inherit salvation?" (NIV). In the Bible, there is a continuity of teaching on angels, which emphasizes their *function*, how they "minister" or serve, as:

- *messengers*. This is the original meaning of both Hebrew and Greek words. Thus, the angel announces to Mary the birth of JESUS CHRIST, and to Gideon (Judges 6:12), telling him to raise an army. The Gideon incident shows that they can hold a dialogue and elucidate.
- *interpreters or revealers of God's will*. Both Zechariah 1:9 and Revelation 10:9 show angels instructing the visionaries. They have understanding of spiritual matters and the future, especially in APOCALYPTIC WRITING.
- *fighters* and active in human and spiritual warfare. It is an angel who kills the Assyrian army (2 Kings 19:35). Apocalyptic literature emphasizes this role.
- *guardians* (Psalm 91:11), including children (Matthew 18:10), churches (Revelation 2:1), and nations. In Daniel 12:1, an angel guards Israel.

Angels have natures, and some have names. They are able to make themselves visible or invisible; they possess glory; they often appear in visions but can appear as humans in everyday reality. There is some suggestion there is a hierarchy of orders of angels. Seraphim and cherubim are mentioned as two orders, and Michael is termed an archangel (Jude 9), *arch-*, meaning "chief," and "the great prince" (Daniel 12:1). Another named archangel is Gabriel (Daniel 8:16), best known for his role in the Annunciation to Mary (Luke 1:19).

Satan, according to Christian tradition, is an archangel who rebelled against God and led unfallen angels into rebellion. There is a realm of "evil spirits" in the Bible, whom many equate with the lesser orders of fallen angels, sometimes also termed devils.

See also REVELATION, GOD'S; SATAN.

anthropomorphism See PERSONIFICATION.

Antichrist The term *Antichrist* only occurs in 1 John 2:18, 22; 4:3, and in 2 John 7; in the first of these verses we find the plural as well as the singular. The word refers to false teachers who form a threat to the churches to which John is writing; John accuses them of teaching heresy about JESUS CHRIST.

In the EARLY CHURCH and ever since the word has been used in a slightly different way, i.e., to refer to a human leader who will deceive the Christians in the end times (see LAST THINGS). The precursor

The beast with seven heads (Revelation 13:1–2), woodcut by Albrecht Dürer

of such a person was King Antiochus Epiphanes (see 1, 2, 3, and 4 Maccabees in Part II).

A figure like this Antichrist is called "the man of lawlessness" in 2 Thessalonians 2:3–12, and in Revelation 13 two demonic beasts appear that are generally identified as the Antichrist and his helper. As does "the man of lawlessness," the first beast derives his power from SATAN (Revelation 13:2, 4), blasphemes against God (Revelation 13:5), allows himself to be worshipped (Revelation 13:8), and is finally defeated by Christ (Revelation 19:20). A difference between the two is that the "man of lawlessness" would *not* seem to be a political power, whereas the beast is. The beast also has traits of the four beasts described in Daniel 7 and forms a parody of the Lamb, which is mentioned elsewhere in Revelation:

The Lamb	The Sea Beast
Power from God (5:6, 12, 13)	Power from the Devil (13:2)
Slaughtered (5:6, 9, 12)	Head wound (slaughtered) (13:3)
Many diadems (19:12)	Ten diadems (13:1)
Worship of God (1:6)	Worship of the dragon (Satan, 13:4)
Holy name (19:11–16)	Blasphemous name (13:1)
Died and lived again (5:9, 12)	Mortal wound, dies, and lives again (13:3, 12, 14)

Thus Antichrist, whether or not called by that name, is the adversary of Christ, the summit of evil, with features of the emperor Nero (Revelation 13:18). He personifies the threats and deceptions from which Christians have suffered in history and will yet suffer.

antithesis   See IMAGERY, BIBLICAL.

apocalyptic writing   The term *apocalypse* is a Greek word meaning an "unveiling" or "revelation." As a genre (see GENRES, BIBLICAL), it refers to that type of writing that claims to unveil the future, usually by means of visions, dreams, and heavenly jour-

neys of visionaries or PROPHETS, who are often not named. These may have been real visions, but often they are a literary device, as in dream literature.

The writing is highly symbolic. Sometimes ANGELS give interpretation of the symbolism, but sometimes it is seen as a mystery, something only the initiated can understand. Symbols can be lengths of time, animals, or elements of the cosmos or traditional. Symbolic actions tend to be catastrophic, for instance: darkness falling, stars falling into the sea, earthquakes and storms, mountains sliding over inhabited places.

Such devastation is often seen as the precursor of some new earth and heaven, where the righteous will reign and evil will have been eliminated in some final judgment by God. The events are predestined, and although repentance is called for, such catastrophes rarely produce it in the wicked. There is moral exhortation, not in the specific and everyday reality of prophetic writing, but more to be patient, since the purpose is often consolatory to believers in a time of desperate hardship or persecution.

The best examples of apocalyptic writing in the Bible are the latter parts of Daniel and Zechariah, and the book of Revelation. Parts of Isaiah, Ezekiel, the Minor Prophets, and the four Gospels also contain elements of apocalyptic writing.

See also LAST THINGS; PROPHECY; REVELATION, GOD'S.

Apocrypha and Pseudepigrapha   Besides the Bible, other religious literature of the Jewish and Early Christian cultures has been handed down to us. Some of these texts were considered by some as truly belonging to the Bible or to have a biblical author.

The early Greek translation of the Hebrew Bible, the Septuagint (see BIBLE, EARLY TRANSLATIONS OF), includes some books that are not part of the Hebrew Bible. These books mostly originated in the late pre-Christian times and were neither accepted as authoritative Scriptures by the Jews nor quoted as such in the New Testament. Among them are, for example, Sirach, Wisdom, Maccabees, Judith, and Tobit.

The Catholic Church recognizes these books as "deuterocanonical," i.e., being of secondary canonical importance. In the Protestant tradition, however, they are not recognized and form the group of the Old Testament Apocrypha. This term means "the hidden ones" and originally refers to the notion that these books contain advanced divine revelation accessible only for a chosen few. Later on, however, the term took on the meaning of "lesser reliable books." In the Protestant realm, the statement of the church reformer Martin Luther is still valid, that the Apocrypha are "not on the same level as the Holy Scriptures, but still good and useful to read." For complete lists of canonical books of the different churches, see Part IV.

Some of the Apocrypha/deuterocanonical books are also Pseudepigrapha, meaning they are pseudonymous. For example, the book of Wisdom is written as if from Solomon (10th century B.C.E.) but contains first-century Hellenistic thinking.

As with the Hebrew Bible, many Christian books were not accepted into the New Testament by the church; as a result the heterogeneous members of this group came to be called "New Testament Apocrypha." These books are available in translation in many editions, including J. K. Elliott's *The Apocryphal New Testament* (Oxford: Clarendon, 1993).

Many apocryphal writings were composed under the name of an apostle of Christ, but these are all pseudonymous. They all date from the second century C.E. and later, after the books of the New Testament had been written, and they reflect the reception of the books that were later canonized (see FORMATION OF THE CANON: THE NEW TESTAMENT). Some authors of Apocrypha wanted to supplement an existing text in order to satisfy the curiosity of the believers concerning Jesus or an apostle; others wanted to express their own doctrinal bias (Acts of John and Acts of Thomas).

There are apocryphal gospels such as those of Thomas, Peter, Philip, Judas, Mary, and Nicodemus. The apocryphal Acts include those of Paul, Peter, John, Andrew, and Thomas. We have a third epistle by Paul to the Corinthians, an epistle to the Laodiceans (cf. Colossians 4:16), and an Epistle of the Apostles, which includes a fictitious dialogue between Jesus and his disciples about future events. Apocryphal apocalypses exist in the names of Peter

and Paul. A large manuscript discovery at Nag Hammadi in Egypt in 1945 considerably enlarged the group of Apocrypha.

Some contemporary scholars promote the gospel of Thomas, found at Nag Hammadi, as the fifth gospel of the New Testament, but Orthodox Christians do not accept this. From a literary point of view many Apocrypha are artless, but the Acts of Thomas contains some beautiful scenes and poetry.

apostles   See TWELVE DISCIPLES.

apostrophe   See IMAGERY, BIBLICAL.

Aramaic   See BIBLE, EARLY TRANSLATIONS OF.

ark of the covenant   See HEBREW BIBLE, WORSHIP AND RITUAL.

Armageddon   Or Harmagedon, the enigmatic name of a location that only occurs in Revelation 16:16. Here large armies gather to do battle, but the battle itself is not described; for the outcome see 17:14 and 19:11–21. The name probably literally means "Mountain of Megiddo" (a town in the north of Israel). According to the Hebrew Bible, Israel was twice attacked near Megiddo (Judges 5:19; 2 Kings 23:29). However, there is no mountain at Megiddo, and most interpreters think that the name is the place that symbolizes God's final victory over his enemies (see LAST THINGS). The likely literary background to Revelation 16:16 is a conflation of Ezekiel 39:2, 4, 17 and Zechariah 12:11.

Assyria   Assyria lies in what is now northwest Iraq, along the River Tigris. Its civilization extends back many thousands of years, with periods of dominance in the region, often known as Mesopotamia, and periods of decline. One such period of dominance was from 1365 B.C.E., when it was a rival to its neighboring kingdom to the south, Babylon, and finally overcame it. This period lasted till about 1000 B.C.E., at which time it fell under constant attack from desert tribes. This was the period of King David's expansion of Israel.

A second and final period of dominance occurred in the ninth century B.C.E. Ashurbanipal II (885–860 B.C.E.) and his son, Shalmaneser III (859–824 B.C.E.), extended the southern borders, though united resistance that included King Ahab of Israel prevented invasion of the HOLY LAND. Tiglath-Pileser III (745–727 B.C.E.), however, conquered Babylon, having himself installed as king, then SYRIA and Jordan. His successors Shalmaneser V (727–722 B.C.E.) and Sargon II (722–705 B.C.E.) invaded the northern kingdom, sacking Samaria, its capital city, in 722 B.C.E. and deporting its citizens.

Sennacherib (705–681 B.C.E.) reconquered Babylon in 701, then marched south to besiege Lachish and JERUSALEM in JUDAH. 2 Kings 18–19 recounts the story of his withdrawal and final death. At its greatest extent, the empire consisted of parts of Turkey, Iran, Arabia, and EGYPT, and all of Iraq, Syria, Jordan, and Israel. The empire declined from 650 B.C.E., allowing Judah independence again, and finally fell to the renascent Babylonians in 612 B.C.E., when its capital, Nineveh, was sacked. The Assyrians were feared for their cruelty to their captives. For example, Ashurbanipal boasts in his records in detail the mutilations of civilian as well as military populations.

See also BABYLON; SAMARIA; SYRIA.

Babylon Babylonia lay in what is now southeastern Iraq. Babylon was its capital, lying on the River Euphrates, south of modern Baghdad. In the Hebrew Bible, the area was first known as Shinar or Sumer, Akkad, and Ur. It later became identified with Chaldea, though all these are areas lying closer to the Persian Gulf, in the area of modern Basra. Its inhabitants are often called Chaldeans.

Its earliest period of greatness, the Sumerian period, dates from ca. 2800 to 2500 B.C.E., when it was a collection of city-states. The Epic of Gilgamesh is associated with this period. Then followed the Akkadian (2371–2191 B.C.E.) and Ur dynasties (2113–2006 B.C.E.), the period of Abraham and the ziggurats. Archaeology has revealed advanced techniques, a system of writing and of laws. The Hammurabi legal code was set down in the next dynasty, between 1894 and 1595 B.C.E.

From then on, there was a steady decline till the Assyrian Empire absorbed it in the mid-eighth century B.C.E. The Assyrian Tiglath-Pileser had himself crowned King Pul (see 1 Chronicles 5:26). Marduk-apla-iddina (Merodach-baladan of the Bible) gained brief independence in 721 and again in 705 B.C.E.

There was one final resurgence of power in 626–539 B.C.E. A Chaldean dynasty arose, conquered Assyria in 612, and Egypt in 605 B.C.E. at the battle of Carchemish under Nebuchadnezzar. Further campaigns in the south led to sieges of Jerusalem in 598 and 586 B.C.E., resulting in the city's destruction and the deportation of its inhabitants. After Nebuchadnezzar's death, the empire became disunited and fell quite suddenly to the Medes and Persians in 539 B.C.E. (see Daniel 5).

In the Hebrew Bible, Babylon is depicted as an archetype of the enemy of God's people. Its first occurrence is in Genesis 11, the tower of Babel. In the New Testament, the term is used in apocryphal writing to denote the type of evil city or civilization, standing in opposition to Jerusalem, the city of God (Revelation 17:5). In 1 Peter 5:13 it is used as a synonym for Rome.

See also EUPHRATES, RIVER; EXILE; JERUSALEM; PERSIA.

baptism From Greek *baptizō*, the washing of humans with or in water as a sign or means of forgiveness of sins. The practice does not occur in the Hebrew Bible, but by New Testament times Gentile converts to Judaism had to undergo a ritual bath, although circumcision remained the most important element of the conversion ceremony. The Jewish sect of Essenes had its own lustrations.

JOHN THE BAPTIST, Jesus' cousin, called the Jews to repentance in preparation for the new things God was going to do and baptized them as a sign of this decision (Luke 3:1–18; John 1:26–28). At the beginning of his public ministry Jesus, too, had himself baptized by John and then started baptizing others (John 3:22–26; 4:1–2). We hear no more about this until the very end of his ministry, when Jesus commands his apostles (see TWELVE DISCIPLES) to baptize all his followers (Matthew 28:18–20).

Consequently the EARLY CHURCH baptized those who professed faith in Jesus and joined the church (Acts 2:37–41; 8:35–38; 10:44–48). In some way the receipt of the Holy Spirit was connected with this event. In postbiblical times the custom of baptizing infants arose for theological reasons.

The meaning of baptism is indicated in diverse ways: It symbolizes the believers' dying to sin and resurrection to a new life with God (Romans 6:1–11), so their rebirth (Titus 3:5; John 3:5) and the forging of a mystic relationship with Jesus Christ (Galatians 3:27). It is an act of confession (1 Peter 3:21).

Nearly all Christian churches practice baptism, either of adults or of infants.

Bethlehem   A small town in the hill country of Judea south of JERUSALEM, which is mentioned as early as Genesis 35:19 but rose to fame as the birthplace of King DAVID. It is also the setting of the book of Ruth. As predicted by the prophet Micah (5:2), JESUS CHRIST was born here (Matthew 2; Luke 2), but the town did not play a role in his later ministry as he grew up in NAZARETH.

Bible, early translations of   One of the earliest translations of any piece of literature was that of the Hebrew Bible into Greek. The resulting Old Testament in Greek was named *Septuagint* after the Greek word for 70. The name was given on the authority of a legend according to which the translation was made in 70 days by 70 scholars who, locked away separately from one another, miraculously produced 70 exactly identical translations. In reality, the translation was done book by book by anonymous people over a period of at least 100 years in the third and second centuries B.C.E., probably in the region of the Egyptian metropolis of Alexandria. Here lived a Jewish population of more than a million people, most of whom no longer knew Hebrew. The Septuagint was their only access to the Holy Scriptures.

Later it was used by many of the earliest Christians, for example, when New Testament authors quote from the Scriptures. Whether the Hebrew Bible or the Septuagint is being quoted in the New Testament can often be established because the Septuagint is not always a literal translation but contains some interpretative bias and shows influences of the contemporary culture. At other times, for example, in Samuel, it seems to be based on a slightly different version of the Hebrew Bible.

Another translation of just the Hebrew Bible is the Targum, a rendering into Aramaic, the vernacular of many Jews in Israel around the time of the New Testament. The Targum replaced the original Hebrew text for the majority of the Jews in Jesus' days, when only the scribes still studied the Hebrew.

In the first Christian centuries the whole Bible was translated into languages such as Latin (the official language of the Roman Empire), Coptic (the language of Egypt at the time), Syriac, Ethiopic, Armenian, Georgian, Slavonic, and Gothic. Together with Bible quotations by the fathers of the church, these translations support the reliability of the transmission of the text. In places where the manuscripts are divided over what the original text says, these translations can tip the balance in favor of a particular reading. So, although the ancient translations of the Bible have little immediate relevance for the contemporary reader, they are of great value for biblical scholars and translators.

The Vulgate, a thorough revision of previous Latin translations by the church father Jerome around the year 400, became over time the official Bible of the church in Rome; its influence increased with the position of the pope, the bishop of Rome. For the Roman Catholic Church the Vulgate is still the official text of the Scriptures.

Bible, English editions of   For a long time the Latin translation (Vulgate) of the Bible was the dominant Bible version of the church in the West (see BIBLE, EARLY TRANSLATIONS OF). The arrival of the Renaissance at the end of the Middle Ages led to two developments: a return to the Bible in the original languages Hebrew and Greek, and a desire to translate the Bible into the languages of the people. The first attempts at English translations were made by scholars such as John Wycliffe (died 1384); William Tyndale, who finished his in 1526; and Miles Coverdale, who in 1539 produced the Great Bible.

All previous versions were outclassed by the translation first published in 1611, which became known as Authorized (King James) Version (AV). It was the work of a large group of translators, and its literary quality was such that it had a formative influence on the English language. Until far into the 19th century it was the undisputed standard.

After several attempts at new translations by individual scholars, the year 1885 saw the publication in England of the Revised Version (RV), based on the latest state of research into the manuscripts that had effectively begun earlier in the nineteenth century. In the United States the RV was adapted to become the American Standard Version (ASV) (1901). Neither was ever very popular, and both were succeeded in 1952 by the Revised Standard Version, which in turn was followed by the New Revised Standard Version (American 1989, Anglicized version 1995). A still popular successor to the ASV as a literal translation is the New American Standard Bible (NASB, 1961; revised 1995).

The most popular version of the Bible in English is currently the New International Version (1978), and its non-gender-specific variant Today's New International Version (TNIV). These two are less literal renderings of the original texts than the NRSV. This makes for easier reading but hinders study of words, concepts, and structures. Still more free renderings are the New English Bible (1970, followed by the Revised English Bible) and the Good News Bible (1976). On the other hand, advocates of the Authorized (King James) Version have produced the New King James Version (1982), which maintains many of the characteristics of the original.

In addition to translations, which are more or less literal (see TRANSLATION THEORIES), an increasing number of "dynamic translations" or paraphrases has appeared on the market. Their value for the reader is that they appeal more easily to people unfamiliar with the Bible and its world, and the characteristic that text and message can to some extent be contextualized. The disadvantage is that the maker's interpretation can dominate the original text and that study of words and concepts becomes impossible. A well-known paraphrase of the previous generation was The Living Bible (1971); a recent best seller is Eugene Peterson's *The Message*, which was completed in 2002.

The current generation sees a proliferation of translations and paraphrases that cannot be enumerated here. In contrast to this plethora of different translations into English, many ethnic groups all over the world still do not even have one translation in their own language.

It is important to emphasize that professional new translations are never just based on previous versions but on a fresh study of the original Hebrew and Greek texts.

Bible, languages of The Bible is largely written in two languages: The Hebrew Bible is in Hebrew, the New Testament in Greek. However, small parts of the Hebrew Bible are in Aramaic (Ezra 4:8–6:18 and 7:12–26; Daniel 2:4–7:28; Jeremiah 10:11).

Hebrew and Aramaic are closely related Semitic languages that are written from right to left in a script different from the Latin alphabet. In fact, in biblical times an older type of script was used for Hebrew, which was later replaced by the Aramaic script. In both languages only the 22 consonants are written, and the reader has to add the appropriate vowels. After the completion of the Hebrew Bible, Jewish scribes, the Masoretes, edited the text and added vowel signs for convenience. The Hebrew of the later rabbis and the Ivrit of modern Israel are developed from ancient Classical Hebrew. The Septuagint is a version of the Hebrew Bible in Greek (see BIBLE, EARLY TRANSLATIONS OF).

As the Hebrew Bible is by far the longest text we have in ancient Hebrew, there are uncertainties about the meaning of rare words. Sometimes comparison with related languages like Akkadian, Ugaritic, or Arabic, or with the Septuagint, sheds light on such cases.

In contrast, we have numerous texts in ancient Greek so that the New Testament is only a very small part of all literature in Greek. The New Testament is written in the language of the Hellenistic period (see CULTURES OF THE BIBLE), also known as Koinē or Hellenistic Greek, which is a relatively late form of the Classical Greek, an Indo-European language used by authors such as Homer, Plato, and Aristotle. Koinē Greek was the world language of

New Testament times. Modern Greek has evolved much further. Greek is written from left to right in an alphabet that differs not much from our own Latin alphabet. The first and last letters are *alpha* and *omega* (Revelation 1:8; 21:6; 22:13); most of the 24 Greek letters are used as symbols in physics.

Note that no part of the Bible was written in Latin; it was due to the dominant position of the church of Rome that Latin became the language of the medieval church and the Latin translation the official Bible of the Roman Catholic Church.

See also BIBLE, ENGLISH EDITIONS OF; GENRES, BIBLICAL; MANUSCRIPTS.

Canaan See HOLY LAND.

Canaan, conquest of According to the Genesis narrative, God promises the PATRIARCHS that their descendants will inhabit the land of Canaan. This promise is fulfilled when the people of Israel conquer the HOLY LAND after the EXODUS from Egypt and 40 years of wilderness wandering.

Under the leadership of MOSES, the Israelites first conquer the sparsely populated eastern Jordan region, preparing for the attack on the Canaanite heartland. Then Moses dies, and Joshua is appointed as his successor. Under his leadership, the people cross the Jordan and defeat JERICHO. Then they move farther west, splitting the heartland into a northern and a southern part, which are then taken one after the other. After that, the land is distributed to the 12 tribes. However, the former inhabitants of Canaan are only partly driven out. This leads to conflicts lasting for centuries, during the time of the judges (see JUDGES, PERIOD OF).

For the dating of the conquest, scholars propose two different dates: either around 1400 B.C.E., relying on a literal understanding of numbers given in the biblical text (especially 1 Kings 6:1), or the middle of the 13th century: Archaeological excavations produced evidence that several cities in the central area of Canaan were destroyed in the middle or near the end of the 13th century, which could be brought into relationship with Joshua's campaigns.

The conquest of Canaan is described as a holy war (the only one in the Bible). The Canaanites are said to be driven out because of their wickedness. For a detailed discussion of this issue, see JOSHUA in Part II.

canon See FORMATION OF THE CANON: THE HEBREW BIBLE; FORMATION OF THE CANON: THE NEW TESTAMENT.

captivity See EXILE, THE.

chapters and verses Most biblical books are divided into chapters. Each chapter is further divided into "verses," which roughly equate to sentences in the Hebrew and Greek originals. This system was invented for easier referencing. For example, Matthew 5:1 refers to the book of Matthew, chapter 5, verse 1. The system developed in medieval times and is therefore not original to the texts. Regarding the verses in the Hebrew Bible, however, the medieval numbering follows an older Jewish system of verse divisions.

The chapter divisions were made for practical purposes mostly and do not always reflect the inner literary organization of a book. For example, in the creation account, the first chapter of Genesis ends after the sixth day, putting the seventh and last day of the account into a new chapter. From a literary point of view, the "chapter" should end after Genesis 2:3.

Concerning the Hebrew Bible, there are some discrepancies between the verse numbering of the Hebrew and modern English versions. For example, in many psalms the superscriptions are counted as verse 1 in the Hebrew but are left uncounted in the English translations, making all following verse numbers be shifted by 1 (what is verse 1 in the English, is verse 2 in the Hebrew, etc.). Another example: Malachi 4:1–6 is counted as 3:19–24 in the Hebrew Bible. Many of these differences already go back to differences in the older Hebrew, Greek, and Latin traditions (see BIBLE, EARLY TRANSLATIONS OF).

In total, the Hebrew Bible has 929 chapters, the New Testament 260. The number of verses in the Hebrew Bible is 23,145 and in the New Testament, 7,957.

chiastic structure See STRUCTURES, LITERARY.

chosen people   In the Hebrew Bible, the expression *chosen people* (Isaiah 65:9) is based on the role of the nation of Israel in God's plan with the world (e.g., Deuteronomy 7:6; 14:2). Israel was meant to be God's model people, so as to be a blessing to the world. In the New Testament the expression is basic to the self-understanding of the Church, which thought of itself as consisting of Jews and Gentiles and as being called to proclaim the mighty deeds of God (Colossians 3:12; cf. 1 Peter 2:4, 9). God took the initiative in calling people to believe in him before they ever thought of him, as described in Ephesians 1.

Christianity   Christianity, like Judaism and Islam, is a monotheistic religion, that is, it believes in only one God, who is the creator of the universe (see GOD). It began with Jesus of Nazareth in the first century C.E. and is seen by its adherents as the natural successor to Judaism. Its main distinctive feature is that it believes that Jesus is the mediator between humanity and God and that he is the Savior of the world, being completely divine and yet also fully human. Other core beliefs are that Jesus died by crucifixion but rose from the dead. His death is regarded as the means of restoring the broken relationship between God and humanity caused by the sin of humanity.

For Christianity, the Bible is the single most important book. Whereas Judaism recognizes (only) the Hebrew Bible as God's revelation, Christians also regard the New Testament as inspired Scripture. Yet Christianity is about belief in God, not in a book; the Bible is merely seen as important insofar as it speaks about God and his self-revelation in history and nature. Christians typically meet on Sundays, usually in purpose-built buildings called churches or chapels. They often sing and pray together and listen to an explanation and application of the Bible. Their main rituals are BAPTISM and the LORD'S SUPPER, which is also called communion.

Followers of Jesus were called Christians by outsiders (Acts 11:26; cf. 1 Peter 4:16); however, the word *Christianity* is not found in the Bible. It appears from the early second century onward. Christianity is now the largest religion on earth, with some 2 billion adherents, living in almost every country. As do all major religions, Christianity includes a variety of different groups, the main ones being the Roman Catholics, Orthodox, and Protestants. Protestants are themselves divided into further subgroups, such as Anglicans, Methodists, Baptists, Reformed, and Pentecostals. See also JESUS CHRIST.

church   The totality of the followers of Jesus Christ, whether seen as a worldwide body or as a local manifestation of it. As such it does not yet occur in the Hebrew Bible, where Israel is the people of God. All 27 documents that make up the New Testament are, directly or indirectly, addressed to the church with the intention to inform, build, instruct, and rebuke it.

In the New Testament, the word *church* (Greek *ekklēsia*) is used in both meanings, worldwide and local, but it never refers to a building and in fact the earliest Christians met in private homes. In the Gospels the word occurs only twice (Matthew 16:18 and 18:17), but it is frequent in Acts and the epistles. However, many other telling words and expressions are used to refer to the Christian church, such as "God's beloved" (Romans 1:7), "brothers and sisters" (Romans 7:1), "those who are in Christ Jesus" (Romans 8:1), "the saints" (Ephesians 1:1), "the body of Christ" (1 Corinthians 12:12–26), "God's own people" (1 Peter 2:9–10), "temple" (1 Corinthians 3:16–17), "flock" or "herd" (1 Peter 5:1–4), "the bride of Christ" (Revelation 19:7; 21:9), and "priesthood" (Revelation 1:6; 5:10). Each of these carries its own connotations and implications for the behavior of the believers.

In the New Testament relatively little attention is paid to church leadership and leadership structures. For example, in Acts 20 the words *elders, overseers* (Greek *episkopoi,* which evolved into "bishops"), and *shepherds* are used for the same group of people. One point is clear, however: Jesus Christ is seen both as the founder and as the leader of the church, and he exercises the latter through the presence of the Holy Spirit. As his authorized witnesses, the apostles have leading roles.

The most important local churches in the New Testament period are those in Jerusalem and Antioch.

concentric structures   See STRUCTURES, LITERARY.

covenant   In the Hebrew Bible, the relationship between God and human beings is often expressed in the form of covenants. The most important of the covenants is the Sinai covenant, in which God makes Israel his chosen people, giving them the LAW (see especially Exodus 19:4–6). The Sinai covenant is based on the covenant made with the PATRIARCHS (Genesis 12:1–3 and others) and is later somewhat extended by the covenant with DAVID (2 Samuel 7). The Sinai describes the basic relationship between God and his people and defines laws and covenant duties for both sides. All the other books of the Hebrew Bible are more or less based on this covenant structure. Therefore, the Sinaitic covenant contained in the PENTATEUCH forms the core of the Hebrew Bible religion.

Apart from the covenants made with Israel, there is also a covenant relating to all nations and even to the animals: the covenant made with Noah after THE FLOOD (Genesis 9).

Jesus Christ is said to have established a "new covenant" in his blood, i.e., by sacrificing himself, paying for the sins of the people (Luke 22:20; 1 Corinthians 11:25; Hebrews 9:15). Therefore, Christians call the Hebrew Bible covenant the "old" covenant. However, the new covenant does not just replace the old but also "fulfills" it (Matthew 5:17; see NEW TESTAMENT, RELATIONSHIP WITH THE HEBREW BIBLE). In the course of time, the expressions *old covenant* and *new covenant* changed to *Old Testament* and *New Testament* via the Latin language.

creation   According to the Bible, the world has neither originated from a battle of gods—as was believed in the time of writing the Bible—nor via the processes of physical sciences—as is believed today. Rather, in the way described by the biblical authors, it has come into existence by the will of a transcendent, almighty God.

Genesis 1–3 records that in the beginning God created the world. Other passages enhance the image by describing creation as an ongoing process, e.g., Psalm 104:28–30. Furthermore, creation is sometimes described as a transformation from chaos to cosmos (especially Genesis 1); other passages convey the notion of creation out of nothing, e.g., Psalm 33:6, 9; Hebrews 11:3. The purpose of creation is that animals as well as human beings find their place for living. The creation also witnesses to the power and wisdom of God (see especially Job 38–41).

Human beings themselves are God's creatures. They can only fully find their true selves when they become conscious of their role as creatures and as the creator's counterparts. God ordains human beings to multiply, fill the earth, cultivate, and keep the land. The statement of Genesis 1:26–27 that humanity is made "in the image of God" includes the task of ruling the earth as God's deputy.

Did God create the world in six days? Christian groups called creationists believe this, basing their belief on a literal interpretation of the creation account in Genesis 1. Other groups make room for different ideas, such as the big bang and evolutionist models, but hold that creation evolved not by chance but by design. Others again leave the "how" of creation fully to the sciences and only explain the "why" from biblical texts. Independent of the particular approach, however, the belief in a Creator means a fundamental shift of perspective in contrast to a worldview depending only on laws of nature.

Important biblical passages on the subject: Genesis 1–3; Job 38–41; Psalms 8; 19; 104; 139:13–16; Romans 1:18–23; Colossians 1:15–17.

cultures of the Bible   The authors of the books of the Bible did not live in a cultural vacuum but in the leading cultures of their time. The Hebrew Bible originated in a world that was dominated by the cultures of EGYPT and Mesopotamia (modern Iraq). The Egyptian civilization predates that of ancient Israel, and it existed all during the period of the Hebrew Bible with great continuity. Among its important literary achievements is the Book of the Dead, an extensive guide for the afterlife. Egypt's religion was characterized by the worship of a multitude of gods, many of them in animal form. Early on Israel had close relations with Egypt, which are reflected in Genesis and Exodus, but throughout the period of the Hebrew Bible the two neighbor nations remained in contact.

To the other side of Israel the cultural heartland was Mesopotamia, where the period of the Hebrew Bible saw a succession of civilizations: Sumerians,

Akkadians, Babylonians (see BABYLON), and Assyrians (see ASSYRIA). Toward the end of the period the Persian culture (see PERSIA) became dominant and with it the Aramaic language. Some of these cultures had stories about the CREATION of the world and about a great flood that have both similarities with and differences from the stories in Genesis. The laws of the Babylonian king Hammurabi bear comparison to the laws given to Moses, which are roughly contemporary.

When the Israelites settled down in the HOLY LAND, they encountered the existing Canaanite cultures, which were characterized by life in cities and by the worship of fertility gods and goddesses such as Baal. As Israel also depended on rain and sun for its agriculture, these forms of worship proved very attractive to them. The PHILISTINES, who arrived in the region at roughly the same time as Israel, had a superior material culture that enabled them to dominate Israel for a while. Israel's own culture flourished during the reigns of David (see the books of Samuel) and Solomon (see the books of Chronicles), and again under the kings of the eighth century B.C.E. It was characterized by the prohibition of divine images, which came to be interpreted as the prohibition of images as such. The Hebrew Bible is by far the most important product of the Israelite culture.

The conquest of the entire Middle East by Alexander the Great in the fourth century B.C.E. resulted in the culture of Hellenism, a mixture of oriental and Greek civilizations. The later rise of the Roman Empire produced little cultural change as culturally the Romans were dependent on the Greeks. However, Hellenism was often confined to the cities, as the countryside was more conservative. Hellenism introduced theaters, rhetoric, and sport to Israel; the apostle PAUL uses illustrations from sport several times. Another effect was the use of the Greek language across the civilized world and in Israel; hence the fact that the New Testament was written in Greek.

It was Greek-speaking Jews who first took the message of Jesus outside Israel (Acts 8), and Greek became the first language of the church. The books of the New Testament, with the exception of Revelation, roughly fit within Hellenistic descriptions of genre (see GENRES, BIBLICAL), with Luke writing Hellenistic-style prefaces.

Whereas the Jewish scheme of thinking is more horizontal, in terms of this world and the world to come, the Greek/Hellenistic scheme tends to be more vertical: heavenly versus earthly and light versus darkness. We also find this way of thinking in the DEAD SEA SCROLLS.

In the New Testament era, the official religion of the Roman Empire was used to promote loyalty to the emperor and the state. Among the popular philosophies of the time were Stoicism and Epicurism, which occur in Acts 17.

David   Most important king of Israel, descending from the tribe of JUDAH and reigning from about 1010 to 971 B.C.E. Among his military achievements are conquering the strategically important town of JERUSALEM, which he made Israel's capital, and permanently freeing Israel from the threat of the PHILISTINES. God promises to make his dynasty everlasting. The books of Samuel provide us with numerous details, positive and negative, from his life. Among the latter are the adultery with Bathsheba and the contract killing of her husband. But since David truly repents his sins, God continues being with him. Later, David becomes an example or type (see TYPES) of the ideal king. Particularly after the destruction of the Israelite kingdom by the Babylonians (see BABYLON), the prophets begin announcing a future savior king who is a descendant of David.

The New Testament sees these expectations fulfilled in JESUS CHRIST (see Matthew 1:1). This line of thinking is also reflected in terminology: In Israel, kings were appointed by anointing them with oil. The Hebrew word for the anointed one is *mashiach*, "Messiah"; the Greek word is *christos*, "Christ." For the historical David, see also 1 and 2 Samuel and 1 and 2 Chronicles in Part II.

Dead Sea   The body of water, known in Hebrew as the Salt Sea, that forms the southernmost part of the rift valley that runs down the eastern border of Israel and Palestine and forms the course of the River Jordan. The Jordan empties into it. It is some 1,378 feet (420 meters) below sea level, making its shores the lowest dry land on earth. At present, its size is shrinking, being now some 42 miles (67 kilometers) long and 11 miles (17.5 kilometers) at its widest. It is 30 percent saline, as no water flows out of it, but there is constant evaporation.

In biblical times, it formed the southeastern border between Israel and Moab and Edom. Because it is a wilderness area, little is recorded of its history. The "cities of the plain" including Sodom and Gomorrah were nearby, perhaps even now under its waters (Genesis 19:24–29; Deuteronomy 29:23). It was the site of an ancient battle (Genesis 14:3) when it was known as the Valley of Siddim. David sought refuge at En-gedi (1 Samuel 24:1), in roughly the area of Qumran, where the DEAD SEA SCROLLS were found in the middle of the last century.

Ezekiel 47 and Zechariah 14:8 see a much more fertile future for the area, though Ezekiel is careful to reserve an area for salt, as one of life's essential ingredients.

Dead Sea Scrolls   Ten miles (15 kilometers) south of Jericho, on mountain slopes near the DEAD SEA, are situated the so-called caves of Qumran. When the Romans approached that area in 70 C.E., a Jewish community living nearby hid all their scriptures—more than 800 scrolls—in these caves. From that time the scrolls stayed unspoiled until they were rediscovered in 1947. The Dead Sea Scrolls are the most important archaeological discovery of all times relating to the transmission of the Bible.

In the caves, manuscripts of virtually all books of the Hebrew Bible have been found. However, only small fragments are extant of some of the manuscripts. One scroll especially has become famous; it is a complete scroll of the book of Isaiah, 22 feet (seven meters) in length, originating from about 300–100 B.C.E. Scholars compared the text with the oldest manuscripts known up to that time (from the 10th century C.E.) and were able to verify that the biblical text had been transmitted very accurately—the texts, separated by a millennium from each other, are practically identical.

Interestingly, different versions of the biblical texts were found in the caves. One group of texts corresponds to the later official Jewish tradition; another group turned out to be the Hebrew basis on which some Septuagint texts were translated

(see BIBLE, EARLY TRANSLATIONS OF); still another group of texts is written in a simplified style and grammar. However, there are no important deviations with regard to content.

Nonbiblical texts have also been found at Qumran. Many of them probably originate from the Jewish community itself. It can be inferred from them that the Qumran people were a Jewish sect standing in relationship to the Essenes movement but separate from them.

Decalogue   See TEN COMMANDMENTS.

deliverance   Deliverance is one of the central biblical images that denote salvation. Others are redemption and healing. Various Bible translations employ a variety of terms to cover the concept, including *being saved*, *victory*, and *release*. In English, the word also has the meaning of "handing over to," but this is not discussed here.

The great model of deliverance in the Hebrew Bible is that of the Israelites from EGYPT. That occurred in two parts: the PASSOVER (Exodus 12:27) and the crossing of the Red Sea (see RED SEA, CROSSING) (Exodus 18:10). A parallel deliverance is seen in the RETURN FROM EXILE (Jeremiah 32:21, 36–44). Deliverance can be from calamities (Genesis 45:7), enemies (1 Chronicles 11:14, and famously Esther 4:14), evil men (Psalm 82:4), even false prophets (Ezekiel 13:21, 23). Ultimately, God is the deliverer, as the exchange in Isaiah 36:20 and 37:20, 36 establishes. Only God can deliver in this miraculous way, as Daniel 3:29 points up also. But often he delivers salvation through a human agency, such as Gideon (Judges 7:7), however unlikely the person might seem.

The ultimate deliverance is from death (Job 33:28; Psalm 22:20; 33:19, etc.). In the New Testament, the prayer is to "deliver us from evil" (Matthew 6:13). Specific miraculous rescues are not unknown, for example, from prison (Acts 12:1–18; 16:25–34), but are subordinate to spiritual deliverance from evil, as well as the law and the insistence on salvation by works (Romans 7:6). The modern use of *deliverance* to mean a specific releasing from evil spirits or demonization is not used in the Bible.

See also SALVATION.

denunciations See WOES AND DENUNCIATIONS.

devil, the See SATAN.

diaspora A Greek word meaning "dispersion, scattering," which denotes the fact that many Jews did not and do not live in the land of Israel.

When the Jews were allowed to return home from the EXILE in BABYLON in 539/8 B.C.E. (see RETURN FROM EXILE), the majority probably stayed behind, and there continued to be a large Jewish community in Babylon in New Testament times and beyond. Others settled in other parts of the Middle East such as EGYPT and Asia Minor (see also INTERTESTAMENTAL PERIOD). From the sixth to the fourth century B.C.E. there was a Jewish colony in Elephantine, an island in the RIVER NILE near modern Aswan in Egypt. A sizable Jewish community lived in Alexandria, the capital city of Egypt.

In New Testament times, thanks to the peace and the expansion of trade under the Roman Empire, Jewish craftsmen and merchants left Israel and settled in ports and cities. Aquila and Priscilla had left Pontus for Rome and then for Corinth (Acts 18:1–2). It is estimated that in New Testament times about two-thirds of the Jews, some 5 million, lived outside Israel. Some of them were Roman citizens (Acts 22:25–28).

The SYNAGOGUE was the center of the Jewish community in the diaspora (cf. Acts 16:13). The links with Jerusalem were generally maintained because many Jews from the diaspora attended the three annual festivals and paid the temple tax. Jews in the diaspora were generally Greek-speaking, whereas the Jews in Israel would speak Aramaic with Greek as a second language for many.

disciples See TWELVE DISCIPLES.

documents Writings that have official, permanent, and binding significance, which have to be recorded and preserved as part of their status. In the Bible, there are references to and examples of legal, official, ritual, and COVENANT formulations in written form. In fact, throughout the ancient Middle East, empires became increasingly dependent on documents to carry on their everyday busi-

ness. One of the most famous of such documents is the Code of Hammurabi, a new codification of Babylonian law compiled by King Hammurabi (ca. 1792–1750 B.C.E.). It contains 282 laws carved in stone. Jeremiah 32:44 is an excellent example of a land transaction, complete with title deeds, seal, and witnesses.

A very good set of documents recorded in the Hebrew Bible is contained in Ezra-Nehemiah. Half the text is documentation: from census and genealogical documents (Ezra 2:2–62; 8:1–14; Nehemiah 7:5–69), to inventories (Ezra 1:9), royal edicts (Ezra 1:2–4; 6:1–12), official letters (Ezra 4:6–16, 17–23; 5:6–17; 7:11–26; Nehemiah 2:7, 9; 6:5–8), and the book of the Mosaic Law (Nehemiah 8:5, 13–18; 13:1f.). All the paraphernalia of documents are described, from scribes (Ezra 4:17–23) to details of original languages, archives, and archival research (Ezra 5:6–17; 6:1–12). Clearly the Persian Empire was bureaucratically very sophisticated in its documentation. The whole of Ezra-Nehemiah is self-consciously written as a historical document.

The Mosaic covenant document, recorded in Exodus 19–24 and Deuteronomy 5ff., was particularly important (see SINAI, MOUNT). The setting in tablets of stone of the TEN COMMANDMENTS emphasized their permanence, and each copy of the Mosaic Law was a solemn document read with care (as Exodus 24:7; 34:28; Deuteronomy 29:21; Joshua 24:25–26; 2 Kings 23:2, 21). Similar formulations have been found throughout documents in the Middle East. For example, second-millennium B.C.E. vassal treaties from the Hittite Empire contain the same six elements as the Sinaitic covenant: a preamble, historical introduction, the agreement itself, blessings and cursings for keeping or breaking it, witnesses, and provisions for depositing the document together with regular public readings.

The sealing of documents gave them their ultimate legitimacy, as in 1 Kings 21:8–10. In the Bible the term *seal* takes on figurative force, as in John 3:33; Romans 4:11; 1 Corinthians 9:2; 2 Timothy 2:19. In APOCALYPTIC WRITING, the idea of sealing the future means it is as assured as any sealed document on history (see Daniel 9:24; 12:4; Revelation 5:1–5; 6:5–9; 8:1; 9:4; 20:3). Just as the term *sealing* became metaphoric and symbolic, so did the very idea of writing a document. Jeremiah 31:33 talks of writing the law "on their hearts," and this is taken up in the New Testament (Hebrews 8:10; Romans 2:15; 2 Corinthians 3:2).

early church   The history of the Christian Church begins with the coming of the Holy Spirit at Pentecost (Acts 2; 30 or 33 C.E.). The transition from early church to medieval church was gradual, but scholars use the term *early church* for the period until at least Augustine of Hippo (died 430). By that time the canon of the Bible had been closed, and the number of Christians with a pagan background far exceeded that of Jewish Christians.

The first century C.E. was the period when the books of the New Testament were written and preserved. Our main source for events up to the year 62 C.E. is Acts of the Apostles; for later events the *Church History* of Eusebius of Caesarea (early fourth century) is useful. For the church in Israel the Jewish war that resulted in the destruction of Jerusalem in 70 C.E. was traumatic, but the church elsewhere was hardly affected. Our knowledge of the second century is quite sketchy. By the year 180 we see the contours of the canon of the New Testament in the writings of the church father Irenaeus.

Initially the spread of Christianity was slow and largely limited to Jews in Israel and in the DIASPORA. Acts 8 and 9 show spontaneous growth even in cities such as Damascus. A notable acceleration took place when PAUL began to make missionary trips in 47 C.E. (Acts 13). From then on the percentage of Christians from a pagan background must have increased rapidly. Nothing is known about how the Christian message reached countries such as EGYPT and PERSIA. For centuries growth through conversion far outnumbered growth through birth. The egalitarian message of Christianity was especially attractive for women and for the lower classes. Even so, by the year 300 the church was still largely limited to the Middle East and countries around the Mediterranean Sea.

Initially, persecution came from Jews who did not accept Jesus as their Messiah (e.g., Acts 7). Emperor Nero was the first Roman official to kill Christians for their faith after the fire of Rome in 64 C.E., but systematic persecution only began in

the third century. This did not hinder the growth of the church, however, for in the words of the church father Tertullian "the blood of the martyrs was the seed of the church." The same Tertullian (ca. 200) also noted that the outsider said about Christians, "See how they love one another," which must have added to the attractiveness. The conversion of the emperor Constantine (313) started off a process that led to the church's becoming the religion of the state.

From the very beginning there were wrong ideas that threatened the "orthodox" teaching of the apostles and their successors, as can be seen, e.g., in Colossians 2; 1 John; and Jude. In this sense there never was an ideal golden age of the church. In the second and third centuries the heresy of Gnosticism was a great danger to the church.

As far as we can see, initially there were various leadership structures side by side: In Jerusalem the apostles were in control, followed by James and other elders (Acts 21:18); in his letters to the Corinthians Paul mentions no leaders at all, and the same is true of 1 John; in Philippians 1:1 Paul refers to "overseers and deacons," and in 1 Timothy he gives criteria for such officials. In the second century the role of the overseer or bishop (Greek *episkopos*) gradually developed into a position of single leadership. Leading cities were Jerusalem, Antioch, Alexandria, and Rome. Initially, the believers met in houses or in rented halls; the earliest known church buildings date from the third century.

See also FORMATION OF THE CANON: THE NEW TESTAMENT; ROME.

edition, editor   See REDACTION.

Egypt   Israel's neighbor to the southwest during the whole period of biblical history. From before 3000 B.C.E. it was a highly civilized country, ruled by kings whose title was *Pharaoh*. ABRAHAM had already traveled to Egypt, and his great-grandson, Joseph, who had been sold to Egypt as a slave, became the country's second in command in charge of food supplies. As a result, Joseph's father, JACOB, settled there with all his descendants, the first Israelites. The book of Exodus describes the persecution and the difficult departure of a later generation of Israelites from Egypt under the leadership of MOSES, on which occasion the pharaoh and his army drowned. The later parts of the Hebrew Bible contain numerous references to this core moment of freedom from servitude.

In the subsequent period there was little contact between Israel and Egypt, but under King Rehoboam of Judah, Pharaoh Shishak invaded and plundered the temple (1 Kings 14:25–26). Some 300 years later Pharaoh Neco killed Judah's king, Josiah, when he interfered in his affairs (2 Kings 23:29). Prophets such as Isaiah warned the Israelites not to form an alliance with Egypt against enemies on the other side of the country, such as ASSYRIA and BABYLON (e.g., Isaiah 30:1–7). After the destruction of Jerusalem in 586 B.C.E, many Israelites fled to Egypt and took the prophet Jeremiah with them. There was a large Jewish population in the country ever after, particularly in the then-capital city of Alexandria (see DIASPORA; 1, 2, 3, and 4 Maccabees in Part II).

In the New Testament the role of Egypt (now part of the Roman Empire) is much smaller. Apart from the temporary stay of Jesus and his parents in Egypt (Matthew 2:13–21), there are just allusions to the narratives in the Hebrew Bible. The early church grew in Egypt, and Alexandria became a major Christian city. The descendants of these early Christians are to be found in the Coptic Church.

Thanks to the dry climate, in our time Egypt is the only region where ancient manuscripts, among them biblical texts, that have survived the centuries in good condition are found.

See BIBLE, EARLY TRANSLATIONS OF; CULTURES OF THE BIBLE; EXODUS, THE; HOLY LAND.

election See CHOSEN PEOPLE.

Elijah Prophet in the northern kingdom of Israel at the time of King Ahab (time of reign 874–853 B.C.E.). Elijah personifies the fight for God and against Baal. He not only proclaims the word of God, as most of the other prophets do, but also performs several signs and wonders on God's behalf—a tradition carried on by his successor, Elisha. At the end of his life, he ascends into heaven. Therefore, in later writing, Elijah becomes a symbol and

type of powerful prophecy. Malachi 4:5 predicts that he will return to prepare the people for the coming of the Lord. In the New Testament, JOHN THE BAPTIST is said to have spoken "with the spirit and power of Elijah" (Luke 1:17). Also, on the Mount of Transfiguration, Elijah appears together with Moses (Matthew 17). See also 1 and 2 Kings in Part II.

epistle The Latin word *epistola* means "letter." The term is used in the Bible to refer to those books in the New Testament written in letter form: 21 of the 27. Letters are common to all literate cultures. Most do not attain literary status, however. Those that do have particular historical significance, or are written by important people, or are found by chance in archaeological digs or musty libraries.

In the Hebrew Bible, references to letters date back to Davidic times. Fateful battle instructions (2 Samuel 11:14–15), official letters between kings (2 Kings 5:5; Isaiah 37:14; 39:1), and other official business of the state, as in Ezra-Nehemiah and Esther. But the book of Jeremiah contains a series of letters between Jerusalem and the exiles in Babylon (Jeremiah 29), which anticipates some of the New Testament letters, containing religious advice and debate.

The Acts of the Apostles mentions similar letters, including official business (Acts 23:33–34), but also church business (Acts 15:23–29), where the Council of Jerusalem make known their decisions. The majority of the other letters of the EARLY CHURCH are epistles written by Paul. He takes the typical structures of Greek, Roman, and Jewish letter writing to form a new sort of letter capable of personal expressions of friendship and concern, theological treatise and debate, and instructions on moral behavior. Each letter begins with a salutation, combining the Greek greeting of "grace" (*charis*) and the Hebrew "peace" (*shalom*); then his message, both personal, theological, and moral; then further greetings and commendations; concluding with his signature. All were probably dictated to a trained scribe. Sometimes we know the bearer of the letter. The supposition is that the letters will be read publicly in a specific church, since the concerns and needs of that church have been addressed. There is often a sense that Paul would prefer presence to epistle.

Other epistles in the New Testament were written by Peter, James, Jude, and John, but the recipients are not always so clearly indicated. The writer to Hebrews does not include an opening salutation—only at the end does it appear it is a letter at all. In Revelation, the letters become angelic messages, and we see the form moving in a more obviously literary direction.

eschatology   See LAST THINGS.

ethics   Ethics are a reflection on what a good life is, how one should live, and what one should (or should not) do. In the Bible, these issues are often at the heart of the message. The belief in God as the creator of the earth (see CREATION) makes him its owner and humans his subservient tenants or stewards; likewise, the belief that God created humankind implies that he knows what is good for them and can instruct them accordingly (see LAW).

In the Hebrew Bible, the TEN COMMANDMENTS are the summary of God's ethical guidance. In the New Testament the Sermon on the Mount (Matthew 5–7) and Jesus' summary of the law as "love for God and the neighbor" (Matthew 22:34–40) have the same role. By extension, in the Hebrew Bible the whole Pentateuch is God's foundational guidance for life, which the prophets apply to ever-changing circumstances. In several of Paul's letters (e.g., Romans) the second half consists of ethical guidance, while other letters such as James are almost wholly ethical. In many places JESUS CHRIST is presented as an example for his followers, in particular in 1 John. Particularly difficult ethical areas are sexuality and money and possessions; on the first, Proverbs has much to say; on the second, Luke and James. One frequent New Testament position is that God's people are no more than resident aliens on earth (see PILGRIMS AND WANDERERS), so they should not "store up treasures for themselves" (Luke 12:21). Not everything in the Bible is countercultural, however. A major concern of Paul and Peter is that Christians should not unnecessarily stand out negatively from their fellow humans. The two adopted and edited conventional lists of sound advice; see, e.g., Ephesians 5:21–6:9; Colossians 3:18–4:1; and 1 Peter 2:13–3:7.

See CHOSEN PEOPLE; HOLINESS; SABBATH.

Euphrates, River   The longest river in western Asia, which rises in Turkey and flows through Syria before entering Iraq, where it flows out to sea in the Persian Gulf near Basra. It is the more southerly of the two rivers that provide the Fertile Crescent with its water, the other being the River Tigris. Mythically, it arose in the Garden of Eden (Genesis 2:14) with the River Tigris, hence its being seen as the source of civilization.

It is along this fertile crescent that Abraham left Ur to journey to Canaan, later to be called Israel. The main civilizations of Bible times that benefited from its waters were the Babylonians, Sumerians, and Chaldeans. Babylon was built on the river, though changes in its course have left its site inland, south of modern-day Baghdad. The Assyrian Empire (see ASSYRIA), though centered on the Tigris, also used its waters.

The river marked the farthest extent of the Promised Land (Deuteronomy 11:24), which was realized under King David (2 Samuel 8:3; 1 Chronicles 18:3) just after 1000 B.C.E. It then marked the northern boundary of Egyptian suzerainty (2 Kings 24:7), until the battle of Carchemish (a fortress city in its northerly section) in 605 B.C.E. returned control to the Babylonians (Jeremiah 46:2).

The river also symbolized the boundary of the Jewish exile. Psalm 137 records the lament of the exiles along the river.

In the New Testament, the name is used in APOCALYPTIC WRITING to denote the boundaries of evil empire in the spiritual warfare between good and evil forces (Revelation 9:14; 16:12).

See also BABYLON; EXILE.

Eve   See ADAM AND EVE.

exile   The forced removal from homeland, as deportees or refugees, as opposed to sojourning or voluntary travel abroad, however long the period. Although the term is not used as such in the Bible, Israel had the experience of it deeply etched into its national psyche.

The first time Israel had to face such a catastrophe occurred when the Assyrians conquered the northern kingdom of Israel in 722 B.C.E. and deported many people, none of whom, as far as we know, ever returned. The Babylonian exile had three stages, the first after the siege of JERUSALEM in 597 B.C.E., when it seems likely the prophets Ezekiel and Daniel were taken. The second and main deportation occurred after the second siege and final sacking of Jerusalem in 586 B.C.E. A third deportation occurred after sporadic resistance, around 581 B.C.E. The exile lasted till Babylonia fell to the Persians under Cyrus in 539 B.C.E.

The Babylonian exile had been prophesied as punishment for Israel's idolatry, injustice, and empty religion (e.g., Isaiah 5:13; Jeremiah 13:19; Micah 1:16), just as the earlier Assyrian captivity had been (Hosea 9:3; Amos 5:5). The length and end of the exile were equally fully predicted (e.g., Hosea 11:11; Amos 9:14; Jeremiah 29:14; 51; Isaiah 45:13).

The exile provided an extremely formative period in Jewish thinking. The earlier exile experience is recorded in Daniel and Ezekiel, and the later Persian experience in Esther and several apocryphal works (see APOCRYPHA AND PSEUDEPIGRAPHA). The book of Lamentations records the grief felt over the exile, as does Psalm 137.

For the New Testament usage of the term, see PILGRIMS AND WANDERERS.

See also BABYLON; PERSIA; RETURN FROM EXILE.

Exodus, the According to the biblical narrative, the family of the PATRIARCHS settles in the Nile delta in EGYPT in approximately 1840 B.C.E. There they multiply and become a strong nation. However, the Egyptian pharaoh oppresses the people and subjects them to forced labor. God therefore appoints MOSES to lead the people out of Egypt. This act of deliverance turns out to be the first great demonstration of the power of God, including 10 plagues and the dividing of the Red Sea (see RED SEA, CROSSING). Therefore, in the Hebrew Bible, the Exodus forms the basis for trusting in God as the powerful liberator.

So far no firm evidence for the Exodus has been found in either Egypt or the HOLY LAND. However,

the experience of the Exodus of Egypt is so foundational to Israelite thinking and to the Hebrew Bible that many scholars assume that there must be at least some historical core to the story. In addition, unlike in the other ancient Near Eastern people groups, there were no class distinctions in Israelite society; this indirectly supports the Exodus narrative, according to which Israel came into being as a community of freed slaves. More generally, the fundamental biblical skepticism against human rule points in a similar direction.

For the dating of the Exodus of Egypt, scholars propose two different dates: either the 15th century B.C.E., relying on a literal understanding of numbers given in the biblical text (especially 1 Kings 6:1), or the 13th century, relying on certain interpretations of archaeological observations made in the country of Canaan (cities that were destroyed as a result of Israel's conquest of the land). For a more detailed discussion, see Exodus in Part II.

Fall, the According to biblical presentation, the world is God's CREATION. The creation is said to have been "very good" (Genesis 1:31) in the beginning. However, very soon human beings began to disobey God's good regulations. The prototype of SIN against God is the arrogant attempt to become like God (Genesis 3), and the prototype of sin against the brother is the fratricide of Abel by Cain (Genesis 4).

Probably no scene of the Bible is more famous than the one with the woman, the fruit, and the serpent. However, the origin of the serpent and, therefore, the origin of evil, are consciously concealed in the text. Nonetheless, it is clear that human sin distorts the order of creation. To the divine blessing (mentioned three times in Genesis 1:22, 1:28, and 2:3) the divine curse is added (three times in Genesis 3:14, 3:17, and 4:11). The results are, among others, the tasks of man and woman, to work at the field and to have children, respectively, are burdened with toil. The relationship between man and woman is distorted, the access to eternal life is blocked, the death penalty is introduced (Genesis 4:15); and animals may be killed for eating (Genesis 9:2–4). The Fall is the biblical answer

The fall of humanity (Genesis 3:1–6), engraving by Julius Schnorr von Carolsfeld

to the question of suffering in the world (for the suffering of the individual, see JOB in Part II).

The brokenness of creation is also treated in the New Testament (e.g., Romans 1:18–32; 8:18–24). The sin of Adam, which affects all humanity, is countered there by the redeeming act of Jesus Christ (Romans 5:12–21), with whom a new era of the world begins (Romans 8:23–24), finally leading to a total renewal of the creation (Revelation 21:1–5).

feasts   See HEBREW BIBLE, WORSHIP AND RITUAL.

Flood, the   Genesis 6–9 tells about an enormous flood that God sent to destroy the earth as a punish-

ment for the sins of humankind. Only eight people were saved in a large boat, the ark, including Noah, its builder. Also on board were representatives of all animals. Afterward God promised that such a radical punishment would never happen again.

The Flood is mentioned remarkably little in the rest of the Bible. In the New Testament it is an image of sudden disaster (Matthew 24:37–39) as well as a prefiguration of the end times (2 Peter 2:5; see LAST THINGS). In the difficult passage 1 Peter 3:20–22, the Flood is used as a symbol of Christian BAPTISM.

Many peoples around the world, e.g., in Mexico, tell stories about worldwide floods that wiped out ancient societies. The Sumerians and Babylonians of ancient Iraq (see CULTURES OF THE BIBLE) have left Flood stories that have interesting similarities with the biblical story, in the Epics of Gilgamesh and of Atrahasis, written between 2000 and 1500 B.C.E. The differences are numerous, however, so the biblical story is by no means only an imitation of those stories.

formation of the canon: the Hebrew Bible

The word *canon* refers to a fixed group of recognized books, in our case, the books of the Bible. The origins of the Hebrew Bible canon are shrouded in mystery. We have to rely on supposition, especially for the early stages of canonical development. Conservative scholars traditionally assumed that each of the biblical books was canonized shortly after its completion. After Malachi, the last book, had been written, the canon was closed, in about 400 to 350 B.C.E. Liberal, historical-critical scholarship for a long time assumed that the canon developed in three stages, according to the three parts of the Hebrew Bible, the "Law," the "Prophets," and the "Writings" (see Appendixes for a list of canonical books). The Law, according to this position, was canonized around 450 B.C.E., the Prophets about 200 B.C.E., and the scope of the Writings was finally fixed around 100 C.E.

Newer research in this area from the 1970s onward, however, draws a still different picture. Scholars point to the fact that the canonizing of biblical texts was not an arbitrary decision taken after the completion of certain text blocks. Rather, the texts were considered canonical as they developed. It is assumed that a "canonical core" came into being at an early time and was soon assigned special dignity. When other texts were added, they were shaped in the sense and style of what was already there. This can explain, for example, the overarching chronological and theological unity of the great narrative of Genesis to Kings stretching over more than a millennium of history. Correspondingly, for the group of the Writing Prophets, it can be assumed that later prophets used the books of their predecessors (which were already canonical) as examples to follow. This explains the stylistic and thematic unity of the prophetic books.

Probably, the sections of the canon grew in parallel with each other. Some scholars also assume that the canonical blocks of narrative and of prophecy each underwent a final overall redaction.

According to the Hebrew book order, the third part of the canon, the "Writings," is closed by the book of Chronicles. Chronicles comprises the whole biblical history from Adam (see ADAM AND EVE) until the return from the Babylonian Exile (see EXILE; RETURN FROM EXILE). Some scholars, therefore, assume that the book of Chronicles was deliberately written to summarize, conclude, and seal off the canon of the Hebrew Bible.

Conservative scholars date this event to the time about 400 to 350 B.C.E. It was the time of the national restoration of Judah after the Babylonian Exile. As we know from extrabiblical sources, the Persian overlords gave instruction to reestablish local cults and local laws in the provinces they controlled. It was in this context that Ezra reinstated the Mosaic Law in Judah—and it is possible that in this context also the whole canon of the Hebrew Bible was closed. If Chronicles was written in order to close the canon, this could explain why the book ends mentioning a Persian king of all people. The dating of the closure of the canon in the Persian era corresponds to the fact that the biblical history does not reach beyond this time.

Other scholars, however, date the closure of the canon around 163 B.C.E. The reason for this is mainly that a dating around 350 B.C.E. seems to be too early for some of the books, when considered from a historical-critical point of view. In particular, the book of Daniel contains quite detailed prophecies for the time of around 163 B.C.E. The dating of the book of Daniel then depends on the question whether one takes these passages as genuine (divinely inspired) prophecies or as prophecies written down after the fact. The restoration of Judah's political independence in the Maccabean wars around 163 B.C.E. would then be another appropriate background for closing the canon.

From about this time, the first reliable historical information about the canon is also extant. Around 190 B.C.E., the book of Jesus Ben Sira was written. It contains many references to biblical persons and texts. From that it can be inferred that Ben Sira's

"Bible" roughly equates with today's Hebrew Bible. However, there are uncertainties with some of the books of the "Writings."

The foreword to the Greek translation of Jesus Ben Sira, around 132 B.C.E., refers to the Hebrew Bible three times, using the tripartite formula "the Law of Moses, the Prophets, and the other books of the fathers" in each of the instances. This is a strong hint that the canon was a clearly defined entity by that time. This tripartite formula is found again in the Jewish tradition (Talmud). It is still the common designation for the Hebrew Bible used by the Jews, who call it *TaNaK = Torah, Neviim,* and *Ketuvim,* which means "Law, Prophets, and [Other] Writings."

The authors of the New Testament (around 50–100 C.E.) see the Hebrew Bible as inspired Scripture without exception. They quote from virtually all books of the Hebrew Bible, the quotes introduced with formulas like "Scripture says" or "God says." We know that Jesus had several discussions with the scribes of his time. The question of the canonicity of the Scripture, however, was not among their topics. Therefore, the canon seems to have been clearly defined at the time of Jesus and the apostles.

In the New Testament, as in some other ancient documents, the Hebrew Bible is often called "Law and Prophets" or "Moses and the Prophets." In this expression, the Writings are not mentioned. However, that does not mean that they were not canonical. Rather, the two-part formula "Law and Prophets" is a different way of describing the Bible that points especially to a canonical differentiation: The Pentateuch, the "Law," forms the basis of the Hebrew Bible. All other divinely inspired writers ("prophets" in a wider sense) follow it. The Writings are therefore subsumed here under the heading "prophets." The New Testament makes no distinction in quoting from the Prophets and from the Writings.

From the time of about 100 C.E., we have statements made by the Jewish writer Josephus and in 2 Esdras confirming that the canon of the Hebrew Bible was a clearly defined entity by that time.

In the course of history, time and again people disputed the canonicity of one or the other book of the canon. Many of the Christian church fathers of the third century, for example, doubted the canonicity of the book of Esther. Again, the church reformer Martin Luther questioned the canonicity of the New Testament letter of James. However, these discussions did not have any real influence on the form of the canon itself.

formation of the canon: the New Testament

The 27 books that form the New Testament were all written within the first century C.E., but their collection and recognition took much longer. This process of so-called canonization was not so much the result of the decision of one or more church councils as well of the local churches that used certain Christian writings in their worship meetings but not others. The criterion used by the churches was perceived divine inspiration, which became evident in apostolic authorship, inspirational contents, agreement with the other Scriptures, and general use.

Early in the second century there is evidence for a collection of the Pauline letters, and from the mid-second century the four Gospels appear as a fixed corpus. By the year 200 the canon had by and large assumed its later shape, but the church took nearly another 200 years to finalize the details. A letter by Bishop Athanasius of Alexandria, written in 367, in which he lists the 27 books, is usually seen as the decisive act, although some regional churches continued to dispute some books (Hebrews, Revelation) even afterward.

The order in which the books appear in printed Bibles was never agreed by the church and is a matter of convention. As (the life of) JESUS CHRIST is the heart of the New Testament, it is logical that the four Gospels are first despite the fact that they were written after most of the letters. The separation of Luke and Acts, however, is unfortunate. This was probably done in order to keep the three Synoptic Gospels together, giving the Gospel of John, which has a different character, the fourth position. While the four Gospels and Acts give a historical foundation of the life of Jesus and the beginning of the Christian Church, the letters give the theological reflection and the practical outworking. The letters are ordered in decreasing length, the Pauline letters to churches first, then his letters to individuals, after that the letters of other authors. The prophetic book of Revelation gives a fitting conclusion to the New Testament so that it ends with the expression of hope for Jesus Christ's return.

genealogy For the modern reader, the biblical practice of including lengthy passages of genealogical material in their narratives is sometimes simply boring. This changes, however, when one considers the literary, theological, and sociological implications genealogies have.

Genealogies, first of all, tell the individual where he or she belongs. They provide an individual of rank or office with a connection to a worthy family. They define social relationships of individuals, tribes, and peoples to one another. Biblical genealogies, in particular, demonstrate the fulfillment of God's promise that they will be fruitful and multiply (Genesis 1:28); they trace lines of divine promises, for example, the promise to the descendants of ABRAHAM (Genesis 12:2) or of DAVID (2 Samuel 7:16); and they exhibit a sense of movement within history toward a divine goal (Ruth 4:18–22; Matthew 1:1–17). To the informed reader, some of the genealogies even recall whole historical epochs (1 Chronicles 1:1–4).

Genealogies can be either linear, i.e., moving from one generation to the next, or segmented, describing a family tree. Mostly, only the male descendants are given, though there are notable exceptions (e.g., Matthew 1:5). Genealogies can skip one or more generations; accordingly, in genealogical context, *father* can also mean "ancestor," *son* can also mean "descendant." An example of skipping several generations would be "Jesus, Son of David" (Matthew 1:1), where the function is to show the connection of Jesus to the Davidic promise in 2 Samuel 7.

genres, biblical An understanding of genre is vital for evaluating any literature, and for reading it aright in terms of how its truth is presented. But many readers find themselves confused in reading the Bible because they apply criteria applicable to Western genres but not to biblical literature.

Western genre traditions go back to the Greeks. The main genre divisions that have emerged are poetry, drama, and prose. With prose, the obvious distinction is between fiction and nonfiction, and then numerous subgenres within each. Over the course of time, some of these subgenres have traveled, so that we now refer to epic novels and epic movies as well as epic poetry, which was the original designation. It is important to realize truth claims cannot be resolved in terms of fictionality against nonfictionality. Aristotle, for example, claimed that tragedy was truer than history, in that drama typically writes about what is most likely to happen rather than what has happened. Other modern ways of categorizing literature cut across these divisions, for example, the modal division of realism versus romance-fantasy.

When we consider biblical literature, we must set aside these categories and look at the Bible in its own terms. In the past, biblical scholars have attempted to do this, under the title of *form criticism*. But much form criticism had to do with production, that is, hypotheses over editorship and transmission of the text, including its oral transmission before it was written, topics in which genre criticism is not interested. Some form criticism has coincided with genre criticism, for example, in describing the parable form, which Jesus used extensively in his teaching. We notice, too, the omission of any drama in the Bible, as the theater was not a cultural institution in the Middle East. Erich Auerbach's *Mimesis*, comparing Western and biblical literature, makes the case that biblical literature is far more representational, democratic, and realistic than classical Western literature.

We notice two characteristics as we examine biblical genres. First, there is no sense at all of fiction or nonfiction in the narrative forms, and within each broad category, subgenres are used in a very mixed way, whereas until very recently, Western literature has stuck rigidly to one subgenre per text, apart from what has been called "the anatomy." A prophetic text, such as Jeremiah, contains straight prophetic utterances but also historic and autobiographical narrative, prayers, curses and consolations, letters, dreams and visions, inner dialogues, and confessional utterances. And it is partly in prose, partly in poetry.

The Hebrew Bible is divided into the Law, the Prophets (Former and Latter), and the Writings, which includes poetry (the Psalms) and some Wisdom books. The Christian Old Testament has a somewhat different arrangement: the History books (Genesis and Esther), Wisdom (Job and Song of Solomon), and the Prophets (Isaiah to the end). The New Testament could be seen to fall into three similar categories. But none of these categories easily fits into Western ideas of genre.

Within the genre called the history books, we have mainly narrative, though, puzzlingly for us, also three and a half books of the Law, and a variety of subgenres, many poetic, such as blessings. Nor is there any distinction between what we would see as history and what might be termed mythology (the early chapters of Genesis) or legends (e.g., stories of the patriarchs). In the Bible, it is a single genre, with perhaps a term like *historicized mythology* as a subgenre. The term *Chronicles* is frequently used of some of these narratives, reminding us of an older form of history within the Western tradition that cannot be evaluated as post-Enlightenment history. We have to see three elements or strands binding this narrative together: its truth claims, its artistic unity, and its theological interpretation, which is a different sort of unity.

In the wisdom literature, a text like Job represents a mixed form: narrative, dialogue, and discourse all used to convey wisdom. The Prophets mostly employ a poetic form, though not consistently; and some, such as parts of Daniel, are visionary or apocalyptic, a structure that might seem to Western minds akin to moving from realism to fantasy.

Within the New Testament, the law/history finds its equivalence in the Gospels and Acts, a new genre form, containing subgenres of historical narrative, biography, poetry, prophecy, and didactic forms, even redefinitions of the Law. They are foundational accounts of God's great deeds, as in the Pentateuch. The Acts become an equivalent of the Former Prophets, a prophetic narrative of the first outworking of God's new revelation and redemption in history. The epistles become the

new Wisdom literature, using a preexisting Western subgenre to convey teaching about the new; and Revelation, the equivalent of the Prophets, using the subgenre of the apocalyptic to take us into the end times.

See also APOCALYPTIC WRITING; EPISTLE; GOSPEL (GENRE); HYMNS; LAMENT; LAW; NARRATIVE; PARABLES; PASTORAL; PRAYER; PROPHECY; PROVERBS (GENRE); PSALMS (GENRE); SERMON; WISDOM LITERATURE; WOES AND DENUNCIATIONS.

God   The Bible can be seen as a book in which God is the main protagonist. The Bible is confident within itself that it is a revelation of God by God himself. Any such revelation must necessarily be gradual and must also be made in language, which is a human construct. The Genesis picture is that God allows Adam to name the creation: That is, God gives man the gift of making language (Genesis 2:19).

The Bible rarely talks of God in negative abstracts (i.e., the qualities that God does not possess), such as immortality, impassibility, or invisibility, but rather in concrete figures, such as Lord, king, father. God is called the provider, not providence. The Hebrew language often emphasizes verbal forms over nouns, so it talks not so much of the Creator but of the God who creates. Nor does the Bible discuss abstractly the qualities of God, such as transcendence and immanence, but instead deals in actual instances of incarnation and visions of glory, however much tension is caused in the language. For example, the temple is seen as God's dwelling place, the site of presence, and yet only as his footstool, since he cannot be contained by human constructs. Such tensions become paradoxes but are inevitable.

The one quality of God that is perhaps abstract and that is also mentioned frequently is God's holiness. But even that at first takes concrete expression in the rituals specified in the Pentateuch: We can see that holiness means otherness, separation from the ordinary. Later this is further concretized in the temple and the vision of transcendence at its dedication. Later still, the prophetic witness shows that God's holiness is ultimately moral and linked to the concept of righteousness and justice. It is in the light of this we can understand earlier anthropomorphic terms such as *anger* and *jealousy* (see PERSONIFICATION).

Similarly the revelation of God as love is through the loving care manifested historically in the covenant relationship of God with a chosen people. This is recorded as it happens in the Bible, being celebrated in the Psalms as song. Typical terms for it are *mercy, compassion,* and *blessing.* The prophetic witness, especially of Isaiah, relies upon historical evidence to support this revelation of God's nature. Isaiah 40–66 is one of the high points for God's revelation of himself. In the New Testament, this love is again seen revealed materially, both in the nature of Jesus Christ as pure loving action and in Christ as God's gift to mankind as their redeemer.

This latter term, *Redeemer,* is a good example of language that begins as figurative and ends as a theological concept. The redeemer-kinsman of the Hebrew Bible had a role to play in saving members of his family. God is seen as that Redeemer. In the New Testament the role is performed by the Son, but the word is not used as such, since its original metaphoric force has been lost. Instead the cognate forms of *Redemption* and *Redeemed* are used as theological signifiers of salvation.

This raises the further point about gradual revelation. The movement of thought in the Hebrew Bible is from seeing God as merely the Israelites' personal deity, whose existence only became fully apparent in the land he had promised them, to God as universal orderer of empires, Assyrian, Babylonian, Persian; as Creator of the cosmos; as Lord of history and the future. The New Testament claims further revelation in the threefold nature of God, known technically as the TRINITY. In this unfolding revelation, the image of God as father, hitherto one image among many, now becomes central. Other aspects of God are seen as belonging to God the Son, Jesus Christ, such as Redeemer, judge, husband (of the church). Other aspects are ascribed to the Holy Spirit, such as creator and regenerator of life, and of presence, healing, and comfort.

Tables 1 and 2 seek to set out some of the names, attributes, and images of God used throughout the Bible, giving a few examples of each. By far the most common term for God in the Hebrew Bible is *Yahweh,* a name revealed to Moses (Exodus 3:14–15) as meaning "I AM" or "I AM WHO I AM." This name was considered too holy to say in later Judaism, so the vowels from *Adonai,* another word for God, meaning "Lord," were added between the

---

TABLE 1: SOME NAMES AND ATTRIBUTES OF GOD THROUGHOUT THE BIBLE

Name or Attribute (Hebrew term; Greek term)	Hebrew Bible	New Testament
God (*El, Elohim, Eloi; Theos*)	Genesis 1:1	John 1:1
God Almighty (*El Shaddai; Pantokratōr*)	Genesis 17:1–2	Revelation 4:8; 11:17
The LORD (*YHWH; Kurios*)	Numbers 14:14	Luke 1:45; Acts 2:36
(as meaning "I AM")	Exodus 3:14–15	John 18:5–6
Lord God (*Elohim; kurios ho theos*)	Genesis 9:26	1 Peter 3:15
(or typically: The Lord [my/our/his] God)	Deuteronomy 4:5	Acts 2:39
The LORD of Hosts (*YHWH Tsebaoth; Pantokratōr*) (or LORD Almighty)	1 Samuel 17:45–46	2 Corinthians 6:18
Creator (*Qoneh, yotser; ktistēs*)	Genesis 14:19, 22: Isaiah 40:28; 43:15	1 Peter 4:19
The Name (*Hashem; to onoma*)	1 Kings 8:28–29; Isaiah 50:10–11	John 17:6, 26; Philippians 2:29–10

(Table continues)

(Table 1 continued)

Name or Attribute (Hebrew term; Greek term)	Hebrew Bible	New Testament
The Lord *(Adonai; kurios)*	Psalm 16:2; Exodus 4:1–5	Luke 5:12
Holy One of Israel *(Qedosh Yisrael; ho hagios)*	Isaiah 37:23	1 Peter 1:14–16
The Living God *(El Chay; theos zōn)*	Deuteronomy 5:26	2 Corinthians 3:2–3
The LORD our righteousness *(YHWH Tsidqenu)* (also a number of other forms of *YHWH + attribute,* such as *YHWH Yireh; YHWH Rapheh; YHWH Shalom, etc.,* meaning God our Provider, Healer, Peace, etc.)	Jeremiah 23:6	1 Corinthians 1:30
Hope of Israel *(Miqweh Yisrael; elpis)*	Jeremiah 17:13	Hebrews 6:18–19
God Most High or the High God *(El Elyon;* Aramaic *Illaya; hupsistos)*	Psalm 57:2; Daniel 4:24–34, 37	Luke 1:30–32; Acts 16:17; Hebrews 1:3–4; 7:1
God of Heaven (and Earth) *(El Shamayim; theos tou ouranou)*	Ezra 5:1	Revelation 11:13
Everlasting God *(El Olam; aionios theos)*	Isaiah 40:28	Romans 16:26
Father *(Ab, abba; pater)*	Psalm 68:5–6	Mark 14:36; John 10:27–30
God with us *(Immanu el; Emmanuel)*	Isaiah 8:8, 10 (cf. Ezekiel 48:35)	Matthew 1:23

TABLE 2: SOME IMAGES OF GOD USED THROUGHOUT THE BIBLE

Image	Hebrew Bible	New Testament
Shepherd	Psalm 23; Isaiah 40:10–11	John 10:11; Revelation 7:17
Rock	Psalm 144:1	1 Corinthian 10:4
Refuge	Psalms 59:16; 91:2	Hebrews 6:18
Shield	Genesis 15:1; Psalm 3:3	
Fortress	Psalm 91:2	
King	Psalms 47:7; 97:1–4	1 Timothy 6:15; Revelation 17:14
Judge	Psalm 94:2–15	Hebrews 12:23
Redeemer	Isaiah 63:16	Hebrews 9:15
Husband	Hosea 2:16, 19–20; Isaiah 54:5–8	Ephesians 5:32
Warrior	Exodus 15:3; Nahum 1:2–5	Revelation 19:11–16
Fire	Deuteronomy 4:24	Luke 3:16; Acts 2:3
Alpha and Omega		Revelation 1:8

transliterated consonants to give the word *Jehovah*, the name that occurs in the Authorized (King James) Version. Later English versions translate *Yahweh* as "the LORD." As the chart makes plain, the New Testament quite consciously adapts the terms and images from the Hebrew Bible.

See also CHOSEN PEOPLE; HOLY SPIRIT; JESUS CHRIST; KINGDOM OF GOD (KINGDOM OF HEAVEN); REVELATION, GOD'S; TRINITY.

gospel (genre)   The four Gospels are a subgenre of the genre of ancient biographies, which described the lives of great men for the benefit of later generations. Ancient biographies were highly selective narratives, avoiding allegedly irrelevant parts of their hero's life. Thus Mark's gospel does not even tell us where Jesus was from or what he did before as an adult he started his ministry. Instead, Mark begins at the start of Jesus' public ministry.

The four Gospels are composite texts consisting of numerous short narrative units belonging to various genres such as miracle stories (healings, exorcisms, provisions, rescues, and epiphany), pronouncement stories, independent words, parables, teaching, and reports of personal contacts. It is likely that much of this material was transmitted orally for some time before being committed to writing. The disciplines of study form history, and tradition history look at the prehistory of these units in their oral and written forms, respectively, but they do not often lead to agreed results. Redaction criticism is the discipline that studies the editorial activity of the evangelists in weaving together the small units and putting their own mark on the material. In the case of Mark, this is a rather theoretical exercise as we do not have any of his alleged sources. On the other hand, we can see how Matthew and Luke worked with Mark.

Greece   Greece appears in the Bible under this name but also as *Javan* (Genesis 10:2, 4) and as *Macedonia and Achaia*, its two constituent provinces in Roman times (Acts 19:21; 1 Thessalonians 1:7–8).

The PHILISTINES probably originated in Greece, although the Bible never makes that connection. Greece's involvement in the history of the HOLY LAND begins in earnest with the arrival of Alexander the Great, who between 336 and 323 B.C.E. conquered the entire Middle East and who is alluded to in Daniel 8:21 and 11:2–4. The empire he founded forms the background to most of the APOCRYPHA and gave the Greek language its dominant position in the eastern part of the Roman Empire (see BIBLE, LANGUAGES OF).

Paul's second and third missionary journeys took him to Greece (Acts 16–20), and some of his letters were written to Greek and Macedonian churches. The leading classes in Greece's capital, Athens, found Paul's message quite unconvincing (Acts 17:22–34), but Luke mocks their elitism (verse 21).

See also CULTURES OF THE BIBLE.

Greek   See BIBLE, LANGUAGES OF.

healing   A central biblical image for SALVATION. Some of the Hebrew and Greek words used for healing also carry the idea of being saved and made whole.

Records of physical healing are found throughout the Bible. Numbers 12:1–15 records Miriam's healing from leprosy, which had been caused by her rebellion against her brother, Moses. But not all healing was as forgiveness for SIN. Naaman's leprosy was healed gratuitously by Elisha even though he was an enemy soldier (2 Kings 5:8–14). Elisha and his mentor, Elijah, both seem to have had extensive healing ministries, the only two prophets to have possessed them, though Isaiah was given revelation as to how King Hezekiah should be healed (Isaiah 38).

In the New Testament, JESUS CHRIST resumed the healing role of Elijah, though it drew him greater popularity than he always desired (for example, Mark 3:9–10). The early church continued this miraculous healing (Acts 3:1–15), which included raising from the dead (Acts 20:9–12) and casting out evil spirits (Acts 16:16–18). Paul taught that such gifts of healing were to be expected in the CHURCH (1 Corinthians 12:28), and James mentions healing through anointing with oil (James 5:14–15).

More importantly, healing became a metaphor for spiritual recovery (Isaiah 58:8). Isaiah 53:5

suggests a healing from the effects of sin, which is how 1 Peter 2:24 interprets it. Some, however, would argue that in the light of the previous verse, it also applies to physical healing. Spiritual healing, or the refusal of it, is mentioned in Isaiah 6:9–10 and quoted by Paul in Acts 28:27. The refusal of healing represents a drastically hardened state of heart, more appropriate to enemies (Jeremiah 51:9).

See also DELIVERANCE; SALVATION; SIN.

heaven The word *heaven* occurs more than 600 times in the Bible and is used to denote such diverse things as (1) the area over the earth in general (see Genesis 1 and Ephesians 4:10); (2) the visible sky, often admired for its glory, which reflect's God's glory (e.g., Psalm 8:1, 3); and (3) the place or sphere where God and his attendant beings reside. This last usage occurs throughout the Bible, such as in Psalm 80:14 and Hebrews 8:1. More elaborate—but still very restrained—descriptions of proceedings in heaven can be found in Isaiah 6; Revelation 4–5; and parts of Job 1–2 (see SATAN). In a spiritual sense, according to the New Testament, those who believe in Christ Jesus already live in heaven (Ephesians 2:4–6; Philippians 3:20).

However, the word *heaven* is *not* used in the Bible to indicate the future abode of humankind. Whereas the Hebrew Bible only has a vague expectation of personal life after death, this developed in the INTERTESTAMENTAL PERIOD, and by the time of the New Testament the resurrection of the dead was accepted by most Jews (see PHARISEES AND SADDUCEES). However, the term *heaven* is not used for this concept; nor is a person's death in the Bible described as "going to heaven." Instead concepts such as "eternal life" and the images of the city (Hebrews) and the festive or wedding meal (Isaiah 25; Revelation 19:6–9) are used to describe future bliss.

It is also said that at the end of time God will create a new heaven and earth and essentially eliminate the separation between the two (Revelation 21:1–6). Christians expect a renewal of the entire cosmos (Romans 8:19–22).

The word *paradise* only occurs three times in the New Testament (Luke 23:43; 2 Corinthians 12:4; Revelation 2:7) as a synonym for (3).

See also KINGDOM OF GOD (KINGDOM OF HEAVEN).

Hebrew See BIBLE, LANGUAGES OF.

Hebrew Bible, worship and ritual Israelite worship in the Hebrew Bible contains a strong ceremonial aspect. The theological background to this is given in the Sinai COVENANT, according to which the people of Israel are God's "own possession" and a "kingdom of priests" (Exodus 19:5–6). The people, therefore, have to act according to the holiness of God. A further aspect of the covenant is that God wants to live in the midst of his people (Exodus 29:45). However, as the narrative of Exodus, Leviticus, and Numbers shows, the presence of God's holiness among his people is a challenge as well as a privilege.

The symbolic place where God wants to be among his people is the tabernacle, and later, the temple. The splendor of the sanctuary reflects God's majesty. The threefold structure of a court area, the holy place, and the most holy place enables people to approach God's holiness step by step. In contrast to other ancient Near Eastern temples, the most holy place does not contain any idol: God cannot be visualized using a human or animal form. Instead, the ark of the covenant, the most holy object Israel possesses, is placed there. The ark was basically a wooden chest with gold overlay and two cherubim (see ANGELS) on top. The instructions concerning the construction of the tabernacle are very detailed (Exodus 25–31). Afterward, the actual construction is again described in great detail (Exodus 35–40). This exactness and meticulousness express respect to God. In contrast, a careless handling of ceremonial aspects means a disregard of God's holiness and, therefore, a sacrilege.

One important aspect of the old Israelite worship was the sacrificial offering of animals. Again, respect shown to God demands that the instructions be followed meticulously. In Leviticus 1–7, different kinds of offerings are described: For example, to give a burnt offering means that the whole animal has to be burned. From the peace offering, however, only the fat and the kidneys are burned. The flesh is eaten by the family in a festive meal. Apart from animals, bread offerings are given. From the bread, only a small part is burned. The rest is given to the priests.

Most of the sacrifices have the function of making atonement for sin. At least some of them mean that a financial burden is incurred by those making them, in the sense of paying a penalty. Furthermore, the offerings demonstrate that sins are a grave problem: Blood has to be shed in order to pay for them. However, the principle of substitution is also introduced, since animal blood is shed on behalf of human sin. The shedding of blood is of particular significance, since blood is seen as the carrier of the God-given life (Genesis 9:4–6).

The offering procedures do not have any magical meaning in the sense that they automatically cleanse from sin. They are symbolic acts that are meaningful only as long as the people making them have the right attitude of repentance and respect to God.

Another important aspect of the old Israelite worship are the feasts, such as the weekly Sabbath. The purpose of this day is to rest from one's work and to worship God. Besides the Sabbath, there is a yearly cycle of feasts, most of them connected to events of Israel's history. Deuteronomy 16 collects them together in an overview.

One of the feasts is the PASSOVER, the historical background to which is given in Exodus 12: The Egyptians still do not allow Israel to leave. God therefore decides to kill all the firstborn of the Egyptians in one night. The evening before, in each Israelite family a lamb is slaughtered. Some of the lamb's blood is sprinkled on the doorposts and the lintel, as a sign for the angel of God to "pass over" the doors of the Israelites when striking down the firstborn.

The Passover lamb is roasted over the fire and eaten. While eating, the people are clothed ready for the journey with sandals on their feet as a sign that the deliverance is coming. This feast is held annually as a remembrance of THE EXODUS.

Another feast is the Day of Atonement (Leviticus 16). On this day, the people give two male goats to the high priest. One of them is sacrificed as a sin offering. On the head of the other, the high priest has to lay both his hands, confessing all the sins of the people, so putting them (symbolically) on the head of the goat. After that, the scapegoat is sent out into the wilderness. This symbolizes that

there is a necessity for sin to be taken out of Israel. The Day of Atonement, furthermore, is the only day of the year when the high priest is allowed to enter the most holy place of the sanctuary.

Five days after the Day of Atonement is the Festival of Booths (see Leviticus 23). In remembrance of the wilderness wandering, huts are made of branches and leaves, in which the Israelites live for one week of celebrating.

hell The concept of hell as a place or state of eternal punishment and suffering for the unrighteous in the afterlife only fully emerges in the Gospels, in the teachings of Jesus Christ. The term itself is not used in the Bible at all—it is a Germanic word used by translators to render the original Hebrew and Greek terms.

In the Hebrew Bible, concepts of the afterlife develop very gradually. The term used most often is *sheol,* sometimes "the pit." In many places it suggests a shadowy and unconscious state of being after death (Psalm 6:5; Isaiah 38:18–19). At times there is an idea it is more for the unrighteous than the righteous (Psalm 31:17) and that it may involve some punishment (Isaiah 14:11). Isaiah 66:24 uses the idea of undying fire, and Ezekiel's apocalyptic vision (Ezekiel 38:22) also talks of burning bodies. Jeremiah names a particular place—the valley of Ben Hinnom (Jeremiah 7:31–34)—which was a place of dreadful pagan child sacrifice (2 Chronicles 28:3; 33:6). This place outside Jerusalem became in later times the city's garbage pile and was called *Gehenna.*

This is one of the terms used in the New Testament (e.g., Matthew 10:28; 23:15; James 3:6). Another term is the Greek word for the underworld, *hades* (e.g., Matthew 16:18; Luke 10:15). The terms are used interchangeably. The dramatic parable of the rich man and Lazarus in Luke 16:19–31 gives us a clear idea of Jesus' teaching, with burning, torment, and irrevocable judgment. Matthew 25:41 suggests the fire and torment were actually first meant for the devil (see SATAN) and his ANGELS. Other verses speak of hell as separation (2 Thessalonians 1:9) and darkness (2 Peter 2:17). God's "wrath and fury" (Romans 2:8–9) lie behind such harsh punishments. APOCALYPTIC WRITING enlarges on the pictorial quality of hell, as in the lake of fire of Revelation 20:14–15.

See also HEAVEN; LAST THINGS.

hermeneutics On different approaches to the Bible, see Part I.

Herod Several kings of Israel in the time of the New Testament bear the name *Herod,* and they are easily confused.

From a historical perspective the most important is Herod "the Great." He was not a Jew but an Idumean (Edomite), who was appointed client king (a native ruler subject to the empire) of Israel in the year 40 B.C.E. He had the power to appoint and depose high priests and carried out an expensive building program, including a new city and port at Caesarea (later the residence of Pilate, Felix, and Festus); an amphitheater, a theater, and a hippodrome in Jerusalem; and the reconstruction of the temple (cf. John 2:20). This and more gained him the epithet "the Great." In his private life he was unhappy, and he had many relatives put to death on suspicion of plotting against him. He is mentioned in Matthew 2. After his death in 4 B.C.E. the Romans divided his territory between his sons.

The son of Herod "the Great," Archelaus, inherited Judea with Samaria and Idumea (Matthew 2:22) but was deposed in 6 C.E.; Judea was then turned into a Roman province governed by *procurators* such as Pilate (26–36 C.E.).

Another son, (Herod) Antipas, was given Galilee, where he built Tiberias as his capital city. He is mentioned in Luke 3:1 and Matthew 14:1, 9. This is the Herod who was rebuked by JOHN THE BAPTIST and who had John killed (Mark 6:16–29).

Finally, Herod Agrippa I, grandson of Herod "the Great," was born ca. 10 B.C.E. As a favorite of the emperor Claudius he ruled over nearly all territories of his grandfather in the years 41–44 C.E. and was very popular (Acts 12:1–5, 19–23). After Agrippa's death, Rome once more appointed governors, of whom Felix (52–60) and Festus (60–62) are mentioned in Acts 23–26.

history Both Judaism and Christianity are historical faiths. Biblical history is often called *salvation history,* since it focuses preeminently on how God has saved a people out of all peoples in the world and called them his, whether they be defined as a nation or as a group of believers. He is thus the god of their history, since all people inevitably live in time and record that time as history.

The main mode of recording history in the Bible is narrative, as much secular history is also recorded. But unlike in secular history, God is the main character. As with most narratives, there are not only time frames but also explanations of connections and happenings, of cause and effect. But unlike in secular history, the explanations are in terms of covenant keeping or breaking; of divine blessing and protection or of divine punishment, directly or through withdrawal of blessing and protection. These explanations are given both within the narrative and by way of commentary. This commentary is largely provided by the prophetic writings, though sometimes the prophetic writings also contain extra narrative material. The poetry also contains historical material and commentary, especially the Psalms.

Within the narrative is embedded biography, typically of those leaders who have helped shape the actions, good or bad, of the nation. These are mainly the patriarchs and kings, but the lives of such prophets as Elijah and Elisha are also recorded. The history and the biography are never named by those terms: The typical term is the *chronicle.*

Much of what has been said relates primarily to the Hebrew Bible. But the New Testament is equally historical, claiming the history of the Hebrew Bible to authenticate its own message and the significance of Jesus Christ. The first five books of the New Testament narrate the life of Jesus Christ and the beginnings of the Christian Church. There is a significant shift of emphasis from a people defined racially and nationally to a people defined purely in terms of their faith in Christ, among whom there is to be no inherited hierarchy. Both Jewish and Christian history are extended into the future in APOCALYPTIC WRITING, according to which, ultimately, human history will cease.

See also CHOSEN PEOPLE; COVENANT; EXILE; EXODUS, THE; MONARCHY; RED SEA, CROSSING; RETURN FROM EXILE.

holiness God's moral goodness and according to the Bible, a key attribute of God, which humans are called to reflect. This is a main concern in the book of Leviticus, of which chapters 17–26 have been called "the holiness code," and in many of the prophets (e.g., Zechariah 7:8–10).

The same concern is reflected in the New Testament, e.g., in 1 Peter 1:15: ". . . just as he who called you is holy, so be holy in all you do." The believers are addressed as "those who are sanctified in Christ Jesus, called to be saints" (1 Corinthians 1:2). In the original Greek there is one word for "holy" and "sanctified," *hagios.*

God's holiness means that he cannot tolerate impurity and sin. As a result, humans who want fellowship with him require forgiveness. In the Hebrew Bible forgiveness was the result of sacrifices (see HEBREW BIBLE, WORSHIP AND RITUAL). In the New Testament such forgiveness comes about through the perfect sacrifice of Jesus Christ (Hebrews 9:11–15).

Believers are called to grow in holiness over time and so increasingly reflect God's holiness; this process is called *sanctification.* It is not a matter of self-confidence or a reason for pride but of awareness of sins graciously forgiven, as illustrated in Jesus' parable of the Pharisee and the tax collector (Luke 18:9–14). In the epistles sanctification is seen as the work of the Holy Spirit in the believers (e.g., Galatians 5:16–26).

In a derived sense certain objects and activities can also be seen as holy, that is, "set apart" for God and his service. The Hebrew word for "holy" literally means "separate." Examples of holy items are the temple, the mountain of God, and the Scriptures. Images connected with the theme are, in particular, water and fire.

See also ETHICS; PROPHETS.

Holy Land The term *Holy Land* is only used once in the Bible (Zechariah 2:12) but was the name used from medieval times to denote the traditional "land of Israel." Its geographical features are a narrow coastal plain bordering the Mediterranean and rising hills leading to a plateau, on which is situated the capital, Jerusalem. Arid mountains tumble down eastward to the fertile Jordan valley, lying below sea level. Beyond that east and south stretches further arid country.

However, the term implied a sacred space rather than a geographical or political entity, meaning that land allocated by God for his chosen people under Abraham and Moses, and the site for his most significant activity, both in the Hebrew Bible and the New Testament, though it had to be abandoned by them as punishment during a period of exile.

The following terms are used in the Bible for this area:

- Canaan: used in the earlier books of the Bible to denote the territory occupied by the Canaanites, as listed in Genesis 10:15–19. These were Semitic-speaking peoples, including the Amorites, Jebusites (the original inhabitants of JERUSALEM), and the Phoenicians. Ugaritic literature gives us good documentation of their culture and worship of Baal and Ashtoroth among other deities. Their territory extended into LEBANON and SYRIA.
- The Promised Land: literally promised by God to the patriarchs (Genesis 50:24; Exodus 3:8; Deuteronomy 9:28). Moses' successor, Joshua, occupied this land by military conquest, dividing it among the 12 tribes (Joshua 13–21) (see CANAAN, CONQUEST OF). The Deuteronomic writer felt the original promise was for greater territory (Deuteronomy 11:24), but this was only once attained, by King David (2 Samuel 8:3).
- Israel: see ISRAEL.
- Israel and Judah (the divided kingdoms): see JUDAH.

The term *Palestine* derives from the area occupied by the PHILISTINES. It is not a biblical one. Herodotus and Roman writers used the term, which was adopted later for the Muslim province of the Ottoman Empire, and then after 1947, after the establishment of the state of Israel, for the Arab-speaking territory outside the present Israel proper.

In the New Testament, the Roman provinces of Galilee, Samaria, and Judaea are the terms employed for the political area. In New Testament thinking, the Promised Land ceases to be a geographical concept (see PILGRIMS AND WANDERERS) and becomes a synonym for heaven.

Holy Spirit The term *spirit* is difficult to grasp. It can mean the essence of someone, the life force. But it can have a supernatural meaning also. The older term *Holy Ghost* now conveys, unfortunately, a rather weird supernatural meaning to us, though the term originally meant the same as *spirit*, as it still does in modern German.

The biblical meaning of *Holy Spirit* or *Spirit of God* takes on both meanings: of essence and yet of something beyond the natural or physical. The Holy Spirit is the very essence of GOD, his life force. In Christian theology, he is seen as the third person of the TRINITY.

References to the spirit of God run throughout the Bible, though there are significant differences between the Hebrew Bible and the New Testament. The Hebrew word *ruach* can mean "spirit," "breath," or "wind," and different English translations tend to vary in which term is used, as in Genesis 1:2, the Spirit's involvement with Creation. The Spirit, in the Hebrew Bible, is seen as the source of prophetic inspiration (1 Samuel 10:10; Isaiah 61:1–3; Ezekiel 11:5) and the source of power to accomplish God's will (1 Samuel 16:13; Zechariah 4:6). The Psalmist realizes he cannot do without the spirit (Psalm 51:11). In the New Testament, it is stated that all Scripture, which was then the Hebrew Bible, was inspired by God through the Holy Spirit (2 Peter 1:21).

The New Testament develops a theology of the Holy Spirit. The Spirit is now seen as an integral part of being a Christian. The promise of a universal giving of the Spirit in Joel 2:28–29 is claimed for the early church by Peter in his Pentecost sermon (Acts 2:1–21). Symbols not just of wind but of fire are used here, just as the symbol of the dove is used in Jesus Christ's receiving the Spirit at his baptism (Luke 3:21–22). Jesus was seen as "full of the Holy Spirit" (Luke 4:1,14), which enabled him to perform his miracles and speak with such wisdom. But Luke 3:16 states that Jesus will also baptize his followers with "the Holy Spirit and fire" (Luke 3:16).

In the EARLY CHURCH, the Holy Spirit was said to dwell within believers, to transform their lives (Romans 8:9) through the "new birth" (Titus 3:5–7), to produce "the fruit of the Spirit" (Galatians 5:22–23), to pray through them (Romans 8:23, 26), to give them true understanding (1 Corinthians 2:12–13), and to give them a sense of adoption as part of God's family (Romans 8:15–16). The Spirit also gives them *charismata*, or gifts of grace, to enable them supernaturally to serve in the church (Romans 12:6–8). The Spirit is called a *parakletos*, or an advocate who stands by us (John 14:26; 15:26), and an *arrabon*, or a first deposit of full salvation (Romans 8:24). And the Spirit can be grieved by wrong behavior (Ephesians 4:30).

hymns Ephesians 5:19 and Colossians 3:16 speak of "psalms and hymns and spiritual songs." This threefold division of sung poetry has continued in the Christian Church. Hymns are not, or rarely, mentioned in the Hebrew Bible (the NIV translation of Psalm 40:3 is an unusual one), though references in Matthew 26:30 and Mark 14:26 to an event "after they had sung a hymn" suggest that in Judaism hymn singing had developed as a form of worship. Otherwise the Hebrew Bible contains many psalms and references to songs and singing. The phrase "sing a new song" occurs nine times (e.g., Isaiah 42:10–13).

Fragments of early Christian hymns are to be found in the New Testament, especially Philippians 2:6–11; 1 Timothy 3:16; 2 Timothy 2:11–13. References to actual practice are to be found in 1 Corinthians 14:26, where it would appear individual members of the congregation could suggest a hymn, supposing a collection of hymns on which to draw. Acts 16:25 refers to Paul and Silas's singing hymns, which may have been derived from Judaism or been new compositions by the early Christians.

1 Corinthians 14:14–15 refers to spiritual songs. Probably the differences between hymns and songs is much as it is today in many churches: songs being perhaps more spontaneous, possibly sung many times over, whereas hymns are structured stanzas with a tune repeating for each stanza, and that embody more substantial praise or belief statements. Spiritual songs occur frequently in Revelation (4:8, 11; 5:9–10, 12–13; 7:12; 11:17–18; 15:3–4; 19:6–8). Even if they were not sung congregationally at that time, all of them have now found a place in Christian worship.

hyperbole See IMAGERY, BIBLICAL.

imagery, biblical Imagery works at two levels. At one level, the writer creates pictures with words that we recreate in our imaginations as images. At the other level, the writer uses various language devices called figures of speech, which make us see a certain thing in a certain way. The figures themselves are also called *tropes.*

The Bible is a highly imagistic book at both levels described. It is very visual, even when legal or theological matters are being discussed. And its poetry especially is densely figurative. For example, in Jeremiah 2 many examples of tropes can be located. The most obvious is the *simile,* in which two things are compared, usually by a verbal link such as *like* or *as . . . as* so that features of the first can be highlighted by reference to likenesses in the second. Thus:

> As a thief is shamed when caught,
> so the house of Israel shall be shamed—
> (Jeremiah 2:26)

The thief image is common in the Bible (cf. Luke 12:39). It is a universal image, the reality known in just about every culture.

More common is the *metaphor.* If a simile says A is like B, the metaphor identifies the two: A is B. The point of identity remains hidden, unlike in a simile: It is for us to work it out. In most cases, this is not difficult, but if we live in a different culture, or if the writer is being deliberately obscure, then it can be. For example:

> for my people have committed two evils:
> they have forsaken me [i.e., God],
> the fountain of living water,
> and dug out cisterns for themselves,
> cracked cisterns that can hold no water.
> (Jeremiah 2:13)

The overall image is a universal one, the production of water. God is not literally a "fountain of living water," but figuratively he is the source of life. In the New Testament this image is used specifically to refer to spiritual life (e.g., John 4:10). And while the people may literally be digging cisterns as part of the house construction, what is meant is figurative: They are looking for sources of (spiritual) life that will empty out as soon as filled.

The futility of looking for life outside God is made much more vivid and memorable than a literal statement, since it has emotive and experiential force. Further on, the people are described as "a restive young camel" (verse 23), "a wild ass" (verse 24), while God "planted you as a choice vine from the purest stock" (verse 21), another metaphor that runs through the Bible.

More difficult to grasp, though similar to the metaphor, is *metonymy.* In it an aspect of a thing, or a quality of it, is used to describe the thing as a whole. Thus:

> Your own sword devoured your prophets
> like a ravening lion. (Jeremiah 2:30)

The second line is, of course, a simile. But the sword did not literally jump up and swallow the prophets. The sword represents their persecution of God's messengers, though it is only one small part of the whole process. Metonymy is used typically as *symbolic* language (cf. 2:20, 37) and is used frequently in APOCALYPTIC WRITING (e.g., Revelation 2). Other examples are in 2:27, where *tree* and *stone* represent part of the system of idolatry, the making of artifacts out of certain materials. The linked figure, *synecdoche,* in which a part of a thing represents the whole, is not so frequent.

Another figure is *hyperbole,* or exaggeration:

> How well you direct your course to seek lovers!
> So that even to wicked women you have
> taught your ways. (Jeremiah 2:33)

Their unfaithful behavior has been so outrageous, even prostitutes have learned from them—a forceful expression. Exclamation marks and *even* are telltale signs of exaggeration. The idea is to shock. It is commonly used in prophetic oracles (cf. 2:28).

Antithesis uses verbal formulas like "This . . . yet that . . ." and "Not this . . . but that. . . ," setting side by side two very contrasting items to draw out the difference (as opposed to metaphor). Thus:

> Can a girl forget her ornaments,
> or a bride her attire?
> Yet my people have forgotten me,
> days without number. (Jeremiah 2:32)

Other figures present here are *rhetorical questions,* needing no answers (2:5, 14), and *apostrophe,* addressing a nonpresent audience (2:12). Elsewhere in the Bible we have examples of *irony* (2:36), mocking something or undermining someone's pretensions, as in the incident in 2 Chronicles 18:12–14; *bathos,* or anticlimax, as at the end of book of Jonah; and the Greek device of *litotes,* denying the opposite, as in Acts 12:18; 27:20. These, together with PERSONIFICATION, are usually considered the main biblical tropes.

It is not possible to list the subject matter of the imagery. A standard reference work like *The Dictionary of Biblical Imagery* is needed for this. Even within the one chapter of Jeremiah 2, there are images drawn from nature, history, and the military, as well as legal and sexual images. Certain images recur throughout the Bible, such as water, wine and vineyards, sheep and shepherds: all common to the context of the writers and many universal to human experience.

See also TYPES.

incarnation   See JESUS CHRIST.

inclusio   Often, the end of a narrative or of a text section refers to its beginning. If this is done in a striking way by verbal repetition or taking up of key concepts, this is called *inclusio.* An inclusio helps to bind together a piece of text.

In the original manuscripts of the biblical books, there are no paragraphs or subtitles indicating the structure of the text. Instead, features like inclusio are used to communicate the literary structure to the reader. When analyzing structure, however, not every repetition should automatically be interpreted as an inclusio. Rather, one has to demonstrate that the material bracketed really is a unity in terms of content.

Inclusios occur regularly in biblical texts. Some examples are the statements on "the heavens and the earth" in Genesis 1:1 and 2:1 that frame the six days of creation; the statement "Vanity of vanities! All is vanity," occurring in Ecclesiastes 1:2 and 12:8 framing the whole book; the question "What does man gain from all the toil at which he toils under the sun?" in the same book in 1:3 and 3:9 framing

a section dealing with the question of the meaning of life; the statement of praise at the beginning and ending of Psalm 8.

interpretation   On different approaches to the Bible, see "How to Read the Bible as Literature" in Part I.

intertestamental period   The name given to the period between the writing of the last books of the Hebrew Bible and the life of Jesus. During this time the Jews continued to write books, but these were not incorporated into the Bible; instead they are known as the Apocrypha (see APOCRYPHA AND PSEUDEPIGRAPHA; FORMATION OF THE CANON: THE HEBREW BIBLE). Other sources of information for this period are the Jewish historian Josephus and the DEAD SEA SCROLLS.

The first part of the intertestamental period is that of Persian rule over Israel, which lasted till 331 B.C.E., when Alexander the Great conquered the whole Middle East. The subsequent period of Greek rulers fell between 331 and 140, after which Israel was independent from 140 till 63 B.C.E. under the Maccabees (see 1, 2, 3, and 4 Maccabees, in Part II). In 63 B.C.E. the Romans conquered the area and turned Israel into a vassal state. Their occupation continued throughout the era of the New Testament and beyond. From 40 B.C.E. they let king HEROD and his sons rule over Israel on their behalf.

Alexander and his successors actively encouraged the mingling of European, Asiatic, and Egyptian cultures, which resulted in Hellenism (see CULTURES OF THE BIBLE).

The major event of the era was the uprising of the Maccabees against King Antiochus IV in 167 B.C.E. After three years of war they captured Jerusalem and cleansed the temple, which Antiochus had defiled.

Several elements that are absent from the Hebrew Bible but appear in the New Testament have their roots in the intertestamental period, such as the PHARISEES AND SADDUCEES, the SYNAGOGUE, and APOCALYPTIC WRITING. For this reason the intertestamental period is important for the study of the New Testament.

irony   See IMAGERY, BIBLICAL.

Isaac   Son of ABRAHAM and the second bearer of the divine promise after him. His name, meaning "he laughs," reflects his parents' incredulity at God's announcement of his birth (Genesis 17:17; 18:10–15). Though Isaac sometimes responds positively to God, God is seen as often at work through his passivity, as when he is offered as a sacrifice (Genesis 22) and a wife is found for him (Genesis 24). He is father of Esau and JACOB. Overall, in the Genesis narrative, he is a rather passive figure, overshadowed first by his father and then by his sons.

Israel   In the Bible, the name *Israel* appears in four different contexts:

- Israel is the new name given to JACOB, the patriarch, when he receives the divine blessing (Genesis 32:28).
- Israel is also the name of the nation that originates from Jacob's 12 sons (see ISRAEL, TWELVE TRIBES OF).
- In later times, when the nation is divided into a northern and a southern part, *Israel* often refers to the northern kingdom (whereas JUDAH denotes the southern kingdom).
- In the New Testament, the concept is occasionally used in a figurative sense (see TYPES) referring to the "new" or "second" people of God, which is the worldwide Christian community consisting of Jews and Gentiles who believe in Jesus Christ (see Galatians 3:7, 29; 6:16; James 1:1).

See also HOLY LAND.

Israel, twelve tribes of   The Hebrew Bible consists of the holy tradition of one nation, namely, Israel. Accordingly, Israel is the main (human) protagonist in most of the biblical books. The nation is theologically defined as God's own possession, his chosen people that he delivered from the slavery of Egypt in order to be a "kingdom of priests" for him and to mediate the divine blessing to "all families of the earth" (see Genesis 12:1–3; Exodus 19:4–6).

According to the book of Genesis, the people of Israel originated with JACOB, the PATRIARCH, who is also called Israel. From his 12 sons descend the 12 tribes of Israel. The sons are Reuben, Simeon, Levi, Judah, Dan, Naphtali, Gad, Asher, Issachar, Zebulun, Joseph, and Benjamin (Genesis 29:31–30:24; 35:18; see 35:23–26; 49:1–27).

Some distinctive aspects need to be stated: First of all, there is no tribe called Joseph. Instead, two tribes are called after Joseph's two sons, Ephraim and Manasseh. That means, strictly speaking, there would be 13 tribes. However, the biblical lists tend to sum up to 12 tribes by either counting Ephraim and Manasseh as one or by setting aside the tribe of Levi. The Levites were occupied with the temple service and the rites. That is why they did not possess their own tribal territory but cities throughout the territories of the other tribes. The tribe of Simeon received a territory inside Judah. It seems that this tribe gradually dispersed into Judah.

The Genesis narrative reports unreasonable behavior of Jacob's three oldest sons, Reuben, Simeon, and Levi. Judah, the fourth son, therefore receives the role of the firstborn (see Genesis 49). Accordingly, Israel's great kings DAVID and SOLOMON come from the tribe of Judah.

After Solomon's reign, however, the nation splits into a southern and a northern kingdom. The southern kingdom consists of the tribes of Judah and Benjamin and the Levites living in their territory. The kingdom is together called Judah after the name of its main tribe. The northern kingdom, on the other hand, consists of the remaining tribes of Israel. Sometimes it is called after its main tribe Ephraim; otherwise it is simply Israel.

The northern kingdom is destroyed by the Assyrians when they conquer its capital, Samaria, in 722 B.C.E. The Assyrians follow a policy of forced resettlement: Many of the Israelites are deported to other places, whereas foreign people are settled in the Israelite territory. From this results a mixed population. Though some of the inhabitants of the northern territory still feel they are Israelites, they are not recognized as such by the people of the southern tribes. In New Testament times, they reappear as the "Samaritans."

The southern kingdom is destroyed by the Babylonians (see BABYLON) in 587 B.C.E. However, the people are allowed to resettle around Jerusalem in the time of the Persians, becoming the Persian province of Judah (see RETURN FROM EXILE). From this name also the designation *Jew* has developed. Today, many Jews still assign themselves to one of the Israelite tribes.

Jacob   Ancestor of the people of Israel, son of ISAAC and grandson of ABRAHAM. Characteristic of his life is that he has to wrestle time and again to obtain God's blessing. Cheating and being cheated, he has to learn not to rely on his own cunning but on God. When he finally receives the blessing, God gives him the new name *Israel,* meaning "God-wrestler" (Genesis 32:28). With his two wives, Leah and Rachel, and their two maids, Bilhah and Zilpah, he fathers 12 sons in total. They become the ancestors of the 12 tribes of Israel (see ISRAEL, TWELVE TRIBES OF). See also GENESIS in Part II.

Jericho   The Jericho of the Bible is today's Tell es-Sultan, located to the north of the DEAD SEA. The place was populated from the early Neolithic age (7000 B.C.E.) onward. At the time of Joshua, Jericho was a strategically important fortress since it controlled the access to Canaan from the east from the plains of Moab. Therefore, Jericho is the first city the Israelites have to conquer when they enter the land (see CANAAN, CONQUEST OF). In the book of Joshua, the conquest of Jericho is described as a ceremonial or ritual rather than a military act: priests carrying the ark of the covenant lead the Israelite army. They march around the city, one time each for six days, and seven times on the seventh day, thereby symbolically consecrating the city to God. When they sound the trumpets, God himself makes the city walls collapse.

The destruction of Jericho has been confirmed by archaeological excavations. However, the archaeological dating of this destruction is disputed. The time of Joshua's conquest is one of the options discussed. For a more detailed discussion see Joshua in Part II.

Jerusalem   In religious terms, Jerusalem is one of the world's most sacred cities, containing sites revered by Jews, Christians, and Muslims. In the Bible, it is also known as Zion, from the name of one of its hills.

It lies some 30 miles (about 48 kilometers) inland from the Mediterranean, in the hills of Judea, northwest of the Dead Sea. In the history of the Israelites, it became their capital in the days of King David, who took it from its original inhabitants, the Jebusites (2 Samuel 5:6–8). The part he developed is known as "the city of David," consisting of his palace and a fortified area. He planned the site and construction of a permanent temple for the ark of the covenant, which he had taken to the city (2 Samuel 6).

However, it was David's son, Solomon, who actually built the temple, a full account of which is to be found in 1 Chronicles 23:1–2 Chronicles 7:10. From then on, Jerusalem was seen to be the site where God had placed his presence. Many of the Psalms celebrate this (e.g., Psalm 122).

Jerusalem was attacked by the Egyptians (1 Kings 14:25f.) and Assyrians (2 Kings 18:13–19:36) before being destroyed by the Babylonians in 587 B.C.E. After the EXILE, the temple and city were rebuilt between 536–445 B.C.E., as recorded in Ezra-Nehemiah. The temple was desecrated in the INTERTESTAMENTAL PERIOD and had to be reconsecrated.

In the New Testament, the city, under Roman control from 63 B.C.E., was still the center of Jewish worship in a temple largely rebuilt by HEROD. The Gospels describe various features of the city, including the Mount of Olives, the Garden of Gethsemane, and Golgotha, the site of JESUS CHRIST's death. After Christ's resurrection it became the center of the early Christian Church (Acts 1–8). It was destroyed by the Romans in 70 C.E. and rebuilt some time later but without a temple.

The city features prominently in prophetic writing both as the actual city and as the ideal city of the future, on earth (as Ezekiel 40–48), or in heaven (cf. the "heavenly Jerusalem" of Hebrews 12:22). APOCALYPTIC WRITING, both Jewish and Christian, features a new Jerusalem to which all nations shall come, either in worship or military opposition, or both.

Jesus Christ   Jesus Christ is the central character of the New Testament. The name *Jesus* is the Greek form of the Hebrew *Joshua,* which means

The transfiguration of Jesus (Luke 9:28–36), engraving
by Julius Schnorr von Carolsfeld

"God saves." This entry is subdivided into discussions of the life and the character of Jesus.

JESUS' LIFE

The primary sources for Jesus' life are the GOSPELS. Of these the three SYNOPTIC GOSPELS provide similar outlines, whereas the Gospel of John has its own approach. The rest of the New Testament has just a few data to add, with contemporary extrabiblical sources merely confirming the key facts.

Each gospel begins by making it clear who Jesus really is—a divine person—and subsequently describes how during his life his contemporaries struggled to understand him. The reader is thus privileged over the actors in the stories.

Jesus' cousin and precursor, John (see JOHN THE BAPTIST), was born less than a year before he was; both miraculous births were announced by angel appearances. In the case of Jesus the angel said that his mother would remain a virgin and that he would not have a human father as God himself would conceive him through the Holy Spirit. At that time Mary and her fiancé, Joseph, were still unmarried.

Although they lived in NAZARETH, Jesus was born in BETHLEHEM, the city of King DAVID, probably in the year 6 B.C.E. Because Mary's husband, Joseph, adopted him, Jesus officially became a descendant of David. The Gospel of John adds an extra dimension to Jesus' identity by arguing that Jesus exists as God from eternity, so that his birth as a human being can be described as "incarnation." This term is derived from the Latin word *caro*—which means "flesh, human being"—and it is used to say that Jesus became a true mortal Jewish human being.

Little is known about his youth except one incident when he was 12 years old. Because *Jesus* was a very common name, he was often referred to as *Jesus of Nazareth.* At the age of around 30, in 26 or 29 C.E., he began a wandering ministry of preaching and teaching. Its start was marked by his baptism by John the Baptist, a programmatic speech in the synagogue at Nazareth, and the highly symbolic event of turning water into wine during a wedding.

During a period of some three years, Jesus traveled through the HOLY LAND and occasionally across the borders into neighboring territories to the north. This type of ministry was typical for Jewish religious teachers. Jesus paid occasional visits to Jerusalem, in particular for the main religious festivals. He soon had a large following, but many people also deserted him in view of his radical demands. The group of his close followers gradually developed into a band of 12 named individuals, who were called disciples. Rich people provided material support to this group, and they occasionally stayed with friends in Bethany, called Mary, Martha, and Lazarus. From early on most leaders of the Jewish people did not like Jesus, however, as he threatened their positions and was less scrupulous than they about aspects of the Jewish lifestyle.

Jesus' main activities were preaching to large groups, teaching his followers, and performing diverse MIRACLES. His meetings with individuals set them on a new course in life. Key elements of his teaching were the PARABLES. A well-known collection of his ethical teaching is the so-called Sermon on the Mount in Matthew 5–7, which can be seen as a kind of constitution of the KINGDOM OF GOD (KINGDOM OF HEAVEN). Jesus withdrew regularly from even his disciples to pray in private. A key moment was his transfiguration on a mountain in the north of Israel.

Around the midpoint of his ministry, after the violent death of John the Baptist, Jesus started telling the disciples about his approaching end, but they hardly recognized these signals. However, his foreknowledge indicates that his death was more than a tragic incident or a miscarriage of justice. When he traveled to Jerusalem for the last time, he made a triumphal entry into the capital city as its rightful king. He subsequently challenged the old dispensation by cleansing the temple, its bulwark. His last week was characterized by increased confrontations with the Jewish leaders and public announcements by Jesus that the privileged position of Israel would come to an end unless they would convert to their God, who was now revealing his will through him, Jesus.

With his disciples Jesus celebrated the PASSOVER meal, which he gave a new meaning that revolves around his own achievement. He also used the occasion for a long farewell speech and a beautiful prayer. The same night he was betrayed by one of his disciples, Judas, and put on trial by the Jewish ruling council, which condemned him to death for blasphemy. As the Jews could not execute capital punishment, a Roman trial ensued at which the governor, PILATE, declared Jesus innocent but nonetheless acceded to Jewish pressure to allow the crucifixion of Jesus. Thus on the Friday before Easter, Jesus of Nazareth died in the most cruel way possible. Friends obtained permission to bury him, and the Jews had the tomb sealed and guarded by soldiers, but on the morning of Easter Day his tomb was found open and empty. Christians interpret this as evidence that God had restored him to life. This event is known as his resurrection, which is seen as a divine display of power, the basis for the salvation of humankind, and a prototype for the believers' transformation from death to life.

After that Easter morning Jesus appeared to numerous people on different occasions (in this respect 1 Corinthians 15 is a valuable addition to the gospel stories) but after 40 days returned to heaven (his so-called ascension, Acts 1). Christians live in the expectation of his second coming (see LAST THINGS).

JESUS' CHARACTER AND TITLE

During his lifetime many people, even his disciples, had no clear idea who Jesus was, although spec-ulation abounded. Jesus is credited with normal human emotions and qualities such as sadness, joy, hunger, and thirst. He was generally recognized as a teacher, even a prophet, possibly more than just a prophet. He was compared to Elijah, Elisha, and Moses. Soon after his life his followers acknowledged him as divine, equal to the God of Israel, and worthy of worship and adoration. This recognition was largely due to his resurrection. However, several centuries passed before the church formulated the detailed creeds about his divinity and his humanity, because they did not want to compromise the latter.

John's gospel makes it clear that Jesus claimed divinity by calling himself "the Son" and "the Son of God," and by speaking of God as his Father; see also Matthew 11:25–27. In the Synoptic Gospels, on the other hand, Jesus often refers to himself as "the Son of Man." This often misunderstood title is not explained in the texts and was not used as a title by the Jews. When read against the background of Daniel 7:13–14, it turns out to be a title that marks Jesus out as God's special envoy. Thus "Son of God" and "Son of Man" are not a contrasting pair, for both denote Jesus' special authority and status. On the lips of Jesus, "Son of Man" constitutes a claim to be Israel's leader but also an attempt to avoid the politically laden title *Messiah*.

The title *Messiah* also lays claim to a special identity. *Messiah* is a Hebrew word that means "anointed one" and is translated as "Christ" (Greek *Christos*). In the Hebrew Bible kings, priests, and some prophets were anointed with oil to commission them for their roles. The expectation in the Hebrew Bible and in the INTERTESTAMENTAL PERIOD was that God would one day send an anointed one to save and redeem his people. Over time this expectation acquired political overtones, which explain why Jesus largely avoided it until the end of his life. That Jesus is the Messiah is nonetheless the heart of the message proclaimed in Acts (see 10:34–43). The title is frequent at the beginning of Matthew (1:16–18; 2:4). Note that *Christ* is a title and that its use as a proper name is secondary.

The title *Son of David*, which is frequent in Matthew, more or less equals *Messiah* in that it suggests high honor and has military overtones. It may also imply that Jesus is the one who brings Israel's history to fulfillment.

Another common designation of Jesus is *Lord* (Greek *kurios*). This word can mean "Sir" or "owner," and it was used to address a master. But in the Septuagint (see BIBLE, EARLY TRANSLATIONS OF) it translates God's name *Yahweh,* and some of the usage in relation to Jesus suggests he was seen at the level of God. When the early church worshipped Jesus as "the Lord," the implication was that they saw him as divine. His followers probably began to recognize Jesus as Lord in this sense only at the Resurrection, but what they recognized was a status that Jesus had had all along.

Among Luke's favorite concepts are *Savior* (Greek *sōtēr*) and "Servant of the Lord" (see at Isaiah). *Savior* was a word frequently applied to kings, gods, doctors, and philosophers. In addition Luke often uses the word *salvation* (Greek *sotēria*) to characterize the work of Jesus.

John begins his gospel by calling Jesus "the Word" (Greek *logos*) of God. He is also the one evangelist to use the title *Lamb (of God)*, which is characteristic of the way Revelation refers to Jesus.

JESUS AND THE HEBREW BIBLE

Christian readers find numerous passages in the Hebrew Bible that contain predictions of elements of Jesus' person and ministry. As shown earlier, much of the vocabulary in the New Testament is based on that of the Hebrew Bible. There are countless passages in the New Testament in which the Hebrew Bible is expounded as referring to Jesus Christ.

In parts of the Hebrew Bible the emphasis is on the suffering of the promised one, in others on his ultimate triumph. Messianic passages, taken by Christians to relate to Jesus, include Genesis 3:15; Deuteronomy 18:15–20; 2 Samuel 7:6–16; Psalms 2; 22; 45; 110; Isaiah 9:1–7; 11:1–10; 42:1–7; 49:1–7; 50:4–9; 52:13–53:12; 61:1–3; Daniel 7:13; Zechariah 9:9–10; and Malachi 3:1, among many others.

John the Baptist   John, the forerunner of JESUS CHRIST, was sent by God to prepare the hearts of the Jewish people for Jesus' ministry. John taught

that belonging to the nation of Israel was not enough to please God. People needed to repent of their sins and change their lifestyles. As a sign of this change, people were baptized, i.e., immersed in water. Among those baptized by John was Jesus himself.

John was born the son of an elderly couple in Judea, Zechariah and Elizabeth, who were of priestly descent. Elizabeth was a relative of Mary, and the pregnancies of the women overlapped (Luke 1). The New Testament sees John as the fulfilment of prophecies about a messenger like Elijah (Malachi 3:1; 4:5–6).

Contemporary Judaism practiced periodic ritual immersion, but BAPTISM as a one-time act was an innovation. John was particularly critical of the religious establishment of PHARISEES AND SADDUCEES and scribes. John is mentioned by the contemporary historian Flavius Josephus, who gives a slightly different picture of his ministry.

When Jesus began his ministry, John gradually disappeared into the background (but see Matthew 11:2–15) and Jesus took over some of his disciples. Sometime during Jesus' activity, John was captured by King HEROD Antipas and killed at the request of his wife (Mark 6:16–29).

Certain phrases in John's gospel suggest that for a while there was some rivalry between followers of Jesus and people who clung to John (1:8; 3:30; 4:1–2); this impression is confirmed in Acts 19:1–7 and in later church history. To this day the sect of the Mandaeans worships John and rejects Jesus.

John the Evangelist   Strictly speaking, the Fourth Gospel (see John [Gospel] in Part II) is anonymous, but the tradition of the church unanimously ascribes it to the apostle John, who held the epithet *Evangelist* to distinguish him from JOHN THE BAPTIST. This John, son of Zebedee and brother of James, originally a fisher, was among the first four disciples called by JESUS (Matthew 4:18–22). He is mentioned in the SYNOPTIC GOSPELS and in Acts (e.g., 3:1–11; 8:14–25) but surprisingly not at all in the fourth gospel, in which *John* consistently refers to John the Baptist (e.g., 1:6; 4:1).

However, in the fourth gospel an enigmatic Beloved Disciple appears (13:23; 19:26; 20:2;

21:7, 20), who is assumed to be the work's author, John the evangelist, who also refers to himself as "another disciple" next to Peter (18:15–16; 20:2–8). In chapter 21 Jesus promises this disciple a long life, and, whereas for all other disciples we have extrabiblical stories or legends about their martyrdoms, John the Evangelist is indeed reputed to have died peacefully in old age in Ephesus, having written a gospel and three letters (see 1, 2, and 3 John in Part II).

The contents of the gospel and the first letter also earned John the epithet "apostle of love." Whether he is also the John who authored Revelation (1:1, 4, 9; 22:8) is uncertain.

Jordan, River   The Jordan is a relatively small river that rises in the area of Mount Hermon in LEBANON. It finds its way through the SEA OF GALILEE and the Jordan Valley to the Dead Sea, which is some 1,200 feet (400 meters) below sea level. It thus flows through the lowest-lying area on earth. Its length is some 100 miles (170 km) as the crow flies, but its meandering means the real length is double that distance. In the times of the HEBREW BIBLE the Jordan divided the HOLY LAND in two; nowadays the Kingdom of Jordan is to the east of the river, with Israel and the present West Bank to the west.

The Hebrew Bible regularly mentions the Jordan; in Deuteronomy the expression *cross the Jordan* refers to Israel's coming entry into the Promised Land as the book's perspective is from east of the Jordan. The Jordan plays a major role in the narrative of the entry of the Israelites under Joshua (Joshua 1–4), in the ascension of Elijah (2 Kings 2), and in the ministry of JOHN THE BAPTIST (Matthew 3; John 3:22–26). Consequently, for believers the Jordan became a symbol of transition to a new life, although in popular parlance and song it also represents the "river of death."

Judah   Judah is one of the 12 sons of JACOB and the ancestor of the tribe bearing his name (see ISRAEL, TWELVE TRIBES OF). After the division of Israel into a northern and a southern part, *Judah* also becomes the designation for the southern kingdom as a whole. In still later times, when the north-

ern kingdom has faded, *Judah* is used as a synonym for Israel in general, hence the designation *Jew*. From the tribe of Judah, King DAVID and his successors descended.

Judaism   The term *Judaism* is used to refer to the religion of the Jews in the period after approximately 300 B.C.E., when the Hebrew Bible was more or less complete. (The religion of the period of the Hebrew Bible is known as the Israelite religion.) At this time, the Jews believed that authoritative prophecy had come to an end. A new development beyond the original Israelite religion was the origin of the SYNAGOGUE. The DEAD SEA SCROLLS show how diverse Judaism had become around the turn of the era. Some of the groups, the PHARISEES AND SADDUCEES, are mentioned in the New Testament.

Later on, in particular as a result of the DIASPORA and of the destruction of Jerusalem in 70 C.E., Judaism became increasingly determined by the traditions of the orthodox rabbis. These traditions are reflected in the Mishnah and the Talmud, collections of rabbinic legislation and its interpretation that were codified from 200 C.E. onward. Modern-day Judaism is very diverse, with major groups such as Reform, Conservative, and Orthodox Judaism.

Christianity originated as a faction within Judaism that shared its Scriptures. Over several generations it became an independent religion in its own right, which acknowledges the New Testament as a record of God's further revelation in JESUS CHRIST.

Judges, period of   A period of the history of Israel, about 1380–1030 B.C.E., dealt with in the book of Judges. After the conquest of Canaan (see CANAAN, CONQUEST OF), the nation is politically organized as a rather loose confederation of the cities and villages of the 12 tribes. In situations when other people groups attack and oppress Israel, leaders are appointed to help Israel out of the crisis. These leaders are called "judges," although their main function is a military one. Many of the judges have only regional influence.

The book of Judges analyzes the era theologically, in "cycles of disobedience": first people are disobedient to God, then God sends a punishment in the form of a military threat, then the people cry to God, then God appoints a judge delivering the people, then, after the death of the judge, the people become disobedient again.

To the end of the era, the PHILISTINES become an increasing threat to Israel. They are one of the reasons why the people call for a king. With the installation of Saul as king around 1030 B.C.E., the era of the Israelite MONARCHY begins. For more information, see Judges and 1 and 2 Samuel in Part II.

kingdom of God (kingdom of heaven)   One of the key convictions of the people of Israel is that God is not only Lord over Israel but also king of the whole universe. Yet there is also the awareness that at present the world is in rebellion and that in the future God will bring his kingdom to full realization.

In the New Testament, Jesus Christ makes this kingdom the central subject of his preaching and teaching, proclaiming that in his mission God is realizing the kingdom in the present time. In saying this, he was preceded by John the Baptist, and both purged the concept of its nationalistic associations. According to Jesus, God has begun to perform his final acts in the world, and the bliss of the future age is already experienced. Jesus proclaims God's mercy and brings acceptance, forgiveness, and healing. Those who wish to enter the kingdom must commit themselves to follow him and to love one another. Jesus reveals much about what the kingdom is like through his parables and through the miracles he performs.

God's kingdom does not coincide with a territory or a society, e.g., Israel or the church. The sovereignty of God can rather be described as an *event* (Isaiah 52:7–10), the state of affairs when God's rule is established. To bring this out the term *kingship* could be preferred to *kingdom*.

The mysterious aspect of the kingship is that it originated within the confines of history in the person, deeds, and words of the man Jesus, who was proclaimed king by God. Jesus only partially realized the kingdom, and it will be fully realized in the end times (see LAST THINGS). This mysteriousness implies that God's kingship can be overlooked and resisted, and that the church is only an imperfect

realization of it. This explains why passages that speak about the kingdom as present and passages about a future kingdom can be found side by side in the Gospels.

The preceding discussion is based on Jesus' teaching according to the SYNOPTIC GOSPELS; John's gospel puts different accents and depicts Jesus as empowered by the Spirit. What the Synoptics call entry into the kingdom, John calls birth by the Holy Spirit (John 3:3–5). In the New Testament letters the message of the kingdom gives way to a more direct proclamation of Jesus himself as king and of the work of the Spirit.

Whereas Matthew prefers to speak of the kingdom of heaven—in order to avoid a direct reference to God—Mark and Luke refer to the kingdom of God; no difference in meaning is implied.

kingship   See DAVID; MONARCHY.

lament   In older literatures, a subgenre that expresses grief at some personal or national tragedy, written or sung as poetry. The subgenre in the Bible contains these well-defined features:

- Invoking God through a recital of God's past deeds for his people
- Reminding him of the present dire state
- Pleading for God to act once again
- Confessing sins that have caused the catastrophe
- Praying with confidence and thanks that God will answer
- Often concluding with a question either rhetorical or open

Typical verbal markers of a lament are "How...!"; "How long?"; "Why?"; "Help!"; "Awake O LORD!" The tense is typically past, or past and present interweaving. Often the theological basis is a *theodicy:* trying to understand how an evil event has apparently derived from a good God; or a *confession,* for acknowledged past failure.

Remarkable laments in the Hebrew Bible include the book of Lamentations, over the destruction of JERUSALEM by the Babylonians, and a number of Psalms (12; 44; 60; 79f.; 83; 85; 94:1–11; 126; 137). Individual examples include David's lament over the deaths of Saul and Jonathan (2 Samuel

1:17–27) and Isaiah's over Jerusalem (Isaiah 63:7–64:12). But laments can be over enemies. One of the most remarkable laments is Ezekiel's over Tyre and Sidon in Ezekiel 26–28, a complex interweaving of three laments and three WOES AND DENUNCIATIONS, showing the complex verbal patterning of both subgenres and their interrelatedness. The laments are in the past tense; the woes in the future, though the time reference is the same. It would seem from Ezekiel 32:16 that the lament was often chanted.

A similar subgenre is the *complaint* (as in Job 6–7; 9–10).

The opposite of the lament might be considered *the consolation,* as in Isaiah 40. Both laments and consolations are communal acts (e.g., 1 Chronicles 7:22). Again, there is a close interrelationship.

last things   The events that will occur at the end of this age, also known as *eschatology* (from Greek *eschatos,* "last").

According to the New Testament, the main event in history was the death and resurrection of JESUS CHRIST, which has already taken place. In the same way as in World War II the invasion in Normandy on D-day (1944) effectively broke the power of Nazi Germany, although the final victory (V-day, 1945) was still in the future, so Jesus' resurrection was D-day, whereas the completion of world history will be V-day. Christians believe that they live between these two points and that since the resurrection the world is in the so-called last days. The KINGDOM OF GOD (KINGDOM OF HEAVEN) is already at work in history, but they still await Jesus' return, also called the "second coming" (Greek *parousia*). In the Roman Empire *parousia* denoted the visit of a dignitary, a visit that already had significant impact before the actual event. Two other words used to designate the return of Jesus also point to it as a glorious event. The one is "revelation" (*apokalupsis*), the other "glorious manifestation" (*epiphaneia*). The term *the Day,* which usually occurs in phrases like *the Day of the Lord,* is bleaker; it stems from the Hebrew Bible. There is no material difference in what these four words refer to, but whereas the singular *Day* refers to the actual coming of Christ, the plural *days* or *last days* refers to the preceding period. In this entry both some penultimate events and the Day itself are discussed. The systematic study of the last things is called *eschatology* from the Greek word for last, *eschatos.*

Jesus Christ spoke regularly about his future return (e.g., Mark 13:26; cf. 8:38; 14:62) and several of his PARABLES urge believers to be alert and watchful for it. In Mark 13 he also mentioned events that will precede his return, such as the preaching of the gospel to all nations, persecution of believers, wars, earthquakes, and famines. Likewise, Revelation is largely taken up by events leading up to the return of Jesus, which are here seen as divine judgments over the earth, on the one hand, and increased activity of SATAN, on the other. The central place of Jesus is expressed by the title *Alpha and Omega* (the first and the last letter of the Greek alphabet), which he shares with God the Father (Revelation 22:13; cf. 1:8; 21:6).

In places it looks as if the apostle Paul expected the imminent return of Jesus (e.g., Romans 13:12). However, in 2 Thessalonians 2 he calms the overheated expectations of his readers, which at least in part must have stemmed from his own preaching, by explaining that prior to Jesus' coming there will be a rebellion against God led by his adversary (see ANTICHRIST). 2 Peter 3 also deals with the alleged delay of Jesus' return, arguing that what to human beings seems a long period, for God is only a very brief period: "With the Lord a day is like a thousand years, and a thousand years are like a day."

Several places use imagery of "the last trumpet," which will be blown as a signal of Jesus' return. The trumpet in biblical language is the instrument to announce important events, and it here serves to highlight the public character of Christ's return. In a way, Jesus' coming will be unexpected, and for that reason it is compared to a thief in the night. In 1 Thessalonians 4:13–18 Paul gives some details of the events that will take place at that moment: Jesus himself will appear, and those who are in their graves will rise to join him. Then the living believers will meet him too, and finally they will all be with Jesus forever. The fact that not only those who are alive when Christ comes but also those who died previously are involved has led to the expression "the resurrection of the dead" (1 Corinthians 15:12, 42).

In just one passage, Revelation 20, it is said that after the return of Jesus there will be a prolonged period of peace followed by a final insurrection of his enemies, who will swiftly be defeated. As this period of peace lasts 1,000 years, it is called the millennium. Afterward the unbelievers will return to be judged and receive punishment. The final judgment, mentioned regularly in the New Testament, can be seen as a form of retribution that will not affect the followers of Jesus as they have already been forgiven. Grounds for the retribution are a lack of faith and the absence of good works. Whereas in the Hebrew Bible God was seen as the future judge, in the New Testament this role is ascribed to Jesus. Revelation 19:11–21 is a highly figurative description of the last judgment. Another way to look at the same event is to see it as the final defeat of Satan, when he and his associates will receive their due.

As to the nature of the ensuing punishment, if any, Christians are divided. Traditionally, it is seen as HELL, a fiery place where people will be eternally tormented. This view is best supported by the biblical texts (e.g., Matthew 13:49–50). Some Christians argue, however, that the unbelievers will not be punished eternally but annihilated. Still others hold that in the end the love of God is stronger than human unbelief and that—maybe after a process of purification—all people will still be accepted by God.

Finally, God will renew HEAVEN and earth and there will be no more death (Revelation 20:14; 21:4). The imagery of a new Jerusalem is used to describe the glory of the new creation in Revelation 21. God's original creation will not be destroyed but cleansed, renewed, and glorified. Thus the future brings the liberation of creation from the powers of sin and death, which have reigned from the moment sin entered the world (Romans 8:18–27). It is better to speak of the eternal state of the believers in terms of "being with God" than in terms of "being in heaven."

Elsewhere the image of a festive or bridal meal is used to describe the ultimate situation. The believers will receive a renewed body and live eternally with God and with Jesus in a state of happiness, without grief, pain, illness, death, or any other problem. Thus the return of Jesus will bring world history to completion and vindicate him in the eyes of all humanity. We are not given much detail about the future state. The emphasis in the Bible is on eternal being with God.

law   In the biblical context, *Law* or *Law of Moses* refers to the laws connected to the Sinai covenant and contained in the PENTATEUCH, especially in the books Exodus, Leviticus, Numbers, and Deuteronomy. The Law comprises legal and cultic material as well, since there was no distinction between politics and religion at that time. The most important part of the Law is the TEN COMMANDMENTS.

In comparing the Sinaitic law to other law codes from the ancient Near East, many similarities but also differences emerge. Among the most striking contrasts are that in the Sinaitic law there are (almost) no class distinctions; rather, all people are regarded as equal before the law; and that human life has a high value protected by maximal penalties. The theological key for understanding the Sinaitic laws is to see that they are part of a COVENANT. That means that keeping the commandments is seen as a response by believers to God, who has delivered the people out of EGYPT and promises to bless them.

In the New Testament, God forms a new covenant community, which consists of Jews and Gentiles. It becomes evident that, through the death and Resurrection of JESUS CHRIST, the members of this new community, the Church, are not bound by the letter of the Law. Nonetheless, the Law remains important as guidance for the life of the Church and for the insights it provides into the will of God.

Lebanon   Modern Lebanon is Israel's northwest neighbor, lying along the Mediterranean. Originally, the name applied to the mountain range that runs the length of the country, rising to 10,000 feet (3,300 meters). On its slopes the famous Cedars of Lebanon grew, whose export was economically significant. Even more significant from a literary point of view was their figurative use as an image of strength, beauty, or pride (see Song of Solomon 5:15; Isaiah 2:13; 14:8). In its southern section, Mount Hermon, eternally snow capped, is the main feature.

In the Hebrew Bible, the country is known mainly as two united city-states of Tyre and Sidon, both major ports. They were inhabited by a Semitic people, whose culture and language have been well documented through archaeological work at Ugarit. They grew rich through trade. Ezekiel 26–28 gives a vivid description of their magnificence, using imagery later applied to SATAN.

Relations with Israel were friendly in David's time, with materials and craftsmen for the temple being imported (1 Kings 5). But when the Tyrian princess Jezebel married the Israelite king Ahab and reintroduced a particularly attractive fertility religion, based on Baal and Astarte (1 Kings 16:30–33), prophetic preaching turned against the country, led by Elijah (1 Kings 18–19). WOES AND DENUNCIATIONS followed: Isaiah 23; Jeremiah 27:1–11; Joel 3:4–8; Zechariah 9:2–3 can be added to the Ezekiel passage to exemplify this.

Tyre-Sidon later became known as Phoenicia, and though it did suffer militarily at times, it also planted a number of colonies round the Mediterranean, the most famous of which was Carthage. In the New Testament it was part of the Roman province of SYRIA and became a place of refuge for persecuted Christians, being also mentioned in Paul's travels.

letter See EPISTLE.

litotes See IMAGERY, BIBLICAL.

Lord's Prayer In Matthew 6:9–13 and Luke 11:2–4 we find a prayer that Jesus taught his followers to pray and that has become a standard prayer in the church. By its first words it is also known as the *Paternoster* (Our Father).

The versions of Matthew and Luke differ, probably reflecting the fact that Jesus taught similar subjects several times. The form commonly used in Christian churches follows that of Matthew as found in the King James Version (see BIBLE, ENGLISH EDITIONS OF). This version is longer than that of recent translations in that at the end it reads,

"For thine is the kingdom, and the power, and the glory, for ever. Amen." These additional words are not found in the best manuscripts, and they probably originated in the earliest Church.

The form of the prayer is highly stylized. After the opening "Our Father," the first three petitions contain the word *your* and ascribe glory to God. The last three contain the word *us*, and they ask for the provision of basic human needs. This order reflects the priorities in Jesus' teaching. The prayer as a whole is in the plural so that it can be used by the community of Jesus' followers. Interpreters tend to think that Jesus did not intend the very words of this short prayer to be recited, but that it was rather meant as an example of good practice.

Lord's Supper (Eucharist, Communion) A formal act instituted by JESUS CHRIST himself during his last meal with his TWELVE DISCIPLES (Luke 22:14–20; 1 Corinthians 11:23–26). This meal had begun as a Jewish PASSOVER meal, to which Jesus added the innovation of centering the meaning in himself. As a result, Christians no longer celebrate the PASSOVER festival.

The New Testament, in particular in 1 Corinthians 14:26–32 and Colossians 3:16, gives us limited insights into what happened at the meetings of the early Christians. In additions to the things mentioned in these passages, we know that new believers were baptized (see BAPTISM) and that the Lord's Supper was celebrated. Both practices are confirmed by postbiblical sources.

The Lord's Supper consists of bread and wine, the elements mentioned in the story of its institution, which symbolize the body and the blood of Jesus, who suffered vicariously for those who believe in him (John 6). In Acts the ceremony is referred to as "breaking bread" (2:42, 46; 20:7). Postbiblical names for the same are *Communion, Eucharist,* and *Mass.* The first is based on the fellowship of believers with Jesus and with one another; the second means "thanksgiving" and refers to the thanks given in prayer for the elements of bread and wine (1 Corinthians 10:16 New International Version). The third is used by Roman Catholics, who traditionally believe that bread and wine are transformed into the actual body and blood of Christ.

manuscripts   In the period when the Bible was being written, the art of printing books was unknown. For centuries, the handwritten texts were copied by trained scribes as well as laypeople. The original manuscripts have not been preserved, but we have sufficient manuscripts of good quality to be able to establish the original text. Compared to that for the works of ancient authors such as Plato, Virgil, and Tacitus, the manuscript evidence for the text of the Bible is excellent.

The oldest complete Hebrew Bibles are only from around 1000 C.E. because of the Jewish practice habit of destroying worn manuscripts. But among the DEAD SEA SCROLLS were found two complete scrolls of Isaiah and fragments of other books.

Complete copies of the Septuagint (see BIBLE, EARLY TRANSLATIONS OF) date back to the fourth century, just as complete copies of the New Testament. The oldest manuscripts of the Septuagint date from before the turn of the era. The oldest fragmentary manuscript of the New Testament is known as Papyrus 52. Dating from the first half of the second century, it contains a few verses from John 18 and is kept in the John Rylands Library, Manchester, United Kingdom. The famous Codex Sinaiticus dates from the fourth century and surfaced in the 19th century; it contains both the Septuagint and the New Testament. It is in the British Library, London, United Kingdom.

Archaeologists continue to discover manuscripts from time to time. Occasionally these shed new light on a word, but on the whole the biblical text is well established. The important manuscripts have been published so that they can be studied by scholars all over the world.

Mary (mother of Jesus)   JESUS CHRIST was born from a young woman called Mary who lived in NAZARETH, in the north of Israel (Matthew 1–2; Luke 1–2). Her fiancé and later husband, Joseph, was a descendant of King David, so that Jesus was regarded as being from the line of David. Mary, however, was not a descendant of David but a relative of Elizabeth, who was from the tribe of Levi (Luke 1:5).

As Jewish women married at a young age, the fact that Mary was engaged at the time of Jesus' birth points to her being a teenager. The Bible indicates that God was the father of Jesus through the activity of the Holy Spirit and that Mary was still a virgin when Jesus was born. This miracle is known as "the virgin birth" but should rather be called the virginal conception.

Mary is mentioned several times in the further gospel narratives, sometimes together with other children of hers, the brothers of Jesus. She figures in John 2:1–11, whereas John 19:26–27 tells how Jesus cared for her future after his departure. Here and elsewhere she is only called "the mother of Jesus." In Acts 1:14 she is mentioned among the early nucleus of followers of Jesus, but she plays no further role in the early church. The fact that her husband, Joseph, is never mentioned after the birth of Jesus suggests that he died before Jesus' public activity began.

The name *Mary* was very common in Israel, and the Bible also includes other women called Mary, such as Mary of Bethany, who anointed Jesus (John 11–12), and Mary Magdalene (John 20). The Hebrew version of the name, *Miriam*, was carried by Moses' and Aaron's sister (Exodus 15:20; Numbers 12).

metaphor   See IMAGERY, BIBLICAL.

metonymy   See IMAGERY, BIBLICAL.

miracles   To Jews and Christians the working of the universe and the human body reveals God's constant powerful activity. However, in addition to his "normal" work, he is also believed to intervene in special ways. Throughout the Bible there are many stories about miracles; particularly large numbers occur in Exodus, in the ministries of Elijah and Elisha (see 1 and 2 Kings in Part II), of JESUS CHRIST, and of the apostle PAUL.

In the Hebrew Bible the purpose of most miracles are the well-being and liberation of God's people Israel, whereas in the New Testament miracles are signs of the arrival of the KINGDOM OF GOD (KINGDOM OF HEAVEN.) They are meant to elicit questions and, if possible, faith in the witnesses, although they are not always successful in that respect. Moreover, miracles point to the nature of

God and his purposes, and they confirm the teaching of Jesus. Especially Luke's gospel shows how Jesus' miracles also break down the social and cultural barrier of uncleanness.

Biblical miracles can roughly be classified as nature miracles (e.g., authority over seas and storms), healings, exorcisms, and resurrections. According to the SYNOPTIC GOSPELS, Jesus Christ is the subject of a few special miracles, such as the virgin birth, the transfiguration, the ascension, and supernatural appearances. Belief in demon possession was common among Jews and pagans in that era, and exorcisms also occurred in diverse forms of Judaism.

Jesus sometimes used means to heal people, but sometimes he healed by a mere touch (Luke 4:40; 5:13; 13:13). Whereas some types of miracles have parallels in Greek-Hellenistic religions like the cult of Asclepius, this particular manner of healing is unique to Christianity.

monarchy, period of   An era of the history of Israel, from about 1030 to 586 B.C.E. The era can be divided into three phases: the first heyday of the kingdom under Saul, DAVID, and SOLOMON (1030–931), the time of the divided kingdoms Israel and Judah until the destruction of Israel (931–722), and the time of the sole kingdom of Judah until its destruction (722–586). The time of Saul (1030–1010) marks the transition from the system of the judges (see JUDGES, PERIOD OF) to the monarchy. In some respects, Saul acts more like a judge than like a king, in that for a long time he seems to have no permanent court. In the end, Saul is not successful in defeating the Philistines. Therefore, the narrative presents David (1010–971) as the first "true" king. He sets a standard regarding political power and faithfulness to God. According to 2 Samuel 7, God promises him an everlasting dynasty. Solomon (971–931) stands for the golden time of Israel in terms of economic upturn and peace. In his time, the temple in Jerusalem is built. However, as a result of his turning to idolatry and the high taxes he has imposed upon the people, a rift develops between the northern and southern tribes.

The 10 northern tribes found their own kingdom called *Israel,* choosing Samaria as their capital.

Several dynasties follow each other in the northern kingdom. In 722 B.C.E., the Assyrians conquer Samaria and bring the kingdom to an end. In the southern kingdom of the two tribes of Benjamin and Judah, often called *Judah,* the dynasty of David continues reigning until the destruction of Jerusalem by the Babylonians and the beginning of the Babylonian Exile.

In the Bible, the period of the monarchy is dealt with in the books 1 and 2 Samuel; 1 and 2 Kings; and 1 and 2 Chronicles. Moreover, some of the kings and the events described are also documented in Assyrian, Babylonian, and other extrabiblical documents from the ancient Near East. These texts confirm the basic reliability of the biblical sources. The absolute chronology of the Israelite kings can be established on the basis of Assyrian sources (which, in turn, can be dated in terms of astronomical data mentioned there).

Moses   The most important human character in the Hebrew Bible. Moses is appointed by God to be the leader of the people of Israel, leading them out of Egypt (see EXODUS, THE). Moses also becomes the mediator between God and Israel in making the covenant at Mount SINAI. The stories represent him as a man of strong character, who sometimes reacted wrongly on strong impulses but learned to trust in God for the things he could not do himself. No one ever would be as close to God as Moses was (see Deuteronomy 34:10–12). Therefore, the covenant book of Moses, which is contained in the PENTATEUCH, is seen as the most holy part of the Hebrew Bible. See also Exodus, Leviticus, Numbers, and Deuteronomy in Part II.

narrative   Telling a story or giving an account of events in a storylike way. Narrative can be fictional, as in novels, short stories, or novellas, or nonfictional, as in histories, chronicles, and biographies. It can be of any length. Its language is usually prose, but narrative poetry is also possible.

Narrative needs a narrator, characters, a structured story line, and a setting. An audience is also implied and may be addressed directly. The narrator is not the same as the author, but the two may be close, as in the all-knowing (omniscient) impersonal narrator, or far apart, as when a character in the story tells that story. There are usually a few main characters, who are developed over time and given extensive dialogue, and a number of minor characters. The story line usually gives a train of cause and effect (see STRUCTURES, LITERARY). The setting for the narrative may be primarily historical, geographical, or social.

Biblical narrative is a very flexible form, embracing history, biography, and fiction. It also occurs in nonnarrative material, such as prophecy, and can also contain in itself nonnarrative elements, such as sermons and discourses. It should not be judged anachronistically by the norms of the classic 19th- and 20th-century novel.

Biblical narrative contains a good deal of dialogue and some interior monologue but not usually detailed psychological analyses or descriptions of characters. It is explicit about finding a place for God and includes extensive dialogues between God and the human characters. Ultimately, biblical narrative sees itself as God's story or history, an ordered and unfolding account through time of his dealing with his people, told by a reliable but usually anonymous narrator.

Nazareth   A small town in lower Galilee, which is not mentioned in the Hebrew Bible. According to the New Testament it did not have a high reputation (John 1:46). Nazareth was the residence of both Joseph and MARY, the parents of Jesus. Although Jesus was born in BETHLEHEM, he grew up in Nazareth and was consequently called "Jesus of Nazareth" to distinguish him among the many other males called Jesus.

According to Luke (4:16–30), Jesus gave a programmatic speech in the SYNAGOGUE at Nazareth but was rejected by its inhabitants. He soon moved to Capernaum (Matthew 4:13), although later he seems to have been without a fixed abode (Luke 8:1; 9:58). A later visit to Nazareth was distinctly unsuccessful (Matthew 13:54–57).

New Testament, relationship with the Hebrew Bible   The Hebrew Bible is the Holy Scripture of Jewish believers. For Christian believers, however, it is only one part of it. They often call the Hebrew

Bible the "Old Testament," as opposed to the "New Testament." By doing so, they also reinterpret the Hebrew Bible in a specifically Christian way. This double role of the Hebrew Bible/Old Testament in the Christian canon is an ongoing challenge for interpretation. In the Christian Church, different "solutions" have been followed, ranging from a devaluation or partial rejection of the Old Testament, on the one side, to a total "christianization" by way of a christological allegorical interpretation, on the other side. The real relationship between Old and New Testaments, from the point of view of the first Christians, should be seen more discriminating as follows.

On the one hand, the Hebrew Bible was Holy Scripture for Jesus and the apostles. In no way does the New Testament devalue the Old. On the contrary, the Christian faith is firmly grounded in what is said about God in the Old Testament. God remains the same in descriptions in both the Old and New Testaments, as does the nature of human beings. The apostles do not hesitate to explain and justify even the mission of Jesus Christ by quoting extensively from the Old Testament.

The widespread view that the Old Testament describes a God of revenge and the New Testament a God of love is based on an ignorance of the texts. The Old Testament also speaks about the love and the grace of God, whereas the New Testament also speaks about the judgment of God on all who turn away from him. Jesus' death on the cross is the symbol of God's wrath as well as his love: God's wrath for sin and his love of the sinner. The most important commandment of the New Testament, to love God and one's neighbor, is in fact a quotation from Old Testament passages (Matthew 22:34–40; see Deuteronomy 6:5; Leviticus 19:18, 34).

On the other hand, Jesus is not just a representative of the Old Testament faith. According to Matthew 5:17, Jesus has not come to destroy the "Law and the Prophets" but to "fulfill" them. The Old Testament is a book with an open end, pointing to something beyond, announcing a future "day of the Lord," a time when God will reveal himself and bring judgment and salvation, and a coming kingdom of God that will be established by his Messiah. According to the Christian view, these announcements have been fulfilled in the person of Jesus Christ. He is the fulfillment of the messianic prophecies of the Old Testament, but even more: In him all Old Testament institutions and conceptions have found their complete fulfillment.

This can especially be demonstrated by the covenants God made with human beings at different times, which have come to a typological fulfillment in Jesus Christ.

The most important Old Testament COVENANT is the covenant God made with the people of Israel at Mount Sinai (Exodus 19ff.). After God has liberated the people of Israel from slavery in Egypt, he gives them his commandments, helping them to lead a successful life according to his moral standards. At the same time, the Old Testament worship and ritual are also established, in which sin can be redeemed by sacrificing animals.

According to the New Testament, Jesus Christ is the only one who kept all the commandments of the Sinai covenant. In that way he "fulfilled" the covenant. Moreover, Jesus also "fulfilled" the sacrificial ceremonial system, offering himself as the "true Lamb of God." By his death on the cross, he pays once and for all for sin and reconciles to God all those human beings who believe in him. By his self-sacrifice, he finally validates all the animal sacrifices that have been offered in the past. After the death and Resurrection of Jesus, no more animal offerings are necessary.

Therefore, in the New Testament the Sinai covenant is taken up by a "new covenant": "This cup is the new covenant in my blood that is poured out for you" (Luke 22:20; see Jeremiah 31:31f.). Thereby, the old covenant is transformed into the new: The political shape of Israel as the first people of God is transformed into a spiritual shape of the worldwide Christian Church as the second people of God; the national-political legislation of the Mosaic Law is transformed onto a spiritual level, where the moral values stay the same, but the specific legislation is left over to the secular authorities. The system of temple cult and animal offering is transformed into the New Testament church community having Jesus Christ as their once-for-all sacrifice and their head. (See also LORD'S SUPPER.)

This transformation from the old into the new covenant fundamentally determines the way Christians read the Old Testament. For example, Old Testament promises to Israel are applied to Christians as well (because both are people of God), but leaving aside the political aspects of the promises. From the "old" Sinai covenant and from the new covenant Jesus established, the two designations *Old Testament* and *New Testament* are derived.

There are two more important Old Testament covenants, which relate to the Sinai covenant. According to the New Testament, they are also "fulfilled" in Christ. The Abraham covenant (Genesis 12:1–3) promises among other things that through the descendants of Abraham, blessing would come to all nations. This promise is finally fulfilled by Jesus Christ, the "true Israelite," the son of Abraham (Matthew 1:1). The Davidic covenant (2 Samuel 7:8–16) promises an everlasting dynasty to David. According to the New Testament, Jesus Christ is the expected Son of David (Matthew 1:1), the "true king," establishing the everlasting kingdom of God.

In the New Testament, not only the great covenants, but also all other areas of Old Testament theology are brought into reference with Jesus Christ. Concerning creation theology, for example, Jesus is said to be the mediator of creation (John 1:3; Colossians 1:16; see Genesis 1:1). Concerning wisdom theology, Jesus is the "fulfillment" of divine wisdom (Colossians 2:3; 1 Corinthians 1:24; see Proverbs 8).

A danger of reading the Old Testament according to this Christian way is, however, that the Old Testament is sometimes no longer heard for what it wants to say in itself. In order to prevent this, an Old Testament text should first be understood in itself. Moreover, there are many areas of Christian theology where the Old Testament has more to say than the New, for example, regarding creation, wisdom, government, culture, and sexuality.

From a Christian perspective, both Old Testament and New Testament are revelation of the same God and therefore part of the Holy Scripture. The New Testament directly addresses the Christian Church. The Old Testament, although it first addresses the community of the Sinai covenant, can be applied to the Christian Church insofar as it is the same God who speaks and as the Sinai covenant is taken up in the new covenant of Jesus Christ.

Nile River The Nile is one of the ancient world's great rivers, and the physical source and sustenance of Egyptian civilization. It rises from two sources in East Africa, one branch being 3,500 miles, the other 4,000, as they flow through Ethiopia (*Cush* in the Hebrew Bible) and Uganda, respectively, before joining in the Sudan (*Nubia*) and Egypt, then emptying into the Mediterranean Sea in a huge delta. All the major ancient Egyptian cities lay on its banks: Thebes (Luxor), Memphis, Karnak. Its flood patterns and its canal systems ensured continuing fertility in what would otherwise have been desert (compare Jeremiah 46:7–9; Amos 9:5). The worst WOES AND DENUNCIATIONS the prophets could utter against Egypt threatened the drying up of the Nile (e.g., Isaiah 19:5–10; Ezekiel 29:10, 30:12; Zechariah 10:11).

In the Bible, the Nile is closely associated with the period of history from Joseph to Moses. After Joseph's elevation in the Egyptian court, he settled his father's wider family in Goshen, probably in the eastern delta near Raamses (Genesis 47:6, 27). Moses was hidden in the Nile by his parents to escape the ban on Hebrew baby boys (Exodus 2:1–10). His finding by the Egyptian princess was seen as part of his preparation to lead the Hebrews out of Egypt. Two of the plagues sent against the pharaoh had to do with the Nile: the changing of the waters into blood (Exodus 7:14–24) and the plague of frogs (Exodus 8:1–15).

In the Authorized (King James) Version, mirroring the original Hebrew, the term *Nile* is not used, only *the river* (e.g., Genesis 41:1), though elsewhere this term applies to the RIVER EUPHRATES (Zechariah 9:10).

See also EGYPT.

numbers, significance of Most numbers given in biblical texts are to be understood in a literal sense. Larger numbers, such as 5,000, are often rounded even if that is not stated explicitly. Scholars discuss whether some of the very large numbers, for example, in military contexts, are deliberate exaggerations used in the sense of a literary device. Sometimes, however, numbers of the Bible also carry symbolic levels of meaning.

The number 4, especially in APOCALYPTIC WRITING, stands for the four points of the compass. For example, the four creatures with the four faces in Ezekiel 1 symbolize God's power reaching over the whole earth.

The number 7 derives its symbolic meaning from the seven-day week and from the Sabbath as the seventh day. It stands for the divine, for holiness, and/or for completeness. It often appears in the context of priestly tasks, but it can also be used for a fixed, completed period of time in a more general sense. Its derivations 70, 7,000, and 70,000 carry similar symbolic overtones.

The number 10 symbolizes humankind and the (sinful) human nature: 10 fingers, Ten Commandments, 10 times of disobedience (Numbers 14:22), the beast with 10 horns (Daniel 7:7; Revelation 13:1), 10 virgins (Matthew 25:1), 10 lepers (Luke 17:12), 10 servants (Luke 19:13), etc.

Twelve is the number of the tribes of Israel and the number of Jesus' disciples. Twelve, therefore, stands for the Jews and the Christians as the first and second people of God. The numbers 12,000 and 144,000, the latter being $12 \times 12 \times 1,000$, express the fullness of members of the people of God (Revelation 7:4ff.).

Forty is the number of years Israel had to stay in the wilderness before entering the Promised Land. Forty is also the number of days Jesus fasted in the wilderness before beginning his ministry. Therefore, the number of 40 can stand for a time of preparation or temptation. However, it is also used often to describe a longer, fixed period in a more general sense.

For the number 666, see Revelation in Part II.

parables A form of WISDOM LITERATURE that are basically analogies and involve analogical thinking. In the Bible, parables range from pithy axiomatic sayings (as Luke 12:2–7; 22–29) to extended narratives (as Matthew 20:1–16). Many scholars have tried to classify the various types of parables, especially those recorded in the SYNOPTIC GOSPELS, where the majority are to be found.

In the Hebrew Bible, the form is clearly recognized, though in modern translations the term is often translated as "allegories" or "proverbs" (as Psalm 49:4; Ezekiel 20:49). Probably the most famous parable is that told by the prophet Nathan to King David, which finally convicted David of his guilt over Bathsheba (2 Samuel 12:1–15). This is told in the classic narrative-question-interpretation-judgment form that typifies many of Jesus Christ's parables. Another example of parable in the Hebrew Bible is Ezekiel 17:1–10, which unusually is in poetic form.

In the SYNOPTIC GOSPELS, Jesus' parables are to teach kingdom principles, using the formula "The Kingdom of God is like . . ." (Luke 13:18). It is suggested this teaching is mainly done through parables (Matthew 13:13–15; 34–35; Mark 4:33), though the interpretation is only given to the disciples. In fact, Mark's gospel relegates parabolic teaching, while Matthew groups the parables together. Luke's gospel best sets the parables into a context. By doing this, we can see not only a general meaning but the specific meaning by knowing what occasioned the parable. Only Luke records some of the most famous parables, such as that of the good Samaritan (Luke 10:29–37).

The imagery used in parables is wide-ranging, from everyday situations, such as of losing and finding (Luke 15:8–10) or sowing (Matthew 13:1–32), to familiar situations given unlikely twists, for example, vineyard owners' having their sons murdered (Matthew 21:33–41) or identical wages being paid, despite disparity of hours worked (Matthew 20:1–16); to hyperboles, as the giving of the talents (Matthew 25:14–30) or the unjust steward (Luke 16:1–9) or the selling of everything for just one pearl (Matthew 13:46). The parables were thus to startle, shock, expose, or otherwise confront traditional values and attitudes. In many cases, they raise as many questions as they answer. We as readers are meant to be disturbed by them, as disturbed as the older brother of the so-called prodigal son parable (Luke 15:11–32).

parallelism See POETRY, BIBLICAL.

parousia See LAST THINGS.

Passover Perhaps the most dramatic part of the Hebrew Bible is the liberation of the people of Israel from Egypt, where they had been slaves. The story is described at length in Exodus and resounds in many later books. To commemorate this event, God gave the people the festival of Passover (Exodus 12; Leviticus 23; Deuteronomy 16), which basically consisted of a ceremonial meal with lamb and unleavened bread as main course. The name derives from the fact that the angel who killed Egyptian boys "passed over" (Exodus 12:13) the houses of the Israelites because they had the blood of a lamb on their doorposts. Scholars think the festival was an innovation of an existing spring harvest festival, not least because it also included seven days of eating unleavened bread. In the later history of Israel the festival was not always celebrated (2 Kings 23:21–23).

The New Testament puts much emphasis on the fact that the death of Jesus on the cross coincided with the celebration of Passover. To Jesus and his followers that meant that he was the true Passover lamb, whose blood saves his people from death. Hence Christians do not celebrate Passover, as Jews still do. Their ceremonial meal is the LORD'S SUPPER (or Eucharist), which focuses on Jesus' suffering as the Lamb of God (1 Corinthians 5:7) and is celebrated frequently. However, the Easter

The parable of the Good Samaritan (Luke 10:25–37), engraving by Julius Schnorr von Carolsfeld

celebration of Jesus's resurrection from the dead on Easter corresponds to Passover. Christians have also added Good Friday as a separate day of commemoration three days before this Sunday. The term *Easter* is not found in most translations of the New Testament. (The Greek word is *pascha,* and in most modern languages the name of the Resurrection festival includes the root *pas-*; the English word *easter* is of pagan origin.)

Unlike Christmas, Easter is not celebrated on a fixed date. The date is set in such a way that it will never coincide with the Jewish Passover festival, which itself is not fixed, as the Jewish religious calendar is the lunar calendar.

pastoral   The term *pastoral* derives from the Latin word *pastor,* which means "shepherd." In the Bible, the term is used in two different ways. First, it has to do with instruction to be given to pastors as meaning "church leaders," the term still commonly given in the United States and other countries to ministers of religion and priests. Thus the "pastoral epistles" (1 and 2 Timothy; Titus) have to do with instruction as to how to lead a church.

The other usage is a literary one. The pastoral genre is common to many literatures and is one that deals with primitive but idealized forms of civilization, where a largely rural world is imagined. In fact, pastoral poets are often from the city, contrasting urban corruption with rural innocence. Typical features of the genre are shepherds, sheep, fertile meadows and streams, protection and safety, youth, music, dance and gladness, feasting and celebration. Pastoral poetry can see the shepherd as a lover, a singer, or a poet. More developed forms of the pastoral become allegorical or symbolic, often using irony, developing themes of the true and false shepherd, corruption, deception.

Such literary forms are to be found plentifully in the Bible. The term *sheep* is used more than 400 times; *shepherd,* more than 100, not surprising as Hebrew society was largely rural and pastoral but with many of its writers urban. The Song of Solomon has the shepherd-lover figure, using images of fertility, enclosure ("the garden"), and feasting. Psalm 23 springs immediately to mind as the portrayal of the ideal shepherd, again with images of

fertility, protection, and feasting. Less obviously, Jeremiah 31 is a pastoral, with images of pastoral care, fertility, young men and women, and looking to an ideal future.

Ezekiel 34:7–31 is a crucial discussion in the Hebrew Bible of true and false shepherds, with God the true shepherd of the flock of Israel. This is paralleled in the New Testament by John 10:1–18, where Jesus Christ becomes the true shepherd. This is then put into a wider context of the messianic shepherd (10:19–30), a figure drawn from Ezekiel 37:24.

Other significant pastoral passages include Isaiah 30:23–26, 29, and 65:8–10. The birth of Christ is given a pastoral setting in Luke 2:8. Elsewhere, pastoral imagery is used in a more figurative way, as in Jeremiah 50:19; Micah 2:12; Zephaniah 2:6–7.

patriarchs   In the context of the Hebrew Bible, *patriarchs* refers to the ancestors of the people of ISRAEL, especially ABRAHAM, ISAAC, and JACOB, living in the early second millennium B.C.E. Terah, Abraham's father, and Joseph, one of Jacob's sons, are also occasionally reckoned among the patriarchs. The family of Israel's ancestors is from the city of Ur in Mesopotamia (see BABYLON), but they are called by God to leave their home and move to the land of Canaan (see HOLY LAND). There they live for three generations as seminomads in different places, until they move to EGYPT as a result of a famine. See Genesis in Part II.

Paul   After Jesus Christ, the apostle Paul is the next important character in the New Testament. Some have even called him the founder of Christianity—but he would have disagreed strongly as he always preached Christ (1 Corinthians 1:17, 23; 2 Corinthians 4:5). We have a multidimensional portrait of him because we have both his own letters and the description in Acts, which probably stems from his companion Luke.

Paul was born as Saul in Tarsus in Asia Minor (modern Turkey) but educated in JERUSALEM. He joined the party of the Pharisees (Acts 23:6; Philippians 3:4–6), and when Christianity started, he persecuted the followers of Jesus (Acts 8:1–3; 9:1–2). However, on his way to Damascus to capture more of them, his life was changed by a manifestation of Jesus Christ (Acts 9; 22; 26), and he became a follower of Jesus. The expression "a Damascus Road experience" stems from this event. After many quiet years (Galatians 1:13–2:1), during which much of his theological thinking will have been formed, he became active as a Christian leader, and the church in Antioch sent him out as a missionary together with Barnabas (Acts 13:1–4). From then on he was known as Paul (Acts 13:9).

The book of Acts reports three missionary journeys by Paul (13–20), but on his return from the third he was arrested in Jerusalem (21). After two years in captivity he was taken to Rome to appear before the emperor and lived in the city for two years (28:30). At the end of that period Paul was probably released and made another journey, evidence for which is found in 2 Timothy and Titus. A second-century story tells how he was beheaded as a martyr in Rome. It is unlikely that he managed to travel to Spain, as he intended (Romans 15:24–28).

Paul usually traveled and worked with others, as can be seen in Acts and in the opening and closing passages of his letters. He wrote many letters to churches that he had founded, to other churches (Rome, Colosse), and to individuals, 13 of which have been preserved in the New Testament. To younger workers like Timothy and Titus he was a spiritual father.

Paul's ministry can be characterized as that of a missionary, a church planter, and a pastor. In his letters he attempts to strengthen the faith of the new churches and to preserve them from wrong ideas and practices. As a Jew who recognized Jesus as the Messiah he had many adversaries, such as Jews (1 Thessalonians 2:14–16), Christians who wanted to embrace a law-bound form of the faith (Galatians), and false teachers who had invaded the church in Corinth (2 Corinthians 10–13).

Paul often referred to himself as an example for those who became Christians through him. He reports experiences such as the appearance of the risen Christ (1 Corinthians 15:8), his "speaking in tongues" (see 1 Corinthians), and visions of heaven (2 Corinthians 12:1–5). At times he became excited and angry when the gospel was under threat (see

Galatians), but he could also be tactful (Philemon) and friendly and pastoral (Philippians; 1 Thessalonians). Among his qualities were great courage, faith, humility, and self-discipline.

Although from his earlier to his later letters there is a certain development in his thinking, in particular in the emphasis on church order, Paul's theology stands out as the most mature achievement of the first generation of Christians: Within 30 years after Jesus Christ all key elements of later Christianity are present in his thinking. In particular, Romans, 2 Corinthians, and Ephesians are key theological texts. Both Acts and his own letters (Romans 9–11) show his concern for his own people, the Jews, and his disappointment in their lack of faith in Jesus as the Messiah.

Paul coined or was the first to write down a good number of new Greek words to express elements of the faith. He was a master of irony, he could write poetic passages (1 Corinthians 13), and in Romans he used fictional dialogue (*diatribe*) to good effect. Although generally a good stylist, he would occasionally produce an incomplete sentence (*anacoluthon*), edited out in translation (e.g., Ephesians 2:1–3).

Pentateuch The first five books of the Hebrew Bible, namely, Genesis, Exodus, Leviticus, Numbers, and Deuteronomy. These five books narrate the history of the world from its CREATION and then focus on the history of Israel from its beginning until the arrival at the borders of Canaan. The main emphasis of the Pentateuch is on the COVENANT made between God and Israel at Mount SINAI as mediated by Moses. This covenant describes the relationship between God and his people and defines laws and duties for both sides. The Sinai covenant forms the theological basis for most of the books that follow. Therefore, in Jewish tradition, the Pentateuch, also called Torah or Law of Moses, is regarded as the core of the Hebrew Bible's divine revelation (see REVELATION, GOD'S).

Pentecost Leviticus 23:15–21 contains the command to celebrate a harvest festival seven weeks after the PASSOVER festival. In other words, this festival took place 50 days after Easter, hence the later name *Pentecost,* which means "50th." In the Hebrew Bible it is known as the Festival of Weeks (Exodus 34:22), but it does not play a major role.

John 5 tells that Jesus attended the Festival of Weeks in Jerusalem, and Acts 2 shows that in a later year during this festival the followers of Jesus received the Holy Spirit. Hence for Christians the meaning of Pentecost has changed into a commemoration of that event. In Acts 20:16 and 1 Corinthians 16:8 Pentecost serves as an indication of time. As the day marking the church's original reception of the Holy Spirit, Pentecost entered the church calendar.

In modern times, several churches have taken on the name as a means of showing they emphasize the work of the Holy Spirit today, with the same manifestations as in Acts 2.

Persia   Compared to the antecedent empires of the region, Assyria and Babylon, the Persian Empire was a relative newcomer. Until 680 B.C.E., Persia (modern-day Iran) was a loose confederation of tribes under the Medes, who had their capital at Ecbatana. In 550 B.C.E., Cyrus II rebelled against the Medes and took over their capital before founding his own at Susa.

In 547 B.C.E., Cyrus conquered the midsize states of Anatolia and Lydia in today's Turkey, then moved in the opposite direction to capture some of today's Pakistan. By 540 B.C.E., he felt strong enough to attack the regional superpower, Babylonia, and he conquered it the following year. He divided his new empire into "satrapies" and adopted a policy of allowing exiled peoples to return to their native lands and reconstitute their religions, restoring their idols or gods to them.

This benefited the Jews, exiled by the Babylonians. They were given back some of the temple furniture for a new temple in Jerusalem. The Persians allowed their satrapies a good deal of local autonomy, and this gave stability to the empire. Darius I (522–486 B.C.E.) and Xerxes (or Ahasuerus, 486–465 B.C.E.) tried to extend the empire into Egypt and Greece but were defeated by the Greeks at Marathon in 490 B.C.E. The empire was finally defeated by the Greeks under Alexander in 333 B.C.E.

The workings of the empire are described in the book of Esther in the Hebrew Bible, as well as its high standard of living. In the sixth century B.C.E., Zoroaster proclaimed a monotheistic religion, which was finally adopted by Darius I (522–486 B.C.E.), the first major monotheistic religion outside of Judaism.

See also Babylon; Greece; return from exile.

personification   A type of figurative language in which abstractions or inanimate objects are given personality. It is common in all poetic discourse, and the Bible is no exception. In the book of Proverbs, wisdom is personified as a woman, often referred to as Lady Wisdom (Proverbs 8–9). However, this type of abstract personification is much more rare than the ascribing of personality to geographical features. This is seen plentifully in the Psalms, such as Psalm 98:7–8; 114:3–6; and in prophetic writing, as Isaiah 52:9. Thus the hills and mountains, the sea and rivers, are all seen as responsive to their creator's approach and commands, sometimes more so than humans. In Isaiah 52:9, the ruins of Jerusalem sing.

More significant in the Bible is the personification of God, which is technically called *anthropomorphism,* literally giving human form to God. The Bible not only speaks of God in terms of human qualities, such as love or compassion or justice, but also goes much further than this. Not only are problematic emotions employed of God, such as jealousy or hatred, but he is also given parts of the human body, such as eyes, ears, mouth, hands, and body. Most of these can be taken as metonymic of the divine activity of communicating, protecting, punishing, and so on. However, the body image in the New Testament is also applied to the church, which becomes both the body of Christ (1 Corinthians 12) and the bride of Christ (Revelation 21:2). Similarly, God's living space, his house, footstool, throne, and so forth, are metonymic of his presence, even though at the same time such terms are specifically differentiated from the literal constructs (2 Chronicles 6:18).

For further study, Psalm 104 is an excellent example of both personification and anthropomorphism.

Peter   See Twelve Disciples.

Pharisees and Sadducees   In the INTERTESTA-MENTAL PERIOD the Jews in Israel were divided into several groups. Some of these, such as the Essenes, are not mentioned in the New Testament. The vast majority—more than 90 percent—of the population did not belong to any of the particular groups.

The Pharisees were a party of probably about 6,000 men, most of whom lived in Judea. This movement consisted of laypeople and priests alike. They emerged in the second century B.C.E., and their name probably means "those who kept themselves separate," meaning from the Hellenizing policies of the rulers of the time. They sought to keep the Law in purity, and they understood HOLINESS to mean separation from all that is not holy. They adapted the Mosaic LAW to everyday practice, and so they were effective leaders with a nationwide influence. They respected the oral traditions as equally valuable as the written Hebrew Bible. They were the critics and opponents of Jesus (e.g., Matthew 12:2, 14, 24, 38), and they came in for severe criticism from him (Matthew 23).

The Sadducees were even fewer in number than the Pharisees, and they are even less known. (Neither party left any writings of their own.) Their name may mean "righteous ones." They were generally members of the wealthy aristocratic families of JERUSALEM, and many of them were priests (Acts 5:17). They held the office of high priest from around 100 B.C.E. Their policy was cooperation with the Romans in order to have freedom to practice the temple ceremonies, which they thought essential to maintain the relationship between God and his people. Because their supreme norm was only the PENTATEUCH, they did not believe in the resurrection of the dead or in ANGELS (Acts 23:8; Matthew 22:23–33), as did the Pharisees, their opponents. Mark and Luke mention them only once, Matthew usually in connection with the Pharisees (16:1).

Philistines   The Philistines inhabited the coastal plain running up the Mediterranean northward from the borders of EGYPT, somewhat larger than today's Gaza Strip. At their greatest power, they occupied the Judean foothills and as far north as Carmel. Their political organization was centered round the five cities of Gaza, Ashkelon, Ashdod, Ekron, and Gath.

They were probably part of an invasion of "sea peoples" from the Aegean or Mycenean Crete. Outside the Bible they are not mentioned till ca. 1185 B.C.E., when they occur in Egyptian records. Though there are isolated earlier Bible references in Genesis 21:32–34, most references date back to the occupation of the Promised Land (see HOLY LAND) under Joshua, ca. 1380 B.C.E. Joshua 13:2–3 lists the territory as still to be conquered.

In fact, it never was. The Philistines remained a constant threat both militarily and religiously to the Israelites. Samson led a campaign against them (Judges 13–16), and they briefly captured the sacred ark of the covenant (1 Samuel 4–6). Their god, Dagon, is featured here. King Saul fought against them ineffectually, being killed in battle against them. David's exploits were more successful, from the slaying of their giant warrior Goliath (1 Samuel 17) to fighting for them, to having a bodyguard from them. When David finally fought them, he beat them decisively (2 Samuel 5:25).

But they remained a thorn in the side of the divided monarchy (Isaiah 9:12). The area became a satrapy under the Persians but then disappeared as a separate entity. The term *Palestine* is held to be derived from the name.

Prophetic views on the Philistines were uniformly hostile, as Amos 1:6–8; Zephaniah 2:4–7; Jeremiah 47; and Zechariah 9:5–8 demonstrate.

Pilate   Pontius Pilate was the Roman governor of the provinces of Judea and Samaria from 26 to 36 C.E. He is known from an inscription found in Caesarea in 1961, from the writings of the contemporary Jews Josephus and Philo, and from the Roman historian Tacitus. He was morally weak and could be cruel. Josephus tells that he provoked the religious feelings of the Jews but backed down when they threatened an uprising. He used money destined for the temple in Jerusalem to build an aqueduct and was deposed after murdering many Samaritans.

In the four Gospels he is the judge who condemns Jesus to death on the cross, despite knowing that Jesus is innocent and despite receiving sound

Jesus before Pilate (Matthew 27:11–14; Mark 15:2–5; Luke 23:3–6; John 19:1–11), woodcut by Albrecht Dürer

advice from his wife (Matthew 27:19). The fact that he symbolically washed his hands does not, of course, make him less guilty. Later legends that he converted to Christianity cannot be verified.

pilgrims and wanderers A pilgrim may be defined as someone who sets out on a spiritual journey to a sacred destination. A wanderer has a much less well-defined purpose or destination. As in cases of exiles, the traveling may be involuntary. The Bible uses a number of terms to cover the latter category, such as *sojourner, alien,* or *stranger.* Neither pilgrims nor wanderers "belong" to the territory through which they pass.

The early heroes of the Hebrew Bible were nomadic, as Abraham (Genesis 17:8), or seminomadic, as Isaac and Jacob (Genesis 28:4). Deuteronomy 26:5 describes them as "wandering Arameans" (see SYRIA). However, with this wandering was a sense of a Promised Land (see HOLY LAND). The exodus from EGYPT produced more wandering,

again toward a Promised Land (Exodus 6:4), even though the 40-year wandering was as much punishment as preparation (Numbers 14:43–44). The exile and return from BABYLON had similar features of punishment and release (Isaiah 42:6). In other literatures such wandering might be depicted as an epic journey, as in the Odyssey.

Once the Promised Land was settled, journeys became pilgrimages to the tabernacle shrines (1 Samuel 1:3) or to the temple (Luke 2:41–42; Acts 8:27), especially for the feasts of Passover and Pentecost (Acts 2:5). A subgenre of literature was produced for these journeys, known as Songs of Ascent (Psalms 120–134).

Whereas the Hebrew Bible emphasized settling the land and religious center, the New Testament emphasis began to differ sharply. There were, of course, literal reasons for journeying—to escape persecution (Acts 8:1) or to evangelize (Acts 8:26–40)—but the figure of life as a journey, seen in Psalm 39:12, now becomes a spiritual reality. Hebrews 11:13, 37 sees the heroes of the faith as essentially wanderers and aliens, as do 1 Peter 1:1, 17; 2:11. But strangers on earth become heavenly pilgrims, on a new pilgrimage to a new JERUSALEM (Hebrews 12:22–24).

See also EXILE; RETURN FROM EXILE.

poetry, biblical The Authorized (King James) Version, together with some modern paraphrases of the Bible, translates the original poetry of the Bible into prose. For some readers, therefore, it is a surprise to find so much poetry in the Bible, especially the Hebrew Bible. But in most ancient cultures, it is poetry that is the first genre to emerge in literary form, followed much later by prose. In Greek literature, Homer's epic poems are the oldest texts. What is surprising about the Hebrew Bible is not the amount of its poetry but the wonderful sophistication of its prose.

The most readily acceptable instance of poetry are the PSALMS (GENRE), designed to be sung in the worship services of the temple, and now sung regularly as part of Christian worship also. But the Prophets also uttered many of their oracles as poetry. Other notable instances of poetry in the Hebrew Bible are the sensuous love poetry of the

Song of Solomon and the problematic theodicy of Job. Throughout the remaining books of the Bible, frequent passages of poetry occur. Much of the poetry of the New Testament is quotation from the Hebrew Bible (as Hebrews 1:5–13; 2:6–8, etc.), but there are fragments of early Christian HYMNS (as Philippians 2:6–11), and Luke 1–2 contain psalmlike songs still used in Christian liturgy.

Sometimes these are just fragments embedded within prose narratives, as Genesis 1:27; 2:23; 3;14–19; 24:60; or Ruth 1:16–17, 20–21; or within the Law, as in Exodus 34:6–7; Leviticus 10:3. Sometimes these fragments appear to be from older books of poetry, now lost. Numbers 21:14–15 refer to the Book of the Wars of the Lord, quoting briefly (vv. 17–18). Similarly 2 Samuel 1:18 quotes from the Book of Jashar. Numbers 21:27–30 are clearly old ballads quoted within the prose text.

But besides these unorganized fragments, there are recognized subgenres: hymns, LAMENTs and consolations, songs, and blessings. These latter are often the last words of some famous person: Jacob blessing his sons (Genesis 48:15–16, 20; 49:2–27); Moses blessing the people (Deuteronomy 32–33); David's last words (2 Samuel 23:1–7). One of the most interesting blessings occurs in a series of prophecies, possibly the oldest in the Hebrew Bible, those of Balaam (Numbers 23:7–10,18–24; 24:3–9,15–24).

The songs are usually to celebrate and memorialize some historical moment; thus Deborah's song (Judges 5), a brilliant but obscure piece of poetry celebrating her victory; the Crossing of the Red Sea, a song of triumph (Exodus 15:1–18), the first verse of which was set by Miriam to a dance (Exodus 15:21). Its words are echoed in a later prophecy (Isaiah 12). Other songs entered the Psalms, such as David's song of triumph in 2 Samuel 22, which turns up as Psalm 18. As David wrote many of the psalms, this is hardly surprising.

It is reckoned that all the poetry in the Bible collected would be longer than the New Testament. But what are the main features of biblical poetry? As with genres (see GENRES, BIBLICAL), we have to forget many patterns of Western poetry, such as rhyme, meter, and stanza form. Other features

are universal: the compactness of poetic utterance, much more so in Hebrew poetry than most English translators allow, and imagery, which is discussed at IMAGERY, BIBLICAL.

The main structural feature of Hebrew poetry is parallelism. At its simplest, it is a series of clauses, called *cola* (singular, *colon*), of the same grammatical structure and meaning but using different diction or images. Thus:

> Then our mouth was filled with laughter,
> And our tongue with shouts of joy.
> (Psalm 126:2)

At one time it was thought each colon was a mere repetition, but the cola are clearly more than that. There is a cumulative effect, common in rhetoric. Often the repeating cola add to the original meaning, so it is best to take both parts as a single whole, as:

> If you return, O Israel, says the Lord,
> if you return to me,
> if you remove your abominations from my presence . . .

where a list of unfolding conditions are presented, followed by a climactic:

> Then nations shall be blessed by him,
> and by him they shall boast
> (Jeremiah 4:1, 2)

The New Testament frequently continues this tradition:

> For all the nations have drunk of the wine of the wrath of her fornication,
> and the kings of the earth have committed fornication with her
> (Revelation 18:3)

where the typical two cola form is used.

Sometimes there are more Hebrew or Greek terms than English ones, so the English lacks some of the original variety. For example, in the preceding examples, the Greek has two different terms for "fornication"; in Job 4:10–11, the Hebrew has five different terms for "lion," the English only two. Poetry is notoriously more difficult to translate than prose. Even despite the lack of synonyms, parallelism is the least difficult verse form to translate, being "a rhyme of thought."

One variation of parallelism is *chiasmus,* where the parallel terms are arranged in reverse, so instead of having A-B : A1-B1, we have A-B : B1-A1. A very simple example is that earlier in Jeremiah 4:2.

There are numerous variations, which scholars have variously categorized. Common variations are three cola parallels, antithetical constructions, and what might be termed *concentric* or *circular* structure, i.e., A-B-C-B1-A1. Larger structures tend to be determined by the sense, as in free verse.

prayer   In the Bible, both an activity and a literary form. As an activity, it is seen as normative for all believers and assumes a God who hears, is near and is willing to answer. Various elements of prayer activity are praise, thanksgiving, confession of sin and pleas for forgiveness, intercessions for others, petitions for oneself, and personal expressions of devotion, hope, difficulty, longing, and so on. It often takes the form of dialogue, but it can also be inarticulate, "sighs" of the spirit (Romans 8:26). Prayer is both a very private activity and a public one. There is a contrast in the Bible between spontaneous, genuine, heartfelt prayer, and long, repetitious, formulaic, and ultimately empty praying (Matthew 6:5, 7; Mark 12:40; Proverbs 28:9). Different forms of prayer are described variously as "supplications" (or "requests"), "prayers" (or "petitions"), "intercessions," and "thanksgivings" in 1 Timothy 2:1: The passage sees prayer as a normative activity for a church.

This activity takes on literary form throughout the Bible. A good example is Jeremiah 14:7–9. Jeremiah's prayer is an inclusive one, in that he typically uses the first-person plural. Thus, though it is "private," it is also "public" as he includes the whole nation as addressers of God and as objects of God's mercy. The prayer contains confession; petition, both positive and negative (a plea for God to act, and a plea not to forget them); a naming of God's attributes; and a statement of faith in God's nearness and accessibility. The language uses figurative questions in the parallel form typical of Hebrew poetry, apostrophe (O LORD; O hope . . .), and concessive clauses ("Although we are . . . , yet

you are . . ."), contrasting the sins of the people with the goodness of God.

The book of Psalms is often regarded as a book of prayers. Apart from this collection, there are more than 50 prayers recorded in the Bible. They range from Abraham's dialogues with God (Genesis 15:1–4; 18:23–33), the latter almost bargaining; and Moses' private arguments with God (Exodus 3:13–4:7); through Solomon's majestic public prayer of dedication of the new temple (2 Chronicles 6:12–42). These are one-time prayers. Jesus' prayer of Matthew 6:9–13 and Luke 11:2–4 has become the best known ritual prayer (the Lord's Prayer), whether or not it was intended to become formulaic. Various blessings have similarly become ritual benedictions (Numbers 6:24; Jude 24–25). Jesus' long prayer in John 17, often known as the high-priestly prayer, is a wonderful example of the balanced and spacious rhetoric of the literary form at its highest.

Promised Land   See HOLY LAND.

prophecy   In the Bible, the oral proclaimed message of a prophet or prophetess, which he or she believes is inspired and revealed by God. It can be delivered to a particular person, or to a group, or to a nation as a whole. It demands a response. It can be about past, present, or future events, behavior, or attitudes. It is thus not just predictive of the future. If there is a future dimension, it is usually the result of the present, as a blessing or a punishment. *Because* and *therefore* become connective structures: "Because this is happening now, that will happen soon." Much is not so much predictive as exhortatory, urging change and repentance, and as such is conditional. Future oracles are sometimes called "kingdom oracles" or "salvation oracles."

Biblical prophecy can be written as either poetry or prose: The earlier it is, the more likely is it to be poetic (see POETRY, BIBLICAL). The later development of prophecy called APOCALYPTIC WRITING is almost invariably prose. The language can be highly imaginative and visionary or very realistic; it can be symbolic, figurative, and allegorical, or it can be literal.

Units of prophecy, or speeches, are usually called "oracles," though they can be described as "a burden" or as visions. Frequently, biblical prophets say they "saw" the prophecy. One type of oracle are WOES AND DENUNCIATIONS, often called "judgment speeches." Other types of utterance can be the LAMENT, the SERMON, HYMNS, or PSALMS (GENRE), or taunt songs, where sarcasm and irony are used rather than invective. Sometimes the dramatic nature of prophecy is emphasized by enacted prophecy, as the prophet had to act out his message symbolically (as Ezekiel 4:1–15).

Most biblical prophecy is found in the Hebrew Bible, which is often quoted in the New Testament as now having been fulfilled by Jesus Christ or in the EARLY CHURCH. Although prophetic utterances were made in the New Testament, only a few, mainly those of Jesus Christ himself, have been recorded (e.g., Mark 13:3–37; Acts 21:10) apart from the book of Revelation, which is entirely prophetic and apocalyptic.

prophets   Prophets are very significant figures in the Bible, delivering prophecies or messages from God to his people as his messenger (1 Kings 17:1). There are three main terms used in Hebrew, variously translated as "prophet," "seer," and "visionary." A prophet is sometimes called "the man of God." There are also examples of prophetesses throughout the Bible (e.g., Exodus 15:20; Judges 4:4; Acts 21:9).

The earliest references in the Hebrew Bible to prophets stem from the time of THE EXODUS. Miriam is a prophetess (Exodus 15:20), and her brother, Moses, besides being a leader, is also called a prophet (Numbers 16:6–8; Deuteronomy 18:15–22). Balaam is another early example of a prophet (Numbers 24:3–4). In the time of the judges, Samuel is called a prophet (1 Samuel 3:20), although he is also a priest. Other instances of priest-prophets are Ezekiel and Zechariah, though there was often tension between priests and prophets. There seem to be bands of wandering ecstatic prophets in Samuel's time (1 Samuel 10:10–11; 19:23–24). In David's time, individual prophets emerge who have the ear of the king (Gad, Nathan). From then on, prophets are often caught up in state affairs (as Isaiah 38–39).

The most significant early prophet to emerge was Elijah (1 Kings 17–2 Kings 2), who became the ideal or type of true prophet along with Moses. He and his successor, Elisha, stood out against the mixing of Yahweh worship with elements of Baal worship, which had pagan fertility rituals. We hear of the prophets of Baal (1 Kings 18:4, 20) and groups of true prophets (2 Kings 2:3). From then on, false prophets become a major problem for the true ones.

After Elisha's death, the so-called Writing Prophets emerge, from Amos around 760 B.C.E. to Malachi around 460 B.C.E., a 300-year period. These prophets are usually divided into three Major Prophets (Isaiah, Jeremiah, Ezekiel) and 12 Minor Prophets. They represent a huge diversity of people, some considering themselves as "professional" prophets, others (Amos, for example) refusing that title. The book of Daniel is counted among the prophetic books in the Christian Old Testament but not in the Hebrew Bible, where he is placed in the Ketuvim, since he is seen as wise as well as prophetic. After Malachi, it is reckoned that the office of prophet ceased. Besides the message of true religion, these prophets also stress social justice and God's sovereignty over all the world, including hostile nations.

In the New Testament, we find a revival of the prophet. John the Baptist is seen as a type of Elijah (Matthew 17:9–13), while Anna is described as a prophetess (Luke 2:36). At Pentecost, the giving of the Holy Spirit released prophetic gifts into the early church (e.g., Acts 21:9–10). 1 Corinthians 12 suggests a fulfillment of Numbers 11:29.

Prophets in the Bible have a sense of a calling by God. Some callings are dramatically described (as Isaiah 6:1–6). There is always an urgency in the message, and often a high cost to pay for delivering it. They are confronters of wrong; a social or personal conscience; interpreters of events, past, present and future; and, above all, revealers of the nature, purposes, and will of God to his people (Amos 3:7).

See also JOHN THE BAPTIST; PROPHECY; REVELATION, GOD'S.

proverbs (genre)   A form of WISDOM LITERATURE (Proverbs 7:4). All cultures seem to have their own sets of proverbs, which are best seen as practical short sayings, memorably illustrating truths of everyday life, which give basic guidance as to right attitudes and behavior. There is a range of terms for such sayings, such as *axioms, aphorisms, maxims, saws*. In the Bible, the main collection of proverbs is to be found in the book of Proverbs in the Hebrew Bible and, to a lesser extent, Ecclesiastes.

Typically, proverbs in these books contain a contrast or comparison, often expressed as parallelism or chiasm. Sometimes they take the form of commands, warnings, or good advice. Sometimes they are statements. They use everyday imagery, often metonymies (e.g., eyes, tongue, fruit), personification (wisdom and prudence are seen as people), similes (seduced youths are like oxen or like birds "rushing into a snare"), symbolism (the seven pillars of wisdom's house), and metaphor ("A gentle tongue is a tree of life"). They often occur in list form, but any single proverb can be extracted and meditated on without needing any context.

The prophets sometimes challenge proverbs, partly because proverbs can be reductionist and lead to complacency or limited thinking. Thus the proverb about sour grapes in Jeremiah 31:29–30 is challenged by the prophet because he wants to stress individual responsibility rather than generational sin. Ezekiel 18:2–3 offer exactly the same challenge.

In the New Testament, Jesus Christ also challenges old proverbs or axioms. For example, the "eye for an eye" principle is radically challenged (Matthew 5:38–42). Jesus generated many axioms of his own, such as: "Render unto Caesar . . ." (Mark 12:17, Authorized [King James] Version) or "Let the dead bury their own dead" (Luke 9:60). Other New Testament writers quote proverbs, as 2 Peter 2:22, to memorialize their argument.

psalms (genre) Psalms are one of the two major forms of Hebrew poetry; the other are prophetic oracles. They are basically to be sung as part of religious ritual, the most substantial collection being the book of Psalms itself (see Part II), compiled as part of the temple ritual. However, there are psalms that predate the temple (e.g., Exodus 15:1–21) and others that form part of prophetic literature but are

significantly different from oracular poetry. Such an example is Habakkuk 3:2–19. It is clearly meant to be sung in a ritual setting—3:19 talks of a leader and stringed instruments. It also refers to a mode or style of music called *shigionoth* (3:1) and has the refrain or instruction *selah* (3:13), both of which are typical of the main collection (e.g., Psalm 7).

It would appear most psalms were individually written, as can be seen from their superscriptions, but they were meant to be sung in the first place by the temple singers (1 Chronicles 9:33; 15:16–24) accompanied by skilled musicians (see Psalm 150). When temple ritual was no longer possible, they were used more informally (see Psalm 137). Judaism has developed forms of singing psalms within the synagogue's local congregation, and the Christian Church has developed its own parallel forms.

For the literary form of psalms, see POETRY, BIBLICAL. Their subject matter is primarily praise of a universal creator and his attributes, and thanksgiving for his covenant deeds to his chosen people; then secondarily, explorations of the states of human spirituality and religious experience, both inner and outer, from depression to elation, danger to peace, anxiety to assurance. Psalm 149 is an excellent example in a nutshell of many of these aspects. The use of psalms as meditative PRAYER and as inspiration for HYMNS has been widely recognized.

Pseudepigrapha   See APOCRYPHA AND PSEUDEPIGRAPHA.

Qumran   See DEAD SEA SCROLLS.

quotations   In the Hebrew Bible no quotations from secular sources have been identified. Some texts, however, such as Psalm 104, do display influence from foreign literature, and the author of Kings made ample use of the lost Book of the Annals of the Kings of Judah (e.g., 1 Kings 15:7, 23, 31), which must have been in Hebrew. There are also references to lost books such as the Book of the Acts of Solomon and the Book of the Annals of the Kings of Judah (1 Kings 11:41; 14:29).

There are numerous instances of later texts referring to earlier texts within the Hebrew Bible, but as far as we can see there are no literal quotations. Examples are the fact that some psalms refer back to events in the history of Israel as described in particular in Genesis and Exodus, and that prophets borrowed expressions from each other.

In the New Testament we find the following quotations from Greek literature:

- Acts 17:28 quotes first from Epimenides (?), then from Aratus's *Phaenomena* 5;
- Acts 26:14 uses Euripides, *Bacchae;*
- 1 Corinthians 15:33 quotes from Menander's *Thais;*
- Titus 1:12 uses Epimenedes' (?) *De Oraculis.*

Scholars think that Paul occasionally uses pre-existent Christian texts such as hymns (Ephesians 5:14; Philippians 2:6–11; Colossians 1:15–20), but these texts have not come down to us for verification. More important is the extensive use that the New Testament makes of the Hebrew Bible, sometimes of the Hebrew text, more often of the Greek translation (see BIBLE, EARLY TRANSLATIONS OF). Specific comments on this occur in the entries on most books in Part II. Here it can be said that although nearly all New Testament authors use the Hebrew Bible, they do so in different ways. 1 Peter tops the list in terms of the ratio of quoted to own words. Matthew and Hebrews also contain many explicit quotations, and Matthew often says that the words of the Hebrew prophets were fulfilled in the life of Jesus, and Hebrews points out that the old dispensation is now obsolete. John's use of the Hebrew Bible is largely at the level of themes and symbols, showing how Jesus surpasses God's previous revelation. In a comparable way Luke and Acts show structural influence from passages and characters in the Hebrew Bible. Jude makes use of some of the Apocrypha (see APOCRYPHA AND PSEUDEPIGRAPHA). Revelation, finally, is unique in that it never quotes from the Hebrew Bible but is most heavily dependent upon it in imagery, structure, and countless details.

redaction   It is likely that many books of the Bible are not the work of one person. After an initial text had come into being, one or more editors or redactors probably worked on it. The study of what may have happened in this process, and especially the motifs of the redactors, is called redaction criticism. In the case of the prophetic books, pupils of the prophets probably gathered and edited their messages, which had been delivered orally. However, in the case of Jeremiah, little redaction seems to have taken place. In the case of the SYNOPTIC GOSPELS, we can see clearly how Matthew and Luke independently used Mark to create their own gospels; this is the best-known case of redaction criticism.

Genesis is probably based on older sources, called together by an editor. However, no agreement has been achieved about when and by whom this was done. This process should be distinguished from redactional work. Likewise in the case of Ezra-Nehemiah, an editor found most of the material in written sources and put it together, with few additions of his own. To produce the book of Psalms, the initially independent psalms were gathered and ordered, and formulas of praise were added at the conclusions of the constituent parts (Psalms 41:13; 72:18–19; 89:52; 106:48). In these cases the editors primarily arranged sources and connected them by means of some additional material.

In the absence of copies of the older versions, redactional and editorial work can seldom be distinguished with reasonable certainty in the final text. The exception to this rule is that we do still have Mark, one of the sources of Matthew and Luke. In the past scholars were, nonetheless, often preoccupied with reconstructed older versions of the books of the Bible. More recently the final text has been rehabilitated as the rightful focus of attention by what is called narrative criticism.

Red Sea, crossing   One of the best-known stories of the Hebrew Bible. The people of Israel have just left their place in EGYPT (see EXODUS, THE). Pharaoh gives chase to them with his army. When the people arrive at an inlet, they seem to be trapped. But God divides the water so that Israel can cross it without getting their feet wet. When Pharaoh's army follows them, the water turns back on them, and they drown (Exodus 14).

The dividing of the Red Sea becomes a symbol for the mighty power of God and is mentioned several times throughout the Hebrew Bible. When the people cross the Jordan in order to enter the land of Canaan, the Jordan divides as the Red Sea did (Joshua 3–4). Other texts draw on the symbolism of the event, e.g., Psalm 77:19–20; Isaiah 43:2, 16.

The inlet crossed by the Israelites is literally called "Reed Sea." Although traditionally identified with the Red Sea (Gulf of Suez), it probably refers to one of the lakes that are to the north of it. See also Exodus in Part II.

restoration   See RETURN FROM EXILE.

return from exile   The Jewish exile in Babylonia lasted till 538 B.C.E., after the Persian king Cyrus II overthrew Babylonia. The Persian policy was to allow all exiled peoples to return and to restore their gods or idols to them. The Jews were thus free to return to Judah, and Cyrus restored the temple fittings that had been taken before its destruction (Ezra 1). There were three main stages of return, fully described in the Ezra-Nehemiah narrative:

1. An initial group under Prince Zerubbabel and High Priest Jeshua returned immediately with some 50,000 exiles. They began rebuilding the temple in JERUSALEM, but local opposition to the returnees grew to the extent the work was halted by imperial command. The prophets Zechariah and Haggai preached forcefully against the ensuing inertia. New work began and new representations were made to the Persian government, which finally allowed the work to proceed (Ezra 5:1–6:18). It was completed in 516 B.C.E.
2. A second wave led by Ezra, a priest and government official, about 458 B.C.E. (Ezra 7–8). He had been sent to enforce Jewish laws and rituals. This he did very effectively (Ezra 9–10), before probably returning to Persia.
3. A third wave under Nehemiah ca. 445 B.C.E. Nehemiah had been appointed governor and rebuilt the walls, finally defeating local opposition (Nehemiah 2–6). Ezra may have returned at this time (Nehemiah 8–10), though the observance of the Jewish moral and ritual codes remained an ongoing problem, as Nehemiah found on a return visit (Nehemiah 13; Malachi 1–3).

The restoration from exile had been prophesied more and more specifically by earlier prophets (e.g., Amos 9:11–15; Jeremiah 31:38–40; 32:36–33:26). It was seen as a second Exodus. The second half of Isaiah reflects well the spiritual ideals held concerning the return and its actualities (e.g., Isaiah 40, 59). Not all Jews, however, returned, and the remaining communities formed the first DIASPORA, or scattering of Jews among the nations (see Acts 2:5–11).

See also BABYLON; DELIVERANCE; EXILE; PERSIA.

revelation, God's   The word *revelation* refers to God's making himself known to human beings. In the Bible, God reveals himself and his will by different means, for example, by dreams (Genesis 41), visions (Ezekiel 1), angels (Luke 1), or drawing of lots (Numbers 27:21). He makes himself known through mighty miracles (Exodus 14:4–31) and all kinds of signs (Judges 6:36–40; Acts 9:3–7). At times, storm, fire, and earthquakes represent his power and glory (1 Kings 19:11–13; Exodus 19:18; Job 38:1). The biblical writings themselves are said to be revelation of God, since God inspired the writers (2 Timothy 3:16–17; 2 Peter 1:20–21).

In Christian theology, these ways of revelation are broadly categorized as "direct revelation," which means that God reveals himself in history. Opposed to that is the "indirect revelation" of God through the creation of the world (Romans 1:19–21; Job 38–41).

According to the New Testament, the most significant act of God's revelation is that he revealed himself in JESUS CHRIST, his son (Hebrews 1:1–3; Romans 16:25–27; see also TRINITY). Jesus Christ shows the people the will of God, his love, and his mercy (John 14:6–11).

In a more specific usage of the word, *revelation* refers to receiving a deeper insight into the divine counsel, especially concerning the end of times, by way of dramatic visions (see APOCALYPTIC WRITING). From this context the modern *apocalypse* is derived, although the word originally does not mean anything more than "revelation."

rhetorical question   See IMAGERY, BIBLICAL.

Rome Although founded, according to tradition, in 753 B.C.E., Rome only became an empire in the INTERTESTAMENTAL PERIOD. In the second century B.C.E. it expanded from Italy into the whole of the Mediterranean. By the next century, the HOLY LAND had been included as part of the province of Syria (Luke 2:2).

In New Testament times, the Romans ruled directly, as in Judea, where Pilate was the governor for a time (Matthew 27:2), or through local rulers such as HEROD (Luke 23:7–11), or they set up their own colonies, such as Philippi (Acts 16:12), which were seen as extensions of Rome itself. Decisions from Rome impinged directly on the provinces, such as Augustus's census (Luke 2:1). Roman law prevailed over local law, as in the case of the trials of JESUS CHRIST (Luke 23:1–25) or Paul (Acts 16:37–39; 22:31; 23:25–30), where Paul uses his Roman citizenship to obtain a fair trial and appeal. Roman justice was approved by the governor (Romans 13:5). There were conflicts, however, especially over paying taxes (Luke 20:20–25).

It is widely held that the Pax Romana (Roman peace) enabled the Christian gospel to spread by allowing freedom of travel (Romans 15:24) and by employing Latin and Greek as the official and trade languages throughout the Mediterranean. However, the rule of the emperors devolved into emperor worship, bringing Christians and Jews into direct conflict with it, resulting in sporadic persecution. APOCALYPTIC WRITING reflects this facet. In Revelation 17–18, *Babylon* is a covert term for Rome, including references to its seven hills, wealth, and trade.

Paul ends his days at Rome (Acts 28:30–31). The noncanonical First Epistle of Clement suggests both Paul and Peter died martyrs' deaths in Rome, though later the city was to become the center of Western Christianity. For the church at Rome, see Romans in Part II.

Sabbath From the moment they formed an independent nation, God gave the people of Israel one day of rest per week (Exodus 16:23–29; 20:8–11), in line with his own resting after the six days of creation (Genesis 2:1–3). This institution become one of the hallmarks of Israel, unparalleled in the ancient world. The prophets consistently attacked Sabbath breaking as a major covenant breach. The name *sabbath* is derived from the word "to rest" (i.e., from his work, Genesis 2:2).

Although the intention of the Sabbath was positive, keeping it gradually became a matter of legalism and strict rules. Afraid of breaking the commandment to refrain from all work, Jewish scribes defined exactly what "work" was. Thus a "Sabbath day's journey" (Acts 1:12) was the maximal distance one was allowed to walk on the Sabbath. Jesus, on the other hand, saw the Sabbath as an opportunity to do good things for other people, putting him in conflict with the Jewish authorities. He was regarded as a transgressor of the Sabbath law, whereas he merely ignored their strict interpretations in an attempt to regain and restore the positive elements of the Sabbath.

The Christian Church took over the Sabbath as a day of rest but combined it with the celebrations of the Resurrection of Jesus on Sunday. In Christian cultures, Sunday is still largely observed as a day of rest. In the book of Hebrews "Sabbath rest" takes on symbolic meaning.

sacrifice See HEBREW BIBLE, WORSHIP AND RITUAL.

Sadducees See PHARISEES AND SADDUCEES.

salvation God's salvation is one of the most central concepts to run through the Bible. The salvation to be found in Jesus Christ is the key message of the New Testament. With salvation come its cognate words *save* and *Savior*, with the name *Jesus* meaning "savior" (Matthew 1:21). Linked to it are many other theological concepts: redemption, deliverance, bondage and freedom, regeneration or "being born again," and justification. Salvation is only from God and is an act of God's grace toward his people.

One of the key themes in the Hebrew Bible is salvation from the slavery of EGYPT. God delivered the people of Israel through THE EXODUS, taking them to the Promised Land (Deuteronomy 26:5–9). He then saved them from various enemies, usually when the Israelites repented of their covenant breaking and unfaithfulness. There is thus a national element in the term. But individuals also experience salvation, as David and the prophets testify (e.g., Psalm 18; Jeremiah 31:34).

In the New Testament, this physical element gives way to an emphasis on the need for individual and personal salvation, of new birth (John 3:3), as well as the concept that Jesus Christ is Savior for all people, not just one group. The name *Jesus* actually means "the Lord saves." Salvation is not just from enemies but widened to that release from the bondage of SIN (Romans 6:12–14). But this release has a price (1 Corinthians 6:20). Jesus Christ becomes Savior because his death has paid this release price, or "ransom," as it is sometimes called (Mark 10:45). His healing ministry also shows that salvation is not only from judgment and death but also from disease (Isaiah 53:4) and the oppression of SATAN (e.g., Matthew 9:33).

But salvation is also to and for something. Being saved means repenting of an old life and putting on a new nature (Ephesians 4:24), which involves both being "in Christ" and having "Christ in you" (Colossians 1:27). It is a change of legal status, an adoption into the family of God (Galatians 4:5), with the HOLY SPIRIT the "spirit of adoption" to make that real (Romans 8:15). There is thus a radical new dimension in salvation in terms of personal living, which is meant then to spill over, through the church, into the world.

See also DELIVERANCE; HEAVEN; HISTORY.

Samaria The name of a town and a region in central Israel. The town was founded by King Omri and enlarged by his son, Ahab, in the ninth century B.C.E. (1 Kings 16:24–32). As capital of the northern kingdom of the 10 tribes it succeeded Tirzah and later gave its name to the surrounding landscape. Severe criticism of the townsfolk and their lifestyle arose from the eighth-century prophets Hosea and Amos.

Samaria kept its role as capital until the end of the northern kingdom in 722 B.C.E., when it was destroyed by the Assyrians. After many Israelites had been taken in captivity to Assyria, foreigners were settled in the region of Samaria who mixed with the Jewish population to form a group with a religion that differed from that of the Jews (2 Kings

17). This led to a segregation that was still acutely felt in New Testament times (John 4:9; 8:48) but that JESUS CHRIST tried to overcome (Luke 10:25–37; 17:16; John 4).

In the second century B.C.E. the Jews conquered the region of Samaria. The Romans gave the city of Samaria to HEROD, who renamed it *Sebaste* (= Greek for Augustus). In New Testament times the Samaritans were monotheists who recognized the PENTATEUCH and who worshipped God on Mount Gerizim. Acts 8 tells us about the conversion of Samaritans as the first step of the Jesus movement outside the territory of Israel (cf. Acts 1:8).

sanctification See HOLINESS.

Satan Although the appearance of evil occurs near the beginning of the Bible in the form of the serpent (Genesis 3:1) who tempts Adam and Eve to disobey God, it is not till the very end of the Bible that we have a full description of who that serpent really is. Revelation 12:7–9 describes a war in heaven, where angelic forces fought against God and his ANGELS, were defeated, and fell to earth, where they continually deceive people. They are led by a spiritual personage variously called "the great dragon," "the serpent of old," "the devil," and "the satan." The final defeat of such forces is then depicted in Revelation, as it is in other APOCALYPTIC WRITING.

In the Hebrew Bible, by comparison, there are only fleeting and disorganized references to the leader of evil forces. The serpent does not appear again as such. In Job 1–2, a figure called "the satan," meaning the accuser or even prosecutor, seems to be part of a heavenly council. God allows him to afflict Job to test him. The term is used again in Psalm 109:6 and Zechariah 3:2. In Isaiah 14:12 (Authorized [King James] Version) is the Bible's single reference to the name *Lucifer* as being cast from heaven. The term means "light-bearer" and is referred to again as a deceiving "angel of light" in the New Testament (2 Corinthians 11:14). And in Ezekiel 28:14–17 there is an ambiguous reference to an angelic being cast out of Eden.

By contrast, the teaching of Jesus Christ in the New Testament has plentiful references to a figure who is called "the devil" (Greek *diabolos*), a term not used in the Hebrew Bible. His evil followers are called demons (Greek *daimonoi*), though occasionally the term *devil* is used of these minions too (John 6:70). The word *Satan* is also used, now more as a personal name. It is the devil who tempts Jesus (as Matthew 4:1–11) and who enters into people to make them commit evil acts, as Judas (Luke 22:3) and Ananaias (Acts 5:3). Jesus names him as a murderer and "father of lies" (John 8:44). But he may be resisted (James 4:7). He deceives (Ephesians 6:11), hinders God's purposes (1 Thessalonians 2:18), causes diseases (Luke 13:16), and sends afflictions (2 Corinthians 12:7). John makes clear his evil was "from the beginning" (1 John 1:8) but will have a final defeat (Revelation 20:7–10), though there have been partial defeats before (John 12:31; Luke 10:18).

Sea of Galilee This "sea" is the largest freshwater lake in Israel, fed by the River Jordan, which flows through it. It is not a sea but just called so in tradition. Among its many other names are *Lake of Galilee, Lake of Tiberias* (John 6:1), *Sea of Gennesaret* (Luke 5:1), and *Chinnereth* (= harp, because of its shape, Numbers 34:11). The lake is some 21 kilometers (13 miles) long and 13 kilometers (eight miles) wide, and it lies entirely below sea level. It was and is rich in all kinds of fish so that in New Testament times a lively fish trade existed. Several of Jesus' disciples were fishermen.

Hardly mentioned in the Hebrew Bible, the Sea of Galilee plays a large role in the four Gospels as the setting of many stories about JESUS CHRIST. He found some of his disciples here, taught on its shores, went fishing on it, crossed the lake, stilled a storm on it, and even walked on it. Unexpected storms still occur on the lake. On its shores the villages of Capernaum, Bethsaida, Gergesa, Tiberias, Magdala, and Gennesaret could be found, and tradition points to a mount overlooking the lake as the place where Jesus pronounced the Sermon on the Mount.

Septuagint See BIBLE, EARLY TRANSLATIONS OF.

sermon The sermon is one of the most common features of religious worship today. It is an oral form,

which may sometimes be written down or recorded to give permanency. It is discourse by a preacher to teach, evangelize, reprimand, convict, encourage, or persuade. It presupposes a congregation of listeners, who rarely interact with the speech.

Although the sermon is also a recognized literary subgenre, there is no word for it in the Bible. In the ritual worship of the Hebrew Bible, the emphasis is on sacrifice and celebration, and there seems no room for the sermon. Many of the prophetic oracles do have many of the functions of the sermon—warning, exhortation, teaching, guidance— but they are not set within a liturgy. And the term *preach* is only occasionally used.

By New Testament times, the Jewish SYNAGOGUE had a form of teaching in sermon form. This is the form that Jesus and Paul participated in when invited by the synagogue elders (Luke 4:16–27; Acts 13:16–41) and that was taken over and extended by the early church (1 Timothy 5:17). By comparing these particular two sermons, we can see they were scripturally based, with a ready knowledge of the Hebrew Bible. To some extent, what is said is a commentary on that, but also an extension. It is this extension that causes Jesus and Paul trouble. Acts 13:45 suggests some debate was possible in the synagogue over the sermon. The so-called Sermon on the Mount (Matthew 5–7) is really a collection of teaching material and wisdom literature compiled by Matthew.

In the Acts of the Apostles, there are a number of other addresses recorded. Acts 2:14–40 record Peter's preaching at Pentecost. Again, Scripture is extensively quoted and a response elicited, this time a very favorable one. Acts 7:2–53 constitute Stephen's defense, which takes the form of a survey of Scripture and an attack on the religious forms of the day as part of his extension. Paul also defends himself, but through "testimony" or a narrative of personal experience (Acts 22:1–21), which is normally considered a separate subgenre. When Paul preaches to non-Jews, as at Athens, he quotes Greek literature rather than Scripture (Acts 17:22–31).

The language of the Bible uses verbs, not nouns, for this oral presentation. It is the *act*, rather than the *form*, that is important. The most common

Greek terms are translated "evangelizing" and "proclaiming." But words best translated as "speaking boldly," "lecturing," "persuading," "testifying," "teaching," "exhorting," and "announcing" are also used (e.g., Luke 4:18; Acts 17:2–4; 28:30; Romans 10:15; 1 Timothy 4:13). The theological noun used is *kerugma*, or proclamation.

simile See IMAGERY, BIBLICAL.

sin One of the central concepts of the Bible. Of the various Hebrew and Greek terms used, the meanings conveyed include those of wickedness, being bent or twisted, rebellion and the breaking of the law, missing a mark or standard, overstepping a boundary, being enslaved, and losing one's way. Sin is seen as universal and inborn (see FALL, THE) and incurring God's anger. Thus it is taken most seriously, for the ultimate end of sin is death (Romans 6:23; see HELL) in terms of judgment by God. Although some traditions have divided individual sins into less or more serious, the Bible is more concerned about sin as a principle of a wrong relationship with God.

If sin is taken seriously, so are God's mercy and the possibility of forgiveness (e.g., Psalm 51; 103:12). The ways in which sin can be "covered," "cleansed," or "blotted out" are set out in the Hebrew Bible first in ritual terms (e.g., the sacrificial system of Leviticus 1–7). The principle is that "without the shedding of blood there is no forgiveness of sins" (Hebrews 9:22). Animal death is therefore a substitute for human death. Various theological concepts emanate from this, including those of atonement, expiation, and propitiation.

Later, the higher moral and spiritual principles of forgiveness are set out. The prophets (e.g., Isaiah 1:11–13) stress that sacrifice without repentance is useless. But Isaiah goes further in his "suffering servant" (Isaiah 53), a passage that becomes central for the New Testament writers (e.g., John 1:29; 1 Corinthians 15:3; Hebrews 9:26—among many other verses) as they explain that the death of Jesus Christ was the ultimate sacrifice. It is the one complete and sufficient sacrifice for the sins of the whole world and thus sets his people free of the bondage of sin and its guilt.

Sinai, Mount There are a number of sacred mountains recorded in the Bible: Sinai, Zion, Carmel, Gerizim, Ebal, Moriah, Horeb. But there are two that stand out. One is Mount Zion, on which the temple was built (see JERUSALEM) and that is identified as Mount Moriah, where Abraham sacrificed Isaac (Genesis 22:1–4; 2 Chronicles 3:1). The other is Mount Sinai, which is identified with Mount Horeb, where Moses had the vision of the burning bush (Exodus 3:1–2), and where Elijah, fleeing from Queen Jezebel, heard God speak in a "still, small voice" (1 Kings 19:8–12).

Mount Sinai, in fact, does not lie within the HOLY LAND, being most probably situated near the southern tip of the large triangle of land bordered by the Gulfs of Suez and Aqabah in Egypt. However, Galatians 4:25 suggests it was situated in Arabia. Its particular sacredness lies in the fact that it was here that God appeared to Moses in a theophany (Exodus 33:12–23), and it was here that the Ten Commandments were given as part of the holy covenant God made with his people (Exodus 19–20).

The extreme holiness of the site is stressed as no one except Moses is allowed to step on to it, and it is covered by thick darkness and fire. Although it was thus a place of God's meeting with his people, it was also a place where separation of people from God was stressed. As the Holy Land was settled, Mount Zion, the high place of Jerusalem, became the center of worship and the presence of God, and references to Mount Sinai become limited in the Hebrew Bible.

In the New Testament, the sacred geography becomes metonymic, that is, figurative and symbolic rather than literal. Both Galatians 4:21–31 and Hebrews 12:18–29 juxtapose Sinai and Zion as metonymies of the old and the new covenants, respectively. In the latter passage, Sinai is a place of dread and unapproachability; Zion of joy and access.

See also EXODUS.

Solomon King of Israel, son of DAVID, reigning from about 971 to 931 B.C.E. With Solomon, the Israelite kingdom reaches its zenith in terms of power, material wealth, and peace. Solomon is also described as the "father" of Israel's wisdom; the book of Proverbs and the Song of Songs (and, indirectly, Ecclesiastes) are assigned to him. However, Solomon also has many wives and is enticed to idolatry toward the end of his reign. See also 1 and 2 Kings and 1 and 2 Chronicles in Part II.

structures, literary   Many narrative texts of the Bible are organized as modern narratives are, along a story line. They can be analyzed using such categories as setting, problem, complicating and resolving incidents, sudden turns, climax, resolution, and coda. They employ scenic and straight narrative, speeches, and dialogue.

In addition, however, the Bible uses other types of structures that are uncommon in modern literature. One of these is the chiastic or concentric structure. This means that a text consists of several sections, in which the first corresponds to the last, the second to the second-to-last, the third to the third-to-last, and so on. The resulting forms are often expressed using letters, e.g., A-B-C-C'-B'-A'. An example is Amos 5:1–17:

5:1–3	A	*lament*: Israel fallen
5:4–6	B	*appeal*: Seek the Lord!
5:7	C	*accusation*: justice refused
5:8–9	D	*hymn*: the power of God—Yahweh is his name
5:10–13	C'	*accusation*: justice refused
5:14–15	B'	*appeal*: Seek the good!
5:16–17	A'	*lament*: wailing everywhere—for God will pass through Israel's midst

The final statement that God "will pass through the midst of you" bringing judgment is also expressed by the literary form, where the hymn on God's power is placed at the "midst" of sinful and fallen Israel. The opposition of the two appeals "Seek God!" and "Seek the good!" expresses a basic aspect of Amos's message, namely, that if you believe in God you have to act accordingly. The example shows how these structures are used to transmit and underscore elements of the text's message.

Concentric structures can also be the principle according to which larger sections or even whole books are shaped. In some cases, the structures

are very clear, and the text cannot even be understood properly without referring to the structure. (Amos 5:1–17 would seem quite confusing otherwise.) In other cases, concentricity is more in the background but still communicates deeper levels of meaning of the text. In scholarship, some of the concentric structure analyses are agreed on, while others are disputed.

Further examples of concentric structures include the paradise narrative (Genesis 2:4–3:24), arranged around the central question of God "Where are you?"; the Flood narrative (Genesis 6:8–8:22), arranged around the sentence "God remembered Noah" in 8:1; the Jacob cycle as a whole (Genesis 25:19–35:29); the book of Deuteronomy with three concentric rings around the central section 12–26; furthermore, Joshua 13–21; Ruth; Esther 3–9; Daniel 2–7; 2 Kings 2; 2 Chronicles 1–9.

A simpler variant of this type of structure is the sandwich, an A-B-A' form. See Mark and 1 Corinthians in Part II for examples. The basic form of the chiasm, A-B-B'-A', extending over two poetical lines or verses (e.g., 1 Corinthians 15:12–13), is also common in classical literature.

Another typical pattern according to which biblical texts are organized is in parallel rows, having a form like A-B-C-A'-B'-C'. For example, in Genesis 1–11, a pattern of blessing–curse–new hope is repeated three times; the book of Judges is structured along the pattern of disobedience–threat–appointment of a judge–deliverance–new disobedience that occurs six times throughout the main part of the book. Again, the Song of Solomon is made up of a pattern that it repeated four times: She longs for him–she sees him coming and praises him–he praises her beauty and longs for her–she invites him. These patterns again organize the flow of thoughts the text wants to communicate.

See also "How to Read the Bible as Literature" in Part I; GENRES, BIBLICAL; POETRY, BIBLICAL.

synagogue   In the New Testament the place were Jews meet for worship, presumably on the SABBATH. Elements of such a service were in any case the reading of the Hebrew Bible and an address or sermon based on the readings; we have no information regarding other elements, such as singing. Worship in this context is reflected in Luke 4:16–22 and Acts 13:14–44. Jesus often, but not exclusively, taught in synagogues (John 18:20).

In later times, especially after the destruction of the temple of Jerusalem in 70 C.E., synagogues were local centers for Jewish meetings, worship, and education. It is unknown whether the later requirement that 10 adult males be present already existed in biblical times.

The origin of the synagogue is shrouded in mystery. It is not mentioned in the Hebrew Bible (Psalm 74:8 in the Authorized [King James] Version is incorrectly translated), and it probably originated in the INTERTESTAMENTAL PERIOD in the DIASPORA either in Babylon or in EGYPT. Synagogues were an important means of winning Gentiles to the Jewish faith, the so-called proselytism, a phenomenon unique to Judaism.

By the time of the New Testament there were synagogues in JERUSALEM (Acts 6:9), Nazareth (Matthew 13:54), Capernaum (Mark 1:21), throughout the HOLY LAND (Matthew 4:23; 13:54), and in many cities in the Roman Empire. On his missionary trips PAUL went to synagogues to talk about Jesus before he went to other venues (Acts 13:5, 14; 14:1; 17:2).

Archaeologists have found synagogues dating from the first century B.C.E. onward. The earliest examples are little more than houses; later synagogues were larger and more ornate.

See also JUDAISM.

synecdoche See IMAGERY, BIBLICAL.

Synoptic Gospels The first three Gospels in the New Testament, Matthew, Mark, and Luke, have so many characteristics in common that they are called *Synoptic,* which means "the ones with the same perspective." The Gospel of John offers a different perspective on the life and ministry of JESUS CHRIST.

The story line of the Synoptics consists of four main elements: the activity of John the Baptist culminating in the baptism of Jesus; Jesus' ministry in Galilee, culminating in the confession of Peter and the transfiguration; Jesus' travel to JERUSALEM;

and Jesus' last days in Jerusalem. The length of the Galilean period is unspecified, and much attention is given to the final week of Jesus' life. Each Synoptic Gospel contains many and diverse MIRACLES and PARABLES told by Jesus. Only Matthew and Luke report the birth of Jesus.

In places two or three have (nearly) the same wording, pointing to some form of dependence. Although a common oral tradition will have existed in the EARLY CHURCH, many scholars think of literary dependence as well. The most common hypothesis is that Mark was written first and used as a source by both Matthew and Luke. Only 31 verses of Mark do not also occur in Matthew and/or Luke. In addition, Matthew and Luke may both have used a source with sayings of Jesus that no longer exists and is called Q; thus they share some 235 verses. The name Q is from the German word for source, *Quelle.* Matthew has some 350 unique verses, Luke no fewer than 548.

The Synoptic Gospels display the tension that Jesus Christ is at the same time a human and a divine person (e.g., Mark 3:5; 6:3; 10:14; 13:32 compared to 1:1; 9:7; and 15:39). They present the KINGDOM OF GOD/(KINGDOM OF HEAVEN) as the subject of Jesus' message.

Syria Syria is Israel's northeast neighbor, stretching to the RIVER EUPHRATES, bound by LEBANON in the west and by the deserts of the Arabian peninsula in the east. Its capital is Damascus.

In the Bible it is only known as Syria in the New Testament, the name a Greek one, representing the Roman province formed in 64 B.C.E. In the Hebrew Bible, the area is either known as Aram or by its individual cities, such as Damascus, and the inhabitants as Arameans.

In the Bible they are first mentioned in connection with the search for a wife for Isaac among Abraham's old family living in Aram Naharaim (Genesis 24:10). Deuteronomy 26:5 may refer to this, seeing Israelite origins in the seminomadic Arameans, who had originated in Arabia and moved to ASSYRIA before settling to the south (Amos 9:7).

Only brief mentions are made of Israelite-Aramean contact before King David's time. In 2

Samuel 3:3 he married an Aramean princess from Geshur. His northern conquests led him into conflict with Hadadezer (2 Samuel 8:3–12) before annexing Damascus. From then on, there were border disputes and incursions, the most dramatic of which was the battle of Ramoth Gilead, which saw the death of King Ahab (1 Kings 22:35). The Aramean general Naaman received healing from Elisha (2 Kings 5). The Assyrians deported the Arameans in 732 B.C.E.

Aramean religion was a synthesis of Canaanite and Babylonian religion, a constant threat to the worship of Yahweh. Prophetic WOES AND DENUNCIATIONS are to be found in Isaiah 17 and Jeremiah 49:23–27. By contrast, the Aramean language, Aramaic (or Syriac), became the regional lingua franca (see 2 Kings 18:26) and after the EXILE was adopted by the Jews, being still spoken in the time of the New Testament (Acts 22:2).

tabernacle   See HEBREW BIBLE, WORSHIP AND RITUAL.

temple   See HEBREW BIBLE, WORSHIP AND RITUAL.

Ten Commandments   The Ten Commandments are the most important laws of the Sinai COVENANT. They give basic principles of behavior toward God and toward fellow human beings. The Ten Commandments are seen as obligatory in the Jewish orthodoxy as well as in the Christian Church. In the Bible, they appear in Exodus 20 and in Deuteronomy 5. For detailed information, see the commentary on Exodus 20 in Part II.

Testament   See COVENANT.

Torah   A Hebrew word literally meaning "instruction," mostly referring to divine instruction. The word also refers to the core of the Hebrew Bible, the first five books, which Christians call the PENTATEUCH.

translation theories   Modern translations of the Bible are based on a conscious decision as to whether to give greater privilege to the original

language or the receiving language. In the first case there will be emphasis on maintaining the form and feel of the original text, and the result will be what is called "formal correspondence." In the second case the reader's ability to understand will be central, and the result is called "dynamic equivalence." Some advocates of this approach also attempt to translate the emotive aspects of the text, arguing that the sacred text should be able to provoke similar reactions to the original readers'.

Among the translations mentioned in the entry BIBLE, ENGLISH EDITIONS OF, the Authorized (King James) Version (AV), New American Standard Book (NASB), and New Revised Standard Version (NRSV) are of the formal correspondence type. These versions attempt to maintain the word order of the original text and to translate the same Hebrew or Greek word consistently with one English word. Dynamic-equivalent translations, such as the New Living Translation, the Good News Bible, and The Message, have no such concerns. The New International Version sits somewhere in the middle between these approaches. It could be argued that both approaches have their place, the first for study Bibles, the second for making editions more widely accessible.

By way of example, here are three renderings of John 3:3:

> New King James Version: Jesus answered and said to him, "Most assuredly, I say to you, unless one is born again, he cannot see the kingdom of God."
>
> New International Version: In reply Jesus declared, "I tell you the truth, no one can see the kingdom of God unless he is born again."
>
> New Living Translation: Jesus replied, "I assure you, unless you are born again, you can never see the Kingdom of God."

Trinity   The Christian doctrine is that God has three expressions or *persona*, to use the Latin term. Originally a persona was a mask an actor wore to take on different characters. Thus it was one actor, but a number of characters or "persons." Thus, the

Trinity never denies the oneness of God. But there are three expressions of the one: Father, Son, and Holy Spirit.

The doctrine of the Trinity marks out Christianity as distinctly different from other monotheistic religions, such as Judaism and Islam. It has been the source of much dissent within the church over the centuries, and theistic groups who reject this particular doctrine are known as Unitarians, as opposed to Trinitarians. There is no specific teaching in the Bible that incontrovertibly teaches trinitarianism, but the doctrine emerged over the first few centuries of Christianity as the most logical way to explain certain passages of the New Testament, as well as attaining the fullest possible understanding of the revelation of God through Jesus Christ. It is best to see the doctrine as a philosophical one, using figurative language to make concrete concepts otherwise too abstract to have real force in the lives of individual believers.

The Hebrew Bible does occasionally see God as Father (as Malachi 2:10) and does have an understanding of the spirit of God. Even the term *Son of God* is used, but usually in the sense of angelic beings.

In the New Testament, both the Gospel of John and his letters set out quite explicitly to show that the Father and Jesus Christ, the Son, are to be seen equally as God (e.g., John 10:15, 30; 14:6, 9, 11; 17:21; 1 John 2:23–24; 2 John 3, 9). Jesus Christ becomes God in human form and revealed in human terms that can be comprehended in a way an invisible, unseen God could not be. This is God's grace, to make himself known in terms humans could understand. Even in death, Jesus Christ is still God; the Resurrection demonstrates both that and the profound love of God for humans. Other New Testament references to their equality include Colossians 1:19; Philippians 2:6–11; Titus 1:4; Hebrews 1:3–4.

The understanding of the Holy Spirit as the third person of the Trinity is harder to establish. It was through the Spirit that Jesus was begotten (Luke 1:35) and raised from the dead (Romans 8:11; 1 Peter 3:18). Jesus ascends to the Father in order for the Spirit to descend and be with us (John 14:26, 28; 15:26). The Spirit is thus Jesus' presence to his people and in them now (1 Corinthians 3:16). Other trinitarian references are to be found in the benedictions of Matthew 28:19 and 2 Corinthians 13:13.

See also GOD; HOLY SPIRIT; JESUS CHRIST.

Twelve Disciples (Twelve Apostles, the Twelve)

The word *disciple* translates the Greek word *mathētes*, which means "pupil," "follower," or "student." In the Gospels it refers to those who were close to Jesus Christ during his lifetime, but in Acts, by extension, it is a common designation for all Jesus' later followers.

In both Israel and the rest of the Hellenistic world, religious and philosophical teachers often had groups of disciples (Matthew 22:15–16). In the same way as JOHN THE BAPTIST had, during his ministry in Israel, Jesus had a large following of men and women (Mark 10:32; 15:40–41). Twelve of these men formed an inner circle, and in Christian parlance, they are normally called the disciples. They can also simply be called the Twelve (Luke 8:1; John 6:67). The lists of names (Matthew 10:2–4; Mark 3:16–19; Luke 6:14–16; Acts 1:13) show slight differences, which can be explained by the fact that some persons had two different names (Thaddeus = Simon the Zealot).

Peter is the most prominent of the disciples. Together with the brothers James and John he formed an inner group of three (Mark 9:2; 14:33). John's gospel never mentions John but it does pay particular attention to Thomas and to "the Beloved Disciple." All four Gospels narrate that one of the disciples, Judas Iscariot, was the person who betrayed Jesus to his enemies. Otherwise the Twelve operate as a group rather than as individuals, and they often speak with one voice. They are taught by Jesus and are charged with proclaiming him throughout the world after his departure. Acts shows the reluctant beginning of this task, focusing largely on Peter and Paul, who was not one of the Twelve. We know almost nothing about what most other disciples did after PENTECOST. As a result, from the second century onward many fictitious books were written to supply missing information (see APOCRYPHA AND PSEUDEPIGRAPHA).

types   Although we use the terms *type* and *typically* frequently, we often do so unaware of the theological and philosophical dimensions of the terms. The Greek word *tupos* is only used in the New Testament in Romans 5:14, where Adam is described as a type of Christ. The context is more specific in suggesting that it was in their sinless birth that one was a type or copy of the other. Adam and Christ both "took on" sin voluntarily. That is where the analogical thinking required for typology ceases, since Adam took on sin as rebellion that led to punishment, while Christ's taking on sin was as a voluntary substitute, which led to salvation.

We need to go back to Greek, and specifically Platonic, thinking fully to understand this sort of analogical argument. Plato posited all material things were "copies" or "types" of ideal spiritual "forms"; that we have a sense of the perfection of all created things, but only as lying behind their imperfection or difference. Most New Testament writers were not deeply engaged with this type of thinking, since the Hebrew Bible went no further than to see historical analogies and parallels (e.g., the exodus from Egypt paralleled by the exodus from Babylon). But Paul and the writer to the Hebrews are prepared to use typology as a helpful way of thinking about theological truths. Hebrews argues that certain rituals of the old covenant anticipated the full truth of the new covenant, which is thus a fulfillment of them rather than a simple replacement. In Hebrews 9:9, the high priest's entering the sanctuary on the Day of Atonement is seen as "prefiguring" or anticipating Christ as our high priest sacrificing himself to be a full and complete atoning sacrifice. In 11:19 the author sees the action of Abraham offering up Isaac as a "parable" of the Resurrection. In fact, the writer uses the Greek terms *parabole* and *antitupa*.

From quite early in the Christian Church till the present a much more systematic typology has developed in some quarters, whereby the characters of the Hebrew Bible are seen as prefiguring various aspects of Christ. So besides Adam and Abraham, Jacob, Joseph, David, and many others were described as anticipatory types of the perfect, ideal man, Jesus Christ. This has often become melded with various allegorical and symbolic interpretations of the Bible.

wisdom literature   A generic term that includes PROVERBS and PARABLES, which are considered as separate entries in Part III. In the Hebrew Bible, three books are designated as wisdom books: Job, Proverbs, and Ecclesiastes. Some scholars add Song of Solomon. These are considered as separate entries in Part II, as are the Wisdom of Solomon and Sirach (Ecclesiasticus), which are books in the Apocrypha.

Ecclesiasticus presents one form of wisdom literature, often called "Torah wisdom." Its prologue states that "the reading of the Law and the Prophets and the other books of our ancestors . . . led [the author] to write something pertaining to instruction and wisdom." This suggests the material is a practical understanding of how life should operate derived from the principles set out by the Law and prophets. The other category would be practical wisdom, deriving its principles from direct observation of society and creation. This wisdom, then, is part of general revelation, available to the whole human race. Psalm 19 is an example of both types of wisdom.

King Solomon is seen as the epitome of the wise man. 1 Kings 4:29–34 is informative, suggesting there was a general wisdom literature throughout the Middle East, especially in EGYPT. Certain renowned wise men are mentioned, but Solomon is seen as surpassing them all. Knowledge of Middle Eastern literatures of the time confirms the extent of this wisdom literature.

The wisdom books of the Hebrew Bible apart from Job were thus attributed to Solomon, though Ecclesiastes 12:9 mentions its author only as Qoholeth, or the Preacher, and Proverbs 25:1 suggests many proverbs were copied out in the days of King Hezekiah. The great disparity of form, approach, and subject matter among the books precludes just one author. Proverbs' practicality and assurance stand in great contrast to both the dramatic debate form of Job and Song of Solomon or the pessimism of Ecclesiastes. Perhaps Proverbs is best seen as a beginner's book, whereas Job and Ecclesiastes represent advanced wisdom gained through life's difficult questions. It might be said that Solomon "fathered" such Hebrew literature, though sadly his own life seems to suggest he failed to establish its fundamental premise that "the fear of the LORD is the beginning of wisdom" (Proverbs 1:7; 9:10; Job 28:28).

Wisdom literature pervades other biblical writings. Psalm 37 is a good example of a "wisdom psalm." Written as an acrostic, its pithy statements have all the marks of the Proverbs. Prophetic writing also contains elements of wisdom literature. Jeremiah 7:34; 16:9; 33:11 echo Ecclesiastes 12:1f, for example. Jeremiah 12:5 is set out as a proverb. And Jeremiah 10 takes on the forms of wisdom literature or the psalms. Jeremiah 10:1–5 echo Proverbs; 10:12–16 are more like Job, while 10:6–10, 23–25 are psalmlike. In the New Testament, the book of James is sometimes seen as its wisdom literature, as well as the obvious example of Jesus Christ's Sermon on the Mount (Matthew 5–7; Luke 6:20–49). Such wisdom is often set against Greek wisdom literature derived from secular philosophy (1 Corinthians 1:20–25; Colossians 1:19, 23).

woes and denunciations   Woes and denunciations are often connected to the PROPHETS of the Hebrew Bible, as among the most common forms of their oracles. In fact, they can be seen as a specific literary form, mainly belonging to prophecy and, to a lesser extent, WISDOM LITERATURE and APOCALYPTIC WRITING. They convey the sense of God's judgment on wrong behavior or beliefs. But in the Bible, such judgments are never arbitrary: There are always, as in a law court, evidence presented, a sense of a formal charge, and reasons given for the judgment. There is thus a logical as well as a rhetorical structure.

One of the clearest set of woes is uttered by Jesus Christ as recorded in Matthew 23:13–36 and Luke 11:39–52. The hypocrisy of the religious leaders is ruthlessly exposed in an ordered series of charges, with evidence given, and judgment clearly leading from them. Though outrage and anger are the dominating emotions, there is no hate or desire

for harm for its own sake. This, too, is the case with prophetic woes. Even when the woes are against foreign countries that may have done great harm to Israel (as in Jeremiah 46–51), it is the nations' moral failings or their hubristic pride that is held against them.

While some denunciations are marked by "Woe" (that is, harm), there are many other formulas, such as "O!"; "Alas for . . ."; "Cursed be . . ."; "prophesy against"; even "do not pray for . . ." (Jeremiah 11:14). A "thus says the LORD . . ." formula maintains a sense of objective justice. There is often a direct address, to the accused, with a specific list of failures, and a series of accusatory questions. Then came constructions of reason and consequence: "because . . . therefore/then . . ."; "Thus says . . ."; "I will judge because. . ." But not all prophetic woes remain negative. There is sometimes a time limit for punishment or consequences, followed by the promise of restoration, as in Ezekiel 36:22f.

There are woes in WISDOM LITERATURE, as Ecclesiastes 4:10, and prophetic woes derived from such literature, as Isaiah 3:11; 45:9. Apocryphal woes are exemplified in Revelation 9:12 in "the three woes" or punishments predicted (see also LAST THINGS).

women in the Bible   It has been stated that 170 women are named in the Bible, with a similar number referred to but not named. It needs to be said that all the women in the Bible are presented in specific cultural settings. In the Hebrew Bible, women's importance is a reflection of that Hebrew setting. In the New Testament, however, a somewhat different worldview emerges.

In the Hebrew Bible, women are portrayed in their society in a fully human way, neither stereotyped, demeaned, nor written out of the text. Clearly women had an inferior status, reflected in the smaller space given them. But their influence is affirmed, obviously in the begetting of children, especially male heirs, but also in unusual ways. For example, women use subterfuge, from Rebekah's persuading Jacob to deceive his father in order for him to have the blessing (Genesis 27:5–17), to Potiphar's wife's trying to seduce Joseph, then incriminating him (Genesis 39). Outright idealization or condemnation is avoided. Ruth, though a lovely daughter-in-law, has a risky encounter with Boaz. And Eve's temptation and fall are condemned much less than in later Jewish and Christian writing. Only Jezebel, the wicked queen of Ahab, is fully condemned (1 Kings 21:23–25), but even then much less severely than her husband. The narrative spares no detail about her grisly death. In the New Testament, she becomes a type of spiritual adultery (Revelation 2:20).

No specific instruction is given in the law about the role of women, only aspects of ceremonial purity and legal aspects of marriage and divorce. Nor is there any law concerning concubinage or polygamy; the practice eventually died out culturally rather than as a result of divine prohibition.

Two of the smaller books in the Hebrew Bible are named after women: Ruth and Esther. Interestingly, Ruth was not an Israelite, and Esther was in a foreign country. Both adapt to their new cultures and become heroines rather than victims. A woman shares the central place in the Song of Solomon, where the sensuous descriptions of her beauty reflect the general appreciation of the Hebrew Bible for marriage, human love, and sexuality. But a number of the Genesis narratives suggest similar passion and similar beauty, especially in the wives of the patriarchs: Sarah, Rebekah, Rachel, in particular. In fact, of all the books in the Hebrew Bible, Genesis gives us the most varied narratives of its women, from Eve through Sarah to Tamar. We see the jealousy of Leah for her sister, Rachel (Genesis 29), Dinah's rape and its avenging (Genesis 34). All these narratives have the ring of verisimilitude. They also affirm the importance of women in forming the significant genealogies of the Bible.

Women were not normally allowed to be in power, but it did happen. The prophetess Deborah is a case in point. She finds herself in a position of leadership in the period of the judges (Judges 4–5). Her achievement is recounted in exactly the same way as that of the male judges. The queen of Sheba travels to visit Solomon (1 Kings 10). There is no thought that her position is anomalous, though we have no instance of a queen's reigning in her own right in Israel or Judah. Still, as consorts, they have considerable influence: Bathsheba,

Jezebel, Athaliah, for example. Within the religious context, the priesthood is clearly male, but women are allowed significant roles, particularly as prophetesses, such as Deborah and Huldah. Women act as helpers in the narratives concerning ELIJAH and Elisha, and Hosea's wife forms a highly symbolic role in his prophecies.

One interesting chapter, Proverbs 31, does give us an insight into the power a woman could ideally have. She is able to conduct her own business, run her own household, and make decisions independently. This is the only picture in the Hebrew Bible of the ideal wife. It is descriptive, not prescriptive.

There are many little cameos of women: Rizpah, Saul's concubine, grieving over her slain sons (2 Samuel 21); Abigail dealing with David, excusing her boorish husband (1 Samuel 25); Rahab the prostitute, negotiating for her family's safety (Joshua 2); Zelophehad's daughters' precedent-setting negotiation over their right to inherit and freedom to marry whom they wish (Numbers 27:1–11; 36:1–12); and so on. There is also a significant subset of women who were barren and then have significant miraculous births, from Sarah, through Samuel's mother, Hannah, to Elizabeth, the mother of JOHN THE BAPTIST. Although the cultural condemnation of barrenness was relieved, the biblical narrative emphasizes the births are for God's redemptive purposes.

In the New Testament, some traditional cultural settings dissolve as the gospel enters Greek and Roman culture. In this context, explicit instructions start becoming noticeable about the allowed roles and behavior of women. Although the headship of the husband is maintained (Ephesians 5:22–23), the equality of male and female in the light of the gospel is emphasized (Galatians 3:28). Again, though Jesus chose only male disciples, yet a significant number of women helpers followed him, clearly with his blessing, and Mary and Martha were close friends (John 11:5). Women are welcomed as fellow laborers by Paul (Romans 16). Again, their depiction is normative.

Certain women in the New Testament have key positions, most obviously MARY (MOTHER OF JESUS), who in some way is seen as a second Eve. Women first see Jesus resurrected. Women are allowed some leadership within the church, for example, Phoebe and Priscilla. Lydia appears to be the ideal woman of Proverbs 31, leading her household to faith (Acts 16).

There are significant examples of female PER-SONIFICATION in the Bible. Babylon and Jerusalem are seen as women; so is Wisdom in Proverbs. God is shown as having maternal nurturing characteristics, and Jesus likens himself to a mother hen (Matthew 23:37), reminding us that females as well as males were created in God's image (Genesis 1:27).

worship See HEBREW BIBLE, WORSHIP AND RITUAL; LORD'S SUPPER.

PART IV

Appendixes

CHRONOLOGY

Compiling a chronology of the biblical period is not exact science. Many dates are only known by approximation because of lack of information, as the biblical writers worked in a different way from modern historians. The exact numbers in certain editions of the Bible have little basis in scholarly work. For the period of the Hebrew Bible since 1000 B.C.E., however, Egyptian, Assyrian, and Babylonian sources offer enough parallels to attain some level of certainty. The chronology of the Hebrew kings is complicated by the fact that several kings reigned in coregencies with their father or son, so that the numbers given cannot just be added. The list of kings of Israel and Judah given here is selective. For a full chronology of the rulers of Israel, see page 229.

For the New Testament period Roman historians offer helpful parallels, but the beginning of the common era was only calculated in the sixth century by Dionysius Exiguus, who got the date of the birth of Jesus wrong by approximately five years.

The dates given relate to the years of activity (reign) of the persons, not to their entire life span, which is usually unknown.

	Extrabiblical	Biblical
Early history		
2100–1800 B.C.E. (approx.)		Middle Bronze Age patriarchs: Abraham, Isaac, and Jacob
1900–1800 (approx.)		Joseph
1840–1440 (approx.)		Israelites in Egypt
ca. 1520		Birth of Moses
ca. 1440		Exodus from Egypt and travel to Canaan under Moses; covenant at Mount Sinai
ca. 1400		Death of Moses; crossing of the Jordan; fall of Jericho; subsequent conquest of Canaan
ca. 1380–1030		Period of the judges
ca. 1100		Ruth
ca. 1060–1000		Samuel

(Table continues)

(Table continued)

	Extrabiblical	Biblical	
The monarchy			
ca. 1050–1010		King Saul	
1010–971		King David	
971–931		King Solomon	
962		Completion of the temple	
945–924	Pharaoh Shishak (Shoshenq)		
931–722		Kingdom divided into Israel in the north and Judah in the south	
		Israel (10 tribes)	**Judah (two tribes)**
931–913			King Rehoboam
926			Raid of Pharaoh Shishak on Judah
910–869			King Asa
931–909		King Jeroboam	
885–874		King Omri	
874–853		King Ahab (mentioned in Assyrian records for 853); prophet Elijah	
872–848			King Jehoshaphat
843–805	King Hazael of Aram		
841–835			Queen Athaliah
841–814		King Jehu (mentioned in Assyrian records for 841)	
835–796			King Joash
796–767			King Amaziah
793–753		King Jeroboam II	
792–740			King Azariah (Uzziah)
ca. 760		Prophets Amos and Hosea	
750–ca. 700			Prophet Isaiah
745–727	King Tiglath-Pileser III of Assyria		
735–715			King Ahaz
732		King Tiglath-Pileser III of Assyria conquers the Trans-jordan regions of Israel	
732–722		Hoshea, the last king	

	Extrabiblical	Biblical	
		Israel (10 tribes)	Judah (two tribes)
727–722	King Shalmaneser V of Assyria		
722		Northern kingdom conquered by Shalmaneser; beginning of exile of the 10 tribes	
722–705	King Sargon of Assyria		
715–686			King Hezekiah
705–681	King Sennacherib of Assyria		
701			Sennacherib besieges Jerusalem
ca. 700			Prophet Micah
696–642			King Manasseh
639–609			King Josiah; killed by Pharaoh Necho
627–ca. 580			Prophet Jeremiah
before 612			Prophets Nahum and Zephaniah
612	Fall of Nineveh; Babylonia succeeds Assyria as world power		
610–595	Pharaoh Necho of Egypt		
605–	King Nebuchadnezzar of Babylonia		
600			Prophet Habakkuk
598–597			The Babylonians besiege and take Jerusalem; exile of the leading inhabitants, among them Ezekiel
597–586			Zedekiah, the last king
587			Zedekiah revolts against Babylon; Babylonians besiege Jerusalem
586			Capture of Jerusalem; destruction of the temple; Judah in exile

(Table continues)

(Table continued)

	Extrabiblical	Biblical	
		Israel (10 tribes)	**Judah (two tribes)**
after 586			Prophet Obadiah
605–535		Prophet Daniel	
593–570		Prophet Ezekiel	
559–530	King Cyrus II of Persia		
After the Exile			
539–331	Persia dominates Judea		
539/8		King Cyrus allows the Jews to return	
536		Some building on the second temple	
522–486	King Darius I of Persia		
520–516		The temple completed; prophets Zechariah and Haggai	
486–465	King Xerxes (Ahasuerus) of Persia	Esther	
ca. 480–460		Prophet Malachi	
464–424	King Artaxerxes I of Persia		
458–		Ezra the scribe	
445–		Governor Nehemiah	
Intertestamental period			
336–323	Alexander the Great (of Macedonia)		
331		Alexander the Great conquers Israel	
331–140	Greeks dominate Judea		
from ca. 250		Translation of the Septuagint	
175–	King Antiochus IV Epiphanes		
167		Antiochus bans the Jewish religion	
167–164		Maccabean uprising	
December 164		Dedication of the temple	
164–163		Maccabean rule over Judea	
140–163		Judea independent under the Maccabees or Hasmoneans	
New Testament period			
63 B.C.E.	Romans conquer Judea		
63 B.C.E.–330 C.E.	Romans dominate Judea		
37–4 B.C.E.		King Herod the Great; after his death his kingdom is divided	

	Extrabiblical	Biblical		
27 B.C.E.–14 C.E.	Emperor Augustus			
ca. 5 B.C.E.		Birth of Jesus		
14–37 C.E.	Emperor Tiberius			
		Judea and Samaria	**Galilea**	**Northern areas**
4 B.C.E.–6 C.E.		Archelaus ethnarch		
4 B.C.E.–34 C.E.				Herod Philip tetrarch
4 B.C.E.–39 C.E.			Herod Antipas tetrarch	
37–41 C.E.				Herod Agrippa I
6–40 C.E.		Roman governors (Pilate 26–36)		
26 or 29 C.E.		Jesus begins his ministry		
30 or 33		Crucifixion and Resurrection of Jesus		
ca. 35		Conversion of Paul		
37–41	Emperor Gajus (Caligula)			
41–44		Herod Agrippa I rules all of Israel		
44–70		Roman governors, such as Felix and Festus, rule over Israel		
41–54	Emperor Claudius			
46–58		Missionary journeys of Paul		
47 (?)		Galatians		
48		Meeting in Jerusalem		
50		1 Thessalonians		
51		2 Thessalonians		
55		1 Corinthians		
56		2 Corinthians		
57		Romans		
58		1 Timothy		
54–68	Emperor Nero	Colossians, Philemon		
before 62		James		
60–62		Paul in Rome as prisoner; Ephesians, Philippians, 2 Timothy		
60–67		Mark, 1 and 2 Peter		
62–66		Titus		

(Table continues)

(Table continued)

	Extrabiblical	Biblical
62–70		Matthew, Luke and Acts, Hebrews, Jude (?)
66–73	Jewish revolt against Rome, resulting in the destruction of the second temple by Titus in 70	
68–69	Three Roman emperors	
69–79	Emperor Vespasian	
79–81	Emperor Titus	
81–96	Emperor Domitian	
80–100		John, 1–3 John, Revelation

LISTS OF BIBLICAL BOOKS

The Hebrew Bible / Tanakh
Torah (Law)
- Bereshit (Genesis)
- Shemot (Exodus)
- Wayyiqra (Leviticus)
- Bamidbar (Numbers)
- Devarim (Deuteronomy)

Neviim (Prophets)

Neviim Rishonim (Former Prophets)
- Yehoshua (Joshua)
- Shoftim (Judges)
- Shemuel (1 and 2 Samuel)
- Melachim (1 and 2 Kings)

Neviim Acharonim (Latter Prophets)
- Yirmiyah (Jeremiah)
- Yechezqel (Ezekiel)
- Yeshayah (Isaiah)
- Shenem asar (The Twelve)
  - Hoshea (Hosea)
  - Yoel (Joel)
  - Amos
  - Ovadyah (Obadiah)
  - Yonah (Jonah)
  - Michah (Micah)
  - Nachum (Nahum)
  - Chavaqquq (Habakkuk)
  - Tsefanyah (Zephaniah)
  - Chaggay (Haggai)
  - Zecharyah (Zechariah)
  - Malachi

Ketuvim (Writings)
- Ruth

Sefer Tehillim (Psalms)
Iyyov (Job)
Mishle (Proverbs)
Qohelet (Ecclesiastes)
Shir Hashirim (Song of Songs)
Qinoth (Lamentations)
Daniel
Megillath Ester (Esther)
Ezra (Ezra-Nehemiah)
Divre Hayyamim (1 and 2 Chronicles)

The preceding list gives the Hebrew Bible according to the Babylonian Talmud (Baba Bathra 14b, approximately second century C.E.). In later tradition, Yeshayah is often made the first of the Latter Prophets. The order of the Ketuvim varies. From the 10th century onward, the five books of Ruth, Qohelet, Shir Hashirim, Qinoth, and Esther are grouped together as the so-called Megillot (Scrolls) have special significance for the Jewish liturgical calendar. The name *Tanakh* for the Hebrew Bible is derived from the first letters of each of the main parts, Tora, Neviim, and Ketuvim.

The Christian Bible—Old Testament
Historical books
- Genesis
- Exodus
- Leviticus
- Numbers
- Deuteronomy
- Joshua
- Judges
- Ruth
- 1 and 2 Samuel
- 1 and 2 Kings

1 and 2 Chronicles
Ezra
Nehemiah
Esther

Books of poetry
Job
Psalms
Proverbs
Ecclesiastes
Song of Solomon

Prophetic books
Isaiah
Jeremiah
Lamentations
Ezekiel
Daniel
Hosea
Joel
Amos
Obadiah
Jonah
Micah
Nahum
Habakkuk
Zephaniah
Haggai
Zechariah
Malachi

The Apocryphal books / Deuterocanonical books of the Old Testament

The following books are recognized as deuterocanonical (being of secondary canonical rank) by the Catholic and Orthodox Churches but excluded as apocryphal (outside the canon) by the Protestant churches. See also APOCRYPHA AND PSEUDEPIGRAPHA in Part III.

Books that are recognized by all Catholic and Orthodox Churches
Tobit
Judith
Esther, Greek version containing additional chapters

Wisdom of Solomon
Sirach (Ecclesiasticus)
Baruch
Letter of Jeremiah (sometimes as an appendix to Baruch)
Greek additions to Daniel: the Prayer of Azariah, Susanna, Bel and the Dragon, 1 and 2 Maccabees

Books that are recognized by the Greek and Russian Orthodox Churches only
1 Esdras
Prayer of Manasseh
Psalm 151
3 Maccabees

Other Books
2 Esdras: included in the Slavonic Bible
Book of Enoch: included in the Ethiopian Bible
Book of Jubilees: included in the Ethiopian Bible
Psalms of Solomon: included in some editions of the Septuagint (see BIBLE, EARLY TRANSLATIONS OF), but not accepted by any of the Christian churches
4 Maccabees: included as an appendix in the Septuagint

The Christian Bible—New Testament
Gospels
Matthew
Mark
Luke
John

Historical book
Acts of the Apostles

Letters
Romans
1 and 2 Corinthians
Galatians
Ephesians
Philippians
Colossians
1 and 2 Thessalonians

1 and 2 Timothy
Titus
Philemon
Hebrews
James
1 and 2 Peter

1, 2, and 3 John
Jude

Prophetic book
Revelation

BIBLIOGRAPHY

Selected Bibles

Abegg, Martin, Jr., Peter Flint, and Eugene Ulrich, trans. *The Dead Sea Scrolls Bible*. New York: HarperCollins, 1999.

The Amplified Bible. Updated edition. The Lockman Foundation. Grand Rapids, Mich.: Zondervan Corp., 1987.

The Essential Study Bible: Contemporary English Version. American Bible Society. New York: G.P. Putnam's Sons, 1995.

Good News Bible: The Bible in Today's English Version. 2d ed. American Bible Society. New York: American Bible Society, 1992.

The Holy Bible: Authorized King James Version. Oxford: Oxford University Press, 1967.

Holy Bible: ESV New Testament. Crossway Bibles. Wheaton, Ill.: Crossway Bibles, 2002.

The Holy Bible: New International Version. International Bible Society. Colorado Springs, Colo.: International Bible Society, 1984.

Holy Bible: New Living Translation. Wheaton, Ill.: Tyndale House Publishers, 1996.

The Holy Bible: New Revised Standard Version. 2d ed. Division of Christian Education of the National Council of the Churches of Christ in the United States of America. Nashville, Tenn.: T. Nelson, 1990.

The Holy Bible: Revised Standard Version. 2d ed. Division of Christian Education of the National Council of the Churches of Christ in the United States of America, 1971.

The Holy Bible: Revised Version. Oxford: Oxford University Press, 1885.

The Holy Bible: Today's New International Version. International Bible Society. Colorado Springs, Colo.: International Bible Society, 2005.

The Jerusalem Bible. New York: Doubleday, 1966.

Jewish Publication Society. *Tanakh: The Holy Scriptures: The New JPS Translation According to the Traditional Hebrew Text*. Philadelphia: Jewish Publication Society, 1988.

Jones, Alexander. *The Jerusalem Bible*. Garden City, N.Y.: Doubleday, 1966.

The Living Bible. Wheaton, Ill.: Tyndale House Publishers, 1971.

Lucado, Max. *The Devotional Bible: Experiencing the Heart of Jesus: New Century Version*. Nashville, Tenn.: T. Nelson, 1991.

New American Standard Bible. The Lockman Foundation. Nashville, Tenn.: Broadman Press, 1995.

New Century Version. Nashville, Tenn.: Nelson, 1991.

New English Bible. Joint Committee on the New Translation of the Bible. London: Oxford University Press/Cambridge University Press, 1970.

The New Jerusalem Bible. Garden City, N.Y.: Doubleday, 1985.

New King James Version. Nashville, Tenn.: T. Nelson, 1982.

Peterson, Eugene H. *The Message: The Bible in Contemporary Language*. Colorado Springs, Colo.: NavPress, 2002.

Phillips, J. B. *The New Testament in Modern English*. 2d ed. New York: HarperCollins, 1972.

The Revised English Bible. Cambridge: Cambridge University Press; Oxford: Oxford University Press, 1989.

Works of reference

Douglas, J. D. et al., eds. *The New International Bible Dictionary*. Grand Rapids, Mich.: Zondervan, 1999.

Freedman, David Noel, Allen C. Myers, and B. Beck. *Eerdmans Dictionary of the Bible.* Grand Rapids, Mich.: Eerdmans, 2000.

Lockyer, Herbert. *All the Men of the Bible.* Grand Rapids, Mich.: Zondervan, 1958.

Marshall, I. Howard, et al., eds. *The New Bible Dictionary.* 3d ed. Downers Grove, Ill.: InterVarsity Press, 1996.

Metzger, Bruce M. *The Oxford Guide to People and Places of the Bible.* New York: Oxford University Press, 2004.

Odelain, O, and R. Séguineau. *Dictionary of Proper Names and Places in the Bible.* London: Robert Hale, 1981.

The Oxford Bible Atlas. 4th ed. New York: Oxford University Press, 2007.

Ryken, Leland, et al., eds. *Dictionary of Biblical Imagery.* Downers Grove, Ill.: InterVarsity Press, 1998.

Selman, Martin, and Martin H. Manser, *The Hearthside Bible Dictionary.* Nashville, Tenn.: Cumberland House, 2001.

Water, Mark. *The Baker Encyclopedia of Bible People: A Comprehensive Who's Who from Aaron to Zurishaddai.* Grand Rapids, Mich.: Baker Books, 2006.

Literary approach to the Bible

Alter, Robert. *The Art of Biblical Narrative.* Oshkosh, Wis.: Basic Books, 1983.

———. *The Art of Biblical Poetry.* Oshkosh, Wis.: Basic Books, 1987.

———. *The World of Biblical Literature.* Oshkosh, Wis.: Basic Books, 1992.

———, and Frank Kermode, eds. *The Literary Guide to the Bible.* Cambridge, Mass.: Harvard University Press, 1987.

Auerbach, Eric. *Mimesis: The Representation of Reality in Western Literature.* Princeton, N.J.: Princeton University Press, 1953.

Balentine, Samuel E., and John Barton, eds. *Language, Theology, and The Bible.* Festschrift J. Barr. Oxford: Clarendon, 1994.

Bailey, James L., and Lyle D. Vander Broek. *Literary Forms in the New Testament.* London: SPCK, 1992.

Bar-Efrat, Shimon. *Narrative Art in the Bible.* JSOT. Suppl. no. 70. Sheffield, England: Sheffield Academic Press, 1989.

———. "Some Observations on the Analysis of Structure in Biblical Narrative." *Vetus Testamentum* 30 (1980): 154–173.

Barton, John. *Reading the Old Testament: Method in Biblical Study.* London: Darton, Longman and Todd, 1996.

———, ed. *The Cambridge Companion to Biblical Interpretation.* Cambridge: Cambridge University Press, 1998.

Beale, Gregory K., and D. A. Carson, eds. *Commentary on the New Testament Use of the Old Testament.* Downers Grove, Ill.: InterVarsity Press, 2007.

Beekman, John, John Callow, and Michael Kopesec. *The Semantic Structure of Written Communication.* Dallas, Tex.: Summer Institute of Linguistics, 1981.

Berlin, Adele. *Poetics and Interpretation of Biblical Narrative.* Sheffield, England: Almond, 1983.

Bullinger, Ernest W. *Figures of Speech Used in the Bible Explained and Illustrated.* Grand Rapids, Mich.: Baker, 1968.

Brett, Mark G. *Biblical Criticism in Crisis? The Impact of the Canonical Approach on Old Testament Studies.* Cambridge: Cambridge University, 1991.

Caird, George B. *The Language and Imagery of the Bible.* London: Duckworth, 1988.

Coats, George W., ed. *Saga, Legend, Tale, Novella, Fable: Narrative Forms in Old Testament Literature.* JSOT. Suppl. no. 35. Sheffield, England: JSOT Press, 1985.

Coggins, R. *Who's Who in the Bible.* London: Batsford, 1981.

Crouch, Walter B. *Death and Closure in Biblical Narrative.* Studies in Biblical Literature 7. New York: Lang, 2000.

Dorsay, David A. *The Literary Structure of the Old Testament: A Commentary on Genesis-Malachi.* Grand Rapids, Mich.: Baker, 1999.

Exum, J. Cheryl, and David J. A. Clines, eds. *The New Literary Criticism and the Hebrew Bible.* JSOT. Suppl. no. 143. Sheffield, England: JSOT Press, 1993.

Fokkelman, Jan. *Reading Biblical Narrative: An Introductory Guide.* Louisville, Ky.: Westminster, 1999.

Fokkelman, Jan P. *Reading Biblical Poetry: An Introductory Guide.* Louisville, Ky.: Westminster John Knox, 2001.

Freedman, David N. *The Unity of the Hebrew Bible.* Ann Arbor: University of Michigan, 1991.

Frei, Hans W. *The Eclipse of Biblical Narrative: A Study in Eighteenth and Nineteenth Century Hermeneutics.* New Haven, Conn.: Yale University, 1974.

Frye, Northrop. *The Great Code. The Bible and Literature.* New York: Harcourt Brace Jovanovich, 1982.

Gabel, John B., Charles B. Wheeler, Anthony D. York, and David Citino. *The Bible as Literature: An Introduction.* 5th ed. New York: Oxford University, 2006.

Good, E. M. *Irony in the Old Testament.* Philadelphia: Westminster Press, 1965.

Jeffreys, David L. *A Dictionary of Biblical Tradition in English Literature.* Grand Rapids, Mich.: Eerdmans, 1992.

Josipovici, Gabriel. *The Book of God: A Response to the Bible.* New Haven, Conn.: Yale University Press, 1988.

Kennedy, George A. *New Testament Interpretation through Rhetorical Criticism.* Chapel Hill: University of North Carolina Press, 1984.

Kugel, James. *The Idea of Biblical Poetry: Parallelism and Its History.* New Haven, Conn.: Yale University Press, 1981.

Licht, Jacob. *Storytelling in the Bible.* Jerusalem: Magnes, 1978.

Longman, Tremper, III. *Literary Approaches to Biblical Interpretation.* Downers Grove, Ill.: Apollos, 1987.

Matthews, Victor H. *Old Testament Turning Points: The Narratives That Shaped a Nation.* Grand Rapids, Mich.: Baker, 2006.

McKnight, Edgar V. *Post-Modern Use of the Bible: The Emergence of Reader-Oriented Criticism.* Nashville, Tenn.: Abingdon, 1990.

Morgan, Robert, with John Barton. *Biblical Interpretation.* New York: Oxford University, 1988.

Muilenberg, J. "Form Criticism and Beyond." *Journal of Biblical Literature* 88 (1969): 1–18.

Powell, Mark A. *What Is Narrative Criticism? A New Approach to the Bible.* Minneapolis: Fortress, 1990.

Radday, Yehuda T., and Athalya Brenner, eds. *On Humour and the Comic in the Hebrew Bible.* Sheffield, England: Almond, 1990.

Rendtorff, Rolf. "The Paradigm Is Changing: Hopes—and Fears." *Biblical Interpretation* 1 (1993): 34–53.

Resseguie, James L. *Narrative Criticism of the New Testament: An Introduction.* Grand Rapids, Mich.: Baker, 2005.

Roberts, Ruth ap. *The Biblical Web.* Ann Arbor: University of Michigan Press, 1994.

Ryken, Leland. *How to Read the Bible as Literature.* Grand Rapids, Mich.: Zondervan, 1985.

———. *Words of Delight: A Literary Introduction to the Bible.* Grand Rapids, Mich.: Zondervan, 1987.

———, and Tremper Longman III, eds. *A Complete Literary Guide to the Bible.* Grand Rapids, Mich.: Zondervan, 1993.

Simon, Ulrich. *Story and Faith in the Biblical Narrative.* London: SPCK, 1975.

Sternberg, Meir. *The Poetics of Biblical Narrative: Ideological Literature and the Drama of Reading.* Bloomington: Indiana University, 1987.

Thiselton, Anthony C. *New Horizons in Hermeneutics: The Theory and Practice of Transforming Biblical Reading.* London: HarperCollins, 1992.

Van Gemeren, Willem A., et al., eds. *New International Dictionary of Old Testament Theology and Exegesis.* Carlisle: Paternoster, 1996.

Watson, Duane F., and Alan J. Hauser. *Rhetorical Criticism of the Bible: A Comprehensive Bibliography with Notes on History and Method.* Biblical Interpretation Series 4. Leiden: Brill, 1994.

Weis, Richard D., and David M. Carr, eds. "A Gift of God in Due Season: Essays on Scripture and Community in Honor of James A. Sanders." JSOT Suppl. no. 225. Sheffield, England: Sheffield Academic Press, 1996.

Welch, John W., ed. *Chiasmus in Antiquity: Structures, Analyses, Exegesis.* Hildesheim, Germany: Gerstenberg, 1981.

Wright, Christopher J. H. *The Mission of God: Unlocking the Bible's Grand Narrative.* Nottingham, England: Inter-Varsity Press, 2006.

Historical and theological surveys

Aune, David E. *The New Testament in Its Literary Environment.* Cambridge, England: Clarke, 1988.

Barnett, Paul W. *Jesus and the Rise of Early Christianity: A History of New Testament Times.* Downers Grove, Ill.: IVP, 1999.

Bright, John. *A History of Israel.* 3d ed. Philadelphia: Westminster, 1981.

Caird, George B. *New Testament Theology.* Oxford: Clarendon Press, 1994.

Childs, Brevard S. *Introduction to the Old Testament as Scripture.* Philadelphia: Fortress Press, 1979.

de Silva, David A. *An Introduction to the New Testament*. Downers Grove, Ill.: Apollos, 2004.

Dillard, Raymond B., and Tremper Longman, III. *An Introduction to the Old Testament*. Grand Rapids, Mich.: Zondervan, 1994.

Ferguson, Everett. *Backgrounds of Early Christianity*. 3d ed. Grand Rapids, Mich.: Eerdmans, 2003.

Gower, Ralph. *The New Manners and Customs of Bible Times*. Amersham, England: Scripture Press, 1987.

Hasel, Gerhard F. *Old Testament Theology: Basic Issues in the Current Debate*. 4th ed. Grand Rapids, Mich.: Eerdmans, 1991.

House, Paul R. *Old Testament Theology*. Downers Grove, Ill.: InterVarsity Press, 1998.

Kaiser, Walter C., Jr. *A History of Israel: From the Bronze Age through the Jewish Wars*. Nashville, Tenn.: Broadman & Holman, 1998.

Marshall, I. Howard. *New Testament Theology*. Downers Grove, Ill.: InterVarsity Press, 2004.

Millard, Alan R. *Reading and Writing in the Time of Jesus*. Sheffield, England: Sheffield Academic Press, 2000.

Rendtorff, Rolf. *The Canonical Hebrew Bible: A Theology of the Old Testament*. Leiden: Deo, 2005.

Witherington, Ben. *New Testament History: A Narrative Account*. Grand Rapids, Mich.: Baker, 2001.

Hebrew Bible

Pentateuch

Clines, David J. A. *The Theme of the Pentateuch*. JSOT. Suppl. no. 10. Sheffield, England: JSOT Press, 1994.

McEvenue, Sean E. *Interpreting the Pentateuch*. Old Testament Studies 4. Collegeville, Minn.: Liturgical Press, 1990.

Sailhamer, John H. *The Pentateuch as Narrative: A Biblical-Theological Commentary*. Grand Rapids, Mich.: Zondervan, 1992.

Watts, James W. *Reading Law: The Rhetorical Shaping of the Pentateuch*. Sheffield, England: Sheffield Academic Press, 1999.

Genesis

Anderson, Bernhard W. "From Analysis to Synthesis: The Interpretation of Genesis 1–11." *JBL* 97 (1978): 23–39.

Brueggemann, Walter. *Genesis*. Interpretation. Louisville, Ky.: John Knox Press, 1982.

Cassuto, U. *Genesis: From Adam to Noah / From Noah to Abraham*. Jerusalem: Magnes Press, 1961.

Hamilton, Victor P. *The Book of Genesis: Chapter 1–17*. The New International Commentary on the Old Testament. Grand Rapids, Mich.: Eerdmans, 1990.

Hess, Richard S., Gordon J. Wenham, and Philip E. Satterthwaite, eds. *He Swore an Oath: Biblical Themes from Genesis 12–50*. 2d ed. Carlisle: Paternoster; Grand Rapids, Mich.: Baker, 1994.

Kidner, Derek. *Genesis*. Tyndale Old Testament Commentary 1. Leicester, England: InterVarsity Press, 1967.

Knight, George A. F. *Theology in Pictures: A Commentary on Genesis Chapters One to Eleven*. Edinburgh: Handsel, 1981.

Longacre, Robert E. *Joseph: A Story of Divine Providence: A Text Theoretical and Textlinguistic Analysis of Genesis 37 and 39–48*. Winona Lake, Ind.: Eisenbrauns, 1989.

Niditch, Susan. *Chaos to Cosmos: Studies in Biblical Patterns of Creation*. Chico, Calif.: Scholars Press, 1985.

Robinson, Robert R. "Literary Functions of the Genealogies of Genesis." *Catholic Biblical Quarterly* 48 (1986): 595–608.

Wenham, Gordon. *Genesis 1–15*. Word Biblical Commentary. Waco, Tex.: Word Books, 1987.

———. *Genesis 16–50*. Word Biblical Commentary. Dallas, Tex.: Word Books, 1994.

Exodus

Brenner, Athalya, ed. *A Feminist Companion to Exodus to Deuteronomy*. The Feminist Companion to the Bible 6. Sheffield, England: Sheffield Academic Press, 1994.

Coats, George W. *Exodus 1–18*. The Forms of the Old Testament Literature. Grand Rapids, Mich.: Eerdmans, 1999.

Durham, John I. *Exodus*. Word Biblical Commentary. Dallas, Tex.: Word Books, 1987.

Hauge, Martin Ravndal. *The Descent from the Mountain: Narrative Patterns in Exodus 19–40*. JSOT. Suppl. no. 323. Sheffield, England: Sheffield Academic Press, 2001.

Houtman, C. *Exodus*. Commentaar op het Oude Testament. Kampen, Netherlands: Kok, 1996.

Johnstone, W. *Exodus.* Old Testament Guides. Sheffield, England: JSOT Press, 1995.

Roukema, Riemer. *The Interpretation of Exodus: Studies in Honor of Cornelis Houtman.* Leuven, Belgium: Peeters, 2006.

Sprinkle, Joe M. *The Book of the Covenant: A Literary Approach.* JSOT. Suppl. no. 174. Sheffield, England: JSOT Press, 1994.

Leviticus

Bergen, Wesley, J. *Reading Ritual: Leviticus in Postmodern Culture.* JSOT. Suppl. no. 417. London: Clark, 2005.

Douglas, Mary. *Leviticus as Literature.* Oxford: Oxford University Press, 1999.

Hartley, John E. *Leviticus.* Word Biblical Commentary. Dallas, Tex.: Word Books, 1992.

Rendtorff, Rolf, Robert A. Kugler, and Sarah Smith Bartel, eds. *The Book of Leviticus: Composition and Reception.* Leiden: Brill, 2003.

Numbers

Ahsley, Timothy R. *The Book of Numbers.* The New International Commentary on the Old Testament. Grand Rapids, Mich.: Eerdmans, 1993.

Davies, Eryl W. *Numbers.* New Century Bible Commentary. Grand Rapids, Mich.: Eerdmans, 1995.

Knierim, Rolf P., and George W. Coats. *Numbers.* The Forms of Old Testament Literature 4. Grand Rapids, Mich.: Eerdmans, 2005.

Olson, Dennis T. *Numbers.* Interpretation. Louisville, Ky.: John Knox Press, 1996.

Wenham, Gordon. *Numbers.* Old Testament Gudes. Sheffield, England: Sheffield Academic Press, 1997.

Deuteronomy

Brueggemann, Walter. *Deuteronomy.* Abingdon Old Testament Commentaries. Nashville, Tenn.: Abingdon, 2001.

Christensen, Duane L. *Deuteronomy 1–11.* Word Biblical Commentary. Dallas, Tex.: Word Books, 2002.

Clements, R. E. *Deuteronomy.* Old Testament Guides. Sheffield, England: JSOT Press, 1993.

Lenchak, Timothy A. *Choose Life! A Rhetorical-Critical Investigation of Deuteronomy 28, 69–30, 20.* Analecta Biblica 129. Roma: Pontificio Istituto Biblico, 1993.

McConville, J. G. *Deuteronomy.* Apollos Old Testament Commentary 5. Leicester, England: Apollos, 2002.

Stackert, Jeffrey. *Rewriting the Torah: Literary Revision in Deuteronomy and the Holiness Legislation.* Forschungen zum Alten Testament 52. Tuebingen, Germany: Mohr Siebeck, 2007.

Thompson, John A. *Deuteronomy.* Tyndale Old Testament Commentaries. London: InterVarsity Press, 1974.

Joshua

Butler, Trent C. *Joshua.* Word Biblical Commentary. Dallas, Tex.: Word Books, 1983

Creach, Jerome F. D. *Joshua.* Interpretation. Louisville, Ky.: John Knox Press, 2003.

Kissling, Paul J. *Reliable Characters in the Primary History: Profiles of Moses, Joshua, Elijah and Elisha.* JSOT. Suppl. no. 224. Sheffield, England: Sheffield Academic Press, 1996.

Koorevaar, Hendrik J. *De opbouw van het boek Jozua.* Heverlee: Centrum voor Bijbelse Vorming België, 1990.

Mitchell, Gordon. *Together in the Land: A Reading of the Book of Joshua.* JSOT. Suppl. no. 134. Sheffield, England: JSOT Press, 1993.

Nelson, Richard D. *Joshua: A Commentary.* The Old Testament Library. Louisville, Ky.: Westminster/John Knox Press, 1997.

Judges

Amit, Yairah. *The Book of Judges: The Art of Editing.* Biblical Interpretation Series 38. Leiden: Brill, 1999.

Klein, Lillian R. *The Triumph of Irony in the Book of Judges.* JSOT. Suppl. no. 68. Sheffield, England: Almond, 1988.

McCann, J. Clinton. *Judges.* Interpretation. Louisville, Ky.: John Knox Press, 2002.

O'Connell, Robert H. *The Rhetoric of the Book of Judges.* Vetus Testamentum Supp. 63. Leiden: Brill, 1996.

Wong, Gregory T. K. *Compositional Strategy of the Book of Judges: An Inductive, Rhetorical Study.* Vetus Testamentum Supp. 111. Leiden: Brill, 2006.

Yee, Gale A. *Judges and Method: New Approaches in Biblical Studies.* Minneapolis, Minn.: Fortress Press, 1995.

Ruth

Atkinson, David. *The Message of Ruth: The Wings of Refuge.* Leicester, England: InterVarsity Press, 1993.

Bertman, Stephen. "Symmetrical Design in the Book of Ruth." *Journal of Biblical Literature* 84 (1965): 165–168.

Bush, Frederic W. *Ruth, Esther.* Word Biblical Commentary. Dallas, Tex.: Word Books, 1996.

Green, Barbara. "The Plot of the Biblical Story of Ruth." *Journal for the Study of the Old Testament* 23 (1982): 55–68.

Hamlin, E. John. *Surely There Is a Future: A Commentary on the Book of Ruth.* International Theological Commentary. Grand Rapids, Mich.: Eerdmans; Edinburgh: Handsel, 1996.

Jobling, David. "Ruth Finds a Home: Canon, Politics, Method." *The New Literary Criticism and the Hebrew Bible,* edited by J. Cheryl Exum and David J. A. Clines, 125–139. JSOT. Suppl. no. 143. Sheffield, England: JSOT Press, 1993.

Nielsen, Kirsten. *Ruth: A Commentary.* Louisville, Ky.: Westminster John Knox, 1997.

Porten, Bezalel. "The Scroll of Ruth: A Rhetorical Study." *Gratz College Annual of Jewish Studies* 7 (1978): 23–49.

Rauber, D. F. "Literary Values in the Bible: The Book of Ruth." *Journal of Biblical Literature* 89 (1970): 27–37.

1 and 2 Samuel

Anderson, A. A. *2 Samuel.* Word Biblical Commentary. Dallas, Tex.: Word Books, 1989.

Baldwin, Joyce G. *1 and 2 Samuel.* Tyndale Old Testament Commentaries. Leicester, England: InterVarsity Press, 1988.

Fokkelman, J. P. *Narrative Art and Poetry in the Books of Samuel: A Full Interpretation Based on Stylistic and Structural Analyses.* Studia Semitica Neerlandica 31. Assen, Netherlands: Van Gorcum, 1993.

Heller, Roy L. *Power, Politics, and Prophecy: The Character of Samuel and the Deuteronomistic Evaluation of Prophecy.* New York: T&T Clark, 2006.

Klein, Ralph W. *1 Samuel.* Word Biblical Commentary. Dallas, Tex.: Word Books, 1983.

Klement, Herbert H. *II Samuel 21–24: Context, Structure and Meaning in the Samuel Conclusion.* Europae-ische Hochschulschriften 23/682. Frankfurt/Main: Lang, 2000.

Weiss, Andrea L. *Figurative Language in Biblical Prose Narrative: Metaphor in the Book of Samuel.* Vetus Testamentum Supp. 107. Leiden: Brill, 2006.

1 and 2 Kings

Brodie, Thomas L. *The Crucial Bridge: The Elijah-Elisha Narrative as an Interpretive Synthesis of Genesis—Kings and a Literary Model for the Gospels.* Collegeville, Minn.: Liturgical Press, 2000.

DeVries, Simon J. *1 Kings.* Word Biblical Commentary. Dallas, Tex.: Word Books, 1985.

Grottanelli, Cristiano. *Kings and Prophets: Monarchic Power, Inspired Leadership, and Sacred Text in Biblical Narrative.* New York: Oxford University Press, 1999.

Hobbs, T. R. *2 Kings.* Word Biblical Commentary. Dallas, Tex.: Word Books, 1985.

Murray, Donald F. *Divine Prerogative and Royal Pretension: Pragmatics, Politics and Polemics in a Narrative Sequence about David (2 Samuel 5.17–7.29).* JSOT. Suppl. no. 264. Sheffield, England: Sheffield Academic Press, 1998.

Provan, Iain W. *1 and 2 Kings.* Old Testament Guides. Sheffield, England: Sheffield Academic Press, 2001.

Seibert, Eric A. *Subversive Scribes and the Solomonic Narrative: A Rereading of 1 Kings 1–11.* New York: Clark, 2006.

Wiseman, Donald John. *1 and 2 Kings.* Tyndale Old Testament Commentaries. Leicester, England: InterVarsity Press, 1993.

1 and 2 Chronicles

Ackroyd, Peter R. *The Chronicler in His Age.* JSOT. Suppl. no. 101. Sheffield, England: JSOT Press, 1991.

Braun, Roddy L. *1 Chronicles.* Word Biblical Commentary. Waco, Tex.: Word Books, 1986.

Coggins, Richard J. *The First and Second Book of the Chronicles.* Cambridge: Cambridge University Press, 1976.

Dillard, Raymond B. *2 Chronicles.* Word Biblical Commentary. Waco, Tex.: Word Books, 1987.

———. "The Literary Structure of the Chronicler's Solomon Narrative." *Journal for the Study of the Old Testament* 30 (1984): 85–93.

Duke, Rodney K. *The Persuasive Appeal of the Chronicler: A Rhetorical Analysis.* JSOT. Suppl. no. 88. Sheffield, England: Almond, 1990.

Japhet, Sara. *I and II Chronicles: A Commentary.* Louisville, Ky.: Westminster John Knox, 1993.

Koorevaar, Hendrik J. "Die Chronik als intendierter Abschluss des alttestamentlichen Kanons." *Jahrbuch fuer Evangelikale Theologie* 11 (1997): 42–76.

Riley, William. *King and Cultus in Chronicles: Worship and the Reinterpretation of History.* JSOT. Suppl. no. 160. Sheffield, England: JSOT Press, 1993.

Selman, Martin J. *1/2 Chronicles: An Introduction and Commentary.* Tyndale Old Testament Commentary 10. Leicester, England: InterVarsity Press, 1994.

Steins, Georg. *Die Chronik als kanonisches Abschlussphaenomen.* Bonner Biblische Beitraege 93. Weinheim, Germany: Beltz Athenaeum, 1995.

Williamson, H. G. M. *1 and 2 Chronicles.* The New Century Bible Commentary. Grand Rapids, Mich.: Eerdmans; London: Marshall, Morgan & Scott, 1982.

Ezra and Nehemiah

Blenkinsopp, Joseph. *Ezra-Nehemiah: A Commentary.* London: SCM, 1988.

Breneman, Mervin. *Ezra, Nehemiah, Esther.* The New American Commentary. Nashville, Tenn.: Broadman & Holman, 1993.

Clines, David J. A. *Ezra, Nehemiah, Esther.* The New Century Bible Commentary. Grand Rapids, Mich.: Eerdmans, 1984.

Eskenazi, Tamara C. *In an Age of Prose: A Literary Approach to Ezra-Nehemiah.* Atlanta: Scholars Press, 1988.

Fensham, F. Charles. *The Books of Ezra and Nehemiah.* The New International Commentary on the Old Testament. Grand Rapids, Mich.: Eerdmans, 1982.

Japhet, Sara. "Composition and Chronology in the Book of Ezra-Nehemiah." In *Second Temple Studies 2: Temple and Community in the Persian Period,* edited by Tamara C. Eskenazi and Kent H. Richards, 189–216. JSOT. Suppl. no. 175. Sheffield, England: Sheffield Academic Press, 1994.

Kidner, Derek. *Ezra and Nehemiah: An Introduction and Commentary.* Tyndale Old Testament Commentary. Leicester, England: InterVarsity Press, 1979.

Myers, Jacob M. *Ezra; Nehemia: Introduction, Translation, and Notes.* Anchor Bible. New York: Doubleday, 1965.

Throntveit, Mark A. *Ezra-Nehemiah.* Interpretation. Louisville, Ky.: John Knox Press, 1992.

Esther

Baldwin, Joyce G. *Esther: An Introduction and Commentary.* Tyndale Old Testament Commentary. Leicester, England: InterVarsity Press, 1984.

Berg, Sandra Beth. *The Book of Esther: Motifs, Themes and Structure.* Atlanta: Scholars Press, 1979.

Bronner, Leila L. "Reclaiming Esther: From Sex Object to Sage." *Jewish Bible Quarterly* 26 (1998): 3–10.

Bush, Frederic W. *Ruth, Esther.* Word Biblical Commentary. Dallas, Tex.: Word Books, 1996.

Clines, David J. A. *The Esther Scroll: The Story of the Story.* JSOT. Suppl. no. 30. Sheffield, England: JSOT Press, 1984.

Craig, Kenneth M., Jr. *Reading Esther: A Case for the Literary Carnivalesque.* Louisville, Ky.: Westminster John Knox Press, 1995.

Day, Linda. *Three Faces of a Queen: Characterization in the Books of Esther.* JSOT. Suppl. no. 186. Sheffield, England: JSOT Press, 1995.

Dorothy, Charles V. *The Books of Esther: Structure, Genre, and Textual Integrity.* JSOT. Suppl. no. 187. Sheffield, England: Sheffield Academic Press, 1997.

Fox, Michael V. *Character and Ideology in the Book of Esther.* Columbia: University of South Carolina, 1991.

Gordis, Robert. "Religion, Wisdom and History in the Book of Esther: A New Solution to an Ancient Crux." *Journal of Biblical Literature* 100 (1981): 359–388.

Humphreys, W. Lee. "A Life-Style for Diaspora: A Study of the Tales of Esther and Daniel." *Journal of Biblical Literature* 92 (1973): 211–223.

Laniak, Timothy S. *Shame and Honor in the Book of Esther.* SBL Diss. Series 165. Atlanta: Scholars Press, 1998.

Loader, James A. "Esther as a Novel with Different Levels of Meaning." *Zeitschrift fuer die alttestamentliche Wissenschaft* 90 (1978): 417–421.

Reid, Debra. *Esther.* Tyndale Old Testament Commentary. Leicester, England: InterVarsity Press, 2008.

Wisdom Books

Blocher, Henri. "The Fear of the Lord as the 'Principle' of Wisdom." *Tyndale Bulletin* 28 (1977): 3–28.

Brown, William P. *Character in Crisis: A Fresh Approach to the Wisdom Literature of the Old Testament.* Grand Rapids, Mich.: Eerdmans, 1996.

Crenshaw, James L. *Old Testament Wisdom: An Introduction.* Atlanta: John Knox, 1981.

Garrett, Duane A. *Proverbs, Ecclesiastes, Song of Songs.* The New American Commentary. Nashville, Tenn.: Broadman, 1993.

Kidner, Derek. *Wisdom to Live By: An Introduction to the Old Testament's Wisdom Books of Proverbs, Job and Ecclesiastes.* Leicester, England: InterVarsity Press, 1985.

Kitchen, K. A. "Proverbs and Wisdom Books of the Ancient Near East: The Factual History of a Literary Form." *Tyndale Bulletin* 28 (1977): 69–114.

Murphy, Roland E. *The Tree of Life: An Exploration of Biblical Wisdom Literature.* 2d ed. Grand Rapids, Mich.: Eerdmans, 1996.

Rad, Gerhard von. *Weisheit in Israel.* Neukirchen-Vluyn, Germany: Neukirchener Verlag, 1970.

Skehan, Patrick W. *Studies in Israelite Wisdom and Poetry.* The Catholic Biblical Quarterly Monograph Series 1. Washington D.C.: Catholic Biblical Association, 1971.

Steinberg, Julius. *Die Ketuvim: Ihr Aufbau und ihre Botschaft.* Bonner Biblische Beitraege 152. Hamburg: Philo, 2006.

Job

Alden, Robert L. *Job.* The New American Commentary. Nashville, Tenn.: Broadman & Holman, 1993.

Clines, David J. A. "Deconstructing the Book of Job." In *What Does Eve Do to Help: And Other Readerly Questions to the Old Testament.* JSOT. Suppl. no. 94. Sheffield, England: JSOT Press, 1990, 106–123.

———. *Job 1–20.* Word Biblical Commentary. Dallas, Tex.: Word Books, 1989.

Course, John E. *Speech and Response: A Rhetorical Analysis of the Introductions to the Speeches of the Book of Job (Chaps. 4–24).* The Catholic Biblical Quarterly Monograph Series 25. Washington D.C.: Catholic Biblical Association, 1994.

Dell, Katharine J. *The Book of Job as Sceptical Literature.* Zeitschrift fuer die alttestamentliche Wissenschaft Beihefte 197. Berlin: de Gruyter, 1991.

Eaton, John H. *Job.* Sheffield, England: JSOT Press, 1992.

Hartley, John E. *The Book of Job.* The New International Commentary on the Old Testament. Grand Rapids, Mich.: Eerdmans, 1988.

Lugt, Pieter van der. *Rhetorical Criticism and the Poetry of the Book of Job.* Oudtestamentische Studiën 32. Leiden: Brill, 1995.

Perdue, Leo G., and W. Clark Gilpin, eds. *The Voice from the Whirlwind: Interpreting the Book of Job.* Nashville, Tenn.: Abingdon, 1992.

Pope, Marvin H. *Job: Introduction, Translation, and Notes.* Anchor Bible. New York: Doubleday, 1985.

Steinmann, Andrew E. "The Structure and Message of the Book of Job." *Vetus Testamentum* 46 (1996): 85–100.

Weiss, Meir. *The Story of Job's Beginning: Job 1–2: A Literary Analysis.* Jerusalem: Magnes Press, 1983.

Whedbee, William. "The Comedy of Job." In *Humour and the Comic in the Hebrew Bible,* edited by Yehuda T. Radday and Athalya Brenner, 217–249. Sheffield, England: Almond, 1990.

Whybray, Norman. *Job.* Readings. Sheffield, England: Sheffield Academic Press, 1998.

Zuck, Roy B., ed. *Sitting with Job: Selected Studies on the Book of Job.* Grand Rapids, Mich.: Baker, 1992.

Psalms

Allen, Leslie C. *Psalms 101–150.* Word Biblical Commentary. Waco, Tex.: Word Books, 1983.

Auffret, Pierre. *La sagesse a bâti sa maison: Études de structures littéraires dans l'Ancien Testament et specialement dans les Psaumes.* Orbis Biblicus et Orientalis 49. Goettingen, Germany: Vandenhoeck & Ruprecht; Fribourg, Switzerland: Éditions Universitaires, 1982.

Barbiero, Gianni. *Das erste Psalmenbuch als Einheit: Eine synchrone Analyse von Psalm 1–41.* Oesterreichische Biblische Studien 16. Frankfurt/Main: Lang, 1999.

Brueggemann, Walter. "Bounded by Obedience and Praise: The Psalms as Canon." *Journal for the Study of the Old Testament* 50 (1991): 63–92.

Cole, Robert L. *The Shape and Message of Book III (Psalms 73–89)*. JSOT. Suppl. no. 307. Sheffield, England: Sheffield Academic Press, 2000.

Creach, Jerome F. D. *Yahweh as Refuge and the Editing of the Hebrew Psalter*. JSOT. Suppl. no. 217. Sheffield, England: Sheffield Academic Press, 1996.

Craigie, Peter C. *Psalms 1–50*. Word Biblical Commentary. Waco, Tex.: Word Books, 1983.

Goulder, Michael D. "The Fourth Book of the Psalter." *Journal of Theological Studies* 26 (1975): 269–289.

Hossfeld, Frank-Lothar, and Erich Zenger. *Die Psalmen: Psalm 1–50*. Neue Echter Bibel. Wuerzburg, Germany: Echter, 1993.

———. *Psalmen 51–100*. Herders Theologischer Kommentar zum Alten Testament. Freiburg, Germany: Herder, 2000.

Howard, David M. *The Structure of Psalms 93–100*. Biblical and Judaic Studies from the University of California, San Diego. Winona Lake, Ind.: Eisenbrauns, 1997.

Kidner, Derek. *Psalms*. Tyndale Old Testament Commentary. Leicester, England: InterVarsity Press, 1973, 1975.

Mays, James L. *Psalms*. Interpretation. Louisville, Ky.: John Knox Press, 1994.

McCann, J. Clinton, ed. *The Shape and Shaping of the Psalter*. JSOT. Suppl. no. 159. Sheffield, England: Sheffield Academic Press, 1993.

McCann, J. Clinton, Jr. *A Theological Introduction to the Book of the Psalms: The Psalms as Torah*. Nashville, Tenn.: Abingdon, 1993.

Sheppard, Gerald T. "Theology and the Book of Psalms." *Interpretation* 46 (1992): 143–155.

Smith, Mark S. "The Theology of the Redaction of the Psalter: Some Observations." *Zeitschrift fuer die alttestamentliche Wissenschaft* 104 (1992): 408–412.

Tate, M. E. *Psalms 51–100*. Word Biblical Commentary. Dallas, Tex.: Word Books, 1990.

Wilson, Gerald H. *The Editing of the Hebrew Psalter*. SBL Diss. Series 76. Chico, Calif.: Scholars Press, 1985.

———. "The Shape of the Book of Psalms." *Interpretation* 46 (1992): 129–142.

———. "The Use of 'Untitled' Psalms in the Hebrew Psalter." *Zeitschrift fuer die alttestamentliche Wissenschaft* 97 (1985): 404–413.

Proverbs

Clifford, Richard J. *Proverbs: A Commentary*. Louisville, Ky.: Westminster John Knox Press, 1999.

Cohen, Abraham D. *Proverbs: Hebrew Text and English Translation with an Introduction and Commentary*. London: Soncino, 1976.

Farmer, Kathleen A. *Who Knows What Is Good? A Commentary on the Books of Proverbs and Ecclesiastes*. International Theological Commentary. Grand Rapids, Mich.: Eerdmans; Edinburgh: Handsel, 1991.

Frydrych, Tomáš. *Living under the Sun: Examination of Proverbs and Qoheleth*. Vetus Testamentum Supp. 90. Leiden: Brill, 2002.

Heim, Knut M. *Like Grapes of Gold Set in Silver: An Interpretation of Proverbial Clusters in Proverbs 10:1–22:16*. Berlin: de Gruyter, 2001.

Hurowitz, Victor Avigdor. "The Seventh Pillar: Reconsidering the Literary Structure and Unity of Proverbs 31." *Zeitschrift fuer die alttestamentliche Wissenschaft* 113 (2001): 209–218.

Kidner, Derek. *Proverbs*. Tyndale Old Testament Commentary. Leicester, England: InterVarsity Press, 1964.

Murphy, Roland E. *Proverbs*. Word Biblical Commentary. Nashville, Tenn.: Nelson, 1998.

Perdue, Leo G. *Proverbs*. Interpretation. Louisville, Ky.: Westminster John Knox Press, 2000.

Whybray, Roger N. *The Book of Proverbs: A Survey of Modern Study*. History of Biblical Interpretation Series 1. Leiden: Brill, 1995.

———. *The Composition of the Book of Proverbs*. JSOT. Suppl. no. 168. Sheffield, England: JSOT Press, 1994.

———. *Proverbs*. The New Century Bible Commentary. Grand Rapids, Mich.: Eerdmans, 1994.

Ecclesiastes

Anderson, William H. U. *Qoheleth and Its Pessimistic Theology: Hermeneutical Struggles in Wisdom Literature*. Mellen Biblical Press Series 54. Lewiston, N.Y.: Mellen, 1997.

Bartholomew, Craig G. *Reading Ecclesiastes: Old Testament Exegesis and Hermeneutical Theory*. Analecta Biblica 139. Rome: Pontificio Istituto Biblico, 1998.

Brown, William P. *Ecclesiastes.* Interpretation. Louisville, Ky.: John Knox Press, 2000.

Christianson, Eric S. *A Time to Tell: Narrative Strategies in Ecclesiastes.* JSOT. Suppl. no. 280. Sheffield, England: Sheffield Academic Press, 1998.

Eaton, Michael A. *Ecclesiastes: An Introduction and Commentary.* Tyndale Old Testament Commentary 16. Leicester, England: InterVarsity Press, 1983.

Fox, Michael V. *A Time to Tear Down and a Time to Build Up: A Rereading of Ecclesiastes.* Grand Rapids, Mich.: Eerdmans, 1999.

Frydrych, Tomáš. *Living under the Sun: Examination of Proverbs and Qoheleth. Vetus Testamentum.* Supp. 90. Leiden: Brill, 2002.

Kamano, Naoto. *Cosmology and Character: Qoheleth's Pedagogy from a Rhetorical-Critical Perspective.* Zeitschrift fuer die alttestamentliche Wissenschaft Beihefte 312. Berlin: de Gruyter, 2002.

Kidner, Derek. *A Time to Mourn, and a Time to Dance: Ecclesiastes and the Way of the World.* Leicester, England: InterVarsity Press, 1976.

Loader, James A. *Polar Structures in the Book of Qohelet.* Zeitschrift fuer die alttestamentliche Wissenschaft Beihefte 152. Berlin: de Gruyter, 1979.

Schoors, Antoon, ed. *Qohelet in the Context of Wisdom.* Bibliotheca Ephemeridum Theologicarum Lovaniensium 136. Leuven, Belgium: Leuven University Press, 1998.

Wright, A. G. "Additional Numerical Patterns in the Book of Qohelet." *Catholic Biblical Quarterly* 45 (1983): 32–43.

———. "The Riddle of the Sphinx: The Structure of the Book of Qoheleth." *Catholic Biblical Quarterly* 30 (1968): 313–334.

———. "The Riddle of the Sphinx Revisited: Numerical Patterns in the Book of Qohelet." *Catholic Biblical Quarterly* 42 (1980): 38–51.

Song of Solomon

Carr, G. Lloyd. *The Song of Solomon: An Introduction and Commentary.* Tyndale Old Testament Commentary. Leicester, England: InterVarsity Press, 1984.

Clines, David J. A. "Why Is There a Song of Songs and What Does It to You If You Read It?" In *Interested Parties: The Ideology of Writers and Readers of the Hebrew Bible.* JSOT. Suppl. no. 205. Sheffield, England: Sheffield Academic Press, 1995, 94–121.

Elliott, Mary Timothea. *The Literary Unity of the Canticle.* Europaeische Hochschulschriften 23/371. Frankfurt/Main: Lang, 1989.

Exum, J. Cheryl. "A Literary and Structural Analysis of the Song of Songs." *Zeitschrift fuer die alttestamentliche Wissenschaft* 85 (1973): 47–79.

Falk, Marcia Lee. *Love Lyrics from the Bible: A Translation and Literary Study of The Song of Songs.* Bible and Literature Series 4. Sheffield, England: Almond Press, 1982.

Fox, Michael V. *The Song of Songs and the Ancient Egyptian Love Songs.* Madison: University of Wisconsin, 1985.

Hwang, Andrew. "The New Structure of the Song of Songs and Its Implications for Interpretation." *Westminster Theological Journal* 65 (2003): 97–111.

Landy, Francis. *Paradoxes of Paradise: Identity and Difference in the Song of Songs.* Bible and Literature Series 7. Sheffield, England: Almond Press, 1983.

Longman, Tremper, III. *Song of Songs.* Grand Rapids, Mich.: Eerdmans, 2001.

Murphy, Roland E. *The Song of Songs: A Commentary on the Book of Canticles or The Song of Songs.* Minneapolis: Fortress, 1990.

Pope, Marvin H. *Song of Songs: A New Translation with Introduction and Commentary.* Anchor Bible. Garden City, N.Y.: Doubleday, 1977.

Shea, Williams H. "The Chiastic Structure of the Song of Songs." *Zeitschrift fuer die alttestamentliche Wissenschaft* 92 (1980): 378–396.

Stadelmann, Luis I. J. *Love and Politics: A New Commentary on the Song of Songs.* New York: Paulist, 1992.

Prophets

Childs, Brevard S. "The Canonical Shape of the Prophetic Literature." *Interpretation* 32 (1978): 46–55.

Clements, Ronald E. *Old Testament Prophecy: From Oracles to Canon.* Louisville, Ky.: Westminster John Knox Press, 1996.

Podhoretz, Norman. *The Prophets: Who They Were; What They Are.* New York: The Free Press, 2002.

Sawyer, John F. A. *Prophecy and the Biblical Prophets.* New York: Oxford University Press, 1993.

Watts, James W., and Paul R. House, eds. *Forming Prophetic Literature: Essays on Isaiah and the Twelve in Honor of John D. W. Watts.* JSOT. Suppl. no. 235. Sheffield, England: Sheffield Academic Press, 1996.

Isaiah

Adams, Jim W. *The Performative Nature and Function of Isaiah 40–55.* New York: Clark, 2006.

Brueggemann, Walter. *Isaiah 1–39, Isaiah 40–66,* Louisville, Ky.: Westminster John Knox Press, 1998.

Childs, Brevards. *Isaiah: A Commentary.* Louisville, Ky.: Westminster John Knox Press, 2000.

Motyer, J. A. *The Prophecy of Isaiah: An Introduction and Commentary.* Downers Grove, Ill.: InterVarsity Press, 1993.

Webb, Barry G. *The Message of Isaiah: On Eagles' Wings.* Downers Grove, Ill.: InterVarsity Press, 1997.

Williamson, Hugh G. M. *Variations on a Theme: King, Messiah and Servant in the Book of Isaiah.* Carlisle, Pa.: Paternoster Press, 1998.

Jeremiah

Brueggemann, Walter. *A Commentary on Jeremiah: Exile and Homecoming.* 2d ed. Grand Rapids, Mich.: Wm. B. Eerdmans, 1998.

Clements, R. E. *Jeremiah: Interpretation.* Louisville, Ky.: Westminster John Knox Press, 1989.

Diamond, A. R., ed. *Troubling Jeremiah.* JSOT. Suppl. no. 260. Sheffield, England: Sheffield Academic Press, 1999.

Fretheim, Terence E. *Jeremiah.* Macon, Ga.: Smyth and Helwys, 2002.

Kessler, Martin F. *Reading the Book of Jeremiah: A Search for Coherence.* Winona Lake, Ind.: Eisenbrauns, 2004.

Longman, Tremper III. *Jeremiah, Lamentations.* Peabody, Mass.: Hendrickson, 2008.

Lamentations

Dobbs-Allsopp, F. W. *Lamentations: Interpretation.* Louisville, Ky.: Westminster John Knox Press, 2002.

Garr, W. Randall. "The Qinah: A Study of Poetic Meter, Syntax and Style." *Zeitschrift fuer die alttestamentliche Wissenschaft* 95 (1983): 54–75.

Heater, H. "Structure and Meaning in Lamentations." *Bibliotheca Sacra* 149 (1992): 304–315.

Hillers, Delbert R. *Lamentations: Introduction, Translation, and Notes.* Anchor Bible. Garden City, N.Y.: Doubleday, 1992.

Hunter, Jannie. *Faces of a Lamenting City: The Development of the Book of Lamentations.* Beiträge zur Erforschung des Alten Testaments und des antiken Judentums 39. Frankfurt/Main: Lang, 1996.

Johnson, Bo. "Form and Message in Lamentations." *Zeitschrift fuer die alttestamentliche Wissenschaft* 97 (1985): 58–73.

Kaiser, Walter C., Jr. *A Biblical Approach to Personal Suffering.* Chicago: Moody Press, 1982.

O'Connor, Kathleen M. *Lamentations and the Tears of the World.* Danvers, Mass.: Orbis Books, 2002.

Provan, Iain W. *Lamentations.* The New Century Bible Commentary. Grand Rapids, Mich.: Eerdmans, 1991.

Renkema, Johan. *Lamentations.* Leuven, Belgium: Peeters, 1998.

———. "The Meaning of the Parallel Acrostics in Lamentations." *Vetus Testamentum* 45 (1995): 379–383.

Salters, R. B. *Jonah and Lamentations.* Sheffield, England: JSOT Press, 1994.

Ezekiel

Allen, Leslie C. *Ezekiel.* Word Biblical Commentary. Dallas, Tex.: Word Books, 1994.

Goshen-Gottstein, Moshe H., and Shemaryahu Talmon. *The Book of Ezekiel.* The Hebrew University Bible. Jerusalem: Magnes Press, 2004.

Renz, Thomas. *The Rhetorical Function of the Book of Ezekiel.* Vetus Testamentum Suppl. 76. Leiden: Brill, 1999.

Taylor, John B. *Ezekiel: An Introduction and Commentary.* Downers Grove, Ill.: InterVarsity Press, 1981.

Wright, Christopher J. H. *The Message of Ezekiel: A New Heart and a New Spirit.* Downers Grove, Ill.: InterVarsity Press, 2001.

Daniel

Baldwin, Joyce G. *Daniel.* Downers Grove, Ill.: InterVarsity Press, 1978.

Collins, John J. "The Jewish Apocalypses." *Semeia* 14 (1979): 21–59.

———, and Peter W. Flint, eds. *The Book of Daniel: Composition and Reception. Vetus Testamentum.* Suppl. 83. Leiden: Brill, 2001.

Goldingay, John E. *Daniel.* Word Biblical Commentary. Dallas, Tex.: Word Books, 1989.

Good, E. M. "Apocalyptic as Comedy: The Book of Daniel." *Semeia* 32 (1984): 41–70.

Gooding, D. W. "The Literary Structure of the Book of Daniel and Its Implications." *Tyndale Bulletin* 32 (1981): 43–79.

Hartman, Louis F., and Alexander A. Di Lella. *The Book of Daniel*. Anchor Bible. Garden City, N.Y.: Doubleday, 1978.

Lenglet, A. "La structure littéraire de Daniel 2–7." *Biblica* 53 (1972): 169–190.

Longman, Tremper III. *The NIV Application Bible: Daniel*. Grand Rapids, Mich.: Zondervan, 1999.

Towner, Wayne Sibley. *Daniel*. Interpretation. Atlanta: John Knox Press, 1984.

Woude, Adam S. van der, ed. *The Book of Daniel in the Light of New Findings*. Leuven, Belgium: Leuven University Press, 1993.

The Minor Prophets

Baldwin, Joyce G. *Haggai, Zechariah, Malachi*. Downers Grove, Ill.: InterVarsity Press, 1981.

Baker, David W. *Nahum, Habakkuk, Zephaniah*. Downers Grove, Ill.: InterVarsity Press, 1988.

———. *The NIV Application Bible: Joel, Obadiah, Malachi*. Grand Rapids, Mich.: Zondervan, 2006.

———, T. Desmond Alexander, and Bruce K. Waltke. *Obadiah, Jonah, Micah*. Downers Grove, Ill.: InterVarsity Press, 1988.

Carroll R., and M. Daniel. *Amos: The Prophet and his Oracles*. Louisville, Ky.: Westminster John Knox Press, 2002.

Evary, Douglas. *Hosea-Jonah*. Word Biblical Commentary. Waco, Tex.: Word Books, 1987.

Hanley, Homer. *A Commentary on the Minor Prophets*. Grand Rapids, Mich.: Baker Book House, 1973.

House, Paul R. *The Unity of the Twelve*. JSOT. Suppl. no. 97. Sheffield, England: Almond Press, 1990.

Kidner, Derek. *Message of Hosea: Love the Loveless*. Downers Grove, Ill.: InterVarsity Press, 1984.

Knight, G. A. F., and Friedmann W. Golba. *Revelation of God: A Commentary on the Song of Songs and Jonah*. Grand Rapids, Mich.: Eerdmans, 1988.

Moeller, Karl. *A Prophet in Debate: The Rhetoric of Persuasion in the Book of Amos*. London: Sheffield Academic Press, 2003.

Motyer, J. A. *Message of Amos*. Downers Grove, Ill.: InterVarsity Press, 1984.

Patterson, Richard D. *Nahum, Habakkuk, Zephaniah: An Exegetical Commentary*. Peabody, Mass.: Biblical Studies Press, 1991; revised 2003.

Waltke, Bruce K. *A Commentary on Micah*. Grand Rapids, Mich.: Wm. B. Eerdmans, 2007.

New Testament
The Gospels

Bailey, Kenneth E. *Poet and Peasant; and Through Peasant Eyes*. Grand Rapids, Mich.: Eerdmans, 1983.

Wright, Stephen I. *Tales Jesus Told: An Introduction to the Narrative Parables of Jesus*. Carlisle, Pa.: Paternoster, 2002.

Matthew

Carter, Warren. *Matthew: Storyteller, Interpreter, Evangelist*. Peabody Mass.: Hendrickson, 1996.

Davies, W. D., and Dale C. Allison. *A Critical and Exegetical Commentary on the Gospel According to Saint Matthew*. 3 vols. International Critical Commentary. Edinburgh: T.&T. Clark, 1988–1997.

France, R. T. *The Gospel According to Matthew: An Introduction and Commentary*. Tyndale New Testament Commentaries. Downers Grove, Ill.: IVP, 1986.

Kingsbury, Jack Dean. *Matthew as Story*. 2d ed. Philadelphia: Fortress, 1988.

Mark

France, R. T. *The Gospel of Mark: A Commentary on the Greek Text*. New International Greek Testament Commentary. Grand Rapids, Mich.: Eerdmans, 2002.

Humphrey, Robert L. *Narrative Structure and Message in Mark: A Rhetorical Analysis*. Studies in the Bible and Early Christianity. Vol. 60. Lewiston, N.Y.: Edwin Mellen Press, 2003.

Hurtado, Larry W. *Mark*. New International Biblical Commentary. Peabody, Mass.: Hendrickson, 1989.

Kermode, Frank. *The Sense of an Ending: Studies in the Theory of Fiction*. New York: Oxford University Press, 1968.

Rhoads, David M. *Mark as Story: An Introduction to the Narrative of a Gospel*. 2d ed. Minneapolis: Fortress Press, 1999.

Luke

Green, Joel B. *The Gospel of Luke*. New International Commentary on the New Testament. Grand Rapids, Mich.: Eerdmans, 1997.

Johnson, Luke T. *The Gospel of Luke*. Sacra pagina, vol. 3. Collegeville, Minn.: Liturgical Press, 1991.

Kurz, William S. *Reading Luke-Acts: Dynamics of Biblical Narrative*. Louisville, Ky.: Westminster/John Knox Press, 1993.

Tannehill, Robert C. *The Narrative Unity of Luke-Acts: A Literary Interpretation*. Vol. 1, *The Gospel According to Luke*. Philadelphia: Fortress, 1986.

John

Bruce, F. F. *The Gospel of John: Introduction, Exposition and Notes*. Grand Rapids, Mich.: Eerdmans, 1996.

Carson, D. A. *The Gospel According to John: An Introduction and Commentary*. Pillar New Testament Commentary. Downers Grove, Ill.: IVP, 1991.

Culpepper, R. Alan. *Anatomy of the Fourth Gospel: A Study in Literary Design*. Philadelphia: Fortress, 1983.

Resseguie, James L. *The Strange Gospel: Narrative Design and Point of View in John*. Biblical Interpretation Series, Vol. 56. Leiden: Brill, 2001.

Stibbe, Mark W. G. *John*. Readings. Sheffield, England: Sheffield Academic Press, 1993.

———. *John as Storyteller: Narrative Criticism and the Fourth Gospel*. Cambridge: Cambridge University Press, 1992.

Tovey, Derek. *Narrative Art and Act in the Fourth Gospel*. Journal for the Study of the New Testament, Supplement Series, Vol. 151. Sheffield, England: Sheffield Academic Press, 1997.

Acts of the Apostles

Bock, Darrell L. *Acts*. Baker Exegetical Commentary on the New Testament. Grand Rapids, Mich.: Baker, 2007.

Marshall, I. Howard. *The Acts of the Apostles: An Introduction and Commentary*. Tyndale New Testament Commentaries. Downers Grove Ill.: IVP, 1980.

Spencer, F. Scott. *Acts*. Readings. Sheffield, England: Sheffield Academic Press, 1997.

Talbert, Charles H. *Reading Acts: A Literary and Theological Commentary on the Acts of the Apostles*. New York: Crossroad, 1997.

Tannehill, Robert C. *The Narrative Unity of Luke-Acts: A Literary Interpretation*. Vol. 2, *The Acts of the Apostles*. Minneapolis: Fortress, 1990.

Witherington, Ben. *The Acts of the Apostles: A Socio-Rhetorical Commentary*. Grand Rapids, Mich.: Eerdmans, 1998.

Letters

Doty, William G. *Letters in Primitive Christianity*. Philadelphia: Fortress Press, 1973.

Harvey, John D. *Listening to the Text. Oral Patterning in Paul's Letters*. Grand Rapids, Mich.: Baker, 1998.

Richards, E. Randolph. *The Secretary in the Letters of Paul*. Tübingen, Germany: J. C. B. Mohr (Siebeck), 1991.

Paul

Anderson, R. Dean. *Ancient Rhetorical Theory and Paul*. Leuven, Belgium: Peeters, 1999.

Longenecker, Bruce W. *Narrative Dynamics in Paul: A Critical Assessment*. Louisville, Ky.: Westminster John Knox Press, 2002.

Romans

Bruce, F. F. *The Epistle of Paul to the Romans: An Introduction and Commentary*. 2d ed. Tyndale New Testament Commentaries. Downers Grove, Ill.: IVP, 1985.

Moo, Douglas J. *The Epistle to the Romans*. New International Commentary on the New Testament. Grand Rapids, Mich.: Eerdmans, 1996.

Olyott, Stuart. *The Gospel as It Really Is*. Welwyn, England: Evangelical Press, 1979.

Osborne, Grant R. *Romans*. IVP New Testament Commentary. Downers Grove, Ill.: IVP, 2004.

1 Corinthians

Hays, Richard B. *First Corinthians*. Interpretation. Louisville, Ky.: Westminster/John Knox, 1997.

Mitchell, Margaret M. *Paul and the Rhetoric of Reconciliation: An Exegetical Investigation of the Language and Composition of 1 Corinthians*. Tübingen, Germany: J. C. B. Mohr (Siebeck), 1991.

Talbert, Charles H. *Reading Corinthians: A Literary and Theological Commentary on I and II Corinthians*. New York: Crossroad, 1987.

Thiselton, Anthony C. *The First Epistle to the Corinthians: A Commentary on the Greek text.* New International Greek Testament Commentary. Grand Rapids, Mich.: Eerdmans, 2000.

2 Corinthians

Belleville, Linda L. *2 Corinthians.* IVP New Testament Commentary. Downers Grove, Ill.: Apollos, 1996.

Harris, Murray J. *The Second Epistle to the Corinthians: A Commentary on the Greek Text.* New International Greek Testament Commentary. Grand Rapids, Mich.: Eerdmans, 2005.

Kruse, Colin G. *The Second Epistle of Paul to the Corinthians: Introduction and Commentary.* Tyndale New Testament Commentaries. Downers Grove, Ill.: IVP, 1987.

Talbert, Charles H. *Reading Corinthians: A Literary and Theological Commentary on I and II Corinthians.* New York: Crossroad, 1987.

Galatians

Bruce, F. F. *The Epistle of Paul to the Galatians: A Commentary on the Greek Text.* New International Greek Testament Commentary. Grand Rapids, Mich.: Eerdmans, 1982.

Hansen, G. Walter. *Abraham in Galatians: Epistolary and Rhetorical Contexts.* Sheffield, England: Almond, 1989.

———. *Galatians.* IVP New Testament Commentary. Downers Grove, Ill.: IVP, 1994.

Witherington, Ben. *Grace in Galatia: A Commentary on St. Paul's Letter to the Galatians.* Grand Rapids, Mich.: Eerdmans, 1998.

Ephesians

Liefeld, Walter L. *Ephesians.* IVP New Testament Commentary. Downers Grove, Ill.: IVP, 1997.

O'Brien, Peter T. *The Letter to the Ephesians.* Pillar New Testament Commentary. Grand Rapids, Mich.: Eerdmans, 1999.

Philippians

Bockmuehl, Marcus. *A Commentary on the Epistle to the Philippians.* Harper's New Testament Commentary. Peabody, Mass.: Hendrickson, 1997.

Bruce, F. F. *Philippians.* New International Biblical Commentary. Peabody, Mass.: Hendrickson, 1989.

Fee, Gordon D. *Paul's Letter to the Philippians.* New International Commentary on the New Testament. Grand Rapids, Mich.: Eerdmans, 1995.

Colossians and Philemon

Dunn, James D. G. *The Epistles to the Colossians and to Philemon: A Commentary on the Greek Text.* New International Greek Testament Commentary. Grand Rapids, Mich.: Eerdmans, 1996.

Garland, David E. *Colossians and Philemon.* The NIV Application Commentary. Grand Rapids, Mich.: Zondervan, 1999.

Petersen, Norman R. *Rediscovering Paul: Philemon and the Sociology of Paul's Narrative World.* Philadelphia: Fortress Press, 1985.

Wright, N. T. *The Epistles of Paul to the Colossians and to Philemon: An Introduction and Commentary.* Tyndale New Testament Commentaries. Downers Grove, Ill.: IVP, 1986.

1 and 2 Thessalonians

Marshall, I. Howard. *I and II Thessalonians.* New Century Bible Commentary. Grand Rapids, Mich.: Eerdmans, 1983.

Menken, Maarten J. J. *2 Thessalonians.* Readings. London: Routledge, 1994.

Wanamaker, Charles A. *The Epistles to the Thessalonians: A Commentary on the Greek Text.* New International Greek Testament Commentary. Grand Rapids, Mich.: Eerdmans, 1990.

Williams, David. *1 and 2 Thessalonians.* New International Biblical Commentary. Peabody, Mass.: Hendrickson, 1995.

1 and 2 Timothy, Titus

Guthrie, Donald. *The Pastoral Epistles: An Introduction and Commentary.* Tyndale New Testament Commentaries. Downers Grove, Ill.: IVP, 2007.

Knight, George W. *The Pastoral Epistles: A Commentary on the Greek Text.* New International Greek Testament Commentary. Grand Rapids, Mich.: Eerdmans, 1992.

Stott, John R. W. *The Message of 1 Timothy and Titus.* Downers Grove, Ill.: IVP, 2001.

Wright, Tom. *Paul for Everyone: The Pastoral Epistles.* London: SPCK, 2003.

Philemon (see *Colossians*)

Hebrews

Attridge, Harold W. *The Epistle to the Hebrews: A Commentary.* Hermeneia. Philadelphia: Fortress, 1989.

Guthrie, George H. *The Structure of Hebrews: A Text-Linguistic Approach.* Grand Rapids, Mich.: Baker, 1998.

Hagner, Donald A. *Hebrews.* New International Biblical Commentary. Peabody, Mass.: Hendrickson, 1995.

Koester, Craig R. *Hebrews: A New Translation with Introduction and Commentary.* Anchor Bible. New York: Doubleday, 2001.

Vanhoye, Albert. *Structure and Message of the Epistle to the Hebrews.* Rome: Pontificio Istituto Biblico, 1989.

James

Bauckham, Richard J. *James: Wisdom of James, Disciple of Jesus.* Readings. New York: Routledge, 1999.

Johnson, Luke Timothy. *The Letter of James.* Anchor Bible. New York: Doubleday, 1995.

Moo, Douglas J. *The Letter of James.* Pillar New Testament Commentary. Downers Grove, Ill.: Apollos, 2000.

1 Peter

Davids, Peter H. *The First Epistle of Peter.* New International Commentary on the New Testament. Grand Rapids, Mich.: Eerdmans, 1990.

Jobes, Karen H. *1 Peter.* Baker Exegetical Commentary on the New Testament. Grand Rapids, Mich.: Baker, 2005.

Marshall, I. Howard. *1 Peter.* IVP New Testament Commentary. Downers Grove, Ill.: IVP, 1990.

2 Peter and Jude

Bauckham, Richard J. *Jude, 2 Peter.* Word Biblical Commentary. Waco, Tex.: Word Books, 1983.

Green, E. M. B. *The Second Epistle General of Peter and the General Epistle of Jude: An Introduction and Commentary.* 2d ed. Tyndale New Testament Commentaries. Downers Grove, Ill.: IVP, 1987.

Watson, Duane F. *Invention, Arrangement, and Style: Rhetorical Criticism of Jude and 2 Peter.* Atlanta: Scholars Press, 1988.

1, 2, and 3 John

Johnson, Thomas F. *1, 2, and 3 John.* New International Biblical Commentary. Peabody, Mass.: Hendrickson, 1995.

Kruse, Colin G. *The Letters of John.* Pillar New Testament Commentary. Downers Grove, Ill.: Apollos, 2000.

Marshall, I. Howard. *The Epistles of John.* New International Commentary on the New Testament. Grand Rapids, Mich.: Eerdmans, 1978.

Stott, John R. W. *The Epistles of John.* Tyndale New Testament Commentaries. Downers Grove, Ill.: InterVarsity Press, 1964.

Thompson, Marianne M. *1–3 John.* IVP New Testament Commentary. Downers Grove, Ill.: IVP, 1992.

Jude (see *2 Peter*)

Revelation

Jauhiainen, Marko. "Recapitulation and Chronological Progression in John's Apocalypse" *New Testament Studies* 49 (2003) 543–559.

Mounce, Robert H. *The Book of Revelation.* Rev. ed. New International Commentary on the New Testament. Grand Rapids, Mich.: Eerdmans, 1998.

Moyise, Steve P. *The Old Testament in the Book of Revelation.* Journal for the Study of the New Testament Supplement Series, vol. 115. Sheffield, England: Sheffield Academic Press, 1995.

Osborne, Grant R. *Revelation.* Baker Exegetical Commentary on the New Testament. Grand Rapids, Mich.: Baker, 2002.

Resseguie, James L. *Revelation Unsealed: A Narrative Critical Approach to John's Apocalypse.* Biblical Interpretation Series, vol. 32. Leiden: Brill, 1998.

Sandy, D. B. *Plowshares and Pruning Hooks: Rethinking the Language of Biblical Prophecy and Apocalyptic.* Downers Grove, Ill.: IVP, 2002.

Thomas, Robert L. "The Structure of the Apocalypse: Recapitulation or Progression?" *Masters Seminary Journal* 4 (1993): 45–66.

USEFUL WEB SITES

Ancient Jewish Accounts of Jesus. http://ccat.sas. upenn.edu/~humm/Topics/JewishJesus/ (ancient Jewish accounts of Jesus. Josephus, Celcus, Tertullian, Talmud, Toledoth Yeshu—full texts with introductions)

Bible Gateway. www.biblegateway.com (to search for words of texts)

Christian Resources: Biblical Studies Bulletin. www.ridley.cam.ac.uk/bsb.html (biblical study resources)

Inscriptions from the Land of Israel. http://dev. stg.brown.edu/projects/Inscriptions/index.html (inscriptions from the Land of Israel—aims to collect all inscriptions from Israel 500 B.C.E.–640 C.E.)

Internet Ancient History Sourcebook. www.fordham. edu/halsall/ancient/asbook.html (source for ancient history)

Into His Own. http://virtualreligion.net/iho/index. html (primary Jewish sources for background of the New Testament)

Introduction to Judaism. www.philosophy-religion. org/world/judaism.htm (introduction to Judaism from biblical to modern times by Lee A. Belford)

Jewish Encyclopedia. www.jewishencyclopedia.com/ (Jewish Encyclopaedia—full text and searchable database, including pictures)

Navigating the Bible II. http://bible.ort.org/intro1. asp?lang=1 (bar/bat mitzvah tutor—illustrated encyclopedias of places, people, plants, etc.)

The New Testament Gateway. www.ntgateway.com (scholarly Web site that helps users locate research material quickly)

Old Testament Gateway. www.otgateway.com (directory of Hebrew Bible Web sites)

Omniglot. www.omniglot.com/writing/hebrew.htm (Hebrew alphabet and language)

An Outline of the Talmud. www.jasher.com/Btalmud. htm (outline of contents for Talmuds/Mishnah/ Tosephta [Jewish Tradition])

Resource Pages for Biblical Studies. www.torreys.org/ bible (scholarly resources for studying the historical background of the Bible)

Second Temple Synagogues. www.pohick.org/sts/ index.html (ancient synagogues—primary sources and archaeology for ancient synagogues)

Web Sites on Archaeology

Bible History Online. www.bible-history.com (texts, photographs, maps, links, etc.)

Bible Places. www.bibleplaces.com (photographs and descriptions from archaeological sites)

Exploring Ancient World Cultures. http://eawc.evansville.edu/nepage.htm (exploring ancient world cultures)

The History of the Ancient Near East Electronic Compendium. http://ancientneareast.tripod.com/ (for ancient Near East)

Resource Pages for Biblical Studies. www.torreys.org/ bible (Apocrypha and Pseudepigrapha; Qumran; New Testament; Josephus; Philo; Rabbinica; church fathers; etc.)

Tyndale House: Links for Biblical Studies. www. tyndalehouse.co.uk/links_Biblical.htm (other links for biblical studies)

INDEX